考研英语词汇通

主编：张鑫友

长江出版传媒 湖北科学技术出版社

图书在版编目（CIP）数据

考研英语词汇通 / 张鑫友主编 . —武汉：湖北科学技术出版社，2023.8

ISBN 978-7-5706-2827-8

Ⅰ. ①考…　Ⅱ. ①张…　Ⅲ. ①英语－词汇－研究生－入学考试－自学参考资料　Ⅳ. ①H319.34

中国国家版本馆 CIP 数据核字（2023）第 163906 号

考研英语词汇通
KAOYAN YINGYU CIHUITONG

责任编辑：胡思思
责任校对：童桂清　　　　封面设计：曾雅明

出版发行：湖北科学技术出版社
地　　址：武汉市雄楚大街 268 号（湖北出版文化城 B 座 13—14 层）
电　　话：027-87679468　　　　邮　　编：430070

印　　刷：孝感天宇印务有限公司　　　　邮　　编：432100

880×1230　　1/32　　10 印张　　600 千字
2024 年 8 月第 1 版第 2 次印刷
定　　价：49.80 元

英国语言学家威尔金斯曾经说过："没有语法，人们表达的事物寥寥无几，而没有词汇，人们则无法表达任何事物。"语言学家刘易斯进一步提出："词汇是语言的核心。"可见词汇在英语学习中的重要性。对于准备参加全国硕士研究生入学考试英语科目的考生而言，单词可能是我们考研路上的首要拦路虎。为了帮助广大考生在有限的备考时间里更高效快速地记英语单词，我们编写了此书。本书的主要特点如下。

一、按序分频，层次分明

本书按照词汇在历年真题中出现的频次进行统计、筛选，将单词按高频、中频、低零频等进行标记，依次分为高频词汇(★★★)、中频词汇(★★)、低零频词汇(★)，让考生对词汇重要程度一目了然。

二、派生＋同/近/反义，巧妙助记

本书根据词条的特点，从该词条的派生词、短语用法、近义词、反义词中选取最具有代表性、最能帮助考生提高记忆效率的助记内容。

三、真题再现，真实感知考点难度

本书精选了近年考研英语试卷中出现过的真题语句，并附翻译，以便考生在具体的语境中领会该词的意义和用法。

本书是一本实用性强的考研英语单词备考工具书。希望通过本书，帮助广大考生在有限的时间内，系统高效地学习考研词汇，搭建英语学习的高楼大厦。编者预祝各位考研路上辛勤奋斗的追梦人梦想成真！

Contents
目录

Word List 1

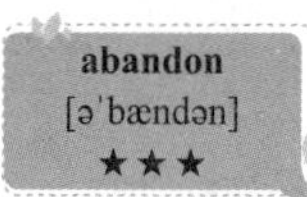

abandon [ə'bændən] ★★★

释义 *v.* 放弃;抛弃

例句 That house was *abandoned* years ago. 那所房子几年前就废弃了。

近义 desert *v.* 抛弃,遗弃

派生 abandoned *adj.* 被抛弃的;废弃的

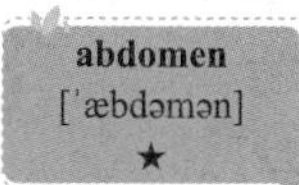

abdomen ['æbdəmən] ★

释义 *n.* 腹部;腹腔

短语 lower *abdomen* 小腹

例句 Spiders usually have silk glands under their *abdomen*. 蜘蛛的腹部下面通常有丝腺。

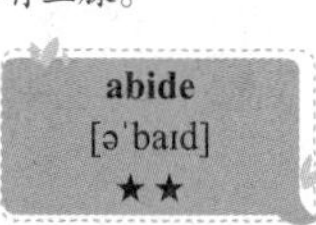

abide [ə'baɪd] ★★

释义 *v.* 忍受;遵守;居住;停留

例句 I've warned him a few times but he couldn't *abide* by the rules. 我警告过他几次,但他就是不遵守规则。

近义 bear *v.* 容忍

派生 abiding *adj.* 持久的

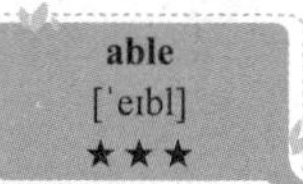

able ['eɪbl] ★★★

释义 *adj.* 有能力的;能干的;能够的

例句 She is *able* to speak French fluently now. 她现在能流利地说法语了。

用法 an *able* person 能人 / be *able* to do 有能力做;能够做

派生 ability *n.* 能力

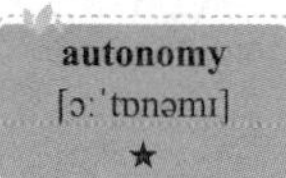

autonomy [ɔː'tɒnəmɪ] ★

释义 *n.* 自治;自治权;自主

例句 In Canada, the Inuit people are delicately guarding their hard-won *autonomy* in the country's newest territory, Nunavut. 在加拿大,因纽特人小心翼翼地维护着他们在该国最新的领土——努纳武特来之不易的自治权。

派生 autonomous *adj.* 自治的;自动的

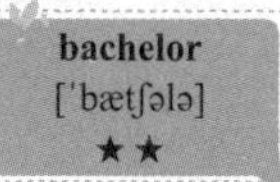

bachelor ['bætʃələ] ★★

释义 *n.* 学士;单身汉

例句 Ellis graduated this summer with a *bachelor* of arts in History. 埃利斯今年夏天毕业,获得了历史学学士学位。

He remained a *bachelor* until he was well into his 40s. 他一直到四十多岁还是单身。

bully ['bʊlɪ] ★

释义 *v.* 霸凌 *n.* 恃强欺弱者

例句 *Bullies* are often cowards. 恶霸往往是懦夫。

He *bullied* his younger brothers. 他欺负弟弟们。

calculate ['kælkjuleɪt] ★★

释义 *v.* 计算;预测

例句 I'll just *calculate* the total. 我来计算一下总数。

We cannot *calculate* on his help. 我们不能指望他的帮助。

派生 calculation *n.* 计算

campaign
[kæmˈpeɪn]
★★★

释义 *n.* 活动；运动 *v.* 参加运动

例句 They launched a *campaign* to raise money for a family in need. 他们发起了一项为贫困家庭筹款的活动。

We have *campaigned* against whaling for the last 15 years. 我们最近 15 年一直参加反对捕鲸的运动。

近义 movement *n.*（有特定目标的）运动

candidate
[ˈkændɪdət]
★★★

释义 *n.* 候选人，候补者；报考者

例句 He stood as a *candidate* in the local elections. 他作为候选人参加地方选举。

用法 a candidate for……的申请人

派生 candidacy *n.* 候选人资格（或身份）

capable
[ˈkeɪpəb(ə)l]
★★★

释义 *adj.* 有能力的，能干的；可以……的

例句 Jason himself was a *capable* but not an outstanding player. 杰森自己是一个有能力的球员，但并不出色。

Young children are often *incapable* of complex abstract reasoning. 幼儿往往不能进行复杂的抽象推理。

反义 incapable *adj.* 不能的

派生 capably *adv.* 能

capacity
[kəˈpæsətɪ]
★★★

释义 *n.* 容量，容积；能力

例句 The fuel tank has a *capacity* of 40 litres. 这个燃料箱的容量为 40 升。

His *capacity* to absorb information is amazing. 他理解信息的能力令人称奇。

近义 ability *n.* 能力

反义 incapacity *n.* 无能力，无能

释义 *v.* 处理；交易 *n.* 协议，交易

例句 We only *deal* with companies which have a good credit record. 我们只与信誉良好的公司做生意。

派生 dealer [ˈdiː lə] *n.* 商人

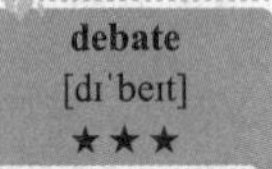

释义 *v./n.* 争论，辩论

例句 Education is the current focus of public *debate*. 教育是目前大众谈论的焦点。

用法 debate with sb. 和某人辩论

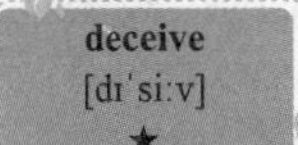

释义 *v.* 欺骗，蒙蔽

例句 The company *deceived* customers by selling old mobile phones as new ones. 该公司用旧手机冒充新手机欺骗顾客。

用法 deceive oneself 自欺

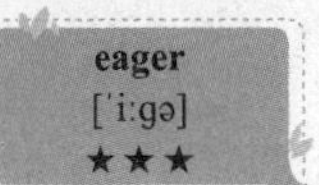

释义 *adj.* 渴望的，热切的

例句 Fans are *eager* for a glimpse of the singer. 歌迷们渴望一睹这位歌手的风采。

用法 eager for 渴望

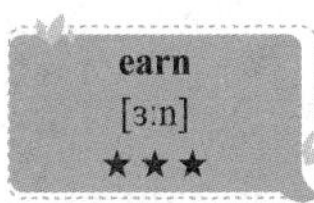

释义 v. 赚得,挣得

例句 Your untiring efforts will *earn* you a good reputation. 你不懈的努力将使你赢得佳誉。

派生 earnings n. 薪水,工资

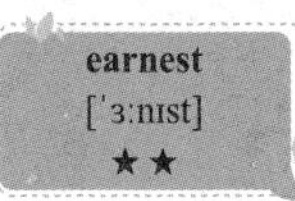

释义 adj. 热心的,诚挚的 n. 定金,认真

例句 When I said I wanted to help you, I was in *earnest*. 当我说我想帮你的时候,我是认真的。

近义 sincere adj. 真挚的

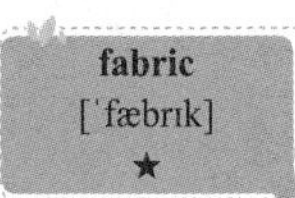

释义 n. 织物,织品;(社会、机构等的)结构

例句 Our new range of *fabrics* are both warm and washable. 我们的新系列面料既暖和又耐洗。

近义 textile n. 纺织物 structure n. 结构

派生 fabricate v. 捏造

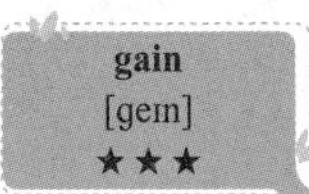

释义 v. 获得,赢得 n. 获益;增加

例句 Her talent and hard work *gained* her success as an artist. 她作为一名艺术家,靠其天资和勤奋获得了成功。

They see *gains* of 5 to 10 percent this spring. 今年春季,他们的利润增长百分之五到百分之十。

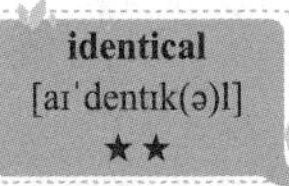

释义 adj. 相同的,同样的

例句 The two pictures are similar, although not *identical*. 这两幅画虽然不完全相同,但是很相似。

派生 identically adv. 相同地

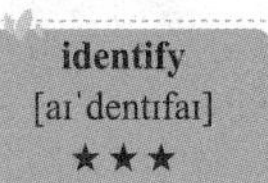

释义 v. 识别,鉴别;确认;发现;认为……等同于

例句 Could you *identify* your sunshade among a hundred others? 你能从100把遮阳伞中认出你的那一把吗?

Scientists have *identified* a link between diet and cancer. 科学家发现了饮食与癌症之间的关联。

近义 recognize v. 认出

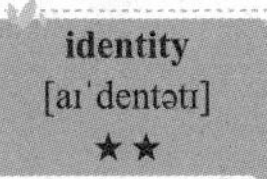

释义 n. 身份;特征;一致

例句 The man's *identity* was being kept secret while he was helping police with enquiries. 这名男子在协助警方调查时身份一直保密。

真题 Today the rapid growth of artificial intelligence (AI) raises fundamental questions:"What is intelligence, *identity*, or consciousness? What makes humans humans?" 今天,人工智能的快速发展提出了一些基本问题:"什么是智能、身份或意识?是什么让人类成为人类?"(2019 阅读理解)

释义 n. 标签,商标 v. 把……称为;用标签标明

例句 Today we have a tendency to *label* obesity as a disgrace. 今天,我们有一种认为肥胖是一种耻辱的倾向。

近义 tag n. 标签

magnificent
[mæɡˈnɪfɪs(ə)nt]
★

释义 *adj.* 华丽的，高尚的，宏伟的

例句 When we reached the top of the hill, a *magnificent* view of the sea greeted us. 当我们抵达山顶时，一片壮丽的海景映入眼帘。

近义 splendid *adj.* 华丽的

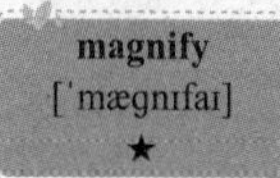

magnify
[ˈmæɡnɪfaɪ]
★

释义 *v.* 放大，扩大，夸大，夸张

例句 One of the easiest ways to segment a market is to *magnify* gender differences or invent them where they did not previously exist. 细分市场最简单的方法之一就是放大性别差异，或创造出之前不存在的差异。

近义 enlarge *v.* 扩大

magnitude
[ˈmæɡnɪtjuːd]
★

释义 *n.* 大小，数量；巨大；规模；星等；星的亮度；震级

短语 signal *magnitude* 信号幅度

例句 Astronomy uses the *magnitude* system to discuss brightness, where larger numbers are fainter. 天文学使用星等系统来讨论亮度，其数值越大亮度越弱。

近义 significance *n.* 重要性，意义

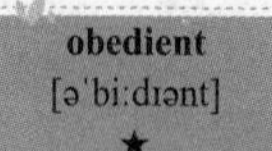

obedient
[əˈbiːdɪənt]
★

释义 *adj.* 顺从的；服从的

短语 an *obedient* child 听话的孩子

例句 Dogs are the most *obedient* animals and they guard our houses as true guardians. 狗是最听话的动物，它们像真正的守护者一样守护着我们的家。

反义 disobedient *adj.* 不服从的

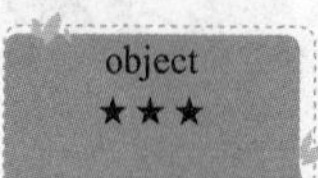

object
★★★

释义 *n.* [ˈɒbdʒɪkt] 物体；目标 *v.* [əbˈdʒekt] 反对

例句 I really *object* to being charged for parking. 我非常反对收停车费。

Her sole *object* in life is to become a travel writer. 她人生的唯一目标就是当游记作家。

派生 objection *n.* 反对

package
[ˈpækɪdʒ]
★★

释义 *n.* 包装，包裹；标准部件，成套设备 *v.* 包装

短语 software *package* 软件包

例句 We *package* our products in recyclable materials. 我们用可回收的材料包装我们的产品。

近义 parcel *n.* 包裹

packet
[ˈpækɪt]
★

释义 *n.* 小包裹，小捆；盒；一捆，一扎 *v.* 打包，包装

例句 A government notice on each *packet* warns the public about the dangers of cigarette smoking. 每包香烟上都有政府告示，警告公众吸烟的危害。

近义 parcel *n.* 包裹

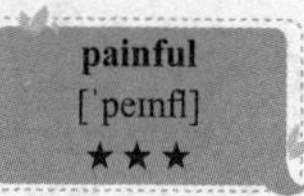

painful
[ˈpeɪnfl]
★★★

释义 *adj.* 疼痛的，使痛苦的，费力的

例句 Given these realities, recovery is likely to be slow and *painful*. 考虑到这些现实情况，经济复苏过程可能会是缓慢而痛苦的。

近义 aching *adj.* 疼痛的 distressing *adj.* 使痛苦的

pamphlet
[ˈpæmflɪt]
★

释义 *n.* 小册子

例句 Over a thousand copies of the *pamphlet* have now been given out. 现在已分发了一千多本小册子。

近义 booklet *n.* 小册子

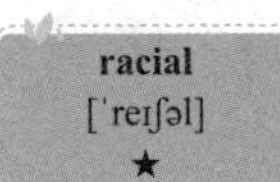

释义 *adj.* 人种的，种族的

短语 *racial* harmony 种族和谐

例句 Dr King's dream of *racial* harmony has never been fully realized. 金博士关于种族和谐的梦想从未完全实现。

派生 racism *n.* 种族主义

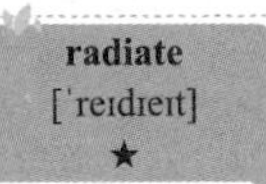

释义 *v.* 辐射；散布，传播

例句 The planet Jupiter *radiates* twice as much heat from inside as it receives from the Sun. 木星内部散发出的热量是它从太阳那吸收到的热量的两倍。

Five roads *radiate* from the square. 五条道路由广场向外延伸。

派生 radiation *n.* 辐射

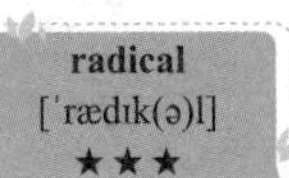

释义 *adj.* 激进的；彻底的；根本的 *n.* 激进分子

短语 *radical* proposals 激进的建议

例句 To paraphrase the great social scientist Joseph Schumpeter: there is no *radical* innovation without creative destruction. 用伟大的社会学家约瑟夫·熊彼特的话来说：没有创造性的破坏，就没有根本性的创新。

派生 radically *adv.* 根本上，彻底地

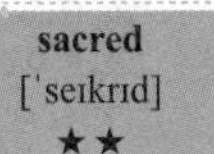

释义 *adj.* 神圣的；宗教的；庄严的

短语 *sacred* flame 圣火

例句 In the most *sacred* room of the temple, clay fragments of fifteen statues were found. 寺庙最神圣的房间里发现了15尊陶制雕像的碎片。

用法 be sacred for sb. 对某人来说是神圣的

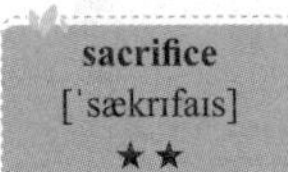

释义 *n.* 牺牲，牺牲品；祭品 *v.* 牺牲，献出

例句 The general public has realized that it's unwise to pursue economic development at the *sacrifice* of the environment. 大众已经意识到，以牺牲环境为代价来追求经济发展并不明智。

派生 sacrificial *adj.* 牺牲的，献祭的

用法 make sacrifices 做出牺牲

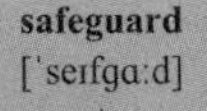

释义 *v.* 维护，保护 *n.* 安全措施

短语 *safeguard* mechanism 保障机制

例句 Local officials are using the levers that are available to them to *safeguard* residents' health in the face of a serious threat. 面对严重的威胁，当地官员正在利用现有的措施来保护居民的健康。

近义 protect *v.* 保护，防护

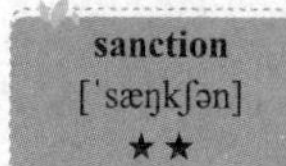

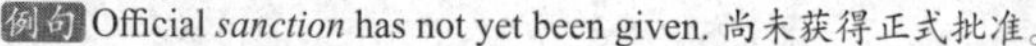

释义 *n.* / *v.* 制裁，处罚；许可，批准

短语 legal *sanction* 法律制裁

例句 Official *sanction* has not yet been given. 尚未获得正式批准。

真题 In contrast to France's actions, Denmark's fashion industry agreed last month on rules and *sanctions* regarding the age, health, and other characteristics of models. 与法国不同的是，丹麦时装界上月就模特的年龄、健康状况等方面的规定和许可达成了一致。（2016 阅读理解）

释义 *v.* 处理，解决；与……交涉；抓获 *n.* 拦截；用具

例句 You would be well advised to *tackle* this problem urgently. 你还是抓紧处理这个问题为好。

近义 seize *v.* 抓住，捉住

用法 tackle sb. about sth. 就某事向某人交涉

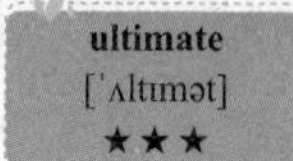

释义 *adj.* 最后的，最终的；根本的 *n.* 最终的事物；最高典范，极致

短语 an *ultimate* goal / aim 终极目标

例句 It is this doubt about *ultimate* outcome that has created your greatest enemy, which is fear. 正是这种对最终结果的怀疑造就了你们的最大敌人——恐惧。

Working from home offers the *ultimate* in flexible life styles. 在家办公为人们提供了极其灵活的生活方式。

近义 final *adj.* 最终的

派生 ultimately *adv.* 最终

释义 *adj.* 空的；空缺的；神情茫然的

短语 *vacant* room 空房

例句 There were many *vacant* seats in the theatre. 剧院里有许多空座位。

She had a kind of *vacant* look on her face. 她脸上有种茫然的神情。

近义 empty *adj.* 空的；空闲的

派生 vacancy *n.* 空缺

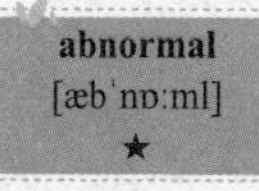

释义 *adj.* 变态的；反常的，异样的；不规则的

短语 *abnormal* phenomena 异常现象

例句 They said that the delay to our flight was due to *abnormal* bad weather conditions. 他们说我们航班的延误是由于异常恶劣的天气条件。

派生 abnormality *n.* 异常；变态

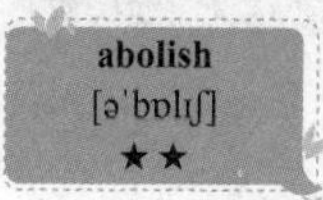

释义 *v.* 废除，废止

短语 *abolish* the death penalty 废除死刑

例句 I think bullfighting should be *abolished*. 我认为斗牛表演应该被废止。

派生 abolition *v.* 废除

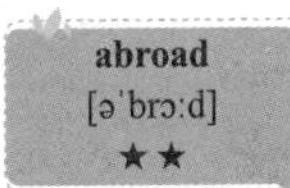
abroad
[əˈbrɔːd]
★★

释义 *adv.* 到国外;在国外;广为人知

短语 market / student *abroad* 海外市场 / 留学生

例句 About half of the company's sales come from *abroad*. 该公司大约一半的销售额来自海外。

The news spread *abroad* that a new factory was going to be built in the county. 将在该县建一座新工厂的消息传开了。

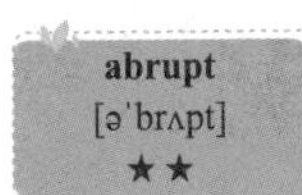
abrupt
[əˈbrʌpt]
★★

释义 *adj.* 突然的;唐突的;意外的

短语 an *abrupt* change 突变

例句 Transitions should connect one paragraph to the next so that there are no *abrupt* or confusing shifts. 过渡段应该将一段与下一段连接起来,这样就不会出现突兀或混淆的转换。

派生 abruptly *adv.* 突然地

aware
[əˈweə]
★★★

释义 *adj.* 察觉到的,意识到的

例句 Smokers are well *aware* of the dangers to their own health. 吸烟者很清楚吸烟对自身健康的危害。

用法 be aware of sth. 意识到某事

派生 awareness *n.* 意识

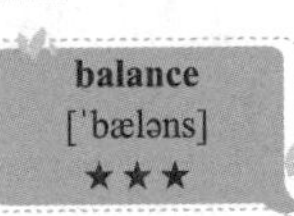
balance
[ˈbæləns]
★★★

释义 *v.* 使平衡 *n.* 平衡;均衡;余额

短语 ecological *balance* 生态平衡

例句 I find it difficult to *balance* on one foot. 我发现单脚站立很难保持平衡。

The skater suddenly lost his *balance* and fell. 滑冰的人突然失去平衡,摔倒了。

drawback
[ˈdrɔːbæk]
★

释义 *n.* 欠缺,缺点

例句 He felt the apartment's only *drawback* was that it was too small. 他感觉这个公寓唯一的缺点就是太小。

近义 disadvantage *n.* 缺点

captive
[ˈkæptɪv]
★★

释义 *adj.* 被俘虏的;受限制的;被迷住的 *n.* 俘虏

例句 They were held *captive* by masked gunmen. 他们被蒙面的持枪歹徒劫持了。

Most of the African *captives* were sent to North America. 大多数非洲俘虏被送往北美。

派生 captivation *n.* 迷惑;魅力

capture
[ˈkæptʃə]
★★★

释义 *v.* 俘虏;占领;引起;记录 *n.* 捕获;占领

例句 They were *captured* by enemy soldiers. 他们被敌军俘虏了。

The show has *captured* the attention of teenagers. 这个节目吸引了青少年的注意。

真题 Spontaneous smiles were relatively easy to *capture* by the 1890s, so we must look elsewhere for an explanation of why Victorians still hesitated to smile. 19世纪90年代时,自然的微笑相对比较容易捕捉,因此我们必须转而寻找“维多利亚时代的人为何仍不愿微笑”的其他原因。(2021 阅读理解)

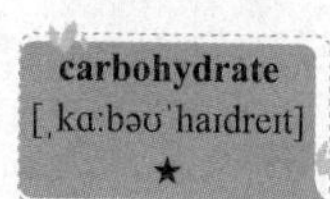

carbohydrate
[ˌkɑːbəʊˈhaɪdreɪt]
★

释义 *n.* 碳水化合物；糖类

短语 *carbohydrate* metabolism 碳水化合物代谢

例句 Athletes usually eat a high *carbohydrate* diet. 运动员通常吃高碳水化合物的食物。

carve
[kɑːv]
★★

释义 *v.* 雕刻，切；减少

例句 He *carved* a doll from a block of wood. 他用一块木头雕刻了一个娃娃。

用法 carve sth. from sth. 从某物中雕刻出某物

近义 cut *v.* 切，割　shape *v.* 塑造

case
[keɪs]
★★★

释义 *n.* 事例；案件；盒子；具体情况　*v.* 把……置于容器中；包围

例句 The rule is applicable to your *case*. 这条规则适用于你这种情况。

It is hard to judge this *case*. 这个案子很难裁决。

短语 in case 万一

真题 In both *cases*, we need a rebalancing of power. 在这两种情况下，我们都需要重新平衡实力。(2020 阅读理解)

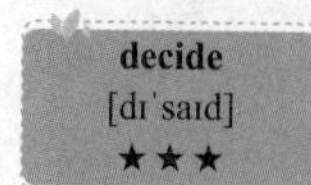

decide
[dɪˈsaɪd]
★★★

释义 *v.* 决定，下决心

例句 After much deliberation, he has *decided* to accept the job offer. 经过再三考虑，他决定接受这份工作。

派生 decision *n.* 决定

declare
[dɪˈkleə]
★

释义 *v.* 宣布，声明；断言，宣称；申报

例句 Have you got anything to *declare*? 你有什么东西需要报关的吗？

派生 declaration *n.* 宣言，宣布，声明

真题 The order also *declared* that state and local governments couldn't regulate broadband providers either. 该指令还宣布，州和地方政府也不能监管宽带提供商。(2021 阅读理解)

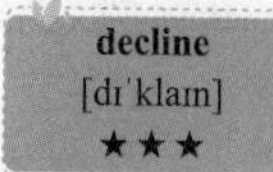

decline
[dɪˈklaɪn]
★★★

释义 *v.* 减少，衰落，降低；下降　*n.* 下降，减少

例句 The unemployment rates in Canada *declined* to 5.5% in February of 2022 from 6.5% in January. 加拿大的失业率从2022 年 1 月份的 6.5% 降至 2 月份的 5.5%。

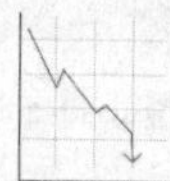

近义 decrease *v.* / *n.*（使）降低，减少　diminish *v.* 减少

eclipse
[ɪˈklɪps]
★

释义 *n.* 日食，月食；暗淡；黯然失色　*v.* 遮住……的光

例句 On Wednesday there will be a partial *eclipse* of the sun. 星期三将会有日偏食。

Her work was in *eclipse* for most of the 20th century. 她的作品在 20 世纪大部分时间里都湮没无闻。

economic
[ˌiːkəˈnɒmɪk]
★★★

释义 *adj.* 经济（上）的，经济学的

例句 New opportunities will emerge as the *economic* climate improves. 随着经济环境的改善，新的机会将出现。

派生 economics *n.* 经济学

真题 One basic weakness in a conservation system based wholly on *economic* motives is that most members of the land community have no *economic* value. 在一个完全以经济目标为基础的（生态）保护系统中，其根本弱点在于陆地群落的大多数成员没有经济价值。（2021 翻译）

释义 v. 教育，培养，训练

例句 Efforts have been made to safeguard the mangroves by government and to *educate* children about their importance. 政府已做出努力保护红树林，并教育孩子们了解它们的重要性。

用法 educate sb. about sth. 教育某人某事

派生 education *n.* 教育，培养

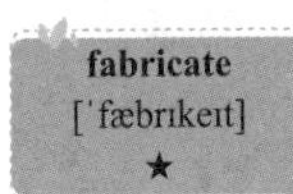

释义 v. 捏造，编造；制造，装配；组装

例句 The evidence used in that trial was *fabricated*. 那场官司提出的证据是被捏造出来的。

Automobile is fabricated from parts made in different factories. 汽车是由各个不同工厂所制的零件装配而成。

用法 be fabricated from... 由……制成

释义 n. 星系；银河系，银河；一群（杰出或著名的人物）

例句 The earth is one of the planets in the *Galaxy*. 地球是银河系中的星球之一。

The company has a *galaxy* of talents. 该公司拥有一批优秀的人才。

用法 a galaxy of 一群……

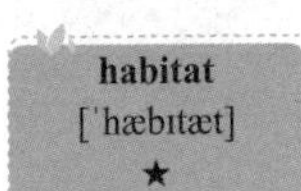

释义 n.（动物的）栖息地，住处

例句 The panda's natural *habitat* is the bamboo forest. 大熊猫的天然栖息地是竹林。

派生 habitation *n.* 住所

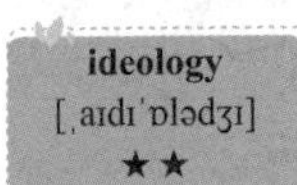

释义 n. 意识形态；思想体系

例句 In the art world after the 1960s, Postmodernism becomes the dominant *ideology*. 在 20 世纪 60 年代以后的西方艺术世界中，后现代主义成为支配性的意识形态。

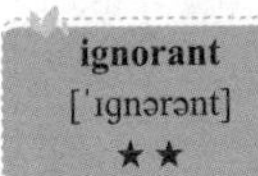

释义 adj. 无知的，不了解的

例句 Both landlords and tenants are often *ignorant* of their rights and obligations. 房东和租客往往都不了解自己的权利和义务。

真题 You can call their views stupid, or joke about how *ignorant* they are. 你可以说他们的观点愚蠢，或者开玩笑说他们多么无知。（2020 翻译）

释义 v. 不理，不顾，忽视

例句 He *ignored* all the No Smoking signs and lit up a cigarette. 他无视所有禁止吸烟的警示，点燃了香烟。

派生 ignorant *adj.* 无知的

释义 v. /n. 落后，滞后 n. 时间间隔

例句 For years, studies have found that first-generation college students those who do not have a parent with a college degree *lag* other students on a range of education achievement factors. 多年来的研究发现，那些父母没有大学学历的第一代大学生，在一系列教育成就方面落后于其他学生。

近义 delay *v.* / *n.* 延期

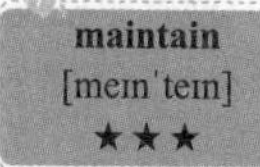
maintain [meɪnˈteɪn] ★★★

释义 *v.* 维修，保养，维持；主张

例句 Sometimes parents get exhausted and frustrated and are unable to *maintain* a tolerant and composed style with their kids. 有时，父母会感到疲惫和沮丧，无法对孩子保持宽容和冷静的态度。

派生 maintenance *n.* 维护；保持

真题 The two highly recommended lifestyle approaches are *maintaining* or increasing your level of aerobic exercise and following a Mediterranean-style diet. 两种强烈推荐的生活方式是保持或增加你的有氧运动水平和地中海式饮食。（2021 完形填空）

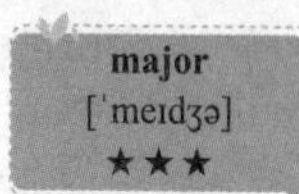
major [ˈmeɪdʒə] ★★★

释义 *adj.* 主要的 *n.* 成年人，主修课程 *v.* 主修

例句 Spain has been one of Cuba's *major* trading partners. 西班牙一直是古巴的主要贸易伙伴之一。

真题 Cattle rearing has been a *major* means of livelihood for the poor. 养牛一直是穷人的主要生计手段。（2021 阅读理解）

narrative [ˈnærətɪv] ★★

释义 *n.* 记叙文；故事 *adj.* 记叙的

短语 a *narrative* poem 叙事诗

例句 His trip through the world made an interesting *narrative*. 他周游世界的旅行是个很有趣的故事。

派生 narration *n.* 叙述

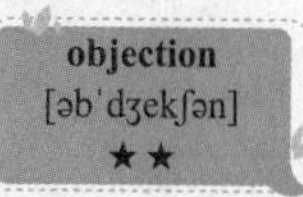
objection [əbˈdʒekʃən] ★★

释义 *n.* 反对，异议；厌恶

例句 We have no *objection* to this change, but doubt that it will significantly improve matters. 我们不反对这种变化，但怀疑这是否将明显地改善情况。

用法 have an objection to sth. 反对某事物

近义 opposition *n.* 反对

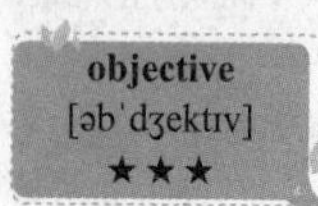
objective [əbˈdʒektɪv] ★★★

释义 *n.* 目标；目的 *adj.* 客观的；不带偏见的

短语 *objective* analysis 客观分析

例句 In order to achieve these *objectives*, we must concentrate more on documentary services and training. 为了实现这些目标，我们必须更加注重文件服务和培训。

反义 subjective *adj.* 主观的

panel [ˈpænl] ★★★

释义 *n.* 面，板；控制板，仪表盘；专门小组

短语 *panel* discussion 专题讨论会 LCD *panel* 液晶显示屏幕

例句 All the writers on the *panel* agreed that Quinn's book deserved special praise. 评委会的所有作家都认为奎因的书值得特别赞扬。

panorama
[ˌpænəˈrɑːmə]
★

释义 *n.* 全景；全景画；全景摄影；全景照片

例句 Horton looked out over a *panorama* of fertile valleys and gentle hills. 霍顿向外望去，肥沃的山谷和平缓的丘陵尽收眼底。

派生 panoramic *adj.* 全景的

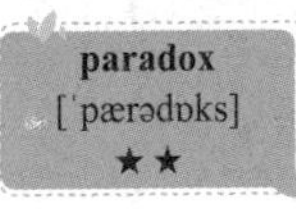

paradox
[ˈpærədɒks]
★★

释义 *n.* 似非而是的话，悖论，反论

例句 The share of information and the security of information are the most *paradox* in computer network. 计算机网络的信息共享与信息安全是网络上最大的悖论。

近义 contradiction *n.* 矛盾

派生 paradoxical *adj.* 自相矛盾的；事与愿违的

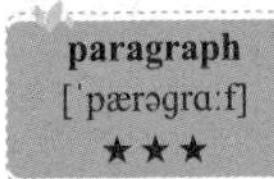

paragraph
[ˈpærəgrɑːf]
★★★

释义 *n.* 段，节；小新闻，短评

短语 opening *paragraph* 首段

例句 What do scientists seem to agree upon, judging from the first two *paragraphs*? 从前两段来看，科学家们似乎达成了什么共识？

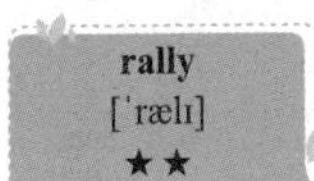

rally
[ˈrælɪ]
★★

释义 *v.* 集合，召集 *n.* 集会，拉力赛

短语 a protest *rally* 抗议集会

例句 About three thousand people held a *rally* to mark International Environment Day. 大约3000人举行集会纪念国际环境日。

用法 rally behind sb. 团结在某人背后

近义 assemble *v.* 集合

random
[ˈrændəm]
★★★

释义 *adj.* 随机的，随意的 *n.* 随机，随意

短语 *random* sampling 随机抽样

例句 Residents in these communities were phoned at *random* and asked the same questions. 我们随机给这些社区的居民打电话，问他们同样的问题。

用法 at random 随便地；任意地

派生 randomly *adv.* 随机地；任意地

rank
[ræŋk]
★★

释义 *n.* 社会阶层；军衔 *v.* 分等级，把……分类

短语 social *rank* 社会等级

例句 Arizona *ranked* second of all states in its growth rate of population. 亚利桑那州的人口增长率在所有州中排名第二。

She was not used to mixing with people of high social *rank*. 她不习惯和社会地位很高的人搅和在一起。

sarcastic
[sɑːˈkæstɪk]
★

释义 *adj.* 讽刺的，挖苦的

短语 a *sarcastic* remark 讽刺的言论

例句 New Yorkers pride themselves on quick quip or a biting *sarcastic* remark. 纽约人以妙语如珠或辛辣的讽刺言论为荣。

用法 have a sarcastic tongue 爱挖苦人

派生 sarcastically *adv.* 讽刺地

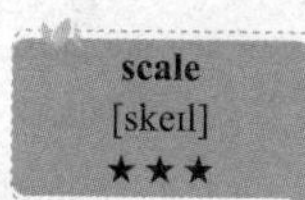

释义 *v.* 使湿透,浸透;使充满,使饱和

短语 *saturate* the markets 使市场饱和

例句 The continuous rain had *saturated* the soil. 连绵不断的雨把土地淋了个透。Japan's electronics industry began to *saturate* the world markets. 日本的电子工业开始使世界市场供大于求。

释义 *n.* 天平;等级;刻度;规模;鱼鳞 *v.* 攀登;去鳞

短语 production *scale* 生产规模

例句 The British aid programme is small in *scale*. 英国的援助项目规模不大。Local schools were ranked on a *scale* of one to five stars. 当地学校按照一到五星的等级进行排名。

用法 on a *scale* of 按……的等级

释义 *n.* 丑闻,流言蜚语;反感,公愤

短语 a financial *scandal* 一桩金融丑闻

例句 If there is the slightest hint of *scandal*, the public will no longer trust us. 只要有丝毫丑闻的迹象,公众就再也不会信任我们。

派生 scandalize *v.* 使震惊;使愤慨

释义 *n.*(tactics) 策略,战术

短语 self-help *tactics* 自助策略

例句 Harry often cleans his room as a *tactic* to avoid doing his homework. 哈里常以打扫房间作为逃避做作业的计策。

近义 strategy *n.* 策略

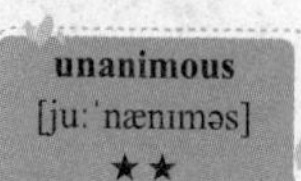

释义 *n.* 标签 *v.* 给……加标签

例句 In Britain, jazz is losing its elitist *tag* and gaining a much broader audience. 在英国,爵士乐不再是精英人物的专利,它正吸引着越来越多的听众。

近义 label *n.* 标签

释义 *adj.* 全体一致的,一致同意的

短语 *unanimous* support 一致的拥护

例句 Most economists are *unanimous* that in the current financial year, India's economy will contract. 大多数经济学家一致认为,在本财政年度,印度经济将出现下滑。

派生 unanimously *adv.* 全体一致地

vacuum
[ˈvækjuəm]
★★

释义 *n.* 真空,真空吸尘器 *v.* 用真空吸尘器清扫

短语 *vacuum* cleaner 吸尘器 fill a *vacuum* 填补空白

例句 Until recently most astronomers believed that the space between the galaxies was a near-perfect *vacuum*. 直到最近,大多数天文学家都认为星系之间的空间是近乎完美的真空。We changed the *sheets*, started the laundry, dusted and *vacuumed* the house. 我们换了床单,开始洗衣服,打扫房间,用吸尘器吸尘。

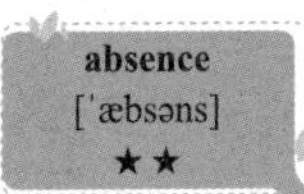

释义 *n.* 缺席；缺乏；不注意

短语 *absence* of mind 心不在焉

例句 Mary acted as supervisor in John's *absence*. 约翰不在时，玛丽担任主管。

反义 presence *n.* 出席，存在

派生 absent *adj.* 缺席的

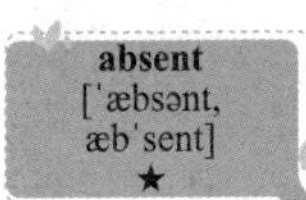

释义 *adj.* 缺席的；心不在焉的 *v.* 缺席

短语 *absent* minded 健忘的；心不在焉的

例句 The teenager, now aged 15, has been *absent* from school for a year. 这名15岁的少年已经旷课一年了。

派生 absence *n.* 缺席

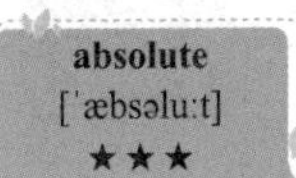

释义 *adj.* 绝对的；完全的；明确的 *n.* 绝对，绝对真理

短语 *absolute* power 绝对权力

例句 Both the *absolute* cost of healthcare and the share of it borne by families have risen. 医疗保健的绝对成本和家庭承担的份额都有所上升。

派生 absolutely *adv.* 绝对地

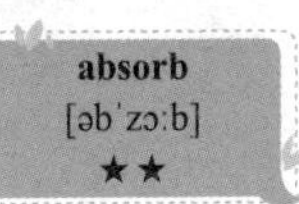

释义 *v.* 吸收；理解；（使）全神贯注于……

例句 During the same period, families have been asked to *absorb* much more risk in their retirement income. 在同一时期，家庭被要求在退休收入方面承担更多的风险。

近义 digest *v.* 理解；消化

释义 *v.* 禁止 *n.* 禁令；禁止

例句 The use of cell phones is *banned* in the restaurant. 餐厅里禁止使用手机。

Swiss voters have backed a *ban* on tobacco advertising anywhere young people might see it. 瑞士选民支持禁止在年轻人可能看到的任何地方出现烟草广告。

短语 *ban* sb. from doing sth. 禁止某人做某事

近义 prohibit *v.* 禁止

释义 *v.* 向……投以（视线、笑容等）；掷、抛；不确信 *n.* 全体演员；铸型，模型

例句 The news *cast* a deep gloom over the whole family. 那个消息使全家笼罩在一片愁云惨雾中。

This movie will be an all-star *cast*. 这部电影将是全明星阵容。

用法 cast a glance at ... 向……瞥一眼

释义 *adj.* 休闲的；随便的，非正式的；漫不经心的

例句 Mary felt more comfortable in *casual* clothes. 玛丽感觉穿便服更舒服。

She tried to make her voice sound *casual*. 她尽力使自己的声音听上去满不在乎。

派生 casually *adv.* 随意地；偶然地

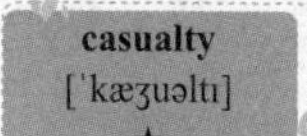

释义 *n.* 伤亡人员；受害者；急诊室；事故，灾难（主要用于保险中）

短语 *casualty* insurance 灾害保险

例句 Our aim is to reduce road *casualties*. 我们的目标是减少道路伤亡。Jean ended up in *casualty* last night. 珍昨晚去了急诊室。

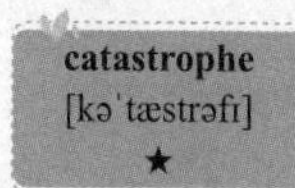

释义 *n.* 大灾难；惨败；大祸

例句 The oil spill was an environmental *catastrophe*. 石油泄漏是一场环境灾难。

近义 disaster *n.* 灾难，灾害

释义 *n.* 目录；一连串（糟糕）事 *v.* 列入目录

例句 The business launched a mail-order *catalogue* in 1987. 该公司于1987年推出了邮购目录。The librarians *catalogued* the new books. 图书管理人员把新书编入目录。

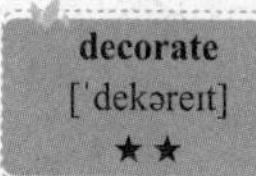

释义 *v.* 装饰；布置

例句 They *decorated* the wedding car with ribbons and flowers. 他们用彩带和鲜花装点婚车。

派生 decoration *n.* 装饰

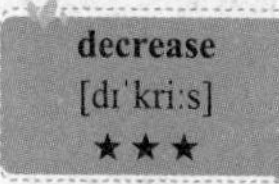

释义 *v./n.* 减少；减小

例句 There has been a sharp *decrease* in the number of visitors. 来访者数量急剧减少。

近义 decline *v.* / *n.* 下降

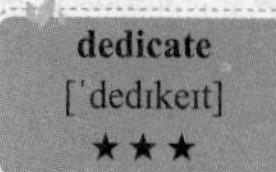

释义 *v.* 献身；致力于；奉献；献给

例句 He has *dedicated* his life to scientific research. 他把自己的一生都献给了科学研究事业。

用法 dedicate to (doing) sth. 致力于（做）某事

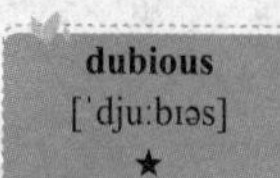

释义 *adj.* 怀疑的，无把握的；靠不住的

例句 I'm *dubious* about his promises to change his ways. 他承诺将改变行事方式，我对此有些怀疑。

近义 doubtful *adj.* 怀疑的，不确定的

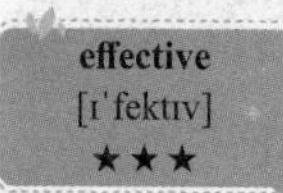

释义 *adj.* 有效的，生效的；给人深刻印象

例句 The new project is very *effective* in encouraging students to enter teacher training. 这个新项目在鼓励学生参加教师培训方面非常有效。

派生 effectiveness *n.* 有效；功效

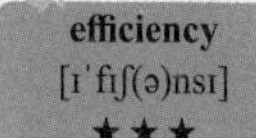

释义 *n.* 效率；效能

例句 What is so impressive about their society is the *efficiency* of the public services. 他们的社会最令人印象深刻的是公共服务的效率。

派生 inefficiency *n.* 效率低下

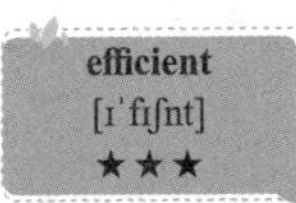

efficient [ɪ'fɪʃnt] ★★★

释义 *adj.* 有效的，效率高的；能胜任的

例句 The city's transport system is one of the most *efficient* in Europe. 这个城市的交通系统是欧洲效率最高的交通系统之一。

反义 inefficient *adj.* 效率低下的

facilitate [fə'sɪlɪteɪt] ★★

释义 *v.* 使变得（更）容易；使便利；推动；帮助；促进

短语 *facilitate* the cultural interchange 促进文化交流

例句 The new underground railway will *facilitate* the journey to all parts of the city. 新的地铁将为去城市各处提供方便。

fortune ['fɔːtʃən, -tʃuːn] ★★★

释义 *n.* 运气；命运；财产；财富 *v.* 给予财富；偶然发生

例句 She suffered mixed *fortunes* during her short life. 在她短暂的一生中，她的命运喜忧参半。

近义 treasure *n.* 财富，宝藏 *v.* 珍视；珍藏

派生 fortunate *adj.* 幸运的

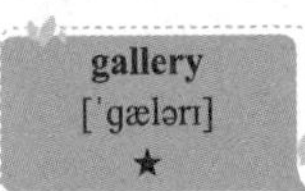

gallery ['gælərɪ] ★

释义 *n.* 画廊，美术馆

短语 art *gallery* 美术馆；画廊 a shooting *gallery* 打靶场

例句 The *gallery* houses 2,000 works of modern art. 美术馆收藏了 2,000 件现代艺术作品。

illegal [ɪ'liːg(ə)l] ★★★

释义 *adj.* 不合法的，非法的

例句 He obtained Monsanto's patented seeds by *illegal* means. 他通过非法手段获得了孟山都公司的专利种子。

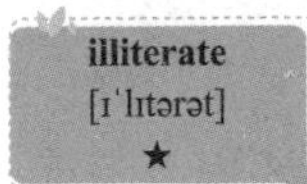

illiterate [ɪ'lɪtərət] ★

释义 *adj.* 文盲的，未受教育的 *n.* 文盲，无知的人

例句 A large percentage of the population is *illiterate*. 文盲人口占有相当高的比例。

反义 literate *adj.* 有读写能力的 *n.* 识字的人；有学问的人

illuminate [ɪ'ljuːmɪneɪt] ★★

释义 *v.* 照亮，照明；用灯光装饰；说明，阐释

例句 The earth is *illuminated* by the sun. 太阳照亮地球。

He *illuminated* a statement with many examples. 他用许多例子来阐明一个论点。

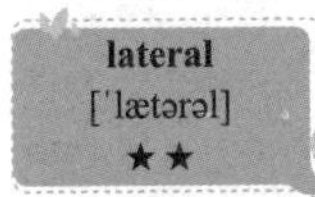

lateral ['lætərəl] ★★

释义 *adj.* 侧面的，旁边的；横向的 *n.* 侧面；边音

短语 *lateral* direction 横向 *lateral* movement 横向运动

例句 The wall is weak and requires *lateral* support. 墙很脆弱，需要横向支撑。

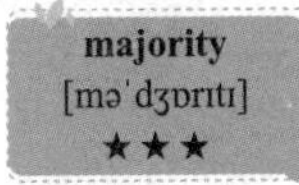

majority [mə'dʒɒrɪtɪ] ★★★

释义 *n.* 大多数；成年；法定年龄

例句 Surveys indicate that supporters of the treaty are still in the *majority*. 调查显示，该条约的支持者仍占多数。

反义 minority *n.* 少数

真题 Among the children who had not been tricked, the *majority* were willing to cooperate with the tester in learning a new skill. 在没有被骗的孩子中，大多数人愿意与测试人员合作学习一项新技能。（2018 完形填空）

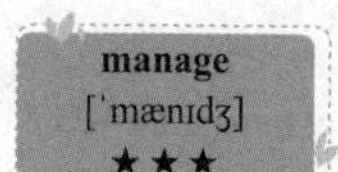

释义 *v.* 经营，管理；设法，对付

短语 *manage* one's life 管理某人的生活

例句 Bill expects me to *manage* all the household expenses on very little. 比尔指望我对每笔家庭支出都精打细算。

派生 manager *n.* 经理；管理者

释义 *n.* 经营，管理；处理；管理层

短语 quality *management* 质量管理

例句 The zoo needed better *management* rather than more money. 这座动物园需要更好的管理，而不是更多的资金。

近义 administration *n.* 管理

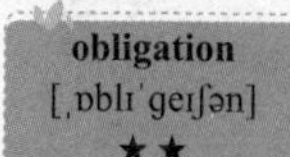

释义 *n.* 义务；责任

短语 moral *obligation* 道义上的责任

例句 Most women today are coping with a lot of *obligations*, with few breaks, and feeling the strain. 今天的大多数女性都要应付很多的责任，很少休息，感到压力。

派生 obligatory *adj.* 必须的

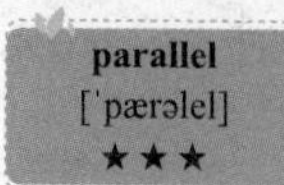

释义 *adj.* 平行的，相同的，类似的 *v.* 与……相似；比得上 *n.* 相似之处；（地球的）纬线

短语 *parallel* line 平行线 in *parallel* with 与……平行

例句 Brain researchers have discovered that when we consciously develop new habits, we create *parallel* synaptic paths, and even entirely new brain cells. 大脑研究人员发现，当我们有意识地养成新习惯，我们会创造出平行的突触路径，甚至是全新的脑细胞。

I'm trying to see if there are any obvious *parallels* between the two cases. 我正试图寻找这两起案件有没有明显的相似之处。

释义 *n.* 包裹，邮包，部分；一块地 *v.* 打包，捆扎，分配

短语 *parcel* post 邮政包裹 *parcel* of land 一片土地

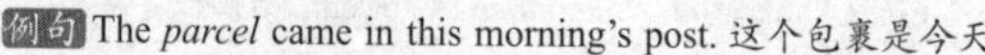

例句 The *parcel* came in this morning's post. 这个包裹是今天上午邮寄来的。

These small *parcels* of land were purchased for the most part by local people. 这些小块土地大多数是当地人买下的。

近义 package *n.* 包裹

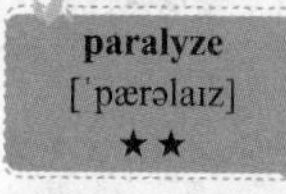

释义 *v.* (paralyse) 使瘫痪（麻痹）；使丧失作用

例句 The snake uses its venom to stun or *paralyze* its victims. 蛇用其毒液使受害者失去知觉或瘫痪。

派生 paralyzed *adj.* 瘫痪的；麻痹的

释义 *n.* 国会，议会

短语 a member of *parliament* 国会议员

例句 The *parliament* agreed to ban websites that incite excessive thinness by promoting extreme dieting. 议会同意禁止那些通过宣传极端节食来煽动过度瘦身的网站。

派生 parliamentary *adj.* 议会的，国会的

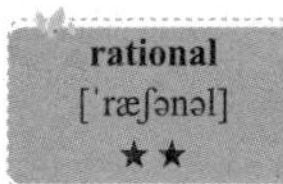

rational ['ræʃənəl] ★★

释义 *adj.* 理性的，合理的 *n.* 合理的事物；有理数

短语 *rational* choice 理性选择

例句 Perhaps, if we continue to improve information-processing machines, we'll soon have helpful *rational* assistants. 也许，如果我们继续改进信息处理机器，我们很快就会有有用的理性助手。

反义 irrational *adj.* 非理性的

派生 rationally *adv.* 理性地

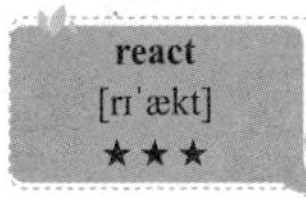

react [rɪ'ækt] ★★★

释义 *v.* 反应，起作用；反对

例句 Under normal circumstances, these two gases *react* readily to produce carbon dioxide and water. 在正常情况下，这两种气体容易发生反应产生二氧化碳和水。

用法 react with 同……起反应

派生 reaction *n.* 反应

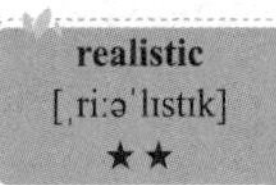

realistic [ˌriːə'lɪstɪk] ★★

释义 *adj.* 现实(主义)的

短语 *realistic* painting 写实绘画

例句 Our income has got smaller, so we must be *realistic* and give up our car. 我们的收入减少了，所以我们得面对现实，把车卖掉。

派生 realistically *adv.* 现实地

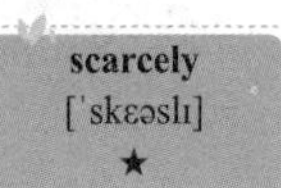

scarcely ['skɛəslɪ] ★

释义 *adv.* 几乎不，简直没有，勉强

短语 *scarcely* relevant 几乎无关

例句 He had *scarcely* put the phone down when the doorbell rang. 他刚放下电话，门铃就响了起来。

近义 hardly *adv.* 几乎不

用法 scarcely... when... 刚……就……

scatter ['skætə] ★★

释义 *v.* 播撒，驱散；撒落

例句 The evidence found in the search was incomplete and *scattered*. 在搜索中发现的证据不完整且分散。

近义 spread *v.* 散布

派生 scattered *adj.* 分散的

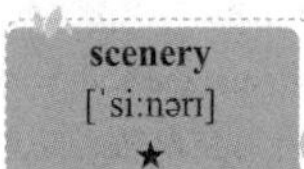

scenery ['siːnərɪ] ★

释义 *n.* 风景，景色；舞台布景

短语 natural *scenery* 自然风光

例句 Sometimes they just drive slowly down the lane enjoying the *scenery*. 有时他们只是沿着小路慢慢地开车，欣赏两旁的风景。

近义 landscape *n.* 风景

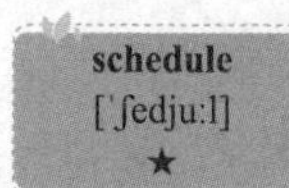

释义 *n.* 时间表，进度表；清单 *v.* 安排，预定

例句 He often attends public events on the weekends and typically keeps a busy *schedule*. 他经常在周末参加公共活动，日程通常很满。

The meeting is *scheduled* for Friday afternoon. 会议安排在星期五下午。

用法 schedule sth. for 为……安排时间

近义 arrange *v.* 安排

释义 *n.* 目标；对象；靶子 *v.* 把……作为目标

例句 The missiles missed their *target*. 导弹没有击中目标。

The company has *targeted* young people as its primary customers. 这家公司把年轻人作为其主要顾客。

近义 goal *n.* 目标

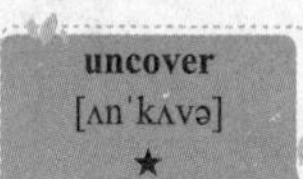

释义 *v.* 揭开，揭露

短语 *uncover* the pan 揭开锅盖 *uncover* a plot 揭露一起阴谋

例句 Archaeologists have *uncovered* an 11,700-year-old hunting camp in Alaska. 考古学家在阿拉斯加发现了一个 11,700 年前的狩猎营地。

近义 discover *v.* 发现

反义 cover *v.* 覆盖，遮盖

派生 uncovered *adj.* 无覆盖的

释义 *adj.* 不明确的，含糊的，暧昧的

短语 a *vague* impression 模糊的印象

例句 Democratic leaders under election pressure tend to respond with *vague* promises of action. 民主党领导人在选举压力下往往用一些含糊其词的行动承诺来予以回应。

近义 ambiguous *adj.* 含糊不清的

派生 vagueness *n.* 模糊

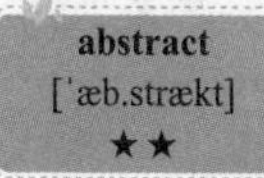

释义 *adj.* 抽象的 *n.* 摘要 *v.* 提取；摘要

例句 Truth and beauty are *abstract* concepts. 真和美都是抽象的概念。

反义 concrete *adj.* 具体的

真题 Fluid intelligence is the type of intelligence that has to do with short-term memory and the ability to think quickly, logically, and *abstractly* in order to solve new problems. 流体智力是一种与短期记忆和快速思考能力、逻辑思考能力、抽象思考能力有关的智力，以解决新问题。（2021 完形填空）

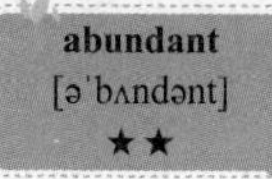

释义 *adj.* 丰富的；大量的；充裕的

短语 *abundant* rainfall 充沛的雨量

例句 Our country has a vast territory and *abundant* resources. 我国土地辽阔，资

源丰富。

派生 abundance *n.* 丰富,充裕;大量

abuse
[ə'bju:s, ə'bju:z]
★★

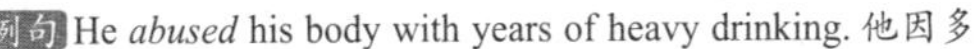

释义 *v.* / *n.* 虐待;辱骂;滥用

短语 drug *abuse* 药物滥用

例句 He *abused* his body with years of heavy drinking. 他因多年酗酒损害了身体。

Abuse can lead to both psychological and emotional problems. 虐待可造成心理和情绪上的问题。

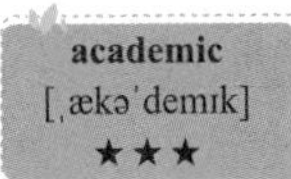
academic
[ˌækə'demɪk]
★★★

释义 *adj.* 学院的;学术的;好学的 *n.* 学者

短语 *academic* research / circles 学术研究 / 学术界

例句 He was offered a teaching job and decided to return to *academic* life. 他得到了一份教学工作,并决定重返学术生活。

派生 academy *n.* 专科院校;研究院

真题 High growth rates increased the chances for *academic* innovation. 高增长率增加了学术创新的机会。(2021 翻译)

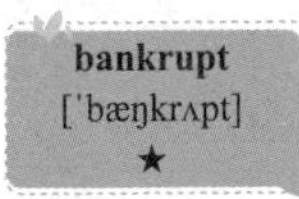
bankrupt
['bæŋkrʌpt]
★

释义 *adj.* 破产的 *v.* 使破产

例句 He went *bankrupt* after only a year in business. 他仅仅做了一年的生意就破产了。

Several risky deals *bankrupted* the company. 几笔冒险的交易使公司破产。

短语 go bankrupt 破产

派生 bankruptcy *n.* 破产,倒闭

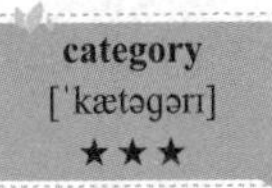
category
['kætəgərɪ]
★★★

释义 *n.* 种类;类别;范畴

例句 The cars belong to the same *category*. 这些汽车属于同一类。

近义 classification *n.* 分类

cater
['keɪtə]
★★

释义 *v.* 提供饮食服务;迎合,满足需要

例句 This five-star hotel can *cater* for receptions of up to 300 people. 这家五星级酒店最多可以同时接待 300 人。

用法 cater for 供应伙食

catholic
['kæθ(ə)lɪk]
★★

释义 *adj.* 广泛的;天主教的 *n.* 天主教教徒

例句 He is (a) *Catholic*. 他是一个天主教徒。

派生 Catholicism *n.* 天主教

cause
[kɔ:z]
★★★

释义 *n.* 原因,起因;事业 *v.* 造成,引起

例句 Smoking is a major *cause* of lung cancer. 吸烟是导致肺癌的主要原因。

真题 Studies have shown that acrylamide can *cause* neurological damage in mice. 研究表明丙烯酰胺会对小鼠造成神经损伤。(2020 完形填空)

cautious
['kɔ:ʃəs]
★★★

释义 *adj.* 小心的,谨慎的

例句 We should not only be bold, but also be *cautious*. 我们不仅要大胆,而且要谨慎。

近义 careful *adj.* 仔细的

反义 bold *adj.* 大胆的；冒失的

释义 *v.* 推断；演绎；推论

例句 We cannot *deduce* very much from these figures. 我们无法从这些数字中推断出太多东西。

用法 deduce from 从……得出结论

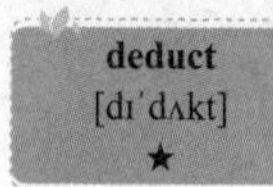

释义 *v.* 扣除；减去

例句 The payments will be *deducted* from your salary. 这笔钱将从你的工资中扣除。

同义 subtract *v.* 减去

派生 deduction *n.* 推论；扣除

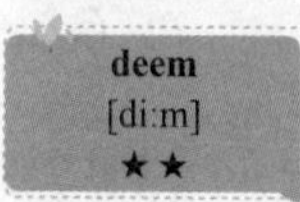

释义 *v.* 认为，觉得

例句 Shouting in the workplace is *deemed* rude. 在工作场所大喊大叫被认为是粗鲁的行为。

近义 consider *v.* 认为

释义 *adj.* 预计的；应支付的；到期的；应得的

例句 *Due* to low investment, industrial output has remained stagnant. 由于投资少，工业生产一直停滞不前。

The next train is *due* in five minutes. 下一班火车预计在五分钟后抵达。

用法 due to 由于，因为……

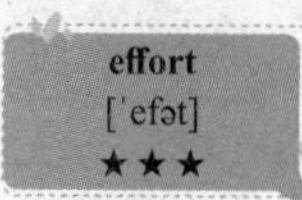

释义 *n.* 努力；成就；艰难的尝试

例句 John lifted the box easily, without using much *effort*. 约翰毫不费力地把箱子举起来了。

用法 make an effort 做出努力

真题 Both figures seem to rise unstoppably despite increasingly desperate *efforts* to change them. 这两个数字似乎都在势不可挡地上升，尽管人们越来越拼命地努力改变它们。（2020 阅读理解）

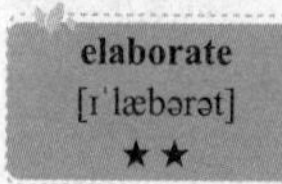

释义 *adj.* 精心制作（的）；详尽的 *v.* 详尽阐述；详细描述；精心制作

例句 The government's new healthcare plan is the most *elaborate* yet. 政府的新医保计划是迄今为止最详尽的。

真题 The *elaborate* French Second Empire style design by Alfred Mullett was selected. 阿尔弗雷德·穆莱特精心设计的法国第二帝国风格被选中。

释义 *adj.* 电的；导电的；电动的

例句 It's expensive to leave the *electric* stove on all day. 整天开着电炉太浪费钱了。

派生 electricity *n.* 电，电流

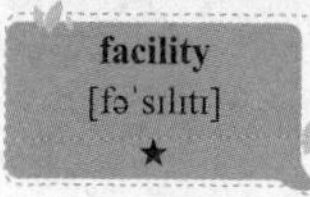

释义 *n.* 灵巧，熟练；(*pl.*) 设备，设施；便利条件

短语 public *facility* 公共设施

例句 The hotel has special *facilities* for welcoming disabled people. 这家旅馆有

专供残疾人使用的设施。

释义 *v.* 促进，培养；领养，收养 *adj.* 收养的 *n.* 养育者

短语 *foster* daughter / family 养女 / 寄养家庭

例句 The club's aim is to *foster* better relations within the community. 俱乐部的宗旨是促进团体内部的关系。

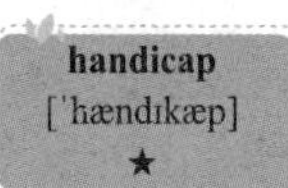

释义 *n.* 障碍；残疾 *v.* 妨碍；使不利

例句 He lost his leg when he was ten, but learnt to overcome his *handicap*. 他十岁时失去了一条腿，但他学会了克服自身的残疾。

His lack of English *handicaps* him. 英语不好对他来说是一件不利的事。

释义 *v.* / *n.* 赌博；冒风险

例句 The federal government *gambled* hundreds of thousands of dollars in research funds to work on the project. 联邦政府为了这项研究计划冒险动用了好几十万美元的资金。

派生 gambler *n.* 赌徒

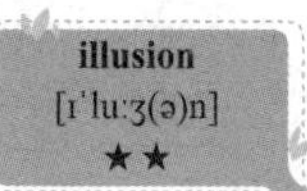

释义 *n.* 幻想；错觉，幻觉，假象

例句 Mirrors in a room often give an *illusion* of space. 房间里的镜子通常给人空间变大的感觉。

用法 give the illusion of sth. 给人以某种假象（或错觉）

释义 *v.* 举例说明，阐明；图解，加插图

例句 The company's bank statements *illustrate* its success. 这家公司的银行报表说明了它的成功。

用法 illustrate sth. with sth. 用某事物说明某事物

派生 illustration *n.* 说明；例证；插图；举例说明

释义 *v.* 想象；设想；料想；猜想

例句 We tend to *imagine* that the Victorians were very prim and proper. 我们倾向于认为维多利亚时代的人非常古板和正派。

用法 imagine doing sth. 想象做某事

释义 *v.* 发起，发动，开始从事；发射；推出 *n.* 发射

短语 *launch* a satellite 发射卫星

真题 The Breakthrough Prize in Life Sciences *launched* this year, takes an unrepresentative view of what the life sciences include. 今年设立的生命科学突破奖将把生命科学中不具有代表性的观点纳入考量范围。（2014 阅读理解）

用法 launch out into sth. 投身于……；着手干……

派生 launcher *n.* 发射器；发射台

释义 *n.* 经理，管理人

短语 general *manager* 总经理

例句 The advertising *manager* is the mastermind of our new

marketing policy. 广告经理是我们新市场政策的策划人。

释义 *v.* 表明,呈现 *adj.* 明白的,显然的 *n.* 货单;名单

例句 The rules and regulations should be made to be *manifest* to all staff. 规章制度应该让全体员工都明白。

派生 manifestation *n.* 表现,显现

真题 The growth of higher education *manifests* itself in at least three quite different ways, and these in turn have given rise to different sets of problems. 高等教育的发展至少以三种截然不同的方式表现出来,而这些方式反过来又引发了一系列不同的问题。(2021 翻译)

释义 *adj.* 令人厌恶的;恶意的;严重的

短语 a *nasty* accident 严重事故 a *nasty* taste 难于入口

例句 A *nasty* incident was prevented by the timely arrival of the police. 警察的及时到来阻止了一次严重事故。

近义 unpleasant *adj.* 不友好的

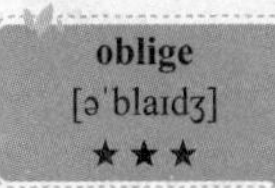

释义 *v.* 迫使做;帮忙

例句 Moreover, the integration of the European community will *oblige* television companies to cooperate more closely. 此外,欧洲共同体的一体化将迫使电视公司进行更密切的合作。

用法 oblige sb. to do sth. 迫使某人做某事

派生 obligation *n.* 义务

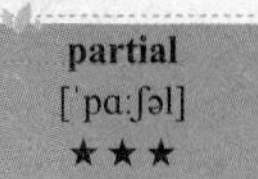

释义 *adj.* 部分的;偏袒的;钟爱的

短语 *partial* loss 部分损失

例句 He managed to reach a *partial* agreement with both republics. 他设法跟两个共和国达成了部分共识。

He is *partial* to sports. 他特别喜欢运动。

Don't be *partial* to your own child. 别护着自己的孩子。

派生 partially *adv.* 不完全地,部分地

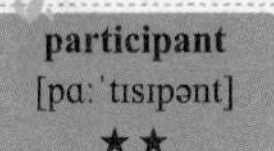

释义 *n.* 参加者,参与者 *adj.* 有份的,参与的

短语 market *participants* 市场参与者

例句 For one trial, each *participant* was shown a pile of pens that the researcher claimed were from a previous experiment. 在一次实验中,研究人员向每个参与者展示了一堆笔,研究人员声称这些笔来自之前的实验。

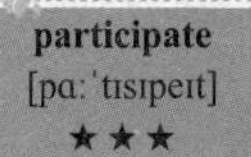

释义 *v.* 参与,参加;分享,分担

例句 Without the ability to think critically, to defend their ideas and understand the ideas of others, they cannot fully *participate* in our democracy. 如果没有能力进行批判性思考,捍卫自己的观点并理解他人的观点,他们就无法充分参与我们的民主。

用法 participate in 参加

派生 participatory *adj.* 参与式的

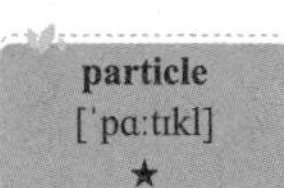

particle
[ˈpɑːtɪkl]
★

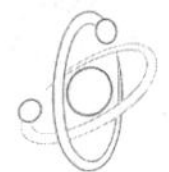

释义 *n.* 粒子，微粒；极小量

短语 *particle* physics 粒子物理学　dust *particles* 尘埃

例句 How can scientists detect a *particle* that interacts so infrequently with other matter? 科学家们是如何探测到一种很少与其他物质相互起作用的粒子的呢？

用法 a particle of 少量

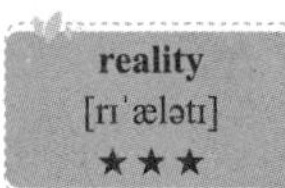

reality
[rɪˈæləti]
★★★

释义 *n.* 现实，实际；真实

短语 virtual *reality* 虚拟现实

例句 Outwardly she seemed confident but in *reality* she felt extremely nervous. 表面上看她显得信心十足，而实际上她紧张得要命。

用法 in reality 实际上；事实上

近义 actuality *n.* 现状，实际情况

realm
[relm]
★

释义 *n.* 王国，国土；领域

短语 within / beyond the *realms* of possibility 在可能的范围内 / 超出了可能的范围

例句 He made outstanding contributions in the *realm* of foreign affairs. 他在外交领域做出了卓越贡献。

用法 in the realm of... 在……领域内

reasonable
[ˈriːzənəbl]
★★★

释义 *adj.* 合理的；通情达理的；适度的

例句 Upcoming reforms might bring the price to a more *reasonable* level. 即将到来的改革可能会使价格降至更合理的水平。

派生 reasonableness *n.* 合理；妥当

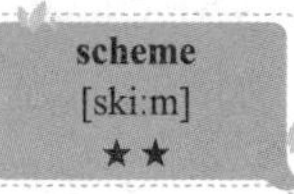

scheme
[skiːm]
★★

释义 *n.* 计划，方案；阴谋 *v.* 策划；阴谋

短语 pilot *scheme* 小规模试验计划；试点方案

例句 He's thought a new *scheme* for making money fast. 他想出了一个快速赚钱的新办法。

近义 plan *n.* 方案；计划，打算

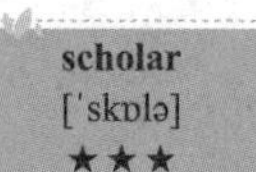

scholar
[ˈskɒlə]
★★★

释义 *n.* 学者

短语 visiting *scholar* 访问学者

例句 He was the most distinguished *scholar* in his field. 他是这一领域最为卓著的学者。

真题 These new forms were at first mainly written by *scholars* and performed by amateurs. 这些新形式最初主要由学者创作，由业余爱好者表演。（2018 翻译）

scholarship
[ˈskɒləʃɪp]
★

释义 *n.* 奖学金；学问，学识

短语 win a *scholarship* 获得奖学金

例句 She won a *scholarship* to study at Stanford. 她获得了奖学金，得以在斯坦福大学求学。

用法 apply for a scholarship 申请奖学金

释义 *v.* 责骂，训斥

例句 She *scolded* her daughter for having talked to her father like that. 她因女儿对她父亲那样讲话而训斥了她。

用法 scold(at)sb. 斥责某人

派生 scolding *n.* 责骂

释义 *adj.* 技术(性)的；工艺的；专业性的

短语 *technical* support / progress 技术支持 / 进步

例句 I missed the first 10 minutes of the show because the network was experiencing *technical* difficulties . 我错过了节目的前 10 分钟，因为网络遇到了技术问题。

派生 technically *adv.* 技术上地

释义 *n.* 技巧，技能，技术

例句 We learned some *techniques* for relieving stress. 我们学习了一些缓解压力的技巧。

真题 To find their sites, archaeologists today rely heavily on systematic survey methods and a variety of high-technology tools and *techniques*. 今天，考古学家在很大程度上依赖系统的调查方法和各种高科技工具和技术来寻找他们的遗址。(2014 阅读理解)

派生 technical *adj.* 技术的

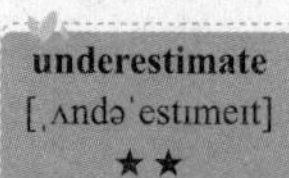

释义 *v.* / *n.* 低估，看轻

短语 *underestimate* one's opponent 低估某人的对手

例句 Psychological research shows we consistently *underestimate* our mental powers. 心理学研究表明，我们总是低估自己的心智能力。

反义 overestimate *v.* 高估

派生 underestimation *n.* 低估

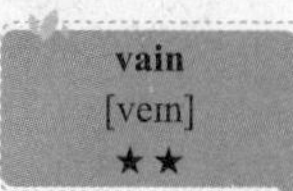

释义 *adj.* 徒劳的；自负的

短语 a *vain* attempt 徒劳的尝试

例句 To get a slim figure, Fanny has tried many ways, but in *vain*. 为了得到苗条的身材，芬妮尝试了许多方法，但都无济于事。

用法 in vain 徒然的

近义 futile *adj.* 徒劳的

释义 *n.* 授权令；正当理由；许可证 *v.* 使有必要；保证，担保

短语 arrest / search *warrant* 逮捕证 / 搜查证

例句 The police must have a search *warrant* to search a house. 警察搜查房屋必须有搜查令。

真题 The Supreme Court will now consider whether police can search the contents of a mobile phone without a *warrant* if the phone is on or around a person during an arrest. 最高法院现在将考虑警察在执行逮捕时是否能在没有授权的情况下搜查犯罪嫌疑人所携带的手机中的内容。(2015 阅读理解)

用法 a warrant for someone's arrest 对某人的逮捕令

派生 warranty *n.* 保修单

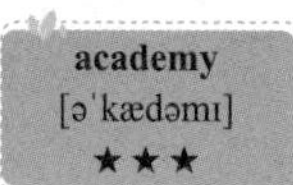

释义 *n.* 学会;研究院;专科院校

短语 *Academy* of Sciences 科学院

例句 He was educated privately at *academies* in Paris. 他曾在巴黎的私立学校接受教育。

派生 academic *adj.* 学业的,学术的

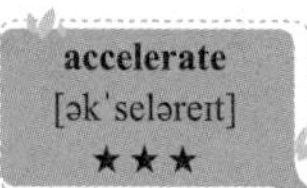

释义 *v.*(使)加速,加快;增加,增长

例句 The pace of change has *accelerated* in recent months. 近几个月来,变化的步伐加快了。

派生 acceleration *n.* 加速

真题 The use of this little-known practice has *accelerated* in recent years, as colleges continue to do their utmost to keep students in school (and paying tuition) and improve their graduation rates. 随着大学继续尽最大努力让学生留在学校(并支付学费),提高毕业率,这种鲜为人知的做法在近年来使用得越来越多。(2019 阅读理解)

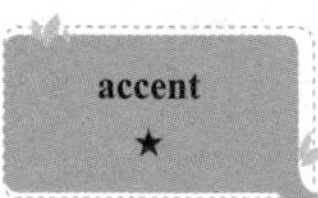

释义 *n.*[ˈæksent] 口音;重音;强调 *v.* [əkˈsent] 强调,突出

例句 He's got a strong southern *accent*. 他说话带有很重的南方口音。

The word "before" has the *accent* on the last syllable. 单词 before 的重音在最后一个音节上。

The tables were *accented* by fresh flower arrangements. 桌子上摆放了鲜花,显得格外醒目。

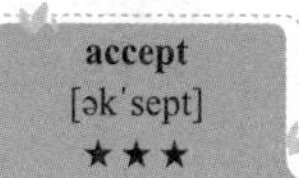

释义 *v.* 接受(建议、邀请等);同意;认可

例句 Rick *accepted* her offer of coffee. 瑞克接受了她提供的咖啡。

反义 refuse *v.* 拒绝

派生 acceptance *n.* 接受

真题 Humility requires you to recognize weakness in your own arguments and sometimes also to *accept* reasons on the opposite side. 谦逊要求你认识到自己论点中的不足,有时也要接受对方的理由。(2019 阅读理解)

释义 *v.* 阻止,禁止 *n.* 酒吧;栏杆;律师职业;块,棒

短语 a *bar* of chocolate 一块巧克力

例句 His rude comments got him *barred* from that website. 他粗鲁的评论使他被那个网站封杀了。

近义 block *v.* 阻止

释义 *v.* 终止 *n.* 停止

例句 At one o'clock the rain had *ceased*. 一点钟时,雨停了。

近义 end *v.* 结束

派生 ceaseless *adj.* 不停的

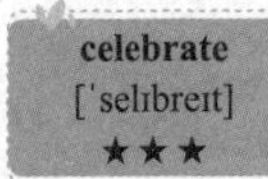
celebrate
[ˈselɪbreɪt]
★★★

释义 *v.* 庆祝,庆贺

例句 The family gathered to *celebrate* Christmas. 一家人聚在一起庆祝圣诞节。

近义 commemorate *v.* 作为……的纪念

派生 celebration *n.* 庆典

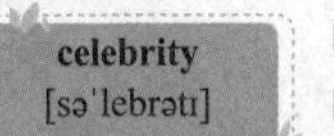
celebrity
[səˈlebrətɪ]
★★★

释义 *n.* 名人;名声,名望

短语 *celebrity* worship 偶像崇拜

例句 The *celebrity* couple have been married since July 2013, and celebrated their ninth wedding anniversary last year. 这对明星夫妇于 2013 年 7 月结婚,去年庆祝了他们的 9 周年结婚纪念日。

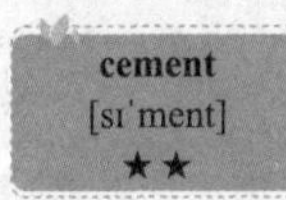
cement
[sɪˈment]
★★

释义 *v.* 胶合;巩固 *n.* 水泥;纽带

短语 a *cement* factory 水泥厂

例句 Our holiday together *cemented* our friendship. 共度假日使我们的友谊更加牢固。

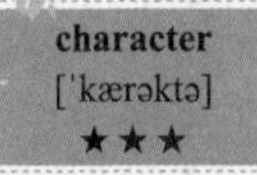
character
[ˈkærəktə]
★★★

释义 *n.* 性格,品质;特色;文字

例句 I can certify to his good *character*. 我可以证明他品德好。

Their house has a lot of *character*. 他们的房子很有特色。

派生 characteristic *n.* 特征,特点

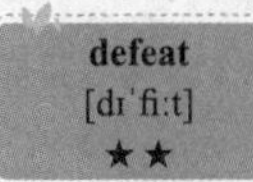
defeat
[dɪˈfiːt]
★★

释义 *v.* / *n.* 击败,战胜

例句 In the last election, they suffered a *defeat*. 在上次大选中,他们遭遇了失败。

He *defeated* the champion in three sets. 他三盘击败了冠军。

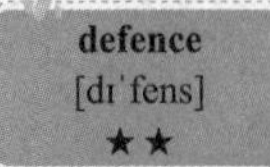
defence
[dɪˈfens]
★★

释义 *n.* (defense) 防御,防御物;辩护

例句 The immune system is our main *defence* against disease. 免疫系统是我们抵御疾病的主要防御系统。

派生 defensive *adj.* 防御的

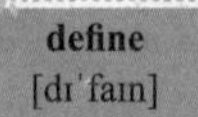
define
[dɪˈfaɪn]
★★★

释义 *v.* 给……下定义;解释;阐明

例句 The powers of a judge are *defined* by law. 法官的权限是由法律规定的。

真题 When the new staff are predominantly young men and women fresh from postgraduate study, they largely *define* the norms of academic life in that faculty and its standards. 当新的员工是刚完成研究生阶段学习的男女青年时,他们很大程度上决定了该学院学术生活的标准。(2021 翻译)

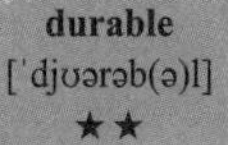
durable
[ˈdjʊərəb(ə)l]
★★

释义 *adj.* 持久的,耐久的

例句 What you need for Africa is a simple, *durable* and inexpensive vehicle. 非洲需要的是一种简单、耐用、便宜的交通工具。

派生 durability *n.* 持久性,耐用性

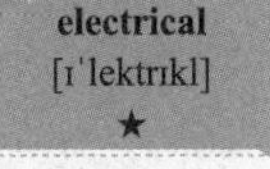
electrical
[ɪˈlektrɪkl]
★

释义 *adj.* 电的,电学的

例句 They sell all kinds of *electrical* equipment and appliances. 他们销售各种各

样的电器设备和用具。

派生 electrically *adv.* 电力地

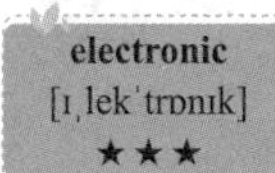

释义 *adj.* 电子的

例句 The airplane has a sophisticated *electronic* guidance system. 这架飞机有一套尖端的电子导航系统。

派生 electronically *adv.* 用电子方法，用电子装置

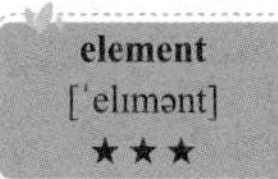

释义 *n.* 元素；要素；成分；自然环境

例句 The movie had all the *elements* of a good thriller. 这部电影具备了一部精彩的惊险片的一切要素。

近义 factor *n.* 要素 substance *n.* 物质

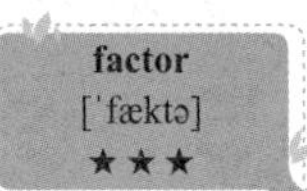

释义 *n.* 因素，要素 *v.* 把……作为因素计入；代理经营

短语 a key *factor* 关键因素

例句 Poverty is only one of the *factors* in crime. 贫穷只是犯罪的因素之一。

近义 element *n.* 要素

释义 易碎的，脆的，易损坏的；虚弱的，脆弱的

例句 The *fragile* economies of several southern African nations could be damaged. 几个南部非洲国家脆弱的经济可能会受到损害。

派生 fragility *n.* 脆弱

释义 *n.* 缺口，裂口；分歧；间隔，间隙 *v.* 裂开；使成缺口

例句 She has a small *gap* between her front teeth. 她的门牙之间有条细缝。

There is a wide *gap* between the views of the two statesmen. 关于这点，两位政治家的政见有很大分歧。

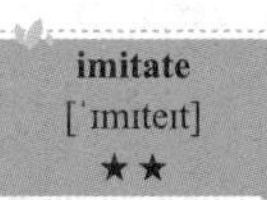

释义 *v.* 模仿，仿效；仿造，伪造

例句 The actors of the Royal Shakespeare Company *imitate* Shakespeare on and off stage. 皇家莎士比亚剧团的演员在舞台上和舞台下都模仿莎士比亚。

派生 imitation *n.* 模仿，仿效；仿制；仿造品

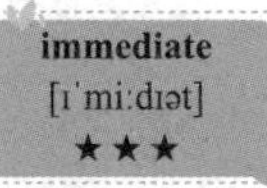

释义 *adj.* 立即的，即时的；直接的，紧迫的

例句 He announced his retirement from rugby league with *immediate* effect. 他宣布从橄榄球联盟退役，立即生效。

派生 immediately *adv.* 立即，马上

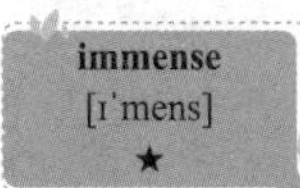

释义 *adj.* 广大的，巨大的

例句 He was a humble and brilliant man who made an *immense* contribution to the show. 他是一个谦逊而聪明的人，为这个节目做出了巨大的贡献。

用法 an immense amount of... 大量的……

派生 enormous *adj.* 巨大的

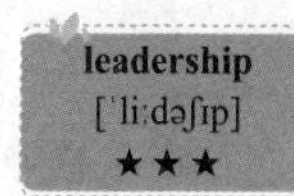

释义 *n.* 领导阶层，领导能力

短语 *leadership* skill 领导技巧

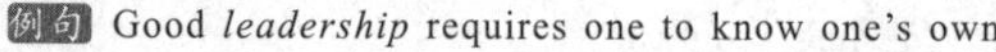

例句 Good *leadership* requires one to know one's own strengths and be able to win people's trust. 好的领导能力需要一个人知道自己的长处，能够赢得人们的信任。

用法 under the leadership of 在……领导下

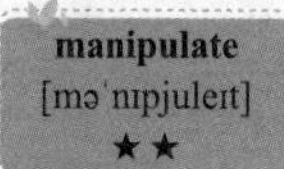

释义 *v.* 操纵；控制；操作

例句 He's accused of trying to *manipulate* the price of the stock. 他被指控试图操纵股票价格。

用法 be manipulated by sb. 被某人控制

近义 operate *v.* 操作

派生 manipulation *n.* 操纵；控制

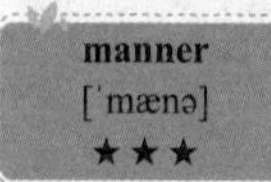

释义 *n.* 方式；举止 (*pl.*) 风度，礼貌；规矩；风俗

例句 For now, we need to interpret the law and its guidelines as accurately as we can and to act in a fair *manner*. 目前，我们需要尽可能准确地解释法律及其指导方针，并以公正的方式行事。

用法 in the manner of... 以……的方式

释义 手工做的；手动的；体力的 *n.* 手册，指南

短语 *manual* work 手工作业

例句 *Manual* accounting system is used only by small businesses. 手工会计系统只适用于小型企业。

近义 handmade *adj.* 手工制作的

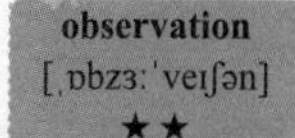

释义 *n.* 注意；观察；观察力；言论；遵守

短语 a scientific *observation* 科学观察

例句 During a separate *observation*, she saw that phones became a source of tension in the family. 在一个独立的观察中，她发现手机成了家庭关系紧张的一个来源。

Is that a criticism or just an *observation*? 那是一种批评，还是一种观察评论而已呢？

派生 observational *adj.* 观测的

释义 *n.* 激情，爱好；强烈感情

短语 *passion* fruit 百香果

例句 His *passion* for collecting ancient coins made him blind to everything else. 他对于收藏古钱币的强烈爱好使他对于别的事情都视而不见。

用法 passion for 对……的强烈爱好

近义 fondness *n.* 爱好；喜爱

释义 *adj.* 被动的，消极的 *n.* 被动形式

短语 *passive* smoking 被动吸烟

例句 She harbors a *passive* attitude and does not actively engage in life. 她态度消

极，不积极参与生活。

反义 active *adj.* 主动地

派生 passively *adv.* 被动地

释义 *n.* 收据，收条；收到

短语 official *receipt* 正式收据

例句 Goods should be supplied within 28 days after the *receipt* of your order. 货物应在收到订单后 28 天内提供。

用法 in receipt of 已收到……

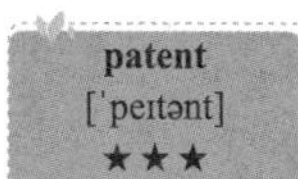

释义 *adj.* 专利的，特许的 *n.* 专利（权、品） *v.* 批准专利

短语 business-method *patents* 商业方法专利

例句 Monsanto accused Bowman of *patent* infringement and won an $84,456 damage award. 孟山都公司指控鲍曼侵犯专利权，从而得到了 84,456 美元的赔偿金。

派生 patentee *n.* 专利权所有人

释义 *adj.* 可怜的，悲惨的

例句 If the future is also *pathetic*, that is truly *pathetic*. 如果未来也很可悲，那才是真正的可悲。

近义 unfortunate *adj.* 不幸的，可怜的

派生 pathetically *adv.* 可怜地

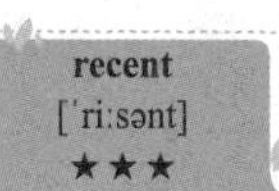

释义 *adj.* 近来的，最近的

短语 *recent* development 最近发展

例句 There have been many changes in *recent* years . 近几年发生了许多变化。

真题 A *recent* paper published on the Royal Society's open science website attempts to answer this important question. 最近发表在英国皇家学会开放的科学网站上的一篇论文试图回答这个重要的问题。（2019 翻译）

派生 recently *adv.* 最近，不久前

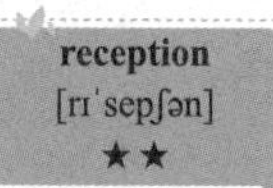

释义 *n.* 接待，招待会；接受

短语 warm / wedding *reception* 热情接待 / 婚宴

例句 The mayor presented him with a gold medal at an official city *reception*. 市长在一次正式的市招待会上给他颁发了一枚金质奖章。

派生 receptionist *n.* 接待员

释义 *n.* 范围，余地；机会；见识

短语 business *scope* 营业范围

例句 The team should see this as an opportunity to broaden their *scope*. 团队应该将此视为扩大其见识的机会。

There's still plenty of *scope* for improvement. 还有很大的改进余地。

近义 range *n.* 范围 opportunity *n.* 机会

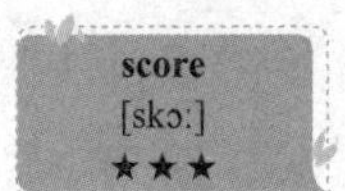

释义 *n.* 得分，分数；成绩 *v.* 得（分），记（……的）分数

短语 a high / low *score* 高分 / 低分 *score* a goal 进球

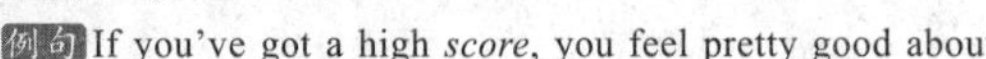

例句 If you've got a high *score*, you feel pretty good about yourself. 如果你得分很高，你对自己感觉就会很好。

Judges will *score* the performances based on their artistic and technical features. 评委将根据他们表演的艺术性和技术特点打分。

释义 *v.* / *n.* 轻蔑，藐视

例句 The idea had been popular among many Americans but drew *scorn* from critics. 这一想法曾在许多美国人中流行，但遭到了批评人士的蔑视。

近义 contempt *n.* 轻视，蔑视

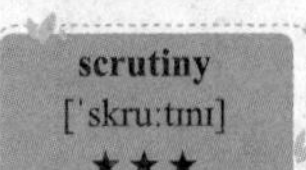

释义 *n.* 仔细检查；监视

短语 public *scrutiny* 群众监督

例句 Manuscripts will be flagged up for additional *scrutiny* by the journal's internal editors. 稿件将被标记出来，由期刊内部编辑做进一步审查。（2015 阅读理解）

近义 examination *n.* 审查

派生 scrutinize *v.* 仔细查看

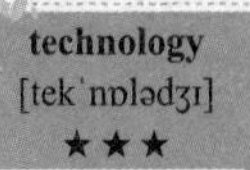

释义 *n.* 科学技术；工业技术；应用科学

短语 information *technology* 信息技术

例句 He always embraced new trends in art and *technology*. 他总是欣然接受艺术和科技的新趋势。

真题 Science and *technology* would cure all the ills of humanity, leading to lives of fulfilment and opportunity for all. 科学和技术将治愈人类的一切弊病，使所有人过上充实的生活并获得机会。（2013 阅读理解）

派生 technique *n.* 技术

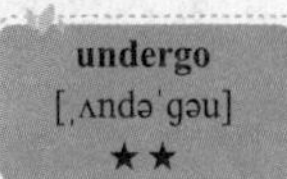

释义 *v.* 遭受，经历，承受

短语 *undergone* hardship 经历苦难

例句 Consequently, our feelings, thoughts and emotions have *undergone* a corresponding change. 因此，我们的感觉、思想和情绪也发生了相应的变化。

近义 experience *v.* 经历 sustain *v.* 承受，经受，维持

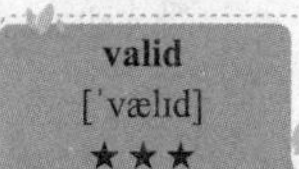

释义 *adj.* 有效的；有根据的；正当的

短语 *valid* data 有效数据

例句 The London Travel Card is a paper ticket that is *valid* on all London public transport. 伦敦旅游卡是一张纸质票，在伦敦所有公共交通工具上都有效。

反义 invalid *adj.*（法律上或官方）不承认的；无效的

派生 validate *v.* 使生效

释义 *n.* 进入;途径;使用权;取得　*v.* 存取,访问;接近,进入

例句 Fire fighters must use door breaching techniques in these situations to gain *access*. 在这种情况下,消防队员必须使用破门技术才能进入。

派生 accessibility *n.*(地方)易于进入性;易使用性

真题 Insurance companies, meanwhile, can base their premiums on AI models that more accurately *access* risk. 与此同时,保险公司可以根据能更准确地评估风险的人工智能模型来计算保费。(2021 阅读理解)

释义 *n.* 事故,意外;偶然

短语 traffic *accident* 交通事故

例句 She was injured in a car *accident*. 她在车祸中受了伤。

Their meeting was an *accident*. 他们的相遇是偶然的。

派生 accidental　*adj.* 意外的

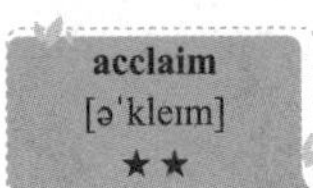

释义 *n.* 欢呼;喝彩;称赞　*v.* 称赞;欢呼

例句 Despite the critical *acclaim*, the novel did not sell well. 虽然这部小说在评论界赢得一片叫好之声,但并不畅销。

The critics have *acclaimed* her performance. 评论家们称赞她的表演。

用法 be highly acclaimed 受到高度赞扬

近义 praise　*v.* 称赞

释义 *v.* 容纳;为……提供住处;适应

例句 The hotel can only *accommodate* about 100 people. 这家旅馆只能容纳大约100人。

New facilities are being added to *accommodate* the special needs of elderly residents. 政府正在增设新的设施,以满足长者的特殊需要。

用法 accommodate oneself to 适应

近义 adapt　*v.* 适应

派生 accommodation　*n.* 住处

释义 *adv.* 几乎不;仅仅;勉强

例句 Mary had *barely* enough money to pay the rent. 玛丽的钱勉强够付房租。

近义 hardly　*adv.* 几乎不

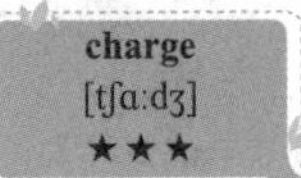

释义 *v.* 收费;控告;充电　*n.* 费用;管理;控告,指控

例句 She's been *charged* with murder. 她被控谋杀。

Customers will face a monthly *charge* of £5. 顾客将面临每月 5 英镑的费用。

用法 be innocent of the charge 无罪

真题 "Before, they might not insure the ones who felt like a high risk or charge them too much," says

Domingos. 多明戈斯说："以前，他们可能不会为那些他们觉得风险很高的人投保，或者向他们收取过高的费用。"（2021 阅读理解）

charity
[ˈtʃærətɪ]
★

释义 *n.* 慈善（团体），仁慈，施舍

例句 They made a generous donation to *charity*. 他们向慈善机构慷慨捐款。

用法 out of charity 出于仁慈

派生 charitable *adj.* 慈善的

charter
[ˈtʃɑːtə]
★★

释义 *n.* 宪章；许可证；租赁 *v.* 租用；特许成立

短语 the United Nations *Charter* 联合国宪章

例句 He has *chartered* a bus and helped the elderly get to their polling places. 他包租了一辆公共汽车，帮助老年人前往投票站点。

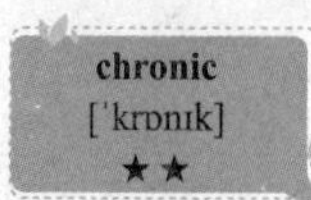

chronic
[ˈkrɒnɪk]
★★

释义 *adj.*（疾病）慢性的，长期的

例句 John suffered from a *chronic* disease. 约翰患有一种慢性病。

派生 chronically *adv.* 慢性地

反义 acute *adj.* 急性的

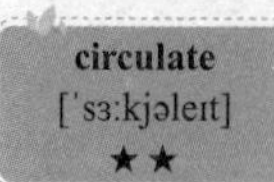

circulate
[ˈsɜːkjəleɪt]
★★

释义 *v.* 环流，循环；传播

例句 Rumors *circulated* rapidly. 谣言迅速散布开来。

用法 circulate sth. (to sb.) 传递；传阅

派生 circulation *n.* 发行量

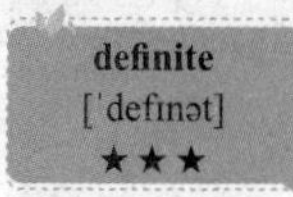

definite
[ˈdefɪnət]
★★★

释义 *adj.* 清晰的；确定的；肯定的

例句 She couldn't give a *definite* answer to the questions. 她无法对这些问题给予明确的回答。

派生 definitely *adv.* 肯定地

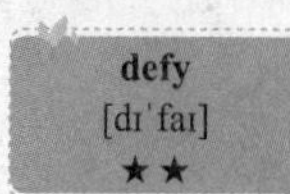

defy
[dɪˈfaɪ]
★★

释义 *v.* 对抗；违抗；反抗

例句 If you *defy* the law, you may find yourself in prison. 如果你不服从法律，就可能会坐牢。

用法 defy sb. to do sth. 激将某人做某事

degree
[dɪˈgriː]
★★★

释义 *n.* 程度；度数；学位；等级

例句 The temperature rose to thirty *degrees* centigrade. 温度上升到三十摄氏度。
By *degrees* the Irish created a classical tradition in their own language. 渐渐地，爱尔兰人用他们自己的语言创造了一种古典传统。

用法 by degrees 逐渐地；渐渐地

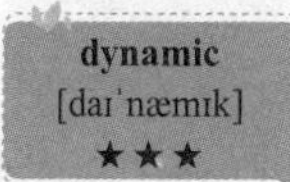

dynamic
[daɪˈnæmɪk]
★★★

释义 *adj.* 动力的，电动的；有生气的；动态的

短语 *dynamic* analysis / balance 动态分析 / 动态平衡

例句 She's young and *dynamic* and will be a great addition to the team. 她年轻而充满活力，将成为团队的一个很好的补充。

elementary [ˌelɪˈmentrɪ] ★

释义 *adj.* 初步的；基本的

短语 *elementary* education 基础教育

例句 Olivia has an *elementary* knowledge of chemistry. 奥利维亚有基本的化学知识。

近义 primary *n.* 初级的

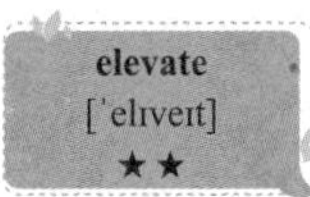

elevate [ˈelɪveɪt] ★★

释义 *v.* 提升；抬起；提高；提拔

例句 Emotional stress can *elevate* blood pressure. 情绪压力可能会导致血压升高。

派生 elevation *n.* 高度，海拔

eligible [ˈelɪdʒəbl] ★★

释义 *adj.* 符合条件的；合格的

例句 Only people over 18 are *eligible* to vote. 只有 18 岁以上的人才有资格投票。

真题 Passengers who pass a background check are *eligible* to use expedited screening lanes. 通过背景调查的乘客可以使用快速安检通道。（2017 阅读理解）

extent [ɪkˈstent] ★★

释义 *n.* 广度；宽度；长度；程度，限度

例句 The newspaper did not mention the *extent* of the damage caused by the fire. 报纸没有提到火灾造成的损失程度。

用法 to a great extent 在很大程度上

fade [feɪd] ★★

释义 *v.* 逐渐消失；（使）褪色；衰退 *n.* 淡入（出）

例句 In the United States, new cases seemed to *fade* as warmer weather arrived. 在美国，随着天气变暖，新增病例似乎有所减少。

用法 fade away 逐渐消失

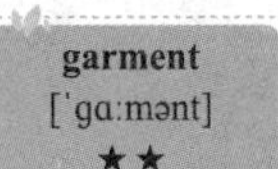

garment [ˈɡɑːmənt] ★★

释义 *n.*（一件）衣服

短语 *garment* industry 服装业

例句 This shop sells *garments* of all kinds. 这个商店出售各种衣服。

harmony [ˈhɑːmənɪ] ★★

释义 *n.* 和睦，融洽，和谐

例句 The couple lives in perfect *harmony*. 这对夫妇生活得非常和谐。

派生 harmonise（harmonize）*v.* 融洽，和睦

immigrant [ˈɪmɪɡrənt] ★★★

释义 *adj.*（从国外）移来的，移民的 *n.* 移民，侨民

短语 *immigrant* visa 移民签证

例句 A century ago, the *immigrants* from across the Atlantic included settlers and sojourners. 一个世纪前，横跨大西洋来到美国的移民包括定居者和旅居者。

派生 immigration *n.* 移民

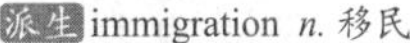

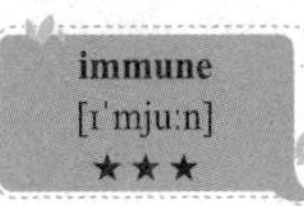

immune [ɪˈmjuːn] ★★★

释义 *adj.* 免疫的，有免疫力的；不受影响的；豁免的

短语 *immune* system 免疫系统

例句 Football is not *immune* to economic recession. 足球不可能不受到经济衰退的影响。

真题 For women, the association may be attributable to changes in *immunity* that resulted from excess abdominal fat; in men, the *immune* system did not appear to be involved . 对于女性，这种关联可能归因于腹部脂肪过多引起的免疫力变化；对于男性来说，（这种关联）似乎并不涉及免疫系统。（2021 完形填空）

释义 *n.*[ˈimpækt] 冲击；影响 *v.* [imˈpækt] 有影响

例句 The better you understand the cultural context, the more control you can have over your *impact*. 你越了解文化背景，你对自己的影响力就越有控制。

Her father's death *impacted* greatly on her childhood years. 父亲去世对她的童年造成巨大影响。

释义 *adj.* 领导的，主要的；首位的

例句 He played a *leading* part in the negotiations. 他在谈判中起到了至关重要的作用。

真题 The gap between the medieval and modern periods had been bridged, *leading* to new and unexplored intellectual territories. 中世纪和现代之间的差距被弥合，带来了新的、未被开发的知识领域。（2020 阅读理解）

近义 major *adj.* 主要的

派生 misleading *adj.* 误导的

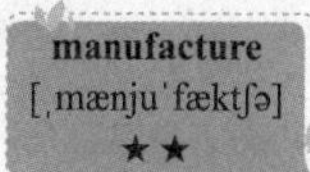

释义 *v.* 制造，加工 *n.* 制造，制造业；产品

短语 steel *manufacture* 钢铁工业

例句 On a global scale, fertilizer *manufacturing* consumes about 3%—5% of the world's annual natural gas supply. 在全球范围内，化肥生产消耗了全球每年 3%~5% 的天然气供应。

派生 manufacturer *n.* 生产商，制造商

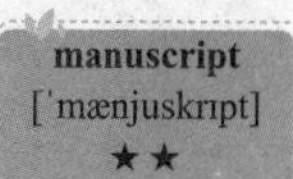

释义 *n.* 手稿，原稿

短语 original *manuscript* 原稿

真题 *Manuscript* will be flagged up for additional scrutiny by the journal's internal editors, or by its existing Board of Reviewing Editors or by outside peer. 稿件将由期刊的内部编辑、其现有的审稿编辑委员会或外部同行做进一步审查。（2015 阅读理解）

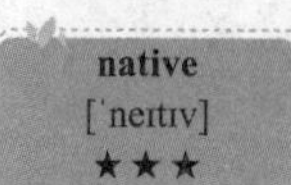

释义 *adj.* 本地的；与生俱来的 *n.* 当地人，本地人

例句 Tobacco is n*ative* to America. 烟草原产于美洲。

They used force to banish the n*atives* from the more fertile land. 他们用武力将土著人驱逐出更加肥沃的土地。

近义 local *adj.* 本地的

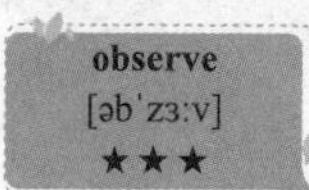

释义 *v.* 观察；注意到；遵守；庆祝

短语 *observe* a rule 遵守规则

例句 Weighing every other week allows me to *observe* and account for any significant weight changes. 每隔一周称一次体重可以让我观察和找出体重显著变化的原因。

Will the rebels *observe* the ceasefire? 叛乱者会遵守停火协议吗？

用法 observe sb. / sth. doing sth. 观察……做某事

obsession
[əbˈseʃən]
★

【释义】*n.* 痴迷，困扰

【短语】chocolate *obsession* 对巧克力的痴迷

【例句】An *obsession* with home ownership is one of the causes of the financial crisis, he says. 他说，对自有住房的痴迷是财务危机的原因之一。

【派生】obsessive *adj.* 着迷的

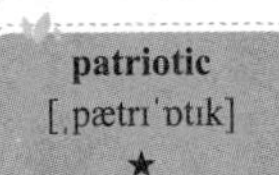

【释义】*adj.* 爱国的

【短语】*patriotic* fervour 爱国热情

【例句】The Duanwu Festival, also called the Dragon Boat Festival, is to commemorate the *patriotic* poet Qu Yuan. 端午节，又叫龙舟节，是为了纪念爱国诗人屈原。

【派生】patriotically *adv.* 爱国地

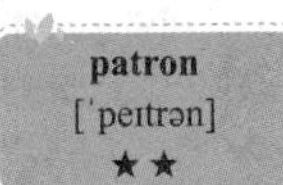

【释义】*n.* 赞助人；资助人；老顾客，老主顾

【短语】*patron* saint 守护神

【例句】She is an active *patron* of several charities and organisations. 她是几个慈善机构和组织的积极赞助人。

【派生】patronal *adj.* 庇佑的；赞助的

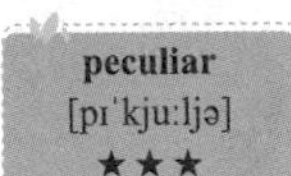

【释义】*adj.* 古怪的，异常的；特殊的，特有的

【例句】It turns out that the *peculiar* way of conducting the experiments may have led to misleading interpretations of what happened. 事实证明，这种特殊的实验方式可能导致了人们对所发生的事情的误导性解读。

【派生】peculiarly *adv.* 特别；尤其

【真题】Each of these manifestations of growth carried its own *peculiar* problems in its wake. 每一种增长的表现都伴随着其特有的问题。（2021 翻译）

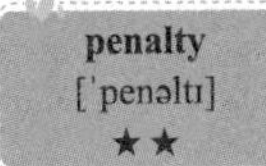

【释义】*n.* 处罚，惩罚；罚金；损失

【短语】*penalty* kick 罚点球

【例句】If you knock the ball with your hand in football, you will suffer a *penalty*. 如果在踢足球时你用手碰到球，你将受到处罚。

【用法】pay the penalty 受惩罚

【派生】penalize *v.* 惩罚，处罚

【释义】*n.* 食谱；诀窍

【短语】*recipe* book 食谱书

【例句】Although this *recipe* looks long, it is actually very quick to prepare. 尽管这个菜谱看上去很长，但做起来很快。

A *recipe* for success is not dreaming about it but doing it. 成功的诀窍不是空想而是实干。

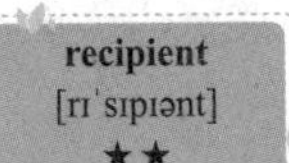

【释义】*adj.* 接受的 *n.* 接受者

【短语】*recipients* of awards 领奖者

【例句】Rosenberg, the *recipient* of a Pulitzer Prize, offers a host of examples of the social cure in action. 获得普利策奖的罗森伯格提供了许多实际的社会治疗的例子。

reckless
[ˈreklɪs]
★

释义 *adj.* 鲁莽的；不计后果的；无所顾忌的

短语 *reckless* driving 鲁莽驾驶

例句 Once again, Pelosi has shown herself to be *reckless* in foreign affairs. 佩洛西再一次证明了自己在外交事务上的不计后果。

secondary
[ˈsekəndərɪ]
★★

释义 *adj.* 次要的；中级的；第二的

短语 *secondary* school 中等学校；中学 *secondary* market 二级市场

例句 There are some *secondary* issues which must be taken into account as well. 还有一些次要问题也必须考虑进去。

近义 unimportant *adj.* 不重要的

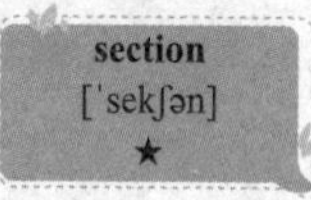

释义 *n.* 段，部分；部门 *v.* 切开，切断

例句 New shelves have been placed in the children's *section*. 儿童专区新设了书架。

A moveable wall is used to *section* off part of the terminal. 用可移动的墙将航站楼的一部分隔开。

用法 a section of sth. 某物的一部分

派生 sectional *adj.* 部分的

释义 *n.* 部门，部分；防御地段，防区；扇形

短语 private / public *sector* 私有 / 国有部门

例句 Salaries in the public *sector* are expected to fall by 15% this year. 今年公共部门的工资预计将下降15%。

Berlin was divided into four *sectors* after the war. 战后，柏林被分成了4个区。

近义 division *n.* 部门

释义 *adj.* 安全的；稳定的；牢固的 *v.* 获得；使安全

例句 Religious associations began, for example, in the desire to *secure* the favor of overruling powers and to ward off evil influences. 比如，宗教团体是为了得到神灵的庇佑、趋避邪魔才产生的。

用法 secure from / secure against 保护……使免于

派生 security *n.* 保障，保证；安全

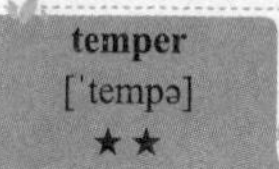

释义 *n.* 脾气 *v.* 调和，使缓和

短语 short *temper* 急性子

例句 I found it hard to keep my *temper* with so many things going wrong. 这么多的事情弄得一团糟，我很难不发脾气。

用法 keep / lose one's temper 忍住性子 / 发脾气

释义 *v.* 实现（计划等）；达到（目的）；完成（任务）

例句 There are several different ways to *accomplish* the same task. 完成同一任务有几种不同的方法。

派生 accomplishment *n.* 成就

真题 We're also giving our customers better channels versus picking up the phone ... to *accomplish* something beyond human scale. 我们也为我们的客户提供了比打电话更好的渠道……来完成一些超出人类能力范围的事情。(2021 阅读理解)

释义 *adj.* 贵重的，有价值的 *n.* (*pl.*) 贵重物品，财宝

短语 *valuable* experience / information 宝贵的经验 / 重要信息

例句 Students can gain *valuable* experience by working on the campus radio or magazine. 学生们通过在校园广播台或校刊工作能够获得宝贵的经验。

近义 precious *adj.* 宝贵的

反义 valueless *adj.* 无价值的

真题 According to Ferraro, the Conditional Cash Transfers program in Indonesia is most *valuable* in that it can protect the environment. 费拉罗认为，印尼的有条件现金转移支付项目最有价值的地方在于它可以保护环境。(2021 阅读理解)

释义 *v.* 陪伴；伴随；伴奏

例句 She will *accompany* me to the store. 她将陪我去商店。

The singer was *accompanied* on the piano by her sister. 由女歌手的姐姐为她钢琴伴奏。

近义 companion *v.* 陪伴

派生 accompanied *adj.* 伴随的；相伴的

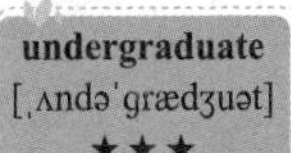

释义 *n.* 本科生 *adj.* 大学本科生的

短语 an *undergraduate* course / student 大学本科课程 / 学生

例句 This section of the book should be required reading for all *undergraduate* students of the drama. 这本书的这一部分应该是所有戏剧专业本科生的必读部分。

释义 *n.* 协议；一致 *v.* 授予；一致；符合

例句 On 1st June, the two leaders signed a peace *accord*. 6 月 1 日，两位领导人签署了一项和平协议。

The competitors should all be *accorded* equal respect. 所有的参赛者都应该得到同等的尊重。

派生 accordance *n.* 一致；和谐；给予

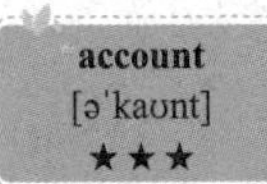

释义 *n.* 账户；报道；描述 *v.* 认为；对……做出解释；占(比例)

例句 We opened new *accounts* at a bank last week. 上周我们在一家银行开了新账户。

She was *accounted* a genius by all who knew her work. 所有知道她作品的人都认为她是个天才。

According to the report, females *account* for 46 percent of Internet users. 该报告称女性网民占网民总数的 46%。

用法 account for 占(比例)；对……负有责任

派生 accountant *n.* 会计师；会计

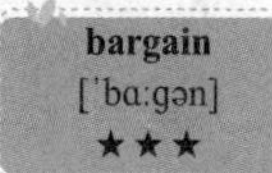

释义 *v.* 讨价还价 *n.* 便宜货

例句 They *bargained* with the shopkeeper for a long time before settling on a price. 他们和店主谈了很长时间才定下价格。

At that price the car is a *bargain*. 按那个价格，这辆汽车很便宜。

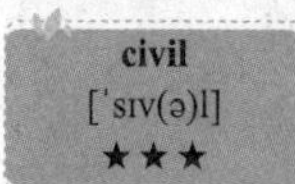

释义 *adj.* 公民的；民用的；文明的

短语 *civil* war 内战 *civil* society 公民社会

例句 There are other forms of *civil* disorder — most notably, football hooliganism. 还有其他形式的民众骚乱，最出名的是足球流氓行为。

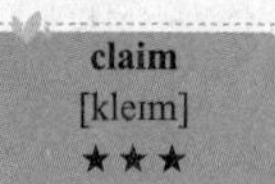

释义 *v.* 要求；声称；索赔 *n.* 要求；断言；索赔

例句 It was *claimed* that some doctors were working 80 hours a week. 据说有些医生每周工作80小时。

用法 claim to do sth. 声称做某事

反义 disclaim *v.* 放弃（财产、头衔等的权利）

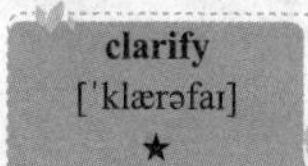

释义 *v.* 澄清；阐明；净化

例句 Could you *clarify* the first point please? 请你把第一点再阐释一下，好吗？

派生 clarity *n.* 清晰，明晰

释义 *v.* / *n.* 碰撞冲突

例句 This shirt *clashes* with your trousers. 这件衬衣和你的裤子不配。

There is a *clash* between two classes at 2 p.m. on Thursday. 星期四下午两点有两堂课是冲突的。

释义 *n.* 杰作；古典作品 *adj.* 经典的；有代表性的

短语 a *classic* novel / study / goal 最佳小说／论文／进球

例句 I had all the *classic* symptoms of flu. 我有流行性感冒的所有典型症状。

释义 *v.*/ *n.* 耽搁，延迟

例句 We *delayed* the celebration for a week. 我们把庆祝活动推迟了一个星期。

近义 postpone *v.* 推迟，延缓

释义 *v.* 删除

例句 He *deleted* the file by accident. 他不小心删除了文件。

派生 deletion *n.* 删除

释义 *adj.* 故意的，蓄意的；深思熟虑的 *v.* 慎重考虑

例句 Ryan made a *deliberate* decision to admit his problem publicly. 瑞安经过深思熟虑，决定公开承认自己的问题。

近义 thoughtful *v.* 深思熟虑的；体贴的

派生 deliberately *adv.* 故意地

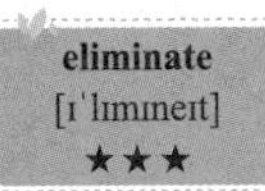

释义 v. 淘汰；把……排除在外；消除

例句 Half of the candidates were *eliminated* after the first round of interviews. 一半的候选人在第一轮面试后就被淘汰了。

真题 Overhead may be high and circulation lower, but rushing to *eliminate* its print edition would be a mistake, says BuzzFeed CEO Jonah Peretti. 美国数学媒体 BuzzFeed 的首席执行官乔纳·佩雷蒂表示，运营费用可能很高，发行量也较低，但急于取消印刷版将是一个错误。（2016 阅读理解）

释义 n. 精英；中坚分子 adj. 精锐的

短语 *elite* education 精英教育

例句 Only a small *elite* among mountaineers can climb these routes. 登山运动员中只有一小部分精英能爬这些路线。

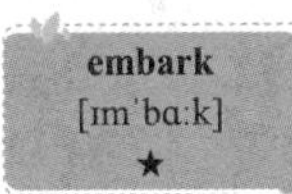

释义 v.（使）上船（或飞机，汽车等）；着手，从事

例句 Many people *embark* for Europe at New York harbor. 许多人从纽约港乘船去欧洲。

The government *embarked* on a programme of radical economic reform. 政府开始实施一项彻底的经济改革计划。

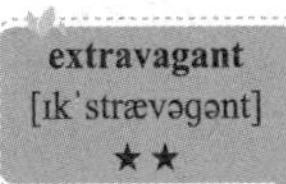

释义 adj. 奢侈的；过分的；放肆的

例句 Fantasies of great wealth often involve visions of fancy cars and *extravagant* homes. 对巨额财富的幻想通常包括豪车和豪华住宅。

近义 luxurious adj. 奢侈的

释义 n. 失败，不及格；失败者；故障，失灵

例句 He ascribed his *failure* to bad luck. 他把失败归咎于运气不好。

反义 success n. 成功

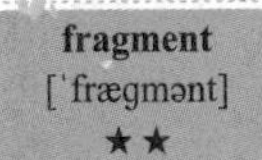

释义 n. 碎片，小部分，片断

例句 They have found several *fragments* of a Roman vase in the area. 他们在这一地区发现了一只罗马瓷瓶的碎片。

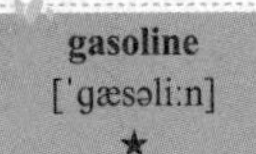

释义 n. 汽油

短语 leaded / unleaded *gasoline* 含铅 / 无铅汽油

例句 This car runs 5 miles on a gallon of *gasoline*. 这部汽车一加仑汽油可以行驶五英里。

释义 n.(pl.) 工具，器具 v. 贯彻，实现

例句 We will *implement* a system for supervising land use. 我们将落实土地使用监督制度。

Shopkeepers are not supposed to sell knives and other sharp *implements* to children. 店主不应该向儿童出售小刀及其他锋利的器具。

派生 implementation n. 实施，执行

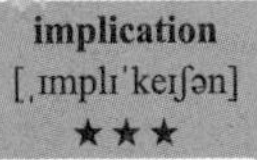

释义 n. 含意，暗示，暗指；牵连；可能的影响（或作用）

例句 It is hard, the state argues, for judges to assess the *implications* of new and rapidly changing technologies. 该州认为，法官很难评估日新月异的技术带来的影响。

近义 hint *n.* 暗示；提示

派生 implicated *adj.* 有牵连的

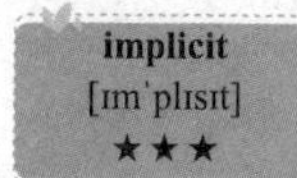
implicit [ɪmˈplɪsɪt] ★★★

释义 *adj.* 含蓄的；固有的；无疑问的；绝对的

例句 This is seen as an *implicit* warning not to continue with military action. 这被视为一个停止军事行动的含蓄警告。

反义 explicit *adj.* 直言的；明确的

派生 implication *n.* 含意；暗指

league [liːg] ★

释义 *n.* 同盟，联盟；联合会，社团；里格（长度单位） *v.*（使）结盟，团结

短语 the football *league* 足球联赛

例句 He won the *league* championship in seven of his last eight full seasons as a professional. 在他职业生涯的最后 8 个完整赛季中，他有 7 个赛季获得了联赛冠军。

近义 alliance *n.* 联盟；结盟

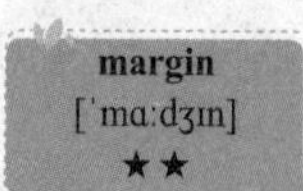
margin [ˈmɑːdʒɪn] ★★

释义 *n.* 页边空白；边缘；盈余，利润；余地；幅度 *v.* 给……镶边，加旁注于

例句 These islands are on the *margins* of human habitation. 这些岛屿位于人类聚居地的边缘。

派生 marginal *adj.* 小的；边际的

真题 Scientific publishers routinely report profit *margins* approaching 40% on their operations at a time when the rest of the publishing industry is in an existential crisis. 在其他出版商陷入生存危机之际，科技出版商的利润率通常接近 40%。（2020 阅读理解）

marine [məˈriːn] ★★

释义 *adj.* 海的；船舶的，航海的 *n.* 海军陆战队士兵

例句 The leopard seal is one of the Antarctic fiercest *marine* predators. 豹纹海豹是南极最凶猛的海洋捕食者之一。

近义 oceanic *adj.* 海洋的

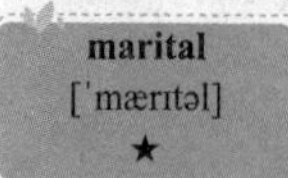
marital [ˈmærɪtəl] ★

释义 *adj.* 婚姻的，夫妻之间的

短语 *marital* breakdown 婚姻破裂

例句 Neither of them ever forgot their *marital* vows, no matter how hard things sometimes got. 无论婚姻有多艰难，他们都没有忘记自己的婚姻誓言。

派生 marriage *n.* 婚姻

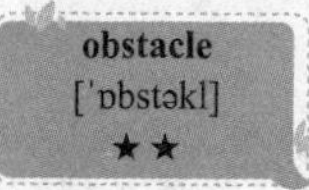
obstacle [ˈɒbstəkl] ★★

释义 *n.* 障碍（物），妨碍

短语 overcome the *obstacles* 克服障碍

例句 The biggest *obstacle* to energy transition is that the present energy system is too expensive to replace. 能源转型的最大障碍是目前的能源体系因过于昂贵而无法替代。

近义 obstruction *n.* 阻碍

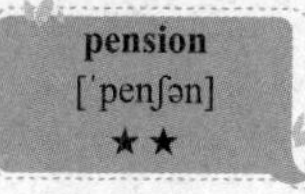
pension [ˈpenʃən] ★★

释义 *n.* 养老金，抚恤金 *v.* 给……发养老金或抚恤金

短语 *pension* insurance 养老保险

例句 The author believes the most effective method to solve the *pension* crisis is to allow people to work longer. 作者认为解决养老金危机最有效的方法是允许人们工作更长时间。

派生 pensionable *adj.* 有享受养老金资格的

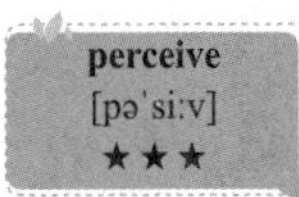

释义 *v.* 察觉，感知；理解，领悟

例句 A key task is to get pupils to *perceive* for themselves the relationship between success and effort. 一个关键的任务是让学生自己认识到成功和努力之间的关系。

近义 realize *v.* 了解，认识到

用法 be perceived by sb. 被某人注意到

派生 perception *n.* 洞察力

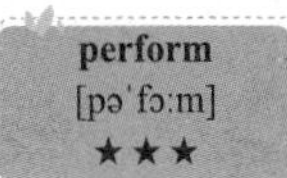

释义 *v.* 履行；表演；完成（事业）

短语 *perform* an operation 动手术

例句 Artists of the National Ballet *perform Emergence*, a contemporary work by Crystal Pite, in Moscow Monday night. 周一晚上，国家芭蕾舞团的艺术家们在莫斯科表演了克丽丝特·派特的当代作品《涌现》。

派生 performance *n.* 表演

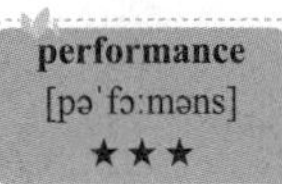

释义 *n.* 履行；表演，演出；性能；成绩

例句 A new study shows that all students including high achievers see a decline in *performance* when they browse the Internet during class for non-academic purposes. 一项新的研究表明，所有的学生，包括成绩好的学生，当他们在课堂上浏览非学业目标的互联网时，学习表现会下降。

真题 The *Wall Street Journal* finds that "a substantial part" of executive pay is now tied to *performance*. 《华尔街日报》发现，高管薪酬的"很大一部分"现在与业绩挂钩。（2019 阅读理解）

释义 *v.* (recognise) 认出；承认；认可

例句 Everybody *recognized* the seriousness of the situation. 谁都看出了局势的严重性。

派生 recognition *n.* 认出，辨认

真题 Now we can understand each other's positions and *recognize* our shared values, since we both care about needy workers. 现在我们可以理解彼此的立场，认识到我们共同的价值观，因为我们都关心需要帮助的员工。（2019 阅读理解）

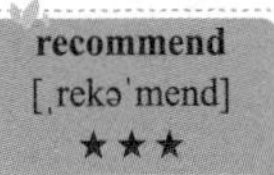

释义 *v.* 推荐，介绍；劝告，建议

短语 *recommend* a product 推荐产品

例句 A panel appointed by the governor will oversee planning and *recommend* prudent investments. 由央行行长任命的一个小组将监督计划，并建议谨慎投资。

用法 recommend for 推荐

派生 recommendation *n.* 提议；推荐

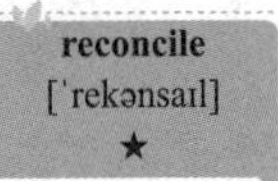

释义 *v.* 使和好，调解，使调和；使一致

例句 They were finally *reconciled* with each other, after not speaking for nearly five years. 他们差不多有 5 年的时间连话都不说，但最后终于重归于好。

用法 reconcile with 与……和解

派生 reconciler 调解人

释义 *n.* 安全(感),防御(物);保证(人),(*pl.*) 证券

短语 public *security* 公共安全

例句 Businesses should enhance their level of accounting *security*. 企业应提高会计安全水平。

真题 It is not yet clear how much more effective airline *security* has become — but the lines are obvious. 目前还不清楚航空公司的安全措施提高了多少,但排队是显而易见的。(2017 阅读理解)

释义 *n.* 部分,片段 *v.* 划分

例句 Lines divided the area into *segments*. 这几条线把这个区域分割成了几个部分。

Market researchers have *segmented* the population into different age groups. 市场研究人员把人口分成不同的年龄组。

近义 section *n.* 段,部分;部门

派生 segmental *adj.* 部分的

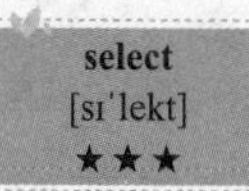

释义 *v.* 选择,挑选 *adj.* 精选的,选择的

例句 She was *selected* as the parliamentary candidate for Bath. 她被选为巴斯选区的议员候选人。

近义 choose *v.* 选择,挑选

派生 selection *n.* 选择,挑选

真题 In December of 1869, Congress appointed a commission to *select* a site and prepare plans and cost estimates for a new State Department Building. 1869 年 12 月,国会任命一个委员会为新国务院大楼选址、准备计划和成本估算。(2018 阅读理解)

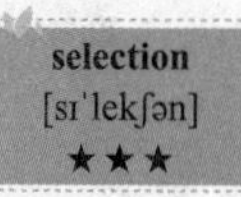

释义 *n.* 选择,挑选;选集

短语 *selection* criteria 选择标准

例句 The showroom has a wide *selection* of home products. 展厅里有各式各样的家居产品可供选择。

真题 Or the young man's parents may make the choice of a spouse, giving the child little to say in the *selection*. 或者,年轻人的父母可能会帮其选择配偶,而孩子在选择时几乎没有发言权。(2016 完形填空)

近义 option *n.* 选择

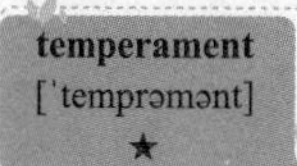

释义 *n.* 气质,性格,性情;资质

短语 artistic *temperament* 艺术气质

例句 You could hardly expect two people of such opposed *temperament* to get on well together. 你很难指望这样两个性格相反的人会和睦相处。

近义 character *n.* 性格

释义 *adj.* 暂时的,临时的

短语 *temporary* work 临时工作

例句 *Temporary* traffic controls are in operation on New Road. 新路正在实施临

时交通管制。

反义 permanent *adj.* 永久的；长期的

派生 temporarily *adv.* 暂时地；临时地

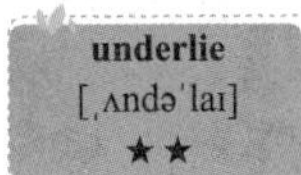

释义 *v.* 位于……之下，成为……的基础

短语 *underlie* one's anger 某人生气的原因

例句 I believe that the most important forces behind the massive merger wave are the same that *underlie* the globalization process. 我相信，大规模并购浪潮背后最重要的力量，正是支撑全球化进程的力量。

派生 underlying *adj.* 潜在的

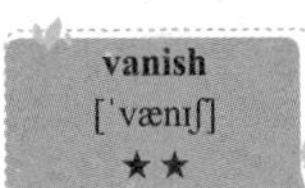

释义 *v.* 突然不见；消失

短语 *vanish* away 消失

例句 Some huge American industries, such as consumer electronics, had shrunk or *vanished* in the face of foreign competition. 美国的一些大型工业，如消费类电子产品，在外国企业的竞争面前已经萎缩或消失。

近义 disappear *v.* 消失

反义 appear *v.* 出现

释义 *n.* 福利；幸福；福利事业

短语 social / public *welfare* 社会 / 公共福利

例句 The *welfare* pension of the aging population becomes a heavy burden for governments at all levels. 老龄人口福利养老金成为各级政府的沉重负担。

近义 benefit *n.* 福利，益处

真题 The principle of British *welfare* is no longer that you can insure yourself against the risk of unemployment and receive unconditional payments if the disaster happens. 英国福利的原则不再允许你为自己的失业风险投保，并在灾难发生时获得无条件的赔偿。（2014 阅读理解）

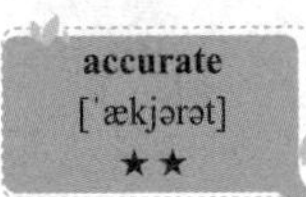

释义 *v.* 积聚；积攒；逐渐增加

短语 the *accumulation* of wealth 财富的积累

例句 During a successful business career, she *accumulated* a great amount of wealth. 在成功的商业生涯中，她积累了大量的财富。

派生 accumulation *n.* 积累，堆积

accurate
[ˈækjərət]
★★

释义 *adj.* 精确的；准确的

例句 Her novel is an *accurate* reflection of life in Spain. 她的小说是西班牙生活的真实写照。

近义 exact *adj.* 精确的

派生 accuracy *n.* 精确(性);准确度

释义 *n.* 桶;一桶;枪管 *v.* 飞驰

例句 They drank a whole *barrel* of beer. 他们喝了整整一桶啤酒。

The truck went *barreling* down Main Street. 卡车沿着主街疾驰。

accuse
[ə'kjuːz]
★★

释义 *v.* 指控;控告

例句 Are you *accusing* me of lying? 你是在指责我撒谎吗?

派生 accusation *n.* 控告,指责

真题 Of course, many discussions are not so successful. Still, we need to be careful not to *accuse* opponents of bad arguments too quickly. 当然,许多讨论并不那么成功。不过,我们需要小心不要太快地指责对手的论点不好。(2019 阅读理解)

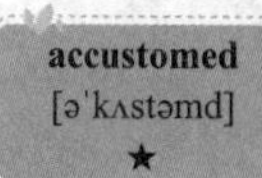

释义 *adj.* 习惯的;一贯的

例句 She is *accustomed* to walking after meals. 她习惯饭后散步。

用法 be accustomed to 习惯于

派生 accustomedly *adv.* 习惯地

释义 *v.* (civilise) 教化;使文明;使开化

例句 Lydia has a *civilizing* effect on her younger brother. 莉迪娅影响了她弟弟,使他变得文明起来。

派生 civilized *adj.* 文明的

释义 *adj.* 经典的,古典的;传统的

短语 *classical* music / literature 古典音乐 / 文学

例句 She listens to *classical* music for relaxation. 她听古典音乐来放松。

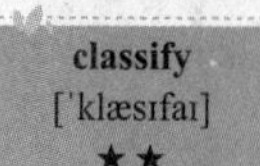

释义 *v.* 分类,分等(级)

例句 The movie is *classified* as a comedy. 这部电影被归类为喜剧。

真题 The US Supreme Court frowns on sex-based *classifications*. 美国最高法院反对基于性别的分类。(2020 阅读理解)

派生 classification *n.* 分类

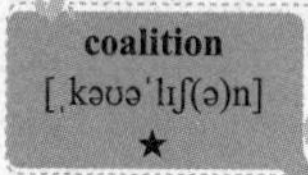

释义 *n.* 联合体;联盟

例句 In 1805, Austria, Russia, and Sweden joined Britain in a *coalition* against France and Spain. 1805 年,奥地利、俄国和瑞典同英国组成了反对法国和西班牙的联盟。

近义 alliance *n.* 联盟 union *n.* 联盟,联合

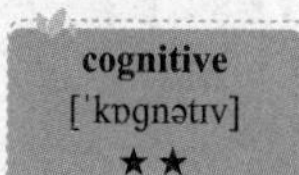

释义 *adj.* 认知的,认识能力的

短语 *cognitive* function 认知功能

例句 *Cognitive* development means how children think, explore and figure things out. 认知发展意思是儿童如何思考、探索和理解事物。

派生 cognition *n.* 认知

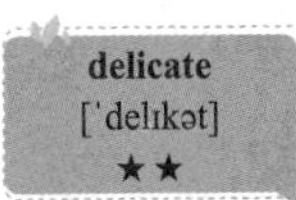

释义 *adj.* 精细的；微妙的；脆弱的；娇嫩的

例句 The pay negotiations have reached a *delicate* point. 工资谈判已经到了微妙的关头。

派生 delicacy *n.* 细致

释义 *n.* 快乐，高兴 *v.*（使）高兴，（使）欣喜

例句 They grinned with *delight* when they heard our news. 他们得知我们的消息时高兴得直咧着嘴笑。

派生 delightful *adj.* 令人愉快的

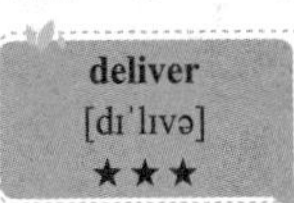

释义 *v.* 交付；递送；发表；分娩；兑现

例句 The goods will be *delivered* at noon tomorrow. 明天中午交货。

用法 deliver sth. to sb. 把某物交付给某人

派生 delivery *n.* 递送；交货；分娩

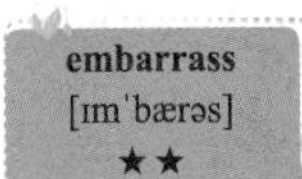

释义 *v.* 使尴尬，使局促不安

例句 I didn't want to *embarrass* her in front of her friends. 我不想在她朋友面前让她难堪。

派生 embarrassment *n.* 尴尬，难堪

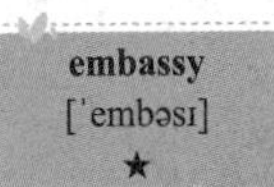

释义 *n.* 大使馆；大使及其随员

短语 *embassy* officials 大使馆官员

例句 He is working at the French *embassy*. 他在法国大使馆工作。

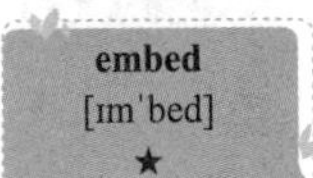

释义 *v.* 使嵌入，使插入；使深留脑中

短语 *embed* watermark 嵌入水印

例句 These facts lie *embedded* in his mind. 这些事实牢牢铭记在他的心中。

The magic sword was *embedded* in the stone. 魔剑牢牢嵌在石头里。

释义 *n.* 假货，赝品 *adj.* 假的，冒充的 *v.* 伪造；伪装

短语 a jacket in *fake* fur 人造毛皮夹克

例句 They were selling *fake* Rolex watches on the market stall. 他们在市场的小摊上卖假劳力士手表。

She *faked* her father's signature on the document. 她伪造了她父亲在文件上的签字。

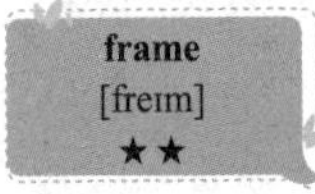

释义 *n.* 框架；体格，骨架；组织，机构 *v.* 设计，制定；做边框

短语 *frame* structure 框架结构

例句 The photograph had been *framed*. 照片已镶了框。

The building has a timber and metal *frame*. 这座建筑有木材和金属框架。

释义 *v./ n.* 喘气，喘息，倒抽气

例句 The exhausted runner threw himself down and *gasped*. 那位筋疲力尽的赛跑运动员一头栽倒，直喘气。

用法 gasp for air / breath 呼吸喘息

释义 *v.* 治理；利用；给（马等）装上挽具 *n.* 马具，挽具

例句 I *harness* the horse to the cart. 我把马套在车上。

The Yellow River has been *harnessed*. 黄河已被治理。

释义 *v.* 使蒙羞，使丢脸

例句 Parents are *humiliated* if their children behave badly when guests are present. 子女在客人面前举止失当，父母也失体面。

派生 humiliation *n.* 耻辱

释义 *v.* 意指，含……意思，暗示

例句 Exports in June rose 1.5%, *implying* that the economy was stronger than many investors had realized. 6 月份的出口量上升了 1.5%，表明经济比许多投资者所认为的更为强劲。

派生 implicit *adj.* 含蓄的

释义 *v.* [imˈpɔːt] 进口，输入 *n.* [ˈimpɔːt] 进口，输入 (*pl.*) 进口商品；要旨，含意

例句 If the *imported* goods became uncompetitive, consumers would shift to buying domestic products. 如果进口商品失去竞争力，消费者就会转而购买国内产品。

反义 export *v.* / *n.* 出口；输出

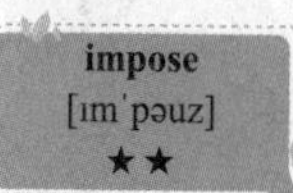

释义 *v.* 征（税）；把……强加给

例句 Britain *imposed* fines on airlines which bring in passengers without proper papers. 英国对运送未携带合法证件的乘客入境的航空公司处以罚款。

派生 imposition *n.*（规章、惩罚、税种等的）实施

用法 impose on 强迫

真题 The FCC also ended the investigations of broadband providers that *imposed* data caps on their rivals' streaming services but not their own. 美国联邦通信委员会还结束了对宽带提供商的调查，这些提供商对竞争对手的流媒体服务设置了数据上限，但对自己的流媒体服务没有设置上限。（2021 阅读理解）

释义 *n.* 遗产，遗赠；先人（或过去）留下的东西

短语 a *legacy* from history 历史遗留问题

例句 The *legacy* of Ancient Rome represented the overwhelming influence on Romanesque architecture. 古罗马的遗产体现在对罗马式建筑的巨大影响上。

派生 heritage *n.* 遗产

释义 *n.* 结婚，婚姻

短语 *marriage* proposal 求婚

例句 He was trapped in an unhappy *marriage*. 他陷入不幸的婚姻之中。

释义 *v.* / *n.* 残杀，大屠杀

短语 *massacre* civilians 屠杀平民

例句 More than 300 civilians are believed to have been *massacred* by the rebels.

据信有超过300位平民被叛乱分子残杀。

She lost a son and husband in the *massacre* along with 22 other close relatives. 她在大屠杀中失去了一个儿子和丈夫，还有其他22名近亲。

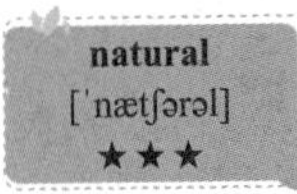

natural
[ˈnætʃərəl]
★★★

释义 *adj.* 自然的，天然的；不做作的

短语 *natural* resources 自然资源

例句 Children are usually more *natural* in their manner than adults. 孩子们的举止通常比成年人自然。

派生 naturally *adv.* 自然地，天然地；当然地，必然地

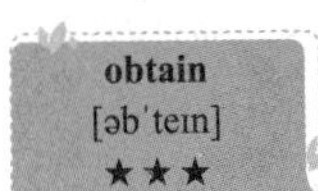

obtain
[əbˈteɪn]
★★★

释义 *v.* 获得，得到

短语 *obtain* a warrant 获得搜查令

例句 In many cases, it would not be overly burdensome for authorities to *obtain* a warrant to search through phone contents. 在许多情况下，对当局来说，获得搜查电话内容的搜查令并不会太烦琐。

近义 acquire *v.* 获得

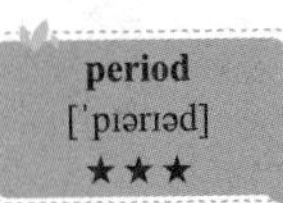

period
[ˈpɪəriəd]
★★★

释义 *n.* 时期；周期；一段时间

短语 *period* of time 一段时间　growth *period* 生长期

例句 Which *period* of history would you most like to have lived in? 你最喜欢生活在哪一个历史时期？

派生 periodical *n.* 期刊 *adj.* 定期的

真题 Shakespeare's lifetime was coincident with a *period* of extraordinary activity and achievement in the drama. 莎士比亚的一生正好赶上戏剧界异常活跃和成就斐然的时期。（2018 阅读理解）

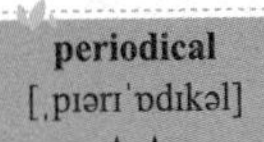

periodical
[ˌpɪəriˈɒdɪkəl]
★★

释义 *n.* 期刊，杂志 *adj.* 周期的，定期的

短语 *periodical* inspection 定期检查

例句 Established in 1887, *The Chinese Medical Journal* is the oldest medical *periodical* in China and is distributed worldwide.《中华医学杂志》创刊于1887年，是中国历史最悠久的医学期刊，在世界范围内发行。

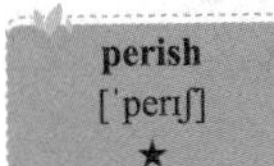

perish
[ˈperɪʃ]
★

释义 *v.* 丧生；凋谢；毁灭，消亡

短语 *perish* the thought 打消念头

例句 They don't understand what it means to adapt, so inevitably their businesses *perish*. 他们不明白适应意味着什么，所以他们的业务不可避免地会消亡。

派生 perishable *adj.* 易腐烂的

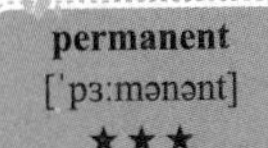

permanent
[ˈpɜːmənənt]
★★★

释义 *adj.* 永久的，持久的

短语 *permanent* resident 永久性居民

例句 They had entered the country and had applied for *permanent* residence. 他们已经入境该国，并申请了永久居留权。

派生 permanently *adv.* 永久地

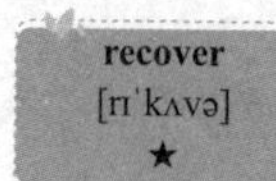

释义 *v.* 收回；恢复，痊愈；寻回

例句 It can take many years to *recover* from a trauma. 从一段痛苦经历中恢复过来可能需要很多年。

The police *recovered* the stolen car. 警察找到被盗的车。

派生 recovery *n.* 痊愈；恢复

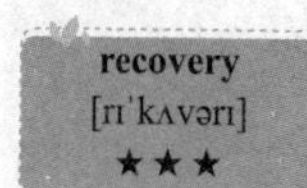

释义 *n.* 痊愈，复原；重获，恢复

短语 economic *recovery* 经济复苏

例句 As the first signs of economic *recovery* begin to take hold, deputy chiefs may be more willing to make the jump without a net. 当经济复苏的迹象开始显现的时候，副总裁们可能更愿意在没有新工作的情况下跳槽。

用法 recovery from 从……中恢复过来

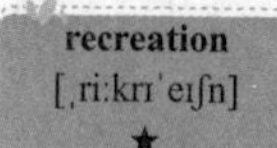

释义 *n.* 娱乐，消遣

短语 *recreation* center 娱乐中心

例句 Wuhan is home to a pleasant mix of manufacturing, high tech and *recreation*. 武汉是一个集制造业、高科技和休闲娱乐于一体的宜人城市。

My only *recreation* has been watching TV or going to the cinema. 我唯一的消遣就是看电视或电影。

派生 recreational *adj.* 娱乐的

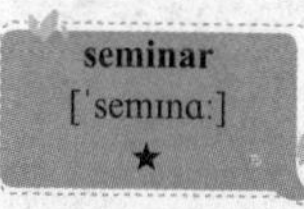

释义 *n.* 研讨会；研讨班

短语 *seminar* course 研究科目 a *seminar* room 研讨室

例句 The *seminar* was to discuss diversification of agriculture. 该研讨会讨论的是农业的多样化问题。

用法 a seminar on... 关于……的研讨会

近义 conference *n.* 研讨会

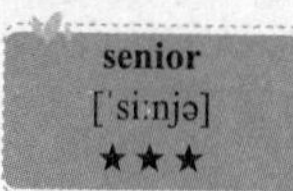

释义 *adj.* 年长的；地位较高的；高级的 *n.*（大学）四年级学生；老年人

短语 *senior* high school 高中 *senior* management 高级管理

例句 The decision to quit a *senior* position to look for a better one is unconventional. 放弃一个高级职位去寻找一个更好职位的决定是反常规的。

反义 youngster *n.* 年轻人；少年

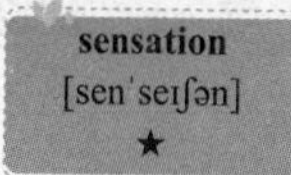

释义 *n.* 感觉，知觉；轰动一时的事情

短语 a burning *sensation* 烧灼感 a pleasant *sensation* 惬意感

例句 Quan Hongchan was just 14 when she caused a *sensation* at the Tokyo Olympics. 全红婵在东京奥运会上引起轰动时才 14 岁。

派生 sensational *adj.* 轰动的

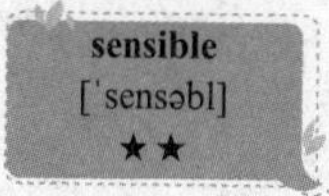

释义 *adj.* 明智的，达理的；可觉察的，明显的

例句 She was *sensible* enough to stop driving when she got too tired. 她很明智，当她太累时就不开车了。

用法 sensible of 察觉；了解

派生 sensibly *adv.* 明显地;容易感知地

释义 *v.* 诱惑,引诱;吸引

例句 Directors may be *tempted* to act in their own self-interest. 董事们可能会出于自身利益行事。

近义 attract *v.* 吸引

派生 temptation *n.* 引诱

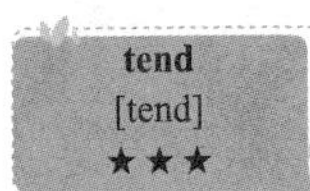

释义 *v.* 趋向,往往是;照料

例句 We *tend* to get cold winters and warm summers in this part of the country. 在我国这个地区,往往冬季寒冷而夏季炎热。

真题 This was also found in high-functioning men with some autistic spectrum symptoms, who may *tend* to avoid eye contact. 这在有一些自闭症谱系症状的高功能男性中也被发现,他们可能倾向于避免眼神接触。(2020 阅读理解)

用法 tend to 倾向于

派生 tendency *n.* 偏好;趋势

释义 *v.* 在……下画线;强调

例句 We *underline* that climate change is one of the greatest challenges of our time. 我们强调,气候变化是我们当今面临最重大的挑战之一。

用法 underline the importance of sth. 强调某事的重要性

近义 highlight *v.* 强调

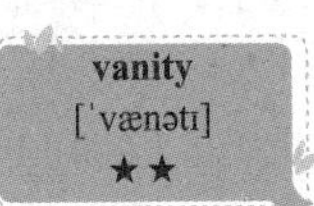

释义 *n.* 虚荣心,自负

短语 *vanity* mirror 化妆镜

例句 *Vanity* is a constant; people will only start shopping more sustainably when they can't afford not to. 虚荣心是永恒的;人们只有在不能承受放纵购物的时候才会开始有所节制。(2013 阅读理解)

用法 out of vanity 出于虚荣心

achieve
[əˈtʃiːv]
★★★

释义 *v.* 达到;实现;获得

例句 We will *achieve* much more by persuasion than by brute force. 我们将通过说服而不是暴力获得更多的成果。

派生 achievement *n.* 成就

释义 *v.* 承认;对……表示感谢;确认收到

例句 He is *acknowledged* as an excellent goalkeeper. 他被认可为一名优秀的守门员。

派生 acknowledgement *n.* 承认;感谢

真题 Any fair-minded assessment of the dangers of the deal between Britain's National Health Service (NHS) and DeepMind must start by *acknowledging* that both sides mean well. 任何关于英国国民医疗服务和深度思考公司之间协议的风险的公正评估都始于承认双方都是有好意的。(2018 阅读理解)

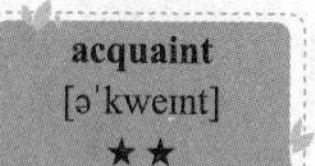

释义 v. 使熟悉；与……结识

例句 You must *acquaint* with your new duties. 你必须熟悉你的新职责。

Are you *acquainted* with my brother? 你跟我兄弟熟吗？

派生 acquaintance *n.* 熟人

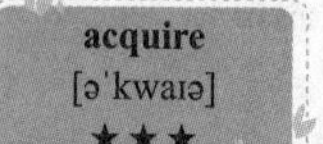

释义 v. 取得；获得

例句 The team *acquired* three new players this year. 这个队今年引进了三名新队员。

近义 obtain *v.* 获得

派生 acquisition *n.* 获得；收购

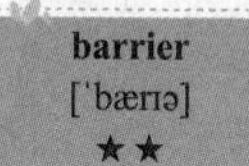

释义 n. 屏障；障碍物；关卡

例句 Lack of confidence is a psychological *barrier* to success.

缺乏信心是阻碍成功的心理因素。

用法 surmount the language barrier 克服语言障碍

近义 obstacle *n.* 障碍

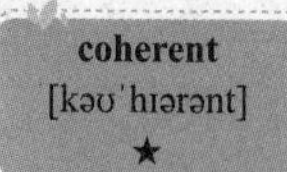

释义 *adj.* 有条理的，连贯的；前后一致的

短语 a *coherent* passage 一个连贯的段落

例句 The subjects of the curriculum form a *coherent* whole. 课程中的科目构成了一个连贯的整体。

派生 coherence *n.* 连贯性

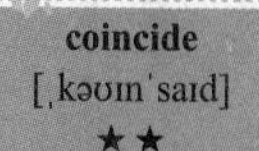

释义 v. 同时发生；巧合；一致

例句 His tastes and habits *coincide* with hers. 他的爱好和习惯与她的一致。

近义 concord *n.* 一致

派生 coincidence *n.* 巧合

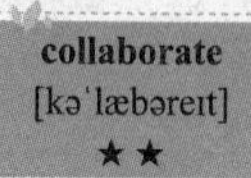

释义 v. 合作；通敌

例句 Andy and I are *collaborating* on a paper for the conference.

安迪和我正在为会议合作写一篇论文。

用法 collaborate on 合作做某事

派生 collaborative *adj.* 合作的，协作的

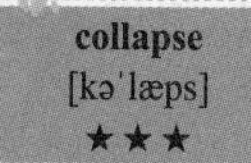

释义 v. / n. 倒塌；瓦解；（价格）暴跌；倒闭

例句 The bridge *collapsed* under the weight of the train. 桥在火车的重压下塌了。

用法 on the verge of collapse 濒于破裂；摇摇欲坠

近义 fall *v.* 倒塌

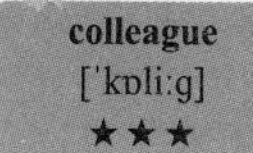

释义 n. 同事，同僚

例句 She discussed the idea with some of her *colleagues*. 她和她的一些同事讨论了这个想法。

近义 co-worker *n.* 同事；合作者

demand
[dɪˈmɑːnd]
★★★

释义 *n.* / *v.* 要求，请求，需要（量）

例句 Consumers *demanded* an immediate explanation from the manufacturer. 消费者要求制造商立即做出解释。

用法 demand sth. of (from) sb. 向某人索取某物

democracy
[dɪˈmɒkrəsɪ]
★★★

释义 *n.* 民主，民主制，民主国家

短语 parliamentary *democracy* 议会民主

例句 The early 1990s saw the spread of *democracy* in Eastern Europe. 20 世纪 90 年代初，民主思想在东欧迅速传播。

democratic
[ˌdeməˈkrætɪk]
★★★

释义 *adj.* 民主的

短语 a *democratic* system / government 民主制度 / 政府

例句 Education is the basis of a *democratic* society. 教育是民主社会的基础。

真题 If connections can be bought, a basic premise of *democratic* society — that all are equal in treatment by government — is undermined. 如果金钱可以买通人脉关系，民主社会的基本前提——人人享有政府平等对待——就遭到了破坏。（2017 阅读理解）

embody
[ɪmˈbɒdɪ]
★★

释义 *v.* 具体表达；包含

例句 She *embodied* good sportsmanship on the playing field. 在运动场上，她展现了优秀运动员的风采。

派生 embodiment *n.* 体现，化身

embrace
[ɪmˈbreɪs]
★★

释义 *v.* 拥抱；包含；采用；围绕；信奉 *n.* 拥抱；接受

例句 Most West European countries have *embraced* the concept of high-speed rail networks with enthusiasm. 大多数西欧国家都热情地接受了高速铁路网的概念。

近义 include *v.* 包含

真题 Believe it or not, a warm *embrace* might even help you avoid getting sick this winter. 信不信由你，一个温暖的拥抱甚至可以帮助你在这个冬天避免生病。（2017 完形填空）

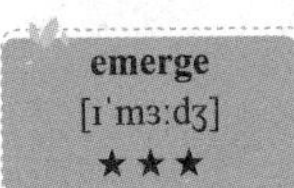

释义 *v.* 显现，出现

例句 After a few weeks, the caterpillar *emerges* from its cocoon. 几周后，毛毛虫破茧而出。

用法 emerge in endlessly 层出不穷

派生 emergence *n.* 出现

释义 *v.* 迷住，强烈吸引

例句 Twenty years after its release, the album continues to inspire and *fascinate* fans like few others. 这张专辑发行二十年后仍像为数不多的专辑那样一如既往地激励和吸引着歌迷。

近义 attract *v.* 吸引

派生 fascination *n.* 着迷；令人着迷的事物

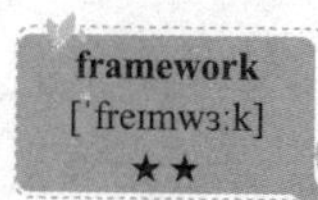

释义 *n.* 构架，框架；结构；组织，机构

短语 the European Union *Framework* 欧盟框架

例句 You can't make decisions without an ethical *framework*. 没有道德框架，你就无法做决定。

释义 *v.*（使）聚集；集合；收集 *n.* 聚集

短语 *gather* information 搜集信息

例句 The teacher *gathered* all the pupils in the auditorium. 老师把全体同学集合在礼堂内。

近义 collect *v.* 聚集；收集

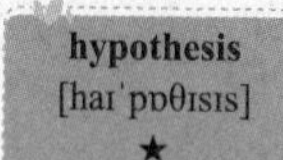

释义 *n.* 假说，假设；前提

例句 The theory is based on the *hypothesis* that all men are born equal. 这个理论建立在人人平等的前提之下。

派生 hypothetical *adj.* 假设的

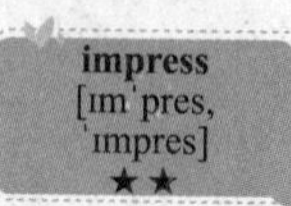

释义 *v.* 给……以深刻印象，引人注目

例句 The speaker tried hard to *impress* the audience but left them cold. 讲演者试图感动听众，但他没有打动听众的心。

用法 impress on 给……留下印象

派生 impression *n.* 印象，感想

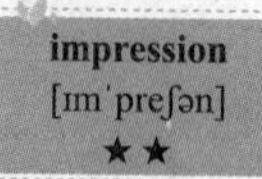

释义 *n.* 印象，感想

例句 The company gave consumers the *impression* that all its products were truly green. 这家公司给消费者的印象是其所有的产品都是真正环保的。

用法 under the impression that... 记得；在印象中

派生 impressive *adj.* 给人深刻印象的，感人的

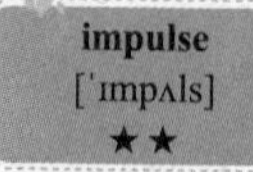

释义 *v.* 推动 *n.* 推动；冲动，刺激

例句 A list can also help you avoid making *impulse* purchases and blowing your budget. 清单还可以帮助你避免冲动购物和超出预算。

近义 urge *n.* 强烈的欲望；冲动

派生 impulsive *adj.* 冲动的

释义 *adj.* 法律的，法定的；合法的，正当的

短语 *legal* status / effect 法律地位 / 效力

例句 More and more women today have learned to arise in defence of their *legal* rights. 现在越来越多的妇女学会了站出来保护她们的合法权利。

派生 legally *adv.* 按照法律，法律上；合法地

真题 The endless *legal* battles and back-and-forth at the FCC cry out for Congress to act. 无休止的法律斗争和联邦通信委员会的反反复复迫切需要国会采取行动。（2021 阅读理解）

释义 *adj.* 大而重的；大规模的，大量的

短语 *massive* investment 大规模投资

例句 I believe that the most important forces behind the *massive* merger wave are the same that underlie the globalization process. 我相信，大规模并购浪潮背后最重要的力量，正是支撑全球化进程的力量。

masterpiece [ˈmɑːstəpiːs] ★

释义 *n.* 杰作，名著

例句 Various ancient architectural *masterpieces* have survived, including palaces, temples and towers. 包括宫殿、寺庙和塔楼在内的各种古代建筑杰作幸存下来。

近义 classic *n.* 经典作品

用法 a masterpiece of... ……的典范

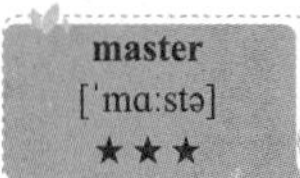

master [ˈmɑːstə] ★★★

释义 *n.* 大师；主人；硕士 *v.* 精通，控制 *adj.* 熟练的，主要的

例句 In 1777, several northern states encouraged white *masters* to free their slaves for military service. 1777 年，几个北方的州鼓励白人奴隶主释放奴隶以服兵役。

用法 master one's temper 控制某人的脾气

派生 spymaster *n.* 间谍组织的首脑

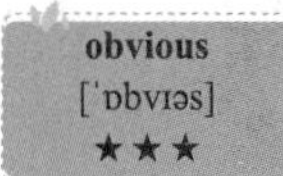

obvious [ˈɒbvɪəs] ★★★

释义 *adj.* 明显的；显而易见的

例句 Huawei has a pretty *obvious* reason for wanting to create its own operating system. 华为想要创建自己的操作系统的原因非常明显。

派生 obviously *adv.* 显然

近义 evident *adj.* 显然的 apparent *adj.* 显而易见的

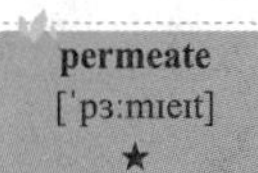

permeate [ˈpɜːmɪeɪt] ★

释义 *v.* 弥漫，遍布，散布；渗入，渗透

例句 With a cheerful atmosphere, laughter and applause *permeate* from start to finish. 伴随着祥和的气氛，晚会自始至终欢声笑语，掌声雷动。

用法 permeate through 渗透入

派生 permeation *n.* 渗透

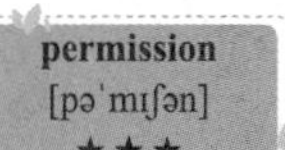

permission [pəˈmɪʃən] ★★★

释义 *n.* 允许，同意

短语 without *permission* 未经许可

例句 Critics allege that by making electronic copies of these books without first seeking the *permission* of copyright holders, Google has committed piracy. 批评人士声称谷歌在没有事先获得版权所有者许可的情况下制作这些书籍的电子副本，已经犯下了盗版罪。

近义 approval *n.* 赞成；批准，许可

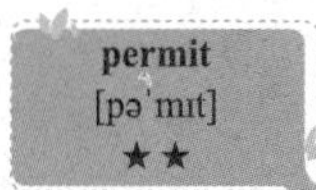

permit [pəˈmɪt] ★★

释义 *v.* 许可，允许 *n.* 许可证，执照

例句 Many museums and art galleries disallow the taking of photographs without a *permit*. 许多博物馆和美术馆不允许未经许可拍照。

Try to go out for a walk at lunchtime, if the weather *permits*. 如果天气条件允许，午饭时尽量出去散散步。

派生 permission *n.* 同意，许可

真题 Successive governments have *permitted* such increases on the grounds that the cost of investing in and running the rail network should be borne by those who use it, rather than the general taxpayer. 历届政府都允许（火车票的）涨价，理由是投资和运营铁路网的成本应该由使用铁路网的人承担，而不是普通纳税人。（2021 阅读理解）

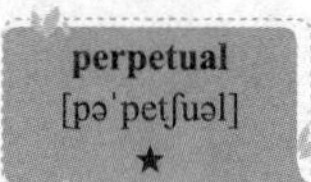

释义 *adj.* 永久的，永恒的，长期的

短语 *perpetual* calendar 万年历 *perpetual* complaints 无休止的抱怨

例句 The p*erpetual* argument is that funds are tight, that we have more pressing problems here on earth. 一个永恒的争论是资金紧张，地球上有更紧迫的问题。

派生 perpetually *adv.* 永恒地

释义 *v.* 征募（新兵），吸收；补充 *n.* 新成员，新兵

例句 Most of the workers will be *recruited* locally. 大多数工人都会在本地被招募。

真题 In South Africa, an HIV-prevention initiative known as loveLife *recruits* young people to promote safe sex among their peers. 在南非，一项名为“爱生活”的艾滋病预防计划招募年轻人在同龄人中推广安全性行为。（2012 阅读理解）

派生 recruitment *n.* 招聘

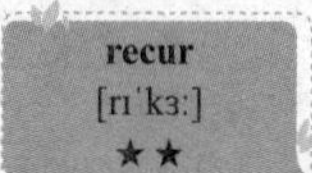

释义 *v.*（尤指不好的事）一再发生；重现

例句 A *recurring* criticism of the UK's university sector is its perceived weakness in translating new knowledge into new products and services. 英国大学经常受到批评，认为其在将新知识转化为新产品和服务方面存在明显短板。

近义 return *v.*（感觉或情况）重新出现，恢复

派生 recurrence *n.* 重现；复发

释义 *v.* / *n.* 再循环，重复利用

短语 *recycle* bin 回收站

例句 More and more Britons buy *recycled* toilet paper to protect the environment. 为了保护环境，越来越多的英国人购买再生卫生纸。

派生 recycling *n.* 回收利用

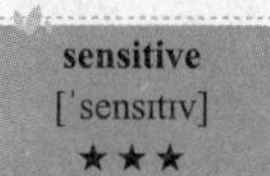

释义 *adj.* 敏感的，易受伤害的；灵敏的

短语 *sensitive* skin 敏感性皮肤

例句 Keeping *sensitive* information on mobile phones is increasingly a requirement of normal life. 在手机上保存敏感信息逐渐成为日常生活的需要。

派生 sensitiveness *n.* 灵敏度；神经过敏

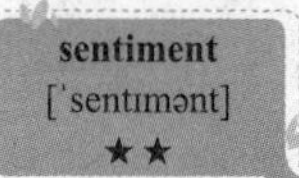

释义 *n.* 感情，柔情；看法；感觉

短语 public *sentiment* 公众意见；公众情绪

例句 You have to be tough to succeed in the business world. There's no room for *sentiment*. 要想在商界取得成功，你必须坚强，不能感情用事。

派生 sentimental *adj.* 多愁善感的

近义 sensibility *n.* 情感；敏感性；感觉

释义 *adj.* 分离的，分开的 *v.*（使）分离，分开 *n.* 抽印本，分开

短语 *separate* bedrooms 独立卧室

例句 Each holiday chalet has its own *separate* garden. 每个度假小屋都有自己独

立的花园。

派生 separation *n.* 分开,分隔;分离

真题 Young people who are digital natives are indeed becoming more skillful at *separating* fact from fiction in cyberspace. 在数字时代下成长的年轻人现在越来越熟练地辨别网络信息的真伪。(2018 阅读理解)

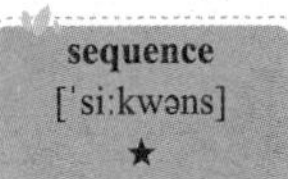

释义 *n.* 先后,次序;连续,数列 *v.* 按顺序排列;测定序列

短语 time *sequence* 时间顺序

例句 Work has to be done on schedule and in a prearranged *sequence*. 工作必须按期并以预先安排好的顺序完成。

The human genome has now been *sequenced*. 人类基因组的序列现已测定。

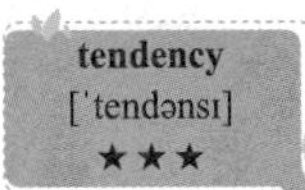

释义 *n.* 趋势,趋向;倾向

短语 development / natural *tendency* 发展 / 自然趋势

例句 This *tendency* in the natural sciences has long been evident in the social sciences too. 自然科学中的这种倾向在社会科学中也一直都很明显。

近义 trend *n.* 趋势

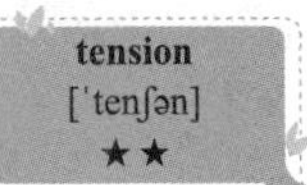

释义 *n.* (紧张)状态;拉(绷)紧;张力,拉力

短语 political *tensions* 政治紧张局势

例句 During a separate observation, she saw that phones became a source of *tension* in the family. 在另一次观察中,她发现手机成了家庭关系紧张的一个因素。

近义 unease *n.* 不安

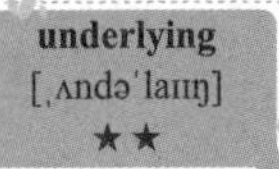

释义 *adj.* 含蓄的,潜在的;在下面的

短语 an *underlying* cause 潜在原因

例句 I think that the *underlying* problem is education, unemployment and bad housing. 我认为深层的问题在于教育、失业和糟糕的住房。

近义 potential *adj.* 潜在的

释义 *adj.* 易变的,可变的;变量的 *n.* 变量

短语 *variable* cost 可变成本

例句 British weather is perhaps at its most *variable* in the spring. 在英国,春季的天气可能是最变幻莫测的。

The *variables* in the equation are X, Y, and Z. 方程式中的变量是 X,Y 和 Z。

派生 variability *n.* 可变性

真题 There is plenty of evidence that the quality of the teachers is the most important *variable*. 有大量证据表明,教师的素质是最重要的变量。(2012 阅读理解)

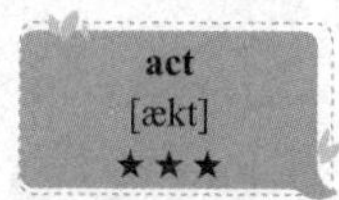

释义 *v.* 行为举止;采取行动;起作用;扮演 *n.* 行为;法案;一段表演

例句 He's taking a dangerous drug: it *acts* very fast on the central nervous system. 他在使用一种危险的药物——这种药物很快作用于中枢神经系统。With the popularity of the car, registration became a must in 1903 with the *Motor Car Act*. 随着汽车的普及,1903 年的《汽车法案》开始要求必须对汽车进行登记。

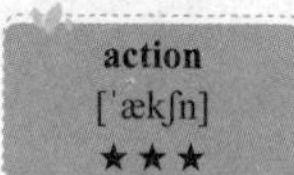

释义 *n.* 行动;行为;作用

例句 The time has come for *action* if these beautiful animals are to survive. 若要使这些美丽的动物能生存下去,现在就要行动起来。Can you be ready to go into *action* with us? 你能准备好跟我们一起行动吗?

用法 go into action 投入战斗;出马

释义 *adj.* 活跃的;积极的

例句 After retirement, he remained *active* in the association, latterly as vice president. 退休后,他仍然活跃在该协会,后来担任副会长。

用法 keep / remain active 保持活跃

派生 activity *n.* 活动

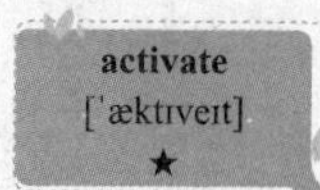

释义 *v.* 启动;激活

例句 The camera is *activated* by pushing a button. 按下按钮就可以启动照相机。

反义 deactivate *v.* 使停止工作;使失去活性

派生 activation *n.* 激活

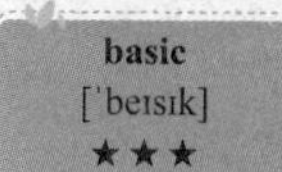

释义 *adj.* 基本的;首要的 *n.* 基本要素,基本原则

例句 People need *basic* education if they are to become employable. 若想要受雇用,人们需要接受基础教育。

真题 Passengers should be able to expect a *basic* level of service for the substantial sums they are now paying to travel. 旅客们应该能够期望他们现在支付的大笔旅行费用保证基本水平的服务。(2021 阅读理解)

释义 *v.* 收集;收藏;募集;领取

短语 *collect* stamps / postcards 集邮 / 收藏明信片

例句 Elizabeth had been *collecting* snails for a school project. 伊丽莎白一直在为完成学校的一份课题作业收集蜗牛。

派生 collection *n.* 收藏(品)

释义 *v.* 碰撞;冲突,抵触

例句 The interests of the two countries *collide*. 两国的利益发生冲突。

近义 clash *n.* / *v.* 冲突

colony ['kɒlənɪ] ★★★

释义 *n.* 殖民地；侨民；群体

例句 Vietnam used to be a *colony* of France. 越南曾是法国的殖民地。

派生 colonist *n.* 殖民者

combat ['kɒmbæt] ★★

释义 *v.* / *n.* 战斗，搏斗

例句 He is determined to *combat* his bad habits. 他决心与自己的坏习惯做斗争。

用法 combat for 为……奋斗

近义 battle *n.* 战斗

combine [kəm'baɪn] ★★★

释义 *v.* 联合；结合；化合 *n.* 集团；联合企业

例句 A number of factors have *combined* to create this difficult situation. 许多因素结合在一起造成了这种困难的局面。

派生 combination *n.* 结合

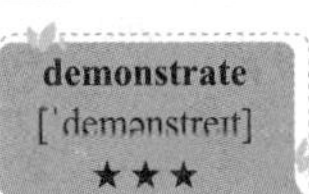

demonstrate ['demənstreɪt] ★★★

释义 *v.* 论证，证实；演示，说明

例句 The salesman *demonstrated* how to use the laptop. 售货员示范如何使用这台笔记本电脑。

真题 During the Renaissance, the great minds of Nicolaus Copernicus, Johannes Kepler and Galileo Galilei *demonstrated* the power of scientific study and discovery. 在文艺复兴时期，哥白尼、开普勒和伽利略等伟大的思想家展示了科学研究和发现的力量。（2020 翻译）

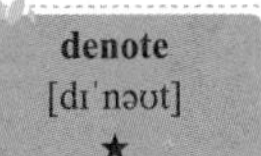

denote [dɪ'nəʊt] ★

释义 *v.* 标志；表示

例句 Crosses on the map *denote* villages. 地图上的叉号表示村庄。

近义 indicate *v.* 表明

denounce [dɪ'naʊns] ★

释义 *v.* 谴责；检举，告发

例句 The government's economic policy has been *denounced* on all sides. 政府的经济政策受到了各方面的谴责。

用法 denounce sb. to the authorities 向当局告发某人

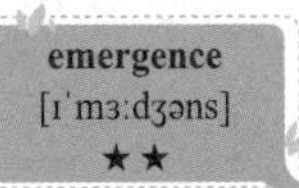

emergence [ɪ'mɜːdʒəns] ★★

释义 *n.* 出现，显现

例句 The *emergence* of small Japanese cars in the 1970s challenged the US and European manufacturers. 20 世纪 70 年代日本小型汽车的出现对美国和欧洲制造商构成了挑战。

近义 appearance *n.* 出现

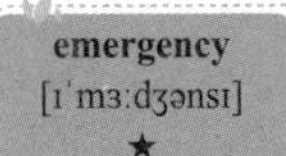

emergency [ɪ'mɜːdʒənsɪ] ★

释义 *n.* 紧急情况，突然事件

例句 You should only use this door in an *emergency*. 在紧急情况下才能使用这扇门。

近义 crisis *n.* 紧要关头

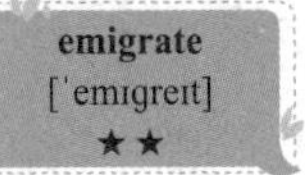

emigrate ['emɪgreɪt] ★★

释义 *v.* 移居外国，移民

例句 Evan's parents *emigrated* to Australia in 2003. 埃文的父母于 2003 年移民到澳大利亚。

反义 immigrate *v.* 移居入境；移民

用法 emigrate from 离开（本国）移居到国外

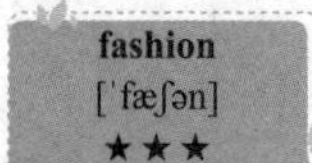

释义 *n.* 流行式样（或货品），风尚，风气；样子，方式 *v.* 制作

例句 Long skirts have come into *fashion* again. 长裙子又流行起来了。

She *fashioned* the clay into a pot. 她用黏土制成一个罐子。

派生 fashionable *adj.* 流行的，时髦的

用法 come into fashion 流行；开始风行

释义 *adj.* 坦白的，直率的

例句 The magazine, which gives *frank* advice about love and romance, is aimed at the teenage market. 这本杂志面向青少年市场，对爱情做出坦率的忠告。

用法 to be frank 坦白说；老实说

释义 *n.* / *v.* 凝视，注视

例句 The climbers stood on the top of the mountain, *gazing* at the splendid view. 登山队员们站在山顶，凝视壮丽的景色。

She felt uncomfortable under the woman's steady *gaze*. 那个女人一直盯着她看，让她觉得不自在。

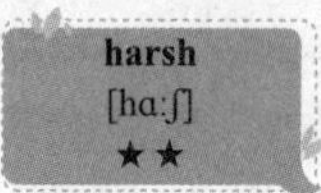

释义 *adj.* 刺耳的；刺眼的；（环境）艰苦的

例句 The sunlight is very *harsh*. 太阳光很刺眼。

Mars has a *harsh* environment when compared with its warmer past. 与温暖的过去相比，火星现在的环境非常恶劣。

派生 harshness *n.* 严肃；刺耳

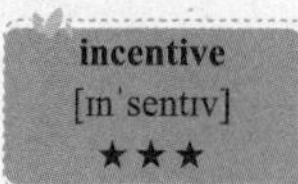

释义 *n.* 刺激；动力；鼓励；诱因；动机

例句 Money is still a major *incentive* in most occupations. 在许多职业中，钱仍是主要的激励因素。

真题 Nostalgia for ink on paper and the rustle of pages aside, there's plenty of *incentive* to ditch print. 抛开对纸质报纸的油墨味和纸张沙沙声的怀念，它们都不能阻止纸质报纸的消失。（2016 阅读理解）

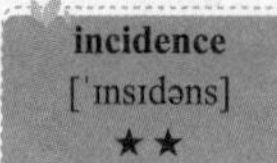

释义 *n.* 影响程度，影响范围；发生率

短语 increase / reduce the *incidence* 提高 / 降低发生率

例句 It has been found that not eating breakfast is related to the *incidence* of certain diseases in some countries. 研究发现，在一些国家，不吃早餐与某些疾病的发病率有关。

释义 *n.* 事件，事变

例句 There was a shooting *incident* near here last night. 昨夜这附近发生了枪击事件。

近义 event *n.* 事件

派生 incidental *adj.* 偶然发生的

释义 *n.* 法律（规）；立法，法律的制定

例句 The assembly voted to delay the *legislation* to allow further consultation to take place. 议会投票决定暂缓立法以便进一步磋商。

真题 *Legislation* is moving through the House that would save USPS an estimated $286 billion over five years, which could help pay for new vehicles, among other survival measures. 立法正在通过众议院的审核，该法案将在5年内为美国邮政局预计节省286亿美元，这将有助于满足其他生存需要，比如购买新车辆。（2018 阅读理解）

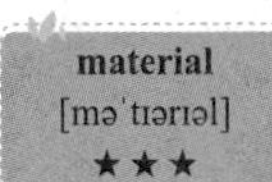

释义 *n.* 材料，原料 *adj.* 物质的

短语 building *material* 建筑材料

例句 Even better would be to help elevate notions of beauty beyond the *material* standards of a particular industry. 更为提倡的则是帮助提升大众的审美，而不仅仅限于对某一特定行业的有形标准。

派生 materialize *v.* 实现

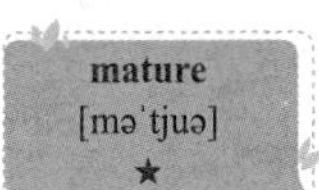

释义 *adj.* 成熟的；成年人的 *v.*（使）成熟

短语 *mature* market economy 成熟的市场经济

例句 Boys *mature* more slowly than girls, both physically and psychologically. 在生理和心理上，男孩比女孩成熟得晚些。

The interview showed her as a self-assured and *mature* student. 从采访中可以看出，她是一个自信而成熟的学生。

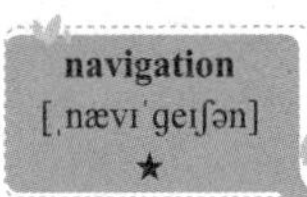

释义 *n.* 航行（学）；航海（术），航空（术）

例句 *Navigation* is difficult on this river because of the hidden rocks. 由于有许多暗礁，在这条河上航行很困难。

真题 Today we live in a world where GPS systems, digital maps, and other *navigation* apps are available on our smartphones. 今天，我们生活在一个智能手机上可以使用GPS系统、数字地图和其他导航应用程序的世界。（2019 完形填空）

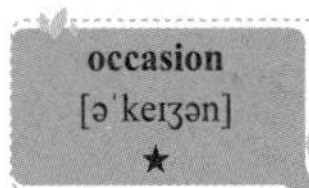

释义 *n.* 时刻；机会；场合 *v.* 引起，惹起

短语 on this / that *occasion* 这 / 那次场合

例句 I only wear a tie on special *occasions*. 我只有在特殊的场合才系领带。

派生 occasional *adj.* 偶尔的

用法 on occasion 有时；偶尔

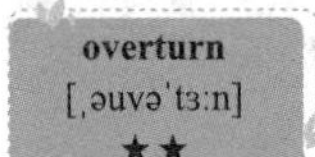

释义 *v.*（使）翻倒；使垮台；推翻 *n.* 倾覆，垮台

短语 *overturn* a conviction 推翻定罪

例句 In Arizona v. United States, the majority *overturned* three of the four contested provisions of Arizona's controversial plan. 在亚利桑那州诉联邦政府一案中，大多数法官投票否决了该方案里受到质疑的四项条款中的三项。

近义 overthrow *v.* 推翻

释义 *v.* 使困惑，使费解，使复杂化

例句 This disease, which only affects young children, has continued to *perplex* doctors. 这种只影响儿童的疾病继续困扰着医生。

近义 puzzle *v.* 使困惑 confuse *v.* 使困惑

派生 perplexing *adj.* 复杂的

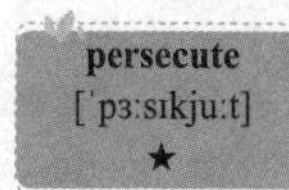
persecute
[ˈpɜːsɪkjuːt]
★

释义 v. 迫害;困扰

例句 Throughout history, people have been *persecuted* for their religious beliefs. 人们因宗教信仰而受迫害的情况贯穿了整个历史。

派生 persecution n. 迫害

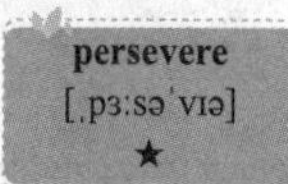
persevere
[ˌpɜːsəˈvɪə]
★

释义 v. 坚持,坚忍,不屈不挠

例句 We were successful not because we were quick-witted but because we *persevered*. 我们之所以成功不是因为我们机智,而是因为我们坚韧不拔。

近义 persist v. 坚持,执意

派生 perseverance n. 毅力

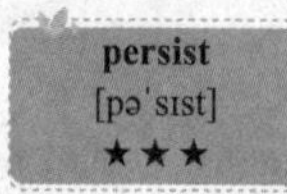
persist
[pəˈsɪst]
★★★

释义 v. 坚持,持续

例句 Cheryl Kaiser holds that people should be constantly reminded that racial inequality still *persists* in American society. 谢丽尔·凯瑟认为应该不断提醒人们美国社会仍然存在着种族不平等。

派生 persistence n. 继续存在,维持;坚持不懈

用法 persist with sth. 坚持某事

qualify
[ˈkwɒlɪfaɪ]
★★★

释义 v.(使)具有资格,(使)合格;限定,修饰

例句 There are certain skills that *qualify* foreigners for work visas. 有一些技能使外国人有资格获得工作签证。

派生 qualification n. 资格,条件

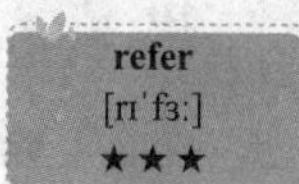
refer
[rɪˈfɜː]
★★★

释义 v. 参考,查询;提到,引用

短语 *refer* a friend 引荐朋友

例句 This, for those as yet unaware of such a disadvantage, *refers* to discrimination against those whose surnames begin with a letter in the lower half of the alphabet. 对于那些尚未意识到这一不利条件的人来说,这指的是对姓氏首字母位于字母表下半部分的人所遭受的歧视。

派生 reference n. 提及;参考

refine
[rɪˈfaɪn]
★

释义 v. 精炼,提纯;改进,完善

例句 The firm is thought to *refine* gold in a process using hazardous chemicals. 这家公司被认为使用危险化学物质提炼黄金。

Online feedback can also be given to help *refine* the bus route network. 在线反馈也可以帮助完善公交线路。

派生 refinery n. 提炼厂

reflect
[rɪˈflekt]
★★★

释义 v. 反射;反映;反省

例句 White clothes are cooler because they *reflect* the heat. 白色衣服比较凉爽,因为它们能反射热量。

派生 reflection n. 反射;反映;反省

真题 How can we make sure that the thinking of intelligent machines *reflects* humanity's highest values? 如何确保智能机器的思维反映人类的最高价值?(2019 阅读理解)

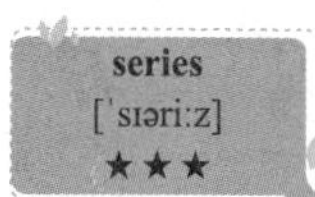

series
['sɪəriːz]
★★★

释义 *n.* 一系列，连续；丛书

例句 They met through a *series* of strange coincidences. 他们因一连串奇妙的巧合而相遇。

真题 A *series* of fires and overcrowded conditions led to the construction of the existing Treasury Building. 一系列的火灾和过度拥挤的环境促使了现有的财政部大楼的兴建。（2018 阅读理解）

用法 *series* of 一系列；一连串

serve
[sɜːv]
★★★

释义 *v.* 服务，尽责；招待，侍候；符合，适用

例句 The only problem here is that they don't *serve* beer — only wine and spirits. 这儿唯一的问题是他们不供应啤酒——只供应葡萄酒和烈酒。

真题 The Small Business & Entrepreneurship Council advocacy group said in a statement,"Small businesses and internet entrepreneurs are not well *served* at all by this decision." 美国小企业与创业委员会倡导组织在一份声明中表示，"这一决定对小企业和互联网创业者根本没有好处。"（2019 阅读理解）

用法 *serve* up 上菜

派生 service *n.* 服务

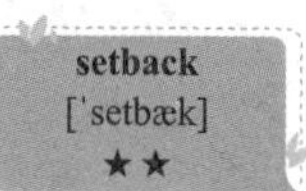

setback
['setbæk]
★★

释义 *n.* 挫折；失效；复发；倒退

短语 a temporary *setback* 暂时的阻碍

例句 The breakdown in talks represents a temporary *setback* in the peace process. 谈判破裂意味着和平进程暂时受阻。

用法 experience a setback 遭受挫折

近义 reverse *n.* 失败，挫折

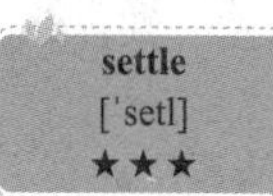

settle
['setl]
★★★

释义 *v.* 安定，安顿；停息；定居；解决，调停

例句 America was first *settled* by people who came across from Asia over 25,000 years ago. 2.5 万年前，从亚洲来的移民首次在美国安家落户。

Both sides are looking for ways to *settle* their differences. 双方都在寻找解决分歧的方法。

派生 settlement *n.* 解决；协议；定居点

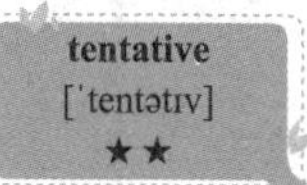

tentative
['tentətɪv]
★★

释义 *adj.* 试探性的，暂时的；犹豫不决的

短语 *tentative* plan 设想；试验性计划

例句 Political leaders have reached a *tentative* agreement to hold a preparatory conference next month. 政治领导人已就下个月举行预备会议达成初步协定。

近义 experimental *adj.* 试验性的

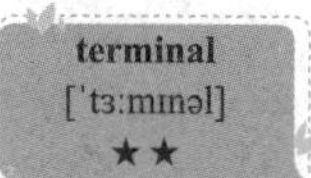

terminal
['tɜːmɪnəl]
★★

释义 *adj.* 晚期的；终点的；期末的 *n.* 终点（站）；航站楼；终端

短语 *terminal* equipment 终端设备 a bus *terminal* 公共汽车终点站

例句 A bus shuttles passengers back and forth from the station to the *terminal*. 一辆公共汽车在火车站和公共汽车终点站之间往返运送旅客。

派生 terminally *adv.*（疾病）晚期地

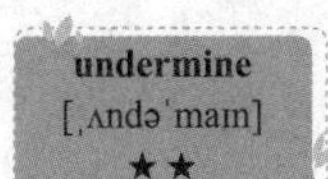

释义 *v.* 暗中破坏，逐渐削弱；侵蚀……的基础

短语 *undermine* one's position / confidence 削弱某人的地位 / 信心

例句 Our confidence in the team has been seriously *undermined* by their recent defeats. 该队最近的几次失败已严重动摇了我们对他们的信心。

近义 weaken *v.*（使）变弱

真题 But demanding too much of air travelers or providing too little security in return *undermines* public support for the process. 然而对飞机旅客要求太高，或者提供的安全保障太低只会使民众对安检流程失去信心。（2017 阅读理解）

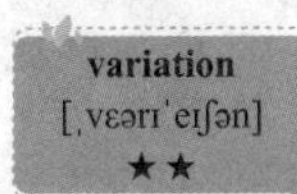

释义 *n.* 变化，变动

短语 temperature / speed *variation* 温度 / 速度变化

例句 Will such *variations* bring about a change in the overall structure of the food and drink market? 这些变化是否会改变食品及饮料市场的整体格局？

用法 variations in...……中的变化

近义 change *n.* 变化

释义 *v.* 出产，生长；屈服，服从 *n.* 产量，收获

短语 product *yield* 产品产量

例句 This research has been in progress since 1961 and has *yielded* a great number of positive results. 这项研究自 1961 年起一直在开展，已取得了不少积极成果。

用法 yield up 被迫放弃；交出；展现

近义 submit *v.* 屈服

真题 Typically, archaeologists survey and sample (make test excavations on) large areas of terrain to determine where excavation will *yield* useful information. 通常情况下，考古学家会对大面积的地形进行调查和取样（进行试验挖掘），以确定在哪里进行挖掘会得到有用的信息。（2014 阅读理解）

释义 *v.*（使）适应；改编

例句 It took Lucy a while to *adapt* to the new job. 露西过了一段时间才适应了新工作。

The play had been *adapted* for children. 这个剧本已被改编成儿童剧。

派生 adaptation *n.* 适应

释义 *v.* 写姓名地址；演说；处理；称呼 *n.* 地址；演讲

例句 Mr King sought to *address* those fears when he spoke at the meeting. 金先生在会上讲话时试图消除那些恐惧。

The former CEO of Google was invited to *address* a conference in Washington, DC, this week. 谷歌的前任总裁本周受邀在华盛顿特区的一个会议上发表演讲。

basis
['beɪsɪs]
★★★

释义 *n.* 基础；依据；基准

例句 Decisions were often made on the *basis* of incorrect information. 决定常常是根据错误的信息做出的。

用法 on the basis of 根据

近义 foundation *n.* 基础

collective
[kə'lektɪv]
★★★

释义 *adj.* 集体的，共同的 *n.* 集体

短语 a *collective* decision / effort 共同的决定 / 努力

例句 This principle of *collective* bargaining has been a mainstay in labor relations in this country. 这一集体谈判原则已经成为该国劳动关系的重要基础。

近义 joint *adj.* 联合的，共同的

释义 *n./v.* 命令；控制 *v.* 赢得 *n.* 掌握

例句 He *commanded* that all the gates be shut. 他命令关闭所有的大门。

He finally felt in *command* of his life. 他终于觉得自己主宰了自己的生活。

She has an impressive *command* of the English language. 她精通英语。

派生 commander *n.* 指挥官

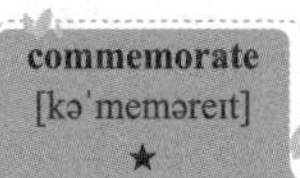

释义 *v.* 纪念，庆祝

例句 This monument *commemorates* our victory. 这座碑是为纪念我们的胜利而建的。

派生 commemoration *n.* 纪念，纪念活动

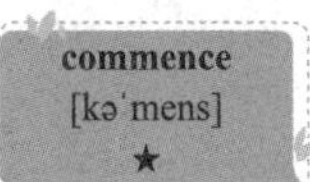

释义 *v.* 开始，着手

例句 A number of new laws have been passed and are due to *commence* this year. 新的法律已经通过，并将于今年开始实施。

派生 commencement *n.* 开始

释义 *v.*（尤指公开地）称赞；推荐

例句 We should *commend* good people and good deeds. 我们应当表扬好人好事。

She is an excellent worker and I *commend* her to you without reservation. 她工作出色，我毫无保留地把她推荐给你。

同义 praise *v.* 赞美

反义 condemn *v.* 谴责

释义 *adj.* 浓厚的，密集的，稠密的

短语 *dense* fog 浓雾

例句 They had to clear a road through an area of *dense* forest. 他们必须在一片茂密的森林中开辟出一条道路。

派生 density *n.* 密集，密度

释义 *v.* 否认；拒绝

例句 In a statement, an FBI spokeswoman wouldn't confirm or *deny* the agency's involvement. 在一份声明中，联邦调查局女发言人对该机构是否参与此事不置

可否。

用法 deny sb. sth. 拒绝给（某人）（某物）

反义 confirm *v.* 确定

释义 *v.* 出发，动身，启程

例句 Flight 79 will *depart* from Tokyo at 11:45 a.m. and arrive in Seattle at 4:12 p.m. 79 号航班将于上午 11:45 从东京起飞，并于下午 4:12 到达西雅图。

派生 departure *n.* 离开，起程

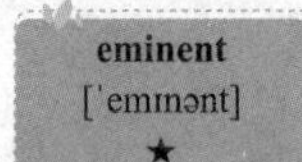

释义 *adj.* 显赫的；杰出的

短语 an *eminent* scholar 著名的学者

例句 The award was established in 1902 as a special distinction for *eminent* men and women. 该奖设立于 1902 年，作为特别荣誉颁发给杰出的男士和女士。

派生 eminence *n.* 著名

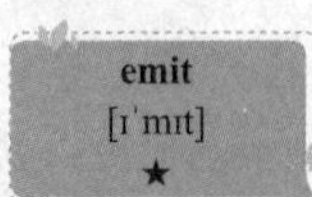

释义 *v.* 发出；放射；散发

例句 The factory has been *emitting* black smoke from its chimney. 这个工厂的烟囱一直冒黑烟。

派生 emission *n.* 散发

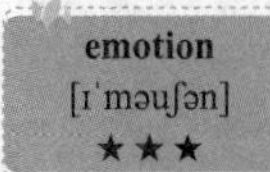

释义 *n.* 情绪，情感，感情

例句 She answered in a voice filled with *emotion*. 她以激动的声音回答。

真题 A more direct finding is that people who scored highly for negative *emotions* like anxiety looked at others for shorter periods of time. 一个更直接的发现是，在焦虑等负面情绪方面得分高的人注视他人的时间较短。（2020 阅读理解）

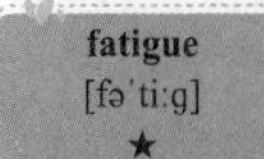

释义 *n.* 疲劳 *adj.* 疲劳的 *v.* 使疲劳

短语 physical / mental *fatigue* 体力 / 精神疲劳

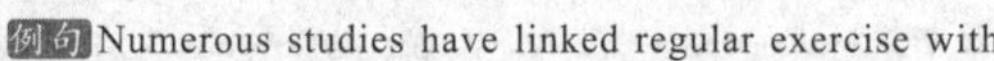

例句 Numerous studies have linked regular exercise with improving *fatigue*, especially among sedentary people. 大量研究表明，定期锻炼可以改善疲劳，尤其是对久坐不动的人。

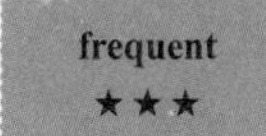

释义 *adj.* [ˈfriːkwənt] 时常发生的，频繁的 *v.* [friˈkwent] 常去，常出入于

例句 She is a *frequent* traveller to Belgium. 她经常到比利时去旅行。

真题 Even among those who got a cold, the ones who felt greater social support and received more *frequent* hugs had less severe symptoms. 即使在感冒的人中，那些感受到更大社会支持和更频繁拥抱的人的症状也不那么严重。（2017 完形填空）

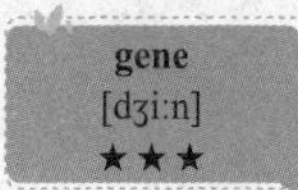

释义 *n.* 基因

短语 *gene* pool 基因库

例句 The illness is believed to be caused by a defective *gene*. 这种疾病被认为是由有缺陷的基因引起的。

派生 genetic *adj.* 基因的，遗传学的

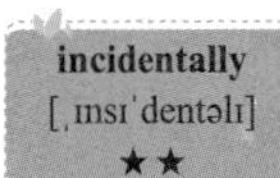

释义 *adv.* 附带地,顺便提及

例句 *Incidentally*, did you read my article in the newspaper? 顺便提一句,你读了我在报纸上发表的文章了吗?

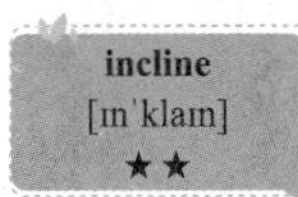

释义 *v.*(使)倾斜;(使)倾向于 *n.* 斜坡,斜面

例句 Compared with younger ones, older societies are less *inclined* to be innovative and take risks than younger ones. 与年轻一代相比,老年社会不太倾向于创新和冒险。

The driver turned off the engine and let the truck coast down the *incline*. 司机关掉了马达让卡车滑下斜坡。

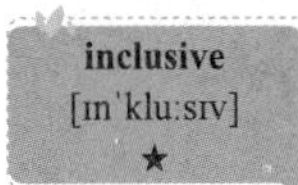

释义 *adj.* 包含的;包容的;范围广的

例句 The monthly rent is $150, *inclusive* of light and water. 每月租金 150 美元,包括水电费在内。

We are trying to provide a more *inclusive* and supportive environment for students. 我们尽力为学生提供一个更具包容性和支持性的环境。

反义 exclusive *adj.* 独有的

派生 inclusively *adv.* 包含地

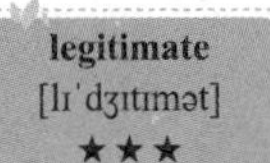

释义 *adj.* 合法的;合理的 *v.* 使合法

短语 *legitimate* authority 法定职权

例句 The government said that it has suspended all aid to Haiti until that country's *legitimate* government is restored. 政府说它已经暂停对海地的所有援助,直到海地恢复合法政府为止。

派生 legitimacy *n.* 合法性,合理性

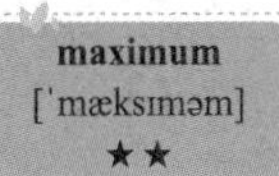

释义 *n.* 最大值,极限 *adj.* 最大的,最高的

例句 The job will acquire you to use all your skills to the *maximum*. 这项工作要求你最大限度地发挥你的技能。

反义 minimum *adj.* 最小的 *n.* 最小值

派生 maximize *v.* 使最大化

释义 *v.* 表示……的意思 *adj.* 吝啬的;平均的 *n.* 平均值

例句 Music *means* different things to different people and sometimes even different things to the same person at different moments of his life. 音乐对不同的人意味着不同的东西,有时甚至对同一个人在他生命的不同时刻意味着不同的东西。

派生 meaning *n.* 意思,意义,含义

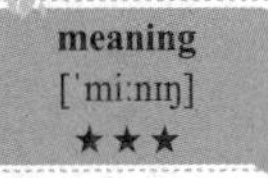

释义 *n.* 意思,含义;重要性,价值

例句 The word "flight" has two different *meanings*: a plane journey, and the act of running away. "flight" 一词有两个不同的意思:航程和逃跑。

派生 meaningful *adj.* 有意义的,重要的

用法 give meaning to sth. 赋予……意义

occupy
[ˈɒkjupaɪ]
★★

释义 v. 占领;占有;使从事;使忙于

例句 The bed seemed to *occupy* most of the room. 床似乎占去了大半个屋子。

Problems at work continued to *occupy* his mind for some time. 工作上的问题继续在他的脑海中萦绕了一段时间。

用法 occupy sb.'s attention 引起某人的注意

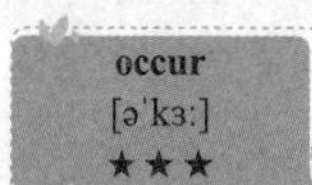

occur
[əˈkɜː]
★★★

释义 v. 发生;存在;突然出现

例句 Something unexpected *occurred*. 发生了一件出乎意料的事。

真题 The Government has pledged to change the law to introduce a minimum service requirement so that, even when strikes *occur*, services can continue to operate. 政府承诺修改法律,引入最低服务要求,以便即使发生罢工,服务也能继续。(2021 阅读理解)

派生 occurrence *n.* 发生,出现

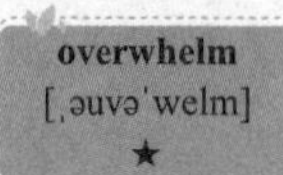

overwhelm
[ˌəuvəˈwelm]
★

释义 v. 覆盖,淹没;压倒,制服

例句 A great wave *overwhelmed* the boat. 一个巨浪吞没了那只小船。

Invading armies *overwhelmed* the town. 入侵的军队控制了这个城镇。

派生 overwhelming *adj.* 难以抗拒的

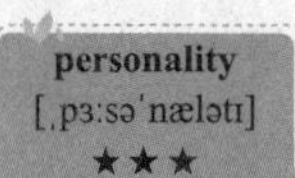

personality
[ˌpɜːsəˈnælətɪ]
★★★

释义 n. 人格,个性

短语 *personality* development 人格发展

例句 The *personality* ethic suggests that people are likely to succeed if they have positive mental attitude. 人格伦理表明,如果人们有积极的精神态度,他们就有可能成功。

近义 character *n.* 性格,品质;特色

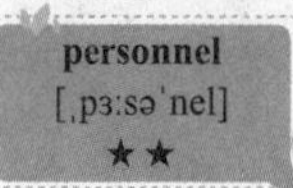

personnel
[ˌpɜːsəˈnel]
★★

释义 n. 全体人员,全体职员;人事(部门)

例句 I want to look at these both from a financial and from a *personnel* point of view and to offer a few hopefully effective solutions. 我想从财务和人事两方面来研究这些问题,并提供一些有望有效的解决方案。

真题 There's no change to collective bargaining at the USPS, a major omission considering that *personnel* accounts for 80 percent of the agency's costs. 美国邮政局的集体契约是不能更改的,考虑到人工成本占该机构成本的 80%,这无疑是重大遗漏。(2018 阅读理解)

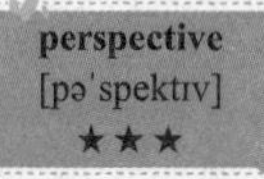

perspective
[pəˈspektɪv]
★★★

释义 n. 观点,看法;远景;透视图

短语 historical *perspective* 历史展望

例句 "It's already a huge problem from a public expenditure *perspective* for the whole country," he says. 他表示:"从公共支出的角度来看,这已经是整个国家的一个巨大问题。"

近义 viewpoint *n.* 观点,看法

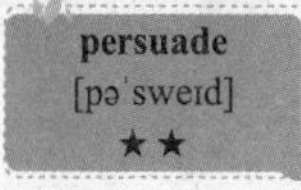

persuade
[pəˈsweɪd]
★★

释义 v. 说服,劝说;使相信

例句 The Conservative Party's victory in April's general election *persuaded* him to run for President again. 保守党在 4 月大选中的胜利使他再次竞选总统。

用法 persuade sb. of sth. 使某人相信某事

近义 convince *v.* 使确信;说服

派生 persuasion *n.* 说服,说服力

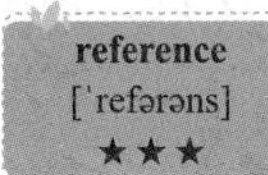

reference
['refərəns]
★★★

释义 *n.* 参考;查询;提及 *adj.* 参考的 *v.* 提及,提到

短语 *reference* value 参考值 *reference* book 参考书

例句 She made no *reference* to her illness but only to her future plans. 她没有提到她的病,只说了她未来的计划。

The book *references* many other authors who have written on this topic. 这本书引用了许多其他作者写过关于这个主题的文章。

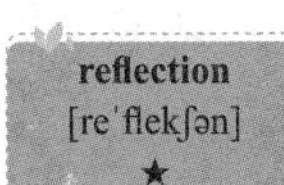

reflection
[re'flekʃən]
★

释义 *n.* (reflexion) 映像,倒影;反省,沉思

短语 mirror *reflection* 镜面反射

例句 Students, your behavior is a *reflection* on this school. At the game this Saturday, I expect there to be no fighting or name-calling. 同学们,你们的行为反映了这所学校的风貌。在这个周六的比赛中,我希望不会有打架或谩骂的发生。

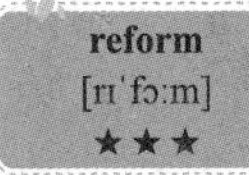

reform
[rɪ'fɔːm]
★★★

释义 *v.* / *n.* 改革,改造,改良

短语 educational / technical *reform* 教育 / 技术改革

例句 Economic *reform* has brought relative wealth to peasant farmers. 经济改革给农民带来了相对的财富。

真题 This is why repeated attempts at *reform* legislation have failed in recent years. 这就是为什么近年来改革立法的多次尝试都失败了。(2018 阅读理解)

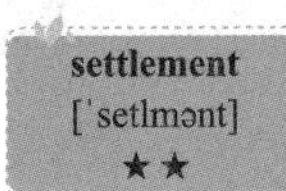

settlement
['setlmənt]
★★

释义 *n.* 解决;协议,和解;定居点

短语 international *settlement* 国际清算 a peace *settlement* 和平协议

例句 Both sides say they want to try to reach a political *settlement* in the embattled north and east of the island. 双方都表示想设法为处于战乱中的北部岛屿和东部岛屿找到政治解决方案。

用法 reach a settlement 达成协议

派生 agreement *n.* 协议

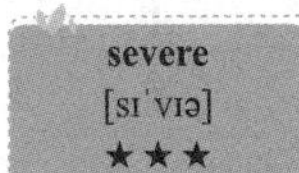

severe
[sɪ'vɪə]
★★★

释义 *adj.* 严厉的;严重的;艰巨的

短语 *severe* punishment 严厉惩罚

例句 The French measures, however, rely too much on *severe* punishment to change a culture that still regards beauty as skin-deep and bone-showing. 然而,法国的措施过于依赖严厉的惩罚来改变一种仍然视美丽为肤浅和骨感的文化。(2016 阅读理解)

用法 be severe with sb. 对某人严厉

派生 severity *n.* 严厉

shelter
['ʃeltə]
★★

释义 *n.* 避难所;住处;掩蔽 *v.* 掩蔽,躲避,庇护

短语 emergency *shelter* 应急避难所

例句 Although horses do not generally mind the cold, *shelter* from rain and wind is important. 尽管马一般不怕冷,但是一定要有个能遮风挡雨的马棚。

Trees *shelter* the house from the wind. 树给房子挡住了风。

用法 shelter from sth. 躲避某物

派生 sheltered *adj.* 受保护的

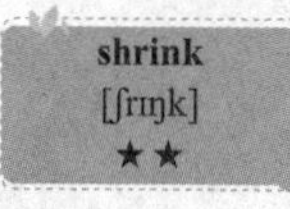

释义 *v.* 收缩，缩小；退缩，畏缩

例句 The town's population *shrank* during the war. 这个城镇的人口在战争期间减少了。

He is decisive and won't *shrink* from a fight. 他很果断，而且不会逃避战斗。

用法 shrink from 退避

派生 shrinkage *n.* 收缩

释义 *v.* 使害怕，使惊恐

例句 He was *terrified* about the pressure of having to do 50 shows for his upcoming tour. 他将在即将到来的巡演中做 50 场演出，这种压力让他感到恐惧。

派生 terrifying *adj.* 吓人的，令人害怕的

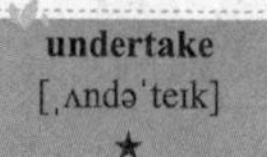

释义 *v.* 承担；许诺，保证；从事

短语 *undertake* a task/project 承担一个任务 / 项目

例句 Do not *undertake* strenuous exercise for a few hours after a meal to allow food to digest. 饭后几个小时不要从事剧烈运动，以便食物能够消化。

近义 commence *v.* 开始 promise *v.* 承诺，保证

派生 undertaking *n.* 任务，企业；许诺，保证

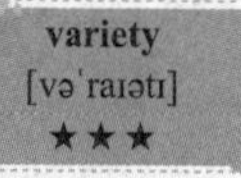

释义 *n.* 种种，多种多样；种类，品种

短语 *variety* show 综艺节目 *variety* store 杂货店

例句 The college offers a wide *variety* of courses for women wanting to return to education. 该大学为有志返校接受教育的女子提供了各种课程。

用法 a great variety of 各种各样的；大量的

近义 diversity *n.* 多样化

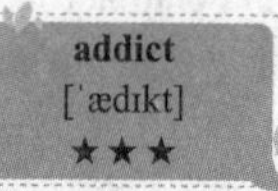

释义 *n.* 上瘾的人 *v.* 使上瘾

短语 a video game *addict* 游戏机迷

例句 She is a TV *addict* and watches as much as she can. 她是个电视迷，看起电视来没完没了。

派生 addiction *n.* 入迷

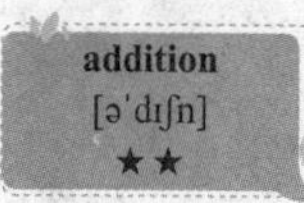

释义 *n.* 增加；增加的人或物

例句 In *addition* to burgers, sandwiches and wraps, we offer a number of signature meals. 除了汉堡、三明治和卷饼，我们还提供许多特色餐。

用法 in addition (to) 除……之外

派生 additional *adj.* 附加的

释义 *n.* 战役；战斗

例句 The *battle* for Kyiv continued late into the night. 基辅的战斗持续到深夜。

近义 fight *v.* 与……做斗争

真题 It was also, and this is unknown even to many people well read about the period, a battle between those who made codes and those who broke them. 这也是一场编写密码者和破译密码者之间的战争，甚至许多熟读这段时期历史的人都不知道。（2022 翻译）

释义 *n.* / *v.* 注释，评论

例句 I'd appreciate your *comments* on this issue. 我将不胜感激您对这个问题的回答。

She *commented* that the service seemed slow. 她评论说服务似乎很慢。

用法 have no comment 无可奉告

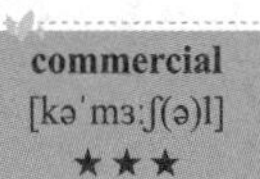

释义 *n.* 商业，贸易；交往

短语 industry and *commerce* 工商业

例句 At least 226 businesses closed within a year, according to an area chamber of *commerce*. 根据一个地区商会的数据，一年内至少有 226 家企业倒闭。

近义 trade *n.* 贸易

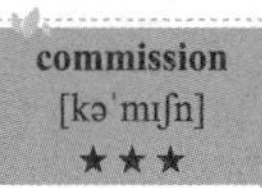

释义 *adj.* 商业的；商务的 *n.* 广告节目

短语 *commercial* use 商业用途

例句 Going forward, the scientists hope to turn their discovery into a *commercial* product. 展望未来，科学家们希望将他们的发现转化为商业产品。

派生 commercially *adv.* 商业上

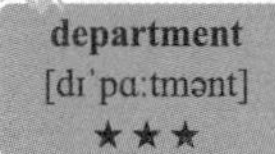

释义 *n.* 委员会；委任；佣金 *v.* 委托

短语 federal communications *commission* 联邦通信委员会

例句 The *commission* is made up of five people. 委员会由五个人组成。

The salesman can get *commission* on everything he sells. 这个售货员能得到每件所售货物的佣金。

派生 commissioner *n.* 委员

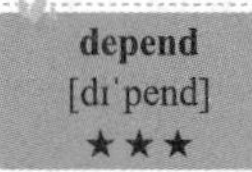

释义 *n.* 部门；科；系

短语 *department* store 百货公司 education *department* 教育部

例句 In 2017, for example, the State *Department* allowed 171,952 Mexicans to become immigrants. 以 2017 年为例，美国国务院允许 171,952 名墨西哥人成为移民。

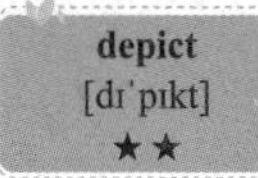

释义 *v.* 取决于，依靠，信赖，相信

例句 They *depend* completely on the land for their livelihood. 他们完全依靠土地为生。

用法 depend on sb. / sth. 取决于；依赖

depict
[dɪˈpɪkt]
★★

释义 *v.* 描绘；描写，描述

例句 The book vividly *depicts* the lives of ordinary French people in the last century. 这本书生动地描绘了上个世纪法国普通人的生活。

真题 In the movies and on television, artificial intelligence (AI) is typically *depicted* as something sinister that will upend our way of life. 在电影和电视中，人工智能通常被描绘成一种会颠覆我们生活方式的不祥之物。（2021 阅读理解）

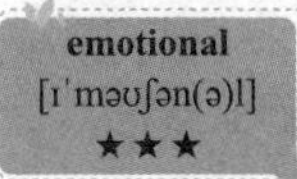

释义 *adj.* 情感的，情绪的；情绪激动的

短语 an *emotional* appeal 情感诉求

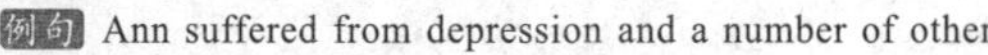

例句 Ann suffered from depression and a number of other *emotional* problems . 安患有抑郁症和许多其他情绪问题。

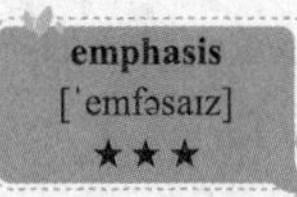

释义 *n.* 强调，重点

例句 The *emphasis* is on developing fitness through exercises and training. 重点在于通过锻炼促进健康。

派生 emphasize *v.* 强调

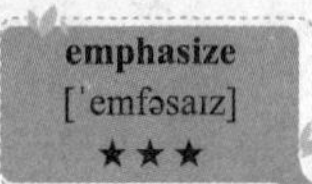

释义 *v.* 强调；重读

短语 *emphasize* creativity 强调创意

例句 Franklin made a speech *emphasizing* the need for more volunteers. 富兰克林做了一个演讲，强调需要更多的志愿者。

派生 emphasis *n.* 强调

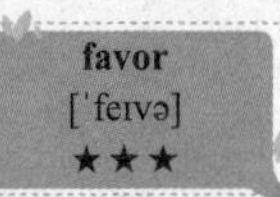

释义 *n.* (favour) 好感；喜爱；关切 *v.* 赞成，支持，偏爱

例句 The women say faculty opportunities in economics *favor* men. 这些女性表示，经济学的教职机会更倾向于给男性。

用法 do sb. a favor 帮某人的忙

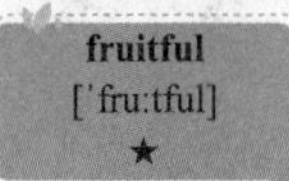

释义 *adj.* 多产的；富有成效的

短语 a *fruitful* discussion 富有成果的讨论

例句 It was a *fruitful* meeting; we made a lot of important decisions. 这是一次很有成效的会议，我们做出了许多重大决定。

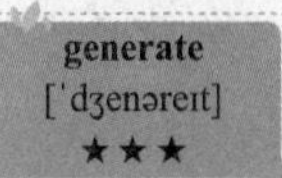

释义 *v.* 生成，产生；引起，导致

短语 *generate* electricity 发电

例句 The advertising campaign *generated* a lot of interest in our work. 广告活动引起了人们对我们工作的极大兴趣。

派生 generation *n.* 一代；产生

释义 *n.* 急忙，匆忙

短语 *haste* makes waste 欲速则不达

例句 While many appreciated the merger, some people said this step had been taken in *haste*. 虽然许多人对合并表示赞赏，但也有人表示，这一举措过于仓促。

派生 hasty *adj.* 仓促的；草率的

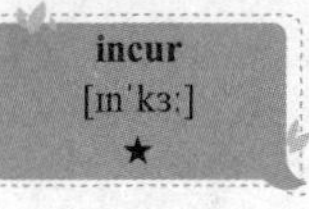

释义 *v.* 招致，遭受，引起

例句 Few students are willing to bear the burden of debt *incurred* at university. 很少有学生愿意承担大学期间的债务负担。

派生 incurrence *n.* 招致；遭受

近义 suffer *v.* 经受，遭受

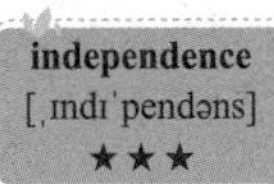

释义 *n.* 独立，自主

短语 financial *independence* 经济独立

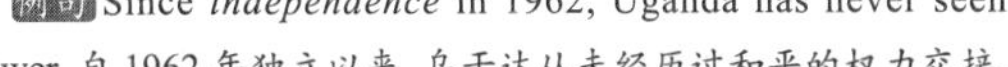

例句 Since *independence* in 1962, Uganda has never seen a peaceful transfer of power. 自1962年独立以来，乌干达从未经历过和平的权力交接。

反义 dependence *n.* 依赖

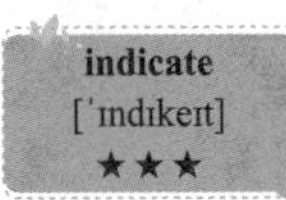

释义 *v.* 指出，指示；表明，暗示

例句 At University of Pennsylvania, students are not asked to *indicate* race when applying for housing. 在宾夕法尼亚大学，学生在申请住房时不要求注明种族。

派生 indication *n.* 指出，指示；表明，暗示

释义 *n.* 空闲，闲暇；悠闲，安逸

短语 *leisure* center 休闲中心 *leisure* time 休闲时间

例句 These days, because *leisure* time is relatively scarce for most workers, people use their free time to counterbalance the intellectual and emotional demands of their jobs. 如今，由于大多数工人的休闲时间相对较少，人们利用闲暇时间来平衡工作中的智力和情感需求。

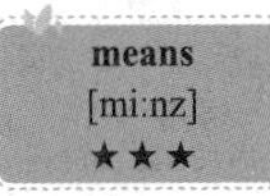

释义 *n.* 方法，手段

例句 Most archaeological sites have been located by *means* of careful searching, while many others have been discovered by accident. 大多数考古遗址是通过仔细搜索确定的，而其他许多是偶然发现的。

用法 by no means 绝不

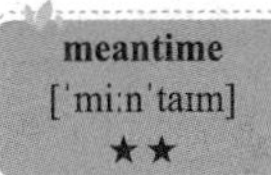

释义 *n.* 其间，其时 *adv.* 同时

短语 in the *meantime* 在此期间

例句 In the *meantime*, anyone planning a trip to the Alps might want to select their winter headgear very carefully. 在此期间，打算去阿尔卑斯山旅行的人恐怕要非常小心地选择冬天的帽子了。

同义 meanwhile *n.* 其间 *adv.* 与此同时

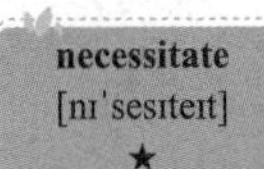

释义 *v.* 使……成为必要，需要

例句 Your proposal *necessitates* borrowing money. 你的提议使借款成为必要。

近义 demand *v.* 需要

派生 necessitation *n.* 迫使；必需

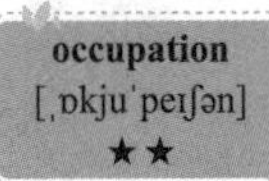

释义 *n.* 工作；职业；消遣；占领

例句 He carried on several *occupations* at a time. 他同时从事几种职业。

Reading is a useful *occupation* to us. 阅读对我们来说是一种有益的消遣。

The areas under *occupation* contained major industrial areas. 被占领地区拥有主要的工业区。

用法 be under occupation 被占领

overwhelming
[ˌəʊvəˈwelmɪŋ]
★★

释义 *adj.* 势不可挡的,压倒一切的;巨大的

短语 an *overwhelming* sense of loss 莫大的失落感

例句 The flood was *overwhelming* and the city was soon drowned. 洪水来势凶猛,很快这个城市就被淹没了。

派生 overwhelmingly *adv.* 压倒性地

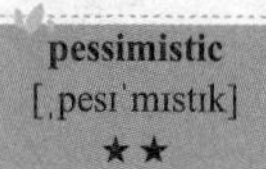

pessimistic
[ˌpesɪˈmɪstɪk]
★★

释义 *adj.* 悲观(主义)的

短语 a *pessimistic* view 悲观的看法

例句 The survey found that most younger voters are *pessimistic* about the outcome. 调查发现,大多数年轻选民对选举结果持悲观态度。

用法 be pessimistic about sth. 对某事很悲观

反义 optimistic *adj.* 乐观的

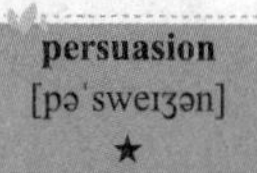

persuasion
[pəˈsweɪʒən]
★

释义 *n.* 说服,说服力

短语 burden of *persuasion* 举证责任

例句 Even administrative regulations must be accompanied by *persuasion* and education. 即使是行政命令也要伴以说服和教育。

派生 persuasive *adj.* 有说服力的

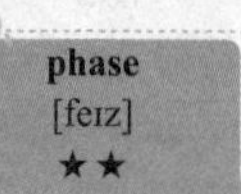

phase
[feɪz]
★★

释义 *n.* 阶段,时期 *v.* 逐步进行

短语 the initial / final *phase* of ... ……的初始/最后阶段

例句 It is not easy to talk about the role of the mass media in this overwhelmingly significant *phase* in European history. 要谈论大众媒体在欧洲历史上这个极其重要的阶段所起的作用是不容易的。

The redundancies will be *phased* over two years. 裁员将在两年内分阶段进行。

近义 stage *n.* 阶段,时期

phenomenon
[fɪˈnɒmɪnən]
★★★

释义 *n.* 现象,杰出人才

短语 social *phenomenon* 社会现象

例句 Staying up late, an increasingly common *phenomenon*, can result in a series of health problems. 熬夜是一种越来越普遍的现象,它会导致一系列健康问题。

refrain
[riːˈfreɪn]
★

释义 *v.* 节制,避免,制止 *n.* 经常重复的评价;叠句,副歌

例句 I was going to make a joke but I *refrained*. 我本想开个玩笑,但我忍住了。

A common *refrain* among teachers these days is that the schools need more funding. 如今,教师们普遍认为学校需要更多的资金。

近义 restrain *v.* 抑制

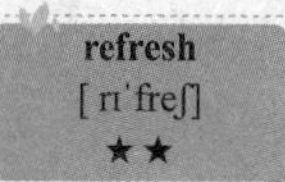

refresh
[rɪˈfreʃ]
★★

释义 *v.* (使)精神振作,(使)精力恢复;刷新,更新(网页)

例句 It was such a hot night that I had a cold shower to *refresh* myself. 那天晚上实在太热,我冲了个凉水澡凉快一下。

There's no need to *refresh* the page as it will automatically update. 不需要刷新页面,因为它会自动更新。

用法 refresh oneself 提神

派生 refreshment *n.* 恢复活力，焕发精神

refuge ['refju:dʒ] ★

释义 *n.* 避难处，藏身处

短语 seek *refuge* 寻求避难

例句 He regarded the room as a *refuge* from the outside world. 他把这个屋子当作是逃避外界的避难所。

派生 refugee *n.* 难民

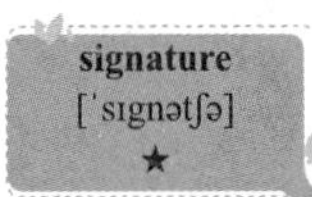

signature ['sɪgnətʃə] ★

释义 *n.* 签名，署名，签字

短语 digital *signature* 数字签名

例句 The package is too big and it needs a *signature* to confirm you have received it. 这个包裹太大了，需要签名确认你收到了。

近义 autograph *n.*（名人的）亲笔签名

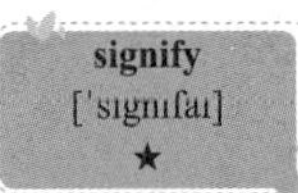

signify ['sɪgnɪfaɪ] ★

释义 *v.* 表示，意味；要紧，有重要性

例句 The contrasting approaches to Europe *signified* a sharp difference between the major parties. 对欧洲截然不同的态度表明两大政党间存在巨大差异。

用法 signify one's dissent 表示异议

近义 indicate *v.* 表明；象征

派生 significant *adj.* 重要的

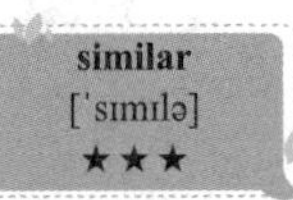

similar ['sɪmɪlə] ★★★

释义 *adj.* 相似的，类似的

短语 *similar* interests 兴趣相仿

例句 Israel's neighbors face a *similar* situation. 以色列的邻国面临着相似的困境。

真题 One of the remarkable findings of the study was that the *similar* genes seem to be evolving faster than other genes. 这项研究的一个巨大发现是，相似的基因似乎比其他基因进化得更快。（2015 完形填空）

派生 similarly *adv.* 相似地

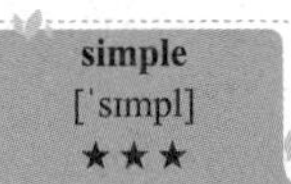

simple ['sɪmpl] ★★★

释义 *adj.* 简单的；单纯的，直率的

短语 in *simple* terms 简言之

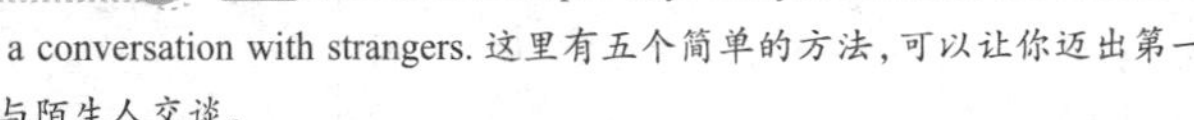

例句 Here are five *simple* ways that you can make the first move and start a conversation with strangers. 这里有五个简单的方法，可以让你迈出第一步，开始与陌生人交谈。

反义 complicated *adj.* 复杂的

territory ['terɪtərɪ] ★★

释义 *n.* 领土；版图；领域，范围

短语 Indian *territory* 印第安人保留区

例句 Peter the Great expands *territory* beyond the Euro mountains along the Caspian Sea. 彼得大帝沿着里海将领土扩展到欧洲山脉之外。

近义 region *n.* 地区，范围 area *n.* 区域，范围

派生 territorial *adj.* 领土的

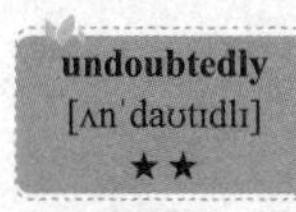

undoubtedly [ʌnˈdaʊtɪdlɪ] ★★

释义 *adv.* 无疑，必定

例句 The most testing time is *undoubtedly* in the early months of your return to work. 最考验人的时候无疑是在你重返工作岗位的头几个月。

近义 certainly *adv.* 无疑

various [ˈvɛərɪəs] ★★★

释义 *adj.* 各种各样的；不同的

短语 *various* options 不同的选择

例句 Dutch students graduate at *various* times of the year. 荷兰学生每年都在不同的时间毕业。

派生 variously *adv.* 不同地；多方面地

真题 Those retailers may face headaches complying with *various* state sales tax laws. 这些零售商可能会面临遵守各州销售税法的难题。(2019 阅读理解)

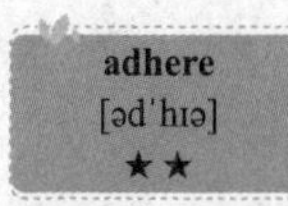

adhere [ədˈhɪə] ★★

释义 *v.* 附着；遵守；坚持

例句 All members of the association *adhere* to a strict code of practice. 协会的所有成员都遵守一套严格的行为规范。

用法 adhere to 坚持；遵守

派生 adherence *n.* 遵守

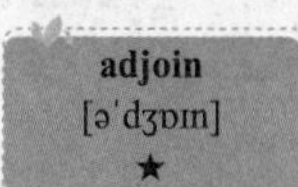

adjoin [əˈdʒɒɪn] ★

释义 *v.* 邻接；毗连

例句 The island nearly *adjoins* the mainland. 这个岛几乎与大陆毗连。

用法 adjoin to 与……毗连

派生 adjoining *adj.* 邻接的

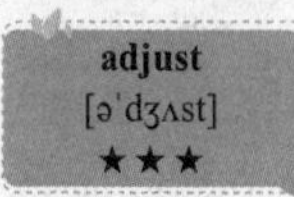

adjust [əˈdʒʌst] ★★★

释义 *v.* 调整；适应

例句 I *adjusted* the volume on the radio. 我调整了收音机的音量。

I can't *adjust* to living on my own. 我不习惯独自生活。

派生 adjustment *n.* 调节；适应

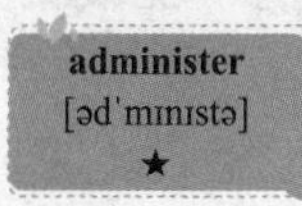

administer [ədˈmɪnɪstə] ★

释义 *v.* 管理；给予；执行

短语 *administer* a charity 管理一家慈善机构

例句 It takes brains to *administer* upon a large corporation. 管理一家大公司需要智慧。

派生 administration *n.* 行政；管理

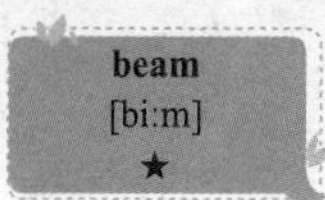

beam [biːm] ★

释义 *n.* 光线；梁 *v.* 笑容满面 *v.* 照射；眉开眼笑；播送

例句 A *beam* of light slices through the darkness. 一道光束划破了黑暗。

She *beamed* as she told us the good news. 当她告诉我们这个好消息时，她微笑着。

The interview was *beamed* live across the state. 这次采访在全州做了现场直播。

释义 *v.* 犯（错误），干（坏事）；（使）致力于；承诺

例句 People who *commit* crimes end up in jail. 犯罪的人最后都进了监狱。

The two governments were *committed* to an enduring friendship. 两国政府致力于建立长久的友谊。

派生 commitment *n.* 忠诚；承诺

释义 *n.* 委员会，全体委员

短语 management *committee* 管理委员会

例句 I was on the parents' *committee* at my kids' school. 我是我孩子学校的家委会成员。

近义 commission *n.* 委员会

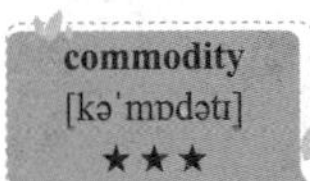

释义 *n.* 日用品；商品；必需品

短语 *commodity* fair 商品展览会

例句 *Commodity* prices remain stable and there are plenty of goods on the market. 商品价格稳定，市场货源充足。

近义 goods *n.* 商品

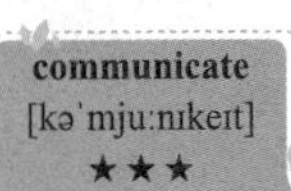

释义 *v.* 交流；传达；通讯，通话

例句 We *communicated* mostly by e-mail. 我们主要通过电子邮件沟通。

派生 communication *n.* 通讯

真题 The growth of the use of English as the world's primary language for international *communication* has obviously been continuing for several decades. 作为国际交流的主要语言，英语的使用人数已经持续几十年上升。（2017 阅读理解）

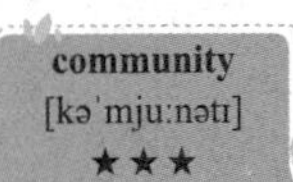

释义 *n.* 界，团体；社区

短语 scientific / academic *community* 科学界 / 学术界

例句 Celebrating the festival was a great way for the local *community* to get together. 庆祝这个节日是当地社区聚会的好方式。

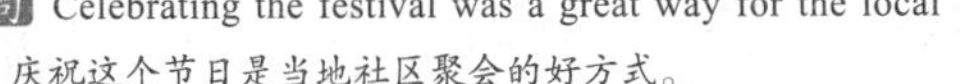

近义 association *n.* 协会，社团

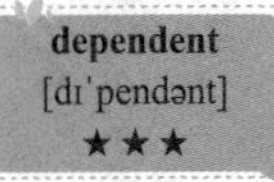

释义 *adj.* 依靠的；从属的；随……而定的

例句 Norway's economy is heavily *dependent* on natural resources. 挪威的经济严重依赖自然资源。

用法 be dependent on 依赖；取决于

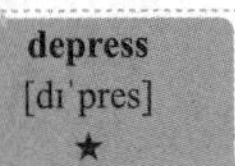

释义 *v.* 使沮丧，降低；使不景气；按下

例句 The rainy days always *depress* me. 雨天总是使我沮丧。

That economic hardship is likely to *depress* consumption, slowing a recovery. 这种经济困难可能会抑制消费，减缓经济复苏。

派生 depressed *adj.* 抑郁的；萧条的

deprive
[dɪˈpraɪv]
★★

释义 *v.* 剥夺，夺去，使丧失

例句 You can't function properly when you're *deprived* of sleep. 当你睡眠不足，你就无法正常工作。

派生 deprived *adj.* 贫困的，穷苦的

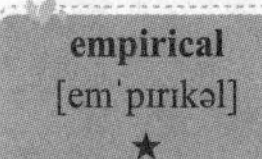

释义 *adj.* 凭经验（或观察）的，经验主义的

短语 *empirical* study 实证研究

例句 *Empirical* studies show that some forms of alternative medicine are extremely effective. 实证研究表明，某些形式的替代医药非常有效。

释义 *n.* / *v.* 雇用；用，使用

例句 A lot of local workers are *employed* in the tourism industry. 许多当地工作人员受雇于旅游业。

用法 be employed as sth. 被雇用为……

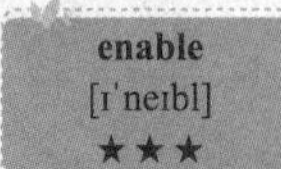

释义 *v.* 使能够，使成为可能；授权

例句 The new test *enables* engineers to detect the problems in time. 这项新测试使工程师能够及时发现问题。

反义 disable *v.* 使丧失能力

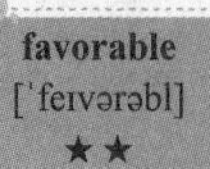

释义 *adj.* (favourable) 赞许的，有利的，讨人喜欢的

短语 *favorable* price 优惠价格

例句 Employees who receive a very *favorable* evaluation may deserve some type of recognition or even a promotion. 得到非常好的评价的员工可能应该得到某种形式的认可，甚至是升职。

派生 favorably *adv.* 有利地

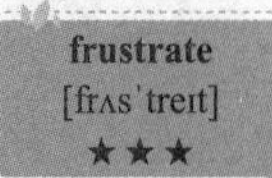

释义 *v.* 挫败，阻挠，使灰心

例句 Thick fog *frustrated* their attempt to land on the tiny island. 浓雾使他们在小岛上登陆的计划失败了。

派生 frustration *n.* 沮丧

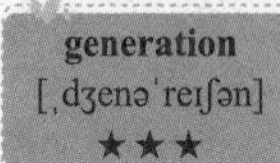

释义 *n.* 一代人，一代；产生

短语 young *generation* 年轻一代

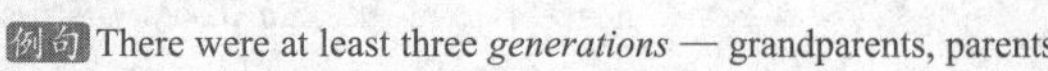

例句 There were at least three *generations* — grandparents, parents and children at the wedding. 婚礼上至少有3代人——祖父母、父母和孩子们。

Steam and water power are used for the *generation* of electricity. 蒸汽和水能可用来发电。

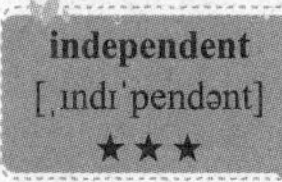

释义 *adj.* 独立的，自主的

真题 Successful markets require *independent* and even combative standard-setters. 健康的市场需要独立甚至富有战斗力的标准制定者。（2010 阅读理解）

反义 dependent *adj.* 依赖的

派生 independently *adv.* 独立地；自立地

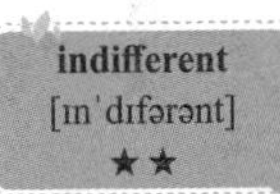

释义 *adj.* 冷漠的，不关心的，不积极的

例句 They are *indifferent* to the inconvenience caused to others. 他们对给别人带来的不便无动于衷。

用法 have become indifferent to sth. 对某事漠不关心，无动于衷

派生 indifference *n.* 漠不关心

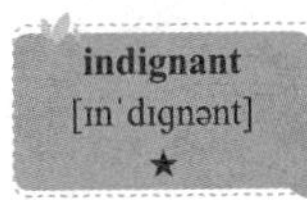

释义 *adj.* 愤慨的，愤慨不平的

例句 They were *indignant* that they hadn't been invited. 他们因没有受到邀请而愤愤不平。

近义 furious *adj.* 狂怒的，暴怒的

派生 indignation *n.* 愤愤不平

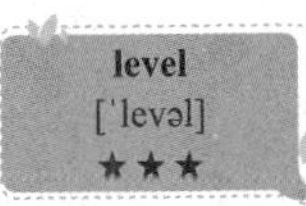

释义 *n.* 水平，水准，等级 *v.* 铺平 *adj.* 水平的

例句 Local citizens boast not only high incomes but also high *levels* of education. 当地居民不仅收入高，而且受教育水平也高。

用法 be level with 跟……相齐

真题 Progressives often support diversity mandates as a path to equality and a way to *level* the playing field. 进步人士往往支持多元化规定，将其当作是通向平等的道路和创造公平竞争环境的途径。(2020阅读理解)

释义 *n.* 其时，其间 *adv.* 当时，与此同时

例句 Carl's starting college in September. *Meanwhile*, he's travelling around Europe. 卡尔9月将开始大学生活。此间他将会环游欧洲。

真题 *Meanwhile*, it has more than $120 billion in unfunded liabilities, mostly for employee health and retirement costs. 与此同时，该公司还有超过1200亿美元的资金负债，主要用于员工健康和退休成本。(2018阅读理解)

同义 meantime *n.* 其间，其时 *adv.* 同时

释义 *v.* 测量，分派，权衡 *n.* 尺寸，量度器，措施，办法

例句 It is difficult to *measure* the success of the campaign at this stage. 现阶段还难以估量这场运动的成败。

派生 measurement *n.* 测量，计算

真题 In signing the *measure*, California Governor Jerry Brown admitted that the law, which expressly classifies people on the basis of sex, is probably unconstitutional. 在签署这项措施时，加州州长杰里·布朗承认，这项以性别为基础明确划分人群的法律可能是违宪的。(2020阅读理解)

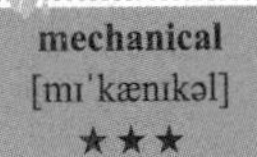

释义 *adj.* 机械的，由机构制成的；机械似的

短语 a *mechanical* device 机械设备 *mechanical* property 机械能

例句 Early in the Industrial Revolution, some *mechanical* devices were built to automate long tedious tasks, such as guiding patterns for looms. 在工业革命的早期，一些机械设备被制造出来以自动执行冗长烦琐的任务，例如织布机的导向模式。

派生 mechanically *adv.* 机械地

释义 *n.* 发生，出现；事件；发生的事

短语 probability of *occurrence* 发生概率

例句 The factors that influence the *occurrence* of disasters are natural, geological environment and human action factors. 影响地质灾害发生的因素有自然因素、地质环境因素及人为因素。

近义 appearance *n.* 出现

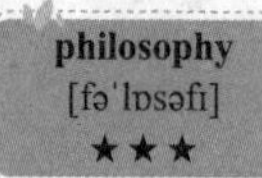

释义 *n.* 所有（权），所有制

短语 land *ownership* 土地拥有权 home *ownership* 自置居所

例句 By 1996 foreign-born immigrants who had arrived before 1970 had a home *ownership* rate of 75.6 percent. 到 1996 年，1970 年之前抵达的外国出生的移民的住房拥有率为 75.6%。

释义 *n.* 哲学，哲理

短语 business *philosophy* 经营理念 natural *philosophy* 自然哲学

例句 Psychology began as a purely academic offshoot of natural *philosophy*. 心理学形成之初是作为自然哲学的一个纯学术分支。

派生 philosopher *n.* 哲学家

释义 *n.* 短语，习语

短语 key *phrase* 关键短语

例句 The *phrase* “less is more” was actually first popularized by a German. “少即是多”这个短语实际上是由一个德国人首先推广的。

派生 phrasal *adj.* 短语的

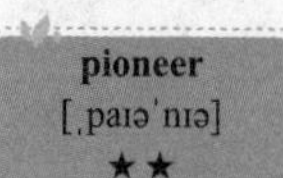

释义 *adj.* 物质的；身体的；物理的

短语 *physical* education 体育课 *physical* quality 身体素质

例句 According to one classical theory of emotion, our feelings are partially rooted in *physical* reactions. 根据一种经典的情绪理论，我们的感觉部分来源于身体反应。

反义 mental *adj.* 精神的，思想的

释义 *n.* 先驱，倡导者，开拓者

短语 young *pioneer* 少先队员

例句 He was a genius, a *pioneer* who moved from one new field to the next. 他是一个天才，从一个新领域进入下一个领域的先锋。

用法 a pioneer of... ……的先锋

派生 pioneering *adj.* 先驱性的

释义 *n.*（政治上的）避难者，难民

短语 a *refugee* camp 难民营 a political *refugee* 政治避难者

例句 She came to the country as a *refugee* from Somalia at age 12. 她 12 岁时，作为难民从索马里来到这个国家。

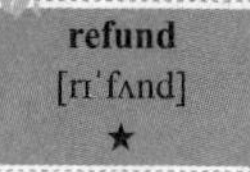

释义 *n.* 退款 *v.* 退还，偿付

例句 Take the goods back to your retailer who will *refund* you the purchase price. 把商品退还给你的零售商，他们会按原价退款的。

Concert attendees can receive a full *refund* if the concert is canceled or rescheduled. 如果演唱会取消或改期，观众可以获得全额退款。

派生 refundable *adj.* 可退还的

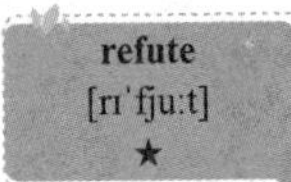

释义 *v.* 反驳，驳斥；否认

短语 *refute* a claim 驳斥一个人说法

例句 The hearing was a chance for Moore to *refute* claims made against her. 听证会是摩尔反驳对她的指控的机会。

同义 contradict *v.* 反驳

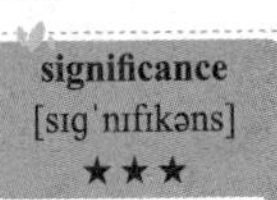

释义 *n.* 意义，含义；重要性，重要的

短语 political *significance* 政治意义

例句 This helped us to appreciate more deeply the *significance* of this work. 这帮助我们更深地理解了这个工作的意义。

用法 the significance of sth. 某事的重要性

近义 importance *n.* 重要，重要性

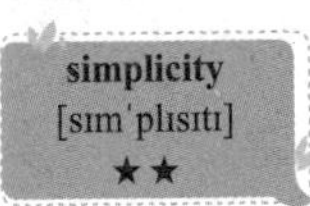

释义 *n.* 简单，简易；直率，单纯

例句 Because of its *simplicity*, this test could be carried out easily by a family doctor. 由于这项测试简单，可以很容易地由家庭医生进行操作。

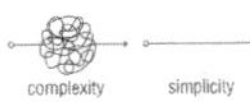

用法 for simplicity 为简单起见

近义 plainness *n.* 简单；朴素

反义 complexity *n.* 复杂性

派生 simplification *n.* 简单化

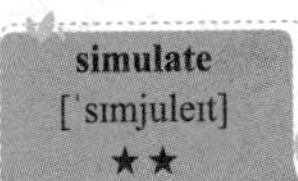

释义 *v.* 模仿，模拟；假装，冒充

短语 *simulate* human behaviour 模拟人类行为

例句 The scientist developed a model to *simulate* a full year of the globe's climate. 这位科学家开发了一个模型来模拟全球全年的气候。

近义 pretend *v.* 伪装，假装；假扮

派生 simulation *n.* 模拟，仿造物；假装

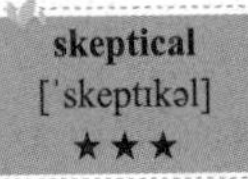

释义 *adj.* (sceptical) 怀疑的

例句 *Sceptical* observers believe that ancestry testing fails to achieve the claimed accuracy. 持怀疑态度的观察人士认为，祖先测试无法达到所宣称的准确性。

用法 skeptical about sth. 对某事表示怀疑

同义 doubtful *adj.* 怀疑的，不确定的

派生 skepticism *n.* 怀疑主义

释义 *n.* 恐怖；可怕的人（事）

例句 These people have been living with *terror* and the threat of *terror* for many years. 这些人多年来一直生活在恐怖和恐怖的威胁中。

用法 in terror 恐惧地

派生 terrorism *n.* 恐怖主义

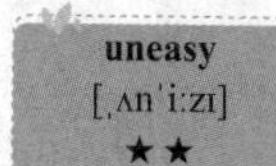
uneasy
[ˌʌnˈiːzɪ]
★★

释义 *adj.* 不安的，焦虑的，不稳定的

短语 an *uneasy* feeling 不安的心情

例句 The fighting of recent days has given way to an *uneasy* truce between the two sides. 最近几天的交战已结束，双方好不容易达成了休战协议。

用法 uneasy about 担忧

派生 uneasily *adv.* 心神不安地

vary
[ˈveərɪ]
★★★

释义 *v.* 改变，变化；使多样化

例句 Those costs would *vary* depending on the size and scale of the businesses. 这些成本将根据企业的规模和大小而有所不同。

用法 vary in 在……方面变化

近义 differ *v.* 不同于

派生 variety *n.* 多样化

Word List 14

admit
[ədˈmɪt]
★★★

释义 *v.* 承认；准许进入；接收入院

例句 They freely *admit* (that) they still have a lot to learn. 他们坦率承认，他们要学的东西还很多。

You will not be *admitted* to the theatre after the performance has started. 演出开始后不许进入剧场。

派生 admission *n.* 准许进入；承认

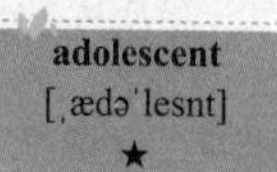
adolescent
[ˌædəˈlesnt]
★

释义 *n.* 青少年 *adj.* 青春期的

例句 He read many books in the *adolescent* stage of his life. 他在青年时期读了很多书。

Young *adolescents* are happiest with small groups of close friends. 青少年在和自己小圈子里的好友待在一起时最为开心。

派生 adolescence *n.* 青春期

adopt
[əˈdɒpt]
★★★

释义 *v.* 收养；采纳；批准

例句 The couple finally happily married and planned to *adopt* a child. 这对夫妇最终幸福地结婚了，并计划收养一个孩子。

The council is expected to *adopt* the new policy at its next meeting. 委员会有望在下次会议上正式通过这项新政策。

派生 adoption *n.* 采用；收养

advance
[ədˈvɑːns]
★★★

释义 *v.*（使）前进；发展；促进 *n.* 进展；提高 *adj.* 预先的

例句 Too much protein in the diet may *advance* the ageing process. 饮食中摄入过量蛋白质可能会加速衰老。

派生 advancement *n.* 进步，进展；提升

真题 A recent paper says that the problem is not merely that people do bad science, but that our current system of career *advancement* positively encourages it. 最近的一篇论文指出，问题不仅在于人们的科学水平低下，还在于我们当前的职业发展体系积极地促进了这一现象。（2019 翻译）

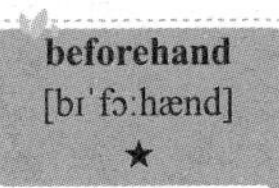

释义 *adv.* 预先；事先

短语 a few hours *beforehand* 几小时前

例句 When you give a speech, it's natural to feel nervous *beforehand*. 当你演讲时，事先感到紧张是很自然的。

释义 *v.* / *n.* 通勤

例句 He lives in the suburb and *commutes* to work every day. 他住在郊区，每天通勤上班。

派生 commuter *n.* 上下班往返的人

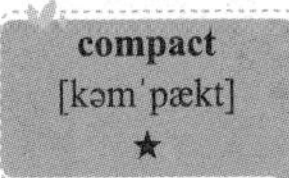

释义 *n.* 协议，契约 *adj.* 紧凑的 *v.* 使紧密结合；把……压实

短语 *compact* car 小型汽车

例句 The apartment was small but *compact*. 这套公寓虽小但紧凑。
They made a global *compact* for migration. 他们制定了全球移民契约。

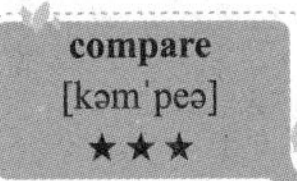

释义 *v.* 比较；把……比作

例句 The police *compared* the suspect's fingerprints with those found at the crime scene. 警察将嫌疑人的指纹与犯罪现场发现的指纹进行了比较。
People *compared* him to Lionel Messi. 人们把他比作里奥内尔·梅西。

近义 contrast *n.* / *v.* 对比

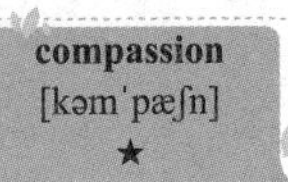

释义 *n.* 同情；怜悯

例句 Being a mom, I felt *compassion* for working moms who won't be able to prepare meals for the children at home. 作为一名母亲，我对那些不能在家为孩子做饭的职场妈妈感到同情。

用法 feel / show compassion 感到 / 表示同情

派生 compassionate *adj.* 有同情心的

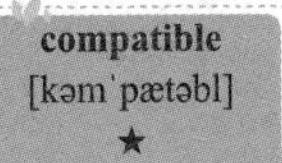

释义 *adj.* 合得来的；兼容的

短语 *compatible* software 可兼容的软件

例句 Their marriage ended because they were simply not *compatible* with each other. 他们的婚姻结束了，因为他们俩根本就合不来。

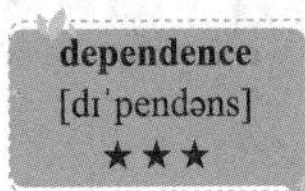

释义 *n.* 依赖，依靠

短语 *dependence* relationship 依存关系

例句 Evan has an unhealthy *dependence* on alcohol. 埃文对酒精有一种不健康的依赖。

用法 dependence on 依赖；依靠

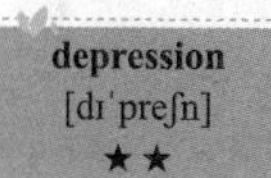

depression [dɪˈpreʃn] ★★

释义 *n.* 抑郁，沮丧；萧条（期）

短语 great *depression* 大萧条

例句 After several years of an economic boom, it looks as though we may be heading toward a *depression*. 在经历了几年的经济繁荣之后，我们似乎正在走向萧条。

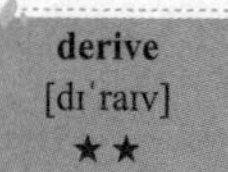

derive [dɪˈraɪv] ★★

释义 *v.* 取得；来自，源自

例句 Paul is one of those happy people who *derive* pleasure from helping others. 保罗是那种从帮助别人中获得快乐的人。

近义 obtain *v.* 获得

派生 derivation *n.* 起源

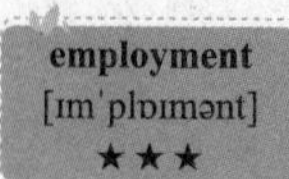

employment [ɪmˈplɔɪmənt] ★★★

释义 *n.* 雇用；使用；工作

短语 without *employment* 失业

例句 After graduation, she found *employment* with a local finance company. 毕业后，她在当地一家金融公司找到了工作。

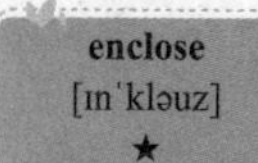

enclose [ɪnˈkləuz] ★

释义 *v.* 围住，圈起；随信附上

例句 The garden was *enclosed* by a small brick wall, bushes and flowers. 花园被小砖墙、灌木和鲜花包围着。

A key was *enclosed* in the envelope. 信封中装有一把钥匙。

派生 enclosure *n.* 围场

encounter [ɪnˈkauntə] ★★

释义 *n.* / *v.* 遇到，遭遇

例句 The theater *encountered* difficulties after its launch, facing budgetary constraints and lacking an appropriate space for performances. 这家剧院开业后遇到困难，预算紧张，又缺乏合适的演出场地。

用法 encounter with sb. 偶然碰到某人

近义 confront *v.* 面对

feasible [ˈfiːzəbl] ★★

释义 *adj.* 可行的；切实可行的；行得通的；可用的

短语 a *feasible* scheme 可行的计划

例句 That may be fine for the US, but it's not *feasible* for a mass European market. 那也许适合美国，但对于庞大的欧洲市场却并不可行。

派生 feasibility *n.* 可行性

fuel [ˈfjuəl] ★★

释义 *n.* 燃料 *v.* 给……加燃料

短语 solid / nuclear *fuel* 固体燃料 / 核燃料

例句 Fossil *fuels* remain the major source of primary energy consumption in today's world. 化石燃料仍然是当今世界一次能源消耗量的主要来源。

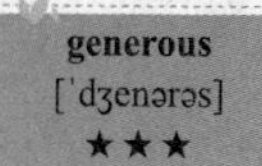

generous [ˈdʒenərəs] ★★★

释义 *adj.* 慷慨的，大方的；宽厚的；丰富的

短语 a *generous* gift 丰厚的礼物

例句 He always sets a *generous* table for guests. 他招待客人吃饭，菜式总是十分丰富。

He was always *generous* in sharing his enormous knowledge. 他总是慷慨地分享他渊博的知识。

派生 generously *adv.* 慷慨地；丰盛地

hazard ['hæzəd] ★

释义 *v.* 冒风险 *n.* 危险；公害

例句 Don't *hazard* your reputation by supporting that proposal. 不要冒着败坏你名声的危险去支持那个提议。

He climbed into the car at the *hazard* of his life. 他冒着生命危险进了汽车。

用法 at the hazard of 冒着……的危险

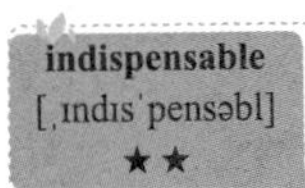

indispensable [ˌɪndɪˈspensəbl] ★★

释义 *adj.* 必不可少的，必需的

例句 The automatic lift is *indispensable* in skyscrapers. 自动电梯在摩天大楼里是不可缺少的。

用法 be indispensable to sb. 对某人必不可少

近义 necessary *adj.* 必要的

反义 dispensable *adj.* 可有可无的

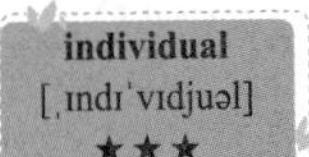

individual [ˌɪndɪˈvɪdjuəl] ★★★

释义 *adj.* 个人的，单独的；独特的 *n.* 个人，个体

短语 *individual* wisdom 个人智慧

例句 The *individual* who promoted this idea was a Stoic philosopher. 提出这一观点的人是斯多葛派哲学家。

用法 write off an individual 忽视个人

派生 individualism *n.* 利己主义

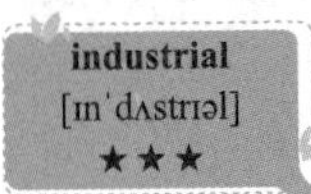

industrial [ɪnˈdʌstrɪəl] ★★★

释义 *adj.* 工业的，产业的

例句 Coal gave the region *industrial* supremacy. 煤炭给这个地区带来了工业上的优势。

真题 There is a strong case that those who have been worst affected by *industrial* action should receive compensation for the disruption they have suffered. 有充分的理由表明，那些受劳工行动影响最严重的人，应该为他们所遭受的破坏获得补偿。（2021 阅读理解）

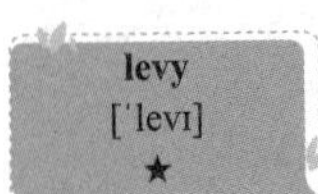

levy ['levɪ] ★

释义 *n.* 征收，征税，征兵 *v.* 征收

例句 A tariff is an import tax countries *levy* on goods entering their borders. 关税是国家对进入其国境的货物征收的税费。

用法 levy on 征税

近义 tax *v.* 对……征税

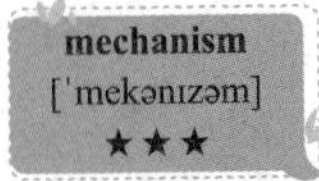

mechanism ['mekənɪzəm] ★★★

释义 *n.* 机械装置，机构；机制

短语 market *mechanism* 市场机制

例句 The peace plan includes a *mechanism* to share power between all four parties. 和平计划包括一个在所有四方之间分享权力的机制。

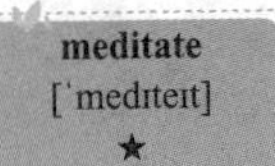

meditate ['medɪteɪt] ★

释义 *v.* 想，考虑；沉思，冥想；谋划

短语 *meditate* revenge 谋划复仇

例句 This way, guests can *meditate* or relax with a good book

without unwanted interruptions. 这样，客人可以通过读一本好书来沉思或放松，没有不必要的打扰。

派生 meditation *n.* 冥想，打坐；沉思

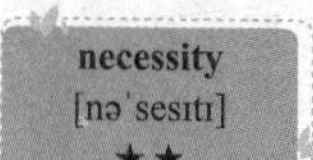

释义 *n.* 必要（性）；必需品

短语 basic *necessities* 基本必需品

例句 Young people must be made aware of the *necessity* to look after the environment. 必须让年轻人意识到保护环境的必要性。

派生 necessitate *v.* 使成为必需

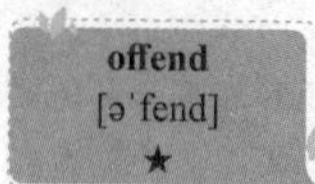

释义 *v.* 触怒；冒犯；犯规，触犯

例句 Frank apologizes for his comments and says he had no intention of *offending* the community. 弗兰克为他的言论道歉，并表示他无意冒犯社区。

用法 offend against 违犯；犯罪

派生 offender *n.* 犯罪者，违法者

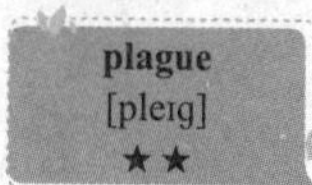

释义 *n.* 瘟疫，灾害 *v.* 折磨，困扰

短语 black *plague* 黑死病

例句 A *plague* of locusts afflicted the land. 农村地区蝗灾为害。

Financial problems are *plaguing* the company. 财政问题使这家公司焦头烂额。

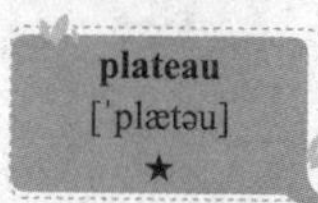

释义 *n.* 高原，平稳状态 *v.* 保持稳定水平，处于停滞状态

短语 *plateau* climate 高原气候

例句 We took a plane south-west across the Anatolian *plateau* to Cappadocia. 我们乘飞机向着西南方向越过安纳托利亚高原，前往卡帕多西亚。

The economic slowdown has caused our sales to *plateau*. 经济发展减速导致我们的产品销量停滞不前。

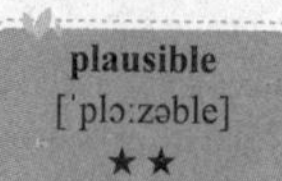

释义 *adj.* 似是而非的，似乎合理的，似乎可信的

短语 a *plausible* explanation 一个合理的解释

例句 A *plausible* explanation would seem to be that people are fed up with the Conservative government. 一个看似合理的解释似乎是，人们已经厌倦了保守党政府。

派生 plausibility *n.* 似乎有理；合理性

释义 *v.* 恳求；为……辩护；提出……为理由

短语 *plead* guilty 认罪

例句 "Dare to be different, please don't smoke!" *Pleads* one billboard campaign aimed at reducing smoking among teenagers. "敢于与众不同，请不要抽烟！"一个旨在减少青少年吸烟的广告牌上这样写道。

用法 plead for sth. 恳求获得某物

近义 beg *v.* 乞求，恳求

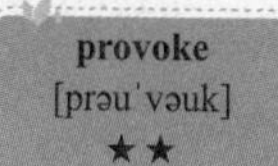

释义 *v.* 挑动；激发；招惹

例句 The announcement *provoked* a storm of protest. 这个声明激起了抗议的风潮。

真题 Unhappy parents rarely are *provoked* to wonder if they shouldn't have had kids, but unhappy childless folks are bothered with the message that children are the single most important thing in the world. 不幸福的父母很少会思考自己是否不该养孩子，但那些不幸福且没有孩子的人却总是受到“孩子是这世上最重要的”这一信息的困扰。（2011 阅读理解）

派生 provocation *n.* 激怒，挑衅

quality [ˈkwɒlɪtɪ] ★★★

释义 *n.* 质量；优点；品质 *adj.* 质优的

短语 product *quality* 产品质量 *quality* control 质量控制

例句 We have been successful because we are offering a *quality* service. 我们之所以成功，是因为我们提供优质的服务。

真题 I find courage an essential *quality* for the understanding, let alone the performance, of his works. 我发现勇气是理解他作品的基本品质，更不用说表演他的作品了。（2014 翻译）

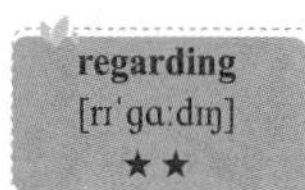
regarding [rɪˈgɑːdɪŋ] ★★

释义 *prep.* 关于，有关，至于

例句 Call me if you have any problems *regarding* your work. 你如果还有什么工作方面的问题就给我打电话。

用法 regarding to 就……而论；关于

派生 regardless *adv.* 不顾，不加理会

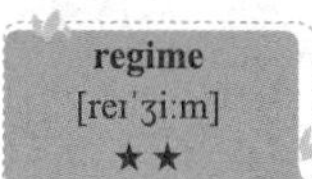
regime [reɪˈʒiːm] ★★

释义 *n.* 政体，政权；组织方法；管理体制

短语 military *regime* 军事政权

例句 Life under a new *regime* has not gone completely to plan. 新政权下的生活并没有完全按照计划进行。

Our tax *regime* is one of the most favourable in Europe. 我们的税收管理体制是欧洲最优惠的税收体制之一。

region [ˈriːdʒən] ★★★

释义 *n.* 地区，地带，行政区；（科学等）领域

短语 administrative *region* 行政区域

例句 This south-west *region* of France is the home of claret. 法国西南部的这个地区是干红葡萄酒的产地。

真题 Europe is the most monarch-infested *region* in the world, with 10 kingdoms. 欧洲是世界上君主最多的地区，有 10 个王国。（2015 阅读理解）

近义 area *n.* 区域，地区

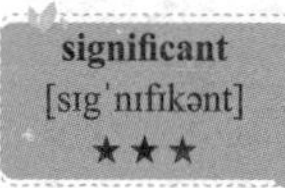
significant [sɪgˈnɪfɪkənt] ★★★

释义 *adj.* 有意义的；重大的，重要的

例句 Food can play a *significant* role in a family or culture's celebrations or traditions. 食物在家庭、文化庆典或传统文化中扮演着重要的角色。

派生 significantly *adv.* 显著地，相当数量地

真题 The building has housed some of the nation's most *significant* diplomats and politicians and has been the scene of many historic events. 这座建筑曾是美国一些最重要的外交官和政治家的住所，也是许多历史事件的发生地。（2018 阅读理解）

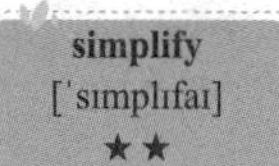
simplify [ˈsɪmplɪfaɪ] ★★

释义 *v.* 简化，使单纯

短语 *simplify* the story 简化故事

例句 While intelligent people can often *simplify* the complex, a fool is more likely to complicate the *simple*. 聪明的人往往能把复杂的事情简单化，而傻瓜更有可能把简单的事情复杂化。

反义 complicate *v.* 使复杂化

派生 simplification *n.* 简单化；单纯化

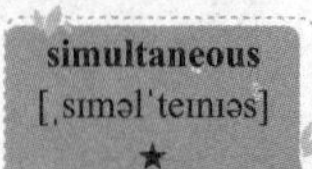

simultaneous [ˌsɪməlˈteɪnɪəs] ★

释义 *adj.* 同时的，同时存在的

短语 *simultaneous* interpretation 同声传译

例句 The theatre will provide *simultaneous* translation in both English and Chinese. 剧院将提供中英文同声传译服务。

派生 simultaneously *adv.* 同时地

sketch [sketʃ] ★★

释义 *n.* 素描；草图；梗概 *v.* 绘略图，速写

短语 design *sketch* 设计图

例句 The artist is making *sketches* for his next painting. 画家正为他的下一幅作品画素描。

He quickly *sketched* the view from the window. 他很快勾勒出了窗外的风景。

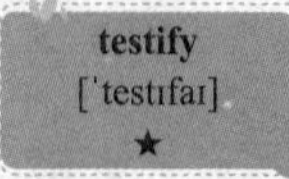

testify [ˈtestɪfaɪ] ★

释义 *v.* 作证，证明；表明，说明

例句 Several eyewitnesses *testified* that they saw the officers hit Miller in the face. 几位目击证人证明他们看见那几个警官打了米勒的脸。

用法 testify under oath 宣誓作证

近义 verify *v.* 证明，证实 declare *v.* 宣布，表明

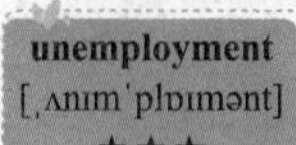

unemployment [ˌʌnɪmˈplɔɪmənt] ★★★

释义 *n.* 失业，失业人数

短语 *unemployment* rate 失业率

例句 *Unemployment* has surged in every major occupational category as a result of the pandemic. 由于疫情的影响，每个主要职业类别的失业率都在飙升。

反义 employment *n.* 就业

真题 The principle of British welfare is no longer that you can insure yourself against the risk of *unemployment* and receive unconditional payments if the disaster happens. 英国福利的原则不再是，你可以确保自己不受失业风险的影响，并在灾难发生时获得无条件的补贴。(2014 阅读理解)

vehicle [ˈviːəkl] ★★

释义 *n.* 车辆；交通工具；媒介，工具

短语 motor / electric *vehicle* 机动 / 电动车辆

例句 People would benefit greatly from a pollution-free *vehicle*. 人们将极大地受益于无污染汽车。

Art may be used as a *vehicle* for propaganda. 艺术可以用作宣传的工具。

近义 transport *n.* 交通工具

派生 vehicular *adj.* 车辆的

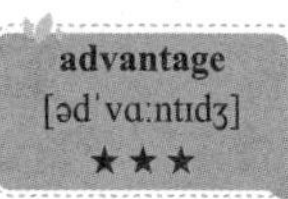

释义 *n.* 优势；好处；利益

例句 The new couple intended to take full *advantage* of this trip to buy the things they need. 这对新婚夫妇打算充分利用这次旅行来购买他们需要的东西。

用法 take advantage of 利用

近义 benefit *n.* 好处，益处

反义 disadvantage *n.* & *v.* 不利条件，劣势

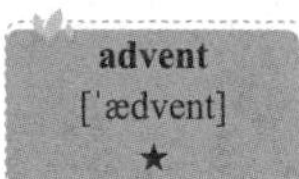

释义 *n.* 出现，来临，到来

例句 Quills were the chief writing implement from the 6th century AD until the *advent* of steel pens in the mid 19th century. 从公元 6 世纪到 19 世纪中期钢笔出现以前，羽毛笔是主要的书写工具。

用法 with the advent of 随着……的出现

近义 arrival *n.* 到来

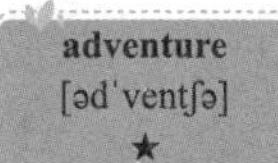

释义 *n.* 冒险；冒险精神 *v.* 冒险

短语 *adventure* film 冒险片 *adventure* tour 探险之旅

例句 Listening to his life story is akin to reading a good *adventure* novel. 听他的生活故事就像读一部好的探险小说。

The group has *adventured* as far as the Austrian Alps. 该团队曾远赴奥地利阿尔卑斯山探险。

派生 adventurous *adj.* 勇于冒险的

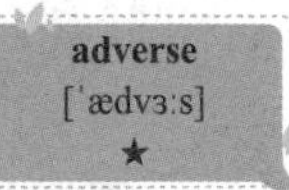

释义 *adj.* 不利的；有害的

例句 The match has been cancelled because of *adverse* weather conditions. 由于天气恶劣，这场比赛已被取消。

近义 favorable *adj.* 有利的

派生 adversity *n.* 逆境

释义 *n.* 代表；为了；就……而言

例句 Helen wasn't able to be present, so I am pleased to accept this award on her *behalf*. 海伦不能出席，所以我很高兴代表她领奖。

用法 on one's behalf 代表某人

comparable
['kɒmpərəb(ə)l]
★

释义 *adj.* 比较的，比得上的；类似的

例句 A car of *comparable* size would cost far more abroad. 同等大小的汽车在国外要贵得多。

There is no play *comparable* with this. 没有比这更好的戏剧了。

反义 incomparable *adj.* 不能比较的

释义 *v.* 强迫，迫使

例句 The rain *compelled* us to stay indoors. 雨迫使我们待在家里。

Mary was *compelled* by circumstances to leave her job. 玛丽因环境所迫而辞去了工作。

近义 oblige *v.* 强迫

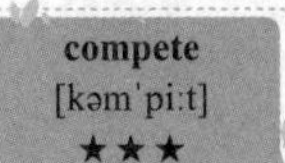

compete
[kəmˈpiːt]
★★★

释义 *v.* 比赛;竞争;对抗

例句 The American economy, and its ability to *compete* abroad, was slowing down according to the report. 报告称,美国经济及其在海外竞争的能力正在放缓和减弱。

派生 competition *n.* 竞争,比赛

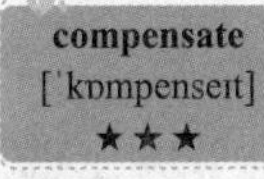

compensate
[ˈkɒmpenseɪt]
★★★

释义 *v.* 补偿,赔偿

例句 I took her swimming to *compensate* for having missed out on the cinema. 为弥补她错过了电影,我带她去游泳。

派生 compensation *n.* 补偿

近义 repay *v.* 偿还

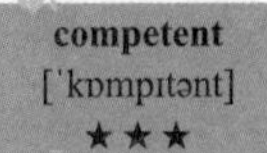

competent
[ˈkɒmpɪtənt]
★★★

释义 *adj.* 有能力的,能胜任的

短语 a *competent* performance 令人满意的表现

例句 Most adults do not feel *competent* to deal with a medical emergency involving a child. 大多数成年人觉得自己没有能力处理涉及儿童的医疗紧急情况。

近义 capable *adj.* 有能力的

派生 competently *adv.* 胜任地

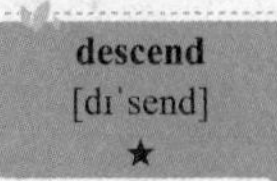

descend
[dɪˈsend]
★

释义 *v.* 下来,下降;突然造访;遗传

例句 The path *descended* steeply into the valley. 这条路很陡,一直通到山谷。

Millions of tourists *descend* on the area every year. 数以百万计的观光客每年都会涌入这个地方。

派生 descendant *n.* 后裔

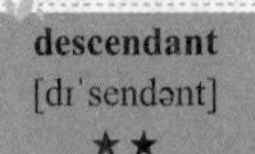

descendant
[dɪˈsendənt]
★★

释义 *n.* 子孙,后代

例句 Elizabeth is a direct *descendant* of Queen Victoria, her great-great-grandmother. 伊丽莎白是维多利亚女王的直系后裔,维多利亚女王是她的曾曾祖母。

用法 a descendant of sb. 某人的后裔

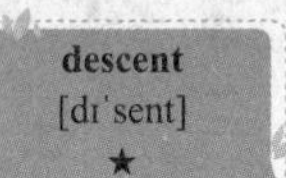

descent
[dɪˈsent]
★

释义 *n.* 下降;斜坡;血统,家世

例句 She's a woman of French *descent*. 她是一个法裔女人。

The plane began its final *descent* into the airport. 飞机开始(做)最终下降,准备在机场着陆。

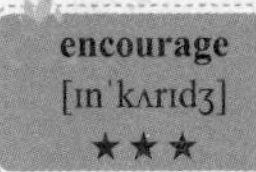

encourage
[ɪnˈkʌrɪdʒ]
★★★

释义 *v.* 鼓励,怂恿;促进

例句 Measures have been taken by government to *encourage* investment. 政府已采取措施鼓励投资。

用法 encourage sb. to do sth. 鼓励某人去做某事

派生 encouragement *n.* 鼓励

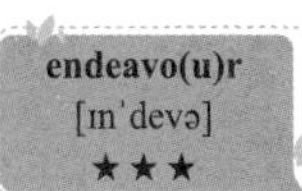

释义 *v./n.* (endeavor) 努力，尽力，力图

例句 Despite their best *endeavours*, they couldn't finish the project before the deadline. 尽管他们尽了最大的努力，他们还是没能在最后期限前完成这个项目。We *endeavour* to make our customers satisfied. 我们力图使顾客都满意。

用法 endeavour to do sth. 努力做……

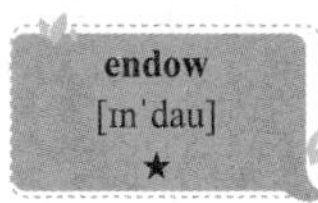

释义 *v.* 资助，捐赠；赋予

例句 Black people are *endowed* with a fantastic sense of rhythm. 黑人生来就有很强的节奏感。This hospital was *endowed* by the citizens of Strasbourg in the 16th century. 这所医院是16世纪斯特拉斯堡市民捐建的。

释义 *adj.* 联邦的；联邦制的；联合的；同盟的

短语 the *federal* government 联邦政府　*federal* court 联邦法院

例句 The U.S. Constitution created the country's *federal* system. 美国宪法建立了联邦制度。

释义 *v.* (fulfil) 完成，履行，实践，满足

短语 *fulfill* the requirement 满足要求

例句 Zoos *fulfil* an important function in the protection of rare species. 动物园起着保护珍稀动物的重要功能。

派生 fulfillment *n.* 履行

释义 *adj.* 遗传（学）的

短语 *genetic* variation 遗传变异

例句 Last year a federal task-force urged reform for patents related to *genetic* tests. 去年，一个联邦工作组敦促对与基因检测相关的专利进行改革。

派生 genetically *adv.* 基因地，遗传地

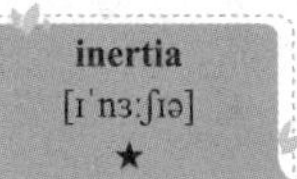

释义 *n.* 不活动，惰性；惯性

短语 force of *inertia* 惯性力

例句 Once you've overcome *inertia*, it's much easier to keep going. 一旦你克服了惰性，接下来就简单得多了。

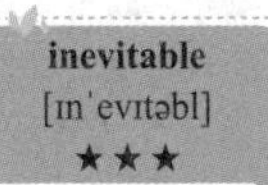

释义 *adj.* 不可避免的，必然发生的

例句 One could interpret much of the work of Beethoven by saying that suffering is *inevitable*, but the courage to fight it renders life worth living. 人们可以这样解读贝多芬的大部分作品：痛苦是不可避免的，但与之斗争的勇气使生命变得有价值。

近义 unavoidable *adj.* 不可避免的

派生 inevitability *n.* 必然性；不可逃避

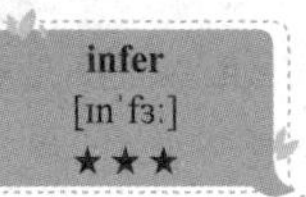

释义 *v.* 推论，推断

例句 By measuring the motion of the galaxies in a cluster, astronomers can *infer* the cluster's mass. 通过测量星系团中星系的运动，天文学家可以推断出星系团

的质量。

派生 inference *n.* 推论

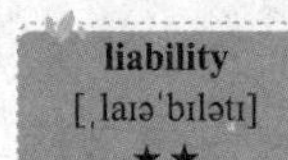

释义 *n.* 责任，义务；(*pl.*) 债务

短语 tax *liability* 纳税义务

例句 The company cannot accept *liability* for any damage caused by natural disasters. 该公司对自然灾害造成的任何损失概不承担责任。

近义 responsibility *n.* 责任

释义 *n.* (*pl.* media) 媒体；方法；媒介 *adj.* 中等的

例句 Frank decided to set up a school where science is taught through the *medium* of English to all classes. 弗兰克决定建立一所学校，在那里所有班级都用英语教授科学。

真题 But in the *medium* term, middle-class workers may need a lot of help adjusting. 但从中期来看，中产阶级工人可能需要很多帮助来调整。（2018 阅读理解）

释义 *adj.* 记忆的，纪念的 *n.* 纪念物，纪念碑，纪念馆

短语 a war *memorial* 战争纪念碑

真题 There is the Royal Shakespeare Company (RSC), which presents superb productions of the plays at the Shakespeare *Memorial* Theatre on the Avon. 还有皇家莎士比亚剧团，他们在埃文河畔的莎士比亚纪念剧院演出精湛的戏剧。（2006 阅读理解）

派生 memorable *adj.* 值得纪念的

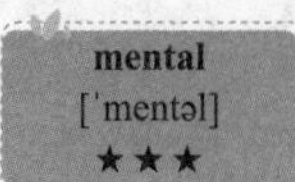

释义 精神的，心理的，智力的，脑力的

短语 *mental* pressure 心理压力

例句 *Mental* health is the seed that contains self-esteem — confidence in ourselves and an ability to trust in our common sense. 心理健康是孕育自尊的种子，即对自己的信心和对常识的信任。

派生 mentally *adv.* 精神上地

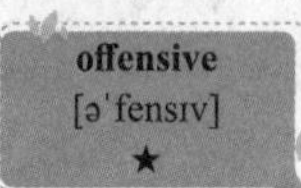

释义 *adj.* 讨厌的；令人不快的；攻击的 *n.* 进攻，攻击

短语 *offensive* weapons 攻击性武器 an *offensive* act 攻击性行为

例句 He was then arrested and charged with possessing an *offensive* weapon. 他之后被逮捕了并被指控拥有攻击性武器。

近义 assault *n.* 攻击

释义 *n.* 誓约；保证 *v.* 发誓；保证

例句 The meeting ended with a *pledge* to step up cooperation between the six states of the region. 会议以承诺加强该地区六国之间的合作而结束。

近义 assure *v.* 使确信，向……保证

真题 On June 7 Google *pledged* not to deploy AI whose use would violate international laws or human rights. 6 月 7 日，谷歌承诺不会部署违反国际法或人权的人工智能。（2019 阅读理解）

plunge
[plʌndʒ]
★★

释义 v. 突然跌落;(使)投入;猛跌 n.(突然的)坠落;骤然下跌

短语 take the *plunge* 冒险尝试

例句 While Thanksgiving, Black Friday and Cyber Monday all saw record spending online, in-store sales *plunged* over the holiday weekend. 虽然感恩节、黑色星期五和网络星期一都创了网上销售的纪录,但实体店内的销售额在假日周末暴跌。

用法 plunge into 跳入;突然或仓促地开始某事

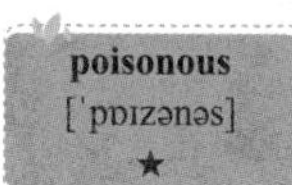

poisonous
[ˈpɒɪzənəs]
★

释义 adj. 有毒的,恶意的,恶毒的,道德败坏的

短语 *poisonous* gas 毒气

例句 If she had been aware that the mushrooms were *poisonous*, she would not have picked them for dinner. 如果她知道蘑菇有毒,她就不会摘下来当晚餐了。

近义 toxic adj. 有毒的

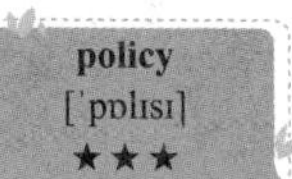

policy
[ˈpɒlɪsɪ]
★★★

释义 n. 政策,方针

短语 basic *policy* 基本方针 trade *policy* 贸易政策

例句 We have always pursued a friendly *policy* towards the people all over the world. 我们一贯奉行对世界各国人民友好的政策。

真题 The US Supreme Court frowns on sex-based classifications unless they are designed to address an"important" *policy* interest. 美国最高法院反对以性别为基础的分类,除非它们旨在解决"重要"的政策利益。(2020 阅读理解)

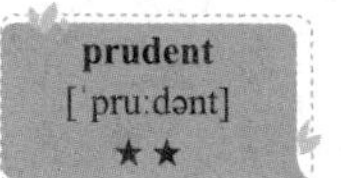

prudent
[ˈpruːdənt]
★★

释义 adj. 谨慎的,智慧的,稳健的,节俭的

短语 a *prudent* decision 审慎的决定

例句 With the risks obvious and growing, a *prudent* people would take out an insurance policy now. 随着风险日益明显,并且不断增长,一个智慧的民族现在就应该制定一些保险的政策。

反义 imprudent adj. 轻率的

派生 prudential adj. 谨慎的

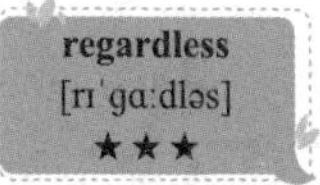

regardless
[rɪˈɡɑːdləs]
★★★

释义 adj. / adv. 不管……的,不顾……的,不注意的

短语 *regardless* of the danger 不顾安危

例句 All children are entitled to a high-quality education regardless of their race, gender or family income. 所有的孩子都有权接受高质量的教育,无论其种族、性别或家庭收入如何。

用法 regardless of 不顾,不管

register
[ˈredʒɪstə]
★★

释义 n. / v. 登记,注册

短语 cash *register* 收银机 company *register* 公司注册

例句 They argue that all Internet users should be forced to *register* and identify themselves, in the same way that drivers must be licensed to drive on public roads. 他们认为,所有的互联网用户都应该被强制注册并确认身份,就像司机必须持有驾驶执照一样。

派生 registration n. 登记,注册

释义 *adj.* 有规律的；定期的；频繁的 *n.* 老主顾；主力队员；经常参加某项活动的人

短语 *regular* customer / bus 常客 / 班车

例句 The *regular* time it takes to get a doctoral degree in the humanities is nine years. 获得人文学科博士学位通常需要九年的时间。

John is one of our *regulars*. 约翰是我们的一位老主顾。

派生 regularly *adv.* 定期地，有规律地

释义 *adj.* 懈怠的，松弛的；萧条的 *n.* 淡季 *v.* 懈怠

短语 *slack* water 缓慢流动的水 *slack* muscles 松弛的肌肉

例句 Discipline in the classroom is very *slack*. 班里纪律十分松懈。

They need to stop *slacking* and get down to work. 他们不能再偷懒了，要认真工作。

派生 slackness *n.* 松弛

释义 *adj.* 轻微的；纤细的，瘦弱的

短语 *a slight* pain / change 轻微疼痛 / 细微变化

例句 There has been a *slight* increase in the consumption of meat. 肉类消费略微增加。

用法 not in the slightest 一点也不；根本不

近义 slim *adj.* 苗条的，纤细的

派生 slightly *adv.* 稍微，轻微地

释义 *v.*（指鸟等）高飞，翱翔；飞涨

短语 *soaring* costs 猛增的成本

例句 In Britain, temperatures are expected to *soar* above 30° Celsius heading into the weekend. 在英国，预计周末气温将飙升至30摄氏度以上。

近义 rise *v.* 上涨，升高

派生 soaring *adj.* 猛增的

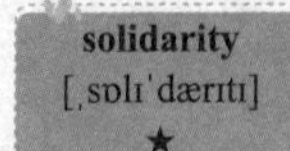

释义 *n.* 团结；休戚相关

短语 community *solidarity* 社群团结

例句 Supporters want to march tomorrow to show *solidarity* with their leaders. 为了显示和领袖的同心同德，支持者们希望明天举行游行。

用法 show solidarity with sb. 表明支持某人

同义 unity *n.* 团结

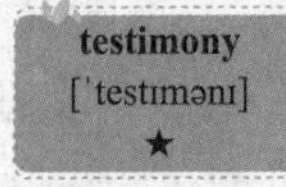

释义 *n.* 证据，证词；表明，说明

短语 a sworn *testimony* 宣誓证词

例句 This increase in exports bears *testimony* to the successes of industry. 出口增长证明了产业的成功。

用法 bear testimony to 证明；担保

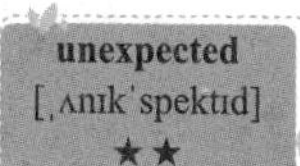

unexpected
[ˌʌnɪkˈspektɪd]
★★

释义 *adj.* 想不到的，意外的，未预料到

短语 *unexpected* accident 不能预料的事故

例句 Failing at something can help you discover your truest friends, or help you find *unexpected* motivation to succeed. 在某件事上的失败可以帮助你找到你最真诚的朋友，或者帮助你找到意想不到走向成功的动力。

派生 expected *adj.* 预料的

venture
[ˈventʃə]
★★

释义 *v.* 冒险；大胆表示 *n.* 风险项目；冒险事业

短语 joint *venture* 合资企业

例句 The island is also a nature reserve, please do not *venture* on to it. 该岛也是自然保护区，请勿冒险前往。

On the *venture* capital side, less than 10 percent of partners are women. 在风险投资方面，只有不到10%的合伙人是女性。

用法 venture on sth. 冒险

派生 venturous *adj.* 好冒险的

Word List 16

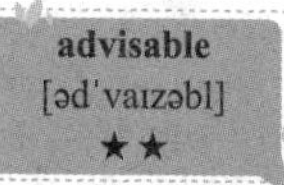

advisable
[ədˈvaɪzəbl]
★★

释义 *adj.* 可取的；明智的；适当的

例句 It's *advisable* to book hotels at least a week in advance. 最好至少提前一周预订酒店。

用法 be advisable to do sth. 做某事是明智的

反义 inadvisable *adj.* 不明智的；不受劝告的

派生 advisability *n.* 明智

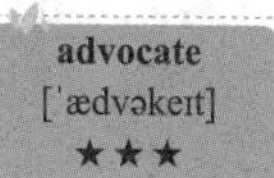

advocate
[ˈædvəkeɪt]
★★★

释义 *v.* 提倡 *n.* 拥护者，提倡者

例句 She's a staunch *advocate* of free trade. 她是自由贸易的忠实拥护者。

We *advocate* solving international dispute by negotiation, instead of appealing to arms. 我们主张通过协商解决国际争端，而不主张诉诸武力。

派生 advocator *n.* 提倡者

aesthetic
[iːsˈθetɪk]
★

释义 *adj.* 美学的；艺术的 *n.* 美学；美感

例句 The furniture on display is both *aesthetic* and functional. 展出的家具既美观又实用。

The students debated the *aesthetic* of the poems. 学生就这些诗的美感展开了辩论。

派生 aesthetically *adv.* 审美地

affair
[əˈfeə]
★★★

释义 *n.* 事情；事件；风流韵事

短语 international / business *affairs* 国际 / 商业事务

例句 In the past, the young have eagerly participated in national service and civic *affairs*, often with lots of energy and idealism. 过去，年轻人热衷于参与国家服务和公民事务，往往充满活力和理想主义。

用法 have an affair with sb. 与某人有暧昧关系

近义 event *n.* 事件

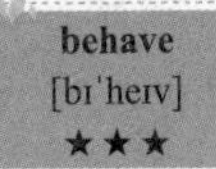

behave
[bɪˈheɪv]
★★★

释义 *v.* 行为；表现；守规矩

例句 The little boy *behaved* as if he was an adult. 这个小男孩表现得像个大人。

She doesn't know how to *behave* in public. 她在公共场合手足无措。

派生 behavior *n.* 行为；举止

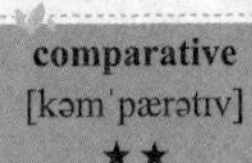

comparative
[kəmˈpærətɪv]
★★

释义 *adj.* 比较的，相比的

短语 *comparative* literature 比较文学

例句 *Comparative* studies, comparing traits across a range of species, was the primary tool used by Darwin. 比较研究是达尔文的主要研究工具，它比较了一系列物种的特征。

派生 comparatively *adv.* 比较地，相对地

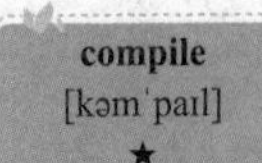

compile
[kəmˈpaɪl]
★

释义 *v.* 编辑，编制，搜集

例句 Subscribers can also *compile* their favorite performances into video "setlists" and watch them anytime. 订阅者还可以将自己喜欢的演出编成视频"节目单"，随时观看。

近义 edit *v.* 编辑

派生 compilation *n.* 编纂，汇编

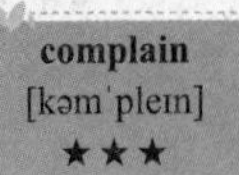

complain
[kəmˈpleɪn]
★★★

释义 *v.* 抱怨；申诉

例句 The American couple *complained* about the high cost of visiting Europe. 那对美国夫妇抱怨去欧洲旅游的费用太高。

派生 complaint *n.* 抱怨

complete
[kəmˈpliːt]
★★★

释义 *adj.* 完全的，彻底的 *v.* 完成，结束

例句 This is a *complete* waste of time. 这完全是浪费时间。

The project took four months to *complete*. 这个项目花了 4 个月才完成。

派生 completely *adv.* 完全地

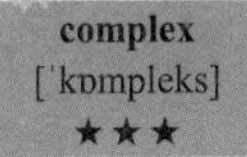

complex
[ˈkɒmpleks]
★★★

释义 *adj.* 复杂的；合成的 *n.* 建筑群；综合体

例句 There is a *complex* network of roads connecting the two cities. 连接这两个城市的道路网络很复杂。

The sports *complex* has six tennis courts. 这个体育综合体有六个网球场。

派生 complexity *n.* 复杂性

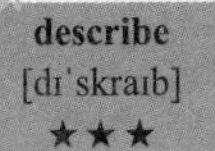

describe
[dɪˈskraɪb]
★★★

释义 *v.* 描述，形容

例句 The witness *described* the robber to the police. 目击者向警方描述了抢劫犯的外貌。

派生 description *n.* 描写

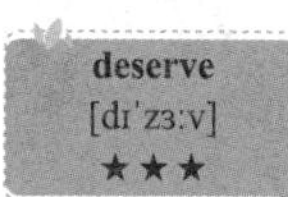

释义 *v.* 应受,值得

短语 *deserve* a medal 值得嘉奖

例句 I think you *deserve* a holiday after all that hard work. 我觉得你辛苦工作了那么久,应该放个假。

释义 *v.* 设计,构思 *n.* 设计;图案

短语 product *design* 产品设计

例句 I like the *design* on your sweatshirt. 我喜欢你运动服上的那个图案。

真题 These social assistance programs are *designed* to reduce inequality and break the cycle of poverty. 这些社会援助项目旨在减少不平等,打破贫困循环。(2021 阅读理解)

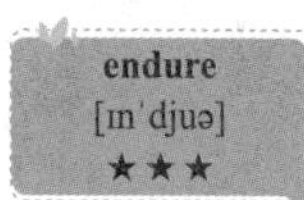

释义 *v.* 忍受;持久,持续

例句 Paul was ready to *endure* any hardship with a will of steel. 保罗准备好用钢铁般的意志忍受任何困难。

The political system established in 1400 *endured* until about 1650. 建立于 1400 年的政治体系一直沿用到 1650 年前后。

派生 endurance *n.* 忍耐力

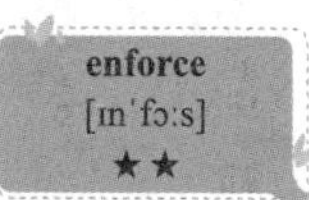

释义 *v.* 实施,执行;强制

例句 New measures are being *enforced* by the local labor department. 当地劳动部门正在实施新的措施。

近义 implement *v.* 执行,贯彻

派生 enforcement *n.* 执行,实施

释义 *v.* 从事;使订婚;保证;雇用;吸引,引起

例句 Even in prison, he continued to *engage* in criminal activities. 他甚至在监狱里还继续从事犯罪活动。

Kate and Larry have just got *engaged*. 凯特和拉里刚刚订婚。

用法 be engaged to sb. 与……订婚

释义 *adj.* 虚弱的,无力的;微弱的

例句 He was a *feeble*, helpless old man. 他是一个虚弱无助的老人。

The little lamp gave only a *feeble* light. 这盏小灯只发出一点微弱的光。

释义 *n.* 功能,作用;(*pl.*)职务;函数 *v.* 起作用

例句 Laughter does produce short-term changes in the *function* of the heart and its blood vessels. 笑确实会对心脏和血管的功能产生短期的改变。

派生 functional *adj.* 实用的;功能的

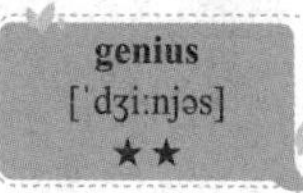

释义 *n.* 天才;天赋

例句 *Genius* is one percent inspiration and ninety-nine percent perspiration. 天才是百分之一的天赋加上百分之九十九的勤奋。

He had a *genius* for picking the right person for the right job. 他有一种能够为合适的工作选择合适的人的本领。

headline
['hedlaɪn]
★★

释义 *n.* 大字标题；新闻提要

短语 *headline* news 标题新闻

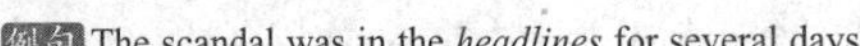

例句 The scandal was in the *headlines* for several days. 这一丑闻连续好几天成为各大报纸的头条新闻。

inference
['ɪnfərəns]
★★

释义 *n.* 推论，推理，推断；结论

例句 It had an extremely tiny head and, by *inference*, a tiny brain. 它的头极小，由此推断其脑容量也非常小。

用法 by inference 根据推理

派生 inferential *adj.* 推理的

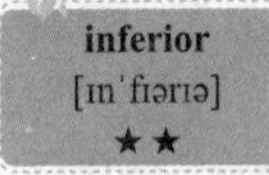

inferior
[ɪn'fɪərɪə]
★★

释义 *adj.* 下等的，下级的；劣等的，差的 *n.* 下级，不如别人的人

例句 If children are made to feel *inferior* to other children their confidence will decline. 如果让孩子觉得自己不如其他孩子，他们的信心就会下降。

派生 inferiority *n.* 低等，劣等

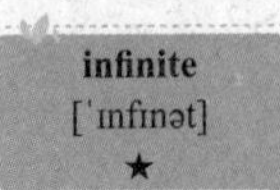

infinite
['ɪnfɪnət]
★

释义 *adj.* 无限的，无穷的 *n.* 无限

短语 *infinite* space 无限空间

例句 The most amazing thing about nature is its *infinite* variety. 大自然最让人惊叹的是它的无限多样性。

派生 finite *adj.* 有限的

journal
['dʒɜːnəl]
★★★

释义 *n.* 杂志；日报；日志，日记

短语 keep a *journal* 写日记

例句 Sara kept a *journal* of his travels across Africa. 萨拉把自己的非洲之旅记录下来了。

派生 journalist *n.* 新闻记者

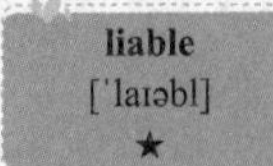

liable
['laɪəbl]
★

释义 *adj.* 有……倾向的；可能遭受……的；有责任的

例句 A recent study of people with HSAM reveals that they are *liable* to fantasy and full absorption in an activity. 最近一项针对"超忆症"患者的研究表明，他们很容易幻想并全神贯注于某项活动。

用法 hold sb. liable for sth. 认为某人对某事负有责任

派生 liability *n.* 责任，义务

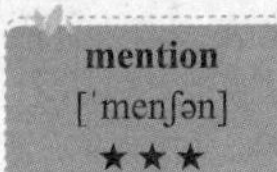

mention
['menʃən]
★★★

释义 *v.* / *n.* 提及，说起

短语 not to *mention* 更不必说

例句 Cooking real food is the best defense not to *mention* that any meal you're likely to eat at home contains about 200 fewer calories than one you would eat in a restaurant. 烹饪真正的食物是最好的防御，更不用说你在家吃的任何一餐都可能比你在餐馆吃的少 200 卡路里。

近义 reference *n.* 提及

merchandise
['mɜːtʃəndaɪz]
★

释义 *n.* 商品，货物 *v.* 推销；推介；买卖

例句 A range of official Disney *merchandise* was on sale. 一系列迪斯尼官方商品

正在出售。

In short, it's a challenge to *merchandise* products like ice cream and cone. 简而言之，对于推销像冰激凌和甜筒这样的商品来说，这是一个挑战。

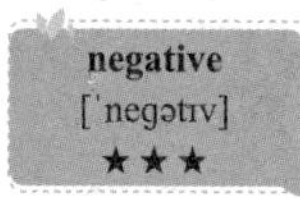

negative
[ˈnegətɪv]
★★★

释义 *adj.* 消极的，否定的；负面的；负的 *n.* 否定；底片

例句 You can't learn anything with *negative* attitude. 你用消极的态度什么也学不到。

反义 positive *adj.* 乐观的；积极地

真题 A more direct finding is that people who scored high for *negative* emotions like anxiety looked at others for shorter periods of time and reported more comfortable feelings when others did not look directly at them. 一个更直接的发现是，在焦虑等负面情绪方面得分高的人看别人的时间更短，当别人不直视他们时，他们感觉更舒服。(2020 阅读理解)

offer
[ˈɒfə]
★★★

释义 *v.* 提供；出价 *n.* 提议，提供

短语 special *offer* 特别优惠 *offer* help 提供帮助

例句 The lesson is not that you should make your personal life an open book, but rather, when given the option to *offer* up details about yourself, you should just be honest. 这不是说你应该把你的个人生活变成一本公开的书，而是说，当有机会提供关于你自己的细节时，你应该诚实。

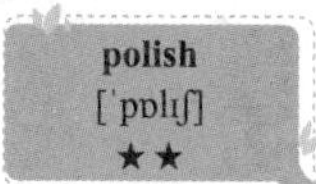

polish
[ˈpɒlɪʃ]
★★

释义 *v.* 磨光，擦亮；润饰 *n.* 擦光剂，上光蜡

短语 shoe *polish* 鞋油

例句 I will give the wardrobe a *polish*. 我要把衣柜擦亮。

He took out a spotless white handkerchief and *polished* his glasses. 他拿出一块一尘不染的白手帕，擦亮了眼镜。

用法 give sth. a polish 给某物抛光；擦亮某物

派生 polished *adj.* 擦亮的

political
[pəˈlɪtɪkəl]
★★★

释义 *adj.* 政治的

短语 *political* party 政党 *political* system 政治制度

例句 Thus poor countries might not be able to escape their poverty traps without *political* changes . 因此，如果不进行政治改革，贫穷的国家可能无法摆脱贫困陷阱。

派生 politician *n.* 政治家

真题 A 2014 survey found that young people's reliance on social media led to greater *political* engagement. 2014 年开展的一项研究发现，年轻人对社交媒体的依赖使其政治参与度大幅提高。(2018 阅读理解)

poll
[pəul]
★

释义 *n.* 民意测验 (*pl.*) 政治选举 *v.* 获得……选票

短语 opinion *poll* 民意测验

例句 Thursday is traditionally the day when Britain goes to the *polls*. 英国传统的投票选举日是星期四。

They *polled* 39% of the vote in the last election. 在上届选举中，他们获得了 39% 的选票。

近义 ballot *n.* 投票选举

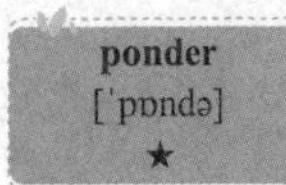

释义 *v.* 沉思，考虑

例句 She sat back for a minute to *ponder* her next move in the game. 她在椅背上靠了一会儿，思考下一步棋该怎么走。

近义 contemplate *v.* 沉思

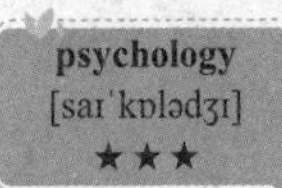

释义 *n.* 心理；心理学；心理状态

短语 consumer / applied *psychology* 消费者心理学 / 应用心理学

例句 With the increasing development of social *psychology*, research topics are also increasingly enriched and expanded. 随着社会心理学的日益发展，研究课题也日益丰富和扩大。

派生 psychologist *n.* 心理学家

释义 *v.* 管制，控制；调节，校准；调整

例句 Such trees provide nesting sites for birds and *regulate* the local water balance. 这些树为鸟类提供筑巢的地方，并调节当地的水平衡。

近义 govern *v.* 统治，管理；控制

派生 regulator *n.* 监管者

真题 The order also declared that state and local governments couldn't *regulate* broadband providers either. 该命令还宣布，州政府和地方政府也不能监管宽带提供商。（2021 阅读理解）

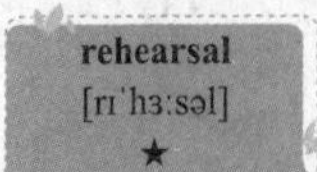

释义 *n.* 排练，排演；演习，试演

短语 dress *rehearsal* 彩排

例句 Our new production of *Hamlet* is currently in *rehearsal*. 我们的新版《哈姆雷特》正在排练之中。

用法 in rehearsal 彩排中

释义 *n.* / *v.* 统治，支配，盛行 *n.* 统治时期 *v.* 占优势

例句 Emperor Taizong died in 649 after *reigning* for 23 years at the age of 51. 唐太宗于 649 年去世，享年 51 岁，在位 23 年。

真题 "The ancient Hawaiians were astronomers," wrote Queen Liliuokalani, Hawaii's last *reigning* monarch, in 1897. "古代夏威夷人是天文学家，"夏威夷最后一位君主利留卡拉尼女王在 1897 年写道。（2017 阅读理解）

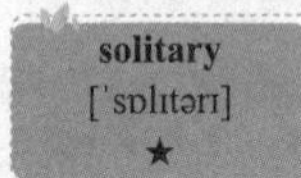

释义 *adj.* 孤独的；偏僻的；单一的，唯一的

短语 a *solitary* life 独居生活

例句 She was a very *solitary* girl who didn't make friends easily. 她是一个非常孤僻的女孩，不容易交到朋友。

近义 isolated *adj.* 孤寂的；单独的

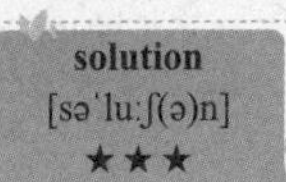

释义 *n.* 解答，解决办法；溶解，溶液

短语 find a *solution* 找到解决办法 water *solution* 水溶液

例句 Although he has sought to find a peaceful *solution*, he is facing pressure to use greater military force. 尽管他试图寻求和平解决的办法，但现在却面临使用更多武装力量的压力。

真题 The *solution* to the ethical issues brought by autonomous vehicles is still beyond our capacity. 自动

驾驶汽车带来的道德问题的解决方案仍然超出了我们的能力。（2019 阅读理解）

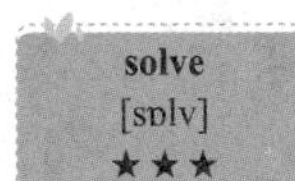

释义 *v.* 解决，解答

短语 *solve* a puzzle 解决一个难题

例句 After studying differential calculus you will be able to *solve* these mathematical problems. 学了微积分之后，你们就能够解这些数学题了。

近义 resolve *v.* 解决

派生 solution *n.* 解决办法

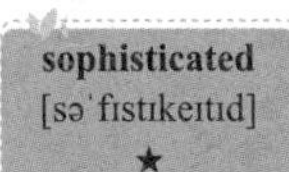

释义 *adj.* 尖端的，复杂的，先进的；老练的

短语 *sophisticated* technology 工艺精良

例句 Advanced equipment, *sophisticated* technology, high quality service is our guarantee of quality. 先进的设备、成熟的技术、优质的服务是我们品质的保证。

派生 sophistication *n.* 精明老练；精密，复杂

释义 *n.* 纺织品 *adj.* 纺织的

短语 *textile* industry 纺织工业

例句 From the 1880s to the 1930s, the *textile* industry in Japan employed over half of all workers. 从 19 世纪 80 年代到 20 世纪 30 年代，日本的纺织业雇佣了超过一半的工人。

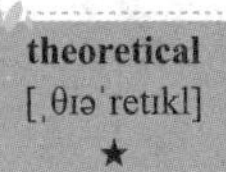

释义 *adj.* 理论（上）的；假设的

短语 *theoretical* foundation 理论基础

例句 She has *theoretical* knowledge of teaching, but no practical experience. 她有教学方面的理论知识，但没有实践经验。

派生 theoretically *adv.* 理论地；理论上

反义 practical *adj.* 实践的

释义 *n.* 联合，联盟；协会；工会

短语 student / trade *union* 学生会 / 工会

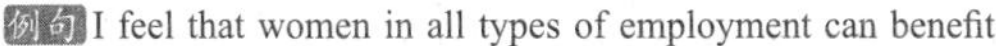

例句 I feel that women in all types of employment can benefit from joining a *union*. 我认为女性无论从事什么工作，加入工会都是有好处的。

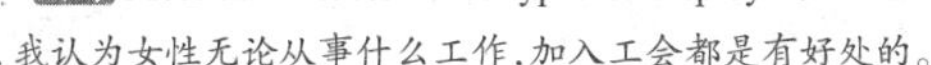

派生 unionist *n.* 工会会员

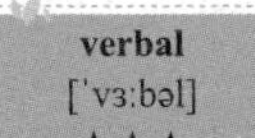

释义 *adj.* 言语的，文字的；口头的；动词的

短语 *verbal* ability 语言能力

例句 The test has scores for *verbal* skills, mathematical skills, and abstract reasoning skills. 该项测试包含对语言能力、数学能力和抽象推理能力的考查。

近义 oral *adj.* 口头的

派生 verbalization *n.* 以言语表现

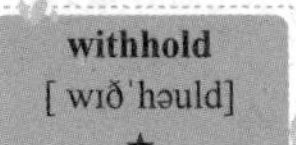

释义 *v.* 拒给；隐瞒，扣留；克制

短语 *withhold* information / support 拒绝提供消息 / 拒绝给予支持

例句 The captain decided to *withhold* the terrible news even from his officers. 船长决定哪怕是对高级船员也要封锁这个可怕的消息。

Financial aid for Zambia has been *withheld*. 向赞比亚提供的经济援助已经被扣。

用法 withhold sth. from sb. 对某人隐瞒某事

近义 conceal *v.* 隐瞒

释义 *v.* 使隶属于 *n.* 成员，附属机构

短语 an international *affiliate* 跨国分公司

例句 The HMO *affiliated* the clinics last year. 医疗保健组织去年将这个诊所列为附属机构。

用法 an affiliate of……的附属机构

派生 affiliation *n.* 从属关系

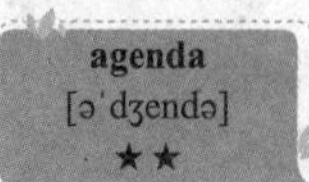

释义 *n.* 议事日程；（待办的）事项

短语 item on the *agenda* 议程项目

例句 The Danish president put environmental issues high on the *agenda*. 丹麦总统把环境问题放在议事日程的重要位置。

近义 schedule *n.* 计划

释义 *v.* 肯定；断言

例句 Numerous studies *affirm* that heat waves are increasing in frequency or intensity as climate changes. 大量研究证实，随着气候变化，热浪的频率和强度都在增加。

反义 deny *v.* 否认

派生 affirmation *n.* 肯定

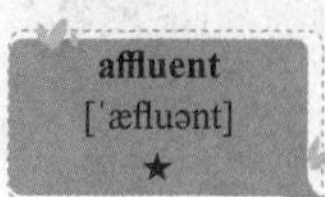

释义 *adj.* 富裕的；富足的 *n.* 支流；富人

短语 *affluent* society 小康社会

例句 The Strand is one of London's busiest and most *affluent* streets. 斯特兰德街是伦敦最繁华、最富足的街道之一。

派生 affluence *n.* 富裕

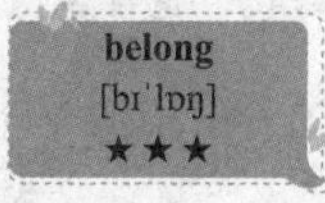

释义 *v.* 属于，归……所有；适合

例句 The house had *belonged* to her family for three generations. 这所房子已经连续三代属于她的家族了。

After three years in Cambridge, I finally feel as if I *belong* here. 在剑桥待了3年以后，我终于找到了归属感。

用法 belong to 属于

派生 belongings *n.* 所有物；财产

comparison
[kəmˈpærɪs(ə)n]
★★★

释义 *n.* 比较，对比，比喻

例句 By *comparison* with London, Paris is small. 与伦敦相比，巴黎较小。

They make a *comparison* of New York to a beehive. 他们把纽约比作一个蜂巢。

用法 by comparison 相比之下

complicate
[ˈkɒmplɪkeɪt]
★★

释义 *v.*（使）复杂；使（疾病）恶化

例句 The continued fighting has *complicated* the peace negotiations. 持续的战斗使和平谈判变得复杂。

派生 complicated *adj.* 复杂的

compliment
[ˈkɒmplɪmənt]
★

释义 *n.* 问候，致意 *n.* / *v.* 称赞，恭维

短语 left-handed *compliment* 假意的恭维

例句 David *complimented* Mary on her new job. 大卫祝贺玛丽找到新工作。

Please accept these flowers with the *compliments* of the manager. 请接受经理送的鲜花。

comply
[kəmˈplaɪ]
★★

释义 *v.* 遵从，服从

例句 She was told to pay the fine, but refused to *comply*. 她被通知交纳罚款，但她拒不服从。

近义 obey *v.* 遵守，服从

反义 refuse *v.* 拒绝

component
[kəmˈpəʊnənt]
★★

释义 *n.* 组成部分，部件 *adj.* 组成的，一部分的

短语 a key / vital *component* 关键 / 至关重要的组成部分

例句 Fresh fruit and vegetables are an essential *component* of a healthy diet. 新鲜水果和蔬菜是健康饮食的一个基本要素。

近义 constituent *n.* 成分

designate
[ˈdezɪgneɪt]
★

释义 *v.* 指明，指出；任命，指派

例句 Vincent has been *designated* (as / to be) the CEO of the company. 文森特已被任命为该公司的首席执行官。

用法 designate sb. to do sth. 指派某人做某事

desirable
[dɪˈzaɪərəb(ə)l]
★★★

释义 *adj.* 值得做的；合意的，称心的

短语 highly *desirable* 非常可取

例句 Being a teacher is a *desirable* job for many people. 对许多人来说，教师是一份理想的工作。

派生 desirability *n.* 愿望；追求

desolate
[ˈdesələt]
★

释义 *adj.* 荒凉的；孤独的 *v.* 使荒芜

短语 a bleak and *desolate* landscape 一片荒凉的景色

例句 Those findings could illuminate how Mars became the *desolate* desert world we see today. 这些发现可以解释火星是如何变成我们今天看到的荒凉沙漠世界的。

派生 desolation *n.* 孤寂；荒芜

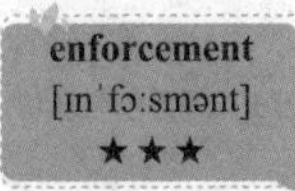

释义 *n.* 忍耐(力),持久(力),耐久(性)

短语 *endurance* test 耐久测试

例句 They are remarkably intelligent, but a bit short on physical strength and *endurance*. 他们非常聪明,但在体力和耐力方面有点不足。

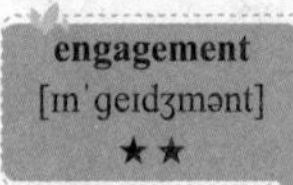

释义 *n.* 执行,实施

短语 compel *enforcement* 强迫执行

例句 The court is ineffective because it lacks the necessary *enforcement* machinery. 法院效率低是因为缺乏必要的执行机制。

释义 *n.* 约定;婚约;参加,从事

例句 Tony was stunned when Debbie suddenly broke off their *engagement*. 当黛比突然取消他们的婚约时,托尼惊呆了。

用法 enter into an engagement with sb. 与某人订婚;与某人约定

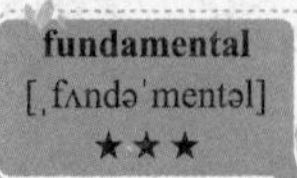

释义 *n.* 反馈;反应

例句 If you're not sure, ask for honest *feedback* from trusted friends, colleagues and professionals. 如果你不确定,可以向你信任的朋友、同事和专业人士寻求诚实的反馈。

用法 feedback on sth. 对……的反馈意见

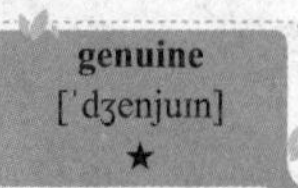

释义 *adj.* 基础的,基本的,必要的 *n.* (*pl.*) 基本原则,基本原理

例句 He believes better relations with China are *fundamental* to the well-being of the area. 他相信和中国建立更加良好的关系对这一地区的繁荣发展至关重要。

用法 be fundamental to sth. 对……来说是基本的(或必需的)

近义 basic *adj.* 基本的

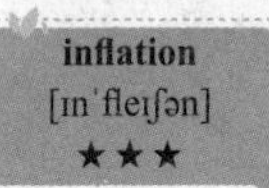

释义 *adj.* 真的,非人造的;真诚的,真心的

短语 *genuine* gold 纯金

例句 They want to show their *genuine* sympathy. 他们想表达他们真诚的同情。

It is not easy to distinguish cultured pearls from *genuine* pearls. 辨别真正的珍珠与人工养殖的珍珠不是一件容易的事。

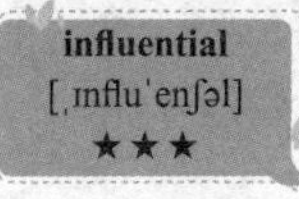

释义 *n.* 通货膨胀

例句 The government hopes these measures will help to bring down *inflation*. 政府希望这些措施将有助于降低通货膨胀。

真题 A report last year pointed out that the costs both of subscriptions and of these "article preparation costs" had been steadily rising at a rate above *inflation*. 去年的一份报告指出,订阅费用和"备读文章费用"一直在以高于通货膨胀的速度稳步上升。(2020 阅读理解)

influential
[ˌɪnfluˈenʃəl]
★★★

释义 *adj.* 有影响的;有权势的

例句 One study shows that our neighbours' actions are *influential* in changing our behaviour. 一项研究表明,我们邻居的行为对改变我们的行为有影响。

派生 influence *n.* 影响

反义 uninfluential *adj.* 不产生影响的

释义 *v.* 通知，告诉；告发

例句 They would *inform* him of any progress they had made. 他们会把他们取得的任何进步都告诉他。

They threatened to *inform* against him unless he left the town at once. 他们威胁说，如果他不立即离开这个城市，他们就要告发他。

派生 information *n.* 信息

释义 *adj.* 慷慨的；自由的，思想开放的 *n.* 思想开明的人

短语 *liberal* party 自由党

例句 Their views on marriage and divorce tend to be more *liberal*. 他们对婚姻和离婚的看法往往更开放。

派生 liberation *n.* 解放，解放运动

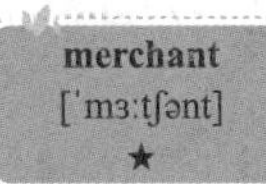

释义 *n.* 商人，零售商

短语 a coal / wine *merchant* 煤炭 / 葡萄酒批发商

例句 Rich *merchants* and factory owners did emerge in Europe, but they seldom had social prestige or political power. 欧洲确实出现了富有的商人和工厂所有者们，但他们很少有社会声望或政治权力。

派生 merchandise *n.* 商品

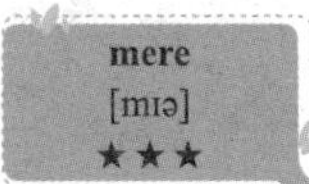

释义 *adj.* 纯粹的；仅仅，只不过

短语 a *mere* nobody 微不足道的人

例句 The *mere* mention of food had trigged off hunger pangs. 一提到食物就引起了阵阵饥饿感。

派生 merely *adv.* 仅仅，只不过

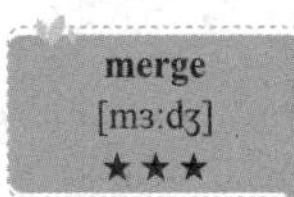

释义 *v.*（使）结合，（使）合并

例句 Nick didn't say anything during the meeting, and it was obvious that he was desperately trying to *merge* into the background. 会议期间，尼克一言未发，很明显，他不想抛头露面。

近义 blend *v.*（使）混合

派生 merger *n.*（公司、组织的）合并

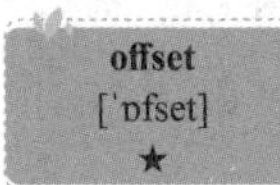

释义 *v.* 抵消，补偿

例句 The slowdown in domestic demand was *offset* by an increase in exports. 国内需求放缓和出口增长互相抵消了。

真题 The latter step would largely *offset* the financial burden of annually pre-funding retiree health care. 后者将极大地抵销每年预拨退休人员医保的财政负担。（2018 阅读理解）

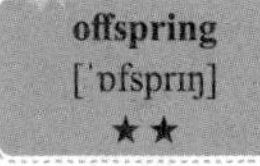

释义 *n.* 子女，子孙，后代；（动物的）崽

短语 human *offspring* 人类的后代

例句 In last week's lecture, we discussed the characteristics of the newly born *offspring* of several mammals. 在上周的课上,我们讨论了几种哺乳动物新生后代的特征。

近义 posterity *n.* 子孙,后裔

politician [ˌpɒlɪˈtɪʃən] ★★★

释义 *n.* 政治家,政客

例句 One reason why pension and health care reforms are slow in coming is that *politicians* are afraid of losing votes in the next election. 养老金和医疗改革进展缓慢的一个原因是,政客们害怕在下一次选举中失去选票。

portable [ˈpɔːtəbl] ★

释义 *adj.* 轻便的,手提(式)的,可移动的

短语 *portable* computer 便携式计算机

例句 A small-screen *portable* TV can be a good investment. 小屏幕的便携式电视机很值得买。

近义 lightweight *adj.* 轻量的

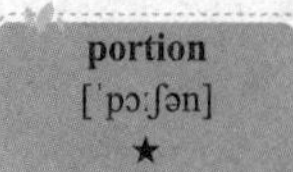

portion [ˈpɔːʃən] ★

释义 *n.* 一部分,一份

短语 main *portion* 主要部分

例句 If homework matters, it should account for a significant *portion* of the grade. 如果家庭作业很重要,那么它应该占分数的很大一部分。

派生 proportion *n.* 部分

用法 portion sth. out 把某物分成若干份

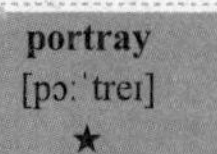

portray [pɔːˈtreɪ] ★

释义 *v.* 描写,描述;画(人物、景象等)

短语 *portray* landscape 描绘风景

例句 Disaster movies often *portray* catastrophes that destroy, or at least threaten to destroy earth's entire population. 灾难电影经常描绘毁灭性的灾难或至少威胁要摧毁地球人类生存的灾难。

近义 depict *v.* 描述,描绘

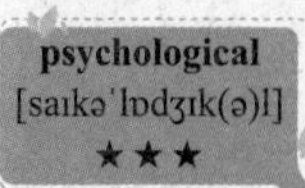

psychological [saɪkəˈlɒdʒɪk(ə)l] ★★★

释义 *adj.* 心理的,精神的

短语 *psychological* development / problems 心理发展 / 心理问题

例句 The constant aircraft noise has a bad *psychological* effect on the residents. 持续不断的飞机噪声给居民造成了不良的心理影响。

派生 psychologically *adv.* 心理上地

regulation [ˌregjuˈleɪʃən] ★★★

释义 *n.* 规则,规章;调节,校准;调整

短语 legal / traffic *regulations* 法律 / 交通条例

例句 Under the new *regulations* spending on office equipment will be strictly controlled. 根据新的规定,办公设备开支将受到严格控制。

用法 under ... regulations 根据……法规

近义 rule *n.* 规章,条例

真题 Journalists need stricter industrial *regulations*. 新闻工作者需要更严格的行业监管。(2015 阅读理解)

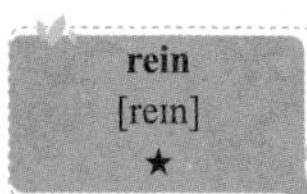

释义 *n.* 缰绳，统治 *v.* 控制，统治

短语 a tight *rein* 严格的控制

例句 She pulled gently on the *reins*. 她轻轻地拉着缰绳。The government gave free *rein* to the private sector in transport. 政府给私营运输业开了绿灯。

用法 give free rein to 对……放任

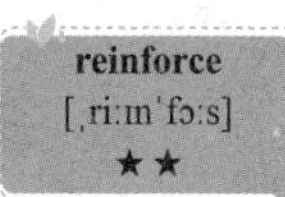

释义 *v.* 增援，加强

例句 A stronger European Parliament would, they fear, only *reinforce* the power of the larger countries. 他们担心，一个更强大的欧洲议会只会强化大国的权力。

近义 strengthen *v.* 加强

派生 reinforcement *n.* 加强

释义 *n.* 种类，类别 *v.* 分类，整理

短语 out of *sorts* 心情不佳

例句 At Harvard, Mr. Menand notes "the great books are read because they have been read"— they form a *sort* of social glue. 在哈佛大学，梅南德发现“学生之所以阅读伟大的著作是因为它们之前一直被人阅读”——这些著作成了一种社会黏合剂。

用法 sort of 有几分地；稍稍

释义 *n.* 来源，出处；根源 *v.*（从……）获得

短语 renewable energy *sources* 可再生能源

例句 Tourism is a major *source* of income for the area. 旅游业是这个地区的主要收入来源。

真题 Mental health is the *source* of creativity for solving problems, resolving conflict, making our surroundings more beautiful. 心理健康是创造力的来源，这种创造力可以让我们解决问题、化解冲突，让我们的环境更美好。（2016 翻译）

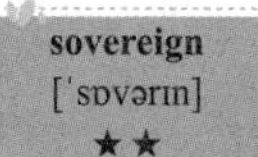

释义 *adj.* 独立的，有主权的 *n.* 君主，国王，统治者

短语 *sovereign* state 主权国

例句 Generally there was a belief that the new nations should be *sovereign* and independent states. 人们普遍认为，新国家应该是主权独立的国家。

近义 monarch *n.* 君主

派生 sovereignty *n.* 主权

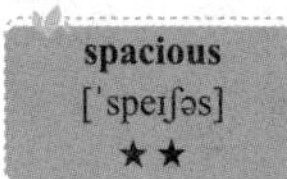

释义 *adj.* 广阔的，宽敞的

短语 a *spacious* living area

例句 Whether they play in small clubs or *spacious* concert halls, jazz musicians are drawing record crowds. 爵士音乐家们无论是在小俱乐部还是在宽敞的音乐厅演奏，都能吸引空前多的听众。

近义 roomy *adj.* 宽敞的；广阔的

派生 spaciousness *n.* 宽敞

释义 *n.* 治疗，疗法

短语 behavior *therapy* 行为疗法

例句 Children may need *therapy* to help them deal with grief and death. 孩子可能需要心理治疗来帮助他们应对悲伤和死亡。

近义 treatment *n.* 治疗

派生 therapist *n.* 治疗专家

释义 *adj.* 唯一的，独一无二的

短语 *unique* style / feature 独特的风格 / 特色

例句 Everyone's fingerprints are *unique*. 每个人的指纹都是独一无二的。

派生 uniquely *adv.* 独特地

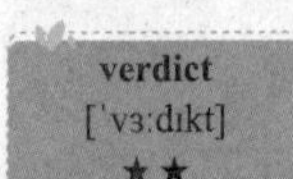

释义 *n.*（陪审团的）裁决，判决；判断；定论

短语 a guilty *verdict* 无罪裁决

例句 The Supreme Court is due to give a *verdict* on a long running legal battle by the end of the year. 最高法院将于今年年底对一场旷日持久的法律战做出裁决。

用法 give a verdict on sth. 对某事做出裁决

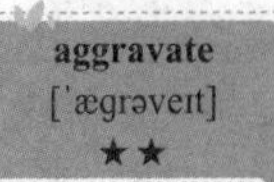

释义 *v.*（使）恶化；严重；惹怒

例句 The incident could *aggravate* relations between the two nations. 这一事件可能使两国关系恶化。

Caroline was *aggravated* by his bossy attitude. 卡洛琳被他专横的态度激怒了。

派生 aggravation *n.* 加重

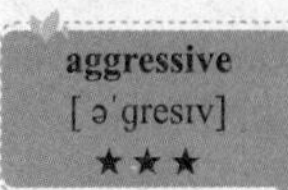

释义 *adj.* 好斗的；侵略的；积极进取的

例句 Men tend to be more *aggressive* than women. 男性往往比女性更具有攻击性。

He is respected as a very *aggressive* and competitive executive. 他被认为是一位非常有进取心和竞争意识的主管。

近义 provocative *adj.* 挑衅的

派生 aggression *n.* 攻击性

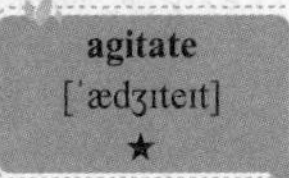

释义 *v.* 使焦虑；煽动，鼓动；搅动

例句 If I talk about the problem with him it just *agitates* him even more. 如果我和他谈论这个问题，他就会更加不安。

As a young man, he had *agitated* against the Vietnam war. 他年轻时曾鼓动反对越南战争。

派生 agitation *n.* 焦虑不安；煽动

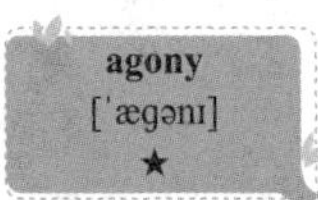

释义 *n.*（肉体或精神的）极度痛苦

短语 an *agony* of doubt 疑虑不安

例句 She was in terrible *agony* after breaking her leg. 她摔断了腿，痛苦万分。

用法 in agony 痛苦地

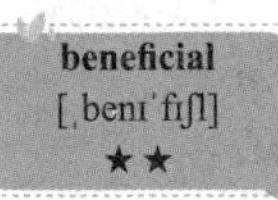

释义 *adj.* 有利的；有益的

例句 Cycling is highly *beneficial* to health and the environment. 骑自行车对健康和环境都非常有益。

近义 advantageous *adj.* 有益的

反义 harmful *adj.* 有害的

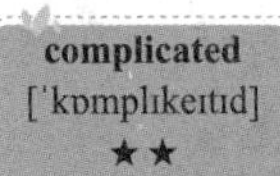

释义 *adj.* 错综复杂的，难解的

短语 a *complicated* system 复杂的系统

例句 The relationship is a bit *complicated*. He's my cousin's nephew's friend's child. 这个关系有点儿复杂，他是我表弟的侄子的朋友的孩子。

反义 simple *adj.* 简单的

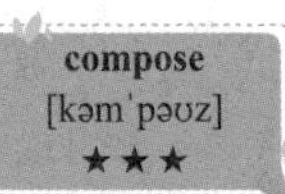

释义 *v.* 组成，构成；作曲；创作（诗歌等）；使镇静

例句 Christians *compose* 40 percent of the state's population. 基督教徒占该国人口的 40%。

Prokofiev started *composing* at the age of five. 普罗科菲耶夫 5 岁时就开始作曲了。

派生 composer *n.* 创作者，作曲家

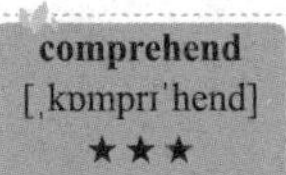

释义 *v.* 理解；了解

例句 I did not fully *comprehend* what had happened. 我不完全明白发生了什么事。

派生 comprehensible *adj.* 可理解的

释义 *v.* 压紧，压缩；浓缩

例句 Some jobs demand an amount of work that's difficult to *compress* into eight hours a day. 有些工作的工作量很难压缩到每天八个小时。

近义 condense *v.* 压缩

反义 expand *v.* 扩展

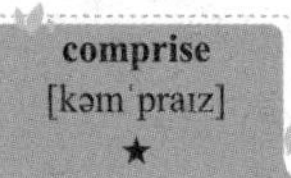

释义 *v.* 包含；由……组成；构成

例句 Older people *comprise* a large proportion of those living in poverty. 在那些生活贫困的人中，老年人占有很大的比例。

近义 constitute *v.* 组成

释义 *n.* / *v.* (despatch) 派遣；发送 *n.* 急件；新闻报道

短语 *dispatch* center 调度中心

例句 The Italian government was preparing to *dispatch* 4,000 soldiers to search the island. 意大利政府正准备派遣 4000 名士兵搜索该岛。

释义 *adj.* 不顾一切的；绝望的；极需要的

短语 *desperate* poverty 赤贫

例句 The situation is *desperate* — we have no food, very little water and no medical supplies. 形势非常严峻——我们没有食物和药品，只有很少的水。

派生 desperately *adv.* 绝望地，拼命地

destination
[ˌdestɪˈneɪʃn]
★

释义 *n.* 目的地，终点

短语 place of *destination* 目的地

例句 Fiji is a popular wedding and honeymoon *destination* with its flawless sandy beaches, year-round warm weather and its incredibly friendly people. 斐济是一个受欢迎的婚礼和蜜月目的地，拥有完美的沙滩，全年温暖的天气和非常友好的居民。

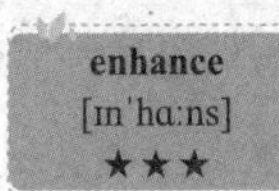

释义 *v.* 提高，增强

例句 Good secretarial skills should *enhance* your chances of getting a job. 出色的秘书工作技能会增加你找工作的机会。

真题 For one person, the goal may be to be taken more seriously and *enhance* their professional image. 对于某个人来说，其目标可能是更被重视，并提升自己的职业形象。（2016 阅读理解）

释义 *v.* 启发，启蒙，教导

例句 TV programs should *enlighten* the audience as well as entertainment. 电视节目既要使观众得到娱乐也要使他们得到启发。

用法 enlighten sb. about sth. 向某人阐明某事

派生 enlightenment *n.* 启迪，启发

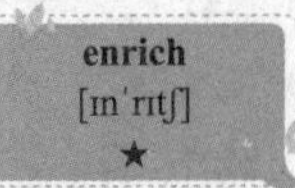

释义 *v.* 使富足；使肥沃；使充实

例句 Instead of just selling products, the brand aims to *enrich* people's lives with technology. 该品牌的目标不仅仅是销售产品，而是用科技丰富人们的生活。

近义 improve *v.* 改善

释义 *adj.* 肥沃的，富饶的；能繁殖的

例句 Farmers left the rocky hills of New England for the *fertile* plains of the Middle West. 农民们离开了新英格兰的多岩石的山丘，来到了中西部肥沃的平原。

派生 fertility *n.* 肥沃

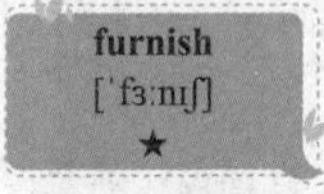

释义 *v.* 供应，提供；装备，布置

例句 The room was *furnished* with a cupboard and some old furniture. 房间里有一个碗柜和几件旧家具。

释义 *n.* 手势，姿势；姿态 *v.* 做手势

例句 Since the waiters spoke only local language, we had to use signs and *gestures* to make ourselves understood. 由于服务员只说当地语言，我们不得不用手势来让他们明白我们的意思。

Let's Rock'n'Roll

近义 wave *v.* 挥手；挥手示意

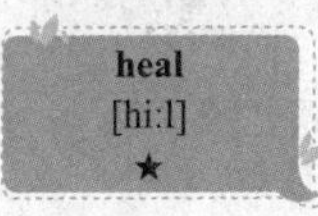

释义 *v.*（使）治愈；调停，消除

例句 The surgeon *healed* the soldier's bullet wound in the leg. 医生治好了那位士兵腿部的枪伤。

The long talk *healed* many of our differences. 那次长谈消除了我们许多分歧。

释义 *n.* 基础结构，基础设施

例句 The government invested $65 billion in *infrastructure*. 政府在基础设施上投资了650亿美元。

派生 infrastructural *adj.* 基础建设的

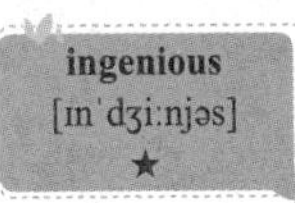

释义 *adj.* 机敏的；有独创性的；精致的

例句 Johnny is so *ingenious* — he can make the most remarkable sculptures from the most ordinary materials. 约翰尼真是手巧——他可以用最普通的材料制作出最棒的雕塑。

派生 ingeniously *adv.* 有才能地

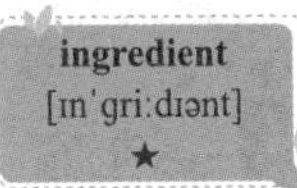

释义 *n.*（混合物的）组成部分，配料；成分，要素

例句 Sesame is an *ingredient* found in a variety of spices, sauces and flavorings. 芝麻是一种配料，广泛用于各种香料、酱汁和调味品中。

近义 element *n.* 基本部分，要素；元素

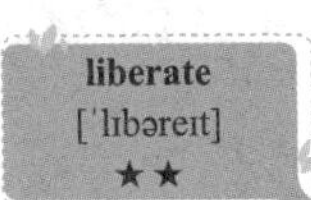

释义 *v.* 解放，释放

例句 He asked how committed the leadership was to *liberating* its people from poverty. 他问领导层对使人民摆脱贫困有多大决心。

近义 release *v.* 释放

派生 liberation *n.* 解放

释义 *n.* 优点，价值 *v.* 值得，应得

例句 The plan has its *merits*. 这计划有它的优点。

真题 Unfortunately, the long-term costs of using simple quantitative metrics to assess researcher *merit* are likely to be quite great. 不幸的是，使用简单的量化指标来评估研究人员的价值，其长期成本可能是相当大的。（2019 翻译）

释义 *n.* 方法，办法

例句 This is a good *method* that might well be adopted by other localities. 这个办法很好，各地可以仿照办理。

真题 The daguerreotype photographic *method* (producing an image on a silvered copper plate) could take several minutes to complete. 银版照相法（在镀银的铜板上照相）可能需要几分钟才能完成。（2021 阅读理解）

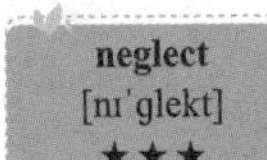

释义 *v.* 疏忽；忽略；遗漏 *n.* 忽视

短语 *neglect* of duty 玩忽职守

例句 But the intention is not to *neglect* social science; rather, the complete opposite. 但其目的不是要忽视社会科学；情况恰恰完全相反。

近义 overlook *v.* 忽略

释义 *v.* 运转；操作；经营，管理；开刀

短语 *operate* a machine 操作机器

例句 The rock salt mine is one of three *operated* by Cargill with the other two in Louisiana and Ohio. 这家岩盐矿是嘉吉公司经营的三家矿之一，另外两家位于路易斯安那州和俄亥俄州。

派生 operation *n.* 操作；手术；经营

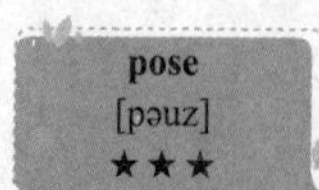

释义 *n.* 政治，政治学；政纲，政见

短语 international *politics* 国际政治

例句 Ultimately, it is likely to reshape our *politics*, our culture, and the character of our society for years. 最终，它可能会在数年内重塑我们的政治、文化和社会特征。

真题 This kind of thinking is why so many people try to avoid arguments, especially about *politics* and religion. 这种想法就是那么多人试图避免争论的原因，尤其是关于政治和宗教的争论。（2019 阅读理解）

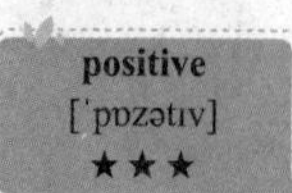

释义 *n.* 姿势，姿态 *v.* 摆姿势

例句 By the time we wake up to the threat *posed* by climate change, it could well be too late. 等到我们意识到气候变化带来的威胁时，可能已经太晚了。

用法 pose a challenge / risk 带来挑战 / 风险

派生 position *n.* 位置

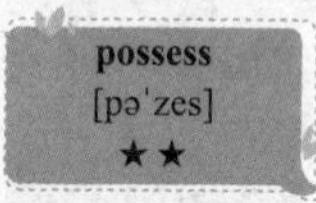

释义 *adj.* 肯定的，积极的，正面的

短语 *positive* attitude 积极态度 *positive* influence 积极影响

例句 Remember, keep a *positive* attitude and good things will happen. 记住：保持乐观的心态，好事自然会发生。

派生 positively *adv.* 绝对地；乐观地

真题 Jeremy Wright, the culture secretary, should welcome this *positive*, hope-filled proposal, and turn it into action. 英国文化大臣杰里米·赖特应该欢迎这种积极、充满希望的提议，并将其转化为行动。（2020 阅读理解）

释义 *v.* 占有，拥有

例句 What she does *possess* is the ability to get straight to the core of a problem. 她确实有直击问题本质的能力。

派生 possession *n.* 拥有，持有

用法 possess of 拥有

publication
[ˌpʌblɪˈkeɪʃən]
★★★

释义 *n.* 出版物；出版，发行；公布，发表

例句 She was in England for the *publication* of her new book. 她在英国准备新书的出版工作。

真题 This year marks exactly two centuries since the *publication* of *Frankenstein*; or, *The Modern Prometheus*, by Mary Shelley. 今年是玛丽·雪莱的《弗兰肯斯坦》，又名《现代普罗米修斯》出版整整两个世纪的一年。（2019 阅读理解）

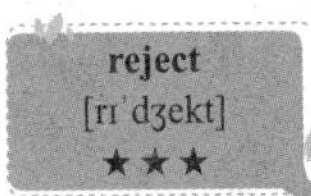

释义 *v.* 拒绝；排斥 *n.* 落选者；次品

例句 I applied for a job as a mechanic in a local garage, but I was *rejected*. 我申请去当地的汽车修理厂当机械师，但被拒绝了。

派生 rejection *n.* 拒绝；拒绝接受

真题 This means that people should avoid crisping their roast potatoes, *reject* thin-crust pizzas and only partially toast their bread. 这意味着人们应该避免把土豆烤脆，拒绝薄皮比萨，把面包只烤到差不多熟。（2020 阅读理解）

释义 *v.* 叙述，讲述；使互相关联

例句 The book breaks down how our success is *related* to interactions with others. 这本书分析了我们的成功与他人的互动是如何相关的。

She *relates* her childhood experiences in the first chapters. 在开始的几章中，她描述了自己童年的经历。

用法 relate with 使相关，使符合

派生 relation *n.* 关系，联系

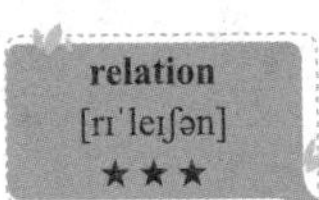

释义 *n.* 关系，联系；亲属，亲戚

短语 public *relation* 公共关系

例句 The incident led to tense international *relations*. 这一事件导致国际关系紧张。

真题 Composure is a state of mind made possible by the structuring of one's *relation* to one's environment. 平静是通过构建人与环境的关系而形成的一种精神状态。（2013 翻译）

近义 link *n.* 联系，关系

派生 relationship *n.* 关系，联系

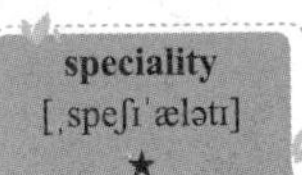

释义 *n.* (specialty) 特性；专长；特产

短语 *speciality* store 专卖店

例句 Foreign language persons of tour *speciality* are greatly in need with the development of tourism. 随着旅游业的迅猛发展，对旅游专业外语人才的需求越来越大。

用法 a speciality of sb. 某人的专长

派生 specialism *n.* 专长

释义 *n.*（物）种，种类

短语 *species* group 种群 an endangered *species* 濒临绝种的生物

例句 Some *species* of trees have been "read out of the party" by economics-minded foresters because they grow too slowly. 有些树种生长太过缓慢，因此被有经济头脑的林业人员"淘汰"。

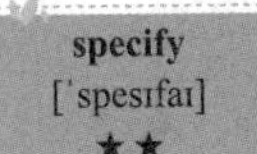

释义 *v.* 指定，详细说明

短语 *specify* a category 指定一个类别

例句 You should *specify* what kind of child you want to help and how you will carry out your plan. 你应该明确说明你想帮助什么样的孩子，以及你将如何实施你的计划。

派生 specific *adj.* 具体的

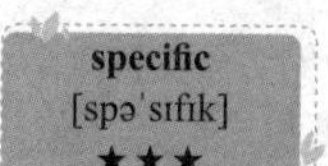

释义 *adj.* 明确的,具体的;特定的,特有的

短语 *specific* function 特殊功能 specific gravity 比重

例句 Surfwatch allows parents to prohibit access to *specific* web sites and newsgroups. 过滤软件可以让父母禁止对特定的网站和新闻组的访问。

派生 specification *n.* 规格,规范

真题 *Specific* brain regions that respond during direct gaze are being explored by other researches, using advanced methods of brain scanning. 其他研究利用先进的大脑扫描方法,正在探索人在直视时做出反应的特定大脑区域。(2020 阅读理解)

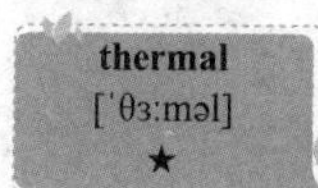

释义 *adj.* 热的,热力的

短语 *thermal* energy / springs 热能 / 温泉

例句 Runners were given *thermal* blankets to prevent heat loss at the end of the race. 运动员们在比赛结束时获得了保暖毯,以防止热量散失。

释义 *v.* (使)联合,团结;统一

短语 the *United* States 美国 the *United* Kingdom 英国

例句 *United* with them, we provide a voice to those experiencing violence at home. 我们与他们团结在一起,为那些在家里遭受暴力的人发声。

用法 unite with 联合

派生 united *adj.* 团结的,统一的

释义 *n.* 边缘;极限;临界点 *v.* 濒临

例句 Many villages either have been deserted, or are on the *verge* of disappearing. 许多村庄要么已被遗弃,要么濒临消失。

用法 on the verge of 处于……的边缘

近义 edge *n.* 边缘

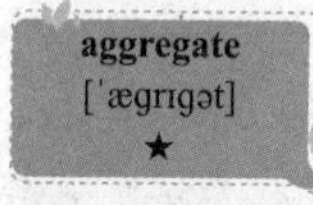

释义 *v.* 合计 *n.* 总数,合计 *adj.* 总数的

例句 The money collected will *aggregate* a thousand dollars. 进账总额将达一千美元。

The rate of growth of GNP will depend upon the rate of growth of *aggregate* demand. 国民生产总值的增长率将取决于总需求的增长率。

派生 aggregation *n.* 聚合;聚集;集合体

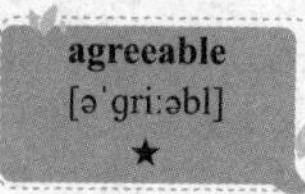

释义 *adj.* 惬意的;欣然同意的

例句 The couple spent a most *agreeable* day together. 这对夫妇在一起度过了非常愉快的一天。

He suggested she go out for a walk with him, and she seemed *agreeable*. 他建议她一起出去散步,她似

乎很乐意。

反义 disagreeable *adj.* 不愉快的

派生 agreement *n.* 协议

释义 *adj.* 陌生的；外国的；外来的 *n.* 外国人；外星人

短语 an *alien* environment 陌生的环境

例句 Fast-food companies brought *alien* foods such as cheese into the Chinese market along with beef burgers and pizzas. 快餐公司将奶酪等外来食品与牛肉汉堡以及比萨一起带入了中国市场。

近义 foreign *adj.* 外国的

反义 native *adj.* 本地的

派生 alienation *n.* 异化

释义 *v.*（未经证实地）指责，宣称，指控

短语 the *alleged* attack / incident 据称的袭击 / 事件

例句 He *alleged* that she stole a large quantity of money. 他声称她偷了一大笔钱。

近义 assert *v.* 宣称 claim *v.* 声称

派生 allegation *n.*（无证据的）说法，指控

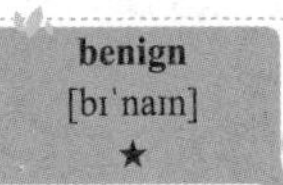

释义 *adj.* 慈祥的；良性的；宜人的；无害的

短语 a *benign* old lady 慈祥的老妇人

例句 The spacecraft provides a *benign* environment for the instruments and on-board equipment. 宇宙飞船为仪器和机载设备提供了一个良好的环境。

近义 affable *adj.* 友善的

派生 benignly *adv.* 亲切地；仁慈地

释义 *n.* / *v.* 妥协，折中

例句 It is hoped that a *compromise* will be reached in today's talks. 希望今天的会谈能达成妥协。

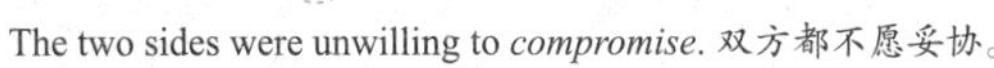

The two sides were unwilling to *compromise*. 双方都不愿妥协。

真题 The astronomy community is making *compromises* to change its use of Mauna Kea. 天文学界正在做出妥协以改变对于莫纳克亚山的使用。（2017 阅读理解）

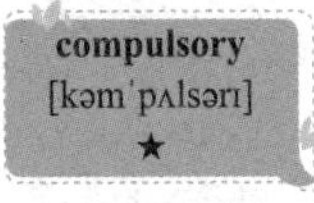

释义 *adj.* 强制性的；（课程）必修的

例句 Norway has *compulsory* military service of nineteen months for men and women between the ages of 19 and 44 . 挪威对 19 岁至 44 岁的男女实行 19 个月的义务兵役制。

派生 compulsion *n.* 强制

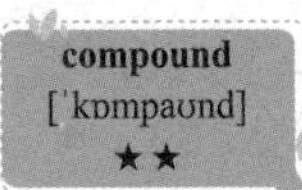

释义 *n.* 混合物 *adj.* 混合的 *v.* 混合；使恶化

例句 Common salt is a *compound* of sodium and chlorine. 普通食盐是钠和氯的化合物。

The problems were *compounded* by severe food shortages. 严重的食物短缺使问题进一步恶化。

释义 *v.* 隐藏，隐瞒

例句 She knew at once that he was *concealing* something from her. 她立刻知道他对她有所隐瞒。

反义 reveal *v.* 揭露

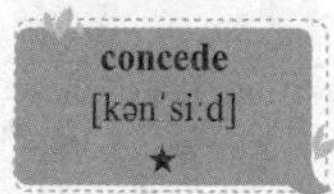

释义 *v.* 承认；容许；认输；让与

例句 He kept on arguing and wouldn't *concede* defeat. 他一直争论个不停，不愿认输。

A strike has ended after the government *conceded* some of their demands. 在政府答应了他们的一些要求后，罢工结束了。

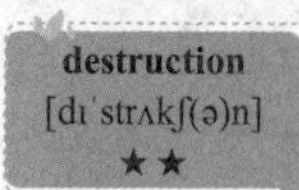

释义 *n.* 毁坏，毁灭

短语 forest / habitat *destruction* 森林 / 栖息地破坏

例句 There is worldwide concern about the *destruction* of the rainforests. 全世界都在关注热带雨林遭到破坏的问题。

派生 destructive *adj.* 破坏性

释义 *v.* 使分离；脱离；派遣

例句 Staff need downtime to *detach* from work, especially in these stressful times. 员工需要休息时间来远离工作，尤其是在压力大的时候。

用法 detach from sth. 脱离……

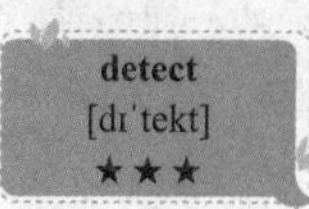

释义 *v.* 察觉，发觉，侦察，探测

例句 Your sense of smell can also help you *detect* weather changes. 你的嗅觉也能帮助你察觉天气的变化。

派生 detective *n.* 侦探

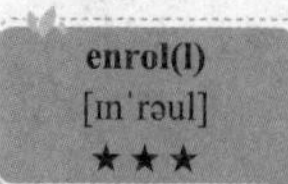

释义 *v.* 招收；登记；入学；参军

例句 You can *enroll* for the courses online. 你可以报名学习我们的在线课程。

真题 The TSA wants to *enroll* 25 million people in PreCheck. 美国运输安全管理局希望将 2500 万人纳入预审计划。（2017 阅读理解）

释义 *v.* 确保，保证；使安全

例句 Officials will *ensure* that the election is carried out fairly. 官员们将确保选举公正地进行。

真题 If we are serious about *ensuring* that our science is both meaningful and reproducible, we must ensure that our institutions encourage that kind of science. 如果我们真的要确保我们的科学既有意义又可复制，我们就必须确保我们的制度鼓励这种科学。（2019 翻译）

释义 *v.* 使承担；需要；导致；限定继承

例句 Such a decision would *entail* a huge political risk. 这样的决定将带来巨大的政治风险。

The land is *entailed* on the eldest son. 土地限定由长子继承。

fierce [fɪəs] ★★

释义 *adj.* 凶猛的，残忍的；狂热的，强烈的

例句 The climbers were trapped by a *fierce* storm which went on for days. 登山者被一场持续了好几天的暴风雨困住了。

近义 violent *adj.* 强烈的，猛烈的

futile [ˈfjuːtaɪl] ★

释义 *adj.* 无效的，无用的，无希望的

例句 After months of *futile* labor, the scientist suddenly had a brainstorm and solved the problem. 数月努力，徒劳无功，科学家突发奇想，问题迎刃而解。

近义 useless *adj.* 无用的

gigantic [dʒaɪˈgæntɪk] ★★

释义 *adj.* 巨大的，庞大的

短语 a *gigantic* statue 巨大的雕像

例句 The earth may be thought of as a *gigantic* magnet. 整个地球可以想象为一块巨大的磁石。

近义 colossal *adj.* 巨大的 massive *adj.* 巨大的

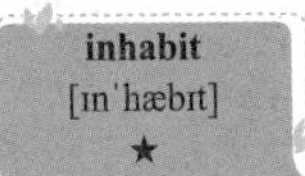

inhabit [ɪnˈhæbɪt] ★

释义 *v.* 居住于，存在于；栖息于

例句 Only rare birds and animals *inhabit* this remote island. 这个偏远的岛屿上只有一些珍禽异兽。

派生 inhabitant *n.* 居民，住户

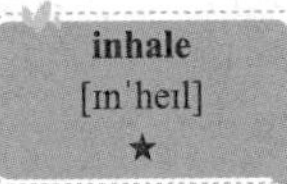

inhale [ɪnˈheɪl] ★

释义 *v.* 吸入(气体等)，吸(烟)

真题 We were taught some basic breathing exercises, such as *inhaling* slowly and deeply through the nose. 我们学了一些基本的呼吸练习，比如用鼻子缓慢地深吸气。

反义 exhale *v.* 呼气

派生 inhalation *v.* 吸气

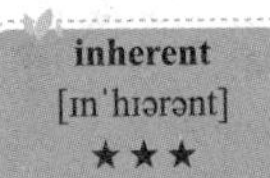

inherent [ɪnˈhɪərənt] ★★★

释义 *adj.* 固有的，内在的，天生的

短语 *inherent* characteristic 固有特性

真题 Good governance rests on an understanding of the *inherent* worth of each individual. 良好的治理依赖于对每个人内在价值的理解。(2017 阅读理解)

用法 be an inherent part of sth. 是某物固有的一部分

派生 inherently *adv.* 内在地

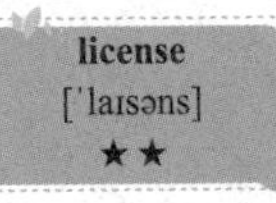

license [ˈlaɪsəns] ★★

释义 *n.* (licence) 许可证，执照 *v.* 准许，认可

短语 a driving *license* 驾照

例句 She was released after posting $100 cash bond and her driver's *license*. 交了100 美元现款保释金及驾驶执照以后，她获得保释了。

近义 permit *v.* 许可 *n.* 执照

metropolitan [ˌmetrəˈpɒlɪtən] ★

释义 *adj.* 大都市的，大城市

短语 *metropolitan* opera 大都会歌剧院

例句 He was drawn to the *metropolitan* glamour and excitement

of Paris. 他被巴黎的大都会魅力与激情所吸引。

近义 urban *adj.* 城市的

释义 *v.* 迁移,移居(国外)

例句 Thousands were forced to *migrate* from rural to urban areas in search of work. 成千上万的人为了寻找工作被迫从农村涌进城市。

派生 migration *n.* 移民,迁徙

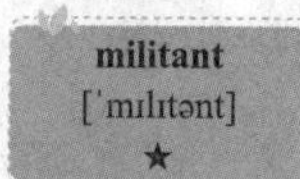

释义 *adj.* 好战的,富于战斗性的 *n.* 斗士

例句 *Militant* mine workers have voted for a one-day stoppage next month. 激进的矿工投票赞成下个月罢工一天。

近义 aggressive *adj.* 好斗的

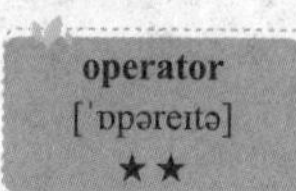

释义 *n.* 操作员;经营者;接线员

短语 telephone *operator* 话务员

例句 She had worked as a call centre *operator* making cold calls to sell life insurance. 她曾经在一个呼叫中心担任话务员,负责推销人寿保险。

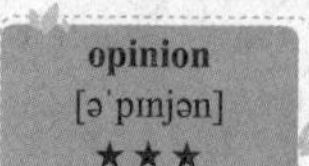

释义 *n.* 意见,看法,主张

短语 *opinion* poll 民意测验 legal *opinion* 法律意见书

例句 The museum is seeking an expert *opinion* on the authenticity of the painting. 博物馆在请专家鉴定那幅画的真伪。

用法 in the opinion of 据……的见解

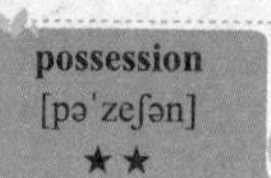

释义 *n.* 持有,拥有;私人物品,财产,财富

例句 You cannot legally take *possession* of the property until three weeks after the contract is signed. 契约签署三周以后,你才能合法取得这份产业的所有权。

真题 But this distinction misses the point that it is processing and aggregation, not the mere *possession* of bits, that gives the data value. 但是,这种区别忽略了一点,赋予数据价值的是数字的处理和整合,而非单单拥有数据。(2018 阅读理解)

用法 take possession of 占有

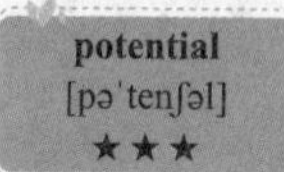

释义 *adj.* 潜在的,可能的 *n.* 潜能,潜力,电位,电势

短语 *potential* market 潜在市场 growth *potential* 增长潜力

例句 The functioning of the market is based on flexible trends dominated by *potential* buyers. 市场的运作基于由潜在买家主导的灵活趋势。

派生 potentially *adv.* 潜在地

真题 The *potential* of this work applied to healthcare is very great. 这个成果应用到医疗保健方面的潜力是非常大的。(2018 阅读理解)

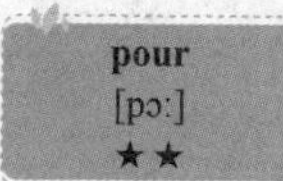

释义 *v.* 灌注,倾泻,涌入,倾盆大雨

短语 *pouring* rain 瓢泼大雨 *pour* out 倾吐,诉说

例句 It has been *pouring* almost non-stop for the past three days, disrupting normal life. 在过去的三天里,倾盆大雨几乎没有停过,扰乱了正常

的生活。

用法 pour cold water over/on sth. 给……泼冷水

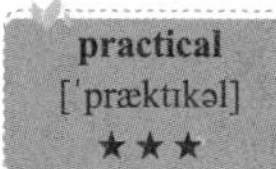

practical [ˈpræktɪkəl] ★★★

释义 *adj.* 实际的，实用的

短语 *practical* application 实际应用 *practical* value 实际价值

例句 Be *practical* and don't waste a lot of time trying to find perfect. 实际一点，不要浪费太多时间去寻找完美。

派生 practically *adv.* 实事求是地，实际地

publicity [pʌbˈlɪsɪtɪ] ★

释义 *n.* 公开；宣传；广告；推销

短语 *publicity* campaign 宣传运动

例句 We have planned an exciting *publicity* campaign with our advertisers. 我们和广告人员一起策划了一场十分精彩的宣传活动。

派生 publicize *v.* 宣传，公布

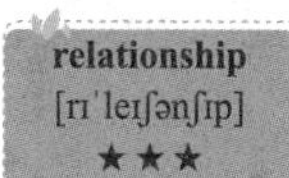

relationship [rɪˈleɪʃənʃɪp] ★★★

释义 *n.* 关系，联系

短语 customer *relationship* management 客户关系管理

例句 Their *relationship* soon went sour. 他们的关系很快有了嫌隙。

真题 If the postgraduate student population also grows rapidly and there is loss of a close apprenticeship *relationship* between faculty members and students ... 如果研究生人数也快速增长，而且教师和学生之间的学徒关系不再密切……（2021 翻译）

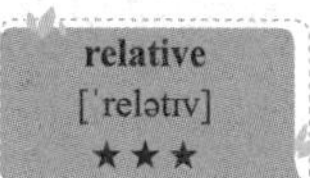

relative [ˈrelətɪv] ★★★

释义 相对的，比较的；有关系的 *n.* 亲戚，关系词

短语 *relative* theory 相对论 a distant *relative* 远亲

例句 They chatted about the *relative* merits of London and Paris as places to live. 他们聊起了伦敦和巴黎两座城市相比较都有哪些宜居的优点。

The ibex is a distant *relative* of the mountain goat. 北山羊与石山羊有较远的亲缘关系。

派生 relativity *n.* 相关（性）；相对论

release [rɪˈliːs] ★★★

释义 *v.* 释放；发行 *n.* 释放；发布；解脱

例句 Exercise *releases* hormones that can improve mood and relieve stress. 运动可以释放改善情绪和缓解压力的激素。

真题 Oxytocin is made primarily in the central lower part of the brain, and some of it is *released* into the bloodstream. 催产素主要在大脑中下部产生，其中一些会释放到血液中。（2017 完形填空）

派生 releasable *adj.* 可免除的；能释放的

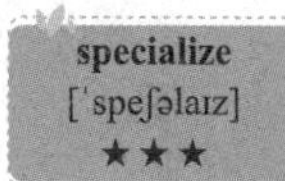

specialize [ˈspeʃəlaɪz] ★★★

释义 *v.* (specialise) 专攻，专门研究，专业化；详细说明

例句 Our company was established in 1990s, which *specializes* in production and service of Auto and Machine Parts. 我公司成立于九十年代，是一家专业生产和服务汽车及机械零部件的公司。

真题 Other scientists perform the *specialised* work of peer review also for free, because it is a central element in the acquisition of status and the production of scientific knowledge. 其他科学家亦无偿进行同行评审的专业性工作，是因为同行评审是获得学术地位以及缔造科学知识的一项核心要素。（2020 阅读理解）

派生 specialist *n.* 专家

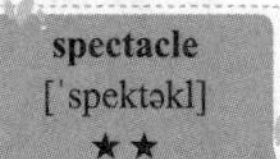

释义 *n.* (*pl.*) 眼镜；场面，景象；奇观，壮观

短语 a pair of *spectacles* 一副眼镜

例句 The sunrise seen from high in the mountains was a tremendous *spectacle*. 从山上居高远望，日出景象蔚为奇观。

派生 spectacular *adj.* 壮观的

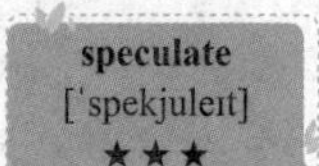

释义 *v.* 思索；推测；投机

例句 They *speculate* that sleep is an attempt by the body to conserve energy. 他们推测睡眠是身体保存能量的一种尝试。

近义 suppose *v.* 推断，猜想

派生 speculation *n.* 猜测，推测

释义 *adj.* 精神（上）的，心灵的

短语 *spiritual* world / leader 精神世界 / 领袖

例句 Buddhism is about the *spiritual* development of the individual. 佛教是关于个人精神发展的。

近义 mental *adj.* 精神的

派生 spiritually *adv.* 在精神上地

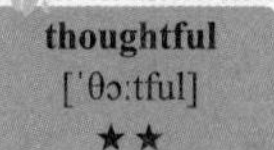

释义 *adj.* 体贴的；认真思考的

短语 a *thoughtful* and caring man 一个体贴入微的男人

例句 Thank you for calling when I was ill — it was very *thoughtful* of you. 谢谢你在我生病的时候打电话来问候，你真是体贴人。

近义 considerate *adj.* 考虑周到的

派生 thoughtfully *adv.* 沉思地；体贴地

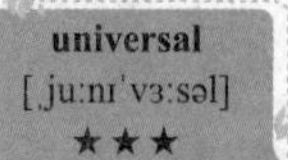

释义 *adj.* 普遍的，全体的；宇宙的，世界的

短语 *universal* language 通用语言

例句 Since the days of Aristotle, a search for *universal* principles has characterized the scientific enterprise. 自亚里士多德时代以来，对普遍原理的探索就是科学事业的特点。

用法 have universal appeal 具有普遍的吸引力

派生 universally *adv.* 普遍地

释义 *v.* 证实，查证；证明

例句 Please *verify* that there is sufficient memory available before loading the program. 请在核实有足够的内存后再安装此程序。

真题 A Knight Foundation focus-group survey of young people between ages 14 and 24 found they use "distributed trust" to *verify* stories. 奈特基金会针对14~24岁年轻人的专题调查发现，这些年轻人利用"分布式信任"验证新闻真伪。（2018 阅读理解）

近义 certify *v.* 证明

派生 verification *n.* 核实

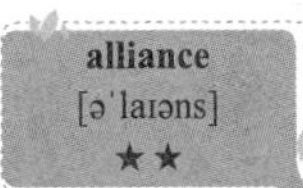

释义 v. 减轻;缓和

例句 You can't cure a common cold, but you can *alleviate* the symptoms. 你不能治愈普通的感冒,但可以减轻症状。

真题 Ferraro wanted to see if Indonesia's *poverty-alleviation* program was affecting deforestation. 费拉罗想知道印尼的扶贫项目是否影响了森林砍伐。(2021 阅读理解)

同义 ease v. 缓和

派生 alleviation n. 减轻,缓和

释义 n. 联盟;结盟;结盟国家

例句 In 1882 Germany, Austria, and Italy formed the Triple *Alliance*.1882 年,德国、奥地利和意大利组成了三国同盟。

用法 form an alliance with 与……结盟

近义 alignment n. 结盟

释义 v. [ə'laɪ](使)结盟 n. ['ælaɪ] 同盟国,盟友

短语 a close *ally* and friend 亲密的盟友和朋友

例句 Russia *allied* itself to France. 俄国与法国结盟。She will regret losing a close political *ally*. 她将为失去一位亲密的政治盟友而后悔。

用法 ally with 与……结盟

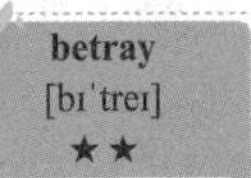

释义 v. 分配;分派

例句 Tickets are limited and will be *allocated* to those who apply first. 门票是有限的,将分配给最先申请的人。

同义 distribute v. 分配

派生 allocation n. 分配,分派

释义 v. 背叛;泄露;出卖

例句 When I tell someone I will not *betray* his confidence, I keep my word. 当我对人说我不会辜负他的信任时,我会说到做到。

用法 betray sb. 背叛某人

派生 betrayal n. 背叛

conceive
[kən'si:v]
★★

释义 v. 想出;设想;怀有(某种感情);怀胎

例句 It is simply a fantastic imagination to *conceive* that one can master a foreign language overnight. 幻想在一天早晨就把外语学好,那只是白日做梦。

派生 conceivable adj. 可想象的

释义 v. 集中;专心;聚集

例句 I can't *concentrate* on my work with all that noise. 噪声这么大,我没法集中精力。

真题 It could also lead to further *concentration* of power in the tech giants. 这也可能导致权力进一步集中在科技巨头手中。(2018 阅读理解)

派生 concentration *n.* 专心,专注

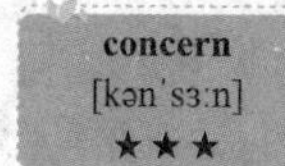

释义 *v.* 使担心;与……有关 *n.* 关心;担心,忧虑

例句 The problem *concerns* us all. 这个问题关系到我们大家。

Refugee problems had become a *concern* to Congress. 难民问题已经成为国会关注的问题。

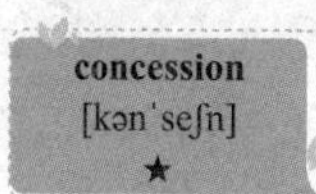

释义 *n.* 让步,妥协;承认;特许(权)

例句 " It is not a *concession* to Russia, but it's a big gesture," he said. 他说:"这不是对俄罗斯的让步,但它是一个重要的姿态。"

近义 compromise *n.* 妥协

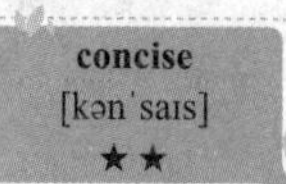

释义 *adj.* 简明的,简洁的

例句 Whatever you are writing make sure you are clear, *concise*, and accurate. 无论你写什么,注意一定要清晰、简练、准确。

近义 brief *adj.* 简短的

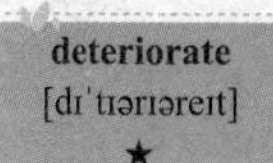

释义 *v.*(使)恶化,(使)变坏

例句 The weather *deteriorated* rapidly so the game was canceled. 天气迅速恶化,所以比赛取消了。

派生 deterioration *n.* 恶化

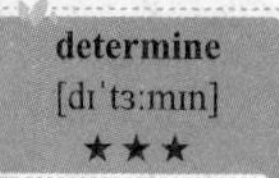

释义 *v.* 下定决心;确定

例句 Genes determine about 80% of a person's height, but other factors can also affect it. 基因决定一个人 80% 的身高,但其他因素也会影响其身高。

用法 be determined by 由……决定

派生 determination *n.* 决心

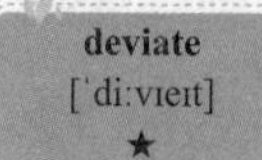

释义 *v.* 背离,偏离

例句 The bus had to *deviate* from its usual route because of a road closure. 因为道路封闭,公共汽车只得绕道而行。

派生 deviation *n.* 偏离,违背

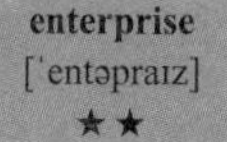

释义 *n.* 企(事)业单位;事业心,进取心

短语 private / state *enterprise* 私有 / 国有企业

例句 The uprising or downfalling of an *enterprise* lies in its management or administration. 企业兴衰取决于经营管理。

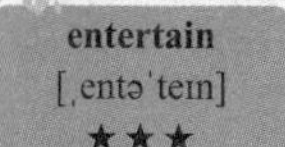

释义 *v.* 招待,款待;使娱乐;接受

例句 He *entertained* us for hours with his stories and jokes. 他既讲故事又说笑话,把我们逗得乐了好几个小时。

We *entertain* a firm belief in the final victory. 我们对最后胜利抱有坚定的信念。

用法 entertain a doubt / suspicion 持怀疑态度

派生 entertainer *n.* 演艺人员，表演者

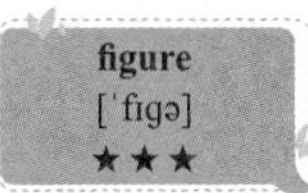

释义 *n.* 热心；热衷；热情

例句 The company eventually lost *enthusiasm* for filmmaking and decided to concentrate on its theatrical endeavours. 该公司最终失去了对电影制作的热情，决定专注于其戏剧事业。

用法 lose enthusiasm for sth. 对某事失去热情

释义 *n.* 体形，轮廓；数字；图形 *v.* 理解，弄懂

例句 It took them about one month to *figure* out how to start the equipment. 他们花了大约1个月的时间才搞清楚如何启动设备。

真题 Many of the most celebrated national *figures* have participated in historical events that have taken place within the Eisehower Executive Office Building's granite walls. 许多最知名的国家级人物参与了发生在艾森豪威尔行政办公楼花岗岩墙壁内的历史事件。(2018 阅读理解)

用法 figure out 解决

释义 *n.* (glamor) 魅力，诱惑力 *v.* 迷惑

例句 What makes television distinctive is its *glamour* and its reach. 电视的独特之处在于它那迷人的魅力和影响力。

派生 glamorous *adj.* 迷人的

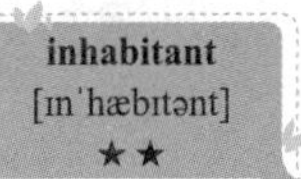

释义 *v.* (使)提高；(使)加强

例句 The case has *heightened* public awareness of the problem of sexual harassment. 这起案件提高了公众对性骚扰问题的认识。

近义 intensify *v.* 增强

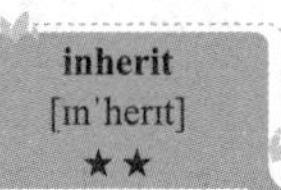

释义 *n.* 居民，住户

短语 local *inhabitants* 本地居民

例句 The current indigenous *inhabitants* seem to have settled here since the 16th century. 现在的土著居民似乎是从16世纪开始在这里定居的。

派生 inhabitancy *n.* 居住

释义 *v.* 继承；经遗传而得

短语 *inherit* a fortune 继承财富

例句 We *inherit* from our parents many of our physical characteristics. 我们的许多身体特征都是从父母那里遗传而来的。

派生 inheritor *n.* 继承人

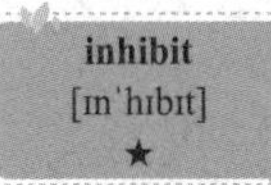

释义 *v.* 抑制，约束

例句 Positive emotions facilitate the creative aspects of learning and negative emotions *inhibit* it. 积极情绪促进学习的创造性，而消极情绪则会对其产生抑制作用。

反义 facilitate *v.* 促进

派生 inhibition *n.* 拘谨；阻止

likelihood
[ˈlaɪklɪhud]
★

释义 *n.* 可能性

例句 The *likelihood* of being named in a federal class-action lawsuit also increases, and the stock is likely to perform worse. 被牵扯到联邦法院所受理的集体起诉案件中的可能性也随之增加，该股的表现可能会更糟。

近义 possibility *n.* 可能性

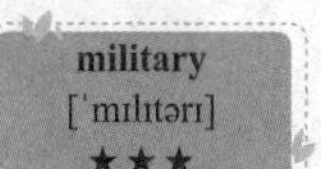

释义 *adj.* 军事的，军用的，军队的 *n.* 军人，军方

短语 *military* officer 军官

例句 The cost for saving our civilization would be considerably less than the world's current *military* spending. 拯救我们文明的成本将大大低于世界目前的军事开支。

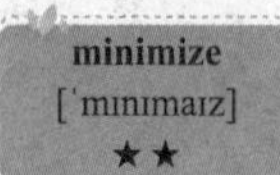

释义 *v.* (minimise) 使减少到最少，使降到最低

例句 You can *minimize* the dangers of driving by taking care to obey the rules of the road. 严格遵守交通规则，你就能把行车危险降到最低点。

真题 Almost all of the interior detail is of cast iron or plaster; the use of wood was *minimized* to insure fire safety. 几乎所有的室内细节都是用铸铁或石膏制成的；木材的使用被减少到最低限度，以确保防火安全。（2018 阅读理解）

反义 maximize *v.* 使最大化

释义 *adj.* 可忽略的，无足轻重的

短语 a *negligible* effect 微不足道的影响

例句 There is a *negligible* difference in meaning between these two words. 这两个词之间在意义上差别是极小的。

近义 minor *adj.* 轻微的

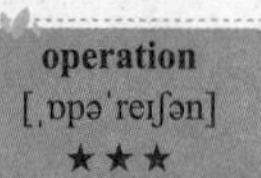

释义 *n.* 操作，运转，经营；手术；行动；活动

短语 mode of *operation* 运行方式 *operation* and management 经营和管理

例句 Regular servicing guarantees the smooth *operation* of the engine. 定期维修可保持发动机的顺畅运转。

派生 operational *adj.* 可使用的；操作的，运营的

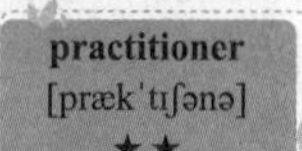

释义 *n.*（医生或律师等）开业者；从业人员

短语 medical *practitioner* 医生 nurse *practitioner* 从业护士

例句 Those who stay on for an additional two years can earn a master's degree that qualifies them as nurse *practitioners* or clinical nurse specialists. 那些在此工作两年以上的人可以获得硕士学位，使他们有资格成为从业护士或临床护理专家。

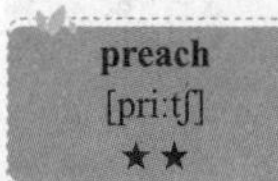

释义 *v.* 宣讲（教义），布道；说教

短语 *preach* a sermon 布道

例句 Many pastors from around the community came to show their respect and *preach* for peace. 社区里的许多牧师前来表达他们的敬意，并为和平布道。

派生 preachment *n.* 长篇大论；说教；讲道

precede
[priːˈsiːd]
★★

【释义】*v.* 领先（于），在（……之前）；优先，先于

【短语】*precede* quarter / year 上一季度 / 上一年度

【例句】The earthquake was *preceded* by several smaller tremors. 这次地震之前有几次较小的震动。

【用法】precede over 优先于

【派生】precedent *n.* 先例，前例

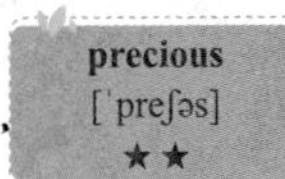

【释义】*adj.* 珍贵的，贵重的

【短语】*precious* moment 珍贵的时刻

【例句】Wasting food means losing not only life-supporting nutrition but also *precious* resources, including land, water and energy. 浪费粮食不仅意味着失去维持生命的营养，也意味着失去宝贵的资源，包括土地、水和能源。

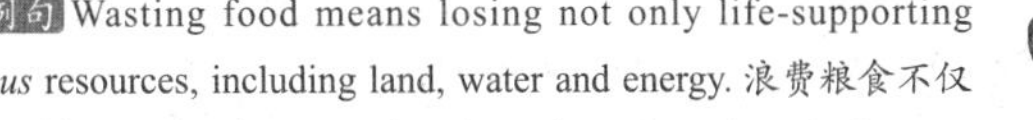

【派生】valuable *adj.* 宝贵的

【释义】*v.* 惩罚，处罚

【例句】If a little boy's male friends are *punished* for crying, he will learn that boys don't cry. 如果一个小男孩的男性朋友因为哭而受到惩罚，他就会知道男孩是不哭的。

【用法】punish with 用……惩罚

【派生】punishment *n.* 惩罚手段，处罚

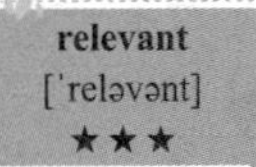

【释义】*adj.* 有关的，有意义的

【短语】*relevant* information 相关信息

【例句】If you have children, this chapter is particularly *relevant* to you. 如果你有孩子，这一章对你特别有意义。

【反义】irrelevant *adj.* 不相关的

【派生】relevance *n.* 相关性

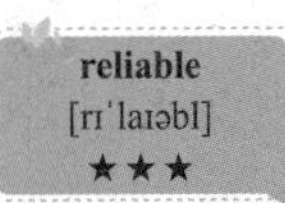

【释义】*adj.* 可靠的，可信赖的

【短语】*reliable* information 可靠信息

【例句】We are looking for someone who is *reliable* and hard-working. 我们在物色可靠而又勤奋的人。

【近义】honest *adj.* 诚实的，正直的

【派生】reliability *n.* 可靠性；可信度

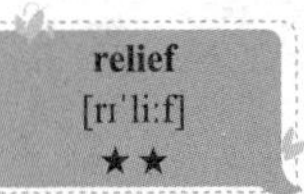

【释义】*n.*（痛苦等）减轻，解除；援救，救济

【短语】disaster *relief* 赈灾

【例句】The calm of the countryside came as a welcome *relief* from the hustle and bustle of city life. 离开喧嚣忙碌的城市生活，来到宁静的乡村，是一种令人愉快的调剂。

【派生】relieve *v.* 缓解；减轻

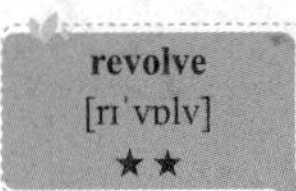

【释义】*v.*（使）旋转；以……为中心；公转；循环

【例句】The book *revolves* around a youngster who is shown various stages of his life. 这本书围绕着一个年轻人展开，描述了他人生的各个阶段。

近义 orbit *v.* 环绕……运行

用法 revolve around 围绕……转动

派生 revolvable *adj.* 可旋转的

释义 *v.* 分裂，分开 *n.* 分裂，裂口 *adj.* 劈开的

例句 By *splitting* up the subject matter into smaller units, one man could continue to handle the information and use it as the basis for further research. 通过将主题进行细分，一个人就能够继续处理这些信息，并且将它作为进一步研究的基础。

用法 split up into 使分裂成

近义 divide *v.*（使）分开

释义 *n.* 发起人，保证人 *v.* 发起，主办

短语 a *sponsored* swim 慈善游泳活动

例句 They want to know if we'd be interested in *sponsoring* a tour they want to make to East Asia. 他们想知道我们是否有兴趣赞助他们去东亚的旅行。

真题 A pair of bills *sponsored* by Massachusetts state Senator Jason Lewis and House Speaker Pro Tempore Patricia Haddad provide a case in point. 马萨诸塞州参议员杰森·刘易斯和众议院临时议长帕特里夏·哈达德提出的两项法案就是一个很好的例子。（2020 阅读理解）

派生 sponsorship *n.* 赞助，赞助款

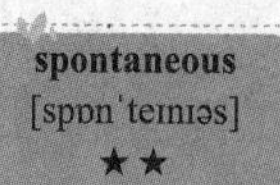

释义 *adj.* 自发的，自然产生的

短语 *spontaneous* applause 自发的鼓掌

例句 Some of the audience broke into *spontaneous* applause, countered by boos from others. 一些观众自发地鼓掌，另一些人则报以嘘声。

派生 spontaneously *adv.* 自发地

释义 *n.* 斑点；地点 *v.* 认出；发现

短语 on the *spot* 立刻，当场 a *spot* of 少量，一点儿

例句 They stayed at several of the island's top tourist *spots*. 他们在岛上几个最好的旅游景点待过。

Can you *spot* the difference between these two pictures? 你能不能看出这两幅画有什么不同？

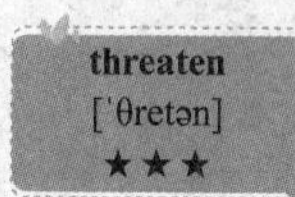

释义 *v.* 恐吓，威胁

例句 We are now knowledgeable enough to reduce many of the risks that *threatened* the existence of earlier humans. 我们现在有足够的知识来减少许多威胁早期人类生存的风险。

用法 threaten to do sth. 威胁做某事

派生 threatening *adj.* 威胁的

释义 *n.* 宇宙，万物；领域

短语 the centre of the *universe* 宇宙的中心 the moral *universe* 道德体系

例句 Early astronomers thought that our planet was the centre of the *universe*. 早期的天文学家认为我们的星球是宇宙的中心。

派生 universal *adj.* 普遍的

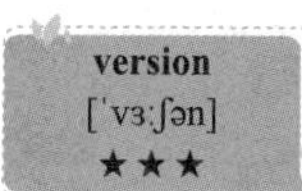

释义 *n.* 版本；说法；译文

短语 English *version* 英文版本 latest *version* 最新版本

例句 She gave us her *version* of what had happened that day. 她从她的角度向我们描述了那天发生的事情。

真题 On May 31st Microsoft set off the row. It said that Internet Explorer 10, the *version* due to appear with Windows 8, would have DNT as a default. 5 月 31 日，微软公司率先发布公告，配置于 Win8 操作系统的 IE 10 浏览器将会把“禁止追踪”设置为一个默认设置选项。（2013 阅读理解）

近义 edition *n.* 版本

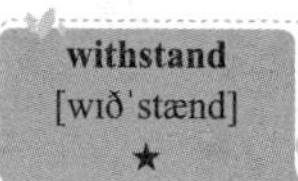

释义 *v.* 抵抗，经受住

短语 *withstand* hunger / stresses 经受住饥饿 / 压力

例句 The plants were unable to *withstand* the rigours of a harsh winter. 这些植物经受不住严冬的考验。

Our troops *withstand* the onset of the enemy. 我们的部队抵挡住了敌人的进攻。

近义 endure *v.* 忍受

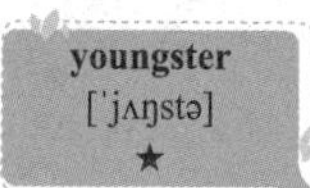

释义 *n.* 年轻人，少年

短语 a wide-eyed *youngster* 一个天真的孩子

例句 We know the promise is there—this is a well-grounded, talented, warm-hearted group of *youngsters*. 我们知道希望就在那里——这是一群全面发展、才华横溢、热心肠的年轻人。

近义 youth *n.* 年轻人

反义 senior *n.* 老年人

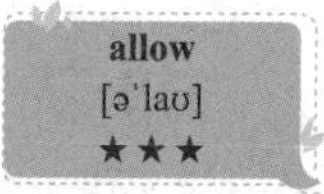

释义 *v.* 允许；承认；接受

例句 Dictionaries are not *allowed* in the exam. 考试时不允许使用字典。

She *allowed* that she might have been too suspicious. 她承认自己可能太多心了。

派生 allowance *n.* 津贴；零用钱

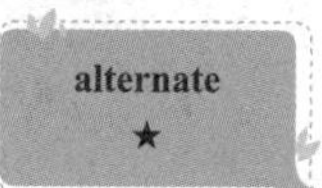

释义 *v.* [ˈɔːltəneɪt]（使）交替 *adj.* [ɒlˈtɜːnət] 交替的；间隔的 *n.*[ˈɒltənət] 替换物；代替者

例句 The poem *alternates* fear and hope. 这首诗交织着恐惧和希望。

He works on *alternate* days. 他每隔一天工作。

The town has elected five councilors and two *alternates*. 这个镇选出了五名议员和两名候补议员。

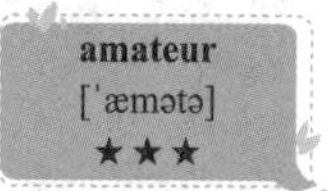

释义 *adj.* 业余的；非专业的 *n.* 外行；业余爱好者

例句 Taylor began his playing career as an *amateur* goalkeeper. 泰勒的足球生涯是从业余守门员开始的。

He thinks the drawings could be the work of an *amateur*. 他认为这些画可能是业余画家的作品。

反义 professional *adj.* 职业的

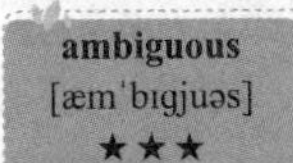

释义 *adj.* 含糊不清的；引起歧义的；不明确的

例句 His attitude to environmental issues was sometimes quite *ambiguous*. 他对环境问题的态度有时相当模棱两可。

反义 unambiguous *adj.* 不含糊的；清楚的

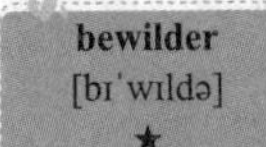

释义 *v.* 使迷惑

例句 She was totally *bewildered* by his sudden change of mood.

他的情绪突变搞得她全然不知所措。

近义 confuse *v.* 使迷惑；混淆

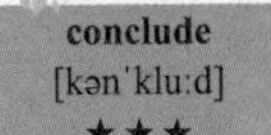

释义 *v.* 结束，终止；下结论

例句 The film *concludes* with the heroine's death. 影片以女主角之死结束。

What can we *conclude* from this debate? 我们能从这场辩论中推断出什么呢？

用法 conclude with 以……结束

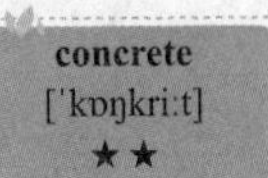

释义 *adj.* 具体的；确实的 *n.* 混凝土 *v.* 浇混凝土

例句 We have a general idea of what we want, but nothing *concrete* at the moment.

我们对需要什么有个大致的想法，可是具体的东西目前还没有想好。

派生 concretely *adv.* 具体地

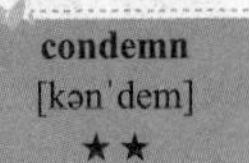

释义 *v.* 谴责；判刑，宣告有罪

例句 Some praise him, whereas others *condemn* him. 一些人赞扬他，而另一些人谴责他。

He was *condemned* to death for murder . 他因凶杀罪被判处死刑。

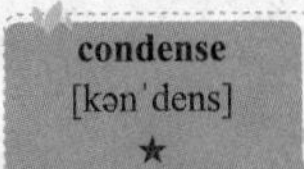

释义 *v.*（使）凝结；浓缩

例句 As the air rises it becomes colder and moisture *condenses* out of it. 当空气上升时，它变得更冷，水分从空气中凝结出来。

近义 compress *v.*（使）压缩

释义 *n.* 状况；条件；情况；疾病；条款 *v.* 使适应

用法 living / working *conditions* 生活 / 工作环境

例句 The car has been well maintained and is in excellent *condition*. 这辆车保养得很好，状态极佳。

On the *condition* that I get a scholarship, I would consider studying abroad. 如果能得到奖学金，我就会考虑出国留学。

用法 on (the) condition that 只要

派生 conditional *adj.* 有条件的

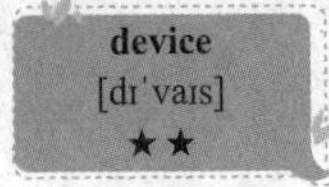

释义 *n.* 装置，设备，仪表；手段，方法

短语 a marketing *device* 营销手段 medical *device* 医疗设备

例句 The store sells phones, tablets and other electronic *devices*.

这家商店出售手机、平板电脑和其他电子设备。

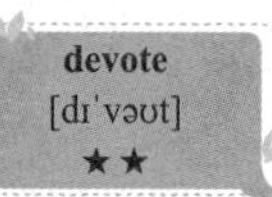

devise
[dɪˈvaɪz]
★

释义 v. 设计;发明;想出(办法)

短语 *devise* a scheme 想出一个办法

例句 They've *devised* a plan to allow employees to work from home. 他们制订了一项允许员工在家工作的计划。

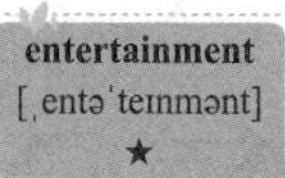

devote
[dɪˈvəʊt]
★★

释义 v. 奉献,致力

例句 He has *devoted* much of his time and energy to the study of American literature . 他把大部分时间和精力都投入到美国文学研究上。

用法 devote sth. to (doing) sth. 致力于

entertainment
[ˌentəˈteɪnmənt]
★

释义 n. 招待,款待;娱乐表演

短语 *entertainment* industry 娱乐业

例句 There will be *entertainment* and a buffet luncheon for a cost of $30. 届时将有娱乐活动和自助午餐,费用为 30 美元。

enthusiastic
[ɪnˌθjuːzɪˈæstɪk]
★★

释义 adj. 热情的,热心的

例句 She doesn't sound very *enthusiastic* about the idea. 她好像对这个想法不太感兴趣。

派生 enthusiasm *n.* 热情,热忱

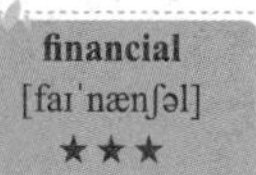

entire
[ɪnˈtaɪə]
★★★

释义 adj. 完全的,全部的,完整的

例句 The dam broke and its water drowned the *entire* valley. 水坝倒塌了,水淹没了整个山谷。

派生 entirely *adv.* 完全地

financial
[faɪˈnænʃəl]
★★★

释义 adj. 财政的,金融的

短语 *financial* regulations 财务条例

例句 Brexit can help free Britain from the *financial* burden. 英国脱欧可以帮助英国摆脱财政负担。

用法 be in financial difficulties 陷入财务困境

派生 financially *adv.* 财政上,金融上

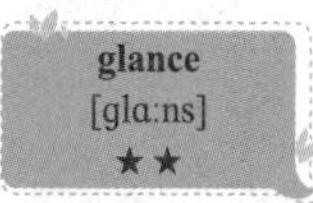

glance
[glɑːns]
★★

释义 v. 瞥一眼;扫视 n. 一瞥;(光的)闪烁

例句 He walked away without a backward *glance*. 他头也不回地扬长而去。

She took her eyes off the road to *glance* at me. 她把视线从公路上移开,扫了我一眼。

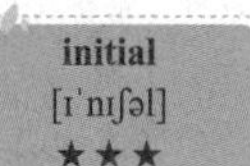

initial
[ɪˈnɪʃəl]
★★★

释义 adj. 最初的,开头的;词首的 n.(名字的)首字母

短语 *initial* period / state 初始期 / 起始状态

例句 In the *initial* stage, the current economic crisis is likely to tear many troubled families apart. 在最初阶段,目前的经济危机可能会使许多陷入困境的家庭破裂。

派生 initially *adv.* 开始

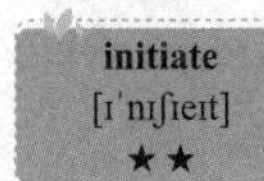

initiate
[ɪˈnɪʃieɪt]
★★

释义 *v.* 开始，发动；使加入

短语 *initiate* a reform 开始改革

例句 The government has *initiated* a programme of economic reform. 政府已开始实施经济改革方案。

派生 initiation *n.* 开始，创始

innocent
[ˈɪnəsənt]
★★

释义 *adj.* 清白的，无罪的；单纯的，无知的 *n.* 无辜者

短语 *innocent* party 无过失之一方

例句 The jury concluded from the evidence that the defendant was *innocent*. 陪审团根据证据断定被告是无辜的。

用法 be innocent of the charge 无罪

派生 innocence *n.* 清白

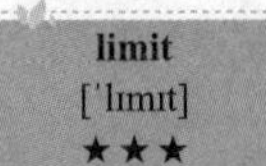

limit
[ˈlɪmɪt]
★★★

释义 *n.* 界限，限度，范围 *v.* 限制，限定

短语 time *limit* 期限

例句 To *limit* the number of telescopes on Mauna Kea, old ones will be removed at the end of their lifetimes. 为了限制莫纳克亚山上的望远镜数量，旧的望远镜将在寿命结束时被移除。

派生 limitation *n.* 限制

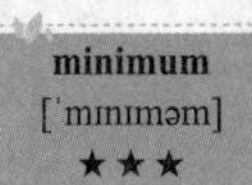

minimum
[ˈmɪnɪməm]
★★★

释义 *n.* 最小值，最低限度 *adj.* 最小的，最低的

例句 Some of them earn below *minimum* wage. 他们中的一些人挣的钱低于最低工资。

派生 minimal *adj.* 最小的

minister
[ˈmɪnɪstə]
★★★

释义 *n.* 部长，大臣

短语 prime *minister* 首相

例句 European *ministers* instantly demanded that the International Accounting Standards Board (IASB) do likewise. 欧洲的部长们立即要求国际会计准则委员会也这样做。

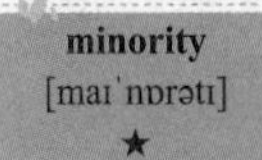

minority
[maɪˈnɒrətɪ]
★

释义 *n.* 少数，少数派，少数民族

短语 *minority* group 少数群体

例句 Students have called for greater numbers of women and *minorities* on the faculty. 学生们呼吁在教师中增加更多的女性和少数族裔。

反义 majority *n.* 大多数

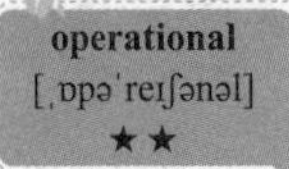

operational
[ˌɒpəˈreɪʃənəl]
★★

释义 *adj.* 正常运转的，可使用的；（用于）操作的，经营的

短语 *operational* management 运营管理 *Operational* Research 运筹学

例句 The whole system will be fully *operational* by December. 整个系统将于12月全面投入使用。

派生 operationally *adv.* 运作上；操作上

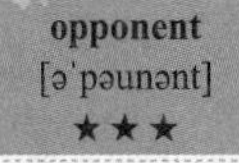

opponent
[əˈpəunənt]
★★★

释义 *n.* 对手，敌手；反对者

短语 a political *opponent* 政敌

例句 The Celtics beat a worthy *opponent*, one that pushed them to be better. 凯尔

特人队击败了一个强有力的对手，一个促使他们变得更好的对手。

He was an *opponent* of Conservatism. 他是保守主义的反对者。

近义 rival *n.* 对手

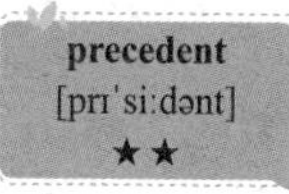

precedent
[prɪˈsiːdənt]
★★

释义 *n.* 先例，前例

短语 condition *precedent* 先决条件 a historical *precedent* 历史先例

例句 If he is allowed to do this, it will be a *precedent* for others. 如果允许他这样做，这就会是其他人的先例。

用法 a precedent for sth. 某事物的先例

派生 precedence *n.* 优先权

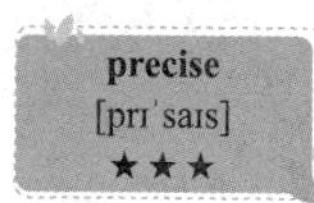

precise
[prɪˈsaɪs]
★★★

释义 *adj.* 精确的，准确的

例句 More than a week ago, Thursday evening to be *precise*, Susanne was at her evening class. 一个多星期前，确切地说是周四晚上，苏珊娜在上晚班。

用法 to be precise 确切地讲

近义 accurate *adj.* 精确的，准确的

派生 precision *n.* 精确

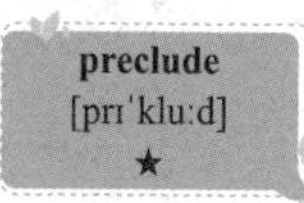

preclude
[prɪˈkluːd]
★

释义 *v.* 排除；阻止，妨碍

例句 The fact that your application was not successful this time does not *preclude* the possibility of you applying again next time. 这次申请失败并不妨碍你下次再申请。

近义 prevent *v.* 阻止，阻碍

派生 preclusion *n.* 排除；阻止

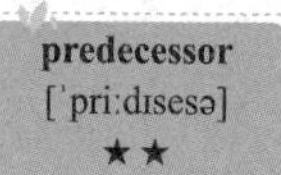

predecessor
[ˈpriːdɪsesə]
★★

释义 *n.* 前辈，前任

短语 a *predecessor* of modern computers 现代计算机的前身

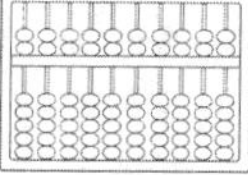

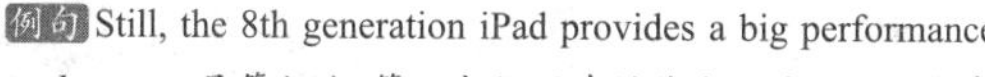

例句 Still, the 8th generation iPad provides a big performance improvement over its *predecessor*. 尽管如此，第八代 iPad 在性能上还是比上一代有了很大的提升。

近义 forerunner *n.* 先驱

purchase
[ˈpɜːtʃəs]
★★★

释义 *v.* 买，购买 *n.* 购买的物品

短语 *purchase* price / order 买价 / 订购单

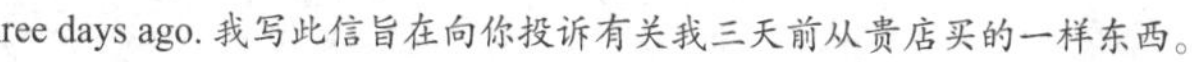

例句 I'm writing to complain about a *purchase* that I made at your store three days ago. 我写此信旨在向你投诉有关我三天前从贵店买的一样东西。

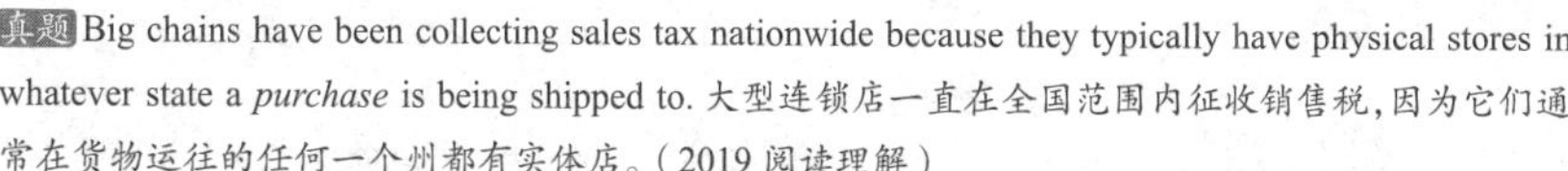

真题 Big chains have been collecting sales tax nationwide because they typically have physical stores in whatever state a *purchase* is being shipped to. 大型连锁店一直在全国范围内征收销售税，因为它们通常在货物运往的任何一个州都有实体店。（2019 阅读理解）

reliance
[rɪˈlaɪəns]
★★

释义 *n.* 信任，依靠，依靠的人或物

例句 China will reduce its *reliance* on petroleum imports by basing its energy supply on developing new energies. 中国将把能源供应建立在开发新能源的基础上，从而减少对石油进口的依赖。

近义 dependence *n.* 依赖,依靠

派生 reliant *adj.* 依赖的

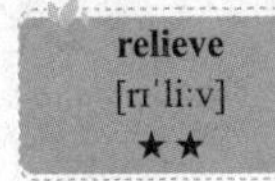

relieve
[rɪˈliːv]
★★

释义 *v.* 减轻,解除;救济,换班

短语 pain-*relieving* medication 止痛药

例句 She *relieved* her boredom at home by watching TV. 她在家里看电视来打发无聊。

At seven o'clock the night nurse came in to *relieve* her. 7 点钟,夜班护士进来给她换班。

派生 relieved *adj.* 宽慰的

religious
[rɪˈlɪdʒəs]
★★★

释义 *adj.* 宗教的,信教的,虔诚的

短语 *religious* belief 宗教信仰

例句 He's deeply *religious* and goes to church twice a week. 他非常虔诚,每周都去教堂做两次礼拜。

真题 By the date of his birth, Europe was witnessing the passing of the *religious* drama, and the creation of new forms. 在他出生的时候,欧洲见证了宗教戏剧的消逝和新形式的创造。(2018 翻译)

派生 religion *n.* 宗教

squeeze
[skwiːz]
★★

释义 *v.* 压榨,挤 *n.* 榨取,勒索

例句 The investigators complained about the difficulties of *squeezing* information out of residents. 调查人员抱怨很难从居民口中获取信息。

用法 squeeze out 挤出

近义 press *v.* 压,挤

派生 squeezable *adj.* 可压榨的

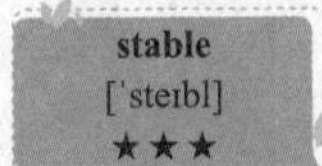

stable
[ˈsteɪbl]
★★★

释义 *adj.* 稳定的,安定的 *n.* 马厩,马棚

短语 *stable* price 稳定价格

例句 Some people regard professional change as an unpleasant experience that disturbs their *stable* careers. 有些人认为转行是一种不愉快的经历,会影响他们稳定的职业生涯。

反义 unstable *adj.* 不稳定的

近义 strong *adj.* 稳固的,持久的

派生 stability *n.* 稳定,安定

staff
[stɑːf]
★★★

释义 *n.* 全体职工 *v.* 配备工作人员

短语 technical *staff* 技术人员

例句 The hotel *staff* are friendly and attentive. 酒店的工作人员很友好而且照顾周到。

The advice centre is *staffed* entirely by volunteers. 在咨询中心工作的全部是志愿者。

近义 crew *n.* 一组工作人员;全体船员

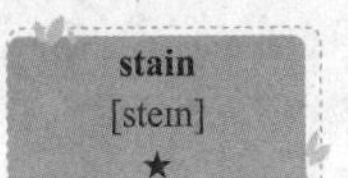

stain
[steɪn]
★

释义 *n.* 污点,瑕疵 *v.* 玷污;染色

短语 blood *stain* 血痕

例句 This carpet is ideal for the kitchen because it doesn't *stain* easily. 这块地毯

很适合在厨房里用，因为它很耐脏。

This washing powder will work miracles on those difficult *stains*. 这种洗衣粉对付顽渍有奇效。

suspect ★★★

释义 *v.* [səˈspekt] 猜想；怀疑；察觉 *n.* [ˈsʌspekt] 犯罪嫌疑人 *adj.* 可疑的

例句 If you *suspect* a gas leak, do not strike a match or even turn on an electric light. 假如你怀疑有煤气泄漏，不要划火柴，甚至连电灯都不要开。

近义 doubt *v.* 怀疑；不信任

派生 suspectable *adj.* 值得怀疑的；可疑的

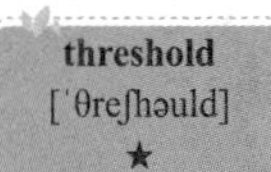

threshold [ˈθreʃhəuld] ★

释义 *n.* 门槛；入门，开端

短语 tax *threshold* 所得税起征点

例句 If your income rises above a certain *threshold*, your tax rate also rises. 如果你的收入超过了某个阈值，你的税率也会提高。

用法 on the threshold of 在……初期 / 开端

近义 beginning *n.* 开端

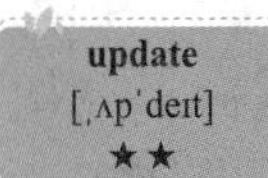

update [ˌʌpˈdeɪt] ★★

释义 *v.* / *n.* 更新

短语 news *update* 新闻快讯

例句 It's about time we *updated* our software. 我们的软件应该更新了。

真题 The justices can and should provide *updated* guidelines to police, lawyers and defendants. 法官可以也应该向警察、律师和被告提供最新的指导方针。（2015 阅读理解）

近义 renew *v.* 更新

vessel [ˈvesəl] ★★

释义 *n.* 容器，器皿；船，舰；血管

短语 blood *vessel* 血管 cargo *vessel* 货轮

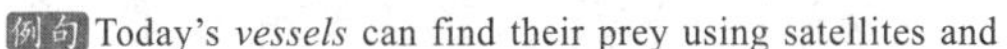

例句 Today's *vessels* can find their prey using satellites and sonar, which were not available 50 years ago. 当今的渔船可以利用卫星和声呐来寻找猎物，这些技术在 50 年前是没有的。

近义 ship *n.*（大）船，舰

Word List 22

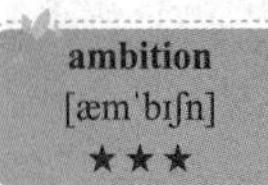

alternative [ɔːlˈtɜːnətɪv] ★★★

释义 *adj.* 可供选择的；不寻常的，非传统性的 *n.* 可供选择的事物

例句 The child-minding service provides an *alternative* to parents. 儿童看护服务为父母提供了另一种选择。

They had no *alternative* but to protest. 除了抗议，他们别无选择。

派生 alternatively *adv.* 要不，或者

ambition [æmˈbɪʃn] ★★★

释义 *n.* 抱负；雄心；野心

例句 His *ambition* is to win gold at the Paris Olympics Games in 2024. 他的志向是在 2024 年巴黎奥运会上夺取金牌。

派生 ambitious *adj.* 野心勃勃的

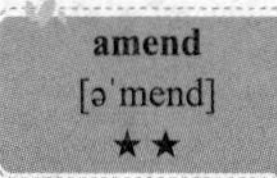

释义 *v.* 修订,修正

例句 He *amended* his speech by making some additions and deletions. 他对演讲稿做了些增删修改。

派生 amendment *n.* 修正;修正条款

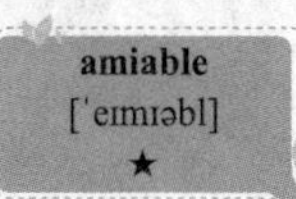

释义 *adj.* 和蔼可亲的;亲切的

短语 an *amiable* old woman 和蔼可亲的老妇人

例句 Everyone knew that he was a nice guy, very *amiable* and there was always a smile on his face. 每个人都知道他是个好人,非常和蔼可亲,脸上总是挂着微笑。

近义 friendly *adj.* 友善的

派生 amiably *adv.* 亲切地

释义 *v.* 使偏心;使有偏见 *n.* 偏见;偏爱

例句 Some institutions still have a strong *bias* against women. 有些机构仍然对妇女持有很大偏见。

真题 The author believes that the bills sponsored by Lewis and Haddad will help little to reduce gender *bias*. 作者认为,刘易斯和哈达德提出的法案对减少性别偏见几乎没有帮助。(2020 阅读理解)

近义 prejudice *n.* 偏见

派生 biased *adj.* 有偏见的

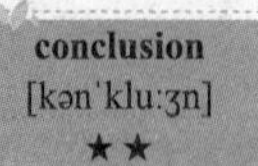

释义 *n.* 结论;结尾;缔结

例句 We should not jump to *conclusions*. Let's investigate first. 我们不应该草率下结论。让我们先调查。

用法 jump to conclusions 匆匆做出结论

释义 *n.* 行为,举止 *v.* 进行,实施;引导;指挥

例句 The interview was *conducted* in English. 面试是用英语进行的。

The orchestra is *conducted* by Herbert Von Karajan. 管弦乐团由赫伯特·冯·卡拉扬指挥。

释义 *v.* 商讨;颁给(勋衔,学位等);赋予

例句 The union plans to *confer* with the workers before deciding on a next step. 工会计划与工人协商后再决定下一步行动。

Diplomas were *conferred* on the students who had completed all courses of study. 完成所有课程的学生被授予毕业证书。

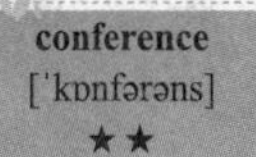

释义 *n.* 会议;讨论

例句 The World Meteorological Organization held its annual *conference* in Copenhagen in December. 世界气象组织于 12 月在哥本哈根举行了年度会议。

近义 seminar *n.* 研讨会

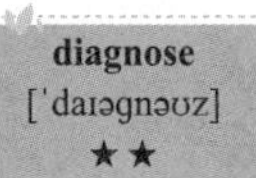

confess [kən'fes] ★

释义 *v.* 供认，坦白，忏悔

例句 She *confessed* to her husband that she had sold her wedding ring to help pay for their new house. 她向丈夫坦白，她卖掉了结婚戒指，以帮助支付他们的新房子。

派生 confession *n.* 供认；承认

diagnose ['daɪəgnəʊz] ★★

释义 *v.* 诊断（疾病）；判断（问题）

例句 She was *diagnosed* as having mental disorder. 她被诊断患有精神障碍。

用法 diagnose sb. with sth.

派生 diagnosis *n.* 诊断，判断

dictate [dɪk'teɪt] ★

释义 *v.* 口授；听写；指示，命令；影响

例句 You can't *dictate* to people how they should live. 你不能强行规定人们应该怎样生活。

用法 dictate to sb. 对某人口述；对某人发号施令

派生 dictation *n.* 听写；命令

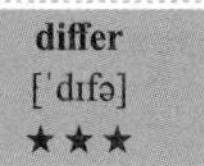

differ ['dɪfə] ★★★

释义 *v.* 与……不同；与……意见不同

例句 Table manners might *differ* from one culture to another. 餐桌礼仪因文化不同而异。

真题 Our findings indicate that people do not only feel different when they are the centre of attention but that their brain reactions also *differ*. 我们的研究结果表明，当人们成为注意力的中心时，他们不仅感觉不同，而且他们的大脑反应也不同。（2020 阅读理解）

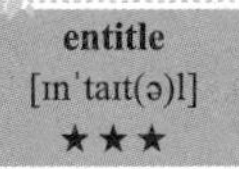

entitle [ɪn'taɪt(ə)l] ★★★

释义 *v.* 使享有权利，使符合资格；给……命名

例句 The voucher is valid between July and December and *entitles* you to 10% off all overseas flights. 此券有效期为 7 月至 12 月，可享受海外航班 9 折优惠。

用法 entitle sb. to (do) sth. 授权某人做某事

派生 entitlement *n.* 权力

entrepreneur [ˌɒntrəprə'nɜː] ★★★

释义 *n.* 企业家，主办人

短语 *entrepreneur* spirit 企业家精神

例句 You cannot buy class, as the old saying goes, and these upstart *entrepreneurs* cannot buy their prizes the prestige of the Nobels. 俗话说，金钱买不到社会地位，而这些新贵企业家们也不可能为他们的奖项买到诺贝尔奖的威望。

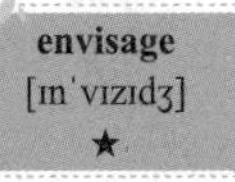

envisage [ɪn'vɪzɪdʒ] ★

释义 *v.* 想象，设想，展望

例句 As the quality of 3D printers continues to improve, we *envisage* this issue rapidly disappearing. 随着 3D 打印机的质量不断提高，我们设想这个问题会迅速消失。

用法 envisage sth. happening 预想某事将要发生

释义 *adj.* 有限的；（数）有穷的，限定的

例句 However, pressure will grow on *finite* resources of land, energy and water. 然而，有限的土地、能源和水资源将面临越来越大的压力。

反义 infinite *adj.* 无限的

释义 *v.* 瞥见 *n.* 一瞥，一看

例句 She catches a *glimpse* of a car in the distance. 她一眼就瞥见了远处的汽车。We *glimpsed* the ruined church from the windows of the train. 透过火车车窗，我们瞥见了教堂的废墟。

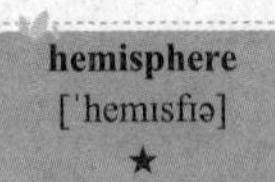

释义 *n.* 半球；地球的半球

短语 the northern *hemisphere* 北半球

例句 This animal is to be found only in the Southern *Hemisphere*. 这种动物只有在南半球才能找到。

释义 *n.* 倡议；积极性；主动权

短语 a peace *initiative* 和平倡议 take the *initiative* 带头

例句 The UN called on all parties in the conflict to take a positive stance towards the new peace *initiative*. 联合国呼吁冲突各方对新的和平倡议采取积极的立场。

用法 launch an initiative 发起一项活动

释义 *n.* 改革，革新

短语 social *innovation* 社会创新

例句 Anthropologists believed that cultural *innovations*, such as inventions, had a single origin and passed from society to society. 人类学家认为，文化创新如发明一样，有一个单一的起源，并从一个社会传递到另一个社会。

派生 innovative *adj.* 创新的

释义 *v.* (enquire) 询问，打听；调查，查问

例句 The HR department has been *inquiring* into complaints of unequal pay in the sales department. 人力资源部一直在调查销售部门关于不平等薪酬的投诉。

用法 inquire into 调查

派生 inquirer *n.* 调查者；询问者

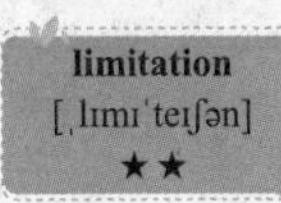

释义 *n.* 限制，局限性

例句 Living in an apartment is fine, but it does have its *limitations* — for example, you don't have your own garden. 住公寓不错，但也有其局限性——如没有自己的花园。

近义 restriction *n.* 限制规定

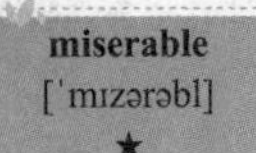

释义 *adj.* 痛苦的，悲惨的

例句 I always feel down when I see others accomplishing things and I feel *miserable* about my own achievements. 当我看到别人取得成就时，我总是感到沮丧，我对自己的成就感到悲哀。

反义 fortunate *adj.* 好运的

派生 miserably *adv.* 可悲地

释义 *v.* 把……带错路，使误入歧途

例句 The guide *misled* the tourists in the woods. 向导在森林里给旅游者带错了路。

People are easily *misled* by false advertisements. 人们很容易上虚假广告的当。

派生 misleading *adj.* 误导的

释义 *v.* 谈判；协商；议定

短语 *negotiating* skills 谈判技巧

例句 The government *negotiated* with the opposition party over the new law. 政府就新法与反对党进行了协商。

派生 negotiation *n.* 谈判，协商；转让

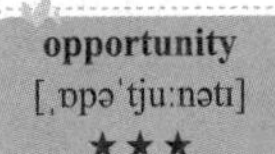

释义 *n.* 机会，时机

短语 golden *opportunity* 绝好的机会

例句 Each set of circumstances, however bad, offers a unique *opportunity* for growth. 每一种情况，无论多么糟糕，都为成长提供了独特的机会。

用法 offer an opportunity 提供机会

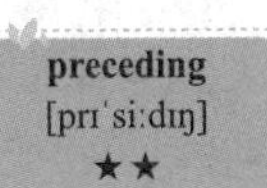

释义 *adj.* 在前的，在先的

短语 the *preceding* months 前几个月

例句 The plots of this novel in the *preceding* chapters are so complicated that I couldn't follow them. 这本小说前几章的情节如此复杂，以至于我都看不懂。

近义 prior *adj.* 在前的

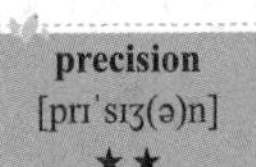

释义 *n.* 精确，精确度

短语 *precision* machinery 精密机械

例句 She doesn't express her thoughts with *precision*, so people often misunderstand what she says. 她不能准确地表达自己的想法，所以人们经常误解她说的话。

用法 with precision 准确地；确切地

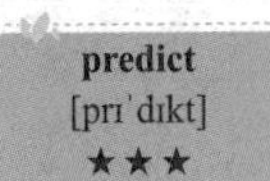

释义 *v.* 预言；预测；预告

例句 In a final experiment, participants were encouraged to *predict* how they would feel after viewing an unpleasant picture. 在最后一个实验中，研究人员鼓励参与者预测他们在看到不愉快的图片后的感受。

真题 You want to *predict* if something needs attention now and point to where it's useful for employees to go to. 你需要预测现在是否需要关注某件事，并指出哪些地方对员工有用。（2021 阅读理解）

派生 prediction *n.* 预测；预言之事

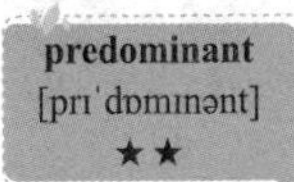

释义 *adj.* 占优势的；主要的，突出的

短语 *predominant* use 主要用途

例句 Yellow is the *predominant* colour this spring in the fashion world. 黄色是今

春时装界的流行颜色。

反义 subordinate *adj.* 从属的，次要的

派生 predominantly *adv.* 绝大多数

purpose [ˈpɜːpəs] ★★★

释义 *n.* 目的，意图；用途，效果 *v.* 打算，企图

例句 The *purpose* of the book is to provide a complete guide to the university. 本书旨在全面介绍这所大学。

真题 The main *purpose* of this "clawback" rule is to hold bankers accountable for harmful risk-taking and to restore public trust in financial institutions. 这项"追回"规定的主要目的是让银行家对有害的冒险行为负责，并恢复公众对金融机构的信任。（2019 阅读理解）

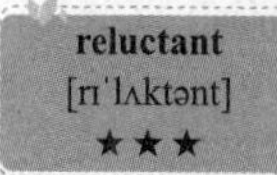
reluctant [rɪˈlʌktənt] ★★★

释义 *adj.* 不愿的，勉强的

例句 The witness was *reluctant* to give evidence in court at first. 证人起初不愿在法庭上作证。

真题 Despite these factors, many social scientists seem *reluctant* to tackle such problems. 尽管有这些因素，许多社会科学家似乎不愿意解决这些问题。（2013 阅读理解）

近义 unwilling *adj.* 不愿意的；不情愿的

派生 reluctantly *adv.* 不情愿地

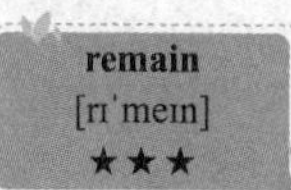
remain [rɪˈmeɪn] ★★★

释义 *v.* 留下；保持；剩余 *n.* 剩余（物），遗迹

短语 *remain* silent 保持沉默

例句 The police made an appeal to the public to *remain* calm. 警方吁请公众保持镇静。

真题 Yet humans *remain* fascinated by the idea of robots that would look, move, and respond like humans. 然而，人类仍然对机器人的外形、动作和像人类一样的反应的想法着迷。（2019 阅读理解）

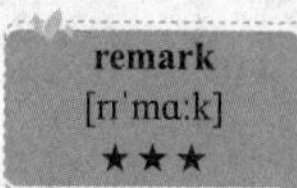
remark [rɪˈmɑːk] ★★★

释义 *n.* 评语，意见 *v.* 评论；说起

例句 Many people have been outraged by Trump's *remarks* on immigration. 很多人对特朗普关于移民的言论感到愤怒。

Many people who have met and worked with Melissa *remark* on her kindness. 许多与梅丽莎见过面并一起工作过的人都称赞她的善良。

派生 remarkable *adj.* 引人注目的，非凡的

reward [rɪˈwɔːd] ★★★

释义 *n.* 报酬，赏金 *v.* 酬劳；酬谢

短语 financial *reward* 物质奖励

例句 You deserve a *reward* for being so helpful. 你帮了这么大的忙，理应受到奖励。

用法 in *reward* for 作为……报答

stability [stəˈbɪlɪtɪ] ★★

释义 *n.* 稳定，安定

短语 economic *stability* 经济稳定

例句 A loving family environment gives children that sense of *stability* which they need. 一个充满爱的家庭环境能给孩子们所需要的稳定感。

派生 stabilize *v.*（使）稳定

释义 *n.* 桩；赌注；股份 *v.* 以……下赌注；系……于桩上

短语 at *stake* 处于危险中

例句 We cannot afford to take risks when peoples' lives are at *stake*. 当人民的生命危在旦夕时，我们不能冒险。

She *staked* her political career on tax reform, and lost. 她把自己的政治生涯押在税制改革上，结果赌输了。

释义 *n.* 标准，规则 *adj.* 标准的

例句 Televisions are a *standard* feature in most hotel rooms. 电视机是多数旅馆房间里的标准设施。

真题 We also need to admit good arguments by opponents and to apply the same critical *standards* to ourselves. 我们也需要承认对手的正确论点，并将同样的评判标准要求我们自己。（2019 阅读理解）

派生 standardize *v.* (standardise) 使……标准化

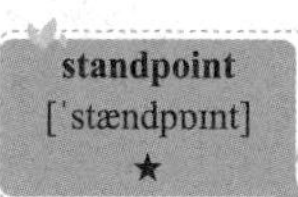

释义 *n.* 立场，观点

短语 a political *standpoint* 政治的角度来看

例句 He believes that from a military *standpoint*, the situation is under control. 他认为从军事角度看，形势已得到了控制。

用法 from the *standpoint* of 从……角度来看

释义 *n.* 节约，节俭

短语 virtues of *thrift* and hard work 节俭和勤奋的美德

例句 We must spread the idea of building our country through diligence and *thrift*. 我们要提倡勤俭建国。

近义 frugality *n.* 节俭

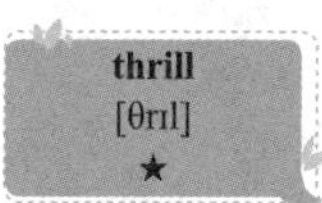

释义 *n.* 一阵激动 *v.*（使）激动；颤抖

短语 a *thrill* of joy 一阵喜悦

例句 I can remember the *thrill* of not knowing what I would get on Christmas morning. 我还记得自己在圣诞节早晨期待礼物时内心有多么激动。

近义 pleasure *n.* 快乐

派生 thrilling *adj.* 令人激动的，惊险的

释义 *v.* [ˌʌpˈgreɪd] 提升，使升级 *n.* [ˈʌpgreid] 升级

短语 image *upgrades* 形象提升

例句 We're going to *upgrade* you and your friend to first class. 我们会将您和您的朋友升等到头等舱。

Stadium *upgrades* were undertaken in preparation for the tournament. 为了准备比赛，体育场进行了升级。

真题 The current international tax system needs *upgrading*. 当前国际税收体系需要升级。（2020 阅读理解）

用法 upgrade oneself 提升自我

派生 upgradation *n.* 升级

释义 *n.* 老手,老兵 *adj.* 经验丰富的

短语 military *veterans* 退伍军人

例句 He is a *veteran* parliamentarian whose views enjoy widespread respect. 他是个资深议员,其观点受到广泛尊重。

近义 experienced *adj.* 熟练的,有经验的

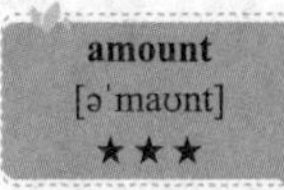

释义 *n.* 量;总额 *v.* 达到……之多;总计

例句 He knows an enormous *amount* about Italian paintings. 他对意大利绘画非常了解。

Consumer spending on sports-related items *amounted* to £9.75 billion. 消费者在体育相关项目上的支出达到 97.5 亿英镑。

用法 amount to 总计为

释义 *adj.* 宽敞的;丰富的;充足的

例句 They had *ample* money for the trip. 他们有足够的钱去旅行。

The police found *ample* evidence of wrongdoing. 警方发现了大量不法行为的证据。

近义 abundant *adj.* 大量的,充足的

派生 amply *adv.* 充足地;广大地

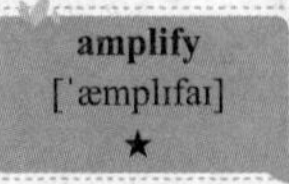

释义 *v.* 扩大;增强;阐述

例句 These stories only *amplified* her fears. 这些故事只会加剧她的恐惧。

Would you care to *amplify* that remark? 你愿意详述一下那句话吗?

派生 amplifier *n.* 扩音器

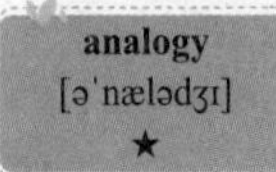

释义 *n.* 类比;类似;类推;相似

例句 She drew an *analogy* between learning English and building a house. 她打了个比方,把学英语比作建房子。

用法 draw an analogy between 把(二者)加以比较

派生 analogous *adj.* 相似的

释义 *v.* / *n.* 出价;投标;努力争取;打招呼

例句 I'll *bid* $100 for the table but no higher. 这张桌子我出 100 美元,但不能再高了。

The team is *bidding* to retain its place in the league. 这个队正争取保住它在联赛中的位置。

They *bade* her good morning. 他们向她道了早安。

派生 bidder *n.* 出价者

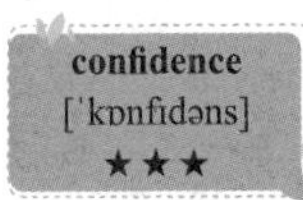

释义 *n.* 信任；信心；秘密

例句 I don't share your *confidence* that the market will improve next year. 对于明年市场会好转这件事，我可没有你那么有信心。

The girls sat in a cafe until 3 a.m., exchanging *confidences* . 女孩们在咖啡馆里一直坐到凌晨 3 点，互相吐露心声。

用法 confidence in 对……的信任

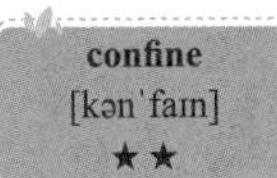

释义 *v.* 限制；禁闭 *n.* 界限，范围

例句 Firefighters managed to *confine* the fire to the living room. 消防队员设法将火控制在客厅内。

派生 confined *adj.* 有限的

真题 Cooper and her colleagues argue that the success of the crown for Hull ought not to be *confined* to cities. 库珀和她的同事认为，赫尔市成功取得这项荣誉不应仅仅局限于城市范围。（2020 阅读理解）

释义 *v.* 确认；证实；批准

例句 These new statistics *confirm* our fears about the depth of the recession. 这些新的统计数据证实了我们对经济衰退程度的担忧。

同义 prove *v.* 证实

派生 confirmed *adj.* 根深蒂固的；已被证实的

释义 *n.* 冲突；矛盾 *v.* 冲突

短语 border *conflict* 边界冲突

例句 Workers are in *conflict* with management over job cuts. 工人们在裁员问题上与管理层发生了冲突。

The results of the new research *conflict* with existing theories. 新的研究结果和已有的理论相抵触。

近义 dispute *n.* / *v.* 争论

释义 *v.* 遵守，适应；符合

例句 This mark signifies that the products *conform* to the European standards. 该标志表示产品符合欧洲标准。

近义 comply *v.* 遵从

反义 oppose *v.* 反抗，作对

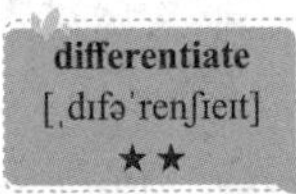

释义 *v.* 区分；（使）不同

例句 You can *differentiate* between the houses by their styles. 你可以根据房子的风格来区分它们。

派生 differentiation *n.* 区分，差异化

释义 *v.* 扩散；传播；减弱 *adj.* 弥漫的；（文章等）冗长的

例句 Cloudy days are better for photos than bright sunny days because the clouds *diffuse* the sun's light. 多云的天气会比万里无云的晴朗天气更适合拍照，因为云彩可以使太阳光线变得很柔和。

派生 diffusion *n.* 扩散，传播

digital [ˈdɪdʒɪt(ə)l] ★★★

释义 *adj.* 数字的;数码的

短语 *digital* library 数字图书馆 *digital* image 数字图像

真题 *Digital* services include everything from providing a platform for selling goods and services online to targeting advertising based on user data. 数字服务包括提供一个在线销售商品和服务的平台,以及基于用户数据的定向广告。(2020 阅读理解)

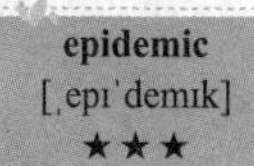

epidemic [ˌepɪˈdemɪk] ★★★

释义 *adj.* 流行性的;传染的 *n.* 流行病;传播

例句 The major impact of this *epidemic* worldwide is yet to come. 这种传染病在世界范围内的重大影响还未完全显现。

近义 pandemic *n.* 流行病

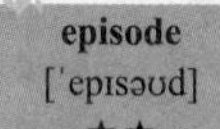

episode [ˈepɪsəʊd] ★★

释义 *n.* 一段情节;片段;(连续剧的)一集

短语 the final *episode* 连续剧的最后一集

例句 I really like these old *episodes* of *The Big Bang Theory*, because the stories are fascinating. 我真的很喜欢《生活大爆炸》这些老剧集,因为它们的故事很吸引人。

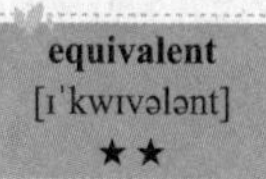

equivalent [ɪˈkwɪvələnt] ★★

释义 *adj.* 相等的,等价的 *n.* 相等物,等价物

例句 Eight kilometers is roughly *equivalent* to five miles. 八公里约等于五英里。

Breathing such polluted air is the *equivalent* of smoking ten cigarettes a day. 呼吸被严重污染的空气等于每天抽十支烟。

firm [ˈfɜːm] ★★★

释义 *adj.* 坚固的;坚决的;坚定的 *n.* 公司,商号 *v.* 使坚固

例句 The *firm's* employees were expecting large bonuses. 这家公司的雇员期待着发放大笔奖金。

She is a *firm* believer in Chinese traditional medicine. 她是中医的忠实信徒。

用法 be firm with sb. 对某人强硬

govern [ˈɡʌvən] ★★

释义 *v.* 统治;控制;支配

例句 The country is *governed* by elected representatives of the people. 这个国家由民选的人民代表统治。

派生 governor *n.* 州长;理事,董事

insight [ˈɪnsaɪt] ★★

释义 *n.* 洞察力,见识

例句 Visiting London gave me an *insight* into the lives of the people who live there. 游伦敦使我对当地居民的生活有深刻的了解。

用法 gain an insight into sth. 深入了解某事

insist [ɪnˈsɪst] ★★★

释义 *v.* 坚持要求,坚决主张

例句 Annas says lawyers can play a key role in *insisting* that these well-meaning medical initiatives translate into better care. 安娜斯说,律师可以在坚持要求将这些善意的医疗方案变成更好的护理行动方面发挥关键性作用。

用法 insist on (doing) sth. 坚持……;坚决主张……

派生 insistent *adj.* 坚持的

释义 *v.* 检查,调查,视察

例句 The customs officer *inspected* his passport suspiciously. 海关官员颇为怀疑地检查了他的护照。

近义 examine *v.* 检查

派生 inspection *n.* 视察

释义 *adj.* 有限的,被限制的

例句 Evidence that the LoveLife program produces lasting changes is *limited* and mixed.
"爱生命"活动产生持久变化的证据是有限的,也是喜忧参半的。

派生 limitation *n.* 限制,制约

释义 *n.* 痛苦,悲惨,不幸

例句 Fame brought her nothing but misery. 名声只给她带来了痛苦。

用法 put sb. out of their misery 使某人摆脱痛苦

派生 miserable *adj.* 痛苦的

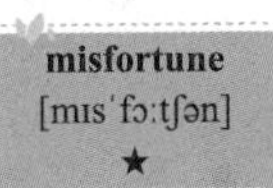

释义 *n.* 不幸,灾祸,灾难

例句 Most of his adult life has been a losing struggle against debt and *misfortune*. 成年后的大部分时间,他都在与债务和不幸作斗争,但最终都以失败告终。

反义 fortune *n.* 好运;财富

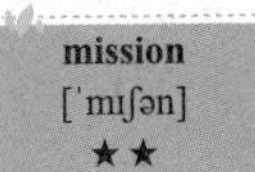

释义 *n.* 使命,任务;使团,代表团

短语 a peace *mission* 和平使命

例句 The exchange of goodwill *missions* greatly contributes to a better understanding between the two countries. 友好代表团的交流大大有助于两国的相互了解。

派生 missionary *adj.* 传教的

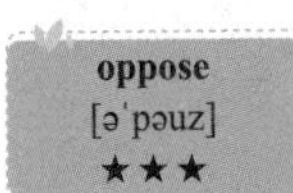

释义 *v.* 反对;使相对

例句 Politically, they belonged to the conservative party and *opposed* reform. 在政治上,他们是保守派,反对改革。

真题 "Many young people assume a great deal of personal responsibility for educating themselves and actively seeking out *opposing* viewpoints," the survey concluded. 这项调查总结:"许多年轻人承担了很大的个人责任来教育自己,并积极寻求相反的观点。"(2018 阅读理解)

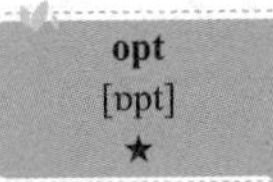

释义 *v.* 选择,挑选

例句 During the recession, the government *opted* for a policy of pay restraint rather than a reduction in public investment. 在经济衰退期间,政府选择了限制薪酬的政策,而不是减少公共投资。

用法 opt for 选择

近义 select *v.* 选择

派生 option *n.* 选择

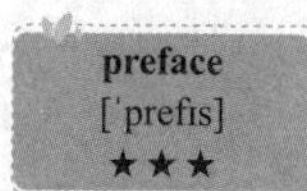

释义 *n.* 序言，引言，前言 *v.* 作序，写前言

例句 This book has a *preface* written by the author. 这本书有作者写的序言。

Today, I'd like to *preface* my remarks with a story from my own life. 今天，我想以我自己生活中的一个故事开始我的发言。

用法 preface sth. with 以……作为开端

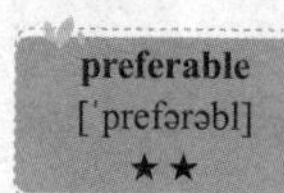

释义 *adj.* 更可取的，更好的

例句 Gradual change is *preferable* to sudden, large-scale change. 渐进的变化比突然、大规模的变化更可取。

用法 far preferable to 远胜于……

派生 preference *n.* 偏爱，偏好

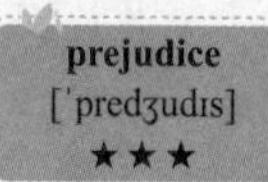

释义 *n.* 偏见，成见 *v.* 使抱偏见，损害

例句 This suggests that British attitudes towards accent have deep roots and are based on class *prejudice*. 这表明英国人对口音的态度有根深蒂固的阶级偏见。

用法 prejudice sb. against... 使某人对……形成偏见

近义 bias *n.* 偏见

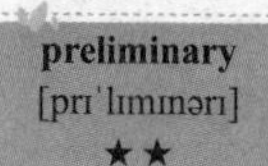

释义 *adj.* 预备的，初步的 *n.* 初步行动，准备工作

短语 *preliminary* study / analysis 初步研究 / 分析

例句 After a few *preliminary* remarks he announced the winners. 说了几句开场白之后，他即宣布优胜者名单。

A background check is normally a *preliminary* to a presidential appointment. 总统任命前通常要进行背景审查的准备工作。

近义 initial *adj.* 开始的，最初的

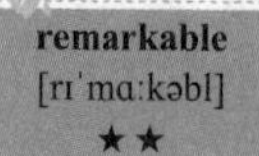

释义 *adj.* 值得注意的；显著的，异常的，非凡的

短语 *remarkable* ability 非凡才能

例句 Owing to the *remarkable* development in mass-communications, people everywhere are being exposed to new customs and ideas. 由于大众通信的显著发展，所有的人都不断接触到新的习俗和思想。

派生 remarkably *adv.* 不寻常地

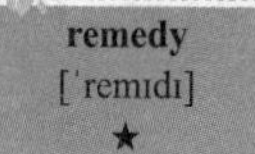

释义 *n.* 药品；治疗措施；解决方法 *v.* 医治；纠正，补救

短语 folk *remedy* 偏方

例句 Sleeping pills, while helpful for some, are not necessarily an effective *remedy* either. 安眠药虽然对一些人有帮助，但也不一定对任何人都有效。

They asked what will be done and if there's a plan to *remedy* the problem. 他们询问将采取什么措施，以及是否有解决这个问题的计划。

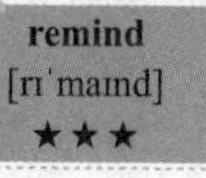

释义 *v.* 提醒，使想起

例句 *Remind* me to buy some groceries after work. 下班后提醒我买些杂货。

真题 The crash of Egypt Air Flight 804, which terrorists may have downed over the Mediterranean Sea, provides another tragic *reminder* of why. 埃及航空 804 航班的坠毁，可能是恐怖分子在地中海上空击落的，这是另一个悲剧的提醒。（2017 阅读理解）

派生 reminder *n.* 提示

释义 *adj.* 刻板的；固执的；僵硬的

短语 *rigid* attitudes 固执的态度

例句 We were disappointed that they insisted on such a *rigid* interpretation of the rules. 他们坚持对规则进行如此刻板的解释，令我们非常失望。

近义 inflexible *adj.* 顽固的

释义 *n.* 主要产品；名产；纤维；主要成分，主食 *v.* 装订，用订书机钉 *adj.* 主要的，常用的

短语 *staple* food / market 主食 / 主要市场

例句 Prices of *staple* foods such as rice, bread and vegetables have also been increasing. 大米、面包和蔬菜等主要食品的价格也一直在上涨。

释义 *v.* 盯，凝视

短语 a blank *stare* 茫然的凝视

例句 We *stare* at our phones when we want to avoid eye contact. 当我们想要避免眼神接触时，我们就会盯着自己的手机。

用法 stare at 凝视，盯住

近义 gaze *v.* 凝视，注视

释义 *v.* 惊吓，使吃惊

例句 The noise of the car *startled* the birds and the whole flock flew up into the air. 汽车声把一大群鸟惊吓得呼啦啦地飞了起来。

用法 be *startled* by sth. 为某事所惊

派生 startling *adj.* 惊人的

释义 *v.*（使）饿死，挨饿；使极其缺乏

短语 *starve* to death 饿死

例句 Some abandoned pets *starve* to death as they are not good hunters. 一些被遗弃的宠物饿死了，因为它们不善于捕猎。

用法 starve for 渴望；急需

派生 starvation *n.* 饥饿

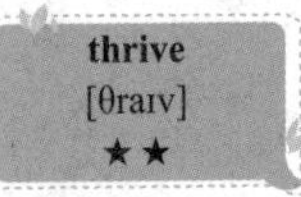

释义 *v.* 兴旺，繁荣

例句 It is still unclear whether electric vehicle companies will continue to *thrive* in the long-term future. 目前还不清楚电动汽车公司是否会在未来长期蓬勃发展。

真题 Websites about dieting would *thrive*. 关于节食的网站将会蓬勃发展。（2016 阅读理解）

近义 flourish *v.* 繁荣，昌盛

派生 thriving *adj.* 繁荣的

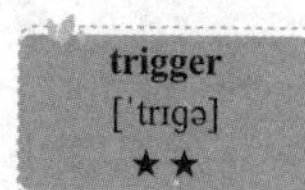

trigger
[ˈtrɪɡə]
★★

释义 *n.* 扳机；诱因 *v.* 触发，引起

例句 Bursting of the credit bubble is *triggering* the biggest recession since the War II. 信贷泡沫的破裂引发了自二战以来最严重的全球经济大萧条。

真题 In people who score high in a test of neuroticism, a personality dimension associated with self-consciousness and anxiety, eye contact *triggered* more activity associated with avoidance. 在神经质（一种与自我意识和焦虑相关的人格维度）测试中得分高的人，目光接触引发的回避活动更多。（2020 阅读理解）

近义 provoke *v.* 引起

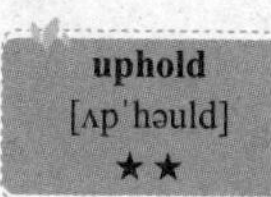

uphold
[ʌpˈhəuld]
★★

释义 *v.* 支持，赞成；举起，坚持

短语 *uphold* the law / decision 维护法律 / 支持决定

例句 It is the responsibility of every government to *uphold* certain basic principles. 维护某些基本原则是每个政府的责任。

真题 Copernicus theorized in 1543 that all of the planets that we knew of revolved not around the Earth, but the Sun, a system that was later *upheld* by Galileo at his own expense. 哥白尼在 1543 年提出了一个理论：我们所知道的所有行星都不是围绕着地球转的，而是绕着太阳转的，后来伽利略自发地维护了这一理论体系。（2020 翻译）

近义 maintain *v.* 保持

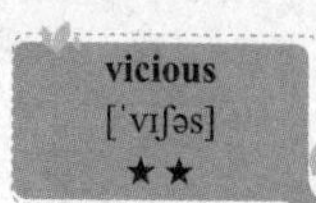

vicious
[ˈvɪʃəs]
★★

释义 *adj.* 恶毒的，恶意的；凶残的，邪恶的

短语 a *vicious* attack / temper 猛烈的攻击 / 脾气暴虐

例句 *Vicious* hate crimes against Asians in the New York City jumped 361 percent from 2020. 纽约市针对亚裔的恶性仇恨犯罪比 2020 年增加了 361%。

近义 brutal *adj.* 凶残的

派生 viciously *adv.* 邪恶地

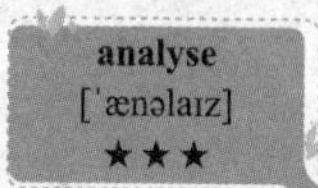

analyse
[ˈænəlaɪz]
★★★

释义 *v.* 分析；分解；解析

例句 The report was written after *analysing* data from the purchases of 6,300 households. 该报告是在分析了 6300 户家庭的购物消费数据后撰写的。

派生 analysis *n.* 分析

ancestor
[ˈænsestə]
★★★

释义 *n.* 祖先；（动植物）原种；原型

例句 My *ancestors* came to America during the 1800s. 我的祖先在 19 世纪来到美国。

This machine is the *ancestor* of the modern computer. 这台机器是现代计算机的前身。

anchor
[ˈæŋkə]
★★

释义 *n.* 锚；主持人 *v.* 抛锚；主持；使固定

例句 We dropped *anchor* and stopped. 我们抛锚后停了下来。

Collins *anchors* the 6 o'clock news. 柯林斯主持 6 点钟新闻节目。

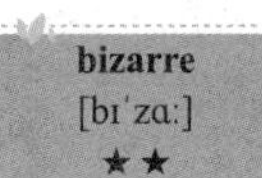
ancient [ˈeɪnʃənt] ★★★

释义 *adj.* 古代的；古老的；老旧的

短语 *ancient* times / city 古代 / 古都

例句 They believed *ancient* Greece and Rome were vital sources of learning. 他们认为古希腊和古罗马是知识的重要发源地。

bizarre [bɪˈzɑː] ★★

释义 *adj.* 奇异的，古怪的

短语 a *bizarre* story 稀奇古怪的故事

例句 Scientists have found hundreds of unique animals that exhibit truly remarkable and *bizarre* features and behaviors. 科学家们发现了数百种独特的动物，它们表现出了真正非凡而奇异的特征和行为。

近义 odd *adj.* 奇怪的，反常的

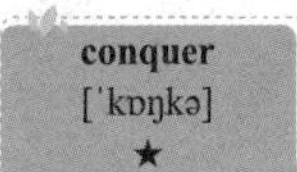
confront [kənˈfrʌnt] ★★★

释义 *v.* 使面临，使遭遇

例句 Their lives were now *confronted* by earthshaking change, by the arrival of the modern world. 随着现代世界的到来，他们的生活正面临着翻天覆地的变化。

派生 confrontation *n.* 对抗，冲突

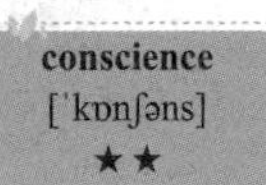
conquer [ˈkɒŋkə] ★

释义 *v.* 征服；占领

例句 The Spanish *conquered* the New World in the 16th century. 西班牙人在16世纪征服了新大陆。

派生 conqueror *n.* 征服者

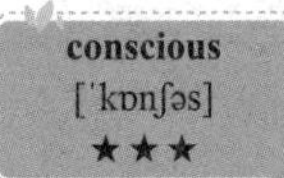
conscience [ˈkɒnʃəns] ★★

释义 *n.* 良心，良知

例句 You didn't do anything wrong — you should have a clear *conscience*. 你没做错什么——你应该觉得问心无愧。

用法 have a clear conscience 问心无愧

派生 conscientious *adj.* 认真的；凭良心的

conscious [ˈkɒnʃəs] ★★★

释义 *adj.* 神志清醒的；意识到的，有意识的

例句 Joanna was fully *conscious* throughout the surgery. 乔安娜在整个手术过程中都是完全清醒的。

We're all becoming increasingly health-*conscious* these days. 如今，我们都变得越来越注重健康。

派生 consciousness *n.* 意识；清醒

connect [kəˈnekt] ★★★

释义 *v.* 连接；与……联系；给……接通电话

例句 The bridge *connects* the island and the land. 这座桥连接了岛和陆地。

派生 connection *n.* 关系

dignity [ˈdɪgnətɪ] ★★

释义 *n.* 庄严，端庄；尊贵，高贵

例句 Prisoners should be treated with regard for human *dignity*. 对待囚犯时应该尊重他们的尊严。

用法 beneath one's dignity 有失尊严

dilute
[daɪˈluːt]
★

释义 *v.* 稀释，冲淡；降低 *adj.* 稀释的，冲淡的

例句 The juice tastes better when *diluted* with a little water. 这果汁加水稀释后味道更好。

Large classes *dilute* the quality of education that children receive. 大班上课会降低孩子所受教育的质量。

派生 dilution *n.* 稀释

diplomatic
[ˌdɪpləˈmætɪk]
★★

释义 *adj.* 外交的；策略的，有手腕的

短语 *diplomatic* immunity 外交豁免权

例句 Chile is the first South American country to establish *diplomatic* relations with China. 智利是第一个同中国建交的南美国家。

派生 diplomatically *adv.* 在外交上

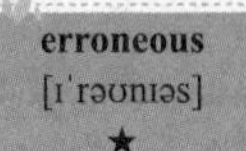

erroneous
[ɪˈrəʊnɪəs]
★

释义 *adj.* 错误的，不正确的

例句 Some people have the *erroneous* notion that one can contract AIDS by giving blood. 一些人错误地认为献血会让人感染艾滋病。

短语 an erroneous belief / impression 一个错误的信念 / 印象

近义 incorrect *adj.* 错误的

escape
[ɪˈskeɪp]
★★★

释义 *n.* 逃跑，逃脱 *v.* 逃跑；避免

短语 a narrow *escape* 侥幸逃脱

例句 They managed to *escape* under cover of darkness. 他们设法在夜色掩护下逃跑了。

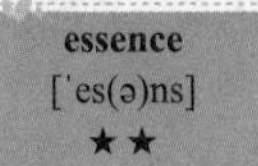

essence
[ˈes(ə)ns]
★★

释义 *n.* 本质，实质

例句 Time is of the *essence* in the fight against the COVID-19 pandemic. 时间是抗击新冠肺炎疫情的关键。

用法 of the essence 必要的，必不可少的

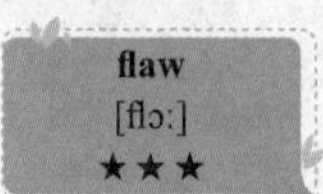

flaw
[flɔː]
★★★

释义 *n.* 裂缝；缺陷 *v.* 使有缺陷

例句 The report reveals fatal *flaws* in security at the airport. 报告揭示了机场安全的致命缺陷。

近义 defect *n.* 缺陷

government
[ˈɡʌvənmənt]
★★★

释义 *n.* 政府；治理，统治

短语 central *government* 中央政府

例句 *Government* of a large city is very difficult. 管理一个大城市是非常困难的。

The local *government* is taking on a greater role in public education. 地方政府正在公共教育中发挥更大的作用。

heritage
[ˈherɪtɪdʒ]
★★

释义 *n.* 遗产，继承物；传统

例句 The ancient buildings are part of the national *heritage*. 这些古建筑是民族遗产的一部分。

真题 The Eisenhower Executive Office Building (EEOB) commands a unique position in both the national history and the architectural *heritage* of the United States. 艾森豪威尔行政办公楼在美国历史和建筑遗

产中都占有独特的地位。(2018 阅读理解)

释义 *v.* 鼓舞,激起;使产生灵感

例句 After her trip to Madrid, she felt *inspired* to learn Spanish. 马德里之行促使她下决心学习西班牙语。

用法 inspire sb. to do sth. 鼓励某人做某事

派生 inspiration *n.* 灵感;启发

释义 *v.* (instal) 安装,设置,安置;使就职,任命

例句 The plumber is coming tomorrow to *install* the new washing machine. 水管工明天来安装新的洗衣机。

She has *installed* a couple of young academics as her advisers. 她任命几名年轻的大学教师作为顾问。

派生 installation *n.* 安装

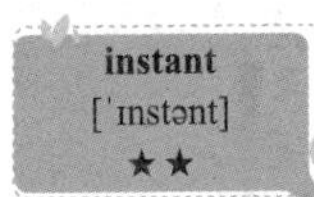

释义 *adj.* 立即的;速食的 *n.* 瞬间

例句 Cell phones provide *instant* access to people. 手机为人们提供了即时联系的方式。

真题 Their reactions may be a complex combination of *instant* reflexes, input from past driving experiences, and what their eyes and ears tell them in that moment. 开车时,凭借过去的驾驶经验,以及在那一刻视觉和听觉输入,让他们能在瞬间整合大量复杂的信息,做出即时判断。(2019 阅读理解)

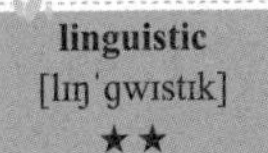

释义 *adj.* 语言的,语言学的

短语 *linguistic* analysis / expression 语言分析 / 表达

例句 *Linguistic* context, situational context and sociocultural context have significant restrictive effects upon speech and its comprehension. 语言语境、情景语境、社会文化语境对语言表达和理解具有重要的制约作用。

释义 *n.* 混合;混合物,混合剂

短语 gas *mixture* 气体混合物

例句 He now looks to the future with a *mixture* of sorrow and hope. 他现在怀着悲伤和希望交织的心情展望未来。

近义 blend *n.* 混合物

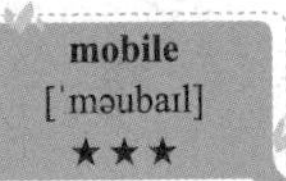

释义 *adj.* 可动的,活动的,运动的 *n.* 移动电话

短语 *mobile* equipment 移动设备

例句 Wechat is becoming increasingly popular on *mobile* among younger users. 微信在年轻的手机用户中越来越受欢迎。

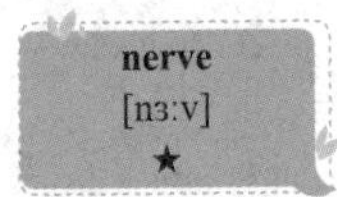

释义 *n.* 神经;神经紧张;胆量

例句 Even after years as a singer, he still suffers from *nerves* before a performance. 尽管当了多年歌手,他在演出前仍然感到紧张。

Malcolm worked up the *nerve* to ask Grandma Rose for some help. 马尔科姆鼓起勇气请罗丝奶奶帮点忙。

用法 suffer from nerves 神经紧张

opposite
[ˈɒpəzɪt]
★★★

释义 *adj.* 相反的；对面的 *n.* 对立面 *prep.* 在……对面

短语 *opposite* view 相反的观点

例句 In fact, instead of straining muscles to build them, as exercise does, laughter apparently accomplishes the *opposite*. 事实上，大笑不像运动那样拉紧肌肉来锻炼肌肉，反而起到明显相反的效果。

近义 contrary *adj.* 相反的

派生 opposition *n.* 反对

preference
[ˈprefərəns]
★★

释义 *n.* 偏爱，喜爱；优惠；优先选择

短语 tax *preference* 税收优惠 color *preference* 色彩的嗜好

例句 Meanwhile, *preference* for private over public services made management even more difficult. 与此同时，对私人服务的偏爱使管理更加困难。

用法 give preference to sb. 优先选择某人

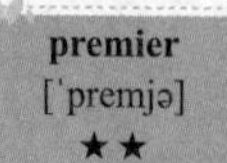

premier
[ˈpremjə]
★★

释义 *n.* 首相，总理；省长 *adj.* 首要的；最佳的

短语 vice *premier* 副总理

例句 A few *premiers* are suspicious of any federal-provincial deal-making. 一些总理对任何联邦和省之间的交易都持怀疑态度。

The company has achieved a *premier* position in the electronics field. 该公司在电子领域取得了领先地位。

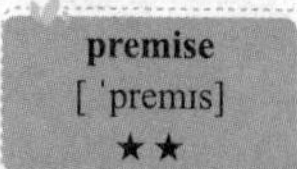

premise
[ˈpremɪs]
★★

释义 *n.* 前提 *v.* 提论，预述，假定

短语 on the *premise* 在……前提下

例句 Let's accept the *premise* that these numbers are somewhat reflective of reality. 让我们接受这样一个前提：这些数字多少反映了现实。

用法 accept one's premise 接受某人的假定

近义 presumption *n.* 推测，设想

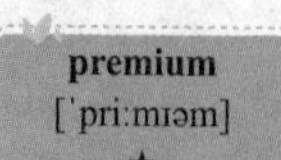

premium
[ˈpriːmɪəm]
★

释义 *n.* 额外费用，奖金，保险费 *adj.* 高昂的；优质的

短语 *premium* quality 一流品质

例句 Americans are deeply concerned about the relentless rise in health care costs and health insurance *premiums*. 美国人对持续上涨的医疗费用和健康保险费用深感忧虑。

remote
[rɪˈməut]
★★

释义 *adj.* 遥远的，疏远的，偏僻的

短语 *remote* education 远程教育

近义 distant *adj.* 遥远的

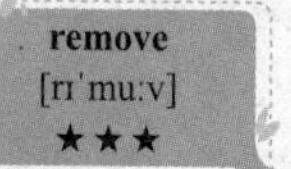

remove
[rɪˈmuːv]
★★★

释义 *v.* 移动；脱掉；除去；远离；免职

例句 Many of these books are far *removed* from the reality of the children's lives. 很多这样的书都跟孩子们的现实生活严重脱节。

真题 Each year the physical presence rule becomes further *removed* from economic reality and results in significant revenue losses to the States. 实际存在的规定每年都在进一步脱离经济现实，给美国带来重大的收入损失。（2019 阅读理解）

派生 removal *n.* 移动；除去

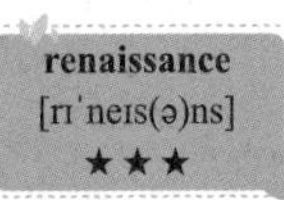

renaissance [rɪˈneɪs(ə)ns] ★★★

释义 *n.* 文艺复兴(时期);新生,复兴

短语 *renaissance* humanism 文艺复兴时期的人文主义

例句 Science took a new and different turn in the *Renaissance.* 科学在文艺复兴时期发生了新的转变。

真题 *Renaissance* ideas had spread throughout Europe well into the 17th century. 直到17世纪,文艺复兴思想才在整个欧洲传播开来。(2020翻译)

statute [ˈstætʃuːt] ★★

释义 *n.* 法令,法规;章程,条例

短语 by *statute* 依照法规

例句 Under the *statutes* of the university, they had no power to dismiss him. 按大学的规章制度,校方无权开除他。

近义 regulation *n.* 规章制度

派生 statutory *adj.* 依照法令的

steady [ˈstedɪ] ★★

释义 *adj.* 稳定的,不变的;坚定的 *v.*(使)稳固/稳定

例句 Since that time, the readership of newspapers has been on a *steady* decline. 从那时起,报纸的读者人数一直在稳步下降。

She breathed in to *steady* her voice. 她吸了一口气,好使自己的声音平静下来。

近义 stable *adj.* 稳定的,牢固的

派生 steadily *adv.* 逐渐地,稳步地

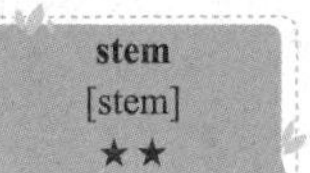

stem [stem] ★★

释义 *n.* 茎,干;船头 *v.* 起源于,由……造成

短语 a *long-stemmed* rose 一枝长茎玫瑰

例句 The researchers' argument stems from a simple observation about social influence. 研究人员的观点源于对社会影响的一个简单观察。

反义 stemless *adj.* 无茎的

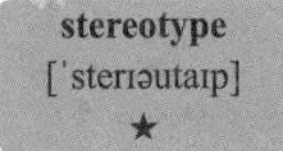

stereotype [ˈsterɪəutaɪp] ★

释义 *n.* 陈规,老套,刻板印象 *v.* 对……形成刻板的看法

短语 a cultural *stereotype* 文化成见

例句 It did not conform to the usual *stereotype* of an industrial city. 这和一座常规的工业城市那种千篇一律的格局不一样。

You are likely to find many people who have *stereotyped* ideas about women. 你可能会发现很多人对女性有刻板印象。

token [ˈtəukən] ★★

释义 *n.* 象征;代币;礼券 *adj.* 象征性的

例句 The researchers spent two years teaching their monkeys to exchange *tokens* for food. 研究人员花了两年时间教他们的猴子用代币换食物。

The government agreed to send a small *token* force to the area. 政府同意派遣一小支象征性的部队到那一地区。

近义 symbol *n.* 象征

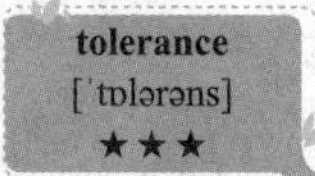

释义 *n.* 宽容；容忍；忍耐

例句 We are all becoming increasingly aware of the importance of modeling *tolerance* and patience for the younger generation. 我们都越来越意识到为年轻一代树立宽容和耐心的榜样的重要性。

近义 resistance *n.* 抵制；抵抗

派生 tolerant *adj.* 宽容的

释义 *adj.* 垂直的，直立的；正直的

短语 an *upright* freezer 立式冰柜 an *upright* man 正直的人

例句 He was sitting on an *upright* chair beside his bed, reading. 他坐在床边的一把直椅子上看书。

He is a very *upright* and trustworthy man who is always willing to help. 他是一个正直可靠的人，总是乐于助人。

近义 straight *adj.* 笔直的 honest *adj.* 正直的

释义 *n.* 牺牲品，受害者

短语 a sacrificial *victim* 祭品

例句 Our local hospital has become the latest *victim* of the cuts in government spending. 我们当地的医院成了政府削减开支的最新牺牲品。

真题 The *victims* of this revolution, of course, are not limited to designers. 当然，这场革命的受害者并不局限于设计师。（2013 阅读理解）

用法 be the victim of sth. 是……的受害者

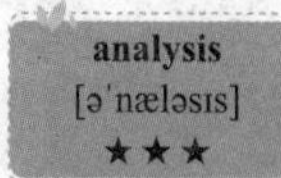

释义 *n.* 分析；解析

例句 They were doing some type of statistical *analysis*. 他们在做某种统计分析。

用法 an analysis of sth. 对……的分析

派生 analytic *adj.* 解析的

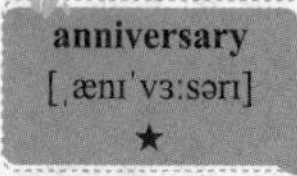

释义 *n.* 周年纪念日

短语 wedding *anniversary* 结婚纪念日

例句 We celebrated our 30th wedding *anniversary* in Paris. 我们在巴黎庆祝结婚 30 周年。

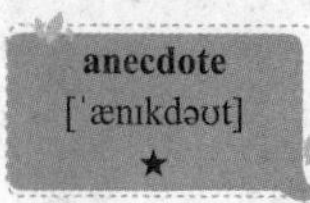

释义 *n.* 轶事；奇闻

例句 She told us some interesting *anecdotes* about the great thinker. 她给我们讲了一些关于这位伟大思想家的趣闻轶事。

近义 tale *n.* 故事，传说

派生 anecdotal *adj.* 轶事的；传闻的

释义 *n.* 极度痛苦 *v.* 感到痛苦

例句 Tears of *anguish* filled her eyes. 她双眸噙满了伤心的泪水。

He *anguished* over his failure. 他因失败而痛苦。

近义 distress *n.* / *v.*（使）悲痛

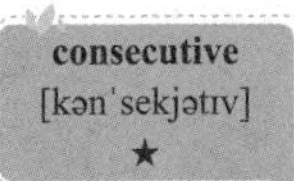

释义 *v.* / *n.* 责备；归咎于

例句 The policy is partly to *blame* for causing the worst unemployment in Europe. 该政策在一定程度上造成了欧洲最严重的失业率。

I always get the *blame* for his mistakes! 我总是因他的错误而受责备！

用法 get the blame 受到责备

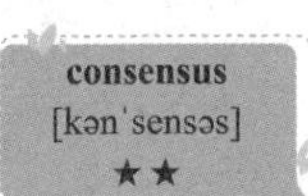

释义 *adj.* 连续的；连贯的

例句 Can they win the title for the third *consecutive* season? 他们能连续第三个赛季夺冠吗?

派生 consecutively *adv.* 连续地

释义 *n.* 一致同意，共识

例句 Could we reach a *consensus* on this matter? Let's take a vote. 我们能在这个问题上达成共识吗？我们来投票吧。

真题 In response to these many unilateral measures, the Organization for Economic Cooperation and Development (OECD) is currently working with 131 countries to reach a *consensus* by the end of 2020 on an international solution. 针对这些单边措施，经济合作与发展组织目前正与131个国家合作，争取在2020年底前就国际解决方案达成共识。（2020 阅读理解）

用法 reach a consensus 达成共识

释义 *v.* / *n.* 同意，赞成，答应

例句 John asked Gina if she would *consent* to a small celebration after the meeting. 约翰问吉娜是否愿意在会后举行一次小型的庆祝活动。

He took the car without the owner's *consent*. 他未经车主同意就把车开走了。

用法 by common *consent* 经一致同意

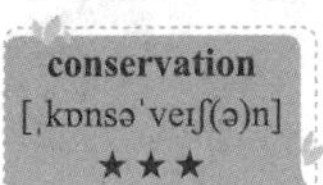

释义 *n.* 结果，后果；重要性

例句 The slightest error can have serious *consequences*. 最轻微的错误都可能造成严重的后果。

真题 We are still at the beginning of this revolution and small choices now may turn out to have gigantic *consequences* later. 我们仍处于这种变革的开端，如今的一个小小选择或许在将来产生巨大影响。（2018 阅读理解）

派生 consequently *adj.* 结果，因此

conservation
[ˌkɒnsəˈveɪʃ(ə)n]
★★★

释义 *n.* 保护；节约

短语 energy / water *conservation* 能量守恒 / 节约用水

例句 The program aims to raise public awareness of *conservation*. 该项目旨在提高公众的环保意识。

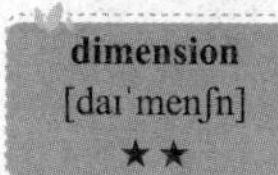

释义 *n.* 尺寸，尺度；维（数），度（数）

例句 It will open a new *dimension* to your life. 它将为你的生活打开一个新的维度。

真题 Two and three-*dimensional* maps are helpful tools in planning excavations. 二维和三维地图是规划（考古）挖掘的有用工具。（2014 阅读理解）

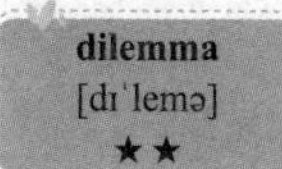

释义 *n.* 窘境，困境

例句 Nowadays many college graduates are facing the *dilemma* of whether to get a job or continue their education. 如今许多大学毕业生正面临着是找工作还是继续读书的两难境地。

用法 in a dilemma 左右为难

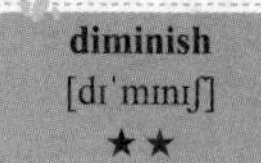

释义 *v.* 缩小，减少

例句 The company tried to *diminish* the cost of production. 公司试图降低生产成本。

真题 Complex international, economic, technological and cultural changes could start to *diminish* the leading position of English as the language of the world market. 复杂的国际、经济、技术和文化变化可能会开始削弱英语作为世界市场语言的主导地位。（2017 翻译）

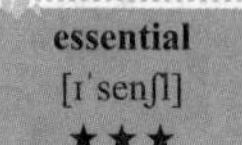

释义 *adj.* 非常重要的；基本的，精髓的 *n.* 本质；要素；必需品

例句 Experience is *essential* for this job. 对于这个工作，经验是非常重要的。

真题 "I think that, for the majority of scientific papers nowadays, statistical review is more *essential* than expert review," he says. 他说："我认为，对于当今的大多数科学论文来说，数据审查比专家审查更重要。"（2015 阅读理解）

派生 essentially *adv.* 本质上，根本上

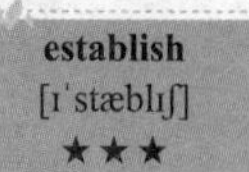

释义 *v.* 建立，设立；确立

例句 Universities and colleges should *establish* close contact with institutes of scientific research. 高等院校应与科研机构建立密切联系。

派生 establishment *n.* 建立

释义 *n.* 地产，不动产；遗产；庄园

短语 real *estate* market 房地产市场

例句 The wedding was held at a luxury seaside *estate* in Majorca, Spain. 婚礼在西班牙马略卡岛的一处豪华海滨庄园举行。

近义 property *n.* 财产

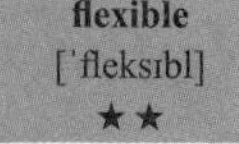

释义 *adj.* 柔韧的，易弯曲的，灵活的，能变形的

例句 You need to be more *flexible* and imaginative in your approach. 你的方法必须更加灵活，更富有想象力。

派生 inflexible *adj.* 不可改变的，不能弯曲的

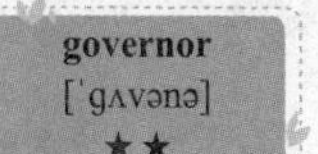

释义 *n.* 统治者，地方长官；州长

短语 a prison / school *governor* 监狱长 / 学校董事

例句 *Governors*, all of whom are popularly elected, serve as the chief executive officers of the fifty states, five commonwealths and territories. 州长都是通过民选产生的，他们是五十个

州、五个联邦和地区的首席执行官。

释义 *n.*(instalment) 分期付款；（连载的）一期；安装

例句 I shall soon pay the last *installment* of my debt. 不久我将偿付我的最后一期债款。

真题 Soon after *Sketches by Boz* appeared, a publishing firm approached Dickens to write a story in monthly *installments*. 《博兹速写》出版后不久，一家出版公司找到狄更斯，让他以每月分期的方式写故事。（2017 阅读理解）

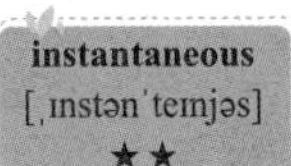

释义 *adj.* 瞬间的，即刻的

短语 an *instantaneous* response 即时的响应

例句 AI could eliminate the risk of human error and provide *instantaneous* decisions. 人工智能可以消除人为失误的风险，并提供即时决策。

近义 immediate *adj.* 立刻的，即时的

派生 instantaneously *adv.* 即刻

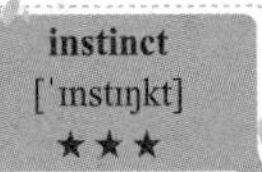

释义 *n.* 本能，直觉，天性 *adj.* 充满的

短语 animal *instinct* 动物本能 by *instinct* 出于本能

例句 Even at an early age, he showed he had an *instinct* for music. 在很小的时候，他就表现出了音乐的天赋。

真题 We know that a typical infant will *instinctively* gaze into its mother's eyes, and she will look back. 我们知道，通常婴儿会本能地注视母亲的眼睛，母亲也会回以注视。（2020 阅读理解）

派生 instinctively *adv.* 本能地

释义 *adv.* 同样地；也，而且

例句 He lent money, made donations and encouraged others to do *likewise*. 他又借钱又捐款捐物，并且鼓励别人也这样做。

近义 also *adv.* 此外，而且；也

释义 *v.* (mobilise) 动员；组织

例句 The purpose of the journey is to *mobilize* public opinion on the controversial issue. 此行的目的就是动员公众对这个备受争议的问题发表意见。

派生 mobilization *n.* 动员；调动

释义 *v.* 嘲笑 *adj.* 假的，模拟的 *n.* 仿制品；嘲笑；（英国）模拟考试

短语 *mock* cream 人造奶油

例句 They *mocked* his way of speaking. 他们嘲弄他的说话方式。

What did you get in the *mock*? 你的模拟考试得了多少分？

释义 *n.* 方式，式样

例句 Most people do not realise that there are strong commercial agendas at work to keep them in passive consumption *mode*. 大多数人意识不到，强大的商业工作议程让他们处在被动消费的模式中。

用法 be in panic *mode* 感到惊恐；感到惊慌

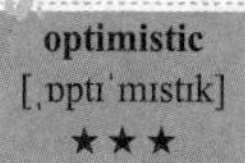

释义 *adj.* 乐观的，乐观主义的

短语 cautiously *optimistic* 审慎乐观 an *optimistic* view 乐观态度

例句 The President says she is *optimistic* that an agreement can be worked out soon. 总统说，她对很快就能达成协议感到乐观。

反义 pessimistic *adj.* 悲观的

派生 optimistically *adv.* 乐观地

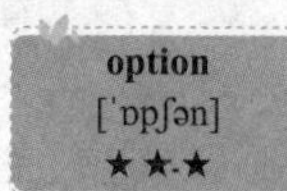

释义 *n.* 选择；选修课；选项

短语 alternative *option* 替代物

例句 The government has two *options*: to reduce spending or to increase taxes. 政府有两种选择：或是减少开支，或是增加税收。

There are four *options* in our college. 我们大学里有四门选修科。

派生 optional *adj.* 可选择的

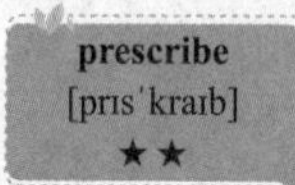

释义 *v.* 指示，规定；处（方），开（药）

例句 The physician may *prescribe* but not administer the drug. 内科医师可以开处方但不可发药。

用法 prescribe for 开处方，开药方

派生 prescription *n.* 药方，处方

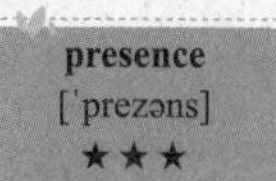

释义 *n.* 出席，到场，存在

例句 Men should watch their language when in the *presence* of ladies. 在女士面前，男士应该注意自己的语言。

真题 The ruling is a victory for big chains with a *presence* in many states, since they usually collect sales tax on online purchases already. 这项裁决对在许多州都有业务的大型连锁店来说是一个胜利，因为他们通常已经对网上购物征收销售税。（2019 阅读理解）

用法 in the presence of 在……面前；有某人在场

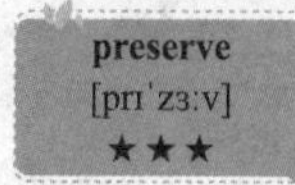

释义 *v.* 保护，维持；保存，保藏 *n.* 果酱；专属领域

例句 One of the purposes for the development of writing was to *preserve* human communication. 文字发展的目的之一，就是保存人类的信息。

真题 In the meantime, the court threw out the FCC's attempt to block all state rules on net neutrality, while *preserving* the commission's power to pre-empt individual state laws that undermine its order. 与此同时，法院驳回了联邦通信委员会试图阻止所有有关网络中立性的州规定的企图，同时保留了委员会先发制人的权力，以防止个别州的法律破坏其秩序。（2021 阅读理解）

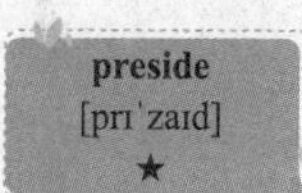

释义 *v.* 主持；掌管（局势）

例句 The mayor's principal function is to *preside* at meetings of the city council. 市长的主要职责是主持市议会的会议。

用法 preside at / over 主持 / 负责

派生 presider *n.* 主持者

repel
[rɪˈpel]
★

释义 v. 击退,抵制;使厌恶;抵制

例句 Only after a long hard struggle were we able to *repel* the enemy from our shores. 经过长期的艰苦战斗,我们才把敌人从我们的海岸击退。

近义 repulse v. 拒绝;驱逐

派生 repellence n. 抵抗性;排斥性

replace
[rɪˈpleɪs]
★★★

释义 v. 取代,替换,代替;把……放回原处

例句 Teachers will never be *replaced* by computers in the classroom. 课堂上,电脑永远不会取代老师。

真题 Here are a few other ways, AI is aiding companies without *replacing* employees. 以下是人工智能在不取代员工的情况下,帮助公司的其他一些方式。(2021 阅读理解)

用法 be replaced by 被……所取代

派生 replaceable adj. 可替换的

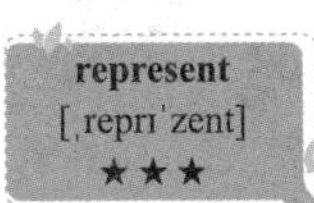
represent
[ˌreprɪˈzent]
★★★

释义 v. 描述;代表;阐明;体现

例句 A group of four teachers were delegated to *represent* the school at the union conference. 四名教师被委派代表学校参加工会会议。

真题 On June 7 Google pledged not to "design or deploy AI" that would cause "overall harm". While the statement is vague, it *represents* one starting point. 6 月 7 日,谷歌承诺不会"设计或部署会造成'全面伤害'的人工智能"。虽然这个说法很模糊,但它代表了一个起点。(2019 阅读理解)

派生 representation n. 代表

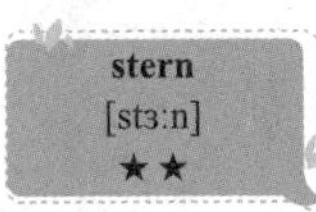
stern
[stɜːn]
★★

释义 adj. 严厉的;坚决的 n. 船尾,舟尾

短语 a *stern* face 严厉的面容 the *stern* of a ship 船尾

例句 The headmaster ruled the school with a *stern* discipline. 校长治校严谨。

真题 Most Victorians look *stern* in photographs. 大多数维多利亚时代的人在照片里看起来都很严肃。(2021 阅读理解)

用法 sternness n. 严厉

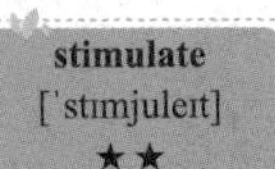
stimulate
[ˈstɪmjuleɪt]
★★

释义 v. 刺激,使兴奋;激励,鼓舞

短语 *stimulate* economic growth 拉动经济增长

例句 This exercise will *stimulate* your creativity, increase your energy and unlock your potential. 这个练习将激发你的创造力,增加你的能量,释放你的潜能。

近义 inspire v. 激发,激励

派生 stimulation n. 刺激,激励

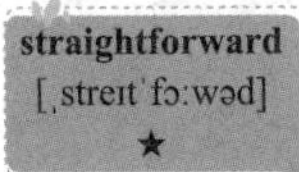
straightforward
[ˌstreɪtˈfɔːwəd]
★

释义 adj. 简单的,易懂的;坦率的

短语 a *straightforward* process 简单的过程

例句 Just follow the signs to Bradford — it's very *straightforward*. 顺着路标走就到布拉德福德了——非常简单。

Roz is *straightforward* and lets you know what she's thinking. 罗兹很坦诚,她会告诉你她的想法。

派生 straightforwardly adv. 直截了当地

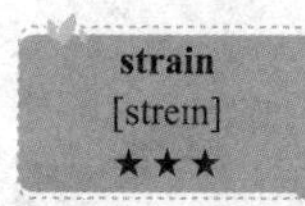

释义 v. 拉紧；损伤；过度使用 n. 压力；拉紧；劳损；负担

例句 Their marriage is under great *strain* at the moment. 眼下他们的婚姻关系非常紧张。

Resources will be further *strained* by new demands for housing. 新的住房需求将使资源变得更紧张。

用法 under the strain 处于紧张状态

近义 pressure *n.* 压力

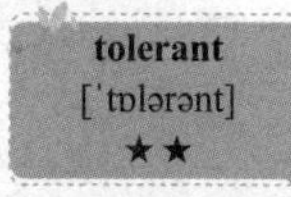

释义 *adj.* 容忍的，宽容的；有耐力的

例句 A well educated man usually has a *tolerant* attitude towards people with different ideas. 一个受过良好教育的人，通常对持有不同理念的人持宽容的态度。

反义 intolerant *adj.* 无法忍受的

派生 tolerance *n.* 宽容；忍耐

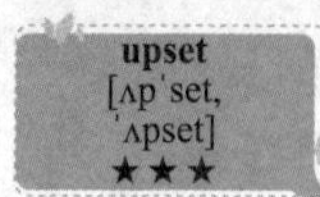

释义 v. 使……心烦意乱 *adj.* 难过的；不安的 *n.* 烦恼

短语 stomach *upset* 肠胃不适

例句 Don't *upset* yourself about it — let's just forget it ever happened. 你别为这事烦恼了——咱们就只当它没发生过。

The turmoil has already *upset* the established order of the old regime. 这场动乱已经打乱了旧政权的既定秩序。

真题 "Figuring out a way to accelerate that transition would make sense for them," he said, "but if you discontinue it, you're going to have your most loyal customers really *upset* with you." "想办法加速这种转变对他们来说是有意义的，"他说，"但如果你停止这种做法，你最忠实的客户就会对你感到不满。"（2016 阅读理解）

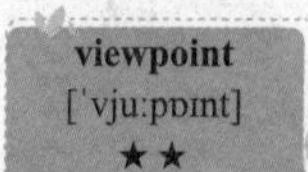

释义 *n.* 观点，意见

短语 opposing *viewpoint* 相反观点

例句 The story is told from the *viewpoint* of someone who grew up during the Great Depression. 这个故事是从一个成长于大萧条时期的人的角度来讲述的。

用法 from someone's viewpoint 从某人的角度来看

近义 standpoint *n.* 观点

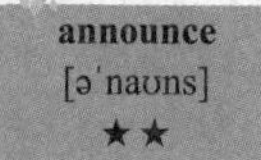

释义 v. 宣布；通知；宣称；显示

例句 The government has *announced* plans to create 10,000 new jobs. 政府宣布计划创造 10,000 个新工作岗位。

Footsteps *announced* her return. 听见脚步声，知道她回来了。

近义 declare *v.* 宣布

派生 announcement *n.* 公告

annual
[ˈænjuəl]
★★★

释义 *adj.* 每年的；年度的 *n.* 年刊；年鉴；一年生植物

例句 The school trip has become an *annual* event. 学校旅行已经成为一年一度的活动。

I looked for Jane's picture in my high-school *annual*. 我在高中年鉴上找简的照片。

派生 annually *adv.* 每年地

anonymous
[əˈnɒnɪməs]
★

释义 *adj.* 匿名的；无名的；无特色的

例句 An *anonymous* buyer purchased the painting. 一位匿名买家买下了这幅画。

His car was an *anonymous-looking* Ford. 他的车是一辆平平无奇的福特车。

近义 unnamed *adj.* 无名的

派生 anonymity *n.* 匿名

antique
[ænˈtiːk]
★

释义 *adj.* 古老的；古董的 *n.* 古董

例句 That car is an *antique*. 那辆汽车是古董。

The Sunday *antique* market is a happy hunting ground for collectors. 周日的古董市场是收藏家的淘物乐园。

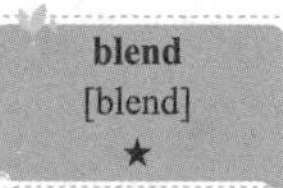

blend
[blend]
★

释义 *v.* 混合 *n.* 混合；混合物

例句 The music *blends* traditional and modern melodies. 这音乐融合了传统和现代的旋律。

Musically, the album was a *blend* of blues, country and folk. 音乐上，这张专辑融合了布鲁斯、乡村和民间音乐。

conservative
[kənˈsɜːvətɪv]
★★★

释义 *adj.* 保守的，守旧的 *n.* 保守主义者

短语 *conservative* party / force 保守党 / 守恒力

例句 Older people tend to be more *conservative* and a bit suspicious of anything new. 上年纪的人往往很保守，对任何新的东西都有些怀疑。

派生 conservatively *adv.* 谨慎地；适当地

considerable
[kənˈsɪdərəbl]
★★

释义 *adj.* 相当大（或多）的，相当重要的；值得考虑的

例句 The recent slowdown in the US economy is likely to have a *considerable* impact on the rest of the world. 最近美国经济的放缓，可能会对世界其他地区产生相当大的影响。

用法 a considerable amount of sth. 大量的

派生 considerably *adv.* 非常，相当多地

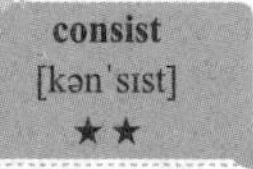

consist
[kənˈsɪst]
★★

释义 *v.* 在于；由……组成，由……构成

例句 The beauty of the plan *consists* in its simplicity. 该计划的妙处在于简洁明了。

There is a large art collection, *consisting* of over 300 paintings. 这里有大量的艺术收藏品，包括 300 多幅绘画作品。

consistent
[kənˈsɪstənt]
★★

释义 *adj.* 一贯的；一致的，持续的

例句 This result is *consistent* with earlier findings. 这一结果与以前的发现一致。

反义 inconsistent *adj.* 不一致的

派生 consistently *adv.* 一贯地

释义 *v.* 安慰，慰藉 *n.* 控制台，仪表盘

例句 Harry *consoled* himself with the thought that he had at least solved part of the mystery. 哈利安慰自己说，他至少解开了一部分秘密。

派生 consolation *n.* 慰藉

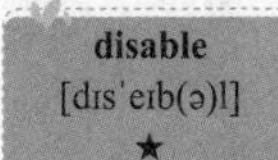

释义 *v.* 使残废；使失去能力；丧失能力

例句 Viruses can delete your files and *disable* your computer. 病毒可以删除你的文件并使你的电脑瘫痪。

派生 disabled *adj.* 丧失能力的，有残疾的

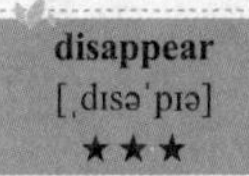

释义 *v.* 不见，消失

例句 I watched the train leaving the station until it *disappeared* from sight. 我看着火车驶离车站，直到看不见为止。

近义 vanish *v.* 突然不见，消失

反义 appear *v.* 出现，呈现

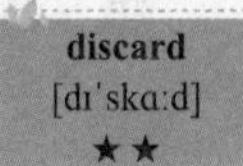

释义 *v.* 丢弃，抛弃，遗弃

例句 We should *discard* old beliefs and adopt new ones. 我们应该摒弃旧观念，接受新观念。

Consumers *discard* a lot of food every year. 消费者每年丢弃很多食物。

近义 abandon *v.* 抛弃

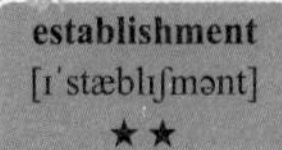

释义 *n.* 建立，设立，建立的机构（或组织）

短语 the medical / military *establishment* 医疗 / 军事机构

例句 The *establishment* of new international economic order is the essence of his article. 他文章的主题是建立国际经济新秩序。

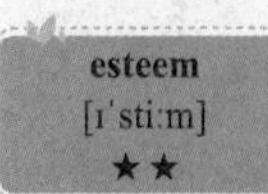

释义 *n.* 尊敬，尊重 *v.* 尊重；把……看作

例句 She was *esteemed* the perfect novelist. 她被认为是最完美的小说家。

She has won *esteem* for her work with cancer patients. 她为癌症患者所做的工作赢得了尊重。

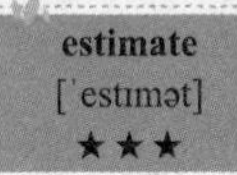

释义 *v.* / *n.* 估计，估价；评估

例句 His personal wealth is *estimated* at around $3 million. 他的个人财富估计在300万美元左右。

At a rough *estimate* the equipment's cost price is about $ 120,000 and will fetch at least $250,000. 粗略估计，该设备的成本价约为12万美元，它至少能卖到25万美元。

用法 at a rough estimate 据粗略估算

派生 estimation *n.* 估计，估算

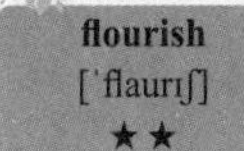

释义 *n.* / *v.* 繁荣，茂盛，兴旺

例句 Due to the pandemic, few businesses are *flourishing*. 由于疫情影响，很少有企业蓬勃发展。

These plants *flourish* in a sunny position. 这些植物在向阳的地方长得特别茂盛。

释义 *adj.* 渐渐的，逐步的

短语 a *gradual* change 逐渐变化

例句 The doctor noticed a *gradual* improvement in his patient. 医生注意到病人在逐渐恢复健康。

派生 gradually *adv.* 逐渐地，逐步地

释义 *v.* 犹豫；不情愿

例句 If you *hesitate* too long, you will miss the opportunity. 如果你老是犹豫不决，那就会错失良机。

派生 hesitation *n.* 犹豫

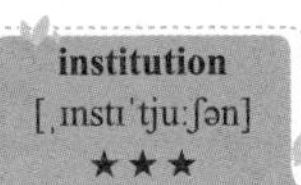

释义 *n.* 公共机构；协会；学校；研究所；制度；惯例

短语 a public *institution* 公共机构

例句 The Hong Kong Bank is Hong Kong's largest financial *institution*. 香港银行是香港最大的金融机构。

真题 When people place their trust in an individual or an *institution*, their brains release oxytocin. 当人们信任一个人或一个机构时，他们的大脑就会释放催产素。（2018 完形填空）

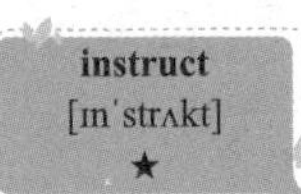

释义 *v.* 教授；命令，指示

例句 The old workers *instruct* the young workers not only in words but in deeds. 老工人对青年工人不仅言传而且身教。

用法 instruct sb. in sth. 指导某人做某事

派生 instruction *n.* 指导；(*pl.*) 说明（书）

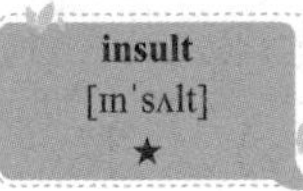

释义 *v.* / *n.* 侮辱，凌辱

例句 I don't want to *insult* him by saying it was a bad play. 我不想说这是一出烂戏来侮辱他。

In some countries, whistling by listeners is a sign of approval while in other courtiers it is a form of *insult*. 在一些国家，听众吹口哨是赞许的标志，而在其他国家，这是一种侮辱。

用法 an insult to sb. / sth. 对……的侮辱

释义 *adv.* 照字面意义，逐字地；确实

短语 *literally* and figuratively 字面上地和象征性地

例句 Translations that are done too *literally* often don't flow well or don't sound natural. 太拘泥于字面意思的翻译往往会不太流畅或不太自然。

There are *literally* hundreds of people involved in the projects. 实际上有数百人参与了这个项目。

近义 indeed *adv.* 确实

释义 *adj.* 中等的，适度的，温和的

短语 *moderate* exercise 适量的运动

例句 The epidemic is "*moderate*" in severity, with the overwhelming majority of patients experiencing only mild symptoms and a full recovery, often in the absence of any medical treatment. 此次疫情的严重程度为“中等”，绝大多数患者症状轻微，往往在没有任何医学治疗的情况下完全康复。

派生 moderation *n.* 适度

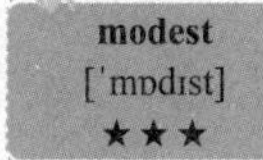

modest
[ˈmɒdɪst]
★★★

释义 *adj.* 谦虚的，有节制的

例句 On a five to three vote, the Supreme Court knocked out much of Arizona's immigration law Monday — a *modest* policy victory for the Obama Administration. 最高法院于周一以五比三的投票结果宣布亚利桑那州移民法多项条款无效，这对奥巴马政府来说算是一场胜利。

近义 moderate *adj.* 适度的

反义 immodest *adj.* 不谦虚的

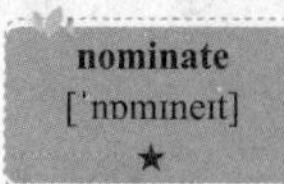

nominate
[ˈnɒmɪneɪt]
★

释义 *v.* 提名，推荐；任命

例句 The movie was *nominated* for an Oscar. 这部电影获奥斯卡金像奖提名。

He has been *nominated* to the committee. 他被任命为委员会委员。

派生 nomination *n.* 推荐；任命

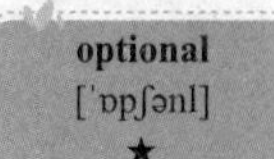

optional
[ˈɒpʃənl]
★

释义 *adj.* 可选择的，非强制的

短语 *optional* course 选修课

例句 By setting Peking Opera as an *optional* course, students may have more freedom to decide whether to take it or not. 通过将京剧设置为选修课，学生们可以有更多的自由去决定是否选修京剧。

近义 elective *adj.* 可选择的

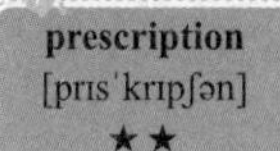

prescription
[prɪsˈkrɪpʃən]
★★

释义 *n.* 药方，处方

短语 *prescription* medicine 处方药

例句 According to the Canadian Institute for Health Information, *prescription* drug costs have risen since 1997 at twice the rate of overall health-care spending. 根据加拿大健康信息研究所的数据，自 1997 年以来，处方药成本的增长速度是整体医疗支出速度的两倍。

用法 make up a prescription 按处方配药

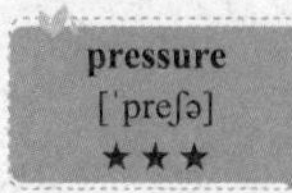

pressure
[ˈpreʃə]
★★★

释义 *n.* 压力，压迫 *v.* 迫使

短语 under *pressure* 在压力之下

例句 Under lobby *pressure*, George Osborne favours rural new-build against urban renovation and renewal. 在游说团体的压力下，乔治·奥斯本倾向于在农村新建房屋，而不是在城市进行改造和更新。（2016 阅读理解）

近义 stress *n.* 压力 compel *v.* 强迫

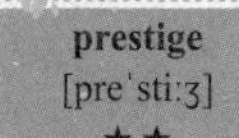

prestige
[preˈstiːʒ]
★★

释义 *n.* 声望，威望，威信

短语 a loss of *prestige* 名誉扫地

例句 It was his competence in foreign affairs that gained him international *prestige*. 正是他处理外交事务的能力为他赢得了国际声望。

派生 prestigious *adj.* 有威望的，有声望的

presume [prɪˈzjuːm] ★★

释义 v. 假定,假设;冒昧

例句 In English law, a person is *presumed* innocent until proved guilty. 英国法律规定,在证明一个人有罪之前,他是推定是无罪的。

近义 assume v. 假定,假设

派生 presumption n. 推测,设想

representative [ˌreprɪˈzentətɪv] ★★★

释义 n. 代表,代理人 adj. 典型的,有代表性的

短语 *representative* office 办事处

例句 The jury is also said to be the best surviving example of direct rather than *representative* democracy. 陪审团制度也被认为是现存的直接民主而非代议制民主的典范。

派生 representation n. 代表

reproduce [ˌriːprəˈdjuːs] ★★★

释义 v. 复制;繁殖;再制造

例句 If we can *reproduce* the form we have shown in the last couple of months, we will be successful. 如果我们能重现前几个月表现出来的状态,我们就会成功。Most reptiles *reproduce* by laying eggs on land. 大多数爬行动物通过在陆地产卵进行繁殖。

派生 reproducible adj. 可再生的;可繁殖的;可复制的

republican [rɪˈpʌblɪkən] ★★★

释义 adj. 共和的 n. 共和主义者

例句 Some families have been *republican* for generations. 有些家庭世代都支持共和党。

真题 Now comes word that everyone involved — Democrats, *Republicans*, the Postal Service, the unions and the system's heaviest users has finally agreed on a plan to fix the system. 现在有消息称,所有参与其中的人——民主党人、共和党人、邮政服务、工会和系统最大的用户终于就修复系统的计划达成共识。(2018 阅读理解)

strategy [ˈstrætɪdʒɪ] ★★★

释义 n. 战略,策略;对策,政策

短语 development *strategy* 发展战略

例句 Next week, health ministers will gather in Amsterdam to agree a *strategy* for controlling malaria. 下周,卫生部部长们将在阿姆斯特丹聚首共商防治疟疾的策略。

近义 policy n. 方针;策略

派生 strategic adj. 战略上的

strengthen [ˈstreŋθən] ★★★

释义 v. 加强,巩固

例句 Obama won the Nobel Peace Prize in 2009 for his efforts to *strengthen* international diplomacy and cooperation between peoples. 2009 年,奥巴马因努力加强国际外交和各国人民之间的合作而获得诺贝尔和平奖。

用法 strengthen one's hand 增强某人的实力

近义 enhance v. 增强,提高

strike [straɪk] ★★★

释义 n. / v. 罢工 v. 打,击;攻击;给……深刻印象

短语 on *strike* 罢工

例句 French air traffic controllers have begun a three-day *strike*

in a dispute over pay. 法国空中交通管制员因工资纠纷开始了为期三天的罢工。

A powerful earthquake *struck* the island early this morning. 今天早上，岛上发生了强烈地震。

派生 striking *adj.* 惊人的

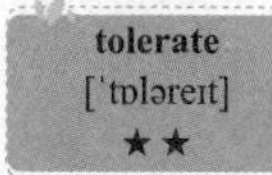

释义 *v.* 容忍；忍受

例句 Women's capacity for *tolerating* stress may even be greater than men's. 女性承受压力的能力甚至可能比男性更强。

Few plants will *tolerate* sudden changes in temperature. 很少植物经受得住气温的突然变化。

近义 stand *v.* 忍受

派生 tolerant *adj.* 忍受的

释义 *n.* 通行费；损失；死伤人数 *v.* 敲钟

短语 death *toll* 死亡人数 *toll* gate 收费站

例句 Since 23 December 2022, a *toll* road to the airport has been opened. 自 2022 年 12 月 23 日起，通往机场的收费公路开通。

The official death *toll* has now reached 100. 官方公布的死亡人数现已达 100 人。

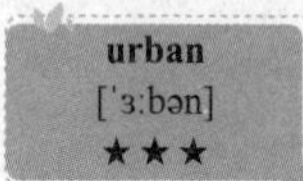

释义 *adj.* 城市的，市内的

短语 *urban* sprawl / development 城市扩张

例句 *Urban* development has led to the ruination of vast areas of countryside. 城市发展导致大片的乡村遭到毁坏。

派生 urbanized *adj.* 城市化的

释义 *v.* 违背；侵犯；亵渎（圣物）

短语 *violate* the law 触犯法律

例句 Those who *violate* traffic regulations should be punished. 那些违反交通规则的人应该受到惩罚。

真题 The court has ruled that police don't *violate* the *Fourth Amendment* when they go through the wallet or pocketbook of an arrestee without a warrant. 法院裁定，警察在没有搜查令的情况下搜查被捕者的钱包或皮夹不违反《第四修正案》。（2015 阅读理解）

派生 violation *n.* 违背，违反

释义 *adj.* 焦虑的；渴望的

例句 There was an *anxious* moment when the plane suddenly dropped. 飞机突然下降时，人们感到一阵焦虑。

I'm *anxious* to get home to open my presents. 我恨不得马上到家去拆开礼物。

派生 anxiety *n.* 焦虑

释义 *adv.* 相距；分开地；成碎片 *adj.* 分离的

例句 He saw Jack standing some distance *apart*. 他看见杰克站在一段距离之外。

Their concept of a performance and our concept were miles *apart*. 他们对表演的看法和我们的截然不同。

用法 apart from 除……之外

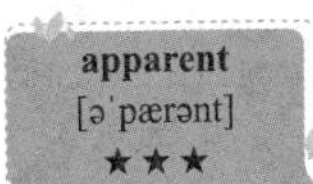

释义 *adj.* 显而易见的；易懂的；表面上的

例句 Her happiness was *apparent* to everyone. 谁都看得出来她很开心。

近义 obvious *adj.* 明显的

派生 apparently *adv.* 显然

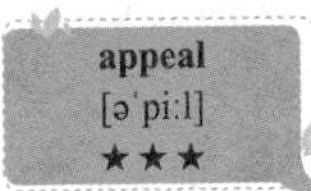

释义 *v.* 呼吁，求助；上诉；对……有吸引力 *n.* 上诉；吸引力；呼吁

例句 Police are *appealing* to women not to go out alone at night. 警方呼吁女性在晚上不要单独外出。

It's a programme designed to *appeal* mainly to 16 to 25 years old. 这个节目的目标观众主要是 16 到 25 岁的年轻人。

The fire service has made an urgent *appeal* for more part-time firefighters. 消防部门紧急呼吁增加兼职消防员。

真题 A federal *appeals* court weighed in again Tuesday. 星期二，一家联邦上诉法院再次介入。（2021 阅读理解）

派生 appealing *adj.* 吸引人的

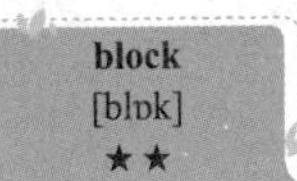

释义 *v.* 阻塞，拦阻 *n.* 街区；大块，一块；大楼；障碍物

例句 The ambulance was *blocked* by cars in the road. 救护车被路上的汽车挡住了。

The museum is just six *blocks* away. 博物馆离这儿只有 6 条街。

派生 blockade *n.* 封锁；阻塞

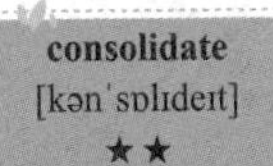

释义 *v.* 使加固；合并

例句 The success of their major product *consolidated* the firm's position in the market. 该公司主打产品取得的成功巩固了该公司在市场上的地位。

派生 consolidation *n.* 巩固

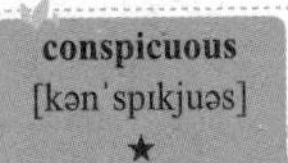

释义 *adj.* 显眼的，明显的

例句 When it came to cleaning up afterwards, Anne was conspicuous by her absence. 后来到做扫除时，本应在场的安妮却因为不在而引起了注意。

同义 obvious *adj.* 明显的

派生 conspicuously *adv.* 显著地，明显

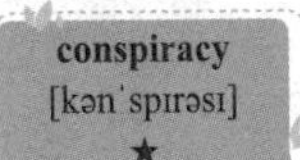

释义 *n.* 阴谋，密谋，共谋

例句 Knowing that hiding is not the answer, Matthew decides to go out into the open and reveal the *conspiracy* to the public. 马修知道藏匿并不能解决问题，于是他决定公开向公众揭露这个阴谋。

用法 reveal one's conspiracy 揭露某人的阴谋

constant
[ˈkɒnstənt]
★★★

释义 *adj.* 固定的;持续不断的;忠实的 *n.* 常数,恒量

用法 *constant* pressure 恒压

例句 The temperature remained *constant* while pressure was a variable in the experiment. 做这实验时温度保持不变,但压力可变。

The dynamic of the market demands *constant* change and adjustment. 市场要有活力,需要不断地去改变和调整。

派生 constantly *adv.* 经常地,不断地

constituent
[kənˈstɪtʃuənt]
★★

释义 *n.* 选民;成分 *adj.* 组成的

短语 the EU and its *constituent* members 欧盟及其成员国

例句 Hydrogen and oxygen are the *constituents* of water. 氢和氧是水的主要成分。

discern
[dɪˈsɜːn]
★★

释义 *v.* 认出,发现;辨别,识别

例句 You need a long series of data to be able to *discern* such a trend. 你需要一长串的数据来认清这种趋势。

近义 recognize *v.* 认识

释义 *n.* 纪律,学科;训练 *v.* 训练,管教

短语 academic *discipline* 学术科目

例句 They acted against the *discipline* of their school. 他们违反了学校的纪律。

Yoga is a good *discipline* for learning to relax. 瑜伽是一种学习放松的有效方法。

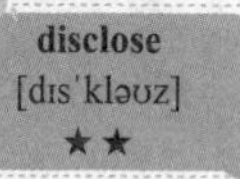

释义 *v.* 揭示,泄露

例句 Most of the people interviewed requested that their identity not be *disclosed*. 大多数受访者要求不透露他们的身份。

近义 reveal *v.* 揭示,透露

派生 disclosure *n.* 披露

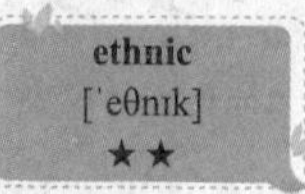

释义 *adj.* 种族的;少数民族的 *n.* 少数民族成员

例句 This music would sound more *ethnic* if it was played on the Erhu. 如果用二胡演奏,这首曲子听起来会更有民族特色。

派生 ethnicity *n.* 种族渊源,种族特点

释义 *v.* 逃避,回避,躲避

短语 *evade* capture 逃脱抓捕

例句 She is trying to *evade* all responsibility for her behaviour. 她在试图逃避应为自己的行为承担的所有责任。

近义 escape *v.* 逃避

派生 evasion *n.* 逃脱,躲避

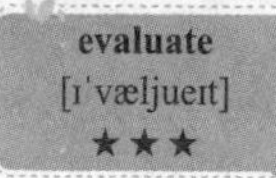

释义 *v.* 估价,评价;估值

例句 It's impossible to *evaluate* these results without knowing more about the research methods employed. 如不能对使用的研究方法有更多了解,就无法对其

结果做出评价。

派生 evaluation *n.* 评估

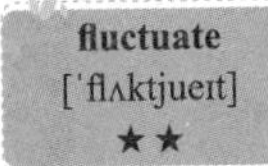

释义 *v.*（使）波动；（使）起伏

例句 Scientists believe that intelligence can expand and *fluctuate* according to mental effort. 科学家们认为，智力可以随着脑力的训练而提升和波动。

派生 fluctuation *n.* 波动

释义 *adj.* 毕业了的，研究生的 *n.* 大学毕业生 *v.*（从……）大学毕业

短语 *graduate* student / school 研究生 / 研究所

例句 *Graduates* from our school are working all over the country. 我们学校的毕业生在全国各地工作。

The university *graduated* 1,600 students last year. 该大学去年有 1,600 位学生毕业。

派生 graduation *n.* 毕业；毕业典礼

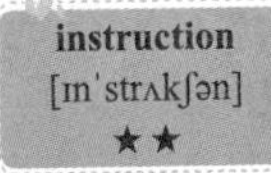

释义 *n.* 教授，指导；(*pl.*) 说明（书）

例句 Please follow the *instructions* on the packet when you take the drug. 吃药时请你按照包装上的说明去服用。

派生 instructional *adj.* 教学的；指导的

释义 *n.* 保险，保险费，保险业

例句 Club members enjoy free travel *insurance* for any flight. 俱乐部会员可享受任何航班的免费旅行保险。

真题 That's likely because the rural poor are using the money as makeshift *insurance* policies against inclement weather, Ferraro says. 费拉罗说，这很可能是因为农村穷人把这笔钱用作应对恶劣天气的临时保险策略。（2021 阅读理解）

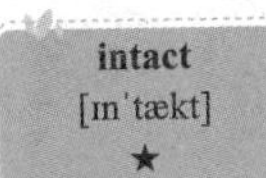

释义 *adj.* 完整无缺的；原封不动的

例句 This is the only example portraying a Roman Emperor which has survived *intact* from such an early age. 这是唯一一个从如此早期完整保存下来的罗马皇帝的画像。

派生 intactness *n.* 完整无缺

释义 *adj.* 文学的；书面的

例句 Camus is considered to be one of the twentieth century's *literary* giants. 加缪被视为 20 世纪的文学巨匠之一。

真题 Plays aiming at *literary* distinction were written for school or court, or for the choir boys of St.Paul's and the royal chapel. 旨在突出文学特色的戏剧是为学校或宫廷，或为圣保罗和皇家教堂的唱诗班男孩创作的。（2018 翻译）

派生 literature *n.* 文学

释义 *v.* 更改，修改，修饰

例句 Furthermore, humans have the ability to *modify* the environment in which they live, thus subjecting all other life forms to their own peculiar ideas and fancies. 而且，人类还有能力改变自己的生存环境，而使所有其他生命形态服从于人类自己独特的想法和想象。

派生 modified *adj.* 改良的

近义 adjust *v.* 调整

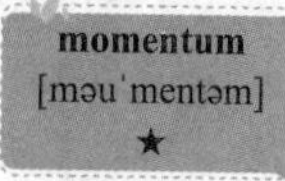

释义 *n.* 动力，要素

短语 *momentum* conservation 动量守恒

例句 Once you push it, it keeps going under its own *momentum*. 一旦你推动了它，它就会在自己的动力作用下持续运动。

近义 impetus *n.* 动力

释义 *n.* 帝王，君主

短语 *monarch* butterfly 帝王蝶

例句 It is this apparent transcendence of politics that explains *monarchs'* continuing popularity as heads of state. 正是这种明显超越政治的地位，解释了君主作为国家首脑将继续受到欢迎的原因。

派生 monarchy *n.* 君主制

释义 *n.* 管弦乐队

短语 symphony *orchestra* 交响乐团

例句 It's the first performance of the State Symphony *Orchestra* in our city, so suit and tie is a must. 这是国家交响乐团在我们市的首场演出，所以穿西装、打领带是必须的。

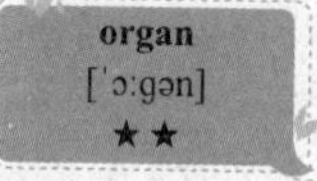

释义 *n.* 器官；风琴；机构

短语 sense *organ* 感觉器官 administrative *organ* 行政机关

例句 He played a beautiful tune on the *organ*. 他用风琴演奏出一支动听的曲子。There are many *organs* in a man's body. 人体中有很多器官。

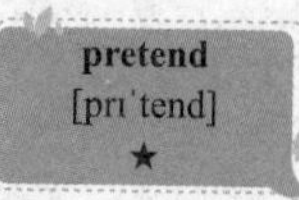

释义 *v.* 假装，借口

例句 Frank tried to *pretend* that nothing unusual had happened. 弗兰克试图假装没有什么不寻常的事情发生。

用法 pretend to do sth. 假装做某事

派生 pretension *n.* 借口

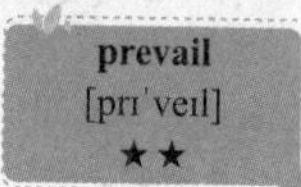

释义 *v.* 取胜，占优势；流行，盛行

例句 If you are at home trying to decide where to go for dinner, however, the knowledge component may *prevail*, and you decide to go where you can eat a healthier meal. 然而，如果你在家试图决定去哪里吃饭，知识因素可能会占上风，你决定去一个可以吃到更健康的饭菜的地方。

用法 prevail over 胜过；占优势

派生 prevailing *adj.* 盛行的

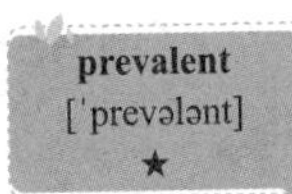

释义 *adj.* 流行的，普遍的

短语 a *prevalent* view 普遍的观点

例句 The tendency to believe that "you are what you buy" is especially *prevalent* among young people. 相信"购物体现品位"的倾向在年轻人中尤其普遍。

派生 prevalence *n.* 普遍

释义 *v.* 预防，阻止，妨碍

例句 Taking a gap year to figure things out initially can help *prevent* stress and save money later on. 在间隔年一开始就把事情弄清楚可以帮助你避免压力，也可以为以后省钱。

真题 Britain's towns, it is true, are not *prevented* from applying, but they generally lack the resources to put together a bid to beat their bigger competitors. 诚然，英国的城镇并没有被阻止申请，但它们普遍缺乏资源来联合竞标击败更大的竞争对手。（2020 阅读理解）

用法 prevent from doing sth. 阻止做某事

近义 stop *v.* 结束；阻拦

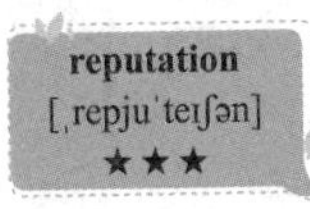

释义 *n.* 名誉，名声，声望

短语 have a good / bad *reputation* 有好 / 坏名声

例句 This college has a good academic *reputation*. 这所大学有良好的学术声誉。

真题 It is only the Queen who has preserved the monarchy's *reputation* with her rather ordinary (if well-heeled) granny style. 只有女王以她相当普通（虽然穿着考究）的奶奶式风格维护了王室的声誉。（2015 阅读理解）

释义 *v./ n.* 请求，要求

短语 service *request* 服务请求

例句 Researchers have found that nearly half of the social networking sites don't immediately delete pictures when a user *requests* they be removed. 研究人员发现，近一半的社交网站不会在用户请求删除照片时立即将其删除。

用法 at one's request 依照某人的请求

释义 *v.* 需要；要求，命令

例句 Such policies would *require* unprecedented cooperation between nations. 这样的政策会要求国家间进行史无前例的合作。

真题 If the bills become law, state boards and commissions will be *required* to set aside 50 percent of board seats for women by 2022. 如果这些法案成为法律，到 2022 年，州董事会和委员会将被要求为女性预留 50% 的董事会席位。（2020 阅读理解）

派生 requirement *n.* 需要，需要的东西

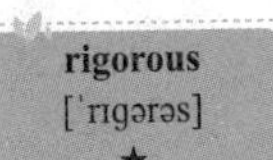

释义 *adj.* 严格，严密的，严谨的

短语 *rigorous* standards 严格的标准

例句 By most measures, corporate governance has become a lot tighter and more *rigorous* since the 1970s. 从大多数标准来看，自 20 世纪 70 年代以来，公司治理已经变得更加严格。

近义 strict *adj.* 严格的

stretch
[stretʃ]
★

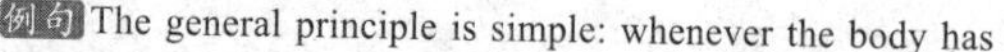

释义 *v.* 伸展，延伸 *n.* 拉长；伸展；一段时间 / 路程 *adj.* 有弹力的

短语 *stretch* fabrics 弹性织布

例句 The general principle is simple: whenever the body has been in one position for a while, it is good to briefly *stretch* it in an opposite position. 基本原理很简单：当身体处于一个姿势一段时间后，最好以相反的姿势进行短暂的拉伸。

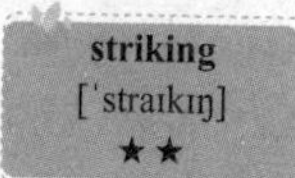

striking
[ˈstraɪkɪŋ]
★★

释义 *adj.* 显著的；惹人注目的，容貌出众的

短语 *striking* contrast 显著对比

例句 There's a *striking* contrast between what he does and what he says. 他的所作所为和他所说的大相径庭。

近义 noticeable *adj.* 显而易见的，明显的

派生 strikingness *n.* 惊人；显著

strive
[straɪv]
★★

释义 *v.* 奋斗，努力

短语 *strive* for freedom 力争自由 strive against 反抗

例句 Tony has been *striving* to achieve musical recognition for the past ten years. 在过去的十年里，托尼一直在努力获得音乐上的认可。

近义 exert *v.* 努力，尽力

用法 strive to do 努力做

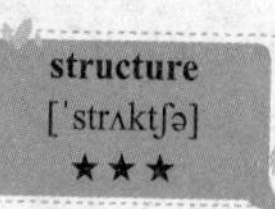

structure
[ˈstrʌktʃə]
★★★

释义 *n.* 结构，构造；建筑物 *v.* 构造，建造

短语 industrial *structure* 产业结构

例句 About half of those funds has gone to repair public roads, *structures* and bridges. 大约一半的资金被用于修复公共道路、建筑和桥梁。

近义 construction *n.* 建造，建筑

派生 structured *adj.* 有结构的；有组织的

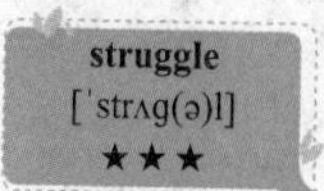

struggle
[ˈstrʌg(ə)l]
★★★

释义 *n.* / *v.* 斗争，奋斗，努力

短语 a *struggle* for survival 为生存而斗争

例句 Her husband lost his job so it would be a *struggle* to pay the rent. 她丈夫失业了，所以现在房租也难以负担得起。

真题 The court's ruling is a step forward in the *struggle* against both corruption and official favoritism. 最高法院的裁决是在打击腐败和官员偏袒的斗争中向前迈出的一步。（2017 阅读理解）

用法 struggle against 与……做斗争

近义 fight *v.* 与……做斗争

suspicious
[səˈspɪʃəs]
★★

释义 可疑的，多疑的，疑心的

短语 a *suspicious* look 怀疑的神情

例句 We were instructed to report any *suspicious* activity in the neighborhood. 我们接到指示要报告附近任何可疑的活动。

近义 distrustful *adj.* 怀疑的

派生 suspicion *n.* 怀疑；猜想

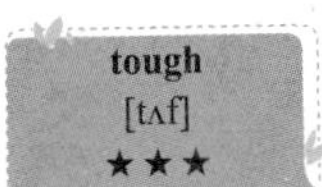

释义 *adj.* 坚韧的；强硬的；难熬的

短语 *tough* luck 坏运气

例句 Sometimes it is easy to feel bad because you are going through *tough* times. 有时很容易感到难过，因为你正在经历艰难的时期。

近义 hardy *adj.* 坚强的

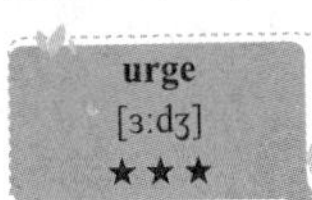

释义 *v.* 催促；怂恿 *n.* 强烈欲望，迫切要求

例句 He had an *urge* to open a shop of his own. 他很想自己开一家店。

Experts *urged* the public to receive seasonal flu *vaccines*. 专家呼吁公众接种季节性流感疫苗。

派生 urger *n.* 推进者

释义 *n.* 猛烈，强烈；暴力，暴行

短语 physical *violence* 肢体暴力

例句 The kinds of interpersonal *violence* that women are exposed to tend to be in domestic situations. 女性遭遇的人际关系的暴力往往来自家庭内部。

用法 violence against sb. 对某人施加暴行

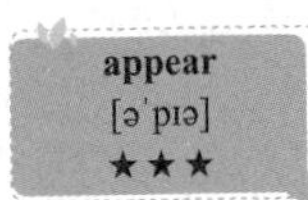

释义 *v.* 出现；显现；似乎

例句 The sun began to *appear* from behind the clouds. 太阳开始从云层后面露出来了。

Jason didn't *appear* surprised at the news. 杰森听到这消息时一点也没有显得吃惊。

派生 appearance *n.* 出现；外貌

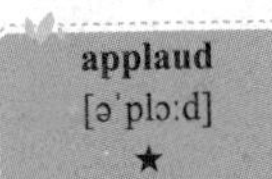

释义 *v.* 鼓掌；称赞；赞成

例句 A crowd of 300 supporters warmly *applauded* her speech. 300 名支持者为她的演讲热烈鼓掌。

I *applaud* their efforts to clean up the city. 我赞赏他们为净化城市所做的努力。

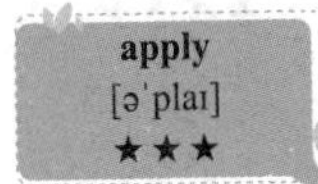

释义 *v.* 申请；适用；应用；涂，敷

例句 I *applied* to four universities and was accepted by all of them. 我申请了四所大学，并且都被录取了。

These ideas are often difficult to *apply* in practice. 这些想法通常很难付诸实践。

真题 The potential of this work *applied* to healthcare is very great, but it could also lead to further concentration of power in the tech giants. 这个成果应用到医疗保健方面的潜力是非常大的，但是它也会导致权力进一步集中于科技巨头手中。（2018 阅读理解）

派生 application *n.* 申请；应用程序

applicable [ə'plɪkəb(ə)l] ★★

释义 *adj.* 适用的

例句 This part of the law is *applicable* to all public and private companies in the EU. 这部分法律适用于欧盟的所有公共和私营公司。

用法 if applicable 如果适用；若可以

近义 suitable *adj.* 合适的

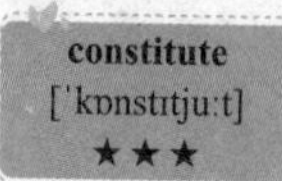

bloom [bluːm] ★

释义 *v.* 开花；繁荣 *n.* 花朵；花期

例句 The apple trees are in full *bloom*. 苹果树开满了花。

These flowers will *bloom* all through the summer. 这些花会绽放整个夏天。

用法 in full bloom 盛开

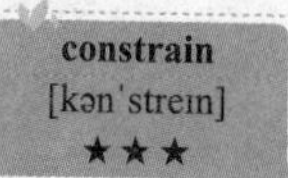

constitute ['kɒnstɪtjuːt] ★★★

释义 *v.* 组成，构成；设立

例句 Volunteers *constitute* more than 95% of the Center's work force. 志愿者占中心工作人员的95%以上。

派生 constitution *n.* 构成；宪法

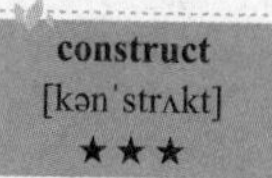

constrain [kən'streɪn] ★★★

释义 *v.* 限制；抑制

例句 Women's employment opportunities are often severely *constrained* by family commitments. 妇女的就业机会往往严重受限于家庭责任。

派生 constraint *n.* 限制

construct [kən'strʌkt] ★★★

释义 *v.* 建设；创立，建立

例句 The house was *constructed* out of wood. 这幢房子是用木头建造的。

He has *constructed* a new theory. 他建立了一种新理论。

派生 construction *n.* 建造，建筑；创立

consult [kən'sʌlt] ★★★

释义 *v.* 咨询，商量，商议

例句 He made the decision to quit his job without *consulting* his parents. 他没有和父母商量就决定辞职了。

派生 consultant *n.* 顾问

consume [kən'sjuːm] ★★★

释义 *v.* 消耗；吃；消费

例句 Some energy-efficient air conditioners *consume* 50 percent less electricity than traditional models. 一些节能空调比传统空调耗电量少50%。

Classically, overweight people underestimate the volume of food that they *consume*. 一般来说，超重的人往往低估自己摄入食物的量。

派生 consumer *n.* 消费者

discourse ['dɪskɔːs] ★★

释义 *n.* 论文；演说；谈话 *v.* 讲述，著述

例句 He *discoursed* for several hours on French and English prose. 他就法国和英国散文谈了几个小时。

He likes to engage in lively *discourse* with his visitors. 他喜欢与访客进行生动的交谈。

释义 v. 发现，显示

例句 Several new species of plants have recently been *discovered*. 最近发现了几种新的植物。

真题 The first published sketch, *A Dinner at Poplar Walk* brought tears to Dickens's eyes when he *discovered* it in the pages of *The Monthly Magazine*. 狄更斯在《每月杂志》上发现了他发表的第一篇随笔《白杨庄晚宴》，不禁潸然泪下。（2017 阅读理解）

派生 discovery *n.* 发现

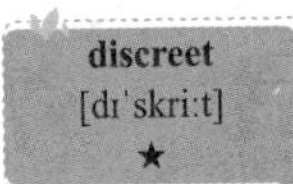

释义 *adj.*（言行）谨慎的；慎重的；不引人注意的

例句 They were very *discreet* and professional at the office. 他们在办公室很低调而且很专业。

派生 discreetly *adv.* 谨慎地

释义 *n.* 明显，显著；证据；迹象 *v.* 证明

例句 There is a lot of *evidence* that stress is partly responsible for disease. 有很多证据证明压力是造成疾病的原因之一。

真题 People have been surprised to see *evidence* that Victorians had fun and could, and did, laugh. 人们惊讶地发现，有证据表明，维多利亚时代的人也有自己的乐趣，会笑，也确实笑过。（2021 阅读理解）

用法 in evidence 明显的，显而易见的

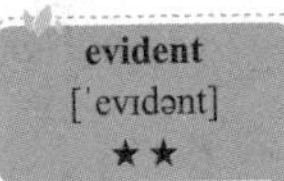

释义 *adj.* 明显的，明白的

例句 By 1952, it was *evident* that television would replace radio as the major entertainment medium. 到 1952 年，很明显，电视将取代广播成为主要的娱乐媒介。

近义 clear *adj.* 明显的

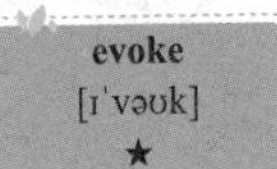

释义 v. 唤起；引起；产生

例句 David hardly needed any encouragement to get involved in volunteer work, since it *evoked* for him the happiest memories. 大卫参与志愿者工作几乎不需要任何鼓励，因为这唤起了他最快乐的回忆。

用法 *evoke* one's memory 唤起某人的记忆

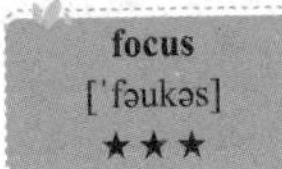

释义 *n.* 焦点，（活动，兴趣等的）中心 *v.* 使聚集

例句 Today, the social sciences are largely *focused* on disciplinary problems and internal scholarly debates. 今天，社会科学主要集中于学科问题和内部学术辩论。

用法 be in focus 保持专注

out of focus 焦点没对准的；模糊不清的

释义 v. 准许；给予；承认 *n.* 补助金

短语 research *grant* 研究补助

例句 They'd got a special *grant* to encourage research. 他们已得到了一笔用来支持研究的特别补助金。

The mayor refused to *grant* my request for an interview. 市长拒绝了我的采访请求。

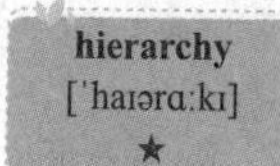

释义 *n.* 等级制度；统治集团；层次

短语 social *hierarchy* 社会等级；社会阶层

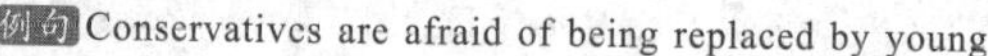

例句 Conservatives are afraid of being replaced by young people in America's social *hierarchy*. 保守派害怕被美国社会阶层中的年轻人取代。

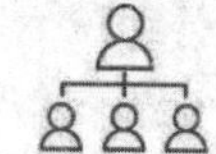

派生 hierarchical *adj.* 等级制度的

释义 *v.* 保险，给……保险；保证

例句 It is wise to *insure* your property against storm damage. 为你的财产投保风暴损失险是明智的。

派生 insurance *n.* 保险

释义 *adj.* 构成整体所必需的；完整的

短语 an *integral* system 完整的系统

例句 Music has been an *integral* part of his life since childhood, especially singing. 音乐是他从小生活中不可分割的一部分，尤其是唱歌。

派生 integrally *adv.* 完整地

释义 *n.* 知识分子 *adj.* 智力的，理智的

短语 an *intellectual* elite 知识精英

例句 Looking after a baby at home all day is nice but it doesn't provide much *intellectual* stimulation. 整天在家照看婴儿虽然不错，但让人不怎么动脑子。

释义 *n.* 记者，新闻工作者

短语 a political *journalist* 政治记者

例句 He moved to England in 1980 where, among other things, he worked as a *journalist*. 他 1980 年移居英格兰，期间从事过包括记者在内的很多工作。

释义 *n.* 文学，文学作品；文献

短语 *literature* review 文献回顾

例句 The girls were given a well-rounded education in science, *literature*, language, and history. 这些女孩们接受了科学、文学、语言和历史的全面教育。

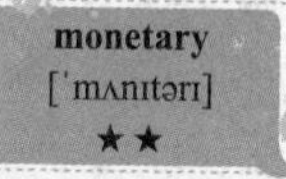

释义 *adj.* 金融的，货币的

例句 Some countries tighten *monetary* policy to avoid inflation. 一些国家收紧货币政策以避免通货膨胀。

真题 Scientists need journals in which to publish their research, so they will supply the articles without *monetary* reward. 科学家们需要在期刊上发表他们的研究成果，所以他们愿意无偿提供论文。（2020 阅读理解）

释义 *n.* 垄断，垄断企业

例句 A good education should not be the *monopoly* of the rich. 良好的教育不应该成为富人的专利。

真题 What matters is that they will belong to a private *monopoly* which developed them using public resources. 重要的是，它们属于一家利用公共资源进行开发的私营垄断企业。（2018 阅读理解）

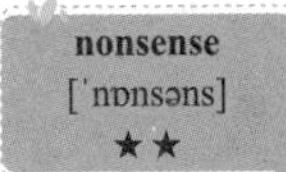

nonsense [ˈnɒnsəns] ★★

释义 *n.* 胡说；废话；愚蠢的行为；无聊的事物

短语 talk *nonsense* 胡说八道

例句 I understood so few of the words they were using that the conversation sounded like *nonsense* to me. 他们说的话我几乎听不懂，这段谈话对我来说听起来像是无稽之谈。

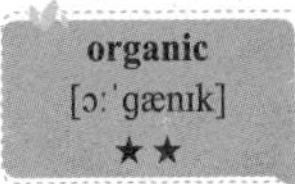

organic [ɔːˈɡænɪk] ★★

释义 *adj.* 器官的；器质性的；有机（体）的，有机物的

短语 *organic* food 有机食品

例句 There's also a farm shop selling eggs, *organic* vegetables and other locally produced food. 这里还有一家农家商店，出售鸡蛋、有机蔬菜和当地生产的其他食品。

派生 organically *adv.* 有机地

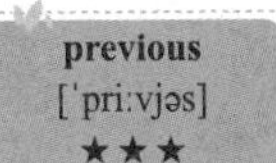

previous [ˈpriːvjəs] ★★★

释义 *adj.* 先前的，以前的

短语 *previous* study / research 以前的研究

例句 The majority of *previous* research has focused on how we learn and remember new information. 之前的大部分研究都集中在我们如何学习和记忆新信息上。

派生 previously *adv.* 先前地；在以前

prey [preɪ] ★★

释义 *n.* 猎物，掠食 *v.* 捕食，掠夺

短语 easy prey 容易捕获的猎物；头脑简单的人

例句 When a predator always eats huge numbers of a single *prey*, the two species are strongly linked. 当一种掠食动物一直大量吃单一猎物时，这两个物种就是紧密相连的。

用法 be the prey of sth. 被……捕食；成为……的猎物

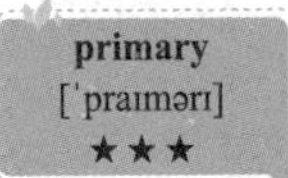

primary [ˈpraɪmərɪ] ★★★

释义 *adj.* 最初的，初级的；首要的

短语 *primary* purpose 主要目的

例句 The primary aim of this course is to improve your spoken English. 这门课的主要目的是提高你的英语会话能力。

派生 primarily *adv.* 主要地；根本地

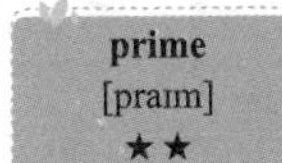

prime [praɪm] ★★

释义 *adj.* 首要的；第一流的；基础的 *n.* 青春，全盛期 *v.* 做准备

短语 *prime* time 黄金时间

例句 Maths is no longer a *prime* requirement for a career in accountancy. 数学不再是从事会计工作的首要条件。

派生 primary *adj.* 主要的，首要的

pursue [pəˈsjuː] ★★

释义 *v.* 追赶，追踪；继续，从事

例句 She returned to London to *pursue* her acting career. 她返回伦敦去从事她的表演事业。

近义 seek *v.* 寻找；寻求

派生 pursuit *n.* 追求

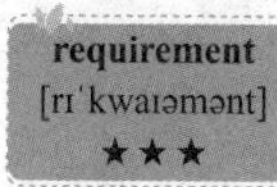

requirement
[rɪˈkwaɪəmənt]
★★★

释义 *n.* 需要，需要的东西；要求

短语 design / technical *requirement* 设计 / 技术需求

例句 Our immediate *requirement* is extra staff. 我们亟须增加人手。

真题 Keeping sensitive information on these devices is increasingly a *requirement* of normal life. 在这些设备上保存敏感信息越来越成为日常生活的一项要求。（2015 阅读理解）

rescue
[ˈreskjuː]
★★

释义 *v.* / *n.* 营救，援救

短语 a *rescue* mission 营救任务　*rescue* operation 救护工作

例句 A *rescue* operation involving the navy has been ongoing. 海军参与的救援行动正在进行中。

They were eventually *rescued* by helicopter. 他们最后被直升机救走了。

派生 rescuer *n.* 救助者

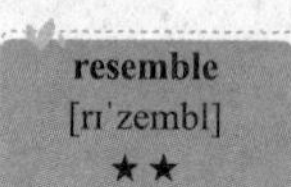

resemble
[rɪˈzembl]
★★

释义 *v.* 像，类似

短语 *resemble* closely 极像

例句 He strongly *resembles* his father in appearance and in temperament. 他在外貌和气质上都很像他的父亲。

真题 In some ways, the scientific publishing model *resembles* the economy of the social internet. 在某些方面，科学杂志的出版模式类似于社交媒体的经济。（2020 阅读理解）

派生 resemblance *n.* 相似

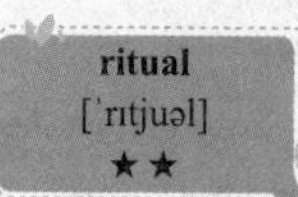

ritual
[ˈrɪtjuəl]
★★

释义 *adj.* 宗教仪式的，典礼的；常规的 *n.*（宗教）仪式；习惯

短语 *ritual* dance 仪式之舞；祭祀之舞

例句 They also focused on important *rituals* that appeared to preserve a people's social structure. 他们还关注那些似乎能保存一个民族社会结构的重要仪式。

近义 rite *n.*（宗教等的）仪式；礼节，惯例

sturdy
[ˈstɜːdɪ]
★

释义 *adj.* 坚定的，不屈不挠的；强健的，结实的

短语 a *sturdy* table 结实的桌子

例句 Due to its *sturdy* structure, it is especially well-suited for outdoor use. 由于其坚固的结构，它特别适合户外使用。

近义 durable *adj.* 耐用的

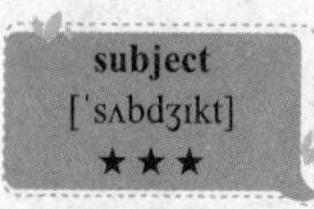

subject
[ˈsʌbdʒɪkt]
★★★

释义 *n.* 主题；学科；实验对象 *adj.* 隶属的；易遭……的 *v.* 使经受；遭受；使臣服

短语 *subject* matter 主题

例句 Flights are *subject* to delay because of the fog. 由于有雾，航班可能延误。

"White noise" was played into the *subject's* ears through headphones. 研究人员通过耳机让受试者听"白噪声"。

派生 subjective *adj.* 主观（上）的

submit
[səbˈmɪt]
★★

释义 *v.* 使服从，屈服；送，提交

短语 *submit* applications 提交申请

例句 When he *submitted* his papers in 1905, Einstein was little known in academic circles. 当他在 1905 年提交论文时，爱因斯坦在学术圈中还鲜为人知。

She refused to *submit* to threats. 她面对威胁，拒不低头。

近义 surrender *v.* 屈服

派生 submission *n.* 提交；屈服

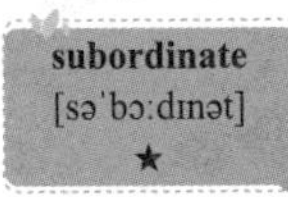

subordinate [səˈbɔːdɪnət] ★

释义 *adj.* 次要的，从属的；下级的

短语 *subordinate* staff 下属人员

例句 Modern women do not consider themselves *subordinate* to man, because they have been able to get success in almost all the departments of life. 现代女性不认为自己是男人的附属，因为她们几乎在生活的各个方面都取得了成功。

派生 subordination *n.* 从属

toxic [ˈtɒksɪk] ★★

释义 *adj.* 有毒的；中毒的

短语 *toxic* gases 毒气

例句 Up to 10 million tonnes of *toxic* wastes are produced every year in the UK. 英国每年会产生多达 1000 万吨的有毒废弃物。

近义 poisonous *adj.* 有毒的

派生 toxicity *n.* 毒性

urgent [ˈɜːdʒənt] ★★

释义 急迫的，紧要的，紧急的

短语 *urgent* need 迫切需要

例句 Mr. Smith is seeing people all morning, but if the matter is *urgent*, I'll see if I can crowd you in. 整个上午史密斯先生都在接待来客，但如果你的事情紧急，我就看看能不能为你安排一下会面。

派生 urgency *n.* 紧急

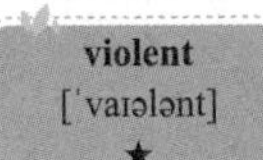

violent [ˈvaɪələnt] ★

释义 暴力的；猛烈的，强烈的

短语 *violent* storm / earthquake 暴风 / 大地震

例句 There isn't much *violent* crime in a small town like Green Ville, or at least not as much as in the large urban areas. 像格林维尔这样的小镇没有太多的暴力犯罪，或者至少没有大城市那么多。

派生 violence *n.* 暴力

Word List 29

applicant [ˈæplɪkənt] ★★★

释义 *n.* 申请人

例句 In my estimation, the *applicant* is well qualified for this job. 据我看，这位应征者很适合这份工作。

近义 candidate *n.* 候选人，申请者

派生 application *n.* 正式申请；应用

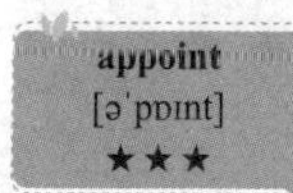

释义 *v.* 指定；任命；约定

例句 She was *appointed* a U.S. delegate to the United Nations. 她被任命为美国驻联合国代表。

A date has been *appointed* for the election. 选举日期已定。

派生 appointment *n.* 预约

释义 *v.* 欣赏；感激；理解；增值

例句 I *appreciate* your kindness. 非常感激你关心。

Anyone can *appreciate* our music. 任何人都能欣赏我们的音乐。

He did not fully *appreciate* the importance of responsibility. 他没有充分认识到责任的重要性。

派生 appreciation *n.* 欣赏；感激

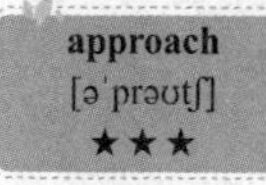

释义 *v.* 靠近；接近；n. 方法；途径；靠近

例句 The cat *approached* the baby cautiously. 猫小心翼翼地靠近婴儿。

Many kinds of birds fly south at the *approach* of winter. 很多鸟在冬天来临之际飞向南方。

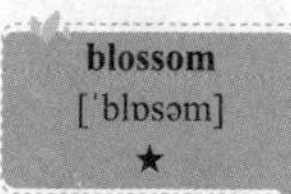

释义 *v.* 开花；兴旺 *n.* 花；兴旺期

例句 The cherry *blossom* came out early in Washington this year. 今年华盛顿的樱花开得早。

The peach tree is beginning to *blossom*. 桃树开始开花了。

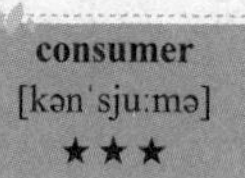

释义 *n.* 消费者，用户

短语 a *consumer* era 消费时代

例句 Low *consumer* demand has forced us to mark down a wide range of goods, sometimes by as much as 30%. 消费者需求低迷迫使我们对很多商品降价，有时降价幅度高达 30%。

释义 *v./n.*（使）接触，联系

例句 The two tribes have had little *contact*, but this is beginning to change. 这两个部落几乎没有接触，但这种情况正在开始改变。

Contact the Tourist Information Bureau for further details. 如欲查询更多详情，请与旅游资讯局联络。

用法 have contact with 和……有联系

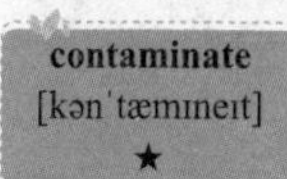

释义 *v.* 弄脏；污染；毒害

例句 The food was *contaminated* during the production process. 食品在生产过程中被污染了。

派生 contamination *n.* 污染

释义 *v.* 深思熟虑；打算；凝视

短语 *contemplate* your future 考虑你的未来

例句 She stood and quietly *contemplated* the scene that lay before her. 她站在那里，静静地注视着眼前的情景。

派生 contemplation *n.* 沉思

近义 consider *v.* 考虑

contempt
[kən'tempt]
★★★

释义 *n.* 轻视，藐视；忽视

例句 I feel nothing but *contempt* for people who are obsessed with fast cars and designer clothes. 我对那些迷恋跑车和名牌服装的人只有鄙视。

用法 a contempt for sb. 对某人的轻视

派生 contemptuous *adj.* 轻蔑的，鄙视的

discriminate
[dɪ'skrɪmɪneɪt]
★★

释义 *v.* 区别，辨别；有差别地对待；歧视

例句 Employers are not allowed to *discriminate* on the basis of gender. 雇主不允许有性别歧视。

同义 distinguish *v.* 使有别于

派生 discrimination *n.* 区别对待

discuss
[dɪ'skʌs]
★★★

释义 *v.* 讨论，商议

例句 Small study groups allow people to interact, *discuss* and ask questions, which improves learning efficiency significantly. 小型学习小组允许人们互动、讨论和提问，这大大提高了学习效率。

用法 discuss with 商洽；与……谈论

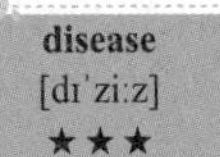

disease
[dɪ'zi:z]
★★★

释义 *n.* 疾病

短语 skin *disease* 皮肤病 occupational *disease* 职业病

例句 Patients with heart *disease*, diabetes and other chronic conditions are at greater risk of dying from COVID-19. 心脏病、糖尿病和其他慢性疾病患者死于新冠病毒感染的风险更大。

evolution
[ˌi:və'lu:ʃ(ə)n]
★★★

释义 *n.* 进化，演变，发展

短语 theory of *evolution* 进化论

例句 In his work, he attempted to show how all aspects of culture changed together in the *evolution* of societies. 在他的作品中，他试图展示文化的各个方面是如何在社会的演变中变化的。

exaggerate
[ɪg'zædʒəreɪt]
★★★

释义 *v.* 夸大，夸张

例句 He has *exaggerated* the whole event to make it sound rather more dramatic than it actually was. 他夸大了整个事件，使其听起来比实际情况更具有戏剧性。

派生 exaggeration *n.* 夸张

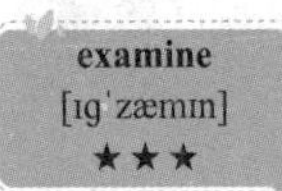

examine
[ɪg'zæmɪn]
★★★

释义 *v.* 检查，调查；测验

例句 We need to *examine* how an accident like this can be avoided in the future. 我们需要研究将来如何能避免类似的事故再次发生。

用法 examine sb. on sth. 在某事上考验某人

近义 inspect *v.* 检查

follow
['fɒləu]
★★★

释义 *v.* 跟随；接着；沿着；遵循

例句 Potatoes are still the most popular food, *followed* by white bread. 土豆仍然是最受欢迎的食品，其次为白面包。

Take care to *follow* the instructions carefully. 注意严格按照说明进行。

用法 followed by sth. 接下来是……;之后是……

真题 If you get lost without a phone or a compass, we have a few tricks to help you navigate back to civilization, one of which is to *follow* the land. 如果你在没有手机或指南针的情况下迷路了,我们有一些技巧可以帮助你导航回到文明世界,其中之一就是沿着陆地走。(2019 完形填空)

释义 *v.* 抓住;理解,领会 *n.* 抓住;理解

例句 She felt a firm *grasp* on her arm. 她感到手臂被紧紧地抓住了。

I could not *grasp* her meaning. 我不懂她的意思。

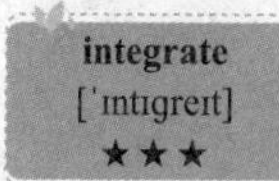

释义 *v.* (使)成为一体,(使)结合在一起

例句 Supporters of the theory viewed culture as a collection of *integrated* parts that work together to keep a society functioning. 该理论的支持者将文化视为一系列综合部分的集合,这些部分共同作用以保持社会的运转。

派生 integration *n.* 结合,融合

用法 integrate with / into sth. 融入……

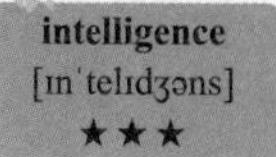

释义 *n.* 智力;理解力;情报,消息

短语 *intelligence* agency 情报局

例句 She seemed to have everything — looks, money, *intelligence*. 她似乎什么都有——美貌、金钱和智慧。

真题 In the movies and on television, artificial *intelligence* (AI) is typically depicted as something sinister that will upend our way of life. 在电影和电视中,人工智能通常被描绘成一种邪恶的东西,它将颠覆我们的生活方式。(2021 阅读理解)

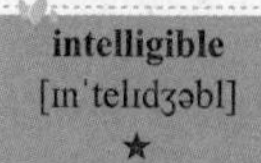

释义 *adj.* 可理解的,明白易懂的,清楚的

例句 She was so upset when she spoke that she was hardly *intelligible*. 她讲话时心烦意乱,导致她的话几乎让人无法理解。

近义 comprehensible *adj.* 可理解的

反义 unintelligible *adj.* 无法了解的

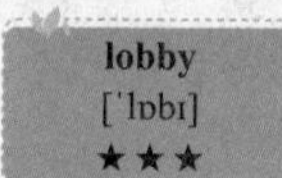

释义 *n.* 门厅,(会议)休息厅;游说团体 *v.* 游说

短语 hotel *lobby* 宾馆大厅

例句 Agricultural interests are some of the most powerful *lobbies* in Washington. 农业利益集团是华盛顿最具影响力的游说团体之一。

派生 lobbyist *n.* 说客

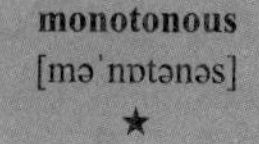

释义 *adj.* 单调的,无变化的

短语 *monotonous* work 单调乏味的工作

例句 The *monotonous* voice of the movement of the train lulled me to sleep. 火车运行的单调声音使我昏昏欲睡。

近义 dull *adj.* 枯燥无聊的

mood
[muːd]
★★

释义 *n.* 心情，情绪；语气

短语 holiday *mood* 假期心情

例句 Now researchers suspect that dreams are part of the mind's emotional thermostat, regulating *moods* while the brain is"off-line". 现在研究人员猜测，梦是大脑中情绪调节器的一部分，当大脑"离线"时，它就在调节情绪。

moral
[ˈmɒrəl]
★★★

释义 *adj.* 道德(上)的，精神上的 *n.* 寓意，教育意义

例句 Beethoven was not interested in daily politics, but concerned with questions of *moral* behavior and the larger questions of right and wrong affecting the entire society. 贝多芬对日常政治不感兴趣，而是关心道德行为的问题，以及影响整个社会的、更大的是非问题。

派生 morally *adv.* 道德上，道义上

近义 ethical *adj.* 道德的

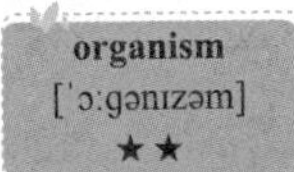

organism
[ˈɔːgənɪzəm]
★★

释义 *n.* 有机体；生物；有机体系

短语 living *organism* 生物体

例句 The army is an extremely complex *organism*. 军队是一个极其复杂的组织。It was an infectious *organism* that he studied. 他研究的是一种可传染病菌的生物。

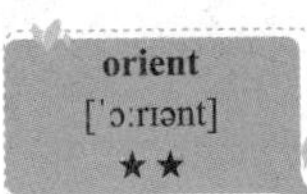

orient
[ˈɔːrɪənt]
★★

释义 *v.* 确定方向；朝向；使适应 *n.* 东方，亚洲

例句 The climbers stopped to *orient* themselves before descending the mountain. 登山者先停下来确定所在的位置，然后再下山。

It took him some time to *orient* himself in his new school. 他经过了一段时间才熟悉新学校的环境。

派生 oriental *adj.* 东方的，东方人的

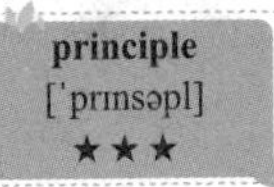

principle
[ˈprɪnsəpl]
★★★

释义 *n.* 原理，原则；主义，信念

短语 basic *principle* 基本原理 precautionary *principle* 预防性原则

例句 These people lack all understanding of scientific *principles*. 这些人完全不懂科学原理。

用法 stick to your principles 坚守你的原则

真题 On the basis of the precautionary *principle*, it could be argued that it is advisable to follow the FSA (Food Standards Authority) advice. 根据预防性原则，可以说采纳食品标准管理局的建议是明智的。(2020 完形填空)

prior
[ˈpraɪə]
★★★

释义 *adj.* 优先的，在前的；在……之前

短语 *prior* condition 先决条件

例句 They had to refuse the dinner invitation because of a *prior* engagement. 因为事先另有约会，他们只好拒绝了吃饭的邀请。

近义 former *adj.* 以前的，前……

派生 priority *n.* 优先事项，最重要的事

privacy
[ˈpraɪvəsɪ]
★★★

释义 *n.* 自由，隐私；私生活

短语 *privacy* protection 隐私保护 *privacy* violation 侵权隐私

例句 There are concerns that government, employers, and marketers might be able to access these data, thereby violating our *privacy*. 人们担心政府、雇主和营销人员可能会访问这些数据，从而侵犯我们的隐私。

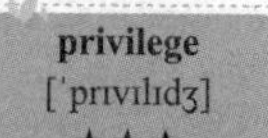

privilege
[ˈprɪvɪlɪdʒ]
★★★

释义 *n.* 特权，优惠，特许 *v.* 给予优惠，给予特权

短语 special *privilege* 特权；特别优惠

例句 One of the *privileges* of belonging to the club is that you can use its tennis courts. 加入这个俱乐部的特权之一是你可以使用它的网球场。

派生 privileged *adj.* 有特权的

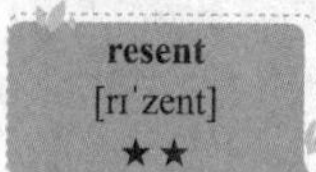

resent
[rɪˈzent]
★★

释义 *v.* 愤恨，怨恨

例句 Though most people *resent* paying taxes, these payments are necessary to facilitate civilization. 虽然大多数人不喜欢纳税，但这些钱对促进文明是必要的。

近义 hate *v.* 厌恶，不喜欢

派生 resentful *adj.* 气愤的，憎恨的

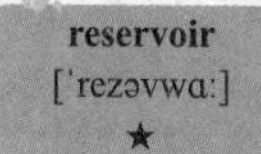

reservoir
[ˈrezəvwɑː]
★

释义 *n.* 水库，蓄水池

短语 gas *reservoir* 气体储备

例句 The benefit which the *reservoir* brings to the villagers is not limited to agriculture. 这水库给村民们带来的好处不止是在农业方面。

近义 store *n.* 储存，储备

rival
[ˈraɪvəl]
★★★

释义 *n.* 竞争者，对手 *v.* 竞争，对抗 *adj.* 竞争的

例句 The world champion finished more than two seconds ahead of his nearest *rival*. 这位世界冠军领先离他最近的对手两秒多钟冲过终点。

真题 Now, *rivals* will be charging sales tax where they hadn't before. 现在，竞争对手们将在此前从未征收过销售税的地方进行征收。（2019 阅读理解）

近义 opponent *n.* 对手，竞争者

派生 rivalry *n.* 竞争，较量

rouse
[rauz]
★

释义 *v.* 唤醒，唤起；激励；激起

例句 The noise *roused* me from a deep sleep. 吵闹声把我从熟睡中惊醒。

用法 rouse one's anger 把某人惹火

近义 awaken *v.* 唤醒 arouse *v.* 引起，激起

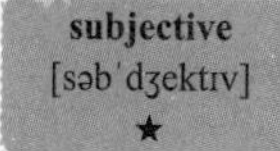

subjective
[səbˈdʒektɪv]
★

释义 *adj.* 主观（上）的，个人的

短语 a *subjective* impression 主观感觉

例句 A 2012 study found that roughly 40% of the time we are talking, we're disclosing *subjective* information about our experience. 2012 年的一项研究发现，在我们谈话的时候，大约有 40% 的时间，我们都在透露自己对于个人经历的主观感受。

反义 objective *adj.* 客观的

派生 subjectively *v.* 主观地

subscribe
[səbˈskraɪb]
★★★

释义 *v.* 订阅,订购;捐助,赞助;赞成

例句 If you *subscribe* to this newspaper, you'll get an extra magazine. 如果你订阅这份报纸,你会得到一本额外的杂志。

She doesn't *subscribe* to his pessimistic view of the state of economy. 她不同意他对经济状况的悲观看法。

用法 subscribe to 订阅

派生 subscriber *n.* 订购者,订阅人

subsequent
[ˈsʌbsɪkwənt]
★★

释义 *adj.* 随后的,后来的

短语 *subsequent* generations 后代

例句 They won only one more game *subsequent* to their Cup semi-final win last year. 继去年在杯赛半决赛中获胜后,他们仅赢过一场比赛。

近义 ensuing *adj.* 因而发生的,随后的

反义 previous *adj.* 以前的,先前的

subsidy
[ˈsʌbsɪdɪ]
★★

释义 *n.* 补助金;津贴费

短语 a state / government *subsidy* 政府补贴

例句 The university will receive a *subsidy* for research in artificial intelligence. 那个大学将得到一笔人工智能研究的补助费。

用法 get / seek a subsidy 获得 / 寻求补贴

派生 subsidize *v.* 补助,给……发津贴

trace
[treɪs]
★★★

释义 *v.* 追溯;追踪;描绘 *n.* 痕迹,踪迹

例句 Police searched the area but found no *trace* of the escaped prisoners. 警方搜索了那一地区,但未发现越狱逃犯的任何踪迹。

派生 traceable *adj.* 可追踪的

真题 In this brief period, we may *trace* the beginning, growth, blossoming, and decay of many kinds of plays, and of many great careers. 在这短暂的时期里,我们可以追溯许多戏剧和许多伟大事业的开始、发展、兴盛和衰落。(2018 翻译)

triple
[ˈtrɪpl]
★★

释义 *n.* 三倍数 *adj.* 三倍的 *v.* 使成三倍

例句 The mine reportedly had an accident rate *triple* the national average. 据报道,该矿的事故发生率是全国平均水平的 3 倍。

近义 threefold *adj.* 三倍的

utilize
[ˈjuːtɪlaɪz]
★★

释义 *v.* (utilise) 利用

例句 Guests can *utilize* these free services while enjoying music, dancing and children's activities. 客人可以在享受音乐、舞蹈和儿童活动的同时使用这些免费服务。

近义 use *v.* 利用

派生 utilization *n.* 利用

释义 *adj.* 实质上的，虚拟的

短语 *virtual* reality / world 虚拟现实 / 世界

例句 New technology has enabled development of an online *virtual* library. 新技术已经使在线虚拟图书馆的发展成为可能。

真题 The best uses of 3D printers and *virtual* reality technology haven't been invented yet, so the U.S. needs the new companies that will invent them. 现在仍未发明出 3D 打印机和虚拟现实技术的最佳用途，而美国需要新的公司将它们发明出来。（2018 阅读理解）

派生 virtually *adv.* 事实上

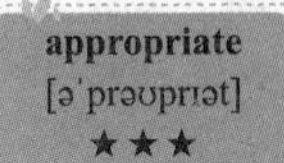

释义 *adj.* 适当的；恰当的；合适的

例句 Is this film *appropriate* for small children? 这部电影适合幼童观看吗？

近义 suitable *adj.* 合适的

反义 inappropriate *adj.* 不合适的

释义 *n.* 批准；认可；同意

例句 The president has already given his *approval* to the plan. 总统已经批准了这个计划。

Children are always seeking *approval* from their parents. 孩子们总是寻求父母的认可。

真题 Mark Twain is quoted to show that the *disapproval* of smiles in pictures was a deep-root belief. 作者引用马克·吐温的话来表明不赞成在照片中笑的观念根深蒂固。（2021 阅读理解）

用法 seek approval 申请批准

反义 disapproval *n.* 反对

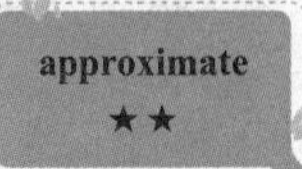

释义 *adj.*[əˈprɒksɪmət] 大约的，大概的 *v.* [əˈprɒksɪmeɪt] 接近，近似

例句 This is the *approximate* location of the ancient city. 这就是那座古城的大致位置。

Student numbers this year are expected to *approximate* 5,000 . 预计今年学生人数将接近 5,000 人。

派生 approximately *adv.* 大约，大概

释义 *adj.* 易于……的；适当的；聪明的

例句 The kitchen roof is *apt* to leak when it rains. 一下雨，厨房屋顶就容易漏。

"Scared stiff" is an *apt* description of how I felt at that moment. "吓得呆若木鸡"是对我当时感受的贴切描述。

He is obviously an *apt* pupil. 他显然是个聪明的学生。

释义 *v.* 犯大错；跌跌撞撞地走 *n.* 大错

例句 The accident was the result of a series of *blunders*. 这次事故是由一连串的失误造成的。

The government *blundered* by not acting sooner. 政府由于没有尽快采取行动而犯了大错。

She had *blundered* into the table, upsetting the flowers. 她不小心撞到桌子上，把花打翻了。

用法 blunder into somewhere 慌张撞上

consumption [kən'sʌmpʃn] ★★★

释义 *n.* 消费(量)，消耗

用法 oxygen / oil *consumption* 氧气消耗量 / 石油消耗量

例句 We need to cut down on our fuel *consumption* by having fewer cars on the road. 我们需要通过减少路上行驶的车辆以降低燃料消耗量。

派生 consume *v.* 消耗

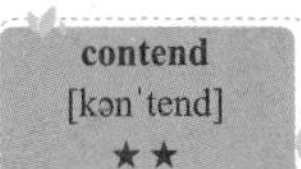

释义 *v.* 声称，主张；竞争；对付

例句 Some researchers *contend* that sleep plays no role in the consolidation of declarative memory. 一些研究者认为，睡眠对于陈述性记忆的巩固没有影响。

The firm is too small to *contend* against large international companies. 这家公司太小，无法与国际性的大公司抗争。

释义 *n.* 内容 (*pl.*) 目录 *adj.* 满足的 *v.* 使满足

例句 I emptied the *contents* of the fridge into carrier bags. 我把冰箱里的东西都倒进购物袋里。

I'm perfectly *content* with the way the campaign has gone. 我对这次活动开展的情况感到心满意足。

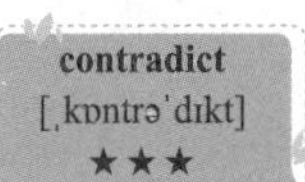

释义 *v.* 反驳；同……矛盾

例句 The witness statements *contradict* each other and the facts remain unclear. 证人的证词相互矛盾，事实仍不清楚。

派生 contradiction *n.* 矛盾

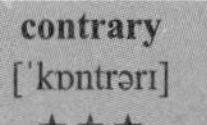

释义 *adj.* / *n.* 相反(的)，矛盾(的)

例句 *Contrary* to all our expectations, he found a well-paid job and a nice girlfriend. 出乎我们的意料，他找到了一份报酬不菲的工作和一个漂亮的女友。

用法 contrary to sth. 与某事相反

近义 opposite *adj.* 相反的

discrimination [dɪˌskrɪmɪ'neɪʃn] ★★★

释义 *n.* 歧视，区别对待；区分，辨别

短语 gender / sex *discrimination* 性别歧视

例句 According to a recent survey, 42% of women in the United States claim that they have faced some type of gender *discrimination* in the workplace. 根据最近的一项调查，42% 的美国女性声称她们在工作中遭遇过某种类型的性别歧视。

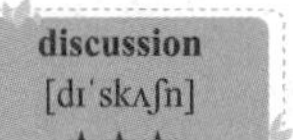

释义 *n.* 讨论；论述

短语 group *discussion* 小组讨论；集体讨论

例句 There was a lot of *discussion* about climate change in the conference. 会议上有很多关于气候变化的讨论。

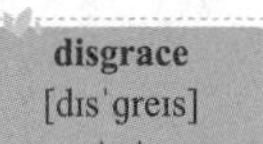

释义 *n.* 耻辱；不光彩 *v.* 使蒙羞

短语 *disgrace* the family name 玷污家族名声

例句 There is no *disgrace* in admitting that you cannot do something — it's always best to ask for help. 承认你不能做某事并不是耻辱——寻求帮助总是上策。

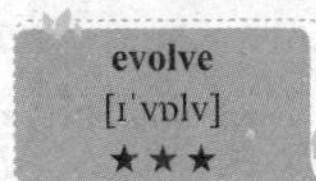

释义 v.（使）发展；（使）进化；（使）进展

例句 Most languages are constantly *evolving* and changing, which is what keeps them alive. 大多数语言都在不断地进化和变化，这是它们保持生命力的原因。

真题 Norms have *evolved* and fragmented. 规范已经演变并支离破碎。（2016 阅读理解）

派生 evolution *n.* 进化

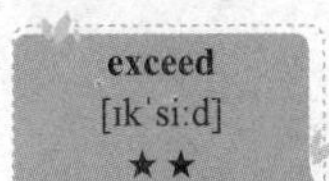

释义 v. 超过，胜过

短语 *exceed* the speed limit 超速

例句 In the Far East, home computer ownership is expected to *exceed* that of the US and Europe combined. 在远东地区，家用电脑的拥有量预计将超过美国和欧洲的总和。

近义 surpass *v.* 超过

释义 v. 胜过，优于；擅长

例句 He *excels* opponents at playing chess. 他的棋艺比对手高。

As a child, he *excelled* at music and art. 他小时候擅长音乐和美术。

用法 excel over sb. 胜过某人

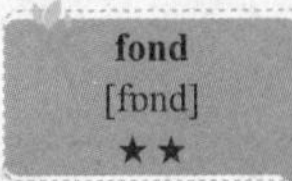

释义 *adj.* 喜爱的，爱好的

例句 I've always been *fond* of poetry and one piece has always stuck in my mind. 我一直喜欢诗歌，有一首诗一直被我铭记于心。

用法 be fond of 喜爱

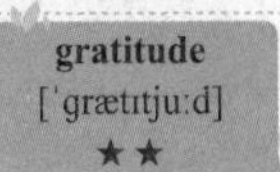

释义 *n.* 感激，感谢

短语 express *gratitude* 表示感谢

例句 She felt a deep sense of *gratitude* to the teacher who had encouraged her to go on to university. 她对鼓励她上大学的老师怀有深深的感激之情。

反义 ingratitude *n.* 忘恩负义

释义 v. 强调，突出 *n.* 最精彩的部分

例句 The report *highlights* the need for improved safety. 那份报告强调了加大安全力度的重要性。

Highlights of the match will be shown after the news. 比赛的精彩部分将在新闻之后播出。

真题 Those realistic possibilities are *highlighted* in the study presented by David Graddol. 大卫·格拉多尔的研究强调了这些现实的可能性。（2017 阅读理解）

释义 *n.* 正直，诚实；完整

例句 These creatures are members of the biotic community and, if its stability depends on its *integrity*, they are entitled to continuance. 这些生物是生物群落的成员，如果生物群落的稳定取决于它的完整性，那么它们有权继续存在。

近义 unity *n.* 整体性，统一性

intelligent
[ɪnˈtelɪdʒənt]
★★★

释义 *adj.* 聪明的，有智力的

短语 *intelligent* system 智能系统 *intelligent* robot 智能机器人

例句 Can you say that dolphins are much more *intelligent* than other animals? 你能说海豚比其他动物聪明得多吗?

真题 We think of it simply as a healthy and helpful flow of intelligent thought. 我们认为它只不过是一种健康的、有益的智慧思想的流动。(2016 翻译)

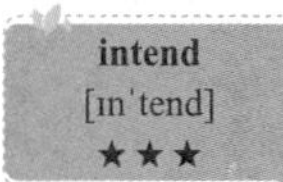

intend
[ɪnˈtend]
★★★

释义 *v.* 想要，打算，企图

例句 Frank has recently graduated from college and *intends* to find a job in China. 弗兰克刚从大学毕业，打算在中国找份工作。

用法 intend to do sth. 想要做某事

派生 intention *n.* 意图，目的

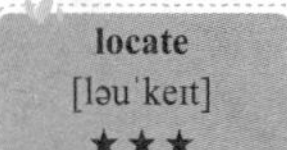

locate
[ləuˈkeɪt]
★★★

释义 *v.* 查找……地点，使……坐落于，位于

例句 Most archaeological sites have been *located* by means of careful searching, while many others have been discovered by accident. 大多数考古遗址是通过仔细搜索确定的，而其他许多是被偶然发现的。

派生 location *n.* 地点，位置

morality
[məˈrælətɪ]
★

释义 *n.* 道德，美德

短语 ideological *morality* 思想品德

例句 Mitsuo Setoyama argued that liberal reforms introduced by the American occupation authorities after World War II had weakened the "Japanese *morality* of respect for parents". 濑户光夫认为，二战后美国占领当局引入的自由主义改革削弱了"日本人尊重父母的道德观"。

反义 immorality *n.* 不道德

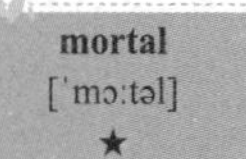

mortal
[ˈmɔːtəl]
★

释义 *adj.* 致命的；终有一死的 *n.* 凡人

短语 a *mortal* blow 致命的一击

例句 The collapse of the business was a *mortal* blow to him and his family. 生意的破产给他和他的家庭以致命的打击。

派生 mortally *adv.* 致命地

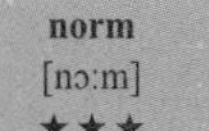

norm
[nɔːm]
★★★

释义 *n.* 标准，规范；准则，行为模式

短语 above the *norm* 高于标准 the *norms* of culture 文化规范

例句 Of his age, the child is above the *norm* in arithmetic. 在他那个年龄，这个孩子的算术能力是超过标准的。

派生 normal *adj.* 正常的

organisation
[ˌɔːgənaɪˈzeɪʃən]
★★★

释义 *n.* (organization) 团体，机构；组织

例句 He is engaged in the *organization* of a new club. 他正忙于组织一个新的俱乐部。

principal
[ˈprɪnsəpəl]
★★

释义 *adj.* 最重要的，主要的 *n.* 校长；资本

短语 *principal* element 主要因素

例句 They found that the *principal* requirement for what is called "global cascades" is the presence of a critical mass of easily influenced people. 他们发现,所谓的"全球连锁反应"形成所需的主要条件是很大一批易受影响的人群的参与。

近义 primary *adj.* 主要的,首要的

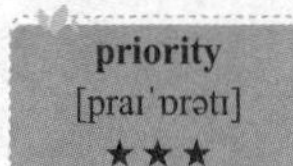

priority [praɪˈɒrətɪ] ★★★

释义 *n.* 优先权,重点

短语 enforcement *priorities* 执行优先权

例句 The White House argued that Arizona's laws conflicted with its enforcement *priorities*. 白宫认为,亚利桑那州的法律与它的执行优先权相冲突。

近义 precedence *n.* 领先,优先权

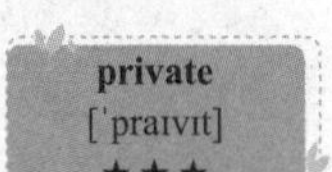

private [ˈpraɪvɪt] ★★★

释义 *adj.* 私人的,个人的

短语 *private* property 私有财产 *private* capital 私人资本

例句 Brazil says its constitution forbids the *private* ownership of energy assets. 巴西称其宪法禁止个人占有能源资产。

真题 Citizens still have a right to expect *private* documents to remain *private* and protected by the Constitution's prohibition on unreasonable searches. 公民仍然有权要求私人文件保持私密性,并受到宪法禁止不合理搜查的法令的保护。(2015 阅读理解)

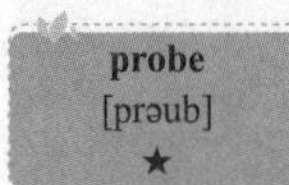

probe [prəub] ★

释义 *n.* 探针,探测器 *v.*(以探针等)探查,穿刺

短语 space *probe* 航天探测器

例句 Chang'e IV is the first lunar *probe* in history that has successfully landed on the "dark" side of the moon. 嫦娥四号是历史上第一个成功登陆月球"暗面"的月球探测器。

用法 probe for sth. 想弄明白某事

residence [ˈrezɪdəns] ★★

释义 *n.* 住处,住宅

短语 *residence* permit 居留证 country of *residence* 居住国

例句 She travels constantly, moving among her several *residences* around the world. 她经常旅行,穿梭于她在世界各地的多处住所。

近义 house *n.* 住宅 mansion *n.* 宅邸

resign [rɪˈzaɪn] ★

释义 *v.* 辞去,辞职;使听从,使顺从

例句 A number of Missouri lawmakers have called on the governor to *resign*. 密苏里州的一些议员已经要求州长辞职。

She didn't *resign* herself to her fate. 她没有屈从于自己的命运。

用法 resign from 辞职

近义 quit *v.* 辞职

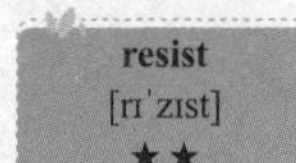

resist [rɪˈzɪst] ★★

释义 *v.* 抵抗,反抗;抵制

短语 *resist* pressure 顶住压力

例句 If you fail at *resisting* a temptation, don't just criticize yourself. Accept that you had a slip-up and move on. 如果你无法抵抗诱惑,不要只批评自己。承认你犯了一个错误,然后继续前进。

近义 oppose *v.* 反抗,阻碍

派生 resistance *n.* 抵抗，反抗；抵抗力

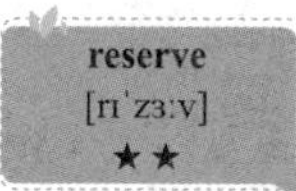

释义 *n.* 预订；保留；储备（物）v. 保留，储备；预订

短语 oil *reserve* 储油量 *reserve* a room 预订房间

例句 According to geologists' estimates, Antarctica has

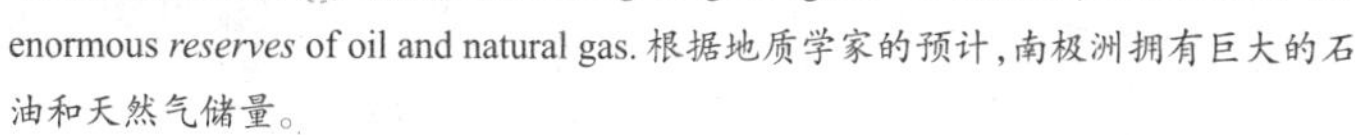
enormous *reserves* of oil and natural gas. 根据地质学家的预计，南极洲拥有巨大的石油和天然气储量。

Staff and faculty can *reserve* the meeting rooms for two hours at a time. 员工和教职员工每次可以预定两个小时的会议室。

派生 reservation *n.* 保留；预订

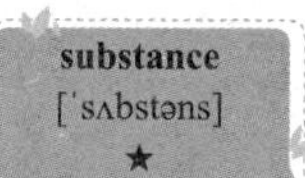

释义 *n.* 物质；实质，本质；主旨

短语 organic *substance* 有机物

例句 The commission's report gives *substance* to these allegations. 委员会的报告为这些说法提供了事实根据。

Nothing of any *substance* was achieved in the meeting. 会议没有取得任何实质性成果。

派生 substantial *adj.* 实质的

释义 *n.* 代替者；代用品 *v.* 代替，替换

短语 *substitute* fuel 代用燃料

例句 In talking to some scientists, particularly younger ones, you might gather the impression that they find the "scientific method" a *substitute* for imaginative thought. 在与一些科学家，尤其是年轻科学家交谈时，你可能会得到这样一种印象：他们认为"科学方法"可以代替想象力。

近义 replace *v.* 取代

派生 substitution *n.* 代替，替换

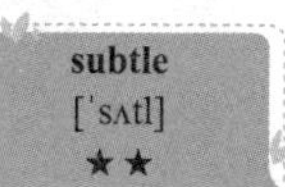

释义 *adj.* 精巧的，巧妙的；细微的

短语 *subtle* differences 细微的差异

例句 There's been a *subtle* change in language as the day has progressed. 随着时间的推移，语言有了微妙的变化。

真题 This is a *subtle* form of peer pressure: we unconsciously imitate the behavior we see every day. 这是同辈压力的一种更为微妙的形式：我们无意识地模仿我们每天看到的行为。（2012 阅读理解）

近义 crafty *adj.* 灵巧的

派生 subtly *adv.* 敏锐地

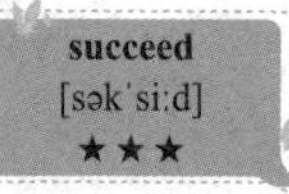

释义 *v.* 成功；继承；接替；继……之后

例句 If Gilbert and the Philharmonic are to *succeed*, they must first change the relationship between America's oldest orchestra and the new audience it hopes to attract. 如果吉尔伯特和爱乐乐团要取得成功，他们必须首先改变这个美国历史最悠久的乐团与其希望吸引的新观众之间的关系。

用法 succeed in 在……方面成功

近义 triumph *v.* 获胜，成功

派生 successful *adj.* 成功的

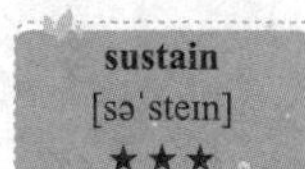

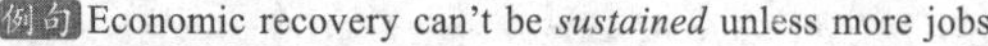

释义 *v.* 支撑；维持；经受，忍耐

短语 *sustain* losses / momentum 蒙受损失 / 保持动力

例句 Economic recovery can't be *sustained* unless more jobs are created. 除非创造更多的就业机会，否则经济复苏无法持续。

真题 The most loyal customers would still get the product they favor, the idea goes, and they'd feel like they were helping *sustain* the quality of something they believe in. 这种想法是：最忠诚的顾客仍然愿意买他们喜欢的产品，他们还会觉得自己在帮助维持他们信任的产品的质量。（2016 阅读理解）

近义 support *v.* 支持

释义 *n.* 跑道；小路；轨迹 *v.* 跟踪，追踪

短语 sound *track* 声道

例句 The research project involves *tracking* the careers of 400 graduates. 这个研究项目对 400 名毕业生的事业发展情况进行跟踪调查。

真题 Conceived in this way, comprehension will not follow exactly the same *track* for each reader. 这样来看，不同的读者就会有不同的理解方式。（2015 阅读理解）

用法 back on track 恢复正常

释义 *adj.* 琐碎的；无足轻重的

短语 *trivial* matters 无关重要的事情

例句 The quarrel was only about a *trivial* matter, but it was years before they made it up. 争吵只是为了一件小事，但是过了多年他们才言归于好。

近义 insignificant *adj.* 无足轻重的

派生 trivially *adv.* 琐碎地

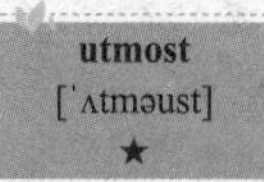

释义 *adj.* 最大的；极度的 *n.* 极限，最大可能

短语 the *utmost* urgency 当务之急

例句 As a matter of the *utmost* urgency, the world has to keep balance between over population and finite resources. 当务之急是，世界必须在过剩的人口和有限的资源之间保持平衡。

用法 do one's utmost 尽某人的全力

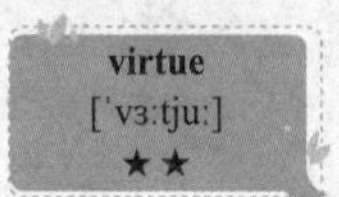

释义 *n.* 美德；优点；好处

短语 *virtue* and vice 善与恶

例句 Among her many *virtues* are loyalty, courage and truthfulness. 她有许多美德，如忠诚、勇敢和诚实。

She got the job by *virtue* of her greater experience. 她由于经验较为丰富而得到了那份工作。

用法 by virtue of 由于，凭借

近义 morality *n.* 道德

派生 virtuous *adj.* 道德高尚的

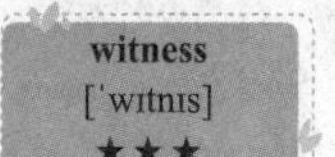

释义 *n.* 目击者，证人；证据 *v.* 目击，目睹；作证

短语 eye *witness* 目击者，见证人

例句 The world is going through the biggest wave of mergers and acquisitions ever *witnessed*. 世界正在经历有史以来最大的并购浪潮。

There must be two *witnesses* present when she signs the document. 她签署文件时必须有两名证人在场。

用法 be (a) witness to sth. 目击，看见（某事发生）

释义 *n.* 热心，热忱，热情

短语 religious / political *zeal* 宗教 / 政治热情

例句 Even as a schoolboy, Elon had an entrepreneurial *zeal*, although his first business ventures failed. 即使在学生时代，埃隆就充满了创业热情，尽管他的第一次商业冒险失败了。

近义 enthusiasm *n.* 热情，热忱

派生 zealous *adj.* 热情的

释义 *v.* 赞成；同意；核准；通过

例句 She doesn't *approve* of my friends. 她不喜欢我的朋友们。

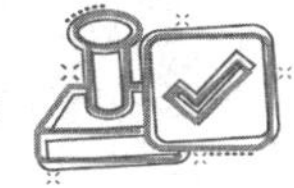

Congress voted not to *approve* the President's plans. 国会投票否决了总统的计划。

反义 disapprove *v.* 不赞成

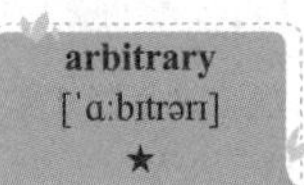

释义 *adj.* 任意的；武断的

例句 The choice of players for the team seemed completely *arbitrary*. 看来这个队的队员完全是随意选定的。

派生 arbiter *n.* 仲裁人；评判人

释义 *n.* 建筑师；创造者；设计师

例句 She resolved to become an *architect*. 她决心成为一名建筑师。

派生 architecture *n.* 建筑学；建筑风格

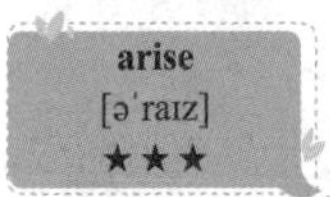

释义 *v.* 起立；发生；出现；起床；上升

例句 Are there any matters *arising* from the last meeting? 上次会议有没有引出什么问题？

He *arose* refreshed after a good night's sleep. 美美地睡了一夜后，他精神焕发。

近义 appear *v.* 出现

反义 vanish *v.* 消失

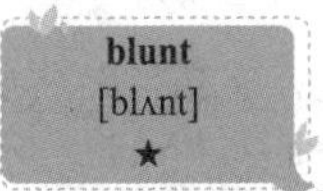

释义 *adj.* 钝的，不锋利的；直率的；*v.* 使变钝；使（情感）减弱

例句 She is *blunt* about her unpleasant feeling. 她对自己不愉快的感觉直言不讳。

The bad traffic has *blunted* his enthusiasm for travel. 糟糕的交通已经使他对旅游的热情减弱了不少。

派生 bluntly *adv.* 直言地

contrast
[ˈkɒntrɑːst]
★★★

释义 *v.* / *n.* 对比,对照

例句 The snow was icy and white, *contrasting* with the brilliant blue sky. 雪是冰冰和白色的,与明亮的蓝天形成鲜明的对比。

用法 contrast with sth. 与……形成对比

contribute
[kənˈtrɪbjuːt]
★★★

释义 *v.* 贡献,捐献

例句 The volunteers contribute their own time to the project. 志愿者们为这个项目贡献了自己的时间。

派生 contribution *n.* 贡献

controversial
[ˌkɒntrəˈvɜːʃ(ə)l]
★★★

释义 *adj.* 引起争论的,有争议的

例句 The commission has managed to reach agreement on some *controversial* issues of immigration reform. 委员会设法就移民改革中一些有争议的问题达成了一致意见。

派生 controversy *n.* 争论

convenient
[kənˈviːnɪənt]
★

释义 *adj.* 便利的,方便的

用法 a *convenient* store 便利店

例句 Our house is *convenient* for the shops. 我们家去商店很方便。

派生 convenience *n.* 便利

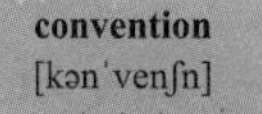

convention
[kənˈvenʃn]
★★★

释义 *n.* 会议;惯例;公约,协定

例句 Each society has its own cultural *conventions*. 每个社会都有自己的文化习俗。Japan has signed a *convention* of peace with a neighboring country. 日本已与邻国签署了一项和平协定。

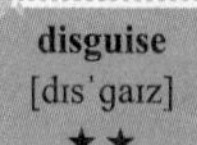

disguise
[dɪsˈgaɪz]
★★

释义 *n.* / *v.* 假装,伪装

例句 The suspect *disguised* himself as a police officer in uniform. 犯罪嫌疑人乔装成身穿制服的警察。

用法 disguise as ... 把……装扮成

dismiss
[dɪsˈmɪs]
★★★

释义 *v.* 免职,解雇;解散;摒弃,不予考虑;驳回

例句 Austin was *dismissed* for playing computer games at work. 奥斯汀因上班时玩电脑游戏而被解雇。

You're fired.

Dismissing her fears, she climbed higher. 她排除了恐惧,爬得更高了。

disorder
[dɪsˈɔːdə]
★★★

释义 *n.* 混乱;骚乱;失调,疾病

短语 eating *disorder* 饮食失调 heart *disorder* 心律失常

例句 Evidence shows that people who diet may be at increased risk for binge eating and eating *disorder*. 有证据表明,节食的人可能会增加暴饮暴食和饮食失调的风险。

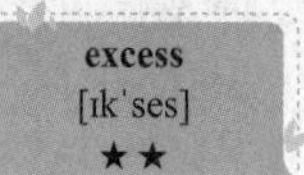

excess
[ɪkˈses]
★★

释义 *adj.* 过量的,额外的 *n.* 过量;过剩

例句 There will be an increase in tax for those earning in *excess* of twice the national average wage. 对于那些收入超过全国平均工资一倍以上的人,税收额

将要增加。

用法 in *excess of* 超过;较……为多

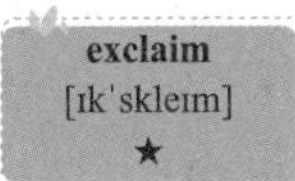

释义 *v.* 呼喊,惊叫,大声说

例句 She *exclaimed* in delight when she got the job offer. 她得到那份工作时高兴得叫了起来。

用法 exclaim against 表示强烈不赞成

释义 *v.* 把……排除在外,排斥;不包括

例句 The shop is open seven days a week *excluding* Christmas Day. 本商店每周营业七天,圣诞节除外。

反义 include *v.* 包括

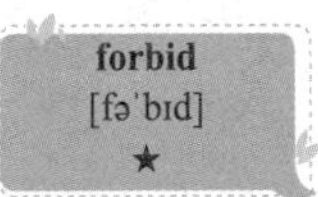

释义 *v.* 禁止;不许

例句 The law *forbids* stealing and robbery. 法律禁止偷盗和抢劫。

My parents *forbade* me to play in the street. 我的父母不准我在街上玩。

近义 prevent *v.* 阻止

释义 *v.* 感到悲痛,伤心

例句 He rejoiced that they had won the battle, but *grieved* that many had been killed. 他为他们打了胜仗而高兴,但又为许多人牺牲而悲伤。

同义 mourn *v.* 悼念,哀悼

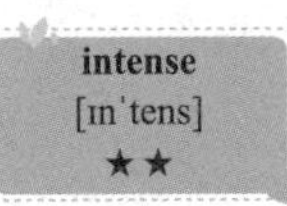

释义 *adj.* 强烈的;热烈的,热情的

短语 *intense* competition / pressure 激烈的竞争 / 巨大的压力

例句 He finally resigned on 20 May 2021 under *intense* pressure from the public. 在公众的巨大压力下,他最终于 2021 年 5 月 20 日辞职。

派生 intensity *n.* 强烈

释义 *n.* 意图,意向,目的

短语 good / evil *intention* 好心 / 歹意　real *intention* 真实意图

例句 She had a firm *intention* within herself to be the best she could be. 她内心坚定地想要做到最好。

派生 intentionally *adv.* 故意地,有意地

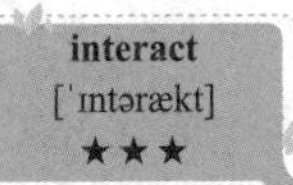

释义 *v.* 互相作用,互相影响

例句 While the other children *interacted* and played together, Ted ignored them. 当其他孩子在一起互动和玩耍时,泰德无视了他们。

派生 interaction *n.* 互动,交流

释义 *n.* 位置,场所;定位

短语 target *location* 目标位置

例句 The satellite enables us to calculate their precise *location* anywhere in the world. 这颗卫星使得我们可以计算出他们在地球上任何地方的准确位置。

派生 position *n.* 位置

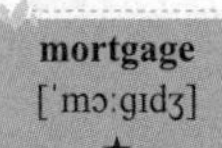

mortgage
[ˈmɔːɡɪdʒ]
★

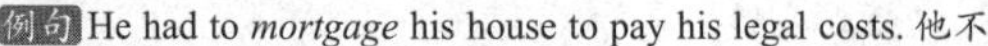

释义 *n.* / *v.* 抵押（借款）

短语 housing *mortgage* 住房按揭

例句 He had to *mortgage* his house to pay his legal costs. 他不得不把房子抵押出去来付诉讼费。

She got behind with her *mortgage* and the house was repossessed. 她拖欠了抵押贷款，房子被收回了。

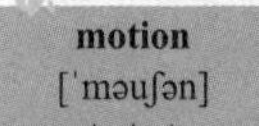

motion
[ˈməʊʃən]
★★★

释义 *n.* 运动，移动；提议，动议 *v.* 提议，动议

短语 law of *motion* 运动定律

例句 The *motion* of one plate with respect to another cannot readily be translated into motion with respect to the earth's interior. 一个板块相对于另一个板块的运动不能轻易地解释为相对于地球内部的运动。

派生 motionless *adj.* 静止的

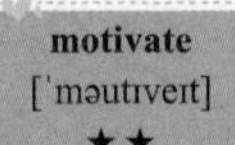

motivate
[ˈməʊtɪveɪt]
★★

释义 *v.* 促动；激励，作为……的动机

例句 What *motivated* him, we were to understand, was his zeal for "fundamental fairness". 我们应该理解，促使他这样做的是他对"基本公平"的热情。

派生 motivation *n.* 动力；诱因

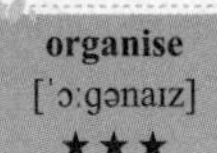

organise
[ˈɔːɡənaɪz]
★★★

释义 *v.* (organize) 组织；使有系统化

短语 *organize* a party 组织聚会

例句 When it was dark, they *organized* an attack a third time. 天黑的时候，他们组织了第三次进攻。

派生 organization *n.* 组织

反义 disorganise *v.* 扰乱；瓦解

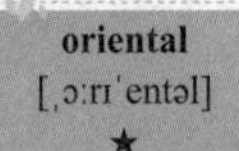

oriental
[ˌɔːrɪˈentəl]
★

释义 *adj.* 东方的，东方人的，东方文化的

短语 *Oriental* rugs 东方地毯 *Oriental* Pearl Tower 东方明珠塔

例句 Do some *oriental* philosophies lean towards fatalism? 有些东方的哲学倾向于宿命论吗？

派生 orientation *n.* 方向；（岗前、学前等的）情况介绍

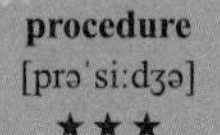

procedure
[prəˈsiːdʒə]
★★★

释义 *n.* 程序；手续；步骤

短语 general *procedure* 通用程序 standard *procedure* 标准程序

例句 The current emphasis on standardized testing highlights analysis and *procedure*. 目前标准化测试的重点是分析和程序。

派生 procedural *adj.* 程序上的

proceed
[prəˈsiːd]
★★

释义 *v.* 进行，继续下去；发生

例句 The teacher should encourage the child to *proceed* as far as he can, and when he is stuck, ask for help. 老师应当鼓励孩子尽可能独立思考，当自己实在无法解决的时候，再寻求帮助。

用法 proceed with 继续进行

派生 proceeding *n.* 行动，进行

proclaim
[prəu'kleɪm]
★

释义 *v.* 宣告，声明

例句 The Boers rebelled against British rule, *proclaiming* their independence on 30 December 1880. 布尔人反对英国统治，并于1880年12月30日宣布独立。

近义 announce *v.* 宣布；声称

派生 proclamatory *adj.* 公告的；宣言的

productive
[prə'dʌktɪv]
★★

释义 能产的，多产的；富有成效的

短语 *productive* capacity 生产能力

例句 Research finds that if employees suffer from high stress, they will be less motivated, less p*roductive* and more likely to quit. 研究发现，如果员工承受着巨大的压力，他们的积极性就会降低，效率也会降低，更有可能辞职。

派生 productivity *n.* 生产率，生产力

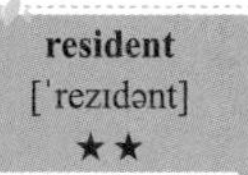

resident
['rezɪdənt]
★★

释义 *n.* 居民，常住者 *adj.* 居住的

短语 city *resident* 城市居民

例句 Local *residents* have reacted angrily to the news. 当地居民对这一消息表示愤怒。

Paul has been *resident* in Brussels since 1990. 保罗自1990年以来一直居住在布鲁塞尔。

派生 residence *n.* 住处

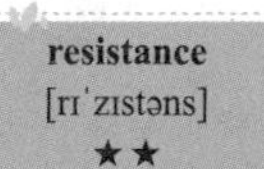

resistance
[rɪ'zɪstəns]
★★

释义 *n.* 抵抗，反抗；抵抗力，阻力；电阻

短语 water *resistance* 防水性

例句 The design of the bicycle has managed to reduce the effects of wind *resistance*. 这种自行车的设计设法减少了风阻的影响。

派生 resistant *adj.* 抵制的

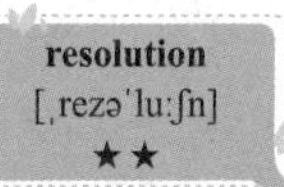

resolution
[ˌrezə'luːʃn]
★★

释义 *n.* 决心；决定；解决

短语 conflict *resolution* 冲突解决

例句 The government is pressing for an early *resolution* of the dispute. 政府正在不断敦促早日解决这起纠纷。

近义 resolve *n.* / *v.* 解决；决心

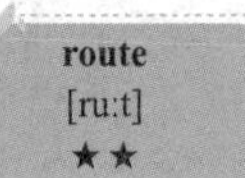

route
[ruːt]
★★

释义 *n.* 路线，路程；途径

短语 air / sea *route* 航线 / 海路

例句 A college education is often the best *route* to a good job. 大学教育常常是获得一份好工作的最佳途径。

The guide contains some of the most popular hiking *routes* for backpackers and nature lovers. 该指南包含了一些最受背包客和大自然爱好者欢迎的徒步路线。

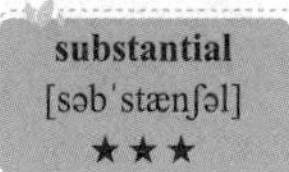

substantial
[səb'stænʃəl]
★★★

释义 *adj.* 实质的；相当的，显著的；坚固的

短语 *substantial* evidence 确实证据

例句 Genetically speaking, there are advantages to avoiding *substantial* height. 从基因上讲，避免过高的身高是有好处的。

近义 considerable *adj.* 相当大的，相当重要的

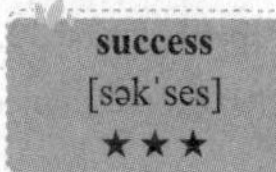

释义 *n.* 成就，成功；成功的事物，有成就的人

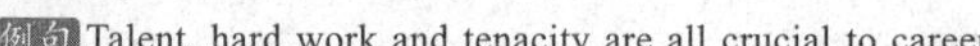

短语 achieve *success* 取得成功

例句 Talent, hard work and tenacity are all crucial to career *success*. 事业要成功，天赋、勤奋和顽强的意志都至关重要。

反义 failure *adj.* 失败

派生 successful *adj.* 成功的

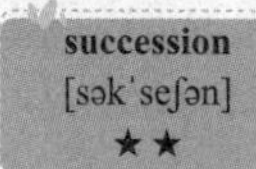

释义 *n.* 连续，系列；继任，继承

短语 a *succession* of visitors 络绎不绝的来访者

例句 She's third in order of *succession* to the throne. 她在王位继承人顺位中排第三。Fraser Clyne has won the Scottish Road Running Championship for the third year in *succession*. 弗雷泽·克莱恩连续第三年获得苏格兰公路跑步锦标赛冠军。

派生 successive *adj.* 连续的

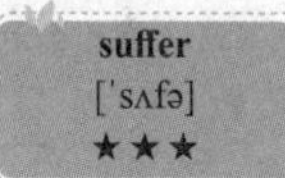

释义 *v.* 受痛苦，患病；受损失；遭受，忍受

短语 *suffer* hunger 挨饿

例句 A number of small businesses *suffered* huge losses during the pandemic when they were forced to close. 许多小企业在疫情期间被迫关闭，遭受了巨大的损失。

近义 experience *v.* 经历，遭遇

派生 sufferer *n.* 患者；受害者

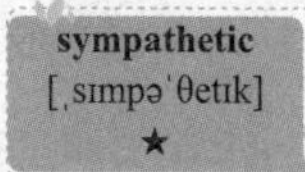

释义 *adj.* 有同情心的；赞同的；合意的

短语 a *sympathetic* listener / character 体恤别人的倾听者 / 一个讨人喜欢的人物

例句 He suffers from test anxiety too, so he was very *sympathetic* about my problem. 他自己也受到考试焦虑的困扰，所以他对我的问题深表同情。

用法 *sympathetic* about 对……同情

派生 sympathetically *adv.* 悲怜地

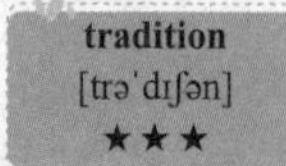

释义 *n.* 传统；惯例；传说

例句 There's a *tradition* in our family that we have a party on New Year's Eve. 我们家有个传统，全家要聚在一起过新年除夕。

近义 custom *n.* 习俗

派生 traditional *adj.* 传统的

释义 *adj.* 悲剧的，悲惨的

短语 a *tragic* accident 不幸的事故

例句 Cuts in the health service could have *tragic* consequences for patients. 减少公共医疗卫生服务可能对患者造成悲惨的影响。

近义 distressing *adj.* 使痛苦的；悲伤的

派生 tragedy *n.* 悲剧

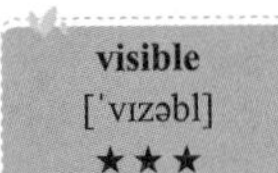
visible
[ˈvɪzəbl]
★★★

释义 *adj.* 看得见的，明显的，显著的

例句 The expulsion of dust from the volcano was *visible* from miles away. 火山喷出的灰尘几英里之外就能看得见。

真题 How do archaeologists know where to find what they are looking for when there is nothing *visible* on the surface of the ground? 在地表什么都看不见的情况下，考古学家怎么知道去哪里寻找他们要找的东西呢？（2014 阅读理解）

近义 obvious *adj.* 明显的

派生 visibility *n.* 能见度

Word List 32

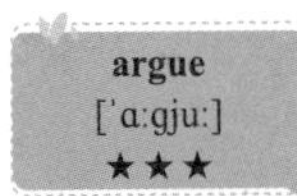
argue
[ˈɑːgjuː]
★★★

释义 *v.* 争论；辩论

例句 The children were *arguing* over / about which TV programme to watch. 孩子们在争论该看哪个电视节目。

派生 argument *n.* 争论；论据

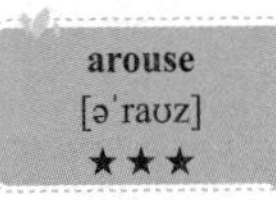
arouse
[əˈraʊz]
★★★

释义 *v.* 引起；唤醒

例句 The report *aroused* a great deal of public interest. 这个报告引起了公众的极大兴趣。

The footsteps *aroused* the dog. 脚步声把狗吵醒了。

用法 arouse sb. from sleep 把某人从睡梦中唤醒

近义 awaken *v.* 叫醒

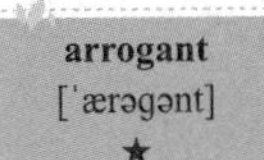
arrogant
[ˈærəgənt]
★

释义 *adj.* 傲慢的；自大的

例句 It's hard to deal with an *arrogant* guy. 和一个傲慢的人打交道是很难的。

近义 humble *adj.* 谦逊的

派生 arrogance *n.* 傲慢

article
[ˈɑːtɪkl]
★★★

释义 *n.* 文章；物品；条款；冠词

例句 Have you seen that *article* about young fashion designers? 你看到了关于年轻时装设计师的那篇文章没有？

She only took a few *articles* of clothing with her. 她只带了几件衣服。

The country appears to be violating several *articles* of the convention. 这个国家看起来违反了公约中的好几项条款。

blur
[blɜː]
★

释义 *v.*（使）变模糊；（使）区别不明显 *n.* 模糊的东西；记不清的东西

例句 I saw the *blur* of the car as it passed in front of me. 那辆汽车从我面前经过时，我看到了模糊的影子。

The street lights were *blurred* by the fog. 路灯笼罩在雾里，变得模糊不清。

派生 blurred *adj.* 模糊的

conventional
[kən'venʃənl]
★★★

释义 *adj.* 惯例的，常规的

例句 Although expensive, it lasts longer and uses less energy than a *conventional* light bulb. 虽然昂贵，但它比传统灯泡寿命更长，耗能更少。

近义 traditional *adj.* 传统的

convert
[kən'vɜ:t]
★★

释义 *v.*（使）转变；改变（信仰等）

例句 Could we *convert* the small bedroom into a second bathroom? 我们能把这间小卧室改造成第二间浴室吗？

派生 conversely *adj.* 相反地

convey
[kən'veɪ]
★★★

释义 *v.* 传达，表达；运输

例句 The best way to *convey* love is with our actions, not just our words. 表达爱的最好方式是用我们的行动，而不仅仅是言语。

Frank's luggage was *conveyed* to his hotel by taxi. 弗兰克的行李由出租车送到他的旅馆。

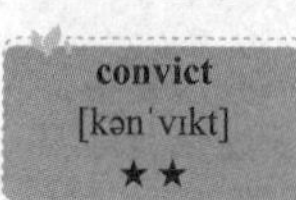

convict
[kən'vɪkt]
★★

释义 *v.* 证明……有罪，宣判……有罪 *n.* 囚犯

例句 In 1977, he was *convicted* of murder and sentenced to life imprisonment. 1977 年，他被判谋杀罪，并判处终身监禁。

派生 conviction *n.* 定罪；确信

convince
[kən'vɪns]
★★★

释义 *v.* 使信服，使确信

例句 Agricultural companies have failed to *convince* consumers that genetically modified foods are safe. 农业公司未能让消费者相信转基因食品是安全的。

近义 persuade *v.* 说服，劝服

disperse
[dɪ'spɜ:s]
★

释义 *v.*（使）分散；（使）散开；疏散

例句 Police *dispersed* the crowd that had gathered around the building. 警察驱散了聚集在大楼周围的人群。

反义 assemble *v.*（使）聚集

派生 dispersal *n.* 分散

displace
[dɪs'pleɪs]
★

释义 *v.* 取代，代替；转移

例句 Investment in the nationalized industries has simply *displaced* private investment. 对国有化工业的投资已经完全取代了私人投资。

派生 displacement *n.* 取代，代替

display
[dɪ'spleɪ]
★★★

释义 *v.* / *n.* 陈列，展览；展示

例句 One of the world's oldest cars has gone on *display* in Brighton today. 今天，世界上最古老的一辆汽车在布赖顿展出。

The chart can *display* the links connecting these groups. 这张图会显示出这些群体之间的关联。

excessive
[ɪk'sesɪv]
★★★

释义 *adj.* 过多的；过分的；额外的

例句 The overwhelming majority of employees attribute their stress mainly to low pay and an *excessive* workload. 绝大多数员工将他们的压力主要归因于低工资

和过度的工作量。

派生 excessively *adv.* 过分地,过量地;极度

释义 *adj.* 独占的;专有的;唯一的 *n.* 独家报道

例句 Skiing weekends cost £108 (*exclusive* of travel and accommodation). 周末滑雪价格为 108 英镑(不包括交通费和住宿费)。

用法 exclusive of 不包括

派生 exclusively *adv.* 专门地

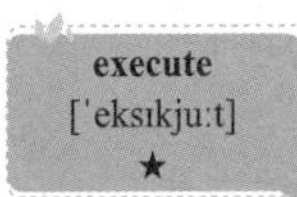

释义 *v.* 实行,实施,执行;完成,履行;处死;制作(艺术作品)

例句 They drew up and *executed* a plan to reduce fuel consumption. 他们制订并实施了一项降低燃料消耗的计划。

Picasso also *executed* several landscapes at Horta de San Juan. 毕加索还在奥尔塔德圣胡安画了几幅风景画。

释义 *v./n.* 预测,预报

例句 Experts forecast a large rise in unemployment over the next two years. 专家预测今后两年失业人口会大幅上升。

近义 predict *v.* 预测

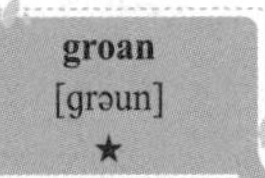

释义 *v.* 呻吟;抱怨 *n.* 呻吟,叹息

例句 His parents were beginning to *groan* about the price of college tuition. 他的父母开始抱怨大学学费太高。

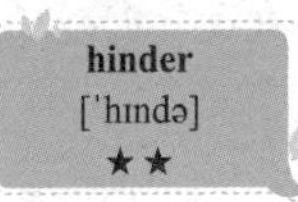

释义 *v.* 阻碍;妨碍

例句 Landslides and bad weather are continuing to *hinder* the arrival of relief supplies to the area. 山体滑坡和恶劣天气继续阻碍救援物资抵达该地区。

近义 hamper *v.* 阻碍

派生 hindrance *n.* 障碍

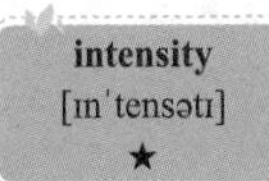

释义 *n.* 强烈,剧烈;强度

短语 sound / rainfall *intensity* 声音 / 降雨强度

例句 The intensity of the hurricane was frightening. 飓风的强度令人恐惧。

派生 intensive *adj.* 加强的

释义 *v.* 干涉;妨碍

例句 Sedentary habits often *interfere* with health. 长坐不动的习惯往往不利于身体健康。

I never *interfere* in his business. 我从不干预他的事。

派生 interference *n.* 干涉

释义 *adj.* 内部的 *n.* 内部,里面

短语 the earth's *interior* 地球内部

例句 When my wife and I chose our Peugeot 405 it was for its comfort, performance and *interior* space. 我和妻子选择我们的标致 405 是因为它的舒适性、性能和内部空间。

反义 exterior *adj.* 外部的 *n.* 外观

logical
[ˈlɒdʒɪkəl]
★★

释义 *adj.* 逻辑的，符合逻辑的

短语 *logical* analysis 逻辑分析

例句 Only when each *logical* step has been checked by other mathematicians will the proof be accepted. 只有每一逻辑步骤都被其他数学家验证之后，证明才能成立。

派生 logicality *n.* 逻辑性；合论理性

释义 *n.* 动机，目的

例句 Police have not been able to establish a *motive* for the attack. 警方还没能确定袭击的动机。

用法 question one's motives 质疑某人的动机

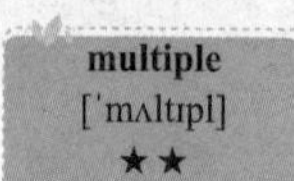

释义 *adj.* 多样的，多重的 *n.* 倍数 *v.* 成倍增加

短语 *multiple* shop 连锁商店

例句 There are also companies like Acquisio, which analyzes advertising performance across *multiple* channels. 还有像艾克斯 (Acquisio) 这样的公司，专门分析多种渠道的广告效果。

派生 multiply *v.* 乘

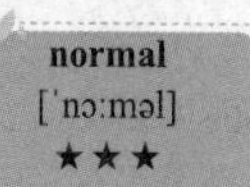

释义 *adj.* 正常的，平常的；正规的；标准的

短语 *normal* university 师范大学

例句 The forecaster said that 2023 was on course to be the 13th consecutive year with an above *normal* temperature for this region. 气象预报员表示，2023 年将是该地区连续第 13 年气温高于正常水平。

派生 normally *adv.* 通常

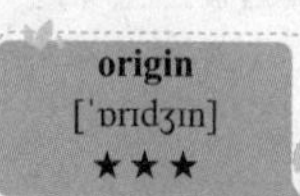

释义 *n.* 起点；来源；出身，血统

短语 humble *origin* 卑微的出身

例句 He is considered to be of noble *origins*. 人们都认为他出身高贵。I'm a Chinese by *origin*. 我是中国血统。

近义 extraction *n.* 血统

派生 originate *v.* 起源，产生

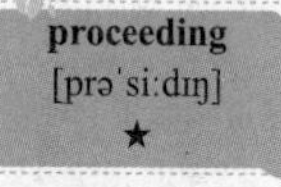

释义 *n.* 行动，进行 (*pl.*) 诉讼，诉讼程序；（会议等的）正式记录

短语 legal *proceeding* 诉讼 civil *proceeding* 民事（诉讼）程序

例句 The Mayor will open the *proceedings* at the City Hall tomorrow. 明天，市长将在市政厅宣布大会开幕。

近义 lawsuit *n.* 诉讼

释义 *n.* 过程；工序，工艺 *v.* 加工，处理

例句 Increasing the number of women in top management jobs will be a slow *process*. 增加女性高管职位的人数将是一个缓慢的过程。

真题 Ms Denham chose to concentrate the blame on the NHS trust, since under existing law it "controlled" the data and DeepMind merely "*processed*" it. 德纳姆女士选择将责任集中在NHS信托公司身上，因为根据现行法律，NHS"控制"数据，而DeepMind只是"处理"数据。(2018 阅读理解)

productivity
[ˌprɒdʌkˈtɪvətɪ]
★★

释义 *n.* 生产率

短语 labor *productivity* 劳动生产率

例句 Wage rates depend on levels of *productivity*. 工资水平取决于生产量的多少。

真题 Likewise, automation should eventually boost *productivity*, stimulate demand by driving down prices, and free workers from hard, boring work. 同样，自动化最终应该会提高生产率，通过压低价格来刺激需求，并将工人从繁重、枯燥的工作中解放出来。(2018 阅读理解)

profession
[prəʊˈfeʃən]
★★★

释义 *n.* 职业，专业；宣布

短语 accounting / teaching *profession* 会计职业 / 教学工作

例句 The majority in the *profession* enjoy their work and are well paid for it. 这个行业的大多数人都很享受他们的工作，而且薪水很高。

派生 professional *adj.* 职业的 *n.* 专业人员

resistant
[rɪˈzɪstənt]
★★★

释义 *adj.* 抵抗的，有抵抗力的

短语 heat *resistant* 耐热的

例句 During this time, she faced opposition from numerous sources who were *resistant* to change. 在此期间，她面临着来自众多抵制变革的人士的反对。

用法 resistant to 对……有抵抗力的

派生 resistance *n.* 抵抗

resolve
[rɪˈzɒlv]
★★

释义 *v.* 决心；决定；分解 *n.* 解决；决心

短语 *resolve* an issue 解决问题

例句 She *resolved* that she would never speak to him again. 她决心再也不理他。

He was to pay dearly for his lack of *resolve*. 他将为自己缺乏决心而付出高昂的代价。

真题 Mental health is the source of creativity for solving problems and *resolving* conflict. 心理健康是创造力的来源，这种创造力可以让我们解决问题和化解冲突。(2016 翻译)

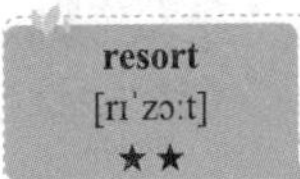

resort
[rɪˈzɔ:t]
★★

释义 *v.* 求助，诉诸 *n.* 度假胜地，凭借；手段

短语 summer *resort* 避暑胜地 last *resort* 最后手段

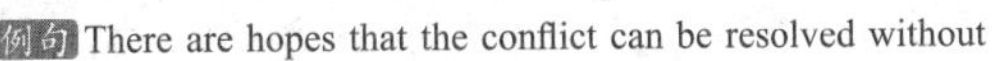

例句 There are hopes that the conflict can be resolved without *resort* to violence. 冲突有望不需要诉诸武力而得到解决。

The ski *resorts* are expanding to meet the growing number of skiers that come here. 该滑雪胜地正在扩建以应对来这里滑雪的不断增长的人数。

近义 adopt *v.* 采用，采纳

routine
[ru:ˈti:n]
★★★

释义 *n.* 例行公事，常规 *adj.* 常规的，例行的

短语 *routine* maintenance 日常维护

例句 The operator carried out *routine* maintenance of the machine. 操作员对机器进行了日常维护。

近义 daily *adj.* 日常的

派生 routinely *adv.* 例行公事地，常规地

successful
[səkˈsesful]
★★★

释义 *adj.* 圆满的；顺利的；成功的

短语 *successful* marriage 成功的婚姻

例句 I am looking forward to a long and *successful* partnership with him. 我期盼着能与他建立长期而有成效的合作关系。

派生 successfully *adv.* 成功地；顺利地

successive
[səkˈsesɪv]
★★

释义 接连的，连续的

短语 *successive* winning / losing 连胜 / 连败

例句 The recession continued, as GDP fell for the third *successive* quarter. 随着GDP连续第三个季度出现下滑，经济衰退仍在持续。

派生 successively *adv.* 相继地

suffice
[səˈfaɪs]
★

释义 *v.* 充足，足够；使满足

例句 A cover letter should never exceed one page; often a far shorter letter will *suffice*. 一封求职信不应超过一页，通常来说，一封相对非常简短的信就足够了。

用法 suffice for 满足……的需要

派生 sufficient *adj.* 足够的

sufficient
[səˈfɪʃənt]
★★★

释义 *adj.* 足够的，充分的

短语 more than *sufficient* 绰绰有余

例句 Price stability is a necessary but not a *sufficient* condition for economic growth. 物价稳定是经济增长的必要条件，但不是充分条件。

真题 A few generative rules are then *sufficient* to unfold the entire fundamental structure of a language, which is why children can learn it so quickly. 几个生成规则就足以展开一门语言的整个基本结构，这就是为什么孩子们能学得这么快。（2012 翻译）

派生 sufficiently *adv.* 充分地，足够地

symposium
[sɪmˈpəuzɪəm]
★

释义 *n.* 讨论会，专题报告会；专题论文集

短语 a *symposium* on... 关于……的研讨会

例句 There will be a company-sponsored *symposium* on degradable plastic and the environment. 公司将赞助主办一个关于可降解塑料与环境的研讨会。

近义 conference *n.* 会议，研讨会

traditional
[trəˈdɪʃən(ə)l]
★★★

释义 *adj.* 传统的；惯例的

例句 Pumpkin pie is a *traditional* American dish served on Thanksgiving. 南瓜馅饼是美国传统的感恩节食物。

真题 Conditional cash transfers programs have helped preserve *traditional* lifestyles. 有条件现金转移支付项目有助于保护传统生活方式。（2021 阅读理解）

派生 traditionally *adv.* 传统上

释义 *n.* 踪迹，痕迹；小路 *v.* 追踪；拖，拉

短语 nature *trail* 通往自然景观的小径

例句 The hot spots and their volcanic *trails* are milestones that

mark the passage of the plates. 热点及其火山痕迹是标记板块移动路径的里程碑。

近义 trace *v.* 追踪

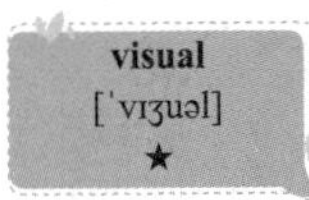

释义 视觉的 *n.* 视觉资料

短语 *visual* field 视野 a *visual* stimulus 视觉刺激

例句 She appreciates the *visual* arts such as painting and film. 她欣赏绘画、电影等视觉艺术。

派生 visually *adv.* 视觉上

Word List 33

释义 *adj.* [ɑːˈtɪkjələt] 善于表达的 *v.* [ɑːˈtɪkjəleɪt] 清楚地表达

例句 You have to be *articulate* to be good at debating. 你必须口齿伶俐才能擅长辩论。

I found myself unable to *articulate* my feelings. 我感到无法用语言来表达我的感情。

派生 inarticulate *adj.* 口齿不清的

释义 *adj.* 人造的；不真诚的；假的

例句 The city is dotted with small lakes, natural and *artificial*. 这个城市小型湖泊星罗棋布，有天然的，也有人工的。

同义 man-made *adj.* 人造的

派生 artificiality *n.* 人工

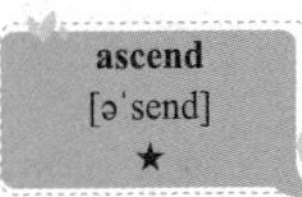

释义 *v.* 上升；攀登；登上；晋级

例句 We watched the balloon *ascending* higher and higher. 我们看着气球升得越来越高。

Before *ascending* to the bench, she was a lawyer in a large New York firm. 在升为法官之前，她是纽约一家大型律所的律师。

用法 ascend to 升至 / 追溯到

近义 rise *v.* 升起

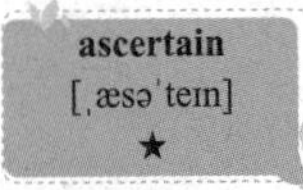

释义 *v.* 弄清，查明；确信

例句 The police have so far been unable to *ascertain* the cause of the explosion. 警方到目前为止还不能确定爆炸的原因。

用法 ascertain sth. from sb. / sth. 从某人那里确定某事

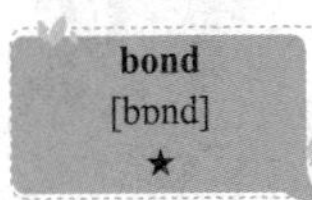

释义 *v.*（使）建立亲密关系；使结合 *n.* 纽带；联系；债券

例句 The agreement strengthened the *bonds* between the two countries. 协议加强了两国间的联系。

Mothers who are depressed sometimes fail to *bond* with their children. 患忧郁症的母亲有时无法和孩子建立亲密关系。

派生 bonding *n.* 黏合

cooperate
[kəʊˈɒpəreɪt]
★★★

释义 *v.* 合作，协作

例句 Both sides agreed to *cooperate* to prevent illegal hunting in the area. 双方同意就防止该地区的非法狩猎进行合作。

派生 cooperative *adj.* 合作的

coordinate
[kəʊˈɔːdɪneɪt]
★★★

释义 *v.* 协调，配合 *n.* 坐标

例句 They are working together to *coordinate* the whole campaign. 他们正在一起协调整个活动。

派生 coordinator *n.* 协调人

释义 *v.* 竞争；对付，处理 *n.* 长袍

例句 It must be really hard to *cope* with three young children and a job. 要照顾3个小孩还要工作肯定不容易。

用法 cope with 处理，应付

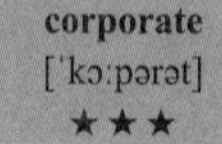

释义 *adj.* 公司的；法人的；全体的

例句 The company plans to relocate its *corporate* headquarters to New York. 这家公司计划把公司总部迁到纽约。

派生 corporation *n.* 公司

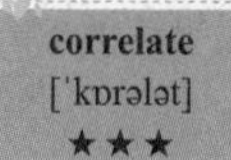

释义 *v.*（使）互相关联

例句 These new conservation laws *correlate* and explain a wide range of physical phenomena. 这些新的守恒定律把极其广泛的物理现象相互联系起来，并对它们做出了说明。

派生 correlation *n.* 相互关系，关联

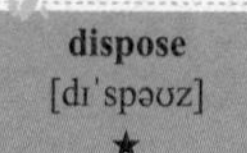

释义 *v.* 处理；布置，安排

例句 Everyone also has a responsibility to ensure they *dispose* of their rubbish appropriately. 每个人都有责任确保他们妥善处理垃圾。

派生 disposal *n.* 处理；安排

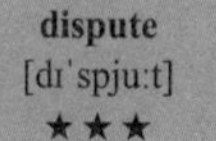

释义 *n.* / *v.* 争论 *n.* 纠纷 *v.* 对……提出质疑

例句 All those matters are in *dispute* and it is not for me to decide them. 所有这些事项都尚无定论，也不是我可以决定的。

派生 disputable *adj.* 有争议的，有待讨论的

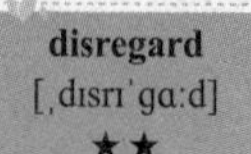

释义 *v.* 不理会；忽视 *n.* 忽视；漠视

例句 Local councillors accused the terrorists of showing a complete *disregard* for human life. 当地议员指责恐怖分子完全漠视生命。

We cannot *disregard* his coming late to work so often. 对他上班经常迟到这件事，我们不能不管。

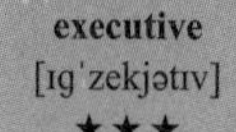

释义 *n.* 总经理，董事，行政负责人 *adj.* 执行的，实施的

短语 executive jobs / positions 行政工作 / 职位

例句 Spark is a young, successful *executive* at an Internet-services company in Tokyo. 斯帕克是东京一家互联网服务公司的一位成功的年轻高管。

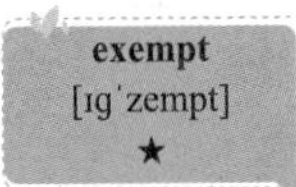

exemplify [ɪgˈzemplɪfaɪ] ★★

释义 *v.* 举例证明;示范

例句 The recent oil price rises *exemplify* the difficulties which the motor industry is now facing. 最近的石油涨价是汽车工业正面临困难的一个例子。

用法 be exemplified by... 以……为代表

exempt [ɪgˈzempt] ★

释义 *adj.* 免除的 *v.* 免除

例句 Companies with twenty-five or fewer employees would be exempted from the tax. 员工人数不超过 25 人的公司将免征该税。

派生 exemption *n.* 豁免

foremost [ˈfɔːməust] ★

释义 *adj.* 最先的;最初的;主要的 *adv.* 首要地

例句 During his lifetime, he was also one of England's *foremost* classical-music critics. 在他的一生中,他也是英国最重要的古典音乐评论家之一。

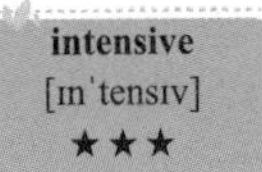

guarantee [ˌgærənˈtiː] ★★★

释义 *v.* 保证;担保 *n.* 保证;保证书

例句 His turning up will *guarantee* the success of the meeting. 他的出席将保证会议成功举办。

The treadmill costs £499 including shipping and a twelve-month *guarantee*. 这台跑步机售价 499 英镑,包括运费和 12 个月的保修期。

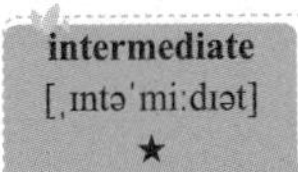

intensive [ɪnˈtensɪv] ★★★

释义 *adj.* 加强的,集中的;集约的

短语 *intensive* agriculture 集约农业 *intensive* training 大强度训练

例句 As capital *intensive* industry, the capital support is needed for the real estate industry. 作为资本密集型行业之一,房地产业的发展离不开资本市场的支持。

派生 intensively *adv.* 强烈地;集中地

intermediate [ˌɪntəˈmiːdɪət] ★

释义 *adj.* 中间的;中级的 *n.* 中间体,媒介物

短语 an intermediate skier / student 中等程度的滑雪者 / 学生

例句 There are three levels of difficulty in this game: low, *intermediate*, and high. 这个游戏有 3 个难度级别:低级、中级和高级。

She often used her father as an *intermediate* in arguments with her mother. 她经常将她的父亲作为与母亲争论的中间人。

internal [ɪnˈtɜːnəl] ★★★

释义 *adj.* 内部的,内的;国内的,内政的

例句 Today, the social sciences are largely focused on disciplinary problems and *internal* scholarly debates, rather than on topics with external impact. 如今,社会科学主要关注学科问题和内部学术辩论,而不是具有外部影响的话题。

反义 external *adj.* 外部的,外面的

loom [luːm] ★★

释义 *n.* 织布机 *v.* 隐现,(危险、忧虑等)迫近

例句 Another government spending crisis is *looming* in the United States. 另一场政府开支危机在美国一触即发。

A *loom* is a machine that is used for weaving thread into cloth. 织布机是用来把线织成布的机器。

派生 looming *adj.* 迫近的

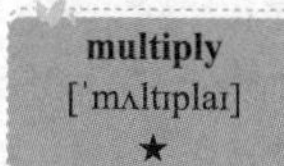

释义 *v.* 使相乘；倍增，繁殖

例句 Without such regulations, tragedies involving water scooters are sure to *multiply*, which makes many beaches unsafe for recreation. 如果没有这样的规定，水上摩托车引发的悲剧肯定会成倍增加，许多海滩会变得不够安全，无法开展娱乐活动。

派生 multiple *n.* 倍数

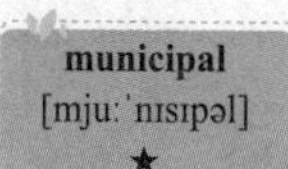

释义 *adj.* 市政的；地方性的，地方自治的

短语 *municipal* engineering 市政工程

例句 The *municipal* government has decided to have a clampdown on building new business centre buildings. 市政府决定不准再建造新的商业中心大楼。

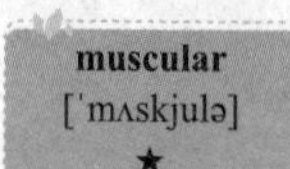

释义 *adj.* 肌肉的；肌肉发达的；强健的

短语 a *muscular* body / build 强壮的身体 / 体格

例句 Police said the man is Hispanic, approximately 6 feet tall, with a *muscular* build. 警方称该男子为西班牙裔，身高约 6 英尺，肌肉发达。

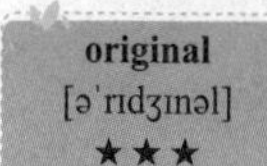

释义 *adj.* 起初的；原来的；独创的；新颖的 *n.* 原文，原稿

例句 *original* design 原设计 *original* data 源数据

例句 It's a fast-moving detective story with strikingly *original* characters. 这是一部情节快速发展的侦探小说，人物都非常有独创性。

Many people expressed a strong preference for the *original* plan. 许多人强烈表示喜欢原计划。

派生 originally *adv.* 起初

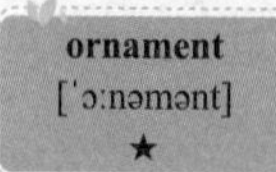

释义 *n.* 装饰；点缀 *v.* 装饰，点缀，美化

例句 The room was full of pictures and other beautiful *ornaments*. 这个房间布满了图画和其他漂亮的装饰品。

The costumes are richly *ornamented* and are made of bright-coloured silk. 这些服装装饰华丽，由色彩鲜艳的丝绸制成。

派生 ornamental *adj.* 装饰性的

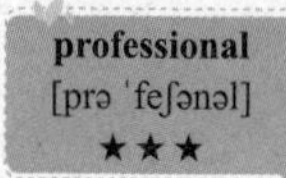

释义 职业的，专门的 *n.* 自由职业者，专业人员

短语 *professional* training 职业培训

例句 He dealt with the problem in a highly *professional* way. 他处理这个问题非常专业。

真题 *Professionals* trying to acquire new skills will be able to do so without going into debt. 想要学习新技能的专业人士可以在不负债的情况下做到这一点。（2018 阅读理解）

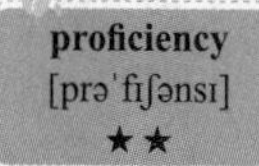

释义 *n.* 熟练，精通

短语 *proficiency* test 水平测试

例句 Because of his Portuguese *proficiency*, Macau became the ideal destination for him. 由于能讲一口流利的葡萄牙语，澳门成了他发挥特长的理想之地。

用法 proficiency in 精通

profile
[ˈprəufaɪl]
★★

释义 *n.* 侧面(像);轮廓,外形;人物简介

短语 personal *profile* 个人档案

例句 An image of the President's *profile* appears on the coin. 总统的头像出现在硬币上。

用法 profile one's career 介绍某人的职业生涯

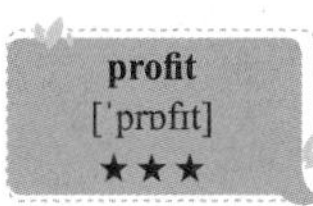

profit
[ˈprɒfɪt]
★★★

释义 *n.* 利润,收益 *v.* 得利,获益;有利于

短语 *profit* margins 利润率 *profit* and loss 损益

例句 You can improve your chances of *profit* by sensible planning. 你可以通过合理的计划增加盈利的机会。

真题 Scientific publishers routinely report *profit* margins approaching 40% on their operations at a time when the rest of the publishing industry is in an existential crisis. 在出版行业陷入生存危机之际,科学出版商的利润率却经常接近40%。(2020 阅读理解)

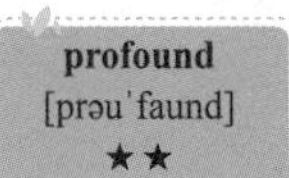

profound
[prəuˈfaund]
★★

释义 *adj.* 深刻的,意义深远的;造诣深的

短语 a *profound* problem / meaning 深刻的问题 / 意义

例句 Many fairy tales have *profound* meanings, and they're not intended for children only. 许多童话故事具有深刻的意义,它们不仅仅是写给儿童的。

真题 This aversion to arguments is common, but it depends on a mistaken view of arguments that causes *profound* problems for our personal and social lives. 这种对争论的厌恶是常见的,但它是基于一种错误的争论观,这一争论观给我们的个人和社会生活带来了深刻的问题。(2019 阅读理解)

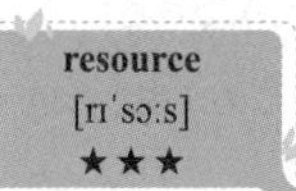

resource
[rɪˈsɔːs]
★★★

释义 *n.* (*pl.*) 资源;资料;财力

短语 human *resource* 人力的源 natural *resources* 自然资源

例句 A country's principal *resource* is its brainpower. 一个国家最重要的资源是其人才库。

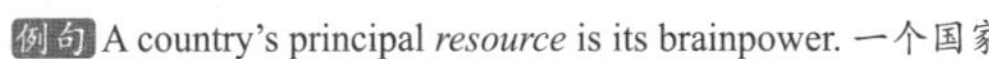

真题 What matters is that all the data will belong to a private monopoly which developed them using public *resources*. 重要的是,所有数据将属于利用公共资源开发它们的私人垄断企业。(2018 阅读理解)

respond
[rɪˈspɒnd]
★★★

释义 *v.* 回答,响应,做出反应

例句 This modest group size allows our teachers to *respond* to the needs of each student. 这样的小组规模适中,可以使老师照顾到每一个学生的需求。

用法 respond with sth. 以……回应

派生 respondent *n.* 答卷人,调查对象;被告

真题 The NHS trust *responded* to Denham's verdict with necessary adjustments. NHS 信托基金对德纳姆的判决做出了必要的调整。(2018 阅读理解)

responsibility
[rɪˌspɒnsəˈbɪlətɪ]
★★★

释义 *n.* 责任,责任心;职责

短语 social *responsibility* 社会责任

例句 We are recruiting a sales manager with *responsibility* for the European market. 我们正在招聘负责欧洲市场的销售经理。

真题 " This indicates there is a real personal *responsibility* in counteracting this problem," says Roxanne

Stone, editor in chief at Barna Group. 巴纳集团总编辑罗克珊·斯通表示："这表明,应对这个问题,个人确实有责任。"(2018 阅读理解)

释义 *adj.* 王室的;盛大的 *n.*(非正式)王室成员

短语 *royal* palace / family 皇家宫殿 / 皇室

例句 The castle, which is located on 11,700 acres, was leased to members of the *royal* family between 1848 and 1970. 这座城堡占地 11700 英亩,在 1848 年至 1970 年间租给了英国王室成员。

近义 regal *adj.* 王室的

释义 *n.* 自杀 *v.* 自杀

短语 *suicide* rate 自杀率

例句 After the scandal was exposed, Dr Bailey committed *suicide*. 丑闻曝光后,贝利博士自杀了。

用法 commit suicide 自杀

派生 suicidal *adj.* 有自杀倾向的

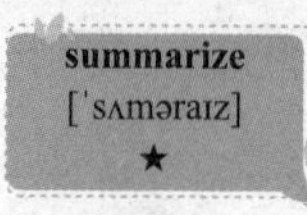

释义 *adj.* 合适的,适宜的

短语 *suitable* candidate 合适人选

例句 Employers usually decide within five minutes whether someone is *suitable* for the job. 雇主通常在 5 分钟内就能决定一个人是否适合这份工作。

派生 suitability *n.* 适合;适当

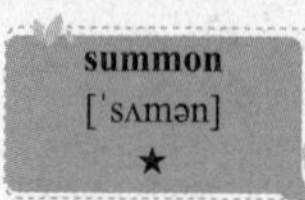

释义 *v.* (summarise) 概括,总结

短语 to *summarize* 简而言之

例句 Basically, the article can be *summarized* in three sentences. 这篇文章基本上可以概括为三句话。

近义 outline *v.* 概述

派生 summarization *n.* 概要

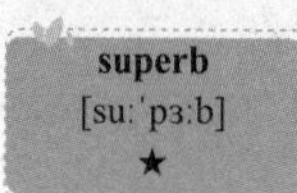

释义 *v.* 召唤;传讯;鼓起(勇气)

短语 *summon* a meeting 召集会议 *summon* assistance 请求援助

例句 The general *summoned* all his officers. 将军把所有的军官召集在一起。Though she felt low, she *summoned* the courage to rebuild her life. 虽然她感到低落,但她鼓起勇气重新开始生活。

superb
[suːˈpɜːb]
★

释义 *adj.* 极好的,杰出的;华丽的

短语 a *superb* performance 一场精彩演出

例句 There is the Royal Shakespeare Company (RSC), which presents *superb* productions of the plays at the Shakespeare Memorial Theatre on the Avon. 其中一个是皇家莎士比亚剧团,它在埃文河河畔的莎士比亚纪念剧院里上演很多高品质的戏剧作品。

近义 magnificent *adj.* 宏伟的,壮丽的

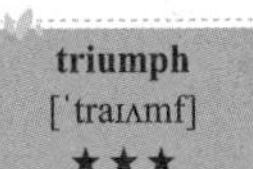

trait [treɪt] ★★★

释义 *n.* 特征，特点，特性

短语 behavioral *trait* 行为特性

例句 Their work makes a rather startling assertion: the *trait* we commonly call talent is highly overrated. 他们的研究得出了一个让人相当吃惊的论断：我们通常称为天赋的特质被严重高估了。

近义 feature *n.* 特点

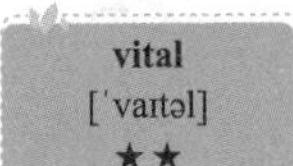

triumph [ˈtraɪʌmf] ★★★

释义 *n.* 胜利，成功 *v.* 得胜，战胜

短语 a shout of *triumph* 喜悦的欢呼声

例句 All her life, Kelly had stuck with difficult tasks and challenges, and *triumphed*. 凯莉一生经历了各种艰巨的任务与挑战，她都一一成功应对了。

真题 By the time that Shakespeare was twenty-five, Kyd had written a tragedy that crowded the pit; and Marlowe had brought poetry and genius to *triumph* on the common stage. 到莎士比亚 25 岁时，基德写出了一部让剧场爆满的悲剧；马洛让诗歌和创造力在普通舞台上大放异彩。（2018 翻译）

vital [ˈvaɪtəl] ★★

释义 *adj.* 生死攸关的；至关重要的

短语 *vital* force 生命力

例句 Only recently have they come to see the *vital* part forests will have to play in storing carbon. 直到最近，他们才看到森林在储存碳方面所发挥的重要作用。

近义 crucial *adj.* 至关重要的

派生 vitality *n.* 活力

Word List 34

aspire [əˈspaɪə] ★★

释义 *v.* 立志；渴望；追求

例句 We hope that more young people can be encouraged to *aspire* after the better future. 我们希望能鼓励更多的年轻人去追求更美好的未来。

词组 aspire after 追求；渴求

派生 aspiration *n.* 抱负，志向

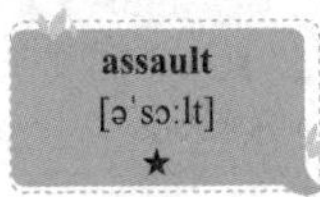

assault [əˈsɔːlt] ★

释义 *v.* & *n.* 攻击；袭击

例句 He was jailed for *assault*. 他因人身攻击而入狱。

Two men *assaulted* him after he left the bar. 他离开酒吧后，两名男子袭击了他。

近义 attack *v.* 袭击，攻击

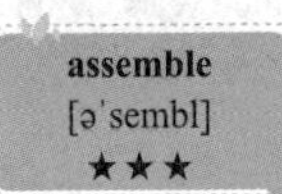

assemble [əˈsembl] ★★★

释义 *v.* 集合；收集；装配

例句 They *assembled* a team of experts to solve the problem. 他们召集了一个专家小组来解决这个问题。

Their father helped them *assemble* their new bicycles in the garage. 他们的父亲在车库里帮他们组装新自行车。

派生 assembly *n.* 装配;集会

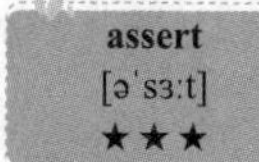

assert [ə'sɜːt] ★★★

释义 *v.* 断言;主张;维护

例句 He *asserted* that nuclear power was a safe and non-polluting energy source. 他断言核能是一种安全、无污染的能源。

派生 assertion *n.* 断言;主张

bonus ['bəʊnəs] ★★

释义 *n.* 红利;奖金;额外好处

例句 The salary was set at £12,000, plus a *bonus* if the company had a good year. 工资定为12000英镑,如果公司一年的业绩好,还会有奖金。

We felt we might finish third, and any better would be a *bonus*. 我们感觉我们可能会获得第三名,要是能比这个名次更好那就是意外的惊喜了。

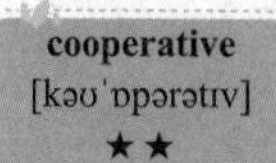

cooperative [kəʊ'ɒpərətɪv] ★★

释义 *adj.* 合作的,协作的

例句 Everyone in the team is very *cooperative*, so the project goes on smoothly. 团队里的每个人都很配合,所以项目进展顺利。

派生 cooperation *n.* 合作

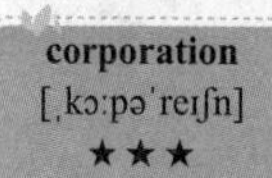

corporation [ˌkɔːpə'reɪʃn] ★★★

释义 *n.* 社团,公司,法人

例句 Microsoft is one of the biggest *corporations* in the world. 微软公司是世界上最大的公司之一。

真题 According to a study by Catalyst, between 2010 and 2015 the share of women on the boards of global *corporations* increased by 54 percent. 根据Catalyst的一项研究,2010年至2015年,全球企业董事会中的女性比例增加了54%。(2020阅读理解)

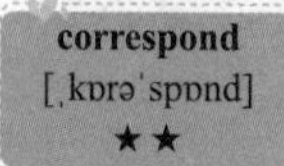

correspond [ˌkɒrə'spɒnd] ★★

释义 *v.* 通信,相符,相当

例句 The written record of the conversation doesn't *correspond* to what was actually said. 那次谈话的文字记录与原话不符。

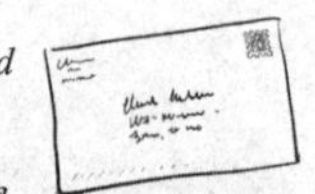

Judy still *corresponds* with British friends she met in Newcastle three years ago. 朱迪仍然和三年前在纽卡斯尔认识的英国朋友们通信。

派生 correspondence *n.* 通信

corrupt [kə'rʌpt] ★★★

释义 *v.* 贿赂,收买 *adj.* 腐败的,贪污的

例句 The company is under investigation for *corrupt* practices. 这家公司因有腐败行为而接受调查。

派生 corruptive *adj.* 使堕落的;腐败性的

cosmic ['kɒzmɪk] ★★

释义 *adj.* 宇宙的;无比巨大的

用法 cosmic ray 宇宙线 cosmic dust 宇宙尘埃

例句 The universe is believed to have been created about 15 billion years ago in a *cosmic* explosion. 宇宙被认为是在150亿年前的一次宇宙爆炸中形成的。

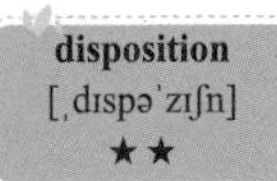

disposition
[ˌdɪspəˈzɪʃn]
★★

释义 *n.* 性情;倾向;布置;支配权

例句 He was a nice lad — bright and with a sunny *disposition*. 他是个不错的小伙子——聪明伶俐而且性格开朗。

He is considering the *disposition* of furniture in his new house. 他在考虑怎样在新居所中布置家具。

disrupt
[dɪsˈrʌpt]
★★

释义 *v.* 扰乱;使中断;妨碍;使分裂

例句 The quarrels of the different political parties seemed likely to *disrupt* the state. 各政党的争执可能导致国家分裂。

派生 disruption *n.* 扰乱;破坏

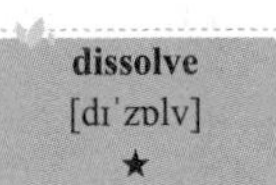

dissolve
[dɪˈzɒlv]
★

释义 *v.* (使)溶解,(使)融化;解散,解除

例句 We have to keep stirring until all the cubes of jelly have *dissolved*. 我们不得不一直搅拌,直到所有的果冻块都溶解。

Diana's marriage was *dissolved* after three years of separation with her husband. 黛安娜与丈夫分居三年后离婚了。

派生 dissolvable *adj.* 可溶解的

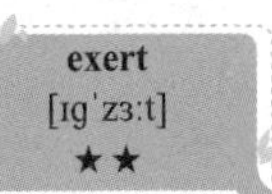

exert
[ɪgˈzɜːt]
★★

释义 *v.* 尽(力),努力;施加(压力等);发挥

例句 The Europeans failed to *exert* some influence over the region. 欧洲未能成功对该地区施加影响。

用法 exert oneself 努力,尽力

派生 exertion *n.* 努力

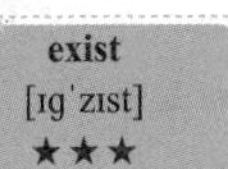

exist
[ɪgˈzɪst]
★★★

释义 *v.* 存在;生存,生活

例句 They say the first way to treat a problem is to admit the problem *exists*. 他们说,解决问题的第一种方法是承认问题的存在。

用法 exist with 与……共存

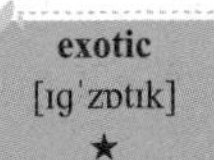

exotic
[ɪgˈzɒtɪk]
★

释义 *adj.* 奇异的;异国情调的;外(国)来的

词组 *exotic* flowers/plants 异国花卉 / 植物

例句 She travels to all kinds of *exotic* locations all over the world. 她走遍了全世界所有具有奇异风情的地方。

expand
[ɪkˈspænd]
★★★

释义 *v.* (使)扩张;增加;扩展;详述

例句 Tyler seized the opportunity to *expand* the market for his goods. 泰勒抓住这个机会为他的商品扩大市场。

I repeated the question and waited for her to *expand* on the details. 我把问题重复了一遍,等着她详细回答。

用法 expand on / upon sth. 详述……;阐述……

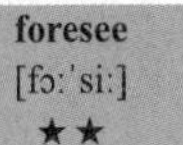

foresee
[fɔːˈsiː]
★★

释义 *v.* 预见,预知

例句 It is difficult for city designers to *foresee* what will happen in the future. 城市设计者很难预见未来会发生什么。

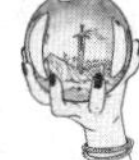

近义 forecast *v./n.* 预测

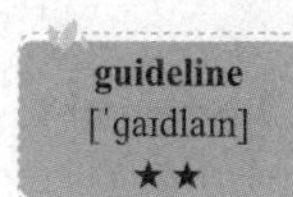

guideline
[ˈgaɪdlaɪn]
★★

释义 *n.* 指导方针，准则

短语 operational *guidelines* 操作指南

例句 The economic policy *guidelines* are scheduled to be compiled in June. 经济政策指导方针计划在6月份制定。

hint
[hɪnt]
★

释义 *v.* / *n.* 暗示，示意

例句 They *hinted* to us that they would take our suggestion. 他们向我们暗示说，他们将采纳我们的建议。

I've tipped him a wink and given him a *hint*, but he didn't get it. 我向他眨眨眼，给了他一个暗示，但他没有领会。

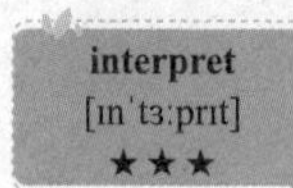

interpret
[ɪnˈtɜːprɪt]
★★★

释义 *v.* 解释，说明；口译

短语 right to *interpret* 解释权

例句 I didn't know whether to *interpret* her silence as acceptance or refusal. 我不知该把她的沉默看作是接受还是拒绝。

She couldn't speak much English so her children had to *interpret* for her. 她讲不了几句英语，所以她的孩子们得给她翻译。

派生 interpretation *n.* 解释，理解

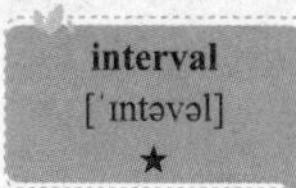

interval
[ˈɪntəvəl]
★

释义 *n.* 间隔，间歇；（幕间或工间）休息

短语 time *interval* 时间间隔

例句 The ferry service has restarted after an *interval* of 2 years. 轮渡服务在中断2年后重新开始。

There will be two 20-minute *intervals* during the opera. 歌剧演出期间有两次20分钟的幕间休息。

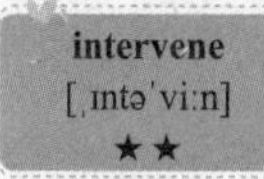

intervene
[ˌɪntəˈviːn]
★★

释义 *v.* 干涉，干预；介入；阻挠

例句 The headmaster had to *intervene* before the situation got worse. 在情况恶化之前，校长及时出面调解了。

We enjoyed the picnic until a thunderstorm *intervened*. 那次野餐我们玩得很痛快，后来一场暴风雨使它中断了。

派生 intervention *n.* 干预

loyal
[ˈlɔɪəl]
★★

释义 *adj.* 忠诚的，忠贞的

例句 He's determined to remain *loyal* to the team whatever comes his way. 他决心不管发生什么事都忠于球队。

派生 loyalty *n.* 忠诚，忠心

mute
[mjuːt]
★

释义 *adj.* 哑的，缄默的 *n.* 哑巴 *v.* 减弱……的声音

短语 a *mute* child 沉默寡言的孩子

例句 The child has been *mute* since birth. 这孩子从生下来就不能讲话。

When someone asked her something she felt pointless, she often remained *mute*. 当有人问她一些她觉得毫无意义的问题时，她经常保持沉默。

mutual [ˈmjuːtʃuəl] ★★

释义 *adj.* 相互的；共同的，共有的

短语 *mutual* trust / respect 相互信任 / 尊重

例句 Positive long-term acceptance of the child involves the parents' *mutual* support throughout the time after birth. 对孩子的长期积极接纳包括父母在孩子出生后的整个时期的相互支持。

派生 mutually *adv.* 相互地

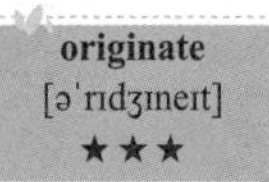

notion [ˈnəuʃən] ★★★

释义 *n.* 概念，观念，看法

例句 It's time to reinvent the formula for how work is conducted, since we are still relying on a very 20th century *notion* of work, Hagel says. 哈格尔认为，是时候重新设计工作方式了，这是因为我们目前仍依赖于 20 世纪的工作理念。

派生 notional *adj.* 理论上的；概念的

originate [əˈrɪdʒɪneɪt] ★★★

释义 *v.* 发源，起源；发明，创立

例句 His book *originated* from a short story. 他的书是根据一个短篇小说撰写的。

真题 A publishing firm approached Dickens to write a story in monthly installments, as a backdrop for a series of woodcuts by the then-famous artist Robert Seymour, who had *originated* the idea for the story. 一家出版公司找到狄更斯，让他以每月一期的方式写一个故事，作为当时著名的艺术家罗伯特·西摩创作一系列木刻作品的背景故事，这个故事的灵感就是源于西蒙。（2017 阅读理解）

派生 origination *n.* 起源

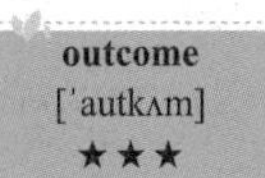

outcome [ˈautkʌm] ★★★

释义 *n.* 结果

短语 learning *outcome* 学习结果

例句 We are anxiously awaiting the *outcome* of their discussion. 我们急切地等待着他们讨论的结果。

近义 result *n.* 结果

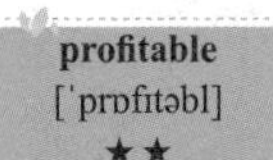

profitable [ˈprɒfɪtəbl] ★★

释义 *adj.* 有利可图的，有益的

短语 a *profitable* business 有利可图的生意

例句 Most of the changes that companies make are intended to keep them *profitable*, and this need not always mean increasing productivity. 公司做出的大多数改变都是为了保持盈利，而这并不总是意味着提高生产率。

派生 profitably *adv.* 有利地

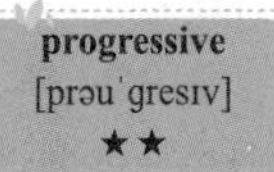

progressive [prəuˈgresɪv] ★★

释义 *adj.* 进步的，先进的；前进的

短语 *progressive* forces 进步力量

例句 How can *progressive* and significant change in the construction industry be achieved at a national policy level? 在国家政策层面上，如何才能使建筑业逐步实现重大变革？

派生 advanced *adj.* 先进的；高级的

prohibit [prəˈhɪbɪt] ★★

释义 *v.* 禁止，不准；阻止

短语 strictly *prohibit* 严禁

例句 The use of cameras or video equipment is *prohibited* in the theatre. 剧院内禁止使用照相机或录像设备。

近义 forbid *v.* 禁止

派生 prohibition *n.* 禁令，禁律；禁止

释义 *n.* [ˈprɒdʒekt] 方案，工程，项目 *v.* [prəˈdʒekt] 投射，放映；设计，规划

短语 graduation *project* 毕业设计

例句 This *project* is designed to help people who have been out of work for a long time. 这个项目旨在帮助那些长期失业的人。

The unemployment rate has been *projected* to rise by 10 %. 据预测，失业率将上升 10%。

派生 projection *n.* 预测；投影

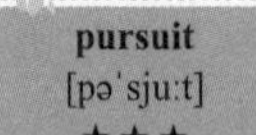

释义 *n.* 追赶，追求；追逐，追捕

短语 in hot *pursuit* 穷追不舍；紧随其后

例句 Good writing most often occurs when you are in hot *pursuit* of an idea rather than in a nervous search for errors. 优秀的写作通常发生在你对一个想法的热切追求中，而不是紧张地寻找错误的时候。

近义 chase *v.* 追逐，追赶；追求

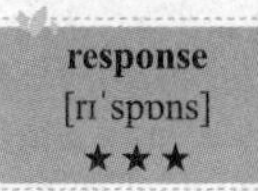

释义 *n.* 回答，响应，反应

短语 emergency *response* 应急响应

例句 I received an encouraging *response* to my project. 我的项目得到了令人鼓舞的回应。

真题 In *response*, the American Academy formed the Commission on the Humanities and Social Sciences. 作为回应，美国科学院成立了人文社会科学委员会。（2014 阅读理解）

近义 reply *n.* 回答，答复

派生 responsible *adj.* 负责的

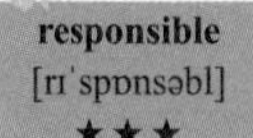

释义 *adj.* 有责任心的；负有责任的

短语 *responsible* stakeholder 有责任的利益相关者

例句 A person is held *responsible* for his conduct and given credit for his achievements. 一个人对其行为负责，并因其成就而受到赞扬。

用法 be held responsible for sth. 对……负责；追究责任

派生 responsibility *n.* 责任

释义 *v.* 恢复，使复原；修复，重建

短语 *restore* public confidence 恢复公众信心

例句 After the shooting, it was some hours before the police could *restore* calm to the neighbourhood. 枪击事件后，警察花了好几个小时才使那个地区重新平静下来。

真题 The main purpose of this "clawback" rule is to hold bankers accountable for harmful risk-taking and to *restore* public trust in financial institutions. 这项"追回"规定的主要目的是让银行家对有害的冒险行为负责，并恢复公众对金融机构的信任。（2019 阅读理解）

近义 recover *v.* 恢复；康复

summary
['sʌmərɪ]
★

释义 *n.* 摘要，概要 *adj.* 概括的，简略的

短语 annual *summary* 年度总结

例句 At the end of the news, they often give you a *summary* of the main stories. 在新闻结束的时候，他们常常会总结一下主要的新闻内容。

用法 in summary 总之

派生 summarize *v.* 总结

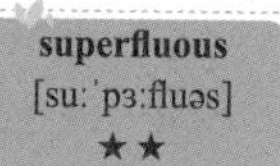

superficial
[ˌsuːpə'fɪʃ(ə)l]
★

释义 *adj.* 表面的；肤浅的，浅薄的

短语 a *superficial* analysis 粗略的分析 a *superficial* injury 皮外伤

例句 When you first meet her, she gives a *superficial* impression of warmth and friendliness. 初次见面时，她总给人以热情亲切的表面印象。

反义 deep *adj.* 深的

派生 superficiality *n.* 肤浅

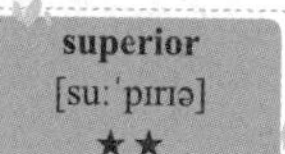

superfluous
[suː'pɜːfluəs]
★★

释义 *adj.* 多余的，过剩的

短语 *superfluous* information 多余的信息

例句 She gave him a look that made words *superfluous*. 她看了他一眼，这已表明一切，无须多言了。

近义 redundant *adj.* 多余的

派生 superfluously *adv.* 过剩地

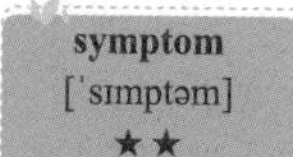

superior
[suː'pɪrɪə]
★★

释义 *adj.* 优良的，卓越的；上级的 *n.* 上级；长者；高手

短语 *superior* goods 优等物品

例句 A few years ago, it was virtually impossible to find *superior* quality coffee in local shops. 几年前，在当地商店里几乎买不到优质咖啡。

用法 be superior to sb. 比某人更好

派生 superiority *n.* 优势

symptom
['sɪmptəm]
★★

释义 *n.*（疾病的）症状；（不好事情的）征兆，表征

短语 a *severe* symptom 严重的症状

例句 The rise in inflation was just one *symptom* of the poor state of the economy. 通货膨胀率上升不过是经济不景气的一个征兆。

用法 a symptom of... ……的症状 / 征兆

近义 sign *n.* 迹象，征兆

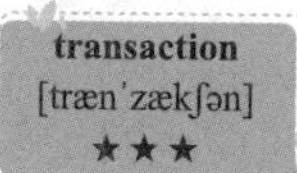

transaction
[træn'zækʃən]
★★★

释义 *n.* 交易，买卖

短语 a business *transaction* 商业交易

例句 Some companies are limiting the risk by conducting online *transactions* only with established business partners. 有些公司为了降低风险，只与那些已经熟识的固定贸易伙伴进行在线贸易。

用法 conduct a transaction 进行交易

近义 deal *n.* 交易

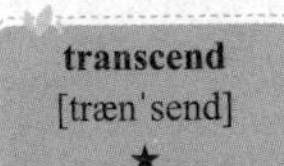

释义 *v.* 超出，超越

短语 *transcend* reality 超越现实

例句 The underlying message of the film is that love *transcends* everything else. 这部电影的根本意义是爱超越一切。

近义 exceed *v.* 超越

派生 transcendence *n.* 超越

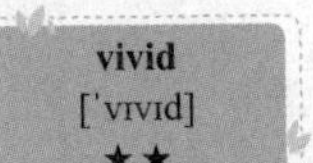

释义 *adj.* 鲜艳的；生动的，栩栩如生的

短语 *vivid* description 生动的描述

例句 The walls had been painted with *vivid* flowers, dark green trees, a silver blue lake. 墙壁上画着鲜艳的花朵、深绿色的树木和一个银蓝色的湖泊。

用法 a vivid account of... 对……的生动描述

派生 vividly *adv.* 生动地

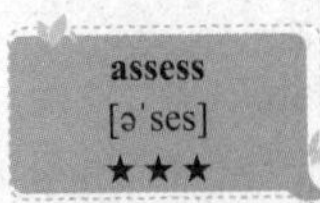

释义 *v.* 评价；评定；对……估价

例句 We need to *assess* whether or not the system is working. 我们需要评估这个系统有效。

The value of the business was *assessed* at £1.25 million. 该企业的价值估计为 125 万英镑。

派生 assessment *n.* 评估

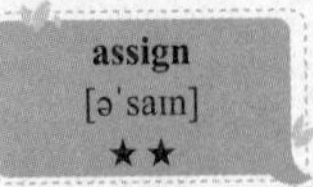

释义 *v.* 分配；分派，布置（工作、任务等）

例句 The teacher *assigned* us 10 math problems for homework. 老师给我们布置了 10 道数学题作为家庭作业。

The new teacher was *assigned* to the science lab. 新老师被分配到科学实验室工作。

近义 allocate *v.* 分配，划拨

派生 assignment *n.* 任务；分配

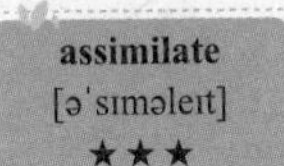

释义 *v.* 吸收；学习；融入；（使）同化

例句 It's hard to *assimilate* so much information in such a short time. 在这么短的时间内吸收这么多的信息是很困难的。

Many of these religious traditions have been *assimilated* into the culture. 这些宗教传统中有许多已被文化同化了。

近义 absorb *v.* 吸收

派生 assimilation *n.* 吸收

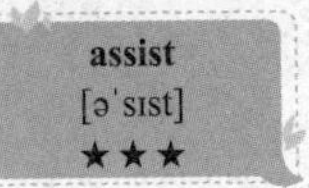

释义 *v.* / *n.* 帮助；协助

例句 The device *assists* those who can't climb stairs. 这个设备可以帮助那些不能爬楼梯的人。

She finished her homework without an *assist* from her father. 她不需要父亲的帮助就完成了家庭作业。

同义 help *v./ n.* 帮助

派生 assistance *n.* 援助

释义 *n.* 繁荣；隆隆声 *v.* 使兴旺

例句 The energy crisis is fueling a *boom* in alternative energy. 能源危机正在推动替代能源的发展。

People migrated into the towns where business was *booming.* 人们移居到商业繁荣的城镇。

近义 flourish *v.* 繁荣

派生 booming *adj.* 繁荣的

释义 *v./n.* 劝告，忠告 *n.* 法律顾问

例句 Randy *counsels* people who are trying to quit smoking. 兰迪为想戒烟的人提供咨询。

I should have listened to my father's wise *counsel*, and saved some money instead of spending it all. 我本该听从父亲的明智忠告，把钱省下一些而不是挥霍一空。

释义 *n.* 对应的人（或物）

例句 German officials are discussing this with their British *counterparts*. 德国官员正在与英国官员讨论此事。

释义 *n.* 赠券，优惠券

短语 a money-saving *coupon* 一张省钱的优惠券

例句 I'm always clipping *coupons* from the newspaper to use at the grocery store. 我总是从报纸上剪下优惠券在杂货店里用。

释义 *v.* 覆盖；包括；掩护；走完（一段路程） *n.* 盖子；封面

例句 The bird may *cover* thousands of miles during its migration. 这种鸟在迁徙过程中可能要飞数千英里。

派生 coverage *n.* 覆盖范围；新闻报道

释义 *v.* 创造，创作

例句 William Hanna and Joseph Barbera *created* the characters "Tom" and "Jerry". 威廉·汉纳和约瑟夫·巴贝拉创造了动画角色"汤姆"和"杰瑞"。

派生 creation *n.* 创造

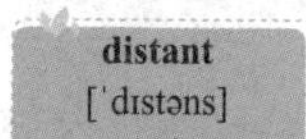

释义 *adj.* 远的；遥远的；疏远的

短语 *distant* view 远景

例句 Occasionally, he would holiday with his parents, but their relationship remained *distant.* 他偶尔会和父母一起度假，但他们的关系仍然很疏远。

She could hear the *distant* sound of fireworks exploding. 她能听到远处的烟花爆炸声。

派生 distantly *adv.* 远离地，遥远地；疏远地

distinct [dɪˈstɪŋkt] ★★★

释义 *adj.* 清楚的，明显的；截然不同的

例句 There is a *distinct* improvement in your spoken English. 你的英语口语有明显的进步。

The results of the survey fell into two *distinct* groups. 调查结果分为截然不同的两组。

派生 distinction *n.* 区别

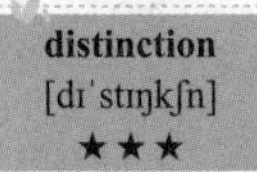

distinction [dɪˈstɪŋkʃn] ★★★

释义 *n.* 区别，差别；杰出；荣誉

例句 Once commercial promotion begins to fill the screen uninvited, the *distinction* between the Web and television fades. 一旦商业推广开始不请自来地充斥屏幕，网络和电视之间的区别就消失了。

用法 distinction between 区别

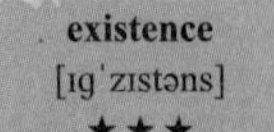

existence [ɪɡˈzɪstəns] ★★★

释义 *n.* 存在；生存，生活

例句 We cannot presume the *existence* of life on other planets. 我们不能推定其他行星上有生命存在。

用法 in existence 现存的

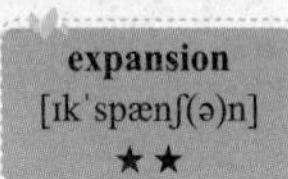

expansion [ɪkˈspænʃ(ə)n] ★★

释义 *n.* 扩张，膨胀；张开，伸展

例句 Despite the recession the company is confident of further *expansion*. 尽管经济衰退，公司对进一步扩张仍充满信心。

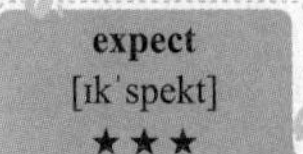

expect [ɪkˈspekt] ★★★

释义 *v.* 预期；期望，指望

例句 We didn't *expect* Madrid to lose. 我们没想到皇马会输掉这场比赛。

真题 Since students and parents *expect* a college degree to lead to a job, it is in the best interest of a school to turn out graduates who are as qualified as possible — or at least appear to be. 由于学生本人和他们的父母都希望大学的学位能帮他们找到工作，因此学校培养出最合格的毕业生或至少看起来是合格的毕业生是符合学校最大利益的。（2019 阅读理解）

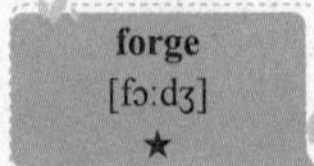

forge [fɔːdʒ] ★

释义 *v.* 形成；锻造，伪造 *n.* 锻工车间；锻炉

例句 A key part of the strategy is to *forge* partnerships with major European companies. 该战略的一个关键部分是与欧洲主要公司建立伙伴关系。

He admitted seven charges including *forging* passports. 他承认了包括伪造护照在内的 7 项指控。

guilty [ˈɡɪltɪ] ★★★

释义 *adj.* 内疚的；有罪的

例句 I feel so *guilty* about forgetting her birthday. 我忘记了她的生日，感到很内疚。

The man was found *guilty* of armed robbery. 那人犯有持械抢劫罪。

用法 feel guilty about 感到愧疚

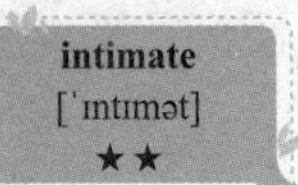

intimate [ˈɪntɪmət] ★★

释义 *adj.* 亲密的，密切的；详尽的 *n.* 熟人

短语 an *intimate* relationship 亲密的关系

例句 An *intimate* friendship grew up between them. 他们之间渐渐产生了亲密的友情。

Intimates of the star say that he has been upset by the personal attacks on him. 这位明星的密友说，他对

这些针对他的人身攻击感到不安。

派生 intimately *adv.* 密切地

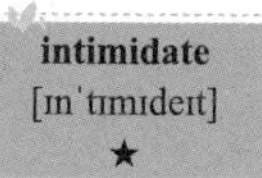

intimidate [ɪnˈtɪmɪdeɪt] ★

释义 *v.* 胁迫，威胁（某人做某事）

例句 They were *intimidated* into accepting a pay cut by the threat of losing their jobs. 他们因为受到失去工作的威胁而被迫同意减薪。

近义 frighten *v.* 使惊吓

派生 intimidating *adj.* 令人紧张不安的

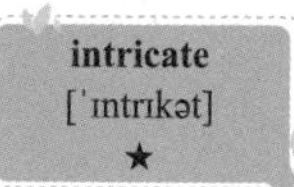

intricate [ˈɪntrɪkət] ★

释义 *adj.* 复杂的，错综的，难以理解的

例句 The watch mechanism is extremely *intricate* and very difficult to repair. 手表的机械结构非常复杂精细，很难修理。

近义 complicated *adj.* 复杂的

派生 intricately *adv.* 杂乱地

judge [dʒʌdʒ] ★★★

释义 *n.* 法官；裁判员 *v.* 审判；评论，裁判

例句 It will take a few more years to *judge* the impact of the Covid-19 pandemic. 要判断新冠肺炎疫情的影响还需要几年的时间。

派生 judgement *n.* 意见；判断力；审判；评论

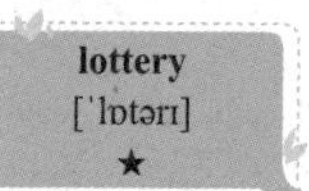

lottery [ˈlɒtərɪ] ★

释义 *n.* 碰运气的事，难于算计的事

例句 You may think that once people win the *lottery*, they live happily ever after. 你也许会想，他们一旦中了大奖，从此就会过着幸福快乐的日子。

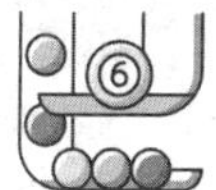

用法 win the lottery 中彩票

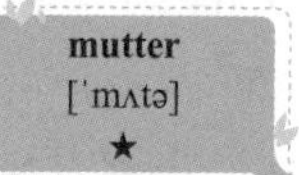

mutter [ˈmʌtə] ★

释义 *n.* 喃喃而语，小声低语；抱怨 *v.* 低声说，抱怨

短语 the soft *mutter* of voices 柔和的低语声

例句 "He's such an unpleasant man," Catherine *muttered* under her breath. "他真是个讨厌的人。"凯瑟琳低声嘀咕着。

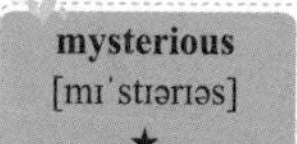

mysterious [mɪˈstɪərɪəs] ★

释义 *adj.* 神秘的，可疑的，难理解的

短语 a *mysterious* illness 一种怪病

例句 By opening a novel, I can leave behind my burdens and enter into a wonderful and *mysterious* world where I am a new character. 通过翻开一部小说，我可以放下我的负担，进入一个美妙而神秘的世界，在那里我是一个新角色。

派生 mysteriously *adv.* 神秘地

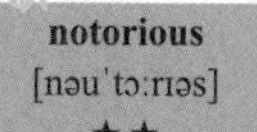

notorious [nəuˈtɔːrɪəs] ★★

释义 *adj.* 臭名昭著的，声名狼藉的

例句 In the 1980s, the company was *notorious* for shady deals. 在20世纪80年代，这个公司因不法交易而臭名昭著。

近义 infamous *adj.* 声名狼藉的；无耻的

用法 be notorious for sth. 因某事而臭名远扬

释义 *n.* 出口，出路；发泄的途径；经销店

短语 air *outlet* 排气口 a fast-food *outlet* 快餐专卖店

例句 The *outlet* of a water pipe was blocked. 水管的出水口堵住了。Running is a good *outlet* for his energy. 跑步是他发泄过剩精力的好方法。

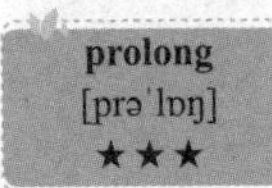

释义 *v.* 拉长，延长，拖延

短语 *prolong* life 延年

例句 The delegation decided to *prolong* their visit by one week. 代表团决定把访问延长一个星期。

派生 prolonged *adj.* 长期的

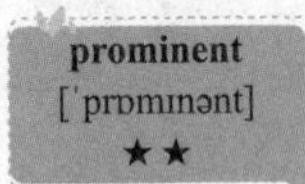

释义 *adj.* 突起的，凸出的；突出的，杰出的

例句 A number of *prominent* economists have argued that it's harder for the poor to climb the economic ladder today. 一些著名的经济学家认为，如今的穷人更难提高经济地位。

近义 conspicuous *adj.* 出色的，引人注目的

派生 prominently *adv.* 显著地

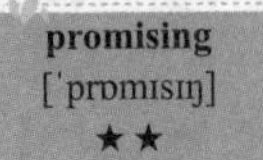

释义 *adj.* 有希望的，有前途的

短语 a *promising* market 发展潜力大的市场

例句 A bill by Democratic Senator Robert Byrd of West Virginia, which would offer financial incentives for private industry, is a *promising* start. 西弗吉尼亚州民主党参议员罗伯特·伯德提出的一项为私营企业提供财政激励的法案是一个有希望的开始。

派生 promisingly *adv.* 良好地

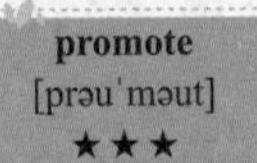

释义 *v.* 促进；提升；增进；促销

例句 We have to suspect that continuing economic growth *promotes* the development of education even when governments don't force it. 我们不得不这样猜测，即便政府不强制推行教育，持续的经济增长也会促进教育发展。

派生 promotion *n.* 晋升；促销；促进

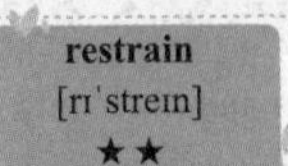

释义 *v.* 抑制，制止

短语 *restrain* oneself 自制

例句 You should try to *restrain* your ambitions and be more realistic. 你应该尽量控制自己的野心，更现实一些。

用法 restrain yourself 克制你自己

派生 restraint *n.* 克制，抑制

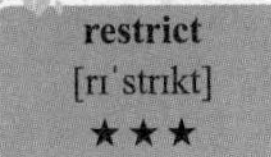

释义 *v.* 限制，约束

短语 *restrict* a road 限制在公路上的速度 *restrict* one's power 限制某人的权力

例句 The invitation list was *restricted* to a few of the host's most intimate friends. 邀请名单仅限于主人最亲密的几个朋友。

派生 restriction *n.* 限制规定，限制法规

释义 *n.*[ˈrezjumeɪ] 个人简历 *v.* [riˈzuːm] 重新开始；恢复

短语 personal *resume* 个人简历

例句 Some hiring managers may be drawn to candidates with a particular educational *resume*. 一些招聘经理可能会被某些具有特定教育背景的求职者吸引。

Talks between the two countries *resumed* in Baghdad after more than six weeks of pause. 在中断6个多星期之后，两国之间的谈判在巴格达恢复。

派生 resumption *n.* 重新开始，恢复

释义 *adj.* 乡村的，农村的

短语 *rural* area / population 农村地区 / 农村人口

例句 *Rural* communities are widely separated and often small. 乡村村落彼此离得很远，而且通常规模很小。

真题 Under lobby pressure, George Osborne favours *rural* new-build against urban renovation and renewal. 在游说团体的压力下，乔治·奥斯本倾向于在农村新建房屋，而不是在城市进行改造和更新。(2016 阅读理解)

反义 urban *adj.* 城市的

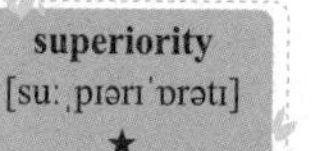

释义 *n.* 优越(性)，优势，优等；高傲，傲慢

短语 overwhelming *superiority* 绝对优势

例句 His sense of *superiority* convinces him that Elizabeth will accept his proposal. 他的优越感使他相信伊丽莎白会接受他的求婚。

用法 have air / naval *superiority* 拥有空军 / 海军优势

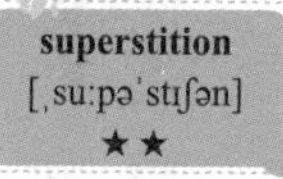

释义 *n.* 迷信，迷信的观念习俗

例句 A common *superstition* considered it bad luck to sleep in a room numbered 13.(西方)一种普遍的迷信观念认为在13号房间睡觉是不吉利的。

用法 be against superstition 反对迷信

派生 superstitious *adj.* 迷信的

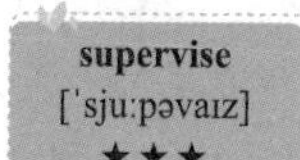

释义 *v.* 管理，监督

短语 *supervise* the market 市场监管

真题 In 1924, America's National Research Council sent two engineers to *supervise* a series of experiments at a telephone-parts factory. 1924年，美国国家研究委员会派出两名工程师到一家电话零部件工厂监督一系列实验。(2010 完形填空)

近义 oversee *v.* 监管，监督

派生 supervision *n.* 监督，管理

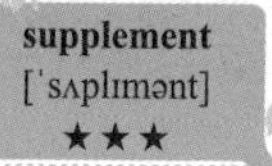

释义 *n.* 增刊；附录 *v.* 补充

短语 nutritional *supplement* 营养补充品

例句 Danish farmers were paid a *supplement* to cover the additional cost of rearing UK pigs. 丹麦农民获得了一笔补助，以支付饲养英国猪的额外费用。

He *supplements* his income by giving private lessons. 他当家庭教师以补充收入。

真题 Typically, if rains are delayed, people may clear land to plant more rice to *supplement* their harvests. 通常情况下，如果降雨推迟，人们会清理土地以种植更多的水稻来补充他们的收成。（2021 阅读理解）

用法 pay a supplement 额外付款

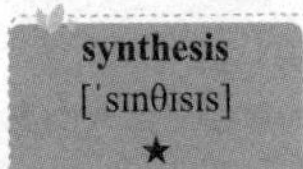

释义 *n.*(*pl.* syntheses) 综合；合成

短语 protein *synthesis* 蛋白质合成

例句 His novels are a rich *synthesis* of Roman history and mythology. 他的小说是对罗马历史和神话的大量综合。

This kind of lighting encourages vitamin D *synthesis* in the skin. 这种光照能促进皮肤中维生素D的合成。

用法 a synthesis of... ……的综合

派生 synthetic *adj.* 合成的，人造的；综合的

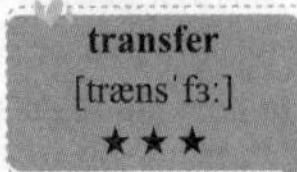

释义 *v.* / *n.* 转移；转让；改乘

例句 She was able to *transfer* her organizational skills to her new job. 她能够把她的组织能力运用到她的新工作中。

派生 transferability *n.* 可转让性

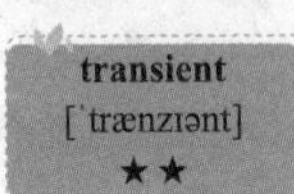

释义 *adj.* 短暂的；临时的，暂住的

短语 the *transient* nature of speech 言语的即逝性

例句 Customer loyalty in the health drinks market appears *transient* at the best of times. 健康饮料市场的顾客忠诚度即使在最好的情况下也是短暂的。

近义 temporary *adj.* 短暂的

释义 *adj.* 声音的；歌唱的；大声表达的 *n.* 声乐作品

短语 a *vocal* opponent 直言不讳的反对者

例句 He has been very *vocal* in his criticism of the government's policy. 他对政府政策的批评一直是直言不讳。

真题 A small but *vocal* group of Hawaiians and environmentalists have long viewed their presence as disrespect for sacred land. 有少数但直言不讳的夏威夷人和环境学家长期以来一直将它们（莫纳克亚山上的望远镜）的存在视为对神圣土地的不尊重。（2017 阅读理解）

派生 vocally *adv.* 用声音；口头地

释义 *v.* 漫步，闲逛；走神 *n.* 游荡，漫步

例句 Respondents' minds tended to *wander* more when they felt upset rather than happy. 当受访者感到不安而不是快乐时，他们更容易走神。

I went to the park and had a *wander* around. 我去公园转了一圈。

近义 ramble *v.* 闲逛

用法 wander about 漫步

释义 v. [əˈsəʊʃieɪt] 联系；交往 n. [əˈsəʊʃiət] 同事；伙伴 adj. [əˈsəʊʃiət] 副的

例句 There are many health risks *associated* with alcohol and tobacco use. 有许多健康风险与饮酒和吸烟有关。

Her *associates* respected her for her hard work. 她的同事因她的努力工作而尊敬她。

真题 We see that the program (Conditional Cash Transfers) is *associated* with a 30 percent reduction in deforestation. 我们看到，有条件现金转移方案与森林砍伐减少 30% 有关。（2021 阅读理解）

派生 association n. 协会；社团

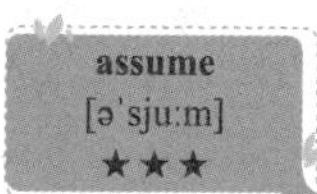

释义 v. 假定；认为；假装，装出；承担；就（职）；显露（特征）

例句 It seems reasonable to *assume* that the book was written around 70 AD. 有理由认为这本书写于公元 70 年左右。

Tina *assumed* an air of confidence in spite of her nervousness. 尽管蒂娜很紧张，但她还是装出了自信的样子。

The new president *assumes* office at midnight tonight. 新总统在今晚午夜就职。

派生 assumption n. 假设；承担

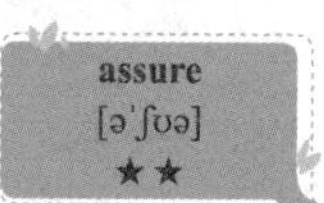

释义 v.（向）保证；确保；使确信

例句 Her doctor has *assured* us that she'll be fine. 她的医生向我们保证她会没事的。

The dealer had *assured* me of its quality. 经销商向我保证它的质量。

同义 ensure v. 确保

派生 assurance n. 保证

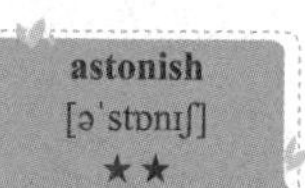

释义 v. 使惊讶；吃惊

例句 Despite the hype, there was nothing in the book to *astonish* readers. 尽管大肆宣传，但书中并没有让读者感到惊讶的内容。

派生 astonishing adj. 惊人的

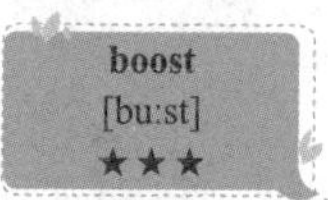

释义 v. / n. 增加；促进；提高

例句 The new resort area has *boosted* tourism. 新的度假区促进了旅游业的发展。

The win gave us a big *boost*. 这场胜利给了我们很大的鼓舞。

真题 So better grades can, by *boosting* figures like graduation rates and student retention, mean more money. 因此，通过提高毕业率和学生保有率等数据，更好的成绩意味着（学校获得的州）经费会更多。（2019 阅读理解）

近义 bolster v. 增强，激励

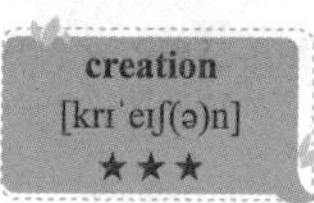

释义 n. 创造，创建

例句 These changes will lead to the *creation* of new businesses. 这些变化将导致新业务的诞生。

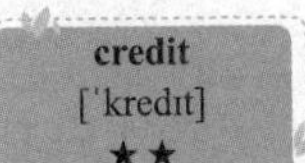

释义 *v.* / *n.* 信用，信任 *n.* 赞扬；名誉，学分

短语 *credit* card 信用卡

例句 They never give Gene any *credit* for all the extra work he does. 他们从不表扬吉恩所做的额外工作。

Each of these classes is worth three *credits*. 这些课程每门 3 个学分。

派生 creditable *adj.* 值得赞扬的

释义 *n.* 罪行，犯罪 *v.* 指控犯罪

例句 There needs to be a partnership between police and public in the fight against *crime*. 在打击犯罪的斗争中，警察和公众之间需要建立伙伴关系。

用法 commit a crime 犯罪

派生 criminal *adj.* 犯罪的

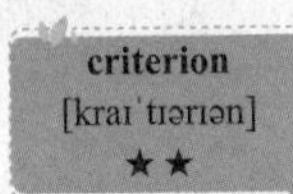

释义 *n.* 标准，尺度

例句 What *criteria* do you use to decide whether he is the best person for the job? 你用什么标准来判定他是否是这份工作的最佳人选？

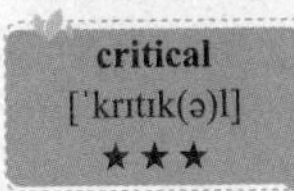

释义 *adj.* 批判性的；爱挑剔的；关键的；严重的

例句 Parents who are too *critical* make their children anxious. 过于挑剔的父母会使孩子焦虑。

派生 critically *adv.* 严重地；批判性地

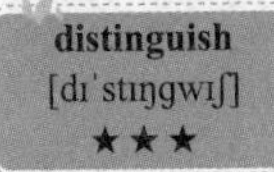

释义 *v.* 区别；辨认出；使杰出

例句 She could not *distinguish* the make and colour of the car in the fading light. 在昏暗的灯光下，她分不清汽车的牌子和颜色。

用法 distinguish oneself 表现自己；使杰出

近义 differentiate *v.* 区分

释义 *v.* 扭曲；歪曲

例句 This report gives a somewhat *distorted* impression of what actually happened. 这份报告对实际发生的事情有点歪曲。

用法 distort one's view 曲解了某人的观点

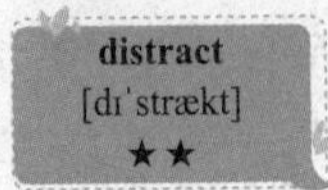

释义 *v.* 分散，使分心；打扰

例句 Coverage of the war was used to *distract* attention from other matters. 对战争的报道被用来转移人们对其他事情的注意力。

派生 distraction *n.* 使人分心的事物

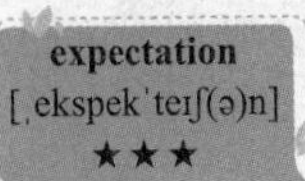

释义 *n.* 预期，期望，指望

例句 Some parents have unrealistic *expectations* of their children. 有的父母对孩子的期望不切实际。

用法 above/below expectations 高于 / 低于预期

派生 expectancy *n.* 期待

释义 *v.* 消费，花费

例句 Children *expend* a lot of energy and may need more high-energy food than adults. 孩子们消耗很多能量，可能比成年人需要更多高能量的食物。

派生 expense *n.* 费用

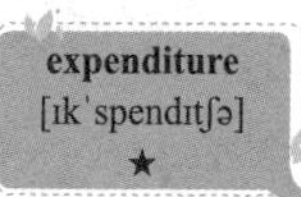

释义 *n.* 花费；支出，消耗

例句 The government's annual *expenditure* on arms has been reduced. 政府已经削减了年度军费开支。

用法 increase / cut expenditure on sth. 增加 / 削减……支出

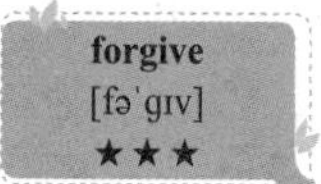

释义 *v.* 原谅，饶恕

例句 Please *forgive* for any inconveniences caused. 给您带来的不便，敬请原谅。

派生 forgiveness *n.* 宽恕

释义 *v.* 雇用 *n.* 租用，雇用

例句 No ordinary families can afford to *hire* servants. 普通人家雇不起仆人。

The day's *hire* for the car is ten dollars. 汽车每日的租金是十美元。

释义 *adj.* 历史上重要的；历史性的

短语 a *historic* event / moment 历史性事件 / 时刻

例句 The ceremony, which will last three days, is a *historic* moment for Thailand. 这场仪式将持续三天，对泰国来说是一个历史性的时刻。

派生 historical *adj.* 历史上的

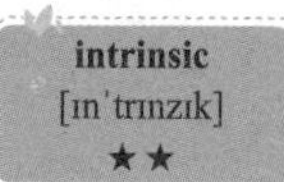

释义 *adj.* 固有的，本质的，内在的

短语 *intrinsic* quality 内在质量

例句 There is nothing in the *intrinsic* nature of the work that makes it more suitable for women. 这项工作的本质并没有让它更适合女性。

反义 extrinsic *adj.* 外在的

派生 intrinsically *adv.* 本质上

释义 *v.* 闯入，侵入；扰乱

例句 The press has been blamed for *intruding* into people's personal lives in an unacceptable way. 人们指责新闻界以一种不可接受的方式侵入人们的个人生活。

派生 intruder *n.* 闯入者

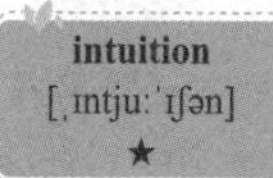

释义 *n.* 直觉；直觉感知

短语 *intuition* thinking 直觉思维

例句 Often there's no clear evidence one way or the other and you just have to base your judgment on *intuition*. 很多时候，往往没有这样或那样的确凿证据，你只得凭直觉进行判断。

近义 instinct *n.* 本能

释义 *n.* 忠诚，忠心

例句 Newspapers are often the most important form of news for a local community, and they develop a high degree of *loyalty* from local readers. 报纸通常是当地社区最重要的新闻形式，它们在当地读者中形成了高度的忠诚度。

派生 loyalist *n.* 忠诚的人

释义 *n.* 神秘，神秘的事物；神秘小说，侦探小说

短语 a *mystery* tour 漫游

例句 Modern weather forecasts try to take the *mystery* out of the meteorology. 现代天气预报试图揭开气象学的神秘面纱。

派生 mysterious *adj.* 神秘的

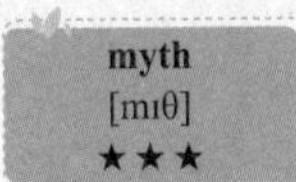

释义 *n.* 神话；虚构的理论

短语 a *myth* of sb. 关于某人的神话

例句 When you are dealing with *myths*, it is hard to be either proper, or scientific. 当你与神话打交道时，很难做到既正确又科学。

派生 mythology *n.* 神话

释义 *n.* 新颖；新奇 *adj.* 新奇的

短语 a *novelty* teapot 新颖独特的茶壶

例句 It was quite a *novelty* to spend my holidays working on a boat. 在船上工作来度过我的假期是件相当新奇的事。

近义 originality *n.* 独创性

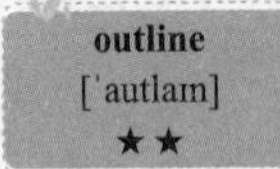

释义 *n.* 提纲，要点；外形，轮廓 *v.* 概述，列提纲

短语 general *outline* 大纲

例句 Make an *outline* before trying to write a composition. 写作文之前先写个提纲。He *outlined* his responsibilities. 他概述了自己的职责。

用法 give sb. an outline of sth. 向某人概述某事

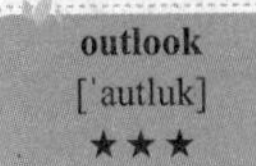

释义 *n.* 景色；观点，见解；前景，展望

短语 market *outlook* 市场前景

例句 The house has a pleasant *outlook* over the valley. 房子俯瞰山谷，景色宜人。The *outlook* for jobs is bleak. 就业市场前景暗淡。

用法 be liberal in *outlook* 观念开放

释义 *adj.* 敏捷的，迅速的 *v.* 激起，促进

例句 Successful team leaders know exactly where the team should go and are able to take *prompt* action. 成功的团队领导者确切地知道团队应该走向何方，并能够迅速采取行动。

用法 prompt sb. to do sth. 催促某人做某事

近义 immediate *adj.* 立刻的，即时的

释义 *adj.* 倾向于；倾斜的，陡的

短语 scandal prone 负面消息多

例句 Tired drivers were found to be particularly *prone* to ignore warning signs. 据调查，疲劳驾车时特别容易忽视警示标志。

用法 prone to 有……倾向的

派生 proneness *n.* 倾向

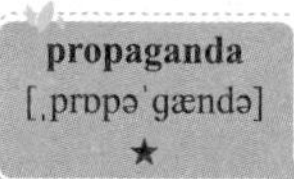

释义 *n.* 宣传（机构）；（天主教）传道总会

短语 enemy *propaganda* 敌方的宣传 *propaganda* tool 宣传工具

例句 During the elections, they have massive *propaganda* against their political opponents at that time. 在选举期间，他们对政敌进行大规模的负面宣传。

释义 *v.* 推进，推动；激励，驱使

例句 The tiny rocket is attached to the spacecraft and is designed to *propel* it toward Mars. 小火箭捆绑在宇宙飞船上，用于推动飞船飞向火星。

用法 propel sb. into sth. 推动某人进入某种状态

近义 stimulate *v.* 促进

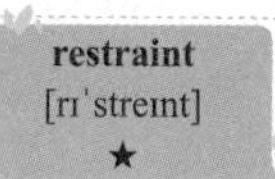

释义 *n.* 抑制，制止；约束

短语 without *restraint* 无拘无束地

例句 The parties involved should exercise *restraint* and prevent the situation from getting worse. 有关各方应采取克制态度，防止事态扩大。

用法 exercise restraint 厉行克制

近义 inhibition *n.* 阻止，抑制

释义 *n.* 零售

短语 *retail* trade 零售业

例句 The shoe company has six *retail* outlets in Paris. 这家鞋业公司在巴黎开设了6家零售店。

真题 *Retail* trade groups praised the ruling, saying it levels the playing field for local and online businesses. 零售贸易组织赞扬了这一裁决，称它为本地和线上企业提供了公平的竞争环境。（2019 阅读理解）

派生 retailer *n.* 零售商

释义 *v.* 保持，保留

例句 High-quality newspapers *retain* a large body of readers. 高质量的报纸拥有大量的读者。

真题 Each spouse *retains* whatever property he or she brought into the marriage, and jointly-acquired property is divided equally.（离婚时）配偶双方都可持有各自婚前的财产，婚后的共同财产平均分配。（2016 完形填空）

近义 keep *v.* 保持，处于

派生 retention *n.* 保留，保持

释义 *v.*（使）冲；奔 *n.* 匆忙，赶紧 *adj.*（交通）繁忙的

短语 gold *rush* 淘金热

例句 I've been *rushing* all day trying to get everything done. 我忙了整整一天，想把所有的事情都做完。

The shop's opening coincided with the Christmas *rush*. 这家商店的开张正赶上圣诞节购物高峰。

用法 in a *rush* 急急忙忙地

释义 *v.* 供给，供应，补足 *n.* 供应，供应量

例句 Prices change according to *supply* and demand. 价格根据供应量和需求量而变化。

真题 Scientists need journals in which to publish their research, so they will *supply* the articles without monetary reward. 科学家们需要在期刊上发表他们的研究，所以他们会无偿提供论文。（2020 阅读理解）

近义 provide *v.* 提供

派生 supplier *n.* 供应商

释义 *n.* / *v.* 支撑；支持

例句 These measures are strongly *supported* by environmental groups. 这些措施得到环境保护组织的大力支持。

真题 That common-sense change enjoys wide public *support* and would save the U.S. Postal Service $2 billion per year. 这一常见性的改变得到了公众的广泛支持，并将为美国邮政总局每年节省20亿美元。（2018 阅读理解）

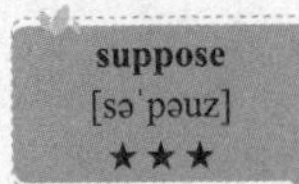

释义 *v.* 料想，猜想；假定

例句 Getting a visa isn't as simple as you might *suppose*. 办签证不像你想的那么容易。

真题 At the beginning of the century songbirds were *supposed* to be disappearing. 在本世纪初，人们认为鸣禽即将灭绝。（2010 翻译）

用法 be supposed to 应该；被期望

派生 supposable *adj.* 想像得到的

释义 *v.* 镇压，压制；抑制，忍住

短语 *suppress* inflation 遏止通货膨胀

例句 When we try to *suppress* our negativity, bad things happen. 当我们试图去压抑自身的负面情感时，糟糕的事情就发生了。

派生 suppression *n.* 镇压，压制；压抑

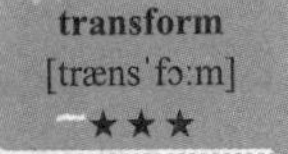

释义 *v.* 改变，转化

例句 Your metabolic rate is the speed at which your body *transforms* food into energy. 新陈代谢率是身体把食物转换为能量的速度。

近义 change *v.* 改变

派生 transformation *n.* 转变

释义 *adj.* 透明的，透光的；易理解的；明显的

短语 a man of *transparent* honesty 显然很诚实的人

例句 It was *transparent* that she was irritated. 显然她是生气了。

Local government announced on Tuesday to introduce electoral reforms to ensure fair and *transparent* elections. 当地政府周二宣布将推行选举改革，以确保选举的公平和透明。

派生 transparency *n.* 透明

释义 *n.* 学费；教学，讲授

短语 *tuition* fee 学费

例句 Angela's $7,000 *tuition* at University this year will be paid for with scholarships. 安杰拉将用奖学金支付今年 7,000 美元的大学学费。

She received private *tuition* in French. 她接受了法语的私人教学。

释义 *n.* 工作；职业；天命

短语 *vocation* training 职业训练

例句 You will not make a good teacher, unless you feel teaching is your *vocation*. 除非你觉得教书是你的天职，否则你不会成为一位好老师。

用法 take vocation 采取使命

近义 occupation *n.* 工作；职业

派生 vocational *adj.* 职业的

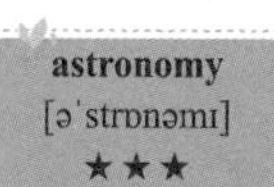

释义 *n.* 天文学

例句 We are on the threshold of a new era in *astronomy*. 我们很快就将迎来天文学的新纪元。

派生 astronomer *n.* 天文学家

释义 *n.* 大气，大气层；氛围

例句 These gases pollute the *atmosphere* of towns and cities. 这些气体污染了城镇的大气。

The food was good but the restaurant has no *atmosphere*. 食物很好，但这家餐馆没有气氛。

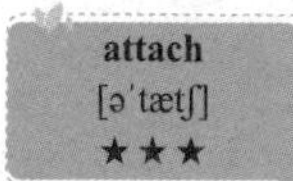

释义 *v.* 附；贴；系；认为……具有；附属；使依恋

例句 I *attached* a photo to my application form. 我在我的申请表上贴了一张照片。

He doesn't *attach* too much importance to fixed ideas. 他不很看重固有的观念。

真题 Oxytocin promotes *attachment* in relationships, including that between mothers and their newborn babies. 催产素可以增强人们之间的依恋之情，包括母亲们和她们刚出生的婴儿之间的依恋之情。（2017 完形填空）

用法 attach importance to 重视

派生 attachment *n.* 附属物；附件；依恋

释义 *v.* / *n.* 攻击；进攻 *n.* 疾病发作

例句 Most wild animals won't *attack* unless they are provoked. 大多数野生动物若非被激怒，是不会主动攻击的。

The company's move came under *attack* Thursday from a wide variety of people. 周四，该公司的这一举措遭到了各界人士的抨击。

派生 attacker *n.* 攻击者；进攻者

释义 *adj.*（与……）密切相关的；必然的；有义务的；开往……的 *v.* 跳；使跳跃；使弹回 *n.* 跳跃

例句 You're *bound* to feel nervous about your interview. 面试时，你很可能会感到紧张。

Andrew felt *bound* to tell Cindy the truth. 安德鲁觉得有必要告诉辛迪真相。

She *bounded* down the stairs. 她蹦蹦跳跳地走下楼梯。

释义 *adj.* 有创造力的，创造性的

例句 They've come up with a *creative* way to give gift cards. 他们想出了一个送贺卡的创意方式。

派生 creativity *n.* 创造力

释义 *n.* 罪犯 *adj.* 犯罪的

短语 *criminal* gang 犯罪集团

例句 There is an old saying, "The problem child of today is the *criminal* of tomorrow." 有句老话说："今天的问题儿童将成为明天的罪犯。"

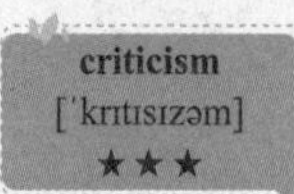

释义 *n.* 评论；批评

短语 literary *criticism* 文艺评论

例句 My only *criticism* of the house is that it is on a main road. 我对这座房子唯一的批评意见是它处于一条主路上。

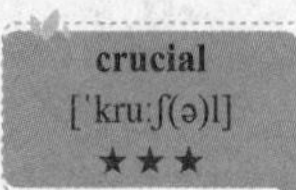

释义 *adj.* 至关重要的，决定性的

例句 The success of this project is *crucial* to the plan as a whole. 这个项目的成功对整个计划至关重要。

用法 be crucial to sth. 对某事至关重要

释义 *adj.* 天然的；粗糙的；简陋的 *n.* 原油

例句 The cottage wears a very *crude* appearance. 那幢农舍外观颇为简陋。

Thousands of gallons of *crude* oil were spilled into the ocean. 成千上万加仑的原油泄漏，流进了海洋。

派生 crudely *adv.* 粗略地

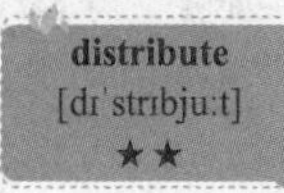

释义 *v.* 分发；分布；分销

例句 Local politicians used to *distribute* Thanksgiving turkeys to needy families. 地方政客们过去常给穷人家分送感恩节火鸡。

派生 distribution *n.* 分发

disturb
[dɪ'stɜːb]
★

释义 *v.* 扰乱，妨碍；使不安

例句 I'm sorry to *disturb* you so late, but my car's broken down and I was wondering if I could use your phone. 很抱歉这么晚打扰你，但我的车坏了，我在想能不能用一下你的电话。

近义 interrupt *v.* 打断，打扰

diverse
[daɪ'vɜːs]
★★★

释义 *adj.* 多种多样的，不同的

例句 Society is now much more *diverse* than ever before. 当今社会较之以往任何时候都要丰富多彩得多。

派生 diversity *n.* 多样化

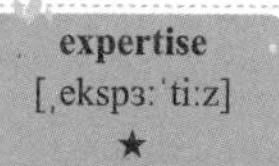
expense
[ɪk'spens]
★★★

释义 *n.* 花费，消费，消耗 *v.* 向……收取费用

例句 Unfortunately, household *expenses* don't go away just because you're out of work. 不幸的是，家庭开支不会因为你失业而减少。

真题 It reported a net loss of $5.6 billion for fiscal 2016, the 10th straight year its *expenses* have exceeded revenue. 该公司公布2016财年净亏损56亿美元，这是连续第10年其支出超过收入。(2018阅读理解)

expertise
[ˌekspɜː'tiːz]
★

释义 *n.* 专门知识(或技能等)，专长

例句 Fred lacks the skills and *expertise* needed for his job. 佛瑞德缺乏他的工作所需的技能和专业知识。

近义 knowledge *n.* 知识，学问

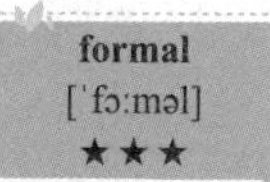
expire
[ɪk'spaɪə]
★

释义 *v.* 期满，(期限)终止；呼气；断气，死亡

例句 He had lived illegally in the United States for five years after his visitor's visa *expired*. 在访问签证到期后，他又在美国非法居住了5年。

派生 expiration *n.* 到期；呼气

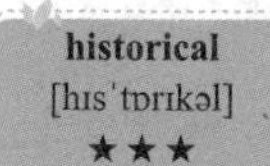
formal
['fɔːməl]
★★★

释义 *adj.* 正式的；形式的

例句 The relationship between *formal* education and economic growth in poor countries is widely misunderstood by economists and politicians alike. 在贫穷国家，正规教育和经济增长之间的关系被经济学家和政治家广泛误解。

派生 formally *adv.* 正式地；形式上的

historical
[hɪs'tɒrɪkəl]
★★★

释义 *adj.* 历史(学)的

短语 *historical* documents 历史文献

例句 The book is based on *historical* events. 这本书是根据历史事件写成的。

invade
[ɪn'veɪd]
★

释义 *v.* 入侵，侵略；大量涌入

例句 In autumn 1944, the allies *invaded* the Italian mainland at Anzio and Salerno. 1944年秋，盟军在安齐奥和萨莱诺入侵意大利本土。

近义 attack *v.* 袭击，攻击

派生 invader *n.* 侵略者

invisible
[ɪn'vɪzəbl]
★★

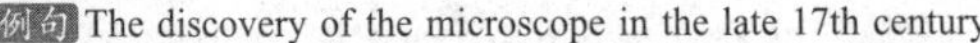

释义 *adj.* 看不见的，无形的

词组 *invisible* assets 无形资产

例句 The discovery of the microscope in the late 17th century caused a revolution in biology by revealing otherwise *invisible* and previously unsuspected worlds. 17世纪末显微镜的发现揭示了不可见的、以前不为人知的世界，从而引发了一场生物学革命。

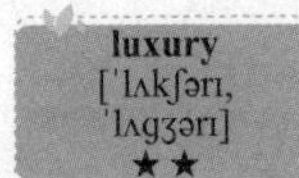
luxury
['lʌkʃərɪ, 'lʌgʒərɪ]
★★

释义 *n.* 奢侈；奢侈品；难得的享受 *adj.* 奢华的，豪华的

短语 *luxury* hotel 豪华饭店

例句 We were going to have the *luxury* of a free weekend, to rest and do whatever we pleased. 我们将有一个奢侈的自由周末，可以休息，做任何我们喜欢的事情。

派生 luxurious *adj.* 奢侈的

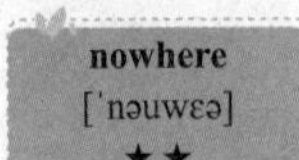
nowhere
['nəuwɛə]
★★

释义 *adv.* 任何地方都不，无处

短语 out of *nowhere* 突然冒出来

例句 Food security and fortunes depend on sufficient rain, and *nowhere* more so than in Africa, where 96% of farmland depends on rain. 粮食安全和财富依赖于充足的雨水，在非洲尤其如此，那里96%的农田依赖雨水灌溉。

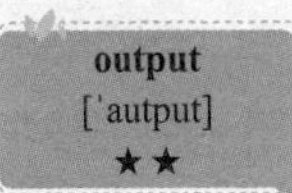
output
['autput]
★★

释义 *n.* 产量；输出，输出功率

短语 annual *output* 年产量

例句 The *output* should be proportional to the input. 输出应当与输入成比例。

近义 yield *n.* 产量

outrage
['aʊtreɪdʒ]
★★

释义 *n.* 义愤，愤慨；暴行 *v.* 引起……的义愤，激怒

短语 public *outrage* 公愤

例句 The use of H-bombs would be an *outrage* against humanity. 使用氢弹是反人道的暴行。

He was *outraged* at the way he had been treated. 他对所遭受的待遇感到非常愤怒。

用法 an outrage *against* sth. 对……的侵犯

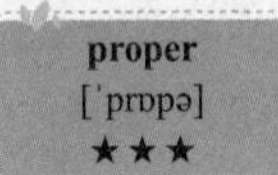
proper
['prɒpə]
★★★

释义 *adj.* 适合的；恰当的；正确的

短语 at a *proper* time 在适当的时候

例句 More than 80% of those cases can be attributed to contact with contaminated water and a lack of *proper* sanitation. 其中80%以上的病例可归因于接触了受污染的水和缺乏适当的卫生设施。

派生 properly *adv.* 适当地

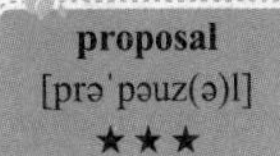
proposal
[prə'pəuz(ə)l]
★★★

释义 *n.* 提议，建议；求婚

例句 The fifth largest city in US passed a significant soda tax *proposal* that will levy 1.5 cents per liquid ounce on distributors. 美国第五大城市通过了一项重要的汽水税提案，将向分销商征收每盎司1.5美分的汽水税。

真题 The *proposal* is that "town of culture" award should sit alongside the existing city of culture title, which was held by Hull in 2017, and has been awarded to Coventry for 2021. 该提议指出“文化之镇”应该与现有的“文化之城”的称号并存，后者于2017年由赫尔市夺得，并将于2021年花落考文垂。(2020阅读理解)

用法 make a proposal to sb. 向某人求婚

释义 *v.* 出版，刊印；公布，发布

例句 An abridgement of the book has been *published* for young readers. 他们为年轻读者出版了这本书的简本。

派生 publication *n.* 出版，发行；出版物

释义 *adj.* 严守时刻的，准时的，正点的

例句 The teacher is very strict about punctuality because she believes that being *punctual* is being polite to others. 这位老师对守时要求严格，因为她认为守时就是对他人礼貌。

用法 be punctual 按时

派生 punctuality *n.* 准时性

释义 *n.* 数目，数量

短语 production / order *quantity* 生产量 / 订货量

例句 People are learning how to organize huge *quantities* of information so that they are able to access it at a later date. 人们正在学习如何整理大量的信息，以便日后使用。

用法 a great quantity of 大量

派生 quantitative *adj.* 数量的

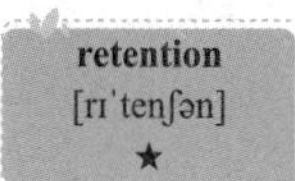

释义 *n.* 保留，保持；记忆力

短语 customer *retention* 顾客维系

例句 The company needs to improve its training and *retention* of staff. 公司需要改进对员工的培训和留用工作。

Visual material aids the *retention* of information. 直观材料有助于加强记忆。

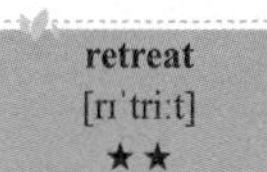

释义 *v.* 撤退，退却 *n.* 撤军；后退

短语 in full *retreat* 全线溃退

例句 Animals also have to adapt to desert conditions, and they may do it through two forms of behavioral adaptation: they either escape or *retreat*. 动物也必须适应沙漠环境，它们可以通过两种形式来适应环境：逃避或撤离。

近义 withdraw *v.* 撤离

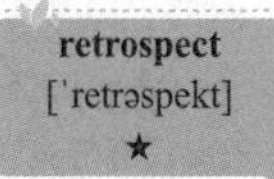

释义 *v.* / *n.* 回顾，回想，追溯

短语 in *retrospect* 回想

例句 It was a decision Peterson admitted, in *retrospect*, he would have done differently. 彼得森承认，现在回想起来，他会做出不同的决定。

近义 remembrance *n.* 怀念；记忆，回忆

释义 *adj.* 残酷的，无情的

短语 a *ruthless* dictator 残酷无情的独裁者

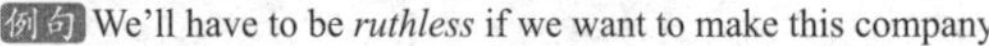

例句 We'll have to be *ruthless* if we want to make this company more efficient. 如果我们想使公司更有效率，我们就必须冷面无情。

近义 cruel *adj.* 残酷的

反义 merciful *adj.* 仁慈的

派生 ruthlessly *adv.* 无情地

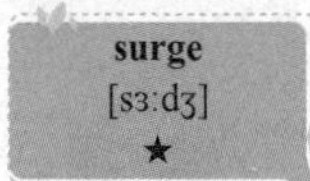

释义 *v.* 汹涌；澎湃；蜂拥而至 *n.* 巨浪；汹涌

短语 a *surge* of anger / excitement 怒火中烧 / 一阵兴奋

例句 The photographers and cameramen *surged* forward. 摄影师和摄像师们蜂拥上前。

Between 2012 and 2017, Sydney's house price *surged* by 68 percent. 2012 年至 2017 年期间，悉尼房价飙升了 68%。

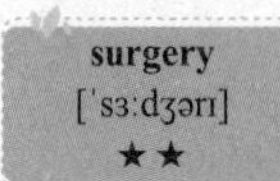

释义 *n.* 外科手术；手术室

短语 cardiovascular *surgery* 心血管外科

例句 He had *surgery* on his right foot after hurting it in a preseason practice. 他的右脚在季前赛训练中受伤后接受了手术。

用法 have / undergo surgery 做手术

派生 surgical *adj.* 外科的

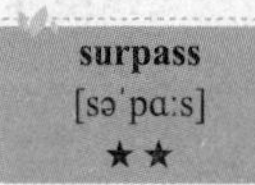

释义 *v.* 超过，胜过

短语 *surpass* the world record 超越世界纪录

例句 He was determined to *surpass* the achievements of his older brothers. 他决心超过他的几位哥哥的成就。

近义 overtake *v.* 追上，赶上并超过

派生 surpasser *n.* 优胜者，超越者

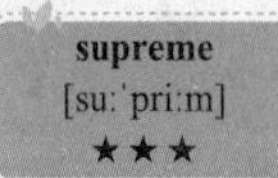

释义 *adj.* 最重要的；至高的，最高的

短语 a *supreme* effort 最大的努力

例句 Winning an Olympic gold medal was, I suppose, the *supreme* moment of his life. 我认为荣获奥运会金牌是他一生中最重要的时刻。

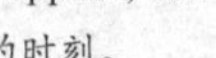

派生 supremely *adv.* 至上地；崇高地

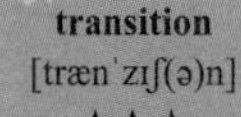

释义 *n.* 转变，变迁，过渡（时期）

短语 *transition* period 过渡时期

例句 *Transitions* should connect one paragraph to the next so that there are no abrupt or confusing shifts. 过渡段应该把上一个段和下一个段连接起来，这样段落之间就没有唐突或者莫名其妙的转换。

派生 transitional *adj.* 暂时的，过渡的

释义 *n.* /*v.* 移植（植物；组织，器官等）；（使）迁移；移居

短语 heart *transplant* 心脏移植

例句 George Washington hired a dentist to *transplant* nine teeth into his jaw—having extracted them from the mouths of his slaves. 乔治·华盛顿雇佣了一名牙医，将9颗牙齿移植到他的下巴上——这些牙齿是从他的奴隶口中取出的。

派生 transplantation *n.* 移植

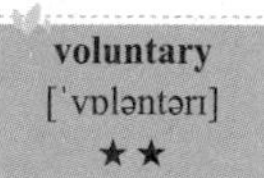

释义 *adj.* 动荡的，无秩序的

例句 The present international situation remains tense and *turbulent*. 当前的国际局势依然紧张且动荡。

反义 peaceful *adj.* 宁静的

派生 turbulence *n.* 骚乱

释义 自愿的，志愿的

短语 *voluntary* services / organizations 志愿服务 / 机构

例句 Some *voluntary* organizations run workshops for disabled people. 一些志愿组织为残障人士开办讲习班。

真题 In Denmark, the United States, and a few other countries, it is trying to set *voluntary* standards for models and fashion images that rely more on peer pressure for enforcement. 丹麦、美国和其他一些国家的时尚产业试图为模特和时尚形象设定一个非强制性标准，该标准更多地依靠同行压力来执行。（2016 阅读理解）

反义 involuntary *adj.* 非自愿的

派生 voluntarily *adv.* 自愿地

wonder
['wʌndə]
★★★

释义 *n.* 惊奇；奇迹 *v.* 惊讶；想知道

例句 I don't *wonder* you're tired. You've had a busy day. 你累了，这我一点儿不奇怪。你已经忙了一整天。

The Grand Canyon is one of the natural *wonders* of the world. 科罗拉多大峡谷是世界自然奇观之一。

真题 Unhappy parents rarely are provoked to *wonder* if they shouldn't have had kids. 不幸福的父母们很少会反思自己是否不该养孩子。（2011 阅读理解）

派生 wonderful *adj.* 绝妙的

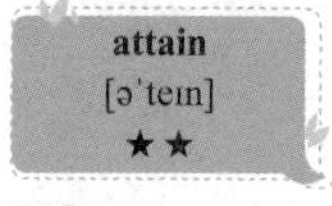

释义 *v.* 获得；达到

例句 This kind of tree can *attain* a height of 20 feet within just a few years. 这种树可以在短短几年内长到20英尺高。

近义 obtain *v.* 获得

派生 attainment *n.* 达到，获得

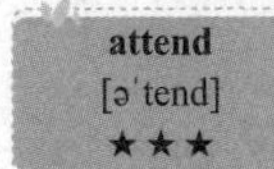

attend [əˈtend] ★★★

释义 *v.* 出席；参加；照料；上（学）

例句 John will *attend* the conference. 约翰将参加会议。

She *attends* a school in the city. 她在城里的一所学校上学。

The nurse *attended* the patient daily. 护士每天照看着这病人。

近义 serve *v.* 服务

派生 attendance *n.* 出勤

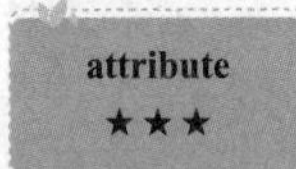

attribute ★★★

释义 *n.* [ˈætrɪbjuːt] 属性；特质 *v.* [əˈtrɪbjuːt] 把……归于

例句 He possesses the *attributes* we want in a leader. 他具备我们想要的领导者的品质。

He *attributed* his failure to a lack of preparation. 他把失败归因于缺乏准备。

短语 be attributed to 归因于……

派生 attribution *n.* 属性

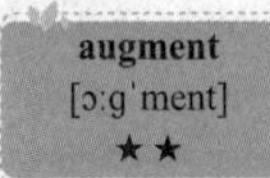

augment [ɔːɡˈment] ★★

释义 *v.* 增加；提高

例句 While searching for a way to *augment* the family income, she began making crafts for tourists. 为了寻找增加家庭收入的方法，她开始为游客制作工艺品。

近义 increase *v.* 增加

派生 augmentation *n.* 增多

boycott [ˈbɔɪkɒt] ★★

释义 *v.* 抵制，拒绝参加 *n.* 抵制行动

例句 They planned to *boycott* products from that company. 他们计划抵制那家公司的产品。

They are now trying to organize a *boycott*. 他们正试图组织一场抵制运动。

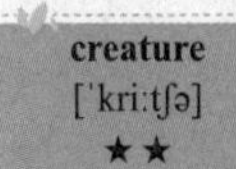

creature [ˈkriːtʃə] ★★

释义 *n.* 人；动物；生物

短语 living *creature* 生物

例句 The Amazon Rainforest is filled with amazing *creatures*. 亚马孙雨林充满了神奇的生物。

criticize [ˈkrɪtɪsaɪz] ★★★

释义 *v.*(criticise) 批评，评论

例句 Traditional programs of higher education were being widely *criticized*. 传统的高等教育项目受到了广泛的批评。

派生 criticism *n.* 批评

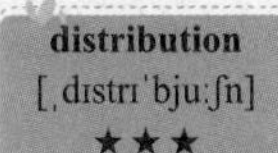

distribution [ˌdɪstrɪˈbjuːʃn] ★★★

释义 *n.* 分发；分销，配送

短语 means of *distribution* 分销方式

例句 Unequal *distribution* of wealth may cause division in society. 财富分配不均会引起社会分裂。

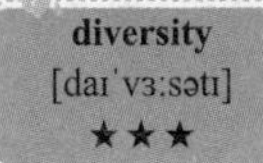

diversity [daɪˈvɜːsətɪ] ★★★

释义 *n.* 多样性，多样化；差异

短语 ecological *diversity* 生态多样性

例句 If I had to choose a slogan it would be "Unity in our *diversity*". 如果非得让

我选个标语，那就是“求同存异”。

divert
[daɪˈvɜːt]
★★

释义 v. 使转向；转移（注意力）

短语 divert one's attention 转移某人的注意力

例句 The war has *diverted* attention from the country's economic problems. 战争转移了人们对该国经济问题的注意力。

近义 switch v. 转移

domain
[dəʊˈmeɪn]
★

释义 n. 领域，范围；领地；（因特网的）域

例句 The Arctic remains the *domain* of the polar bear. 北极仍是北极熊的领地。

As a cricketer, gymnastics is out of his *domain*. 他是个板球运动员，体操非其所长。

domestic
[dəˈmestɪk]
★★★

释义 adj. 家里的；本国的；驯养的 n. 家庭矛盾；佣人

短语 *domestic* product 本地生产 *domestic* trade 国内贸易

例句 The company hopes to attract both foreign and *domestic* investors. 该公司希望吸引国内外投资者。

explicit
[ɪkˈsplɪsɪt]
★★★

释义 adj. 详述的，明确的；坦率的；显然的

例句 He was quite *explicit* as to what he expected us to do for him. 他很明确地要求我们为他做什么。

派生 explicitly adv. 清楚明确地，详述地

explore
[ɪkˈsplɔː]
★★★

释义 v. 勘探，探测；探究，探索

例句 I just wanted to *explore* Paris, read Sartre, listen to Sidney Bechet. 我就想逛逛巴黎，读读萨特的作品，听听西德尼·贝切特的音乐。

真题 Perhaps that is why we *explore* the starry skies, as if answering a primal calling to know ourselves and our true ancestral homes. 也许这就是我们探索星空的原因，就像回应一种原始的召唤，去了解我们自己和我们真正的祖先家园。（2017 阅读理解）

派生 exploration n. 勘探；探究

export
★★

释义 v. [ɪkˈspɔːt] 出口 n. [ˈekspɔːt] 出口；出口商品

例句 A lot of the land is used to grow cotton for *export*. 很多土地被用来种植用于出口的棉花。

反义 import n. / v. 进口；进口商品

expose
[ɪkˈspəʊz]
★★★

释义 v. 使暴露，受到；使曝光

例句 The outer layers of the volcano were worn away until the hard core stood completely *exposed*. 火山的外层已磨损殆尽，直到硬核完全暴露在外。

派生 exposure n. 暴露，揭露；照射量

express
[ɪkˈspres]
★★★

释义 v. 表达；表示 adj. 特快的；快速的 n. 快递服务；特快列车

例句 He found it difficult to *express* himself freely in a foreign language. 他发现很难用外语自由地表达自己的观点。

Henry used to take the *express* train to London at weekends. 亨利过去常常在周末乘特快列车去伦敦。

释义 *adj.* 以前的，在前的 *pron.* 前者 *n.* 模型；起形成作用的人

词组 in *former* times 从前

例句 In *former* times, it was difficult for women to achieve recognition. 在过去，妇女很难获得认可。

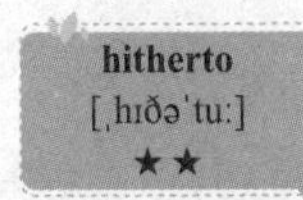

释义 *adv.* 迄今为止；直到某时

例句 *Hitherto*, he had experienced no great success in his attempt. 迄今为止，他的尝试还没取得任何重大的成功。

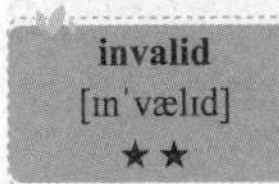

释义 *adj.* 无效的，作废的 *n.* 病人，伤残人 *v.* 使(因伤或病)退役；使伤残

例句 Without the right date stamped on it, your coupon will be *invalid*. 没有盖上正确的日期，您的优惠券将无效。

用法 be declared invalid 被宣布无效

反义 valid *adj.* 有效的；合理的

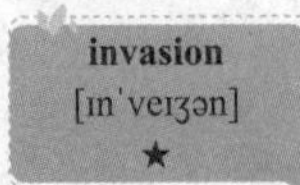

释义 *n.* 入侵；侵略；侵犯

例句 The Beatles were described as a British *invasion* by nationwide newspapers at that time. 那时，全国范围内的报纸都将甲壳虫乐队描述为英国的入侵。

派生 invasive *adj.* 侵入的

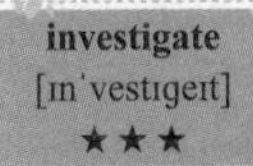

释义 *v.* 调查；调查研究

例句 In a 2011 study, Steinberg and his colleagues turned to functional MRI to *investigate* how the presence of peers affects the activity in the adolescent brain. 在 2011 年的一项研究中，斯坦伯格和他的同事转而使用功能性核磁共振成像来研究同龄人的存在是如何影响青少年大脑活动的。

派生 investigation *n.* 调查，审查

释义 *n.* 陪审团；裁判委员会

短语 *jury* trial 陪审团审案

例句 The *jury* were convinced that he was innocent. 陪审团确信他是无辜的。

派生 juror *n.* 陪审团成员

释义 *n.* 公正，公平；司法；(美)法官

短语 *justice* department 司法部门

例句 He only wants freedom, *justice* and equality. 他只要自由、公正和平等。

真题 *Justice* Anthony Kennedy wrote that the previous decisions were flawed. 大法官安东尼·肯尼迪写道，之前的判决存在缺陷。(2020 阅读理解)

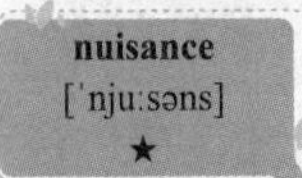

释义 *n.* 讨厌的东西(人，行为)

短语 noise *nuisance* 噪声危害

例句 He could be a bit of a *nuisance* when he was drunk. 他喝醉的时候可能会有点讨厌。

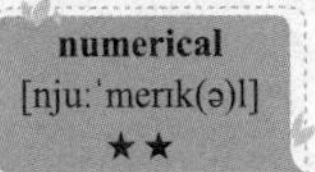

释义 *adj.* 数字的；用数字表示的；数值的

短语 *numerical* model 数值模式

例句 The numbers are in *numerical* order. 这些号码是按数字顺序排列的。

派生 numerically *adv.* 数字上；用数字表示

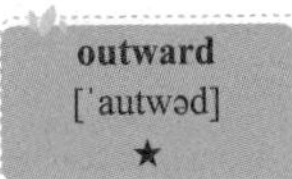

释义 *adj.* 向外的；外表的 *adv.* 向外地

短语 *outward* appearance 外观；外表 fly *outward* 向外飞

例句 The medicine is for *outward* application only. 这药只供外用。

派生 outwardly *adv.* 表面上；向外

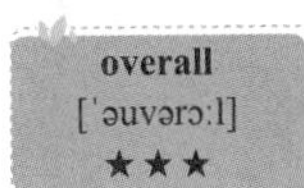

释义 *adj.* 总体的；全部的 *adv.* 全部；总体 *n.* 背带裤

短语 *overall* plan 总体规划

例句 We have finished *overall* homework. 我们已完成所有的家庭作业。
How much will it cost *overall*? 一共多少钱？

近义 total *adj.* 总的

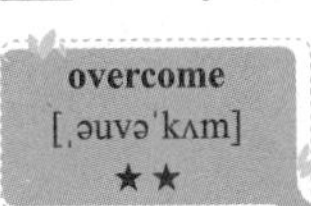

释义 *v.* 战胜；克服；使受不了

短语 *overcome* difficulties 克服困难

例句 He believed the faith that truth would *overcome*. 他相信真理终会战胜一切。
They were *overcome* with sadness. 他们悲痛欲绝。

近义 conquer *v.* 克服

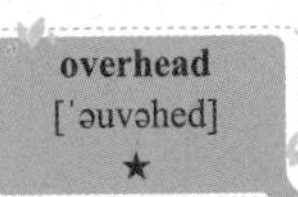

释义 *adj.* 头顶上的；上空的 *adv.* 在头顶上

短语 an *overhead* railway 高架铁路

例句 The *overhead* bird flew away. 头上的鸟飞走了。
The people in the room *overhead* were very noisy yesterday evening. 昨晚，楼上那个房间的人很吵。

释义 *n.* 财产；房地产；所有物；性质，特性

短语 intellectual *property* 知识产权

例句 That car is my *property*, and you mustn't use it without my permission. 这辆车是我的财产，你必须得到我的允许才能使用它。

近义 possession *n.* 个人财产，所有物

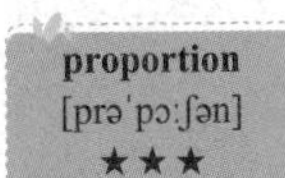

释义 *n.* 比例；部分；均衡，相称 *v.* 使成比例，使相称

短语 out of *proportion* 不成比例

例句 The *proportion* of men to women in the college has changed dramatically over the years. 近年来，这个学院的男女学生比例出现了剧变。

反义 disproportion *n.* 不均衡；不相称

派生 proportionality *n.* 相称；均衡；比例性

释义 *v.* 提议，建议；提名，推荐；求婚

短语 *propose* a toast 敬酒

真题 In December 2010 America's Federal Trade Commission (FTC) *proposed* adding a "do not track (DNT)" option to internet browsers. 2010 年 12 月，美国联邦贸易委员会(FTC)提议在网络浏览器中添加"不跟踪(DNT)"选项。(2013 阅读理解)

用法 propose to sb. 向某人求婚

派生 proposal *n.* 提议；求婚

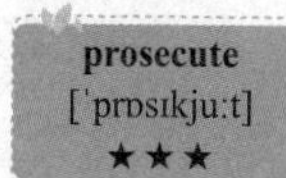

释义 *v.* 起诉，控告，检举；继续从事

例句 The attorney who will *prosecute* the case says he cannot reveal how much money is involved. 负责起诉该案件的律师表示，他不能透露涉案金额。

真题 Elected leaders must be allowed to help supporters deal with bureaucratic problems without fear of *prosecution* for bribery. 民选领袖应该被允许帮助其支持者解决官僚问题，而不用担心被起诉受贿赂。（2017 阅读理解）

派生 prosecution *n.* 起诉，诉讼

释义 *n.* 探求，寻找 *v.* 寻找；探索

例句 Man will suffer many disappointments in his *quest* for truth. 人类在探索真理过程中必然会遭受挫折。

真题 In some ways, this *quest* for commonalities defines science. 在某种程度上，这种对共性的追求定义了科学。（2012 翻译）

用法 in quest of 探寻

释义 *v.* 展现，显示；透露

例句 Pulling up the carpeting *revealed* the home's beautiful hardwood floors. 掀开地毯，可以看到家里漂亮的硬木地板。

近义 disclose *v.* 透露；揭开

反义 conceal *v.* 隐藏；掩盖

派生 revelation *n.* 揭露

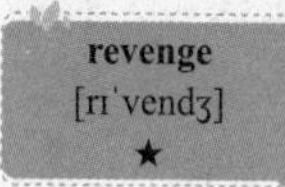

释义 *n.* 报复，复仇 *v.* 替……报仇

用法 be revenged on sb. 向某人复仇 revenge oneself on sb. 向某人复仇

例句 Thoughts of *revenge* kept running through his mind. 报复的念头不断在他的脑子里闪过。

There is no need for you to *revenge* yourself upon Jack. It was an accident. 你没必要向杰克报复。这是个意外。

派生 revenger *n.* 复仇者

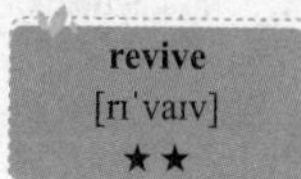

释义 *v.* 恢复；（使）复苏

短语 *revive* a system 恢复系统

例句 Unless banks carry toxic assets at prices that attract buyers, *reviving* the banking system will be difficult. 如果银行不以能够吸引买家的价格卖出不良资产，重振银行系统将会非常困难。

近义 restore *n.* 恢复

派生 revival *n.* 复兴

释义 *n.* 过剩；余额 *adj.* 过剩的，剩余的

短语 economic / trade *surplus* 经济过剩 / 贸易顺差

例句 The manufacturers in some countries dumped their *surplus* commodities abroad. 一些国家的制造商向国外倾销过剩的产品。

近义 superfluous *adj.* 多余的，过剩的

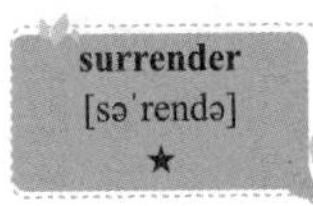

释义 *v.* 投降；放弃 *n.* 投降，认输

短语 unconditional *surrender* 无条件投降

例句 The rebel soldiers were forced to *surrender*. 叛军被迫投降。The victorious army demanded unconditional *surrender*. 胜方要求敌人无条件投降。

近义 submit *v.* 屈服

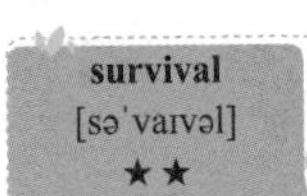

释义 *n.* 幸存，生存；残存物

短语 fight for *survival* 拼搏

例句 If cancers are spotted early there's a high chance of *survival*. 如果癌症在早期发现的话，患者存活的概率会很高。

近义 existence *n.* 存在；生存

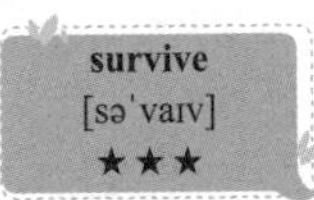

释义 *v.* 幸免于，幸存；比……长寿

例句 These plants cannot *survive* in very cold conditions. 这些植物在严寒中不能存活。

真题 Many of the ships were lost in storms, many passengers died of disease, and infants rarely *survived* the journey. 许多船只在风暴中沉没，许多乘客死于疾病，而婴儿很少能在旅途中幸存下来。（2015翻译）

用法 survive on 靠……活下来

派生 survivor *n.* 幸存者

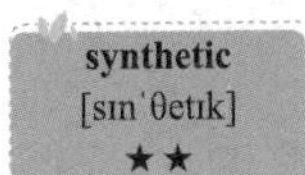

释义 *adj.* 合成的，人造的；综合的

短语 *synthetic* fiber 人造纤维

例句 The rug is made from a mixture of wool and *synthetic* fibers. 这地毯是由羊毛和合成纤维混合制成的。

派生 synthetically *adv.* 综合地；合成地

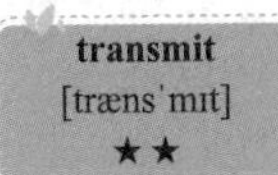

释义 *v.* 传输，传导；发射信号

短语 *transmit* information 传输信息

例句 How do we *transmit* a growth mind-set to our children? One way is by telling stories about achievements that result from hard work. 我们如何将一种成长的心态传递给我们的孩子？一种方法是通过讲述努力工作取得成就的故事。

派生 transmission *n.* 传播

释义 *v.* 运输 *n.* 运输；交通工具

短语 *transport* equipment 运输设备

例句 An efficient *transport* system is critical to the long-term future of London. 高效的交通系统对伦敦的长远未来至关重要。

派生 transportation *n.* 运输

释义 *n.* 营业额；人事变动率；翻覆 *adj.* 可翻转的

短语 an annual *turnover* 年营业额 employee *turnover* 员工流动

例句 In the last calendar year, the company had a *turnover* of $426 million. 在上一个日历年度里，该公司的营业额为 4.26 亿美元。

They've had a lot of *turnover* at the factory recently. 最近他们工厂人员变动很大。

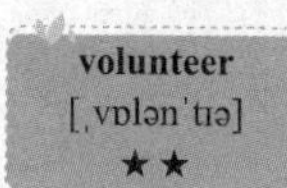

释义 *n.* / *v.* 自愿（者，兵）；自愿（提供）

短语 *volunteer* services 义工服务

例句 She now helps in a local school as a *volunteer* three days a week. 目前，她在当地的一家学校做志愿工作，一周去 3 天。

After dinner, Tom *volunteered* to clean up the kitchen. 晚饭后，汤姆主动要求打扫厨房。

用法 volunteer for sth. 自愿做某事

派生 voluntary *adj.* 自愿的

释义 *adj.* 粗俗的，庸俗的，下流的 *n.* 平民

短语 a *vulgar* man 粗俗的男人

例句 I will not tolerate such *vulgar* language in my home. 我不能容忍这种粗俗的语言出现在我的家里。

派生 coarse *adj.* 粗俗的

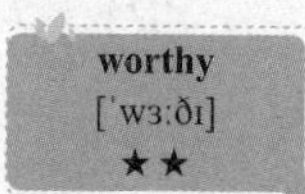

释义 *adj.* 值得……的，配得上……的；有价值的

用法 be worthy of doing sth. 值得做某事

例句 Your diligence is *worthy* of encouragement, but effort does not equal accomplishment. 你的勤奋值得鼓励，但努力不等于成就。

派生 worthwhile *adj.* 值得（做）的；有价值的

反义 unworthy *adj.* 不值得的；无价值的

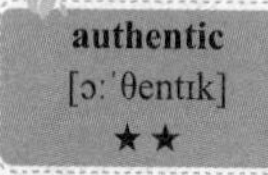

释义 *adj.* 正宗的；真实的；可靠的

例句 Last week, we took the foreign students in our school to experience the *authentic* tea culture. 上周，我们带着我们学校的外国学生去体验真正的茶文化。

近义 genuine *adj.* 真正的

派生 authentically *adv.* 真正地

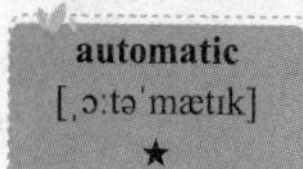

释义 *adj.* 自动的；自动化的；不假思索的 *n.* 自动变速汽车

例句 Citizenship is *automatic* for children born in this country. 孩子出生在这个国家，就自然而然地成为这个国家的公民。

派生 automatically *adv.* 自动地

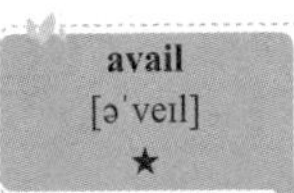

avail
[ə'veɪl]
★

释义 v. 有益；有用 n. 效用；利益

例句 Over a thousand learners have already *availed* the opportunity to study at our college. 已有一千多名学生抓住机会在我校学习。

We opposed the proposal but to no *avail*. 我们反对这个提议，但没用。

用法 to no avail 无效，完全无用

近义 benefit v. / n. 有益 / 益处

available
[ə'veɪləbl]
★★★

释义 adj. 可获得的；可用的；有空的

例句 Fresh fruit is *available* during the summer. 夏天有新鲜水果供应。

真题 More than half of all British scientific research is now published under open access terms: either freely *available* from the moment of publication, or ... 现在，超过一半的英国科学研究是在开放获取条件下发表的：要么从发表之日起就免费提供，要么……（2020 阅读理解）

派生 availability n. 可用性

breach
[bri:tʃ]
★

释义 n./ v. 破坏；违反；中断

例句 The incident caused a *breach* between the two countries. 这一事件引起了两国间的不和。

He was accused of *breaching* the contract. 他被指控违反合同。

brief
[bri:f]
★★★

释义 adj. 简短的，简洁的 n. 概要 v. 给（某人）指示，简报

例句 By the 1950s, most schools required a *brief* personal statement of why the student had chosen to apply to one school over another. 到 20 世纪 50 年代，大多数学校都要求学生提供一份简短的个人陈述，说明为什么选择了这所学校而不是另一所学校。

近义 concise adj. 简明的

派生 briefly adv. 简短地

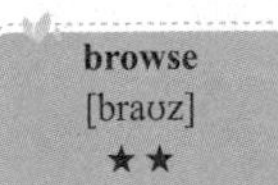

browse
[braʊz]
★★

释义 v. / n. 浏览

例句 Several customers were *browsing* in the bookstore. 几个顾客在书店里浏览。

We went for a *browse* around an antique shop. 我们去一家古董店随便看了看。

派生 browser n. 浏览器

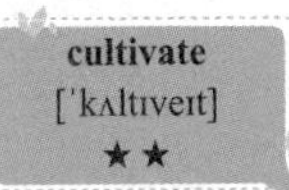

cultivate
['kʌltɪveɪt]
★★

释义 v. 耕作；培育；陶冶

短语 *cultivate* fruits and vegetables 种植水果和蔬菜

例句 *Cultivating* a positive mental attitude towards yourself can reap tremendous benefits. 培养一种自信的积极心态会让人受益匪浅。

派生 cultivation n. 培养；耕种

curb
[kɜ:b]
★★★

释义 v. / n. 控制，抑制

短语 *curb* inflation 抑制通货膨胀

例句 Measures have been taken to *curb* the spread of the virus. 已采取措施遏制病毒的传播。

currency [ˈkʌrənsɪ] ★

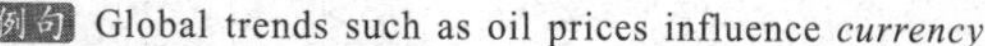

释义 *n.* 通货，货币；通用，流行

短语 foreign *currency* 外币

例句 Global trends such as oil prices influence *currency* movements. 石油价格等全球趋势影响着货币走势。

The qualification has gained *currency* all over the world. 这个学历在全世界都得到了普遍认可。

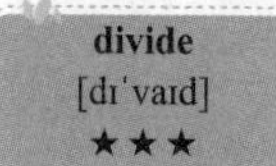

divide [dɪˈvaɪd] ★★★

释义 *v.*（使）分开；分隔；除，除以；分配

例句 She *divides* her time between her apartment in New York and her cottage in Yorkshire. 她经常往返于纽约的公寓和约克郡的小别墅之间。

用法 divide by 用……除以

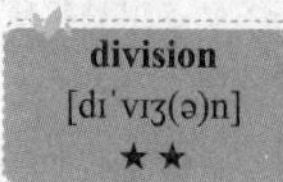

division [dɪˈvɪʒ(ə)n] ★★

释义 *n.* 分割；部门，科，处；除法；分界线

例句 There are deep *divisions* in the party over the war. 党内对于这场战争存在着严重的分歧。

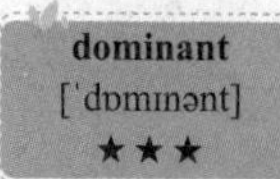

dominant [ˈdɒmɪnənt] ★★★

释义 *adj.* 支配的，统治的；占优势的

短语 *dominant* effect 显性效应 *dominant* role 主要角色

例句 The issue of climate change was the *dominant* theme of the conference. 气候变化问题是这次会议的主要主题。

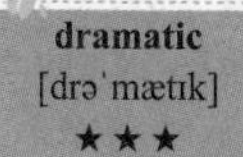

dramatic [drəˈmætɪk] ★★★

释义 *adj.* 戏剧的，戏剧性的；剧烈的

短语 *dramatic* results / news 出人意料的结果 / 令人吃惊的消息

例句 Computers have brought *dramatic* changes to the workplace. 计算机给工作场所带来了巨大的变化。

exploit [ɪkˈsplɔɪt] ★★★

释义 *v.* 开拓；开发；剥削 *n.* 功绩；业绩

例句 Rock is hoping to *exploit* new opportunities in Africa. 洛克希望在非洲开拓新的机会。

What is being done to stop employers from *exploiting* young people?
目前有什么措施制止雇主剥削年轻人呢？

派生 exploitation *n.* 剥削；开发；利用

exposure [ɪkˈspəʊʒə] ★★★

释义 *n.* 暴露，揭露；曝光

例句 After only a short *exposure* to sunlight, he began to turn red. 他在阳光下只晒了一会儿，皮肤就开始变红了。

真题 Scientists have found that *exposure* to this hormone puts us in a trusting mood. 科学家发现，这种激素会让我们处于一种信任的情绪中。（2018 完形填空）

extend [ɪkˈstend] ★★★

释义 *v.* 延长，延伸；扩展；包括；提供

短语 *extend* an invitation 发出邀请 *extend* warm hospitality 给予热情款待

例句 Careful maintenance can *extend* the life of your car. 精心保养可延长你汽车的寿命。

The service also *extends* to wrapping and delivering gifts. 服务项目还包括包装和递送礼物。

派生 extension *n.* 延伸；延期；电话分机

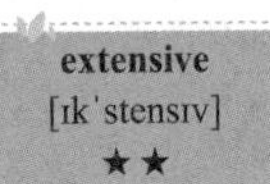

extension [ɪkˈstenʃ(ə)n] ★★

释义 *n.* 延伸；延期；电话分机

短语 *extension* number 分机号码

例句 He first entered Britain on a six-month visa, and was given a further *extension* of six months. 他第一次入境英国时持的是六个月的签证，后来又被延长了六个月。

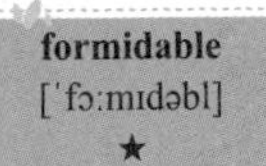

extensive [ɪkˈstensɪv] ★★

释义 *adj.* 广大的，广阔的

短语 *extensive* knowledge 广博的知识

例句 It is quite necessary for a qualified teacher to have good manners and *extensive* knowledge. 对于一个合格的教师来说，有良好的礼貌和广博的知识是非常必要的。

派生 extensively *adv.* 广阔地；广泛地

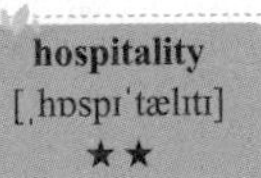

formidable [ˈfɔːmɪdəbl] ★

释义 *adj.* 强大的，令人敬畏的；可怕的；艰难的

例句 Marsalis has a *formidable* reputation in both jazz and classical music. 马萨利斯在爵士乐和古典音乐界都享有极高的声誉。

派生 formidably *adv.* 可怕地；难以应付地

hospitality [ˌhɒspɪˈtælɪtɪ] ★★

释义 *n.* 殷勤，好客；殷勤款待

短语 the *hospitality* industry 酒店业

例句 I received the *hospitality* of the family. 我受到这家人亲切的款待。

hostile [ˈhɒstaɪl] ★★

释义 *adj.* 怀有敌意的，不友善的；敌人的，敌方的

例句 Drinking may make a person feel relaxed and happy, or it may make him *hostile*, or violent. 喝酒可能让人感到放松和愉快，也可能让人变得不友善或暴力。

派生 hostility *n.* 敌意，对抗

involve [ɪnˈvɒlv] ★★★

释义 *v.* 使卷入；包含，含有，涉及

例句 The Bilski case *involves* a claimed patent on a method for hedging risk in the energy market. 比尔斯基案例牵扯到一份已认证的方法专利，即关于能源市场的对冲风险。

真题 Both France and the United States are *involved* in the organization's work. 法国和美国都参与了该组织的工作。（2020 阅读理解）

近义 contain *v.* 包含

派生 involvement *n.* 参与，介入

irrigate [ˈɪrɪgeɪt] ★★

释义 *v.* 灌溉，修水利；进行灌溉

短语 *irrigated* land / fields 经灌溉的土地 / 田野

例句 He also wants to use water to *irrigate* barren desert land. 他还想用水灌溉贫瘠的沙漠土地。

派生 irrigation *n.* 灌溉

issue [ˈɪʃuː, ˈɪsuː] ★★★

释义 *n.* 问题，争端，发行（物），期号 *v.* 发表，颁布；分发；发行

例句 Don't worry about who will do it — that's just a side *issue*. 不要担心这件事由谁来做，那只是次要问题。

The office will be *issuing* permits on Tuesday and Thursday mornings. 办事处将在周二和周四的上午颁

发许可证。

释义 *v.* 证明……正当；为……辩护

例句 The Prime Minister has been asked to *justify* the decision to Parliament. 已请首相向议会说明该决定的合理性。

短语 justify sth. to sb. 向某人证明某事是正当的

派生 justification *n.* 正当理由，合理解释

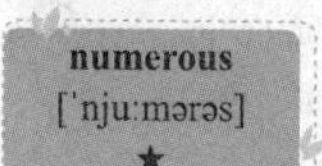

释义 *adj.* 很多的，许多的

短语 *numerous* attempts 多次尝试

例句 I understand there have been *numerous* problems with your holiday arrangements. 我知道你的假期安排有很多问题。

用法 too numerous to mention 不胜枚举

释义 *v.* 养育；培养 *n.* 教养，培育

短语 *nurture* trust 培养起信心

例句 These classes help *nurture* and educate the students to excel in a given artistic area. 这些课程帮助培养和教育学生在特定的艺术领域中脱颖而出。

近义 foster *v.* 培养

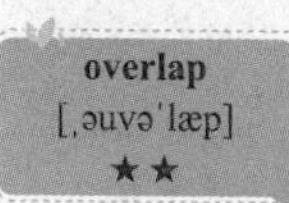

释义 *v.* 重叠 *n.* 重叠的部分

短语 *overlap* region 重叠区

例句 Our jobs *overlap* slightly, which sometimes causes difficulties. 我们的工作略有重叠，所以有时造成一些困难。

The *overlap* between the jacket and the trousers is not good. 夹克和裤子重叠的部分不好看。

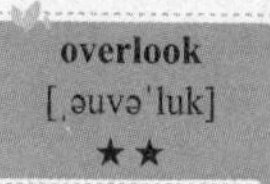

释义 *v.* 忽视；监督，管理；俯视

短语 *overlook* the possibility 忽略可能性 *overlook* the sea 俯瞰大海

例句 The foreman *overlooked* a large number of workers. 工头监督着许多工人。

We *overlooked* the sea. 我们俯瞰大海。

近义 neglect *v.* 忽视

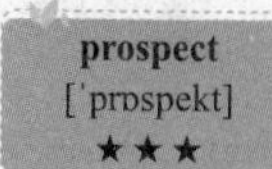

释义 *n.* 景色；前景，前途

短语 market *prospect* 市场前景

例句 Long-term *prospects* for the economy have improved. 长期的经济前景已有所改善。

真题 This long perspective makes the pessimistic view of our *prospects* seem more likely to be a passing fad. 这种长期存在的观点使对我们前景的悲观看法更可能只是昙花一现。（2013 阅读理解）

派生 prospective *adj.* 预期的

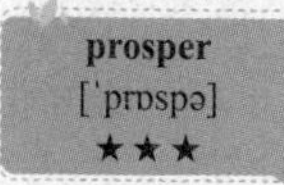

释义 *v.*（使）成功，兴隆，昌盛

例句 Lots of microchip manufacturing companies *prospered* at that time. 许多生产芯片的公司都是在那时候发展起来的。

近义 thrive *v.* 兴旺，繁荣

派生 prosperity *n.* 繁荣,成功

protect [prəˈtekt] ★★★

释义 *v.* 保护,保卫

短语 *protect* the environment 环境保护

例句 She's always chasing cats out of the garden to *protect* her precious birds. 她总是把猫赶出花园,以保护她的宝贝鸟儿。

真题 The Federal Communications Commission argued that other agencies would *protect* against anti-competitive behavior. 联邦通信委员会认为其他机构将会保护自己以免受反竞争行为的侵害。(2021 阅读理解)

用法 protect against 使免受,远离……

派生 protection *n.* 保护

provide [prəuˈvaɪd] ★★★

释义 *v.* 供应,准备

例句 The letter *provided* the answer to what had been troubling him. 这封信回答了一直困扰他的问题。

派生 provided *conj.* 假如,只要

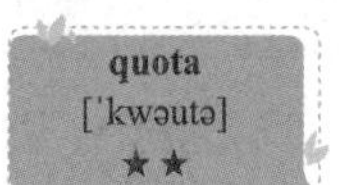
quota [ˈkwəutə] ★★

释义 *n.*(正式限定的)定量,定额,配额

短语 *quota* system / control 配额制 / 配额管制

例句 France belongs to the EU countries, some products are to be the *quota*, some are unwanted. 法国属于欧盟国家,有些产品是要配额的,有些是不要的。

真题 That is exactly what happened when Norway adopted a nationwide corporate gender *quota*. 当挪威在全国范围内实行企业性别配额时,就发生了这种情况。(2020 阅读理解)

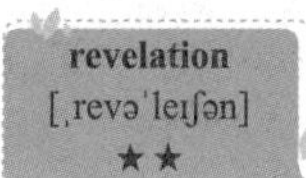
revelation [ˌrevəˈleɪʃən] ★★

释义 *n.* 揭示,透露;显示

短语 a startling / sensational *revelation* 惊人的 / 耸人听闻的发现

例句 The *revelation*, made on Monday, shows a split among the EU bloc's members. 周一披露的这一消息表明,欧盟成员国之间存在分歧。

真题 One of the astonishing *revelations* was how little Rebekah Brooks knew of what went on in her newsroom. 其中一个令人震惊的发现是,丽贝卡·布鲁克斯对她的新闻编辑部发生的事情知之甚少。(2015 阅读理解)

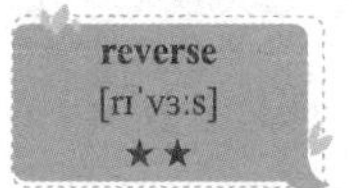
reverse [rɪˈvɜːs] ★★

释义 *n.* 相反;背面 *adj.* 相反的 *v.* 颠倒,倒转

短语 *reverse* side 背面

例句 The rise *reversed* the downward trend in the country's jobless rate. 这一上升扭转了该国失业率下降的趋势。

The truth is just the *reverse*. 真实情况恰好相反。

派生 reversion *n.* 逆转

revolution [ˌrevəˈluːʃn] ★★★

释义 *n.* 革命;变革

例句 There has been a technological *revolution* in the printing industry. 印刷业发生了一场技术革命。

真题 We are still at the beginning of this *revolution* and small choices now may turn out to have gigantic consequences later. 我们仍处于这场革命的开端,现在的小选择可能会在以后产生

巨大的影响。(2018 阅读理解)

派生 revolutionary *adj.* 革命的;突破性的

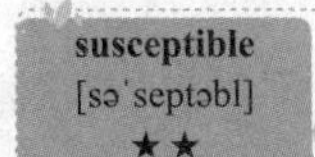

释义 *adj.* 易受影响的;易受感动的;易受感染的

短语 a *susceptible* person 一个敏感的人

例句 Their age and poor health, the doctor said, make them *susceptible* to becoming infected. 医生说,他们的年龄和健康状况不佳,使他们容易受到感染。

用法 be susceptible to 易受……影响

派生 susceptibility *n.* 敏感性

释义 *adj.* 快的;敏捷的;立刻的 *n.* 雨燕

短语 a *swift* decision / current 迅即做出的决定 / 湍急的水流

例句 The gazelle is one of the *swiftes*t and most graceful of animals. 羚羊是最敏捷、最优雅的动物之一。

用法 be swift to do sth. / in doing sth. 迅速做某事

派生 swiftly *adv.* 很快地;敏捷地

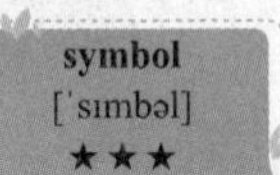

释义 *n.* 符号;标志;象征

短语 Olympic / chemical *symbol* 奥林匹克标志 / 化学符号

例句 The whale, like the dolphin, has become a *symbol* of the marvels of creation. 鲸和海豚一样,已经成为造物杰作的象征。

派生 symbolic *adj.* 有象征意义的

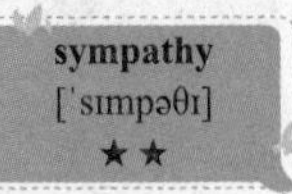

释义 *n.* 同情,同情心;赞同,同感

例句 The flood victims have received both *sympathy* and assistance from the international community during the flood season. 在汛期,受灾人民得到了国际社会的同情和援助。

近义 compassion *n.* 同情

派生 sympathetic *adj.* 同情的;支持的

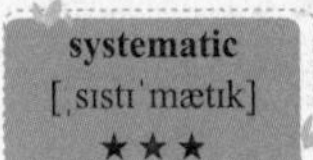

释义 *adj.* (systematical) 系统的,有组织的

短语 *systematic* analysis / study 系统分析 / 研究

例句 Every subject of education in school is *systematic*, such as Chinese, mathematics, science and philosophy. 每一门教育科目都由学校系统地开设,例如语文、数学、科学和哲学。

派生 systematically *adv.* 系统地

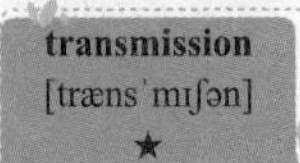

释义 *n.* 播送;传送;传染

短语 power / information *transmission* 电力 / 信息传输

例句 The microphone converts acoustic waves to electrical signals for *transmission*. 麦克风将声波转化成电信号进行传输。

Hand washing is an effective way to prevent disease *transmission*. 洗手是预防疾病传播的一种有效方式。

近义 transfer *n.* 转移

transportation
[ˌtrænspɔːˈteɪʃn]
★★

释义 *n.* 运输，运送；运输工具

短语 forms of transportation 交通方式

例句 Different forms of *transportation* are becoming more popular, particularly for covering short distances. 各种各样的交通工具越来越流行，尤其是短途交通工具。

vulnerable
[ˈvʌlnərəbl]
★★

释义 易受攻击的；脆弱的

短语 leave sb. vulnerable 使某人易受伤害

例句 Plants that are growing vigorously are less likely to be *vulnerable* to disease. 生长旺盛的植物不容易生病。

反义 invulnerable *adj.* 不会受伤害的

派生 vulnerability *n.* 易损性，弱点

worthwhile
[ˌwɜːθˈwaɪl]
★★★

释义 *adj.* 值得（做）的；有价值的

例句 We believe the time and hard work involved in completing such an assignment are *worthwhile*. 我们相信为完成这项任务所需要投入的时间和付出的努力是值得的。

用法 make life worthwhile 使生活有价值

近义 valuable *adj.* 有益的，宝贵的

authority
[ɔːˈθɒrətɪ]
★★★

释义 *n.* 权力；权威；当局；权威人士

例句 The United Nations has used its *authority* to restore peace in the area. 联合国行使其权力以恢复该地区的和平。

派生 authoritative *adj.* 专断的

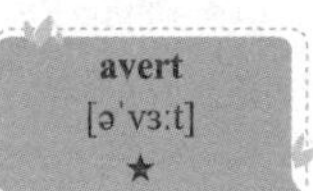

释义 *v.* 防止，避免；转移

例句 Efforts are being made to *avert* war and find a diplomatic solution. 各方正在为避免战争、寻求外交解决途径而做出积极的努力。

近义 avoid *v.* 避免

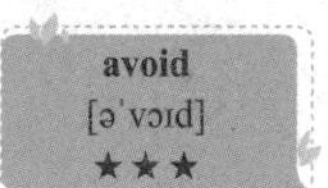

释义 *v.* 避免；避开

例句 I try to *avoid* going shopping on Saturdays. 我尽量不在周六去购物。

用法 avoid doing sth. 避免做某事

近义 avert *v.* 避免

释义 *v.* 授予；颁发 *n.* 奖品

例句 Caroline was *awarded* first prize in the speech contest. 卡洛琳在演讲比赛中获得一等奖。

Ang Lee became the first Asian to win the Academy *Award* for Best Director. 李安成为第一位获得奥斯卡最佳导演奖的亚洲人。

用法 award sb. sth. 给某人颁发

近义 grant *v.* 授予，给予

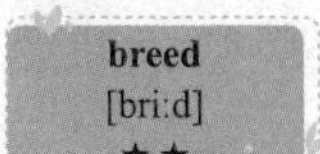

释义 *v.* 饲养；繁殖 *n.* 品种；类型

例句 a *breed* of dog / cat 某一品种的狗 / 猫

Eagles *breed* during the cooler months of the year. 鹰在一年中较冷的月份繁殖。

The plants are *bred* to resist disease and drought. 这些植物能抵抗疾病和抗干旱。

释义 *v.* 做预算 *n.* 预算

例句 The project has a million dollars *budget*. 这个项目的预算是一百万美元。

They *budgeted* millions of dollars to make the film. 他们为拍这部电影编列了数百万美元的预算。

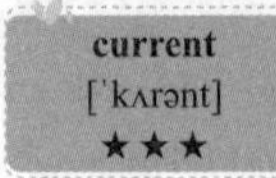

释义 *n.* 电流，水流；潮流，趋势 *adj.* 当前的；流行的

例句 He swam to the shore against a strong *current*. 他逆着急流游向岸边。

In the *current* economic situation, switching careers may not be such a good idea. 在目前的经济形势下，转行也许不是个好主意。

派生 currently *adv.* 现在，目前

释义 *n.* 课程

短语 *curriculum* design 课程设计

例句 Maths is an essential part of the school *curriculum*. 数学是学校课程的重要组成部分。

真题 Alongside that, many countries are introducing English into the primary school *curriculum*. 与此同时，许多国家正在将英语引入小学课程。（2017 阅读理解）

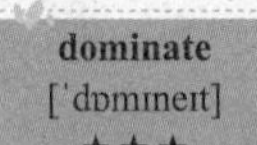

释义 *v.* 支配，控制；占优势；俯视

短语 *dominate* the market 主导市场

例句 Arsenal *dominated* the first half of the match. 阿森纳队在上半场比赛中占据上风。

The cathedral *dominates* the city. 大教堂俯视全城。

派生 domination *n.* 支配；控制

释义 *v.* 捐赠；赠予

例句 They used to *donate* large sum of money to the Red Cross every year. 他们过去每年都向红十字会捐献大笔的钱。

派生 donation *n.* 捐赠

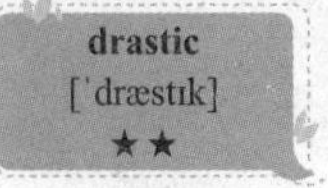

释义 *adj.* 激烈的，严厉的；剧烈的

例句 Scientists have warned that cases of food poisoning will increase unless *drastic* action is taken. 科学家警告说，除非采取严厉措施，否则食物中毒的案例将会增加。

派生 drastically *adv.* 猛烈地；非常

drought
[draʊt]
★

释义 *n.* 旱灾，干旱

短语 *drought* relief 抗旱

例句 The timely rain after a long time of *drought* will certainly bring on the crops. 久旱之后的这场及时雨肯定会有助于作物的生长。

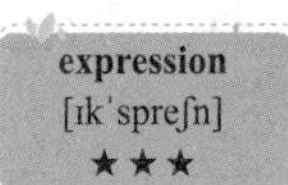

释义 *n.* 表达，表情

例句 Laughter is one of the most infectious *expressions* of emotion. 笑是最具感染力的情感表达方式之一。

用法 give expression to sth. 表达某事

释义 *adj.* 灭绝的；熄灭了的

例句 It is 250 years since the wolf became *extinct* in Britain. 狼在英国灭绝已经有 250 年了。

派生 extinction *n.* 灭绝

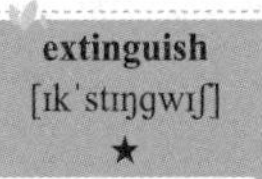

释义 *v.* 熄灭；消灭；使破灭

例句 The lights are *extinguished* as soon as the news conference is over. 新闻发布会一结束，灯光就熄灭了。

派生 extinguished *adj.* 熄灭的；灭绝的

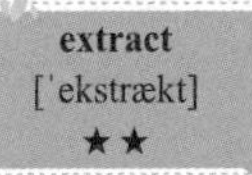

释义 *v.* / *n.* 提取；摘录 *n.* 抽取物；精华；选集

例句 The chef added a few drops of lemon *extract* to the mixture. 厨师在混合物中加了几滴柠檬汁。

用法 extraction *n.* 取出，提炼

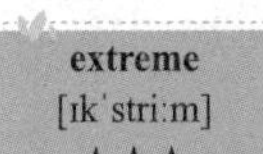

释义 *adj.* 极度的；极端的；尽头的 *n.* 极端；最大程度

例句 He could not tolerate the *extremes* of heat in the desert. 他忍受不了沙漠的酷热。

派生 extremely *adv.* 极度，非常

formulate
[ˈfɔːmjuleɪt]
★★★

释义 *v.* 用公式表示；规划，设计；系统地阐述

例句 She could not *formulate* her ideas in a few words. 她无法用几句话阐明她的思想。

真题 Next time you state your position, *formulate* an argument for what you claim and honestly ask yourself whether your argument is any good. 下次当你表明自己的立场时，为你要提出的主张准备好论据，并且坦诚地问自己，你的论据是否充分。（2019 阅读理解）

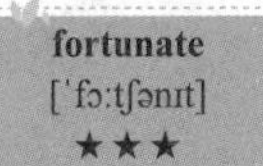

释义 *adj.* 幸运的，侥幸的

例句 I know someone who was in the *fortunate* position of being offered two jobs. 我认识一个人，他很幸运地得到了两份工作机会。

用法 be in the fortunate position of sth. 处于有利的位置；处于幸运的境地

派生 fortunately *adv.* 幸运地

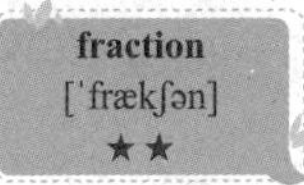

释义 *n.* 碎片，小部分，一点儿；分数

例句 The circle is divided into sections, and each section represents a *fraction* of the data. 圆被分成几个部分，每个部分代表数据的一部分。

释义 *n.* 地平线；范围；界限，眼界

例句 A ship appeared on the *horizon*. 一艘船出现在地平线上。

The company needs new *horizons* now. 公司现在需要开拓新的领域。

用法 beyond the horizon 超越地平线

派生 horizontal *adj.* 水平的；在地平线上的

释义 *adj.* 谦逊的；卑微的；简陋的

例句 He gave a great performance, but he was very *humble*. 他的表演很精彩，但他却很谦逊。

The *humble* cottage, which was built in the late 18th century, has two bedrooms, a lounge and kitchen. 这座简陋的小屋建于18世纪末，有两间卧室、一间客厅和一间厨房。

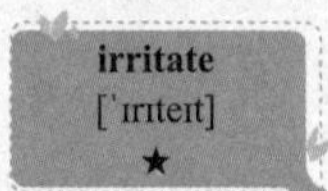

释义 *v.* 激怒，恼火；使急躁；使疼痛

例句 They were *irritated* by the sound of crying. 哭泣声让他们很恼火。

At first, my contact lenses *irritated* my eyes. 起初一戴上隐形眼镜，我的眼睛就疼。

派生 irritation *n.* 恼怒

释义 *n.* 条（款），项目；一则（新闻），（戏剧的）节目

例句 Can we add up this *item* to the agreement? 我们可以把这一条款加入协议吗？

The most valuable *item* on the show is an ancient painted pottery. 展览上展出的最有价值的物品是一件古代彩陶。

Let us go on to the next *item* on the agenda. 让我们继续讨论议程上的下一个项目。

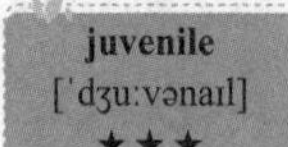

释义 *n.* 青少年，少年读物 *adj.* 青少年的，幼稚的

短语 *juvenile* behaviour 幼稚的行为

例句 This lack of parental supervision is thought to be an influence on *juvenile* crime rates. 这种缺乏父母监督的情况被认为是青少年犯罪率的一个影响因素。

The number of *juveniles* in the general population has fallen by a fifth in the past 10 years. 在过去的10年里，青少年在总人口中的数量下降了五分之一。

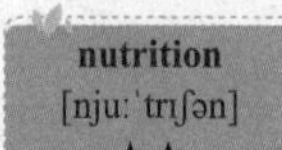

释义 *n.* 营养

短语 *nutrition* and health care 营养与保健

例句 Ruel says in the 1980s Thailand was able to reduce child undernourishment by recruiting a large number of volunteers to travel the countryside teaching about health and *nutrition*. 鲁埃尔说，在20世纪80年代，泰国招募了大量志愿者到农村传授健康和营养知识，从而减少了儿童营养不良的情况。

派生 nutritional *adj.* 营养的

释义 *adv.* 海外的；国外的 *adj.*（在）海外的，（在）国外的

短语 *overseas* Chinese 华侨 *overseas* market 海外市场

例句 The radio station sets up an *overseas* broadcast program. 电台新设置了一个对外广播节目。

近义 abroad *adv.* 在国外，到国外

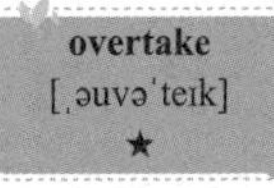

释义 *v.* 追上，赶上，超过

例句 Exports have already *overtaken* last year's figure. 出口量已超过了去年。

It's dangerous to *overtake* on a bend. 在弯道强行超车是危险的。

近义 exceed *v.* 超过

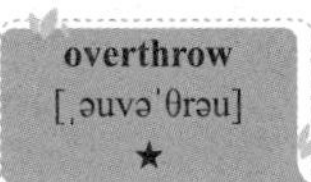

释义 *v.* 打倒；推翻 *n.* 推翻，打倒

例句 They were charged with plotting the *overthrow* of the state. 他们被控密谋颠覆国家。

Several generals formed a conspiracy to *overthrow* the government. 几名将军们密谋颠覆政府。

近义 overturn *v.* 推翻

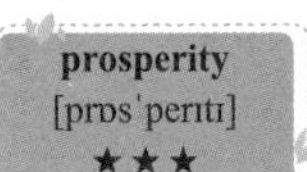

释义 *n.* 繁荣，兴旺

短语 economic *prosperity* 经济繁荣

例句 The town's nineteenth-century *prosperity* was built on steel. 这个城市 19 世纪的繁荣是建立在钢铁工业基础上的。

真题 Here, too, the problems are social: the organization and distribution of food, wealth and *prosperity*. 这里的问题也是社会性的：食物、财富和繁荣的组织和分配。（2013 阅读理解）

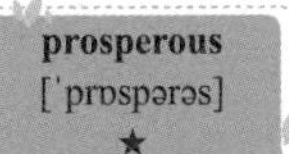

释义 *adj.* 繁荣的，茂盛的，顺利的

短语 thriving and *prosperous* 繁荣昌盛

例句 The peasant household has become *prosperous* through working hard. 这户农家已经通过辛勤劳动变得富裕了。

近义 flourishing *adj.* 繁荣的

派生 prosperously *adv.* 繁荣地

释义 *v.* [prəˈtest]/ *n.* [ˈprəutest] 主张，断言；抗议，反对

例句 Conservation groups have united in *protest* against the planned new road. 自然环境保护组织联合抗议计划建造的新公路。

用法 protest against 反对，对……提出抗议

近义 objection *n.* 反对

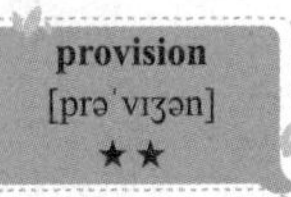

释义 *n.* 供应；条款；准备 (*pl.*) 给养

例句 The department is responsible for the *provision* of residential care services. 该部门负责提供家庭护理服务。

This *provision* gives the president total and unchecked power. 这条规定赋予了总统绝对且不受约束的权力。

近义 supply *v.* 供给

释义 *n.* 财政收入，税收

短语 state *revenue* 财政收入

例句 In fact, the land *revenue* has long been the most important piece of local government *revenue*. 事实上,土地出让收入早已是地方政府最重要的一项财政收入。

真题 It reported a net loss of $5.6 billion for fiscal 2016, the 10th straight year its expenses have exceeded *revenue*. 该公司报告称,公司在2016财年净亏损56亿美元,这是其支出连续第10年超过收入。(2018阅读理解)

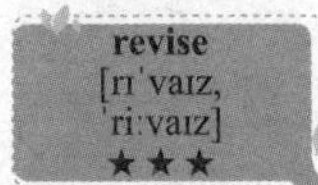

释义 v. 修订,校订;复习 n. 修订,校订

例句 The government may need to *revise* its policy in the light of this report. 政府可能需要根据本报告修订其政策。

真题 The newly *revised Danish Fashion Ethical Charter* clearly states:"..."新修订的《丹麦时尚道德宪章》明确指出:"……"(2016阅读理解)

近义 review n. / v. 复习

派生 revision n. 修改,修订

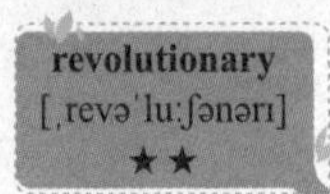

释义 adj. 革命的,革新的 n. 革命者

短语 the *Revolutionary* War 革命战争

例句 Many *revolutionaries* lost their lives for the people. 许多革命者为人民牺牲了生命。

Beethoven's importance in music has been principally defined by the *revolutionary* nature of his compositions. 贝多芬的作品所具有的革命性意义奠定了他在音乐界的重要地位。

释义 n. 节奏,韵律

短语 sense of *rhythm* 节奏感

例句 The boat rocked up and down in *rhythm* with the sea. 小船随着海浪起伏有致。

派生 rhythmic adj. 有节奏的

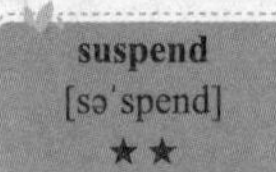

释义 v. 悬(浮),挂;暂停,取消;推迟

短语 *suspend* production 停产

例句 In dreams, a window opens into a world where logic is *suspended* and dead people speak. 在睡梦中,一扇窗户通向一个没有逻辑、死人开始说话的世界。

Some small animals can *suspend* from the branches by their tails. 一些小动物可以用尾巴将自己倒挂在树枝上。

派生 suspension n. 暂停

释义 n. 怀疑,猜疑;一点儿,少量

短语 under *suspicion* 被怀疑

例句 Astronomers will have to collect more spectra from these stars to confirm their *suspicions*. 天文学家们必须要从这些恒星上采集更多的光谱来证实他们的推想。

用法 have a suspicion about 怀疑……

派生 suspicious adj. 怀疑的

释义 n. 开关;转换 v. 转变,转换

例句 When our brains *switch* between being focused and unfocused on a task, they tend to be more efficient. 当我们的大

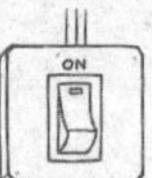

脑就某项工作在“集中注意力”与“分散注意力”之间切换时，它们往往更高效。

用法 switch on / off 开 / 关

近义 shift *v.* 转换

symphony [ˈsɪmfənɪ] ★

释义 *n.* 交响乐，交响曲

短语 *symphony* orchestra 交响乐团

例句 We predict that the *symphony* will flourish in the years to come even without funding from the city. 我们预测，即使没有市政府的资助，交响乐团也会在未来几年蓬勃发展。

派生 symphonic *adj.* 交响乐的

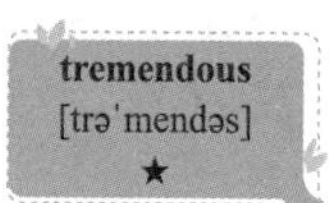

tremendous [trəˈmendəs] ★

释义 *adj.* 巨大的，极大的

短语 a *tremendous* pressure 巨大的压力

例句 This book was the outcome of a *tremendous* amount of scientific work. 这本书是大量科学研究工作的成果。

用法 a tremendous amount of

近义 enormous *adj.* 巨大的

派生 tremendously *adv.* 非常地；极大地

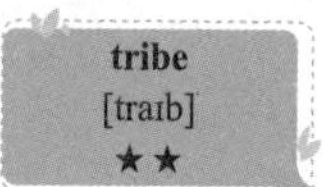

tribe [traɪb] ★★

释义 *n.* 种族，部落；（植物，动物）族，类

短语 a *tribe* of cats 猫族

例句 In ancient times there was a custom which still survives in the Chukchee *tribe* of Asiatic Eskimos. 在古代，亚洲爱斯基摩人的楚克其部落中有一种习俗至今仍在延续。

派生 tribal *adj.* 部落的，部族的

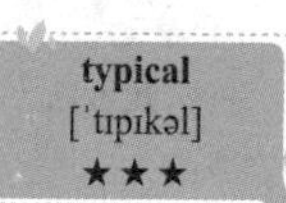

typical [ˈtɪpɪkəl] ★★★

释义 *adj.* 典型的，有代表性的

例句 We wanted him to have the *typical* college experience of living on campus. 我们希望他拥有典型的大学校园生活体验——住校。

真题 We know that a typical infant will instinctively gaze into its mother's eyes, and she will look back. 我们知道，一个典型的婴儿会本能地凝视母亲的眼睛，母亲也会回看孩子。（2020 阅读理解）

派生 typically *adv.* 有代表性地

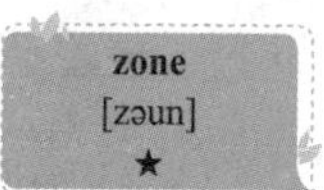

zone [zəun] ★

释义 *n.* 地区，区域 *v.* 分区，划分地带

短语 development / economic *zone* 开发区 / 经济特区

例句 The port, in which many Chinese companies have settled, is to be provided with a free trade *zone*. 许多中国公司已经落户的这个港口将拥有一个自由贸易区。

The town centre was *zoned* for office development. 镇中心被划定为写字楼开发区。

近义 area / district *n.* 地区；区域

派生 zoning *n.* 分区制

A

absurd [əbˈsɜːd] *adj.* / *n.* 荒谬（的）；荒唐（的）

accessory [əkˈsesərɪ] *n.* 配件；附件；（衣服的）配饰

ache [eɪk] *n.* / *v.* 疼痛

acid [ˈæsɪd] *n.* 酸 *adj.* 酸的；刻薄的

acre [ˈeɪkə] *n.* 英亩

acrobat [ˈækrəbæt] *n.* 杂技演员

across [əˈkrɒs] *prep.* / *adv.* 穿过；在对面

actor [ˈæktə] *n.* 男演员；演员

actress [ˈæktrəs] *n.* 女演员

actual [ˈæktʃuəl] *adj.* 实际的；真实的

acute [əˈkjuːt] *adj.* 严重的；急性的；敏锐的

add [æd] *v.* 增加 *n.* 加法

adjacent [əˈdʒeɪsnt] *adj.* 邻近的；毗连的

adjective [ˈædʒɪktɪv] *n.* 形容词 *adj.* 形容词的；附属的

admire [ədˈmaɪə] *v.* 钦佩；欣赏

adult [ˈædʌlt;əˈdʌlt] *n.* 成年人 *adj.* 成年的

adverb [ˈædvɜːb] *n.* 副词 *adj.* 副词的

advertise [ˈædvətaɪz] *v.* 登广告；做广告

advice [ədˈvaɪs] *n.* 建议；劝告；通知

advise [ədˈvaɪz] *v.* 劝（忠）告；建议；通知

aerial [ˈeərɪəl] *adj.* 空中的；航空的 *n.* 天线

aeroplane [ˈeərəpleɪn] *n.* 飞机

affect [əˈfekt] *v.* 影响；（疾病）侵袭

affection [əˈfekʃn] *n.* 喜爱；钟爱

afford [əˈfɔːd] *v.* 提供；买得起

afraid [əˈfreɪd] *adj.* 害怕的

after [ˈɑːftə] *prep.* / *conj.* 在……后 *adv.* / *adj.* 后来（的）

afternoon [ˌɑːftəˈnuːn] *n.* 下午；午后

afterward(s) [ˈɑːftəwəd] *adv.* 以后；后来

again [əˈgen] *adv.* 再一次

against [əˈgenst] *prep.* 反对；违反；紧靠

age [eɪdʒ] *n.* 年龄；时代 *v.*（使）变老

agency [ˈeɪdʒənsɪ] *n.* 代理；经销

agent [ˈeɪdʒənt] *n.* 代理人；药剂；特工

ago [əˈgəʊ] *adv.* 以前

agree [əˈgriː] *v.* 同意；赞成；相符

agriculture [ˈægrɪkʌltʃə] *n.* 农学；农业

ahead [əˈhed] *adj.* 领先；在前的 *adv.* 提前领先地；在前面

aid [eɪd] *n.* 助手；援助 *v.* 帮助

aim [eɪm] *n.* 目标 *v.* 以……为目标；瞄准

air [eə] *n.* 空气；大气；神态 *v.* 使通风

aircraft [ˈeəkrɑːft] *n.* 飞机；航空器

airline [ˈeəlaɪn] *n.* 航空公司；航线

airport [ˈeəpɔːt] *n.* 机场；航空站

aisle [aɪl] *n.* 侧廊；通道；走道

alarm [əˈlɑːm] *n.* 警报；闹钟；惊恐 *v.* 使惊恐

album [ˈælbəm] *n.* 集邮簿；相册；唱片；签名册

alcohol [ˈælkəhɒl] *n.* 酒精；乙醇

alert [əˈlɜːt] *adj.* 警觉的 *n.* 警报 *v.* 使警觉

alike [əˈlaɪk] *adj.* 相似的 *adv.* 同样地；相像地

alive [əˈlaɪv] *adj.* 活着的；有活力的

all [ɔːl] *adj.* 全部的 *adv.* 全部地 *n.* / *pron.* 全部

alloy [ˈælɔɪ, əˈlɔɪ] *n.* 合金 *v.* 把……铸成合金

almost [ˈɔːlməʊst] *adv.* 几乎；差不多

along [əˈlɒŋ] *prep.* 沿着 *adv.* 一起；向前

alongside [əˌlɒŋˈsaɪd] *adv.* / *prep.* 在……旁边

aloud [əˈlaʊd] *adv.* 出声地；大声地

alphabet [ˈælfəbet] *n.* 字母表

already [ɔːlˈredɪ] *adv.* 已经

also [ˈɔːlsəʊ] *adv.* 也；同样；而且 *conj.* 另外

although [ɔːlˈðəʊ] *conj.* 虽然；尽管；然而；但是

altitude [ˈæltɪtjuːd] *n.* 海拔；海拔高度

altogether [ˌɔːltəˈgeðə] *adv.* 总共；完全地

aluminium [ˌæljʊˈmɪnɪəm] *n.* (aluminum) 铝

always [ˈɔːlweɪz] *adv.* 总是；一直

amaze [əˈmeɪz] *v.* 使吃惊

ambassador [æmˈbæsədə] *n.* 大使；使节

ambulance [ˈæmbjələns] *n.* 救护车
amid [əˈmɪd] *prep.* 在其间；在其中
among [əˈmʌŋ] *prep.* 在……之中
amuse [əˈmju:z] *v.* 娱乐；消遣；逗乐
analogue / analog [ˈænəlɒg] *n.* 相似物；类似物 *adj.* 模拟的
analytic(al) [ˌænəˈlɪtɪk] *adj.* 分解的；解析的
analytics [ˌænəˈlɪtɪks] *n.* 分析学；解析学
analyst [ˈænəlɪst] *n.* 化验员；分析者
and [ənd , ænd] *conj.* 和；而且；然后
angel [ˈeɪndʒl] *n.* 天使；善人
anger [ˈæŋgə] *n.* 愤怒 *v.* 激怒；使发怒
animal [ˈænɪml] *n.* 动物 *adj.* 动物的
ankle [ˈæŋkl] *n.* 踝；踝关节
annoy [əˈnɔɪ] *v.* 使恼怒；使烦恼
another [əˈnʌðə] *adj.* 另一的 *pron.* 另一个
answer [ˈɑ:nsə] *v.* 回答；答复 *n.* 答案；回答
ant [ænt] *n.* 蚂蚁
antenna [ænˈtenə] *n.* 触须；天线
anxiety [æŋˈzaɪətɪ] *n.* 焦虑；渴望；担心
any [ˈenɪ] *adj.* / *pron.* 任何的 *adv.* 一点
anybody [ˈenɪbɒdɪ] *pron.* 任何人
anyhow [ˈenɪhaʊ] *adv.* 无论如何；总之
anyone [ˈenɪwʌn] *pron.* 任何人
anything [ˈenɪθɪŋ] *pron.* 任何东西；任何事
anyway [ˈenɪweɪ] *adv.* 无论如何；总之
anywhere [ˈenɪweə] *adv.* 任何地方；无论何处 *n.* 任何的地方
apartment [əˈpɑ:tmənt] *n.* 房间；公寓
apologize(-ise) [əˈpɒlədʒaɪz] *v.* 道歉
apology [əˈpɒlədʒɪ] *n.* 道歉
appal [əˈpɔ:l] *v.* 使惊骇；惊吓
apparatus [ˌæpəˈreɪtəs] *n.* 器官；仪器；装置；机构
appendix [əˈpendɪks] *n.* 阑尾；附录；附加物
apple [ˈæpl] *n.* 苹果
appliance [əˈplaɪəns] *n.* 装置；器械；家用电器
appraisal [əˈpreɪzl] *n.* 评价；估价；鉴定
April [ˈeɪprəl] *n.* 四月
arch [ɑ:tʃ] *n.* 拱门；拱形
area [ˈeərɪə] *n.* 地区；面积；区域；领域
arithmetic [əˈrɪθmətɪk] *n.* 算术
arm [ɑ:m] *n.* 手臂；武器；装备
army [ˈɑ:mɪ] *n.* 陆军；军队
around [əˈraʊnd] *prep.*/ *adv.* 围绕；大约；在周围
arrange [əˈreɪndʒ] *v.* 安排；整理；布置；排列
arrangement [əˈreɪndʒmənt] *n.* 安排；整理；布置；排列
arrest [əˈrest] *v.* / *n.* 逮捕；拘留
arrive [əˈraɪv] *v.* 到达；抵达
arrival [əˈraɪvl] *n.* 到达；到达者
arrow [ˈærəʊ] *n.* 箭头；箭；箭状物
art [ɑ:t] *n.* 美术；艺术 *adj.* 艺术的
artist [ˈɑ:tɪst] *n.* 艺术家；画家
artistic [ɑ:ˈtɪstɪk] *adj.* 艺术的；有艺术才能的
artery [ˈɑ:tərɪ] *n.* 动脉；干线；干流
as [æz] *adv.* 一样；例如 *conj.* 像……一样 *prep.* 作为
ash [æʃ] *n.* 灰；灰烬
ashamed [əˈʃeɪmd] *adj.* 惭愧的；难为情的
ashore [əˈʃɔ:] *adv.* 在岸上 *adj.* 在陆上的
aside [əˈsaɪd] *adv.* 在旁边；除……以外
ask [ɑ:sk] *v.* 邀请；询问；要求
asleep [əˈsli:p] *adj.* 睡着的 *adv.* 熟睡地
astronaut [ˈæstrənɔ:t] *n.* 宇航员；航天员
assassinate [əˈsæsɪneɪt] *v.* 暗杀；行刺
asset [ˈæset] *n.* 资产；财产
at [æt , ət] *prep.* 朝；向；在
athlete [ˈæθli:t] *n.* 运动员
atom [ˈætəm] *n.* 原子；微粒；极小量
attempt [əˈtempt] *v.* / *n.* 努力；尝试；试图
attention [əˈtenʃn] *n.* 注意；照料；兴趣；关心
attitude [ˈætɪtju:d] *n.* 态度；姿势；看法
about [əˈbaʊt] *prep.* 关于；大约 *adv.* 大约；到处
attorney [əˈtɜ:nɪ] *n.* 代理人；律师
attract [əˈtrækt] *v.* 吸引；引起……的兴趣
attractive [əˈtræktɪv] *adj.* 迷人的；有吸引力的
auction [ˈɔ:kʃn] *n.* / *v.* 拍卖；竞卖
audience [ˈɔ:dɪəns] *n.* 观众；听众
audio [ˈɔ:dɪəʊ] *adj.* 声音的；录音的 *n.* 音频
audit [ˈɔ:dɪt] *v.* 旁听；审计 *n.* 审计；查账
auditorium [ˌɔ:dɪˈtɔ:rɪəm] *n.* 礼堂；观众席
August [ɔ:ˈgəst] *n.* 八月

aunt [ɑ:nt] *n.* 伯母；舅妈；姨母；阿姨
author [ˈɔ:θə] *n.* 作者 *v.* 创作
auto [ˈɔ:təʊ] *adj.* 汽车的 *n.* 汽车；自动
automobile [ˈɔ:təməbi:l] *n.* 汽车
autumn [ˈɔ:təm] *n.* 秋天
auxiliary [ɔ:gˈzɪlɪərɪ] *adj.* 辅助的；备用的 *n.* 助手
avenue [ˈævənju:] *n.* 大街；林荫道；途径
average [ˈævərɪdʒ] *adj.* 平均的；一般的 *n.* 平均数；平均水平
aviation [ˌeɪvɪˈeɪʃn] *n.* 航空；飞机制造业
await [əˈweɪt] *v.* 期待；等待
awake [əˈweɪk] *adj.* 醒着的 *v.* 唤起；唤醒
away [əˈweɪ] *adv.* 离开；不在；离开
awe [ɔ:] *n.* / *v.*（使）敬畏；惊叹
awful [ˈɔ:fl] *adj.* 糟糕的；可怕的 *adv.* 非常；极其
awkward [ˈɔ:kwəd] *adj.* 笨拙的；尴尬的
axe [æks] *n.* 斧；*v.* 撤销；解雇
axis [ˈæksɪs] *n.* 轴；轴线；联盟

B

baby [ˈbeɪbɪ] *n.* 婴儿；幼稚的人
back [bæk] *n.* 后面；背面；背部 *adj.* 后面的 *adv.* 向后地
background [ˈbækgraʊnd] *n.* 背景；学历
backward [ˈbækwəd] *adj.* 向后的 *adv.* 向后地
bacon [ˈbeɪkən] *n.* 熏猪肉；培根
bacterium [bækˈtɪərɪəm] *n.*(pl. bacteria) 细菌
bad [bæd] *adj.* 坏的；严重的；有害的；质量差的
badly [ˈbædlɪ] *adv.* 非常；严重地
badge [bædʒ] *n.* 徽章；标记；象征
badminton [ˈbædmɪntən] *n.* 羽毛球
bag [bæg] *n.* 包；袋子
baggage [ˈbægɪdʒ] *n.* 行李
bait [beɪt] *v.* 放诱饵；*n.* 诱饵；饵
bake [beɪk] *v.* 烤；烘；焙
balcony [ˈbælkənɪ] *n.* 阳台；露台
bald [bɔ:ld] *adj.* 光秃的；秃顶的
ball [bɔ:l] *n.* 球；球状物
ballet [ˈbæleɪ] *n.* 芭蕾舞；芭蕾舞剧
balloon [bəˈlu:n] *n.* 气球；热气球
ballot [ˈbælət] *n.* 投票选举；选票
banana [bəˈnɑ:nə] *n.* 香蕉
band [bænd] *n.* 乐队；一群；*v.* 给……分级
bandage [ˈbændɪdʒ] *n.* 绷带 *v.* 用绷带包扎
bang [bæŋ] *v.* 重击；猛摔 *n.* 刘海；巨响；重击
bank [bæŋk] *n.* 银行；岸；库
banner [ˈbænə] *n.* 横幅；旗帜；标语
banquet [ˈbæŋkwɪt] *n.* 宴会；盛宴
barbecue [ˈbɑ:bɪkju:] *n.* 户外烧烤 *v.* 烧烤
barber [ˈbɑ:bə] *n.* 理发师 *v.* 给（男士）理发
bare [beə] *adj.* 赤裸的；空的 *v.* 使暴露
bark [bɑ:k] *v.*（狗）吠；叫 *n.* 树皮；犬吠声
barn [bɑ:n] *n.* 谷仓；畜棚；牲口棚
barren [ˈbærən] *adj.* 贫瘠的；不毛的
base [beɪs] *n.* 基础；基地；根基 *v.* 以……作基础
baseball [ˈbeɪsbɔ:l] *n.* 棒球
basement [ˈbeɪsmənt] *n.* 地下室；地库
basin [ˈbeɪsn] *n.* 盆地；流域；盆
basket [ˈbɑ:skɪt] *n.* 篮子；一篮的量
basketball [ˈbɑ:skɪtbɔ:l] *n.* 篮球；篮球运动
bat [bæt] *n.* 球棒；球拍；蝙蝠 *v.* 用球棒击球
batch [bætʃ] *n.* 一批；一炉 *v.* 分批处理
bath [bɑ:θ] *n.* 沐浴；浴缸；浴室 *v.* 给……洗澡
bathe [beɪð] *v.* 洗澡；游泳
bathroom [ˈbɑ:θru:m] *n.* 浴室；卫生间
battery [ˈbætrɪ] *n.* 电池
bay [beɪ] *n.* 海湾
be [bɪ] *v.* 是；存在；成为
beach [bi:tʃ] *n.* 海滩；海滨
bean [bi:n] *n.* 豆；豆科植物
bear [beə] *n.* 熊 *v.* 忍受；支撑；（树；植物）结（果实）；生育（孩子）
beard [bɪəd] *n.* 胡须 *v.* 公然反对
beast [bi:st] *n.* 野兽
beat [bi:t] *v.* 打；打败；敲打
beautiful [ˈbju:tɪfl] *adj.* 美丽的；美好的
beauty [ˈbju:tɪ] *n.* 美人；美丽；美好
because [bɪˈkɒz] *conj.* 因为
become [bɪˈkʌm] *v.* 变成；成为
bed [bed] *n.* 床；苗圃；花坛；河床
bee [bi:] *n.* 蜜蜂；勤劳的人；聚会
beef [bi:f] *n.* 牛肉；力气

beer [bɪə] *n.* 啤酒；一杯（瓶、罐）啤酒

before [bɪˈfɔː] *prep./ conj.* 在……之前 *adv.* 以前；从前

beg [beg] *v.* 乞讨；恳求

begin [bɪˈgɪn] *v.* 开始

beginning [bɪˈgɪnɪŋ] *n.* 开始；根源；开端

behind [bɪˈhaɪnd] *prep.* 在……后面；落后于

being [ˈbiːɪŋ] *n.* 存在；生物；生命

belief [bɪˈliːf] *n.* 信仰；相信；信念

believe [bɪˈliːv] *v.* 相信；认为；猜想

bell [bel] *n.* 铃；钟；钟声；*v.* 敲钟；鸣钟

belly [ˈbelɪ] *n.* 腹部；肚子

beloved *adj.* [bɪˈlʌvd] 心爱的 *n.* 心爱的人

below [bɪˈləʊ] *prep.* 低于 *adv.* 在下面

belt [belt] *n.* 腰带；地带；传送带

bench [bentʃ] *n.* 长凳；长椅

bend [bend] *n.* 拐弯；弯道；弯曲

beneath [bɪˈniːθ] *prep.* 在……之下 *adv.* 在下方；在底下

benefit [ˈbenɪfɪt] *n.* 利益；好处 *v.* 有益于；得益

beside [bɪˈsaɪd] *prep.* 在……旁边 *adv.* 在附近；此外

besides [bɪˈsaɪdz] *prep.* 除……之外（还） *adv.* 而且；此外

best [best] *adj.* 最好的 *adv.* 最好地 *n.* 最好的人或物

bet [bet] *v.* 打赌 *n.* 下注

better [ˈbetə] *adj.* 更好的 *adv.* 更好的；更多的

between [bɪˈtwiːn] *prep.* 在……中间 *adv.* 在中间

beverage [ˈbevərɪdʒ] *n.* 饮料

beware [bɪˈweə] *v.* 提防；当心

beyond [bɪˈjɒnd] *prep.* 超过；迟于；那一边 *adv.* 在另一边

bible [ˈbaɪbl] *n.* 圣经

bibliography [ˌbɪblɪˈɒgrəfɪ] *n.* 参考书目；书目；索引；文献

bicycle [ˈbaɪsɪkl] *n.* 自行车 *v.* 骑自行车

big [bɪg] *adj.* 大的；重大的；严重的

bill [bɪl] *n.* 账单；议案；法案；钞票；传单；票据

bin [bɪn] *n.* 垃圾箱；储物箱

bind [baɪnd] *v.* 捆绑；系；包扎；装订 *n.* 窘境；约束

biography [baɪˈɒgrəfɪ] *n.* 传记；传记文学；生平

biology [baɪˈɒlədʒɪ] *n.* 生物学；生物

bird [bɜːd] *n.* 鸟

birth [bɜːθ] *n.* 出生；血统；开始；起源

birthday [ˈbɜːθdeɪ] *n.* 生日；诞辰；出生日期

biscuit [ˈbɪskɪt] *n.* 饼干

bite [baɪt] *v.* / *n.* 咬；叮；蛰

bitter [ˈbɪtə] *adj.* 痛苦的；苦的；愤愤不平的

black [blæk] *adj.* 黑色的；黑暗的 *n.* 黑色；黑人

blackboard [ˈblækbɔːd] *n.* 黑板

blackmail [ˈblækmeɪl] *n.* / *v.* 勒索；敲诈

blade [bleɪd] *n.* 刀刃；桨叶；叶片；冰刀

blank [blæŋk] *adj.* 空白的；空的 *n.* 空白处；空格

blanket [ˈblæŋkɪt] *n.* 毯子 *v.* 覆盖 *adj.* 全面的

blast [blɑːst] *v.* 爆破 *n.* 爆炸；强劲的（气或水）流

blaze [bleɪz] *n.* 火焰；烈火 *v.* 燃烧；闪耀

bleed [bliːd] *v.* 出血；流血

bless [bles] *v.* 保佑；祝福；赞美

blind [blaɪnd] *adj.* 盲目的；失明的 *n.* 盲人

blood [blʌd] *n.* 血；血统；出生

bloody [ˈblʌdɪ] *adj.* 血腥的 *adv.* 很；非常

blouse [blaʊz] *n.* 女式衬衫

blow [bləʊ] *v.* 吹；吹气 *n.* 打击；吹

blue [bluː] *adj.* 蓝色的；忧郁的

blueprint [ˈbluːprɪnt] *n.* 蓝图；设计图；计划

blush [blʌʃ] *v.* 脸红；惭愧 *n.* 脸红

board [bɔːd] *n.* 木板；甲板；董事会 *v.* 上（船、飞机、火车等）；寄宿

boast [bəʊst] *v.* / *n.* 自夸；夸耀

boat [bəʊt] *n.* 舟；小船

body [ˈbɒdɪ] *n.* 身体；正文；团体；一群；大量

boil [bɔɪl] *v.* / *n.* 煮沸；沸腾

bold [bəʊld] *adj.* 大胆的；醒目的 *n.* 粗体（字）

bolt [bəʊlt] *n.* 闩；插销；螺栓 *v.* 闩上（门或窗）

bone [bəʊn] *n.* 骨；骨骼

book [bʊk] *n.* 书；卷；账簿 *v.* 预订；登记

boot [buːt] *n.* 靴子

booth [buːð] *n.* 售货棚

border [ˈbɔːdə] *n.* 边界 *v.* 交界

bore [bɔː] *v.* 烦扰；钻（孔） *n.* 讨厌的人；麻烦事

born [bɔːn] *adj.* 天生的；出生的 *v.* 生（孩子）

borrow [ˈbɒrəʊ] *v.* 借；采用
bosom [ˈbʊzəm] *n.* 胸部；胸怀；*adj.* 亲密的
boss [bɒs] *n.* 老板；上司 *v.* 发号施令
both [bəʊθ] *adv.* 和 ；都
bother [ˈbɒðə] *v.* 打扰 ；担心 *n.* 麻烦
bottle [ˈbɒtl] *n.* 瓶子 *v.* 装瓶
bottom [ˈbɒtəm] *n.* 底（部） *adj.* 底部的；最后的
bounce [baʊns] *v.* 弹起 *n.* 活力；弹跳
boundary [ˈbaʊndrɪ] *n.* 分界线；边界
bow [baʊ] *v.* / *n.* 鞠躬；点头 *n.* 蝴蝶结
bowel [ˈbaʊəl] *n.* 肠；内部；深处
bowl [bəʊl] *n.* 碗（状物）；钵
bowling [ˈbəʊlɪŋ] *n.* 保龄球运动
box [bɒks] *n.* 盒；包厢 *v.* 把……装箱；拳击
boy [bɔɪ] *n.* 男孩
brace [breɪs] *v.* 准备；支撑；加固 *n.* 夹子；支架；牙箍
bracket [ˈbrækɪt] *n.*（方）括号
brain [breɪn] *n.*（大）脑 (pl.) 脑力；智能
brake [breɪk] *v.* / *n.* 闸；刹车；阻碍
branch [brɑːntʃ] *n.* 树枝；分支机构；部门
brandy [ˈbrændɪ] *n.* 白兰地酒
brass [brɑːs] *n.* 黄铜；铜器
brave [breɪv] *adj.* 勇敢的 *v.* 勇敢面对
bread [bred] *n.* 面包
breadth [bredθ] *n.* 宽度；广度；广泛性
break [breɪk] *v.* 打破；打碎；断绝 *n.* 间断；休息
breakdown [ˈbreɪkdaʊn] *n.* 故障；精神崩溃；破裂
breakfast [ˈbrekfəst] *n.* 早餐 *v.* 吃早餐
breast [brest] *n.* 胸膛；乳房
breath [breθ] *n.* 呼吸；气息
breathe [briːð] *v.* 呼吸；吸入
breeze [briːz] *n.* 微风；和风 *v.* 吹微风
bribe [braɪb] *n.* 贿赂 *v.* 行贿
brick [brɪk] *n.* 砖块 *v.* 用砖围砌
bride [braɪd] *n.* 新娘；即将（或刚）结婚的女子
bridge [brɪdʒ] *n.* 桥；桥牌 *v.* 架桥；消除（隔阂）
briefcase [ˈbriːfkeɪs] *n.* 手提箱；公事皮包
bright [braɪt] *adj.* 明亮的；鲜艳的；聪明的
brilliant [ˈbrɪlɪənt] *adj.* 杰出的；明亮的；使人印象深的
brim [brɪm] *n.* 边缘
bring [brɪŋ] *v.* 拿来；带来；导致
brisk [brɪsk] *adj.* 快的；敏捷的；麻利的
brittle [ˈbrɪt(ə)l] *adj.* 易碎的；易变的；尖利的；刺耳的
broad [brɔːd] *adj.* 宽的；咧开嘴的；普遍的
broadcast [ˈbrɔːdkɑːst] *v.* / *n.* 广播（节目）
brochure [ˈbrəʊʃə] *n.* 手册 / 宣传小册子
bronze [brɒnz] *n.* 青铜 *adj.* 青铜制的；青铜色的
brook [brʊk] *n.* 小溪；小河
broom [bruːm] *n.* 扫帚
brother [ˈbrʌðə] *n.* 兄弟；同事；战友
brow [braʊ] *n.* 眉（毛）额
brown [braʊn] *n.* / *adj.* 褐色（的）；棕色（的）
bruise [bruːz] *n.* 青肿 *v.* 挫伤
brush [brʌʃ] *n.* 刷（子）；画笔；灌木丛 *v.* 刷；拂去
brutal [ˈbruːt(ə)l] *adj.* 残忍的；残酷的
bubble [ˈbʌb(ə)l] *n.* 泡；气泡 *v.* 冒泡
bucket [ˈbʌkɪt] *n.* 桶
bud [bʌd] *n.* 芽；花蕾 *v.* 发芽
buffet [ˈbʌfeɪ] *n.* 自助餐
bug [bʌg] *n.* 臭虫；漏洞；窃听器 *v.* 窃听；烦扰
build [bɪld] *v.* 建造；建设；建立
building [ˈbɪldɪŋ] *n.* 建筑（物）；房屋；大楼
bulb [bʌlb] *n.* 灯泡；球状物
bulk [bʌlk] *n.* 大批；容积；主体
bull [bʊl] *n.* 公牛
bullet [ˈbʊlɪt] *n.* 子弹；枪弹
bulletin [ˈbʊlətɪn] *n.* 公报；公告；告示
bump [bʌmp] *v.* 碰上；撞上 *n.* 碰撞；肿块；隆起
bunch [bʌntʃ] *n.*（一）簇；束；捆；串
bundle [ˈbʌnd(ə)l] *n.* 捆；包；束 *v.* 捆扎；把……打包
burden [ˈbɜːdn] *n.* 担子；负担
bureau [ˈbjʊərəʊ] *n.* 署；局；司；处
bureaucracy [bjʊəˈrɒkrəsɪ] *n.* 官僚主义；官僚机构；官僚
burglar [ˈbɜːglə] *n.*（入室行窃的）盗贼
burn [bɜːn] *v.* 燃烧；晒伤 *n.* 烧伤；灼伤
burst [bɜːst] *v.* 爆裂；突然发生 *n.* 爆裂
bury [ˈberɪ] *v.* 埋（葬）；埋藏

bus [bʌs] *n.* 公共汽车
bush [bʊʃ] *n.* 灌木(丛)
business [ˈbɪznəs] *n.* 商业;生意;公司;业务
busy [ˈbɪzɪ] *adj.* 忙碌的;热闹的;(电话)占线
but [bʌt] *conj.* 但是 *prep.* 除 ... 以外
butcher [ˈbʊtʃə] *n.* 屠夫;卖肉者
butter [ˈbʌtə] *n.* 黄油 *v.* 涂黄油于……上
butterfly [ˈbʌtəflaɪ] *n.* 蝴蝶
button [ˈbʌt(ə)n] *n.* 纽扣;按钮 *v.* 扣紧
buy [baɪ] *v.* / *n.* 购买;买卖
by [baɪ] *prep.* 被;凭借;通过……方式;在旁边 *adv.* 经过
bypass [ˈbaɪpɑːs] *n.* 旁道;(给心脏接旁通管的)分流术 *v.* 绕过

C

cab [kæb] *n.* 出租车
cabbage [ˈkæbɪdʒ] *n.* 洋白菜;卷心菜
cabin [ˈkæbɪn] *n.* 客舱;机舱;小(木)屋
cabinet [ˈkæbɪnət] *n.* 内阁;储藏柜;陈列柜
cable [ˈkeɪb(ə)l] *n.* 缆绳;索道;电缆 *v.* 给……发电报
cafe [ˈkæfeɪ] *n.* 咖啡馆
cafeteria [ˌkæfəˈtɪərɪə] *n.* 自助餐厅;食堂
cage [keɪdʒ] *n.* 鸟笼
cake [keɪk] *n.* 饼;糕;蛋糕
calcium [ˈkælsɪəm] *n.*(化学元素)钙
calendar [ˈkælɪndə] *n.* 日历;日程表
call [kɔːl] *v.* / *n.* 叫;喊;通话;访问
calm [kɑːm] *adj.* 沉着的;平静的 *n.* 平静 *v.*(使)平静
calorie [ˈkælərɪ] *n.* 卡路里
camel [ˈkæm(ə)l] *n.* 骆驼
camera [ˈkæm(ə)rə] *n.* 照相机;摄影机
camp [kæmp] *n.* 营地;阵营 *v.* 宿营
campus [ˈkæmpəs] *n.*(大学)校园
can [kæn] model *v.* 能;可以;会 *n.* 罐头;容器
canal [kəˈnæl] *n.* 运河;(沟)渠
cancel [ˈkæns(ə)l] *v.* 取消;终止
cancer [ˈkænsə] *n.* 癌
candle [ˈkænd(ə)l] *n.* 蜡烛
candy [ˈkændɪ] *n.* 糖果
cannon [ˈkænən] *n.* 大炮
canoe [kəˈnuː] *n.* 独木舟;小游艇 *vi.* 划独木舟
canteen [kænˈtiːn] *n.* 食堂;餐厅
canvas [ˈkænvəs] *n.* 帆布; 帆布画布;(帆布)油画
cap [kæp] *n.* 帽子 *v.* 覆盖
cape [keɪp] *n.* 海角;岬;斗篷
capital [ˈkæpɪt(ə)l] *n.* 首都;大写字母;资本 *adj.* 主要的;大写字母的;死刑的
capitalism [ˈkæpɪtəlɪzəm] *n.* 资本主义
capsule [ˈkæpsjuːl] *n.* 胶囊;太空舱
captain [ˈkæptɪn] *n.* 首领;队长;船长;上尉 *v.* 指挥;担任……的队长
car [kɑː] *n.* 汽车
carbon [ˈkɑːbən] *n.* 碳;复写纸
card [kɑːd] *n.* 卡片;名片;纸牌
cardinal [ˈkɑːdɪnl] *adj.* 首要的;基本的
care [keə] *n.* 小心;照料 *v.* 照顾;在意;担忧
career [kəˈrɪə] *n.* 事业;职业
careful [ˈkeəf(ə)l] *adj.* 小心的;仔细的
caress [kəˈres] *v.* / *n.* 爱抚;抚摸
cargo [ˈkɑːgəʊ] *n.* 船货;货物
carpenter [ˈkɑːpəntə] *n.* 木工;木匠
carpet [ˈkɑpɪt] *n.* 地毯
carriage [ˈkærɪdʒ] *n.*(四轮)马车;(火车)车厢
carrier [ˈkærɪə] *n.* 搬运人;运输工具;航空公司;带菌者;载体
carrot [ˈkærət] *n.* 胡萝卜
carry [ˈkærɪ] *v.* 运送;搬运;传播
cart [kɑːt] *n.* 马车;购物车
cartoon [kɑːˈtuːn] *n.* 漫画;动画片
cash [kæʃ] *n.* 现金 *v.* 兑现;付现款
cashier [kæˈʃɪə] *n.* 收银员;出纳员
cassette [kəˈset] *n.* 盒子;盒式磁带
cat [kæt] *n.* 猫;猫科
catch [kætʃ] *v.* 捕获;赶上;感染;理解
cattle [ˈkæt(ə)l] *n.* 牛;牲口;家畜
caution [ˈkɔːʃn] *n.* 谨慎;警告 *v.* 警告提醒
cave [keɪv] *n.* 洞;穴
ceiling [ˈsiːlɪŋ] *n.* 天花板

cell [sel] *n.* 细胞；小房间；电池
cellar [ˈselə] *n.* 地窖；地下室
cemetery [ˈsemətrɪ] *n.* 坟墓；墓地
census [ˈsensəs] *n.* 人口普查（调查）
cent [sent] *n.* 分币（美元、欧元等的货币单位）
centigrade [ˈsentɪgreɪd] *n.* / *adj.* 摄氏温度计（的）
centimetre [ˈsentɪmiːtə] *n.* (centimeter) 厘米
central [ˈsentrəl] *adj.* 中心的；中央的；主要的
centre [ˈsentə] *n.* 中心；中央 *v.* 集中；以……为中心
century [ˈsentʃərɪ] *n.* 世纪；一百年
cereal [ˈsɪərɪəl] *n.* 谷类食物；谷类植物；谷物
ceremony [ˈserəmənɪ] *n.* 典礼；仪式；礼节
certain [ˈsɜːt(ə)n] *adj.* 一定的；确信的；某些
certainly [ˈsɜːt(ə)nlɪ] *adv.* 无疑；确定；当然；行（用于回答）
certainty [ˈsɜːt(ə)ntɪ] *n.* 必然；肯定；必然的事
certificate [səˈtɪfɪkət] *n.* 证（明）书；执照
certify [ˈsɜːtɪfaɪ] *v.* 证明；证实；给……颁发合格证书
chain [tʃeɪn] *n.* 链（条）；连锁商店；一连串；镣铐 *v.* 用链条拴住
chair [tʃeə] *n.* 椅子；（会议的）主席 *v.* 当……的主席；主持
chairman [ˈtʃeəmən] *n.* 主席；议长；会长；董事长
chalk [tʃɔːk] *n.* 粉笔；白垩
challenge [ˈtʃælɪndʒ] *n.* 挑战；难题 *v.* 向……挑战；质疑
chamber [ˈtʃeɪmbə] *n.* 房间；室；会议室；议院
champagne [ʃæmˈpeɪn] *n.* 香槟酒
champion [ˈtʃæmpɪən] *n.* 冠军；拥护者
chance [tʃɑːn] *n.* 机会；可能性；运气 *v.* 碰巧；偶然发生
chancellor [ˈtʃɑːnsələ] *n.*（德、奥）总理；（英）财政大臣；（美）大学校长
change [tʃeɪndʒ] *n.* 改变；变化；零钱 *v.* 改变；交换
channel [ˈtʃæn(ə)l] *n.* 海峡；航道；频道；渠道；途径
chaos [ˈkeɪɒs] *n.* 混乱；紊乱
chap [tʃæp] *n.* / *v.*（使）皮肤皲裂 *n.*（皮肤的）皲裂处；小伙子
chapter [ˈtʃæptə] *n.* 章；回；篇
charm [tʃɑːm] *n.* 吸引力；魅力 *v.* 迷人；（使）陶醉
chart [tʃɑːt] *n.* 图表；排行榜 *v.* 绘图表；制图表
chase [tʃeɪs] *v.* / *n.* 追逐；追求
chat [tʃæt] *v.* / *n.* 闲谈；聊天
cheap [tʃiːp] *adj.* 便宜的；低劣的
cheat [tʃiːt] *v.* 欺骗；作弊 *n.* 骗子；欺骗行为
cheek [tʃiːt] *n.* 面颊；脸
cheer [tʃɪə] *v.*（使）振奋；（使）高兴 *v.* / *n.* 喝彩；欢呼
cheese [tʃiːz] *n.* 干酪；乳酪
chef [ʃef] *n.*（餐馆等的）厨师长；厨师
chemical [ˈkemɪkl] *adj.* 化学的 *n.* (pl.) 化学制品
chemist [ˈkemɪst] *n.* 化学家；药剂师
chemistry [ˈkemɪstrɪ] *n.* 化学
cheque [tʃek] *n.*(check) 支票
cherish [ˈtʃerɪʃ] *v.* 珍爱；抱有（希望等）
cherry [ˈtʃerɪ] *n.* 樱桃（树）
chess [tʃes] *n.* 棋；国际象棋
chest [tʃest] *n.* 胸腔；箱；柜
chew [tʃuː] *v.* 咀嚼；思量
chicken [ˈtʃɪkɪn] *n.* 鸡；鸡肉
chief [tʃiːf] *adj.* 主要的；首要的 *n.* 首领
child [ˈtʃaɪld] *n.*(pl. children) 小孩；子女
childhood [ˈtʃaɪldhʊd] *n.* 童年；幼年时代
chill [tʃɪl] *n.* 寒冷；寒意 *v.* 使寒冷；放松
chimney [ˈtʃɪmnɪ] *n.* 烟囱
chin [tʃɪn] *n.* 下巴；颏
china [ˈtʃaɪnə] *n.* 瓷器
chip [tʃɪp] *n.* 炸薯片；芯片
chocolate [ˈtʃɒklət] *n.* 巧克力（糖）；深褐色
choice [tʃɔɪs] *n.* 选择；精选品 *adj.* 上等的；优质的
choke [tʃəʊk] *v.* 窒息；堵塞
choose [tʃuːz] *v.* 选择；挑选
chop [tʃɒp] *v.* / *n.* 砍；劈；斩 *v.* 大幅削减；取消
chorus [ˈkɔːrəs] *n.* 合唱 *v.* 齐声说
Christ [kraɪs] *n.* 基督；救世主
Christian [ˈkrɪstʃən] *n.* 基督教徒 *adj.* 基督教徒的
Christmas [ˈkrɪsməs] *n.* 圣诞节

church [tʃɜːtʃ] *n.* 教堂；教会；教派；礼拜仪式
cigar [sɪˈɡɑ] *n.* 雪茄烟
cigarette [ˌsɪɡəˈret] *n.* 香烟；纸烟；卷烟
cinema [ˈsɪnəmə] *n.* 电影院；电影
circle [ˈsɜːkl] *n.* 圆；周期；循环 *v.* 环绕；旋转
circuit [ˈsɜːkɪt] *n.* 环行；巡回；电路；线路
circular [ˈsɜːkjələ] *adj.* 圆（形）的；环形的；循环的
circumference [səˈkʌmfərəns] *n.* 周长；周围
circus [ˈsɜːkəs] *n.* 马戏团；杂技团
cite [saɪt] *v.* 引用；引证；举（例）
citizen [ˈsɪtɪz(ə)n] *n.* 公民；市民；居民
city [ˈsɪtɪ] *n.* 城市；都市
clap [klæp] *v.* / *n.* 拍手；鼓掌
clasp [klɑːsp] *n.* / *v.* 扣子；扣环；紧握
class [klɑːs] *n.* 班级；等级；类别；（一节）课
classmate [ˈklɑːsmeɪt] *n.* 同班同学
classroom [ˈklɑːsruːm] *n.* 教室
clause [klɔːz] *n.*（法律文件的）条款；从句；分句
claw [klɔː] *n.* 爪；脚爪
clay [kleɪ] *n.* 黏土；泥土
clean [kliːn] *adj.* 清洁的；干净的 *v.*（使）清洁；变干净
clear [klɪə] *adj.* / *adv.* 清晰的（地）*adj.* 明白的 *v.* 清扫；清除；证明……无罪
clergy [ˈklɜːdʒɪ] *n.* 牧师；神职人员
clerk [klɑːk] *n.* 职员；办事员；店员
clever [ˈklevə] *adj.* 聪明的；伶俐的；机敏的
click [klɪk] *n.* 滴答声 *v.* 发出滴答声
client [ˈklaɪənt] *n.* 委托人；顾客
cliff [klɪf] *n.* 悬崖；峭壁
climate [ˈklaɪmət] *n.* 气候；风气；社会思潮
climax [ˈklaɪmæks] *n.* 顶点；高潮
climb [klaɪm] *v.* / *n.* 攀登；爬
cling [klɪŋ] *v.* 粘住；依附；坚持
clinic [ˈklɪnɪk] *n.* 诊所
clip [klɪp] *n.* 夹子；别针；（电影、电视节目等的）片段 *v.* 修剪；夹住
cloak [kləʊk] *n.* 斗篷；掩饰 *v.* 掩盖；掩饰
clock [klɒk] *n.* 钟
clockwise [ˈklɒkwaɪz] *adj.* 顺时针方向
clone [kləʊn] *n.* 克隆；复制品 *v.* 克隆
close [kləʊz] *v.* / *n.* 关；结束 *adj.* / *adv.* 近的（地）；紧密的（地）
closet [ˈklɒzɪt] *n.* 壁橱 *adj.* 秘密的
cloth [klɒθ] *n.*（一块）布；织物；衣料
clothe [kləʊð] *v.* 给……穿衣
clothes [kləʊðz] *n.* 衣服
clothing [ˈkləʊðɪŋ] *n.* 衣服；服装
cloud [klaʊd] *n.* 云；令人忧虑的事
cloudy [ˈklaʊdɪ] *adj.* 多云的；阴（天）的
club [klʌb] *n.* 俱乐部；社团
clue [kluː] *n.* 线索；暗示
clumsy [ˈklʌmzɪ] *adj.* 笨拙的；愚笨的
cluster [ˈklʌstə] *n.* 丛；群；串 *v.* 群集；丛生
clutch [klʌtʃ] *v.* / *n.* 紧握；紧抓
coach [kəʊtʃ] *n.* 长途客车；教练 *v.* 训练；指导
coal [kəʊl] *n.* 煤；煤块
coarse [kɔːs] *adj.* 粗糙的；粗鲁的；粗俗的
coast [kəʊst] *n.* 海岸；海滨
coat [kəʊt] *n.* 外套；大衣；（动物）皮毛；（植物）表皮
cocaine [kəʊˈkeɪn] *n.* 可卡因
cock [kɒk] *n.* 公鸡；龙头；阀门
code [kəʊd] *n.* 代码；编码；道德准则
coffee [ˈkɒfɪ] *n.* 咖啡（色）
cohesive [kəʊˈhiːsɪv] *adj.* 团结的；有凝聚力的
coil [kɔɪl] *v.* 卷；盘绕 *n.* 卷；圈；线圈
coin [kɔɪn] *n.* 硬币 *v.* 铸造（硬币）；创造（新词）
coke [kəʊk] *n.* 可口可乐；焦炭
cold [kəʊld] *adj.* 寒冷的；冷淡的 *n.* 冷；感冒
collar [ˈkɒlə] *n.* 衣领；领口
college [ˈkɒlɪdʒ] *n.* 学院；高等专科学校；大学
colonel [ˈkɜːn(ə)l] *n.*（陆军）上校
color [ˈkʌlə] *n.* (colour) 颜色；颜料；肤色 *v.* 给……着色
column [ˈkɒləm] *n.* 圆柱；柱状物；列；（报刊中的）专栏
comb [kəʊm] *n.* 梳子 *v.* 梳（理）
come [kʌm] *v.* 来；来到；到达；出现
comedy [ˈkɒmədɪ] *n.* 喜剧；喜剧性事件
comfort [ˈkʌmfət] *n.* 舒适；安逸；安慰；慰问 *v.* 安

慰;使舒适

comfortable [ˈkʌmftəbl] *adj.* 舒服的;感到舒适的;安逸的

comic [ˈkɒmɪk] *adj.* 喜剧的;滑稽的 *n.* 连环漫画杂志;喜剧演员

common [ˈkɒmən] *adj.* 普通的;共同的;一般的

commonplace [ˈkɒmənpleɪs] *adj.* 普通的;平庸的 *n.* 司空见惯的事;常见的东西

commonwealth [ˈkɒmənwelθ] *n.* 共和国;联邦;共同体

communism [ˈkɒmjənɪzəm] *n.* 共产主义

companion [kəmˈpænjən] *n.* 同伴;伴侣

company [ˈkʌmpənɪ] *n.* 公司;陪伴

compartment [kəmˈpɑːtmənt] *n.* 隔层;分隔间;车厢;舱

compass [ˈkʌmpəs] *n.* 罗盘;指南针 (pl.) 圆规

complement [ˈkɒmplɪment] *v.* 补充; 补足 *n.* 补足物

composite [ˈkɒmpəzɪt] *adj.* 合成的 *n.* 合成物;复合材料

compound [ˈkɒmpaʊnd] *n.* 混合物; 化合物 *adj.* 混合的;化合的 *v.* 混合

compute [kəmˈpjuːt] *v.* / *n.* 计算;估计

computer [kəmˈpjuːtə] *n.* 计算机

comrade [ˈkɒmreɪd] *n.* 伙伴;战友;同志

concept [ˈkɒnsept] *n.* 概念;观念;设想

concert [ˈkɒnsət] *n.* 音乐会;一致;和谐

confidential [ˌkɒnfɪˈdenʃl] *adj.* 秘(机)密的;授信任的

confuse [kənˈfjuːz] *v.* 使混乱;混淆

confusion [kənˈfjuːʒn] *n.* 困惑;混淆;混乱

congratulate [kənˈgrætʃuleɪt] *v.* 向……道贺

congratulation [kənˌgrætʃuˈleɪʃn] *n.* 祝贺 (pl.) 祝贺词

congress [ˈkɒŋgres] *n.*(代表)大会;(美国等国的)国会;议会

conjunction [kənˈdʒʌŋkʃn] *n.* 结合; 同时发生;连词

consider [kənˈsɪdə] *v.* 认真考虑;体谅;顾及;认为;把……看作

considerate [kənˈsɪdərət] *adj.* 考虑周到的;体谅的

consideration [kənˌsɪdəˈreɪʃn] *n.* 考虑;体谅;照;关心

contain [kənˈteɪn] *v.* 包含;容纳;容忍;抑制

contemporary [kənˈtemprərɪ] *adj.* 现代的; 当代的;同时代的

contest *n.* [ˈkɒntest] / *v.* [kənˈtest] 竞争; 竞赛;比赛

context [ˈkɒntekst] *n.*(文章等)前后关系;(事件等发生的)背景

continent [ˈkɒntɪnənt] *n.* 大陆;洲

continual [kənˈtɪnjuəl] *adj.* 不断的;连续的;频繁的

continue [kənˈtɪnjuː] *v.* 继续;连续;延伸

continuous [kənˈtɪnjuəs] *adj.* 连续的;持续的

contract *n.* [ˈkɒntrækt](承包)合同 / 契约 *v.* [kənˈtrækt] 订合同 / 契约;使缩小

contrive [kənˈtraɪv] *v.* 谋划;设法做到;设计;想出

control [kənˈtrəʊl] *n.* / *v.* 控制;支配

conversation [ˌkɒnvəˈseɪʃn] *n.* 会话;谈话

cop [kɒp] *n.* 警察(俚语)

copper [ˈkɒpə] *n.* 铜;铜币;铜制器

copy [ˈkɒpɪ] *v.* 复印;抄写;抄袭 *n.* 抄本

copyright [ˈkɒpɪraɪt] *n.* / *adj.* 版权(的)

cord [kɔːd] *n.* 绳;索

cordial [ˈkɔːdɪəl] *adj.* 热情友好的;由衷的

core [kɔː] *n.* 果核;中心;核心

corn [kɔːn] *n.* 谷物;庄稼;玉米

corner [kɔːnə] *n.* 角;街角 *v.* 将……逼入困境

correct [kəˈrekt] *adj.* 正确的; 恰当的; 合适的 *v.* 改正;纠正

corridor [ˈkɒrɪdɔː] *n.* 走廊;通路

corrode [kəˈrəʊd] *v.*(受)腐蚀;侵蚀

cost [kɒst] *n.* 成本;费用;代价 *v.* 价值为;花费

costly [kɒstlɪ] *adj.* 昂贵的;价值高的

costume [ˈkɒstjuːm] *n.* 戏装;服装

cosy [ˈkəʊzɪ] *adj.* 温暖舒适的;愉快的

cottage [ˈkɒtɪdʒ] *n.* 村舍;小屋;别墅

cotton [ˈkɒtn] *n.* 棉花;棉制品

couch [kaʊtʃ] *n.* 长沙发

cough [kɒf] *v.* / *n.* 咳嗽

could [kud] aux. / *v.* 能;可以

council [ˈkaʊns(ə)l] *n.* 委员会；地方议会
count [kaʊnt] *v.* 数；计算 *n.* 计数；总数
counter [ˈkaʊntə] *n.* 柜台；计数器 *v.* 反驳；抵消
country [ˈkʌntrɪ] *n.* 国家；农村；乡下
countryside [ˈkʌntrɪsaɪd] *n.* 乡下；农村
county [ˈkaʊntɪ] *n.*（英国）郡；（美国）县
couple [ˈkʌp(ə)l] *n.* 两个；几个；一对夫妇；一对情侣
courage [ˈkʌrɪdʒ] *n.* 勇气；胆量
course [kɔːs] *n.* 课程；过程；进程；路线；航线；一道菜
court [kɔːt] *n.* 法院；法庭；院子；球场
courtesy [ˈkɜːtəsɪ] *n.* 谦恭有礼；有礼貌的举止（言语）
courtyard [ˈkɔːtjɑːd] *n.* 院子；庭院；天井
cousin [ˈkʌzn] *n.* 堂（或表）兄弟；堂（或表）姐妹
cow [kaʊ] *n.* 母牛；奶牛
coward [ˈkaʊəd] *n.* 懦夫；胆怯者
crab [kræb] *n.* 螃蟹；蟹肉
crack [kræk] *n.* 裂纹；缝隙；爆裂声 *v.*（使）破裂；砸开
cradle [ˈkreɪd(ə)l] *n.* 摇篮；发源地
craft [krɑːft] *n.* 工艺；手艺 *v.* 精心制作
crane [kreɪn] *n.* 起重机；鹤
crash [kræʃ] *v.* / *n.* 碰撞 *n.* 撞车事故 *adj.* 应急的
crawl [krɔːl] *v.* / *n.* 爬行；缓慢（的）行进
crazy [ˈkreɪzɪ] *adj.* 疯狂的；狂热的
cream [kriːm] *n.* 奶油；乳脂
credential [krəˈdenʃ(ə)l] *n.* 资格；证明；文凭；资格证书
creep [kriːp] *v.* 爬；爬行；（植物）蔓延
crew [kruː] *n.* 全体船员；全体乘务员
cricket [ˈkrɪkɪt] *n.* 板球；蟋蟀
cripple [ˈkrɪp(ə)l] *n.* 瘸子；残疾人 *v.* 使残疾
crisis [ˈkraɪsɪs] *n.* (pl. crises) 危机；紧要关头
crisp [krɪsp] *adj.* 脆的；易碎的；简明扼要的；（空气）清爽的
critic [ˈkrɪtɪk] *n.* 批评家；评论家
crop [krɒp] *n.* 庄稼；作物；（谷物等）收成 *v.* 剪短；种地
cross [krɒs] *n.* 十字（架）*adj.* 交叉的；发怒的 *v.* 穿过
crow [krəʊ] *n.* 乌鸦 *v.* 欢叫；自鸣得意
crowd [kraʊd] *n.* 人群；一群 *v.* 聚集；拥挤
crown [kraʊn] *n.* 王冠；冕；王位 *v.* 为……加冕
cruel [ˈkruːəl] *adj.* 残忍的；残酷的
cruise [kruːz] *n.* / *v.* 乘船游览；巡游
crush [krʌʃ] *n.* / *v.* 压碎；压坏；挤压 *n.* 拥挤的人群；（对某人短暂的）热恋
crust [krʌst] *n.*（某物的）硬皮；外壳；地壳
cry [kraɪ] *n./v.* 哭；喊；（鸟兽）叫；啼；鸣
crystal [ˈkrɪst(ə)l] *n.* 水晶；结晶 *adj.* 晶莹的；清澈透明的
cube [kjuːb] *n.* 立方形；立方体；立方
cucumber [ˈkjuːkʌmbə] *n.* 黄瓜
cue [kjuː] *n.* 暗示；提示
culture [ˈkʌltʃə] *n.* 文化；文明 *v.* 培育；养殖
cunning [ˈkʌnɪŋ] *adj.* / *n.* 狡猾（的）；狡诈（的）
cup [kʌp] *n.* 杯子；奖杯
cupboard [ˈkʌbəd] *n.* 橱柜
cure [kjʊə] *v.* 治愈；矫正 *n.* 治愈；疗法
curious [ˈkjʊərɪəs] *adj.* 好奇的；不寻常的
curiosity [ˌkjʊərɪˈɒsətɪ] *n.* 好奇心；求知欲；珍品
curl [kɜːl] *v.*（使）卷曲；蜷缩 *n.* 卷发；卷曲物
curse [kɜːs] *n.* / *v.* 诅咒；咒骂
curtain [ˈkɜːt(ə)n] *n.* 窗帘；门帘；幕（布）
curve [kɜːv] *n.* 曲线；转弯 *v.* 弄弯；成曲形
cushion [ˈkʊʃn] *n.* 垫子；坐垫 *v.* 缓冲
custom [ˈkʌstəm] *n.* 习惯；风俗；惯例 (pl.) 海关；关税
customary [ˈkʌstəmərɪ] *adj.* 习惯的；惯例的；典型的
customer [ˈkʌstəmə] *n.* 顾客；主顾
cut [kʌt] *v.* 切；割；削减 *n.* 切口；伤口
cyberspace [ˈsaɪbəspeɪs] *n.* 网络空间
cycle [ˈsaɪk(ə)l] *n.* / *v.*（骑）自行车；循环
cylinder [ˈsɪlɪndə] *n.* 圆筒；圆锥体；汽缸

D

daily [ˈdeɪlɪ] *adj.* 每日的 *adv.* 每日 *n.* 日报
dairy [ˈdeərɪ] *adj.* 奶制的；乳品的 *n.* 乳品店
dam [dæm] *n.* 水；水闸

damage [ˈdæmɪdʒ] *v.* / *n.* 损害；伤害
damn [dæm] int. 可恶 *adj.* 讨厌的 *adv.* 很；非常 *v.* 谴责
damp [dæmp] *n.* 潮湿 *adj.* 潮湿的 *v.* 使潮湿
dance [dɑːns] *n.* 舞（蹈）；舞会 *v.* 跳舞
danger [ˈdeɪndʒə] *n.* 危险；威胁；危险事物
dangerous [ˈdeɪndʒərəs] *adj.* 危险的
dare [deə] *v.* 敢；胆敢
dark [dɑːk] *adj.* 黑暗的；深（色）的；昏暗的 *n.* 黑暗；暗处；暗色
darling [ˈdɑːlɪŋ] *n.* 心爱的人；亲爱的
dash [dæʃ] *v.* / *n.* 猛冲；急奔 *n.* 破折号；（美）短跑
data [ˈdeɪtə] *n.* 资料；数据
database [ˈdeɪtəbeɪs] *n.* 数据库
date [deɪt] *n.* 日期 *v.* 注明日期；过时 *v.* 约会
daughter [ˈdɔːtə] *n.* 女儿
dawn [dɔːn] *n.* 黎明；拂晓 *v.* 破晓；开始
day [deɪ] *n.* 一天；白天；工作日
daylight [ˈdeɪlaɪt] *n.* 日光；白天；黎明
daytime [ˈdeɪtaɪm] *n.* 白天 *adj.* 日间的
dazzle [ˈdæz(ə)l] *v.*（强光）使目眩；使眼花 *n.*（光的）炫目；耀眼
dead [ded] *adj.* 死的；坏了的；失灵的 *adv.* 完全地 *n.* 死者
deadline [ˈdedlaɪn] *n.* 最后期限；截止日期
deadly [ˈdedlɪ] *adj.* 致命的
deaf [def] *adj.* 聋的；置若罔闻的
dean [diːn] *n.*（大学）院长；主持牧师；（基督教）教长
dear [dɪə] *adj.* 亲爱的；珍贵的
death [deθ] *n.* 死；死亡
debt [det] *n.* 债；债务
decade [ˈdekeɪd] *n.* 十年；十进位
decay [dɪˈkeɪ] *v.* / *n.* 腐朽；腐烂；衰减；衰退
deceit [dɪˈsiːt] *n.* 欺骗；欺骗行为
December [dɪˈsembə] *n.* 十二月
decent [ˈdiːs(ə)nt] *adj.* 体面的；得体的
decimal [ˈdesɪm(ə)l] *adj.* 小数的；十进位的 *n.* 小数；十进制
deck [dek] *n.* 甲板
defect [ˈdiːfekt] *n.* 过失；缺点；不足
deep [diːp] *adj.* 深的；低沉的；*adv.* 深深地
deer [dɪə] *n.* 鹿
deficiency [dɪˈfɪʃnsɪ] *n.* 缺乏；不足；缺点
deficit [ˈdefɪsɪt] *n.* 亏损；赤字；不足额
degenerate [dɪˈdʒenəreɪt] *v.* 恶化；堕落；退化 *adj.* 堕落的 *n.* 堕落者
delegate [ˈdelɪgət] *n.* 代表 *v.* 委派……为代表；委托
delicious [dɪˈlɪʃəs] *adj.* 美味的；美妙的
denial [dɪˈnaɪəl] *n.* 否认；拒绝
dental [ˈdent(ə)l] *adj.* 牙齿的；牙科（用）的
dentist [ˈdentɪst] *n.* 牙医
deposit [dɪˈpɒzɪt] *n.* 存款；保证金；沉积物 *v.* 存放；使沉淀；付（保证金）；放置
depth [depθ] *n.* 深度；深奥；深刻
deputy [ˈdepjutɪ] *n.* 代理人；代表 *adj.* 副的；代理的
desert [ˈdezət] *n.* 沙漠；不毛之地 *v.* 抛弃；遗弃
desire [dɪˈzaɪə] *v.* / *n.* 愿望；欲望；要求
desk [desk] *n.* 书桌；办公桌；服务台
despair [dɪˈspeə] *n.* / *v.* 绝望
despise [dɪˈspaɪz] *v.* 轻视；蔑视
despite [dɪˈspaɪt] *prep.* 不管；不顾
dessert [dɪˈzɜːt] *n.* 正餐后的水果或甜食
destiny [ˈdestənɪ] *n.* 命运；天数；天命
destroy [dɪˈstrɔɪ] *v.* 破坏；摧毁；消灭
detail [ˈdiːteɪl] *n.* 细节；详情 *v.* 详述
detain [dɪˈteɪn] *v.* 耽搁；扣押；拘留
develop [dɪˈveləp] *v.* 发展；发育；生长；开发；研制
devil [ˈdev(ə)l] *n.* 魔鬼
dew [djuː] *n.* 露水
diagram [ˈdaɪəgræm] *n.* 图表；图解
dial [ˈdaɪəl] *n.* 钟（表）面；刻度盘；拨号盘 *v.* 拨号；打电话
dialect [ˈdaɪəlekt] *n.* 方言
dialog [ˈdaɪəlɒg] *n.*(dialogue) 对话；对白
diameter [daɪˈæmɪtə] *n.* 直径
diamond [ˈdaɪmənd] *n.* 金刚石；钻石；菱形
diary [ˈdaɪərɪ] *n.* 日记；日记簿
dictionary [ˈdɪkʃən(ə)rɪ] *n.* 词典；字典
die [daɪ] *v.* 死亡；（草木）枯萎；凋谢；渴望

diet [ˈdaɪət] *n.* 饮食；食物
difficult [ˈdɪfɪkəlt] *adj.* 困难的；艰难的
difficulty [ˈdɪfɪkəltɪ] *n.* 困难；困境；难题
dig [dɪg] *v.* 挖；掘
digest [daɪˈdʒest] *v.* 消化；领会 *n.* 文摘
diligent [ˈdɪlɪdʒənt] *adj.* 勤奋的；用功的
dim [dɪm] *adj.* 暗淡的；模糊的
dine [daɪn] *v.* 吃饭；进餐
dinner [ˈdɪnə] *n.* 正餐；宴会
dip [dɪp] *v.* / *n.* 浸；蘸
diploma [dɪˈpləʊmə] *n.* 毕业文凭；学位证书
direct [dəˈrekt] *adj.* / *adv.* 径直的（地） *v.* 管理；指导；指向
direction [dəˈrekʃ(ə)n] *n.* 方向；指令；说明
directly [dəˈrektlɪ] *adv.* 直接地；径直地；马上
director [dəˈrektə] *n.* 指导者；主任；导演
directory [dəˈrektərɪ] *n.* 公司名录；号码簿
dirt [dɜːt] *n.* 污物；污垢
dirty [ˈdɜːtɪ] *adj.* 肮脏的 *v.* 弄脏；玷污
disappoint [ˌdɪsəˈpɔɪnt] *v.* 使失望；使破灭
disaster [dɪˈzɑːstə] *n.* 灾难；大祸
disastrous [dɪˈzɑːstrəs] *adj.* 灾难性的
disc [dɪsk] *n.*(disk) 圆盘；圆面；盘状物
discharge [dɪsˈtʃɑːdʒ] *v.* / *n.* 释放；允许……离开；解雇；开火；放（电）；出院
discount [ˈdɪskaʊnt] *n.* 折扣 *v.* 打折
discourage [dɪsˈkʌrɪdʒ] *v.* 使泄气；失去信心
discrepancy [dɪˈskrepənsɪ] *n.* 相差；差异
disgust [dɪsˈgʌst] *n.* 厌恶；恶心 *v.* 使厌恶
dish [dɪʃ] *n.* 碟子；盘子；菜肴
dislike [dɪsˈlaɪk] *n.* / *v.* 不喜欢；厌恶
dismay [dɪsˈmeɪ] *n.* / *v.*（使）沮丧；（使）惊慌；（使）失望；（使）绝望
dissipate [ˈdɪsɪpeɪt] *v.* 驱散；（使云、雾、疑虑等）消散；挥霍
distance [ˈdɪstəns] *n.* 距离；远方；路程
distill [dɪˈstɪl] *v.* 蒸馏；用蒸馏法提取；提炼
distress [dɪˈstres] *n.* 苦恼；不幸 *v.* 使苦恼
district [ˈdɪstrɪkt] *n.* 地区；行政区
disturbance [dɪˈstɜːbəns] *n.* 动乱；骚乱；干扰
ditch [dɪtʃ] *n.* 沟；沟渠；水沟
dive [daɪv] *v.* / *n.* 潜水；跳水；俯冲
diversion [daɪˈvɜːʃn] *n.* 转移；消遣
dividend [ˈdɪvɪdend] *n.* 红利；股息；被除数
divine [dɪˈvaɪn] *adj.* 神的；天赐的；极好的
divorce [dɪˈvɔːs] *v.* / *n.* 离婚；分离
dizzy [ˈdɪzɪ] *adj.* 头晕目眩的 *v.* 使眩晕
do [duː] aux. / *v.* 做；从事；行动；引起
dock [dɒk] *n.* 船坞；码头
doctor [ˈdɒktə] *n.* 医生；博士
doctorate [ˈdɒktərət] *n.* 博士学位；博士头衔
document [ˈdɒkjumənt] *n.* 公文；文献
documentary [ˌdɒkjuˈment(ə)rɪ] *adj.* 文献的 *n.* 纪录片
dog [dɒg] *n.* 狗 *v.* 尾随；跟踪
doll [dɒl] *n.* 玩偶；玩具娃娃
dollar [ˈdɒlə] *n.* 美元；元（美国、加拿大、澳大利亚以及其他一些地区的货币单位）
dome [dəʊm] *n.* 圆屋顶
donkey [ˈdɒŋkɪ] *n.* 驴子；蠢人；顽固的人
doom [duːm] *n.* 厄运；劫数 *v.* 注定；命定
door [dɔː] *n.* 门；通道
doorway [ˈdɔːweɪ] *n.* 门口
dormitory [ˈdɔːmətrɪ] *n.* (dorm) 宿舍
dose [dəʊs] *n.* 剂量；一剂 *v.* 服药
dot [dɒt] *n.* 点；圆点 *v.* 在……上打点
doubt [daʊt] *n.* / *v.* 怀疑；疑虑
dove [dʌv] *n.* 鸽子
down [daʊn] *adv.* / *adj.* / *prep.* 向下（的）；沿着 *adj.* 沮丧的 *v.* 打倒；下降
downstairs [ˌdaʊnˈsteəz] adj / *adv.* 在楼下 *n.* 楼下
downtown [ˌdaʊnˈtaʊn] *n.* / *adj.* 市中心（的）；商业区的（的） *adv.* 在市中心
downward [ˈdaʊnwəd] *adj.* / *adv.*(downwards) 向下（的）；下降的（地）
doze [dəʊz] *v.* / *n.* 瞌睡；假寐
dozen [ˈdʌzn] *n.* 一打；十二个
draft [drɑːft] *n.* 草案；草图 *v.* 起草；草拟
drag [dræg] *v.* 拖；拖曳
dragon [ˈdrægən] *n.* 龙
drain [dreɪn] *n.* 排水沟；消耗 *v.*（使）排出；使劳累；消耗

drama [ˈdrɑːmə] *n.* 剧本；戏剧；戏剧性事件或场面
draw [drɔː] *v.* 画；拖、拉；引出；吸引 *n.* 平局；抽签
drawer [drɔː] *n.* 抽屉
drawing [ˈdrɔːɪŋ] *n.* 绘图；图样
dread [dred] *v.* / *n.* 恐惧；担心
dreadful [ˈdredf(ə)l] *adj.* 糟糕透顶的；极度的；可怕的
dream [driːm] *n.* / *v.* 梦；梦想；幻想
dress [dres] *n.* 连衣裙 *v.* 穿衣；打扮
drift [drɪft] *v.* / *n.* 漂；漂流（物）
drill [drɪl] *v.* / *n.* 练习；操练；钻孔
drink [drɪŋk] *v.* 喝；饮 *n.* 饮料；喝酒
drip [drɪp] *v.* 滴下 *n.* 滴；水滴；点滴
drive [draɪv] *v.* 开（车）；驱动 *n.* 驾驶
driver [ˈdraɪvə] *n.* 驾驶员
drop [drɒp] *n.* 滴；下降 *v.* 落下；下降
drown [draʊn] *v.* 溺死；淹没
drug [drʌg] *n.* 药物；毒品 *v.* 使服麻醉药
drum [drʌm] *n.* 鼓；圆桶
drunk [drʌŋk] *adj.* 醉酒的；陶醉的 *n.* 醉汉
dry [draɪ] *adj.* 干（旱）的；干燥的 *v.* 使干燥
duck [dʌk] *n.* 鸭；鸭肉 *v.* 迅速俯身；躲避
dull [dʌl] *adj.* 单调的；迟钝的 *v.* 减轻
dumb [dʌm] *adj.* 哑的；无言的
dump [dʌmp] *v.* 倾倒；倾卸 *n.* 垃圾场
duplicate [ˈdjuːplɪkeɪt] *n.* 复制品 *v.* 复印；复制 *adj.* 复制的
duplication [ˌdjuːplɪˈkeɪʃn] *n.* 复印；重复
duration [djuˈreɪʃn] *n.* 持久；期间；持续时间
during [ˈdjʊərɪŋ] *prep.* 在……期间
dusk [dʌsk] *n.* 薄暮；黄昏
dust [dʌst] *n.* 灰尘；尘土 *v.* 拂；掸
duty [ˈdjuːtɪ] *n.* 义务；责任；职务；税
dwarf [dwɔːf] *n.* 矮子；侏儒 *v.* 使……矮小
dwell [dwel] *v.* 住；居留
dwelling [ˈdwelɪŋ] *n.* 住宅；寓所
dye [daɪ] *n.* 染料 *v.* 染；染色

E

each [iːtʃ] *adj.* / *pron.* 各自的；每
eagle [ˈiːg(ə)l] *n.* 鹰
ear [ɪə] *n.* 耳朵；听力
early [ˈɜːlɪ] *adj.* 早的；早期的 *adv.* 提早；在初期
earth [ɜːθ] *n.* 地球；陆地；泥土
earthquake [ˈɜːθkweɪk] *n.* 地震
ease [iːz] *v.* 减轻；使舒适 *n.* 舒适；悠闲
east [iːst] *n.* 东方；东部 *adj.* 东方的
Easter [ˈiːstə] *n.* 复活节
eastern [ˈiːstən] *adj.* 东方的；东部的
easy [ˈiːzɪ] *adj.* 容易的；不费力的；舒适的
eat [iːt] *v.* 吃；喝
ebb [eb] *v.* 衰退；减退 *n.* 处于低潮
eccentric [ɪkˈsentrɪk] *adj.* 古怪的；异乎寻常的 *n.* 古怪的人
echo [ˈekəʊ] *v.* / *n.* 回声；反响；共鸣
ecology [ɪˈkɒlədʒɪ] *n.* 生态学
economical [ˌiːkəˈnɒmɪkl] *adj.* 节约的；经济的
economics [ˌiːkəˈnɒmɪks] *n.* 经济学；经济情况
economy [ɪˈkɒnəmɪ] *n.* 节约；经济
edge [edʒ] *n.* 边；边缘；棱；刀口；刃
edible [ˈedəb(ə)l] *adj.* 可食用的
edit [ˈedɪt] *v.* 编辑；校订
editor [ˈedɪtə] *n.* 编辑；编者
editorial [ˌedɪˈtɔːrɪəl] *n.* 社论 *adj.* 编辑上的
education [ˌedʒuˈkeɪʃn] *n.* 教育；培养；训练
effect [ɪˈfekt] *n.* 效果；影响；生效 *v.* 引起
egg [eg] *n.* 蛋；卵 *v.* 煽动；怂恿
ego [ˈiːgəʊ] *n.* 自我；自负；利己主义；（心理学）自我意识
eight [eɪt] *num.* 八
eighteen [ˌeɪˈtiːn] *num.* 十八
eighty [ˈeɪtɪ] *num.* 八十
either [ˈaɪðə] *pron.* / det.（两者中的）任何一个 *adv.* 也；而且
eject [ɪˈdʒekt] *v.* 喷射；排出；驱逐
elapse [ɪˈlæps] *v.*（时间）溜走；（光阴）逝去
elastic [ɪˈlæstɪk] *adj.* 有弹力的；灵活的 *n.* 松紧带
elbow [ˈelbəʊ] *n.* 肘；肘部 *v.* 用肘推
elder [ˈeldə] *adj.* 年长的；资格老的 *n.* 长辈
elderly [ˈeldəlɪ] *adj.* 年长的 *n.* 老年人
elect [ɪˈlekt] *v.* 选举；推选；选择

electron [ɪˈlektrɒn] *n.* 电子
elegant [ˈelɪgənt] *adj.* 优雅的；端庄的
elephant [ˈelɪfənt] *n.* 大象
elevator [ˈelɪveɪtə] *n.* 电梯；升降机
eleven [ɪˈlevən] *num.* 十一
eloquent [ˈeləkwənt] *adj.* 雄辩的；有说服力的；善辩的；传神的
else [els] *adj.* / *adv.* 其他（的） *adv.* 否则
elsewhere [ˌelsˈwɛə] *adv.* 在别处；去别处
e-mail [ˈiːmeɪl] *n.* 电子信函；电子邮件
emperor [ˈempərə] *n.* 皇帝
empire [ˈempaɪə] *n.* 帝国
employee [ɪmˈplɔɪiː] *n.* 雇工；雇员
employer [ɪmˈplɔɪə] *n.* 雇主
empty [ˈemptɪ] *adj.* 空的；空洞的 *v.* 倒空
enclosure [ɪnˈkləuʒə] *n.* 围墙；圈起；附件
encyclop(a)edia [ɪnˌsaɪkləˈpiːdɪə] *n.* 百科全书
end [end] *n.* 末尾；结束 *v.* 终止；结束
ending [ˈendɪŋ] *n.* 结尾；结局
enemy [ˈenɪmɪ] *n.* 敌人；敌国；反对者
energetic [ˌenəˈdʒetɪk] *adj.* 精力旺盛的；积极的；充满活力的
energy [ˈenədʒɪ] *n.* 活力；精力；能量
engine [ˈendʒɪn] *n.* 发动机；引擎；火车头
engineer [ˌendʒɪˈnɪə] *n.* 工程师
engineering [ˌendʒɪˈnɪərɪŋ] *n.* 工程学
enjoy [ɪnˈdʒɔɪ] *v.* 享受；欣赏；喜爱
enlarge [ɪnˈlɑːdʒ] *v.* 扩大；放大；增大
enormous [ɪˈnɔːməs] *adj.* 巨大的；庞大的
enough [ɪˈnʌf] *adj.* 足够的 *n.* 足够；充分 *adv.* 足够地
enter [ˈentə] *v.* 进入；参加；输入；开始做
entity [ˈentətɪ] *n.* 实体；独立存在体
entrance [ˈentrəns] *n.* 入口；进入；入场
entry [ˈentrɪ] *n.* 进入；进入权；登记；条目
envelope [ˈenvələʊp] *n.* 信封；信皮
environment [ɪnˈvaɪrənmənt] *n.* 环境；周围状况
envy [ˈenvɪ] *v.* / *n.* 羡慕；忌妒
epoch [ˈiːpɒk] *n.* 新纪元；时代；时期
equal [ˈiːkwəl] *adj.* 相等的；平等的；胜任的 *n.* 相等物 *v.* 等于
equality [ɪˈkwɒlətɪ] *n.* 均等；平等；等式
equation [ɪˈkweɪʒ(ə)n] *n.* 等式；方程式；相等
equator [ɪˈkweɪtə] *n.* 赤道
equip [ɪˈkwɪp] *v.* 装备；配备；训练
equipment [ɪˈkwɪpmənt] *n.* 设备；装置；才能
era [ˈɪərə] *n.* 时代；年代；阶段；纪元
erase [ɪˈreɪz] *v.* 擦掉；删去；消磁
erect [ɪˈrekt] *v.* 树立；建立；使竖立 *adj.* 直立的；垂直的
erosion [ɪˈrəʊʒ(ə)n] *n.* 腐蚀；磨损；削弱
erroneous [ɪˈrəʊnɪəs] *adj.* 错误的；不正确的
error [ˈerə] *n.* 错误；过失
erupt [ɪˈrʌpt] *v.*（尤指火山）爆发
escalate [ˈeskəleɪt] *v.*（使）逐步增长（或发展）；（使）逐步升级
escort [ˈeskɔːt] *v.* 护送（卫）；陪同 *n.* 警卫；护送者；仪仗兵
especially [ɪˈspeʃəlɪ] *adv.* 特别；尤其；专门地
essay [ˈeseɪ] *n.* 文章；短文
eternal [ɪˈtɜːn(ə)l] *n.* 永久的；永恒的
evacuate [ɪˈvækjueɪt] *v.* 撤离；疏散；抽空
evaporate [ɪˈvæpəreɪt] *v.* 蒸发；挥发；消失
eve [iːv] *n.*（节日等的）前夜；前夕
even [ˈiːv(ə)n] *adv.* 甚至；更加 *adj.* 均匀的；平的；相等的；偶数的
evening [ˈiːvnɪŋ] *n.* 傍晚；黄昏；晚上
event [ɪˈvent] *n.* 事件；事情
eventually [ɪˈventʃuəlɪ] *adv.* 终于；最后
ever [ˈevə] *adv.* 曾经；在任何时候；究竟
every [ˈevrɪ] *adj.* 每一个的；每个的；每隔
everybody [ˈevrɪbɒdɪ] *pron.* 每人；人人
everyday [ˈevrɪdeɪ] *adj.* 每日的；日常的
everyone [ˈevrɪwʌn] *pron.* 每人；人人
everything [ˈevrɪθɪŋ] *pron.* 每件事；一切；最重要的东西
everywhere [ˈevrɪweə] *adv.* 到处 *n.* 每个地方
evil [ˈiːv(ə)l] *adj.* 邪恶的；罪恶的 *n.* 邪恶；罪恶
exact [ɪgˈzækt] *adj.* 确切的；正确的；精确的
exam [ɪgˈzæm] *n.*(examination) 考试；测验
example [ɪgˈzɑːmp(ə)l] *n.* 例子；模范；榜样
exceedingly [ɪkˈsiːdɪŋlɪ] *adv.* 极端地；非常

excellent [ˈeksələnt] *adj.* 卓越的；极好的
except [ɪkˈsept] *prep.* 除……之外 *v.* 不包括；把……排除在外
exception [ɪkˈsepʃn] *n.* 例外；除外
exceptional [ɪkˈsepʃən(ə)l] *adj.* 卓越的；例外的；异常的
excerpt [ekˈsɜːpt] *n.* / *v.* 摘录；引用
exchange [ɪksˈtʃeɪndʒ] *v.* / *n.* 交换；兑换；交流；交易
excite [ɪkˈsaɪt] *v.* 使激动；激发；激励
excitement [ɪkˈsaɪtmənt] *n.* 刺激；激动；兴奋
exciting [ɪkˈsaɪtɪŋ] *adj.* 令人兴奋的、激动的
excursion [ɪkˈskɜːʃn] *n.* 短途旅行；远足
excuse [ɪkˈskjuːs] *v.* 原谅；宽恕 *n.* 借口
exercise [ˈeksəsaɪz] *n.* 练习；习题；训练；锻炼 *v.* 训练；锻炼
exhaust [ɪgˈzɔːst] *v.* 使筋疲力尽；耗尽 *n.* 排气装置；废气
exhibit [ɪgˈzɪbɪt] *v.* 展出；陈列 *n.* 展览品；陈列品
exhibition [ˌeksɪˈbɪʃ(ə)n] *n.* 展览；陈列
exile [ˈeksaɪl] *n.* 流放；被流放者 *v.* 流放；放逐；把……充军
exit [ˈeksɪt] *n.* 出口；通道
expedition [ˌekspəˈdɪʃ(ə)n] *n.* 远征（队）；考察；探险队
expel [ɪkˈspel] *v.* 开除；驱逐；排出；发射
expensive [ɪkˈspensɪv] *adj.* 花费的；昂贵的
experience [ɪkˈspɪərɪəns] *n.* / *v.* 经验；经历；体验；阅历
experiment [ɪkˈsperɪmənt] *n.* 实验；试验 *v.* 进行实验
experimental [ɪkˌsperɪˈment(ə)l] *adj.* 实验（性）的；试验（性）的
expert [ˈekspɜːt] *n.* 专家；能手 *adj.* 熟练的；有经验的；专门的
explain [ɪkˈspleɪn] *v.* 解释；说明
explanation [ˌekspləˈneɪʃ(ə)n] *n.* 解释；说明
explode [ɪkˈspləʊd] *v.*（使）爆炸；（使）爆发
explosion [ɪkˈspləʊʒ(ə)n] *n.* 爆炸；爆发
explosive [ɪkˈspləʊsɪv] *adj.* 爆炸（性）的；爆发（性）的 *n.* 爆炸物；炸药
exquisite [ɪkˈskwɪzɪt] *adj.* 精致的；精美的；剧烈的；细致的
exterior [ɪkˈstɪərɪə] *adj.* 外部的；外面的 *n.* 外部
external [ɪkˈstɜːn(ə)l] *adj.* 外部的；外来的；对外的；（医）外用的
extra [ˈekstrə] *adj.* 额外的；附加的 *n.* 附加物；额外的东西
extraordinary [ɪkˈstrɔːdnrɪ] *adj.* 异乎寻常的；非凡的；特别的
eye [aɪ] *n.* 眼（睛）；视力 *v.* 注视
eyebrow [ˈaɪbraʊ] *n.* 眉毛
eyesight [ˈaɪsaɪt] *n.* 视力

fable [ˈfeɪbl] *n.* 寓言
fabulous [ˈfæbjələs] *adj.* 极好的；非凡的
face [feɪs] *n.* 脸；面部 *v.* 面对着；朝；面向
fact [fækt] *n.* 事实；实际
factory [ˈfæktərɪ] *n.* 工厂
faculty [ˈfækəltɪ] *n.* 学院；系；（学院或系的）全体教学人员；才能
fail [feɪl] *v.* 失败；不及格；衰退 *n.* 不及格
faint [ˈfeɪnt] *adj.* 微弱的；虚弱的；头晕目眩的 *n.* / *v.* 昏倒；昏晕
fair [fɛə] *adj.* 公平的；合理的；相当的 *n.* 集市；交易会
fairly [ˈfɛəlɪ] *adv.* 公正地；正当地；相当
fairy [ˈfɛərɪ] *n.* 仙子；小精灵
faith [feɪθ] *n.* 信任；信用；信仰；信条
faithful [ˈfeɪθful] *adj.* 守信的；忠实的；可靠的
fall [fɔːl] *v.* 跌倒；落下；下降；减弱 *n.* 落下；秋季
false [fɔːls] *adj.* 谬误的；伪造的；假的
fame [feɪm] *n.* 名声；名望；名气
familiar [fəˈmɪljə] *adj.* 熟悉的；通晓的；亲近的 *n.* 熟客；密友
family [ˈfæmɪlɪ] *n.* 家；家庭成员
famine [ˈfæmɪn] *n.* 饥荒
famous [ˈfeɪməs] *adj.* 著名的
fan [fæn] *n.* 扇子；风扇；（影；球等）迷
fancy [ˈfænsɪ] *v.* 喜欢；想要；爱慕 *n.* 想象；想象力
fantastic [fænˈtæstɪk] *adj.* (fantastical) 奇异的；幻

想的；异想天开的

fantasy [ˈfæntəsɪ] *n.* 幻想；想象

far [fɑː] *adj.* / *adv.* 远；遥远 *adv.* 到……程度；……得多

fare [fɛə] *n.* 交通费用

farewell [ˌfɛəˈwel] *n.* 告别；再会

farm [fɑːm] *n.* 农场 *v.* 种田；经营农牧业

farmer [ˈfɑːmə] *n.* 农民；农场主

farther [ˈfɑːðə] *adv.* 更远地 *adj.* 更远的

fast [fɑːst] *adj.* 快的；迅速的 *adv.* 迅速地

fasten [ˈfɑːsən] *v.* 扣紧；系牢

fat [fæt] *adj.* 肥胖的 *n.* 脂肪

fatal [ˈfeɪtl] *adj.* 致命的；毁灭性的

fate [ˈfeɪt] *n.* 命运

father [ˈfɑːðə] *n.* 父亲；创始人；发明者

fault [fɔːlt] *n.* 过失；过错；缺点；毛病

faulty [ˈfɔːltɪ] *adj.* 有错误的；有缺点的；不完善的

favorite [ˈfeɪvərɪt] *adj.* (favourite) 最喜欢的

fax [fæks] *n.* / *v.* 传真（机）

fear [fɪə] *n.* / *v.* 害怕；恐惧；担心

fearful [ˈfɪəful] *adj.* 害怕的；担心；惊恐的

feast [fiːst] *n.* 节日；宴会

feat [fiːt] *n.* 功绩；伟业；技艺

feather [ˈfeðə] *n.* 羽毛

feature [ˈfiːtʃə] *n.* 特征；特色 *v.* 以……为特色

February [ˈfebruəri] *n.* 二月

federation [ˈfedəreɪʃən] *n.* 同盟；联合（会）

fee [fiː] *n.* 费；酬金

feed [fiːd] *v.* 喂养；饲养；为……供给食物

feel [ˈfiːl] *v.* 感觉；感到；触摸；碰到

feeling [ˈfiːlɪŋ] *n.* 感觉；想法；情感

fell [fel] *v.* 砍伐（树木）；打倒（疾病等） *adj.* 凶恶的

fellow [ˈfeləu] *n.* 小伙子；同事 *adj.* 同类的

fellowship [ˈfeləuʃɪp] *n.* 团体；协会；研究生奖学金；会员资格

female [ˈfiːmeɪl] *n.* / *adj.* 女性（的）；雌性（的）

feminine [ˈfemɪnɪn] *adj.* 女性的；女子气的

fence [ˈfens] *n.* 篱笆；围栏；剑术 *v.* 用篱笆围住；击剑

ferry [ˈferɪ] *n.* 摆渡；渡船；渡口 *v.* 摆渡

fertilizer [ˈfɜːtɪlaɪzə] *n.* (fertiliser) 肥料

festival [ˈfestəvəl] *n.*（音乐或戏剧）节；节庆

fetch [fetʃ] *v.*（去）拿来；（去）找来

feudal [ˈfjuːdl] *adj.* 封建的；过时

fever [ˈfiːvə] *n.* 发热；狂热

few [fjuː] *adj.* 很少的；几乎没有

fiber [ˈfaɪbə] *n.* (fibre) 纤维；构造；纤维制品

fiction [ˈfikʃən] *n.* 虚构；编造；小说

field [ˈfiːld] *n.* 田野；运动场；领域；范围

fifteen [ˈfɪftiːn] *num.* 十五

fifty [ˈfɪftɪ] *num.* 五十

fight [faɪt] *v.* / *n.* 打（仗）；斗争；战斗

file [ˈfaɪl] *n.* 文件；档案

fill [fɪl] *v.* 填满；充满

film [fɪlm] *n.* 电影；胶片 *v.* 把……拍成电影

filter [fɪltə] *n.* 滤器；滤纸

final [ˈfaɪnl] *adj.* 最终的；决定性的 *n.* 结局；决赛；期末考试

finally [ˈfaɪnəlɪ] *adv.* 最后；最终；决定性地

finance [faɪˈnæns] *n.* 财政；金融

find [faɪnd] *v.* 找到；发现；发觉；感到

finding [ˈfaɪndɪŋ] *n.* 发现；发现物；（pl.）调查；研究结果

fine [faɪn] *adj.* 晴朗的；美好的；健康的 *v.* / *n.* 罚金；罚款

finger [ˈfɪŋgə] *n.* 手指；指状物；指针

finish [ˈfɪnɪʃ] *n.* / *v.* 完成；结束

fire [ˈfaɪə] *n.* 火；火灾；炉火 *v.* 开（枪）；解雇

fireman [ˈfaɪəmən] *n.* 消防队员

fireplace [ˈfaɪəpleɪs] *n.* 壁炉

first [fɜːst] det. / *adv.* 第一（的）；首先；最初；首要（的） *n.* 第一个人（或事物）

fish [fɪʃ] *n.* 鱼；鱼肉 *v.* 捕鱼；钓鱼

fisherman [ˈfɪʃəmən] *n.* 渔夫；捕鱼人

fist [fɪst] *n.* 拳头 *v.* 用拳头打；紧握

fit [ˈfɪt] *v.* / *adj.* 合适；试穿；安装

fitting [ˈfɪtɪŋ] *adj.* 适当的；恰当的 *n.*（pl.）配件；附件；装配

five [faɪv] *num.* 五

fix [fiks] *v.*（使）固定；修理；安装；注视

fixture [ˈfɪkstʃə] *n.* 固定设备；体育活动

flag [flæg] *n.* 旗
flame [fleɪm] *n.* 火焰;火苗 *v.* 燃烧
flap [flæp] *n.* / *v.* 拍打;振动(翅)
flare [flɛə] *v.* / *n.* 闪耀;闪烁
flash [flæʃ] *n.* / *adj.* 闪光(的) *v.* 闪亮;闪现
flat [flæt] *adj.* 平坦的;扁平的;平淡的 *n.* 一套房间;平面
flatter [ˈflætə] *v.* 奉承;讨好;使高兴
flavor [ˈfleɪvə] *n.*(flavour) 情味; 风味; 滋味 *v.* 给……调味
flee [fliː] *v.* 逃走;逃避
fleet [fliːt] *n.* 舰队;船队
flesh [fleʃ] *n.* 肉;肉体
flight [flaɪt] *n.* 飞行;航班;楼梯的一段
fling [flɪŋ] *v.*(用力地)扔;抛;丢
float [fləut] *n.* 飘浮;漂流物 *v.* 浮动;漂浮
flock [flɔk] *n.*(禽; 畜等的) 群; 大量 *v.* 群集; 成群
flood [flʌd] *n.* 洪水;水灾 *v.* 淹没;泛滥
floor [flɔː] *n.* 地板;(楼房)的层
flour [ˈflauə] *n.* 面粉
flow [fləu] *v.* 流动 *n.* 流量;流速
flower [ˈflauə] *n.* 花;精华 *v.* 开花
flu [fluː] *n.*(influenza) 流行性感冒
fluent [ˈflu(ː)ənt] *adj.* 流利的;流畅的
fluid [ˈflu(ː)ɪd] *adj.* 流动的;液体的 *n.* 流体;液体
flush [flʌʃ] *n.* 脸红 *v.* 发红;脸红 *adj.* 富裕的
fly [flaɪ] *n.* 飞行;苍蝇 *v.* 飞行;飞
foam [fəum] *v.* / *n.* 泡沫;起泡沫
fog [fɔg] *n.* 雾气;雾 *v.* 被雾笼罩
fold [fəuld] *v.* 折叠 *n.* 褶;褶痕
folk [fəuk] *n.* 人们;亲属 *adj.* 民间的
following [ˈfɔləuɪŋ] *adj.* 下列的;下述的;其次的;接着的
food [fuːd] *n.* 食物;粮食;养料
fool [fuːl] *n.* 傻子;笨蛋 *v.* 欺骗;愚弄
foolish [ˈfuːlɪʃ] *adj.* 愚笨的;愚蠢的
foot [fut] *n.* (pl. feet) 脚;足;英尺;底部
football [ˈfutbɔːl] *n.* 足球
footstep [ˈfutstep] *n.* 脚步(声);足迹
for [fɔː; fə] *prep.* 为了;给;支持;拥护 *conj.* 因为
force [fɔːs] *n.* 力量;力;势力 (*pl.*) 军队 *v.* 强迫
fore [fɔː] *adv.* 在前面 *adj.* 先前的 *n.* 前部
forehead [ˈfɔːhed] *n.* 前额
foreign [ˈfɔrɪn] *adj.* 外国的;外来的;陌生的
foreigner [ˈfɔrɪnə] *n.* 外国人
forest [ˈfɔrɪst] *n.* 森林
forever [fəˈrevə] *adv.* 永远;总是
forget [fəˈget] *v.* 忘记;遗忘
fork [fɔːk] *n.* 餐叉;耙;叉形物
form [fɔːm] *n.* 形状; 形式; 表格 *v.* 组成; 构成; 形成
format [ˈfɔːmæt] *n.* 版式;格式 *v.* 设计;安排
formation [fɔːˈmeɪnʃ(ə)n] *n.* 形成; 构成; 组织; 构造
formula [ˈfɔːmjulə] *n.* (pl.formulae) 公式; 规则; 分子式;药方
forth [fɔːθ] *adv.* 向前;向外;往外
forthcoming [ˌfɔːθˈkʌmɪŋ] *adj.* 即将到来的;准备好的;乐意帮助的 *n.* 来临
fortnight [ˈfɔːtnaɪt] *n.* 两星期
forty [ˈfɔːtɪ] *num.* 四十
forum [ˈfɔːrəm] *n.* 论坛;讨论会
forward [ˈfɔːwəd] *adv.* (forwards) 向前 *adj.* 向前的 *v.* 转交
fossil [ˈfɔsəl] *n.* 化石
foul [faul] *adj.* 难闻的;不道德的;无礼的 *n.* / *v.* 犯规(的)
found [faund] *v.* 建立;创立;铸造;熔制
foundation [faunˈdeɪʃən] *n.* 基础; 根本; 建立; 创立;地基;基金;基金会
fountain [ˈfauntɪn] *n.* 泉水;喷泉;源泉
four [fɔː] *num.* 四
fourteen [ˌfɔːˈtiːn] *num.* 十四
fox [fɔks] *n.* 狐狸
fracture [ˈfræktʃə] *n.* 裂缝(痕); 骨折 *v.*(使) 断裂;(使)折断
fragrant [ˈfreɪgrənt] *adj.* 香的;芬芳的
fraud [frɔːd] *n.* 欺诈;诈骗;骗子;假货
free [friː] *adj.* 自由的;免费的;空闲的 *v.* 释放;使免于
freedom [ˈfriːdəm] *n.* 自由(权);自主(权)

freeze [friːz] *v.* 使结冰；使凝固
freight [freɪt] *n.* 货物；货运；运费
frequency [ˈfrɪkwənsɪ] *n.* 频率
fresh [freʃ] *adj.* 新鲜的；清凉的；新颖的
friction [ˈfrɪkʃən] *n.* 摩擦；摩擦力
Friday [ˈfraɪdeɪ] *n.* 星期五
fridge [frɪdʒ] *n.* (refrigerator 的略语）冰箱
friend [frend] *n.* 朋友
friendly [ˈfrendlɪ] *adj.* 友好的；友谊的
friendship [frendʃɪp] *n.* 友谊；友好
fright [fraɪt] *n.* 恐怖
frighten [ˈfraɪtən] *v.* 使惊恐
fringe [frɪndʒ] *n.* 边缘；（窗帘）缘饰；刘海 *v.* 饰……的边
frog [frɔg] *n.* 蛙；青蛙
from [frɔm] *prep.* 从……起；自从；来自
front [frʌnt] *adj.* 前面的；前部的 *n.* 正面；前线；战线 *v.* 面对
frontier [ˈfrʌntɪə] *n.* 国境；边境；前沿；新领域
frost [frɔst] *n.* 霜；霜冻；严寒
frown [fraun] *v.* 皱眉
fruit [fruːt] *n.* 水果；果实；成果；效果
fry [fraɪ] *v.* 油煎；油炸
full [ful] *adj.* 满的；充满的 *adj.* / *adv.* 完全；充分
fume [fjuːm] *n.* 烟气；烟雾 *v.* 十分恼火
fun [fʌn] *n.* 玩笑；娱乐；有趣的人（或事物）
fund [fʌnd] *n.* 基金；资金；基金会 *v.* 为……提供资金；资助
funeral [ˈfjuːnərəl] *n.* 丧葬；葬礼
funny [ˈfʌnɪ] *adj.* 滑稽的；可笑的
fur [fə] *n.* 毛；毛皮
furious [ˈfjuːrɪəs] *adj.* 狂怒的；猛烈的
furnace [ˈfɜːnɪs] *n.* 炉子；熔炉
furniture [ˈfɜːnɪtʃə] *n.* 家具
further [ˈfɜːðə] *adj.* / *adv.* 更远的（地）；进一步（的） *v.* 促进；增进
furthermore [ˈfɜːðəmɔː] *adv.* 而且；此外
fuse [fjuːz] *n.* 保险丝；导火线 *v.* 熔合
fuss [fʌs] *n.* / *v.* 忙乱；大惊小怪
future [ˈfjuːtʃə] *n.* / *adj.* 将来（的）；未来（的）

G

gallon [ˈgælən] *n.* 加仑
gallop [ˈgæləp] *n.* / *v.*（马等）飞奔；疾驰
game [geɪm] *n.* 游戏
gang [gæŋ] *n.* 帮派；团伙 *v.* 成群；结伙
gaol (jail) [dʒeɪl] *n.* 监狱；拘留所 *v.* 监禁
garage [ˈgærɑːʒ] *n.* 车库
garbage [ˈgɑːbɪdʒ] *n.* 垃圾；废物
garden [ˈgɑːdn] *n.* 花园；菜园 *v.* 从事园艺；种植花木
garlic [ˈgɑːlɪk] *n.* 大蒜
gas [gæs] *n.* 气体；煤气；汽油
gate [geɪt] *n.* 门；栅栏门
gauge [geɪdʒ] *n.* 测量仪器；厚度；（测量或判断的）尺度；标准 *v.* 计量；度量
gay [geɪ] *adj.* 同性恋的；快乐的 *n.* 同性恋者（尤指男性）
gear [gɪə] *n.* 设备；齿轮；装备；服装；（排）挡 *v.* 使变速；使调挡
gender [ˈdʒendə] *n.* 性别
general [ˈdʒenərəl] *adj.* 普遍的；全面的；总体的；整体的 *n.* 上将；将军
generalize [ˈdʒenərəlaɪz] *v.* 概括；归纳；推论；推广；普及
generator [ˈdʒenəreɪtə] *n.* 发电机；发生器
gentle [ˈdʒentl] *adj.* 温和的；和蔼的
gentleman [ˈdʒentlmən] *n.* 绅士；君子；先生
gently [ˈdʒentlɪ] *adv.* 文雅地；有礼貌地
geography [dʒɪˈɔgrəfɪ] *n.* 地理（学）；地形
geology [dʒɪˈɔlədʒɪ] *n.* 地质学；地质情况
geometry [dʒɪˈɔmɪtrɪ] *n.* 几何（学）
germ [dʒɜːm] *n.* 微生物；病菌；细菌
get [get] *v.* 得到；收到；（去）拿来
ghost [gəust] *n.* 鬼；幽灵
giant [ˈdʒaɪənt] *n.* 巨人；巨兽 *adj.* 巨大的
gift [gɪft] *n.* 礼物；赠品；天赋；天才
giggle [ˈgɪgl] *n.* / *vi.* 咯咯地笑；傻笑
girl [gɜːl] *n.* 女孩
give [gɪv] *v.* 给予；赠送；供给；提供
glad [glæd] *adj.* 高兴的；乐意的；情愿的

glare [glɛə] *v.* 怒目而视 *n.* 强光；怒视；瞪眼
glass [glɑːs] *n.* 玻璃；玻璃杯；眼镜
glide [glaɪd] *v.* / *n.* 滑行；滑动；滑翔
glitter [ˈglɪtə] *v.* 闪烁；闪耀 *n.* 闪烁
global [ˈgləubəl] *adj.* 全球的；全世界的；整体的；总括的；全面的
globe [gləub] *n.* 地球；世界；地球仪；球体
gloomy [ˈgluːmɪ] *adj.* 阴暗的；令人沮丧的
glorious [ˈglɔːrɪəs] *adj.* 辉煌的；壮丽的
glory [ˈglɔːrɪ] *n.* 光荣；荣誉；美丽；壮丽
glove [glʌv] *n.* 手套
glow [gləu] *v.* 发出微弱而稳定的光；发热；容光焕发 *n.* 光亮；光辉
glue [gluː] *n.* 胶水；凝聚力 *v.* 黏合
go [gəu] *v.* 去；走；行；驶
goal [gəul] *n.* 目标；球门；进球得分
goat [gəut] *n.* 山羊
God [gɔd] *n.* 神；上帝 *v.* 膜拜；崇拜
gold [gəuld] *n.* 金；黄金；金色 *adj.* 金（制）的；金色的
golden [ˈgəuldən] *adj.* 金子般的；金色的
golf [gɔlf] *n.* 高尔夫球运动
good [gud] *adj.* 好的；优质的；令人满意的
goodbye [ˌgudˈbaɪ] int. 再见；告别
goodness [ˈgudnɪs] *n.* 良好；善良 *int.* 天哪
goods [guds] *n.* (pl.) 货物；商品
goose [guːs] *n.* (pl. geese) 鹅；鹅肉；笨蛋
gorgeous [ˈgɔːdʒəs] *adj.* 美丽的；华美的
gossip [ˈgɔsɪp] *n.* 流言；闲话；爱拨弄是非的人 *v.* 说长道短
gown [gaun] *n.* 女长服；礼服
grab [græb] *v.* / *n.* 抓（住）；夺（得）；攫取
grace [greɪs] *n.* 优美；高雅；魅力
graceful [ˈgreɪsful] *adj.* 优美的；文雅的
gracious [ˈgreɪʃəs] *adj.* 有礼貌的；仁慈的；和蔼的；豪华舒适的
grade [greɪd] *n.* 等级；成绩；年级；*v.* 分类
grain [greɪn] *n.* 谷粒；谷物；谷类
gram [græm] *n.* 克
grammar [ˈgræmə] *n.* 语法
grand [grænd] *adj.* 壮丽的；宏伟的；大的
grandmother [ˈgrændmʌðə] *n.*（外）祖母
grape [greɪp] *n.* 葡萄
graph [grɑːf] *n.* 图表；曲线图
graphic [ˈgræfɪk] *adj.* 绘画的；图表的；形象的 *n.* 图表；绘画作品
grass [grɑːs] *n.* 草；牧草；草地
grateful [ˈgreɪtful] *adj.* 感激的；感谢的
grave [greɪv] *n.* 坟墓
gravity [ˈgrævɪtɪ] *n.* 地心引力；重力
graze [greɪz] *v.*（让动物）吃草；放牧；擦伤 *n.*（表皮）擦伤
grease [griːs] *n.* 动物油脂 *v.* 涂油脂于；用油脂润滑
great [greɪt] *adj.* 伟大的；著名的；极大的；非常的 *adv.* 很好地 *n.* 伟人
greedy [ˈgriːdɪ] *adj.* 贪心的；贪婪的；渴望的
green [griːn] *adj.* / *n.* 绿色（的） *adj.* 未成熟的；没有经验的
greenhouse [ˈgriːnhaus] *n.* 温室；花房
greet [griːt] *v.* 欢迎；迎接；致意；问候
greeting [ˈgriːtɪŋ] *n.* 招呼；问候；祝贺；祝词
grey [greɪ] *adj.* (gray) 灰色（的） *n.* 灰色
grief [griːf] *n.* 悲伤；悲痛
grim [grɪm] *adj.* 严酷的；无情的；严厉的
grin [grɪn] *v.* / *n.* 咧嘴笑
grind [graɪnd] *v.* 磨碎；嚼碎 *n.* 磨；碾
grip [grɪp] *n.* 紧握；抓牢；掌握；控制
grocer [ˈgrəusə] *n.* 食品杂货商
grope [grəup] *v.* 摸索；探索
gross [grəus] *adj.* 总的；毛的；严重的 *adv.* 总共 *v.* 总收入为
ground [graund] *n.* 地面；场地；观点；立场
group [gruːp] *n.* 组；群；团体 *v.* 使成群
grow [grəu] *v.* 种植 *v.* 生长；发育
grown-up [ˈgrəunˈʌp] *adj.* 成人的 *n.* 成年人
growth [grəuθ] *n.* 生长；发育；增加；发展
guard [gɑːd] *v.* 保护；控制 *n.* 卫兵；看守
guess [ges] *v.* 猜想 *n.* 猜测； 猜想
guest [gest] *n.* 客人；宾客
guidance [ˈgaɪdəns] *n.* 指导；引导
guide [gaɪd] *v.* 指导；带领 *n.* 向导；指南

guilt [gɪlt] *n.* 内疚；罪行
guitar [gɪˈtɑː] *n.* 吉他；六弦琴
gulf [gʌlf] *n.* 海湾；鸿沟；分歧
gum [gʌm] *n.* 牙龈；口香糖
gun [gʌn] *n.* 枪；炮 *v.* 开枪；开炮
gut [gʌt] *n.* 勇气；胆量；消化道；肠道
guy [gaɪ] *n.* 家伙；伙计
gymnasium [dʒɪmˈneɪzɪəm] *n.*(gym) 健身房；体育馆

H

habit [ˈhæbɪt] *n.* 习惯；习性
hail [heɪl] *v.* 下雹；欢呼；欢迎 *n.* 雹
hair [hɛə] *n.* 头发；毛发；（动、植物的）毛
half [hɑːf] *adj.* / *adv.* / *n.* 一半（的）；半个（的）
hall [hɔːl] *n.* 门厅；走廊；礼堂
halt [hɔːlt] *v.* / *n.*（使）停止；阻止；中断
ham [hæm] *n.* 火腿
hamburger [ˈhæmbɜːgə] *n.* 汉堡包
hammer [ˈhæmə] *n.* 锤；铁榔头 *v.* 锤打
hand [hænd] *n.* 手；（钟表等的）指针 *v.* 递；交付；传给
handbook [ˈhændbuk] *n.* 手册；便览
handful [ˈhændful] *adj.* 一把；少数
handkerchief [ˈhæŋkətʃɪf] *n.* 手帕；纸巾
handle [ˈhændl] *v.* 处理；应付；对待 *n.* 手柄；把手
handsome [ˈhænsəm] *adj.*（男子）英俊的；（女子）清秀的；端庄健美的；数量多的
handwriting [ˈhændraɪtɪŋ] *n.* 书法；字迹
handy [ˈhændɪ] *adj.* 易使用的；便利的
hang [hæŋ] *v.* 悬；挂；垂下；（被）绞死；吊死
happen [ˈhæpən] *v.* 发生；碰巧；恰巧
happy [ˈhæpɪ] *adj.* 幸福的；愉快的；高兴的
harassment [ˈhærəsmənt] *n.* 骚扰
harbour [ˈhɑːbə] (harbor) *n.* 海港；港口 *v.* 庇护
hard [hɑːd] *adj.* 硬的；坚固的；结实的；艰苦的；努力的；严厉的 *adv.* 努力地；猛烈地
harden [ˈhɑːdn] *v.*（使）变硬；（使）坚固
hardly [ˈhɑːdlɪ] *adv.* 几乎没有；几乎不
hardship [ˈhɑːdʃɪp] *n.* 艰难；困苦
hardware [ˈhɑːdwɛə] *n.* 五金器具；硬件
harm [hɑːm] *n.* 损害；伤害 *v.*（使）受到损害
harvest [ˈhɑːvɪst] *n.* / *v.* 收割；收获
hasty [ˈheɪstɪ] *adj.* 仓促的；草率的
hat [hæt] *n.* 帽子
hatch [hætʃ] *v.* 孵化；孵出；策划；图谋
hate [heɪt] *v.* / *n.* 憎恨；讨厌
hatred [ˈheɪtrɪd] *n.* 仇恨；憎恶
haul [hɔːl] *v.* / *n.* 拖；拉；*v.* 运送
have [hæv] aux. / *v.* 有；持有
hawk [hɔːk] *n.* 鹰 *v.* 沿街叫卖
hay [heɪ] *n.* 干草
he [hiː] *pron.* 他
head [hed] *n.* 头部；领导 *v.* 朝……行进
headache [ˈhedeɪk] *n.* 头痛
heading [ˈhedɪŋ] *n.* 标题
headmaster [ˌhedˈmɑːstə] *n.* 校长
headquarters [ˌhedˈkwɔːtəz] *n.*（机构；企业等的）总部；总店
health [helθ] *n.* 健康（状况）；卫生
healthy [ˈhelθɪ] *adj.* 健康的；健壮的
heap [hiːp] *n.* 大量；许多 *v.* 堆积；堆满
hear [hɪə] *v.* 听到；听见；得知
hearing [ˈhɪərɪŋ] *n.* 听力；听觉
heart [hɑːt] *n.* 心；心脏
heat [hiːt] *n.* 高温；炎热 *v.* 加热
heave [hiːv] *v.*（用力）举起 *v.* / *n.* 拖；拉；抛
heaven [ˈhevn] *n.* 天堂；天国
heavy [ˈhevɪ] *adj.* 重的
hedge [hedʒ] *n.* 树篱 *v.* 用树篱围起；回避
heel [hiːl] *n.* 足跟；踵部；后跟
height [haɪt] *n.* 高度；身高；高处；高地
heir [ɛə] *n.* 继承人；传人
helicopter [ˈhelɪkɔptə] *n.* 直升机
hell [hel] *n.* 地狱；苦难的经历
hello [həˈləu] int. / *n.* 喂
helmet [ˈhelmɪt] *n.* 头盔
help [help] *v.* / *n.* 帮助；援助
helpful [ˈhelpful] *adj.* 有帮助的；有用的
hen [hen] *n.* 母鸡；雌禽
hence [hens] *adv.* 因此；所以
henceforth [ˌhensˈfɔːθ] *adv.* 从此以后

her [hɜː] *pron.* 她；她的
herb [hɜːb] *n.* 草本植物；药草；香草
herd [hɜːd] *n.* 兽群；牧群；人群；群众
here [hɪə] *adv.* 在这里；此时
hero [ˈhɪərəu] *n.* 英雄
heroic [hɪˈrəuɪk] *adj.* 有英雄气概的；英勇的
heroin [ˈherəʊɪn] *n.* 海洛因
heroine [ˈherəuɪn] *n.* 女英雄；女主角
hers [hɜːz] *pron.* 她的
herself [hɜːˈself] *pron.*（反身代词）她自己
hi [haɪ] int.（用作问候语）嘿；喂
hey [heɪ] int. 嘿；喂
hide [haɪd] *v.* 隐藏；隐瞒；掩盖
high [haɪ] *adj.* 高的；高度的
highland [ˈhaɪlənd] *adj.* 高地的；高原（地区）的 *n.* 高地；高原（地区）
highly [ˈhaɪlɪ] *adv.* 高度地；极其；非常
highway [ˈhaɪweɪ] *n.* 公路；交通要道
hijack [ˈhaɪdʒæk] *v.* 劫持；绑架
hike [haɪk] *n.* / *v.* 徒步旅行
hill [hɪl] *n.* 小山；山冈
him [hɪm] *pron.* 他
himself [hɪmˈself] *pron.* 他自己
hinge [hɪndʒ] *n.* 铰链 *v.* 给（某物）装上铰链
hip [hɪp] *n.* 臀部；屁股
his [hɪz] *pron.* 他的
historian [hɪsˈtɔːrɪən] *n.* 历史学家
history [ˈhɪstərɪ] *n.* 历史学；历史
hit [hɪt] *v.* 打；打击；碰撞 *n.* 击中；很受欢迎的人（或事物）
hobby [ˈhɔbɪ] *n.* 业余爱好
hoist [hɔɪst] *v.* / *n.* 吊起；提升 *n.* 起重机
hold [həuld] *v.* 抓住；拿着；托住；举行；继续 *n.* 握住；控制
holder [ˈhəuldə] *n.* 支持物；持有者
hole [həul] *n.* 洞；孔
holiday [ˈhɔlədɪ] *n.* 假期 *v.* 度假；休假
hollow [ˈhɔləu] *adj.* 空的；凹的 *n.* 洞；坑；凹地
holy [ˈhəulɪ] *adj.* 神圣的；圣洁的；虔诚的
home [həum] *n.* 家；住宅 *adv.* 回家；在家 *adj.* 家庭的；家用的；国内的
homework [ˈhəumwɜːk] *n.* 家庭作业
homogeneous [ˌhɒməˈdʒiːnɪəs] *adj.* 同性质的；同类的
honest [ˈɔnɪst] *adj.* 诚实的；正直的；可靠的
honey [ˈhʌnɪ] *n.* 蜂蜜；（口）亲爱的；宝贝
honour [ˈɔnə] (honor) *n.* / *v.* 尊敬 *n.* 荣誉
honourable [ˈɔnərəbl] *adj.* (honorable) 值得敬佩的；品格高尚的；尊敬的
hook [huk] *n.* 钩；吊钩；钩状物 *v.* 钩住
hop [hɔp] vi. 单足蹦跳；跳跃 *n.* 蹦跳；跳跃
hope [həup] *v.* / *n.* 希望；期望
hopeful [ˈhəupful] *adj.* 抱有希望的
horizontal [ˌhɔrɪˈzɔntəl] *adj.* 水平的；一致的；在地平线上的
horn [hɔːn] *n.* 角；触角；号角
horrible [ˈhɔrəbl] *adj.* 可怕的；令人恐惧的；可恶的；不友善的
horror [ˈhɔrə] *n.* 恐怖；恐惧；憎恶；痛恨
horse [hɔːs] *n.* 马
horsepower [ˈhɔːspauə] *n.* 马力
hose [həuz] *n.* 软管；胶管；*v.* 用水管冲洗
hospital [ˈhɔspɪtəl] *n.* 医院
host [həust] *n.* 东道主；主人；节目主持人
hostage [ˈhɔstɪdʒ] *n.* 人质
hostess [ˈhəustɪs] *n.* 女主人；空中小姐
hot [hɔt] *adj.* 热的；烫的；棘手的；争议大的
hotel [həuˈtel] *n.* 酒店；宾馆
hound [haund] *n.* 猎狗；猎犬 *v.* 追踪；纠缠
hour [ˈauə] *n.* 小时
house [haus] *n.* 住宅；房子
household [ˈhaushəuld] *n.* 一家人；户 *adj.* 家庭的；家用的
housewife [ˈhauswaɪf] *n.* 家庭主妇
housework [ˈhauswɜːk] *n.* 家务劳动
housing [ˈhauzɪŋ] *n.* 住房
hover [ˈhɔvə] *v.*（鸟等）盘旋；踌躇
how [hau] *adv.* 怎样；如何；怎么样
however [hauˈevə] *adv.* / *conj.* 然而；可是 不管怎样；无论如何
howl [haul] *n.* 嚎叫 *v.* 嚎叫；咆哮
huddle [ˈhʌdl] *v.* 聚集在一起；蜷缩 *n.* 挤在一起

的人（或事物）
hug [hʌg] v. / n. 拥抱；抱住；紧抱
huge [hjuːdʒ] adj. 巨大的；庞大的
hum [hʌm] v. 发出嗡嗡声；哼唱 n. 嗡嗡声
human [ˈhjuːmən] n. / adj. 人（的）；人类（的）
humanity [hjuːˈmænɪtɪ] n.（总称）人；人类
humid [ˈhjuːmɪd] adj. 潮湿的；湿气重的
humidity [hjuːˈmɪdɪtɪ] n. 湿度；潮湿；湿气
humour [ˈhjuːmə] n. (humor) 幽默；诙谐
humorous [ˈhjuːmərəs] adj. 幽默的；诙谐的
hundred [ˈhʌndrəd] num. 一百
hunger [ˈhʌŋgə] n. 饿；饥饿；欲望；渴望
hungry [ˈhʌŋgrɪ] adj. 饥饿的；渴望的
hunt [hʌnt] v. / n. 打猎；猎取；搜寻
hurl [hɜːl] v. 猛投；用力掷
hurricane [ˈhʌrɪkən] n. 飓风
hurry [ˈhʌrɪ] v. 催促；急忙 n. 匆忙；急忙
hurt [hɜːt] v.（使）受伤 adj. 受伤的 n. 伤、痛
husband [ˈhʌzbənd] n. 丈夫
hut [hʌt] n. 小屋；棚屋
hydrogen [ˈhaɪdrədʒən] n. 氢
hypocrisy [hɪˈpɔkrəsɪ] n. 伪善；虚伪
hysterical [hɪˈsterɪk(ə)l] adj. 歇斯底里的

I [aɪ] pron. 我
ice [aɪs] n. 冰 v. 冰冻；使成冰
ice-cream [ˈaɪskriːm] n. 冰激凌
idea [aɪˈdɪə] n. 想法；观念；主意
ideal [aɪˈdɪəl] adj. 完美的；理想的 n. 理想
identification [aɪˌdentɪfɪˈkeɪʃən] n. 识别；鉴别；证件；认同
idiom [ˈɪdɪəm] n. 习语；成语；方言
idiot [ˈɪdɪət] n. 笨蛋
idle [ˈaɪdl] adj. 懒散的；空闲的 v. 虚度
if [ɪf] conj. 是否；是不是
ignite [ɪgˈnaɪt] v. 点火；引燃
ignorance [ˈɪgnərəns] n. 无知；愚昧；不知道
ill [ɪl] adj. 有病的；坏的；不友好的 adv. 坏地；恶劣地
illness [ˈɪlnɪs] n. 病；疾病
illustration [ˌɪləˈstreɪʃ(ə)n] n. 插图；图解；示例
image [ˈɪmɪdʒ] n. 形象；印象；图像 v. 描绘……的形象
imaginary [ɪˈmædʒɪnərɪ] adj. 想象的；虚构的
imagination [ɪˌmædʒɪˈneɪʃən] n. 想像（力）；幻觉；创作力
imaginative [ɪˈmædʒɪnətɪv] adj. 富有想象力的
imitation [ˌɪmɪˈteɪʃən] n. 模仿；仿效；仿制（品）
immerse [ɪˈmɜːs] v. 使沉浸在；使浸没
impair [ɪmˈpeə] v. 损害；损伤；削弱；减少
impart [ɪmˈpɑːt] v. 传授；给予；告知；通知
impatient [ɪmˈpeɪʃənt] adj. 不耐烦的；急躁的
imperative [ɪmˈperətɪv] adj. 紧急的；极重要的；命令的 n. 紧急的事
imperial [ɪmˈpɪərɪəl] adj. 帝国的；帝王的
impetus [ˈɪmpɪtəs] n. 推动（力）；促进
importance [ɪmˈpɔːtəns] n. 重要；重要性
important [ɪmˈpɔːtənt] adj. 重要的；重大的
impossible [ɪmˈpɔsəbl] adj. 不可能的；难以处理的
impressive [ɪmˈpresɪv] adj. 给人深刻印象的；感人的
improve [ɪmˈpruːv] v. 改善；好转；进步
improvement [ɪmˈpruːvmənt] n. 改进；进步
in [ɪn] prep. 在……里 adv. 进；入
inch [ɪntʃ] n. 英寸
include [ɪnˈkluːd] v. 包括；包含；计入
income [ˈɪnkʌm] n. 收入；收益；所得
incorporate [ɪnˈkɔːpəreɪt] v. 合并；包含
increase [ɪnˈkriːs, ˈɪnkriːs] v. / n. 增加；增长
increasingly [ɪnˈkriːsɪŋlɪ] adv. 不断增加地；日益
incredible [ɪnˈkredəbl] adj. 不可相信的；惊人的；不可思议的
indeed [ɪnˈdiːd] adv. 确实；实在；真正地
index [ˈɪndeks] n. (pl.indexes, indices) 索引
indication [ˌɪndɪˈkeɪʃən] n. 指出；指示；表明
indicative [ɪnˈdɪkətɪv] adj. 指示的；暗示的
indignation [ˌɪndɪgˈneɪʃən] n. 愤怒；愤慨
indoor [ˈɪndɔː] adj. 室内的；户内的
induce [ɪnˈdjuːs] v. 引诱；劝使；引起；导致
indulge [ɪnˈdʌldʒ] v. 放任；纵容；沉迷

industrialize [ɪnˈdʌstrɪəlaɪz] *v.* (industrialise)(使)工业化
industry [ˈɪndəstrɪ] *n.* 工业;产业;勤劳
inertia [ɪˈnɜːʃɪə] *n.* 不活动;惰性;惯性
infant [ˈɪnfənt] *n.* 婴儿
infect [ɪnˈfekt] *v.* 传染;感染;影响(思想等)
infectious [ɪnˈfekʃəs] *adj.* 传染的;传染性的;有感染力的
influence [ˈɪnfluəns] *n.* / *v.* 影响;作用
information [ˌɪnfəˈmeɪʃən] *n.* 通知;报告;情报;资料;消息
infrared [ˌɪnfrəˈred] *adj.* / *n.* 红外线(的)
inject [ɪnˈdʒekt] *v.* 注射(药液等);注入
injure [ˈɪndʒə] *v.* 损害;损伤;伤害
injury [ˈɪndʒərɪ] *n.* 伤害;损害
ink [ɪŋk] *n.* 墨水;油墨
inland [ˈɪnlənd, ɪnˈlænd] *adj.* / *adv.* 国内;内地;内陆 *n.* 内陆;内地
inlet [ˈɪnlet] *n.* 水湾;小湾;入口
inn [ɪn] *n.* 小旅馆;客栈
inner [ˈɪnə] *adj.* 内部的;里面的;内心的
innumerable [ɪˈnjuːmərəbl] *adj.* 无数的;数不清的
input [ˈɪnput] *n.* / *v.* 输入
inquiry [ɪnˈkwaɪərɪ] *n.* (enquiry) 询问;打听;调查
insect [ˈɪnsekt] *n.* 昆虫
insert *v.* [ɪnˈsɜːt] 插入;嵌入 *n.* [ˈɪnsɜːt] 插入物;插页
inside [ˌɪnˈsaɪd] *adj.* 里面的 *adv.* 在里面 *n.* 内部 *prep.* 在……里
inspiration [ˌɪnspəˈreɪʃən] *n.* 灵感;鼓舞;激励
installation [ˌɪnstəˈleɪʃən] *n.* 安装;设置;设备
instance [ˈɪnstəns] *n.* 例子;事例;例证
instead [ɪnˈsted] *adv.* 代替;顶替
institute [ˈɪnstɪtjuːt, -tuːt] *n.* 学会;研究所;学院 *v.* 设立;设置;制定
instrument [ˈɪnstrəmənt] *n.* 工具;仪器;乐器
instrumental [ˌɪnstrəˈmentəl] *adj.* 仪器的;器械的;乐器的;起作用的;有帮助的
insulate [ˈɪnsjuleɪt] *v.* 隔离;孤立;使绝缘
intercourse [ˈɪntəkɔːs] *n.* 交流;交往;交际
interest [ˈɪntrɪst, ˈɪntər-] *n.* 兴趣;重要性;利益 *v.* 使发生兴趣
interesting [ˈɪntrɪstɪŋ, ˈɪntər-] *adj.* 有趣的;引人入胜的
interface [ˈɪntəfeɪs] *n.* 接合部位;分界面 *v.*(使)互相联系
interference [ˌɪntəˈfɪərəns] *n.* 干涉;干预;妨碍;打扰
interim [ˈɪntərɪm] *adj.* 中间的;暂时的;临时的 *n.* 过渡时期;暂定
intermittent [ˌɪntəˈmɪtənt] *adj.* 间歇的;断断续续的
international [ˌɪntəˈnæʃənəl] *adj.* 国际的;世界(性)的;跨国的
internet [ˈɪntənet] *n.* 国际互联网;因特网
interrupt [ɪntəˈrʌpt] *v.* 中断;阻碍;打断(话);打扰
intersection [ˌɪntəˈsekʃən] *n.* 交叉;道路交叉口;十字路口
interview [ˈɪntəvjuː] *v.* / *n.* 接见;会见;采访;面试
into [ˈɪntə] *prep.* 到……里面;进入
intrigue [ɪnˈtriːg] *n.* 阴谋;密谋 *v.* 密谋;激起……的兴趣
introduce [ˌɪntrəˈdjuːs] *v.* 介绍;引进;传入
introduction [ˌɪntrəˈdʌkʃən] *n.* 介绍;引言;传入;采用;引进
invaluable [ɪnˈvæljuəbl] *adj.* 非常宝贵的;无价的
invariably [ɪnˈveərɪəblɪ] *adv.* 不变地;一贯地
invent [ɪnˈvent] *v.* 发明;创造;虚构
invention [ɪnˈvenʃən] *n.* 发明;创造;发明物
inventory [ˈɪnvəntərɪ, -tɔːrɪ] *n.* 详细目录;清单;存货;库存
inverse [ˈɪnvɜːs, ɪnˈvɜːs] *adj.* 相反的;倒转的;反转的 *n.* 相反之物 *v.* 倒转
invert [ɪnˈvɜːt, ˈɪnvɜːt] *v.* 倒置;倒转;颠倒
invest [ɪnˈvest] *v.* 投资;投入(精力、时间等)
investment [ɪnˈvestmənt] *n.* 投资;投入
invitation [ˌɪnvɪˈteɪʃən] *n.* 邀请;招待;请柬
invite [ɪnˈvaɪt, ˈɪnvaɪt] *v.* 邀请;招待
inward [ˈɪnwəd] *adj.* / *adv.* 向内(的) *n.* 内部
iron [ˈaɪən] *n.* 铁;熨斗 *v.* 熨(衣);熨平
irony [ˈaɪrənɪ] *n.* 反语;讽刺

irrespective [ˌɪrɪˈspektɪv] *adj.* 不顾的；不考虑的
island [ˈaɪlənd] *n.* 岛；岛屿
isle [aɪl] *n.* 小岛（常用于诗歌中）
isolate [ˈaɪsəleɪt] *v.* 隔离；孤立
issue [ˈɪʃuː] *n.* 问题；争端；发行（物） *v.* 发行；颁布
it [ɪt] *pron.* 它
its [ɪts] *pron.* 它的
itself [ɪtˈself] *pron.* 它自己；它本身

J

jacket [ˈdʒækɪt] *n.* 夹克衫
jam [dʒæm] *n.* 阻塞；果酱 *v.*（使）阻塞
January [ˈdʒænjuəri] *n.* 一月
jar [dʒɑː] *n.* 罐坛；广口瓶
jargon [ˈdʒɑːgən] *n.* 行话
jaw [dʒɔː] *n.* 颌；颚
jazz [dʒæz] *n.* 爵士乐
jealous [ˈdʒeləs] *adj.* 妒忌的；猜疑的
jeans [dʒinz] *n.* 牛仔裤
jet [dʒet] *n.* 喷气式飞机；喷嘴 *v.* 喷射
jewel [ˈdʒuːəl] *n.* 宝石；宝石饰物
jewelry [ˈdʒuːəlrɪ] *n.* (jewllery) 珠宝
job [dʒɔb] *n.* 工作；职位；任务；职责
jog [dʒɔg] *v.* 慢跑
join [dʒɔɪn] *v.* 参加；加入；联合；连接
joint [dʒɔɪnt] *n.* 接合处；接头；关节 *adj.* 联合的；共同的；连接的
joke [dʒəuk] *n.* 笑话；玩笑 *v.* 开玩笑
jolly [ˈdʒɔlɪ] *adj.* 欢乐的；高兴的
journey [ˈdʒɜːnɪ] *n.* 旅行；旅程 *v.* 旅行
joy [dʒɔɪ] *n.* 欢欣；高兴；乐趣
judgement [ˈdʒʌdʒmənt] *n.* (judgment) 审判；判决；判断（力）；看法；意见
judicial [dʒuːˈdɪʃəl] *adj.* 司法的；法庭的；审判的；明断的；公正的
jug [dʒʌg] *n.*（有柄）大壶；罐；盂
juice [dʒuːs] *n.*（水果等）汁；液
July [dʒuˈlaɪ] *n.* 七月
jump [dʒʌmp] *v.* / *n.* 跳跃；跳动；猛增
junction [ˈdʒʌŋkʃən] *n.*（公路或铁路的）连接点；交叉路口
June [dʒuːn] *n.* 六月
jungle [ˈdʒʌŋg(ə)l] *n.* 丛林；生死地带
junior [ˈdʒuːnjə] *adj.* 年少的；下级（的）地位低下的；青少年的 *n.* 职位较低者；青少年
junk [dʒʌŋk] *n.* 废旧杂物；垃圾
just [dʒʌst] *adv.* 仅仅；正好；刚好 *adj.* 公正的；合适的

K

keen [kiːn] *adj.* 渴望；喜爱的；热情的
keep [kiːp] *v.* 保持；保存；遵守；维持
kettle [ˈketl] *n.* 水壶
key [kiː] *n.* 钥匙；答案；关键；键盘 *adj.* 主要的；关键的
keyboard [ˈkiːbɔːd] *n.* 键盘
kick [kɪk] *n.* / *v.* 踢
kid [kɪd] *n.* 小孩；儿童
kidnap [ˈkɪdnæp] *v.* 诱拐；绑架；劫持
kidney [ˈkɪdnɪ] *n.* 肾；肾脏
kill [kɪl] *v.* 杀死；消灭；毁灭；消磨（时间）
kilo [ˈkiːləu] *n.* (kilogram) 千克；公斤
kilometre [kɪˈlɒmɪtə] *n.* (kilometer) 公里；千米
kin [kɪn] *n.* 家族；亲属 *adj.* 亲属关系的
kind [kaɪnd] *adj.* 仁慈的；友好的 *n.* 种类
kindergarten [ˈkɪndəgɑːt(ə)n] *n.* 幼儿园
kindness [ˈkaɪndnɪs] *n.* 仁慈；亲切；友好
king [kɪŋ] *n.* 君主；国王
kingdom [ˈkɪŋdəm] *n.* 王国；领域
kiss [kɪs] *n.* / *v.* 吻；接吻
kit [kɪt] *n.* 成套工具；用具包；工具箱
kitchen [ˈkɪtʃɪn] *n.* 厨房
kite [kaɪt] *n.* 风筝
knee [niː] *n.* 膝；膝盖
kneel [niːl] *v.* 跪；下跪
knife [naɪf] *n.* 餐刀；刀子；刀具
knit [nɪt] *v.* 编织；编结；接合；黏合
knob [nɔb] *n.* 门把；（球形）把手；旋钮
knock [nɔk] *v.* 敲；敲打；碰撞 *n.* 敲；击
knot [nɔt] *n.*（用绳索等打的）结 *v.* 打结
know [nəu] *v.* 知道；了解；认识

knowledge [ˈnɒlɪdʒ] *n.* 知识；知道；了解

L

lab [læb] *n.* (laboratory) 实验室
labour [ˈleɪbə] *n.* (labor) 劳动；劳动力 *v.* 劳作
lace [leɪs] *n.* 花边；鞋带 *v.* 系带
lack [læk] *n.* / *v.* 缺乏；不足
lad [læd] *n.* 男孩；小伙子
ladder [ˈlædə] *n.* 梯子；阶梯
lady [ˈleɪdɪ] *n.* 女士；夫人
lake [leɪk] *n.* 湖泊；湖水
lamb [læm] *n.* 羔羊；小羊；羔羊肉
lame [leɪm] *adj.* 跛的；（辩解、论据等）无说服力的
lamp [læmp] *n.* 灯
land [lænd] *n.* 陆地；土地 *v.*（使）靠岸
landlady [ˈlændleɪdɪ] *n.* 女房东；女地主
landlord [ˈlændlɔːd] *n.* 房东；地主
lane [leɪn] *n.* 小路；小巷；行车道
language [ˈlæŋgwɪdʒ] *n.* 语言；语言文字
lantern [ˈlæntən] *n.* 灯；灯笼
lap [læp] *n.* 大腿；（跑道的）一圈 *v.* 轻拍；（动物）舔食
lapse [læps] *n.* 过失；小失误；暂停；中断 *v.* 失效；中止；结束
laptop [ˈlæptɒp] *n.* 笔记本电脑
large [lɑːdʒ] *adj.* 大的；广大的；大规模的
largely [ˈlɑːdʒlɪ] *adv.* 很大程度上；主要地
laser [ˈleɪzə] *n.* 激光
lash [læʃ] *v.* 鞭打；猛击；抨击 *n.* 睫毛；鞭打
last [lɑːst] *adj.* 最后的；最近的；上一个的 *adv.* 最近；上次；最后 *n.* 最后 *v.* 持续
late [leɪt] *adj.* 迟的；晚的 *adv.* 迟；晚
lately [ˈleɪtlɪ] *adv.* 最近；不久前
latent [ˈleɪtənt] *adj.* 潜在的；潜伏的
later [ˈleɪtə] *adv.* / *adj.* 后来（的）；以后（的）
Latin [lætɪn] *adj.* 拉丁的；拉丁文的 *n.* 拉丁语
latitude [ˈlætɪtjuːd] *n.* 纬度；纬度地区
latter [ˈlætə] *adj.* 后者的 *n.* 后者
laugh [lɑːf] *v.* 笑；嘲笑 *n.* 笑；笑声
laughter [ˈlɑːftə] *n.* 笑；笑声
laundry [ˈlɔːndrɪ] *n.* 洗衣物；洗衣房（店）
lavatory [ˈlævətərɪ] *n.* 厕所；盥洗室
law [lɔː] *n.* 法律；法规；法学
lawn [lɔːn] *n.* 草地；草坪
lawyer [ˈlɔːjə] *n.* 律师
lay [leɪ] *v.* 放；搁；下（蛋）；铺设；布置
layer [ˈleɪə] *n.* 层；层次；等级；铺设者
layman [ˈleɪmən] *n.* 外行
layoff [ˈleɪɒf] *n.* 解雇；休养；停工期
layout [ˈleɪaʊt] *n.* 安排；布局；设计；布局图
lazy [ˈleɪzɪ] *adj.* 懒惰的；懒散的
lead [liːd] *v.* 引领；通向；导致 *n.* 领先地位；铅
leaf [liːf] *n.* 叶子；（书刊的）一页；一张
leaflet [ˈliːflɪt] *n.* 小叶；嫩叶；传单；活页
leak [liːk] *v.* / *n.* 泄漏 *n.* 漏洞
lean [liːn] *v.* 倾斜；屈身；倚 *adj.* 瘦的；无脂肪的
leap [liːp] *v.* 跳；跳跃 *n.* 跳跃；飞跃
learn [lɜːn] *v.* 学习；学会；听到；获悉
learned [ˈlɜːnɪd] *adj.* 博学的；有学问的
learning [ˈlɜːnɪŋ] *n.* 知识；学问；学习
lease [liːs] *v.* 出租；租用 *n.* 租借；租赁物
least [liːst] *adj.* / *adv.* 最少（的）
leather [ˈleðə] *n.* 皮革；皮革制品
leave [liːv] *v.* 离开；留下；遗忘 *n.* 许可；假期
lecture [ˈlektʃə] *n.* / *v.* 演讲；讲课
left [left] *n.* 左面（方） *adj.* 左边的；剩余的
leg [leg] *n.* 腿部；支柱；（旅程的）一段
legend [ˈledʒənd] *n.* 传说；传奇
lemon [ˈlemən] *n.* 柠檬
lend [lend] *v.* 借给；贷（款）
length [leŋθ] *n.* 长度；细长的一段
lens [lenz] *n.* 透镜；镜头
less [les] *adj.* / *adv.* 更少的（地）
lesson [ˈlesən] *n.*（功）课；课程；教训
lest [lest] *conj.* 唯恐；免得
let [let] *v.* 让；允许；假设；出租；租给
letter [ˈletə] *n.* 信；函件；字母；文字
lever [ˈliːvə] *n.* 杆；杠杆；手段；途径；工具
levy [ˈlevɪ] *n.* 税款；征兵 *v.* 征收；征税
liberty [ˈlɪbətɪ] *n.* 自由；自由权；选择自由
librarian [laɪˈbreərɪən] *n.* 图书管理员

library [ˈlaɪbrərɪ] *n.* 图书馆；藏书；丛书
lick [lɪk] *v.* 舔；掠过；打败 *n.* 舔；少量
lid [lɪd] *n.* 盖
lie [laɪ] *v.* 躺；平卧；位于 *v.* 说谎 *n.* 谎话
life [laɪf] *n.* 生命；生活；生物；寿命 *adj.* 生命的；一生的
lifetime [ˈlaɪftaɪm] *n.* 一生；终生
lift [lɪft] *v.* 升起；举起；撤销 *n.* 电梯；上升；免费搭车
light [ˈlaɪt] *n.* 光；灯 *v.* 点燃；照亮 *adj.* 轻(快)；清淡的；明亮
lightning [ˈlaɪtnɪŋ] *n.* 闪电 *adj.* 闪电般的；快速的
like [laɪk] *v.* 喜欢 *prep.* 像；比如 *adj.* 相像的 *n.* 喜好
likely [ˈlaɪklɪ] *adj.* 很可能的 *adv.* 大概；多半
limb [lɪm] *n.* 肢；翼；大树枝
limp [lɪmp] *adj.* 柔软的；无力的 *v.* / *n.* 蹒跚；跛行
line [laɪn] *n.* 线；路线；航线；排；线路；界线 *v.* 排队；加衬
linear [ˈlɪnɪə] *adj.* 线的；直线的；线状的；长度的；线性的
linen [ˈlɪnɪn] *n.* 亚麻布；亚麻布制品
liner [ˈlaɪnə] *n.* 邮船；内衬；衬里
linger [ˈlɪŋgə] *v.* 逗留；徘徊；消磨
link [lɪŋk] *v.* 连接；联系 *n.* 环节；链环
lion [ˈlaɪən] *n.* 狮子
lip [lɪp] *n.* 嘴唇
liquid [ˈlɪkwɪd] *n.* 液体 *adj.* 液体的；液态的
liquor [ˈlɪkə] *n.* 酒；溶液；液剂
list [lɪst] *n.* 表；名单 *v.* 列清单
listen [ˈlɪsən] *v.* 听；倾听
literacy [ˈlɪtərəsɪ] *n.* 有文化；有读写能力
litre [ˈliːtə] *n.*(liter) 升；公升(容量单位)
litter [ˈlɪtə] *n.* 垃圾 *v.* 乱丢；使杂乱
little [ˈlɪtl] *adj.* 小的；不多的 *adv.* / *n.* 极少；几乎没有
live [lɪv] *v.* 活着；生活；居住 *adj.* 活的；生动的；直播的
lively [ˈlaɪvlɪ] *adj.* 活泼的；活跃的；栩栩如生的；真实的
liver [ˈlɪvə] *n.* 肝；肝脏
living [ˈlɪvɪŋ] *adj.* 活的；居住的 *n.* 生活；生计
living-room [ˈlɪvɪŋ ruːm] *n.* 起居室；客厅
load [ləud] *v.* 装(货)；装载 *n.* 装载(量)；负荷
loaf [ləuf] *n.* 一条；一块(面包)
loan [ləun] *n.* 贷款；出借 *v.* 借出
local [ˈləukəl] *adj.* 地方的；当地的；局部的
locality [ləuˈkælətɪ] *n.* 位置；地点
lock [lɔk] *n.* 锁 *v.* 锁；锁上
locker [ˈlɔkə] *n.* 更衣箱
locomotive [ˌləukəˈməutɪv] *n.* 机车；火车头 *adj.* 运动的；移动的
lodge [lɔdʒ] *v.* 借住；寄住；寄存 *n.* 小屋
lofty [ˈlɔftɪ] *adj.* 巍峨的；高耸的；崇高的
log [lɔg] *n.* 原木；圆木；航海日志
logic [ˈlɔdʒɪk] *n.* 逻辑；逻辑学
lonely [ˈləunlɪ] *adj.* 孤独的；寂寞的；荒凉的
long [lɔŋ] *adj.* 长的；长期的 *adv.* 长久地 *v.* 渴望 *n.* 长时间
longitude [ˈlɔngɪtjuːd] *n.* 经度
look [luk] *v.* / *n.* 看 *v.* 好像 *n.* 外表；脸色
loop [luːp] *n.* 圈；环
loose [luːs] *adj.* 松的；宽松的；不精确的
loosen [ˈluːsən] *v.*(使)变松；放宽
lord [lɔːd] *n.* 领主；君主；贵族；上帝
lorry [ˈlɔːrɪ] *n.* 卡车；运货汽车
lose [luːz] *v.* 丢失；迷路；输掉；失败
loss [lɔs, lɔːs] *n.* 亏损；丧失；损失；损耗
lot [lɔt] *n.* 许多；大量；非常；抽签；场地
loud [laud] *adj.* 大声的；响亮的；吵闹的
loudspeaker [ˌlaudˈspiːkə] *n.* 扬声器；扩音器
lounge [laundʒ] *n.* 休息室；起居室
love [lʌv] *n.* 爱；爱情 *v.* 爱；热爱；喜欢
lovely [ˈlʌvlɪ] *adj.* 可爱的；好看的；美好的
lover [ˈlʌvə] *n.* 情人；爱好者
low [ləu] *adj.* 低的；矮的；低等的；在底部的 *n.* 低点；(人生的)低谷
lower [ˈləuə] *adj.* 较低的；下级的；下游的 *v.* 降下；放低
lubricate [ˈluːbrɪkeɪt] *v.* 润滑；给……加润滑油；促进
luck [lʌk] *n.* 运气；好运；侥幸

lucky [ˈlʌkɪ] *adj.* 幸运的；侥幸的
luggage [ˈlʌɡɪdʒ] *n.* 行李；皮箱
lumber [ˈlʌmbə] *n.* 木材；木料
lump [lʌmp] *n.* 团；块 *v.*（使）成团；（使）成块
lunar [ˈluːnə] *adj.* 月亮的
lunch [lʌntʃ] *n.* 午餐
lung [lʌŋ] *n.* 肺
lure [luə] *n.* 诱惑（物） *v.* 引诱；吸引

M

machine [məˈʃiːn] *n.* 机器；机械
machinery [məˈʃiːnərɪ] *n.* 机器；机械
mad [mæd] *adj.* 发疯的；狂热的；生气的
madame [ˈmædəm] *n.* (madam) 夫人；女士
magazine [ˌmæɡəˈziːn] *n.* 杂志；期刊
magic [ˈmædʒɪk] *n.* 魔术；巫术 *adj.* 有魔力的；魔术的
magistrate [ˈmædʒɪstreɪt] *n.* 地方行政官；地方法官；治安官
magnet [ˈmæɡnɪt] *n.* 磁体；磁铁
magnetic [mæɡˈnetɪk] *adj.* 磁的；有磁性的；有吸引力的
maid [meɪd] *n.* 少女；女仆
maiden [ˈmeɪdən] *n.* 少女 *adj.* 未婚的
mail [meɪl] *n.* 邮件 *v.* 邮寄
main [meɪn] *adj.* 主要的 *n.* 总管道；干线
mainland [ˈmeɪnlənd] *n.* 大陆；本土
maintenance [ˈmeɪntənəns] *n.* 维修；保养；维持；生活费用
majesty [ˈmædʒɪstɪ] *n.* 雄伟；壮丽；王权
make [meɪk] *n.* 品牌；型号；制法 *v.* 制造；做；使变得
male [meɪl] *n.* / *adj.* 男性（的）；雄性（的）
malignant [məˈlɪɡnənt] *adj.* 恶性的；致命的；恶意的；恶毒的
mammal [ˈmæməl] *n.* 哺乳动物
man [mæn] *n.* 人；人类；男人
maneuver [məˈnuːvə] *n.* (manoeuvre) *n.* 策略；手段 *v.* 操纵；部署
mankind [mænˈkaɪnd] *n.* 人类
many [ˈmenɪ] det. / *pron.* /.*adj.* 许多（的）
map [mæp] *n.* 地图 *v.* 绘制地图
marble [ˈmɑːbl] *n.* 大理石；云石
march [mɑːtʃ] *v.* 行军；快步走 *n.* 行军；行程
March [mɑːtʃ] *n.* 三月（略作 Mar.)
marginal [ˈmɑːdʒɪnəl] *adj.* 记在页边的；旁注的；边缘的
mark [mɑːk] *n.* 痕迹；记号；分数 *v.* 标记；打分
market [ˈmɑːkɪt] *n.* 集市；市场 *v.* 销售
married [ˈmærɪd] *adj.* 已婚的；与……结婚的
marry [ˈmærɪ] *v.* 结婚；嫁；娶
marvelous [ˈmɑːvələs] *adj.* (marvellous) 惊人的；奇迹般的；妙极的
Marxist [ˈmɑːksɪst] *adj.* 马克思主义的 *n.* 马克思主义者
masculine [ˈmæskjulɪn] *adj.* 男性的；阳钢的
mask [mɑːsk] *n.* 面具；伪装 *v.* 掩饰；化装
mass [mæs] *n.* 大量；众多；团；块；(pl.) 群众；民众；质量
mat [mæt] *n.* 席子；垫子
match [mætʃ] *n.* 火柴；比赛；竞赛；对手；配偶 *v.* 匹配；相称
mate [meɪt] *n.* 同伴；同事；配偶 *v.* 结伴；配对
mathematical [ˌmæθɪˈmætɪkəl] *adj.* 数有关数学的；具有数学头脑的
maths [mæθs] *n.* (mathematics/ math) 数学
matter [ˈmætə] *n.* 物质；物体；毛病；麻烦；事情 *v.* 有关系；要紧
may [meɪ] aux. / *v.* 可能；也许；祝；愿
May [meɪ] *n.* 五月
maybe [ˈmeɪbɪ] *adv.* 可能；大概；也许
mayor [ˈmeə] *n.* 市长
me [miː] *pron.* 我
meadow [ˈmedəu] *n.* 草地；牧场
meal [miːl] *n.* 膳食；一餐
meat [miːt] *n.*（食用）肉类
mechanic [məˈkænɪk] *n.* 技工；机修工
medal [ˈmedəl] *n.* 奖章；勋章；纪念章
medical [ˈmedɪkəl] *adj.* 医学的；医疗的；内科的 *n.* 健康检查
medicine [ˈmedɪsɪn] *n.* 医药；医学
medieval [ˌmedɪˈiːv(ə)l] *adj.* 中世纪的

meditation [ˌmedɪˈteɪʃən] *n.* 冥想；沉思
meet [miːt] *n.* 会；赛事 *v.* 遇见；会谈
meeting [ˈmiːtɪŋ] *n.* 会议；集合；汇合（点）
melody [ˈmelədɪ] *n.* 旋律；曲调；悦耳的音乐
melon [ˈmelən] *n.* 甜瓜
melt [melt] *v.*（使）融化；（使）熔化
member [ˈmembə] *n.* 成员；会员
membership [ˈmembəʃɪp] *n.* 会员身份
memo [ˈmeməu] *n.* (memorandum) 备忘录
memory [ˈmemərɪ] *n.* 记忆；回忆；存储（器）
menace [ˈmenəs] *v.* / *n.* 有危险性的人（或物）；威胁；威吓
mend [mend] *v.* 修理；缝补；改正；改进
menu [ˈmenjuː] *n.* 菜单
merchandise [ˈmɜːtʃəndaɪz] *n.* 商品；货物
merchant [ˈmɜːtʃənt] *n.* 商人；零售商
mercury [ˈmɜːkjurɪ] *n.* 水银；汞
mercy [ˈmɜːsɪ] *n.* 仁慈；怜悯；宽恕
merely [ˈmɪəlɪ] *adv.* 仅仅；只不过
merry [ˈmerɪ] *adj.* 欢乐的；愉快的
mess [mes] *n.* 混乱；脏乱 *v.* 弄乱；搞糟
message [ˈmesɪdʒ] *n.* 消息；信息
messenger [ˈmesɪndʒə] *n.* 送信者；使者
metal [ˈmetəl] *n.* 金属；金属制品
metaphor [ˈmetəfə] *n.* 隐喻；暗喻
metre [ˈmiːtə] *n.* (meter) 米；计量器
metric [ˈmetrɪk] *adj.* 米制的；公制的
microphone [ˈmaɪkrəfəun] *n.* 话筒；扩音器
microscope [ˈmaɪkrəskəup] *n.* 显微镜
middle [ˈmɪdl] *n.* / *adj.* 中间（的）；当中（的）
midst [mɪdst] *n.* 中间；当中
might [maɪt] aux. / *v.* 可能；也许 *n.* 力量；威力
mild [maɪld] *adj.* 温和的；温暖的；味淡的
mile [maɪl] *n.* 英里
milk [mɪlk] *n.* 牛奶 *v.* 挤奶
mill [mɪl] *n.* 磨粉机；磨坊；作坊；工厂
millimeter [ˈmɪlɪmiːtə] *n.* (millimetre) 毫米
million [ˈmɪljən] *num.* 百万
millionaire [ˌmɪljəˈneə] *n.* 百万富翁
mind [maɪnd] *n.* 精神；理智 *v.* 注意；介意
mine [maɪn] *pron.* 我的 *n.* 矿 *v.* 采矿
mineral [ˈmɪnərəl] *n.* 矿物；矿石 *adj.* 矿物的
mingle [ˈmɪŋgl] *v.*（使）混合
miniature [ˈmɪnɪtʃə] *n.* 缩小的模型；缩图 *adj.* 微型的；缩小的
ministry [ˈmɪnɪstrɪ] *n.*（政府的）部；牧师
minor [ˈmaɪnə] *adj.* 较小的；次要的；轻微的
minus [ˈmaɪnəs] *adj.* 负的；减的 *prep.* 减去
minute [ˈmɪnɪt] *n.* 分钟；片刻
miracle [ˈmɪrək(ə)l] *n.* 奇迹；不可思议的事
mirror [ˈmɪrə] *n.* 镜子；写照 *v.* 反映；反射
mischief [ˈmɪstʃɪf] *n.* 恶作剧；捣乱
miss [mɪs] *n.* 小姐 *v.* 思念；错过；漏掉
missile [ˈmɪsaɪl, -s(ə)l] *n.* 导弹；发射物
missing [ˈmɪsɪŋ] *adj.* 漏掉的；失去的；失踪的
missionary [ˈmɪʃənərɪ] *adj.* 传教的 *n.* 传教士
mist [mɪst] *n.* 薄雾；水汽
mistake [mɪˈsteɪk] *n.* 错误；失误 *v.* 误解；误会
mistress [ˈmɪstrɪs] *n.* 女主人；主妇；女士
misunderstand [ˌmɪsʌndəˈstænd] *v.* 误解；误会
mix [mɪks] *v.* 使混合；混淆
moan [məun] *n.* 呻吟声 *v.* 呻吟；抱怨
mob [mɔb] *n.* 人群；（尤指）暴民 *v.* 围攻
model [ˈmɔdəl] *n.* 样式；型；模范；模型；原型；模特 *v.* 使模仿
modern [ˈmɔdən] *adj.* 现代的；近代的
modernization [ˌmɔdənaɪˈzeɪʃən] *n.*(modernisation) 现代化
module [ˈmɔdjuːl] *n.* 组件；模块；模件；（航天器的）舱
moist [mɔɪst] *adj.* 潮湿的；湿润的；多雨的
moisture [ˈmɔɪstʃə] *n.* 潮气；水分
molecule [ˈmɔlɪkjuːl] *n.* 分子
moment [ˈməumənt] *n.* 片刻；瞬间；时刻
Monday [ˈmʌndɪ] *n.* 星期一
money [ˈmʌnɪ] *n.* 货币；钱
monitor [ˈmɔnɪtə] *n.* 班长；监视器 *v.* 监控
monkey [ˈmʌŋkɪ] *n.* 猴子
monster [ˈmɔnstə] *n.* 怪物；妖怪
month [mʌnθ] *n.* 月；月份
monthly [ˈmʌnθlɪ] *adj.* 每月的 *adv.* 每月一次；按月 *n.* 月刊

monument [ˈmɔnjumənt] *n.* 纪念碑；纪念馆遗址 *v.* 为……树碑

moon [muːn] *n.* 月球；月亮；卫星

more [mɔː] *adj.* / *adv.* / pron 更多（的）；更大（的）*n.* 更多的人（或东西）

moreover [mɔːˈrəuvə] *adv.* 此外；而且

morning [ˈmɔːnɪŋ] *n.* 早晨；上午

mosaic [məuˈzeɪɪk] *n.* 马赛克

mosquito [məˈskiːtəu] *n.* 蚊子

moss [mɔs] *n.* 苔；藓；地衣

most [məust] det. / *pron.* 最多；最大 *adv.* 尤其；最

mostly [ˈməustlɪ] *adv.* 多半；主要地

motel [məuˈtel] *n.*（附有停车场的）汽车旅馆

mother [ˈmʌðə] *n.* 母亲

motor [ˈməutə] *n.* 发动机；电动机

mould [məuld] *n.* 模具；铸型 *v.* 浇铸；塑造

mount [maunt] *v.* 登上；安装 *n.* 山峰；底座

mountain [ˈmauntɪn] *n.* 山

mourn [mɔːn, məun] *v.* 哀悼；忧伤

mouse [maus] *n.* (pl. mice) 鼠；耗子

mouth [mauθ] *n.* 口；嘴

move [muːv] *v.* / *n.* 移动；活动；搬家 *v.* 感动

movement [ˈmuːvmənt] *n.* 运动；移动；迁移

movie [ˈmuːvɪ] *n.* 电影；电影院

much [mʌtʃ] det. / *pron.* 许多；大量 *adv.* 非常；很

mud [mʌd] *n.* 泥；泥浆 *v.* 弄脏；使沾污泥

mug [mʌg] *n.*（有柄的）大茶杯

multitude [ˈmʌltɪtjuːd] *n.* 众多；大量

murder [ˈmɜːdə] *v.* / *n.* 谋杀；凶杀

murmur [ˈmɜːmə] *v.* / *n.* 低语；私下抱怨；咕哝

muscle [ˈmʌsl] *n.* 肌肉；体力

museum [mjuˈziːəm] *n.* 博物馆；展览馆

mushroom [ˈmʌʃrum] *n.* 蘑菇 *v.* 迅速生长

music [ˈmjuːzɪk] *n.* 音乐；乐曲；乐谱

musical [ˈmjuːzɪkəl] *adj.* 音乐的；有音乐才能的 *n.* 音乐剧

musician [mjuːˈzɪʃən] *n.* 音乐家；乐师

must [mʌst] *aux.* 必须；很可能；一定要 *n.* 必须做的事

mute [mjuːt] *adj.* 哑的；缄默的 *n.* 哑巴；弱音器 *v.* 减弱；消音

mutton [ˈmʌtən] *n.* 羊肉

my [maɪ] *pron.* 我的

myself [maɪˈself] *pron.* 我自己；我亲自

N

nail [neɪl] *n.* 钉子；钉状物

naive [nɑːˈiːv] *adj.* 天真的；幼稚的

naked [ˈneɪkɪd] *adj.* 裸露的

name [neɪm] *n.* 名字；名称；名声

namely [ˈneɪmlɪ] *adv.* 即；也就是

nap [næp] *n.* / *v.* 小睡；打盹

napkin [ˈnæpkɪn] *n.* 餐巾

narrow [ˈnærəu] *adj.* 狭窄的；狭隘的 *v.*（使）变窄

nation [ˈneɪʃən] *n.* 国家

national [ˈnæʃənəl] *adj.* 国家的；民族的；全国性的；国民的 *n.* 国民；全国性比赛

nationality [ˌnæʃəˈnælɪtɪ] *n.* 国籍

nature [ˈneɪtʃə] *n.* 大自然；自然界；天性

naughty [ˈnɔːtɪ] *adj.* 顽皮的；不听话的

naval [ˈneɪvəl] *adj.* 海军的

navy [ˈneɪvɪ] *n.* 海军

near [nɪə] *adv.* 在附近 *prep.* 在……附近 *adj.* 近的；不远的

nearby [ˈnɪəbaɪ] *adj.* / *adv.* 附近的（地）

nearly [ˈnɪəlɪ] *adv.* 几乎；差不多

neat [niːt] *adj.* 整洁的；简洁的

necessary [ˈnesɪsərɪ] *adj.* 必要的；必需的 *n.* 必需品

neck [nek] *n.* 颈；脖子；领圈；领口

necklace [ˈneklɪs] *n.* 项链

need [niːd] *v.* 需要 *n.* 需要；需求

needle [ˈniːdl] *n.* 针；针状物

Negro [ˈniːgrəu] *n.*（含歧视）黑人

neighbour [ˈneɪbə] *n.* (neighbor) 邻居

neighbourhood [ˈneɪbəhud] *n.* (neighborhood) 社区；邻近的地方

neither [ˈnɪðə, ˈnaɪ-] *pron.* 两者都不 *adv.* / *conj.* 也不

nephew [ˈnefjuː] *n.* 侄子；外甥

nervous [ˈnɜːvəs] *adj.* 害怕的；神经紧张的

nest [nest] *n.*（鸟）窝；巢 *v.* 筑巢

net [net] *n.* 网；网状物 *v.* 用网捕；净赚 *adj.* 净得的；纯的
network [ˈnetwɜːk] *n.* 网络；广播网；电视网
neutral [ˈnjuːtrəl] *adj.* 中立的；不偏不倚的 *n.* 中立人士；中立国
never [ˈnevə] *adv.* 从不；永不；从来没有
nevertheless [ˌnevəðəˈles] *adv.* 然而；不过
nonetheless [ˌnʌnðəˈles] *adv.* 虽然如此；但是
new [njuː] *adj.* 新的；新出现的
news [njuːz] *n.* 新闻；消息
newspaper [ˈnjuːzpeɪpə] *n.* 报纸
next [nekst] *adj.* 下一个的；接下来的 *adv.* 紧接着 *n.* 下一个
nice [naɪs] *adj.* 美好的；美妙的；好心的
nickel [ˈnɪkəl] *n.* 镍；（美国和加拿大的）五分镍币；五分钱
nickname [ˈnɪkneɪm] *n.* 绰号；诨名；昵称
niece [niːs] *n.* 侄女；外甥女
night [naɪt] *n.* 夜；夜晚
nightmare [ˈnaɪtmeə] *n.* 噩梦；可怕的事情
nine [naɪn] *num.* 九
nineteen [naɪnˈtiːn] *num.* 十九
ninety [ˈnaɪntɪ] *num.* 九十
nitrogen [ˈnaɪtrədʒən] *n.* 氮；氮气
no [nəu] *adv.* 不；毫不 *adj.* 没有 *n.* 否定
noble [ˈnəubl] *adj.* 高尚的；雄伟的 *n.* 贵族
nobody [ˈnəubədɪ] *pron.* 没有人 *n.* 小人物
nod [nɔd] *v.* 点头；打盹；打瞌睡 *n.* 点头
noise [nɔɪz] *n.* 噪声；喧哗声；声音；响声
noisy [ˈnɔɪzɪ] *adj.* 嘈杂的；喧闹的
nominal [ˈnɔmɪnəl] *adj.* 名义上的；有名无实的；很少的
none [nʌn] *adv.* 绝不 *pron.* 没有一个
nonetheless [ˌnʌnðəˈles] *adv.* 虽然如此；但是
nevertheless [ˌnevəðəˈles] *adv.* 然而；不过
noodle [ˈnuːdl] *n.* 面条
noon [nuːn] *n.* 正午；中午
nor [nɔː] *conj.* / *adv.* 也不；也没
normalization [ˌnɔːməlaɪˈzeɪʃn] *n.*(normalisation) 正常化；标准化
north [nɔːθ] *n.* 北方 *adj.* 北方的 *adv.* 向北
northeast [ˌnɔːθˈiːst] *n.* 东北 *adj.* 东北方的 *adv.* 向东北；在东北
northern [ˈnɔːðən] *adj.* 北方的；北部的
northwest [ˌnɔːθˈwest] *n.* 西北方；西北部 *adj.* 西北的 *adv.* 向西北；在西北
nose [nəuz] *n.* 鼻子
not [nɔt] *adv.* 不；没有
notable [ˈnəutəbl] *adj.* 值得注意的；显著的
note [nəut] *n.* 便条；笔记；值得注意之处；纸币 *v.* 记录；注意
notebook [ˈnəutbuk] *n.* 笔记簿
nothing [ˈnʌθɪŋ] *pron.* 没有什么 *n.* 无关紧要的人（或事）
notice [ˈnəutɪs] *n.* 通知；布告；注意 *v.* 注意
noticeable [ˈnəutɪsəbl] *adj.* 显而易见的；明显的；显著的
notify [ˈnəutɪfaɪ] *v.* 通知；告知
notwithstanding [ˌnɔtwɪθˈstændɪŋ] *prep.* 尽管；*adv.* 尽管如此 *conj.* 虽然；尽管
noun [naun] *n.* 名词
nourish [ˈnʌrɪʃ] *v.* 养育；培养；滋养
novel [ˈnɔvəl] *n.*（长篇）小说 *adj.* 新颖的
November [nəuˈvembə] *n.* 十一月
now [nau] *adv.* 现在；目前
nowadays [ˈnauədeɪz] *adv.* 现在；现时
nuclear [ˈnjuːklɪə] *adj.* 核的；原子核的
nucleus [ˈnjuːklɪəs] *n.*（原子）核
numb [nʌm] *adj.* 麻木的；失去感觉的 *v.* 使麻木；使失去知觉
number [ˈnʌmbə] *n.* 数字；号码；数量
nurse [nɜːs] *n.* 护士 *v.* 护理；照料
nursery [ˈnɜːsərɪ] *n.* 托儿所；育儿室
nut [nʌt] *n.* 干果；坚果
nylon [ˈnaɪlɒn] *n.* 尼龙

O

oak [əuk] *n.* 栎树；橡树
oar [ɔː] *n.* 桨；橹
oath [əuθ] *n.* 誓言；誓约；诅咒
obedience [əˈbiːdiəns] *n.* 服从；顺从；听话
obey [əˈbeɪ] *v.* 服从；遵守

obscure [əbˈskjuə] *adj.* 不难以说清楚的；模糊的 *v.* 遮掩；掩盖
obsolete [ˈɔbsəliːt] *adj.* 已不用的；已废弃的；过时的
obstruct [əbˈstrʌkt] *v.* 阻塞；堵塞；阻碍
obstruction [əbˈstrʌkʃən] *n.* 阻碍（物）；堵塞；阻挠
occasional [əˈkeɪʒən(ə)l] *adj.* 偶尔的
ocean [ˈəuʃ(ə)n] *n.* 海洋；大海
o'clock [əˈklɔk] *adv.* ……点钟
October [ɔkˈtəubə] *n.* 十月
odd [ɔd] *adj.* 奇怪的；古怪的；奇数的
odds [ɔdz] *n.* 可能性；机会
odor [ˈəudə] *n.*(odour) 气味；名声
of [əv] *prep.* 属于（某人或物）
off [ɔf] *prep.* / *adv.* 离开；休息 *adj.* 休息的
office [ˈɔfɪs] *n.* 办公室；办公处；事务所
officer [ˈɔfɪsə] *n.* 军官；（政府）官员；警察
official [əˈfɪʃ(ə)l] *n.* 行政官员 *adj.* 公务的；官方的；正式的
often [ˈɔf(ə)n] *adv.* 常常；经常；时常
oil [ɔɪl] *n.* 油；石油
okay [əuˈkeɪ] *adj.* / *adv.* 可以 *int.* 行；好的
old [əuld] *adj.* 老的；年老的 *n.* 老年人
omit [əuˈmɪt] *v.* 省略；遗漏；删掉
on [ɔn] *prep.* 在……上 *adv.* 在上面 *adj.* 开着的；正在播出的
once [wʌns] *adv.* 一次；曾经 *conj.* 一旦
one [wʌn] *num.* 一；一个
oneself [wʌnˈself] *pron.* 自己；亲自
onion [ˈʌnjən] *n.* 洋葱（头）
only [ˈəunlɪ] *adv.* 只有；仅仅 *adj.* 仅有的
onto [ˈɔntu] *prep.*（表示方向）到……之上
opaque [əuˈpeɪk] *adj.* 不透明的；难理解的
open [ˈəupən] *adj.* 开着的；开放的；营业的 *v.* 开；打开
opening [ˈəupənɪŋ] *n.* 开始；开幕；开张 *adj.* 开始的
opera [ˈɔpərə] *n.* 歌剧
oppress [əˈpres] *v.* 使烦恼；压迫；压制
optical [ˈɔptɪkəl] *adj.* 视觉的；视力的；光学的；光的
optimum [ˈɔptɪməm] *adj.* 最适宜的；最优的 *n.* 最佳条件
or [ɔːə；ɔr] *conj.* 或；或者；否则；要不然
oral [ˈɔrəl] *adj.* 口头的；口述的
orange [ˈɔrɪndʒ] *n.* 橙；柑；橘；橘黄色；橙色 *adj.* 橙色的
orbit [ˈɔːbɪt] *n.* 轨道 *v.* 沿轨道运行
orchard [ˈɔːtʃəd] *n.* 果园
order [ˈɔːdə] *n.* 顺序；订购；指令；条理；治安 *v.* 命令；点餐
orderly [ˈɔːdəlɪ] *adj.* 安排好的；整齐的；有秩序的
ordinary [ˈɔːd(ə)n(ə)rɪ] *adj.* 普通的；平常的；平庸的；平淡的
ore [ɔː] *n.* 矿物；矿石
orientation [ˌɔːrɪənˈteɪʃən] *n.* 方向；目标；熟悉情况；培训
orphan [ˈɔːfən] *n.* 孤儿 *v.* 使成为孤儿
orthodox [ˈɔːθədɔks] *adj.* 传统的；正统的
other [ˈʌðə] *pron.* / *adj.* 其他；另外；另一个
otherwise [ˈʌðəwaɪz] *adv.* 否则；不然
ought [ɔːt] *aux.* / *v.* 应该；应当；可能会
ounce [auns] *n.* 盎司
our [ˈauə] *pron.* 我们的
ours [ˈauəz] *pron.* 我们的
ourselves [ˌauəˈselvz] *pron.* 我们自己
out [aut] *adv.* 出去 *adj.* 外面的；往外去的
outbreak [ˈautbreɪk] *n.* 爆发；突然发生
outdoor [ˈautdɔː] *adj.* 户外的；露天的
outer [ˈautə] *adj.* 外面的；外部的
outfit [ˈautfɪt] *n.* 全套工具（设备或服装）
outing [ˈaʊtɪŋ] *n.* 远足；郊游；短途旅行
outset [ˈautset] *n.* 开始；开端
outside [ˌautˈsaɪd] *adv.* 在（向）外面 *n.* 外面；外部 *adj.* 外部的 *prep.* 在……的外面
outskirts [ˈautskɜːts] *n.* 外围地区；郊区
outstanding [autˈstændɪŋ] *adj.* 杰出的；优秀的；显著的
oval [ˈəuvəl] *n.* 椭圆形 *adj.* 椭圆形的
oven [ˈʌvən] *n.* 烤箱；炉
over [ˈəuvə] *prep.* 在……的上方；超过
overcoat [ˈəuvəkəut] *n.* 大衣

overflow [ˌəuvəˈfləu] *v.* 溢出；淹没；充满
overhear [ˌəuvəˈhɪə] *v.* 偶然听到
overnight [ˌəuvəˈnaɪt] *adv.* 一夜之间；突然
overpass [ˈəuvəpɑːs] *n.* 立交桥；天桥
overtime [ˈəʊvətaɪm] *n.* 加班 *adj.* / *adv.* 超时的（地）
owe [əu] *v.* 欠（钱）；应当给予；归功于
owing [ˈəuɪŋ] *adj.* 欠着的；未付的
owl [aʊl] *n.* 猫头鹰
own [əun] *adj.* 属于自己的 *v.* 拥有
owner [ˈəunə] *n.* 物主；所有人
ox [ɔks] *n.* 牛；公牛
oxide [ˈɔksaɪd] *n.* 氧化物
oxygen [ˈɔksɪdʒən] *n.* 氧；氧气
ozone [ˈəuzəun] *n.* 臭氧

P

pace [peɪs] *n.* 步；步伐；步调；速度 *v.* 踱步；节奏；步测
pack [pæk] *v.* 捆扎；打包；塞满 *n.* 背包
pact [pækt] *n.* 合同；条约；公约；协定
pad [pæd] *n.* 垫；衬垫；便笺簿
paddle [ˈpædl] *n.* 桨 *v.* 用桨划
page [peɪdʒ] *n.* 页；版面 *v.* 给……标页码
pail [peɪl] *n.* 桶；提桶；一桶的量
pain [peɪn] *n.* 痛；痛苦 *v.* 使痛苦
paint [peɪnt] *n.* 油漆；颜料 *v.* 涂漆；画
painter [ˈpeɪntə] *n.* 漆工；画家
painting [ˈpeɪntɪŋ] *n.*（一幅）画；绘画作品；绘画；粉刷；上油漆
pair [pɛə] *n.* 一对；一双；一副 *v.* 成对
palace [ˈpælɪs] *n.* 宫；宫殿
pale [peɪl] *adj.* 苍白的；灰白的；暗淡的
palm [pɑːm] *n.* 手掌；掌状物；棕榈
pan [pæn] *n.* 平底锅；盘子；面板
panda [ˈpændə] *n.* 熊猫
panic [ˈpænɪk] *n.* / *adj.* 恐慌（的）；惊慌（的） *v.* 使惊慌；使害怕
pant [pænt] *n.* 喘气 *v.* 喘息；气喘吁吁地说
pants [pænts] *n.* 裤子；短裤
paper [ˈpeɪpə] *n.* 纸；报纸 (pl) 试卷；论文
paperback [ˈpeɪpəbæk] *n.* 平装本；简装本
parachute [ˈpærəʃuːt] *n.* 降落伞 *v.* 跳伞
parade [pəˈreɪd] *n.* / *v.* 游行 *n.* 检阅；阅兵
paradigm [ˈpærədaɪm] *n.* 典范；范例；示例
parameter [pəˈræmɪtə] *n.* 参数；参量
parasite [ˈpærəsaɪt] *n.* 寄生虫；食客
pardon [ˈpɑːdn] *n.* 原谅；请再说一遍 *v.* 原谅
parent [ˈpeərənt] *n.* 父或母 (pl.) 父母
park [pɑːk] *n.* 公园；停车场 *v.* 停放
part [pɑːt] *n.* 部分；成员；零件 *v.* 使分开
particular [pəˈtɪkjulə] *adj.* 特殊的；特定的 *n.* 详情；细节
partly [ˈpɑːtlɪ] *adv.* 部分地；在一定程度上
partner [ˈpɑːtnə] *n.* 合伙人；伙伴；配偶
party [ˈpɑːtɪ] *n.* 聚会；政党 *v.* 举行派对
pass [pɑːs, pæs] *v.* 通过；传递 *n.* 通行证；考试及格
passage [ˈpæsɪdʒ] *n.* 段落；节；通过；经过；通路；走廊
passenger [ˈpæsɪndʒə] *n.* 乘客；旅客
passer-by [pɑːsəˈbaɪ] *n.* (pl.passers-by) 过路人
passport [ˈpɑːspɔːt] *n.* 护照；途径
past [pɑːst] *adj.* 过去的 *n.* 过去 *prep.*（经）过
paste [peɪst] *n.* 糊；浆糊 *v.* 粘；贴
pastime [ˈpɑːstaɪm] *n.* 消遣；娱乐
pasture [ˈpɑːstʃə] *n.* 牧草地；牧场
pat [pæt] *v.* / *n.* 轻拍；轻打；抚摸
patch [pætʃ] *n.* 补丁；碎片小块 *v.* 补；修补
path [pɑːθ] *n.* 小路；小径；路线；轨道
patience [ˈpeɪʃəns] *n.* 耐心；忍耐
patient [ˈpeɪʃənt] *adj.* 有耐心的 *n.* 患者
patrol [pəˈtrəul] *v.* 巡逻 *n.* 巡逻；巡查
pattern [ˈpætən] *n.* 模式；式样；图案；图样
pause [pɔːz] *v.* / *n.* 中止；暂停
pave [peɪv] *v.* 铺砌；铺（路）
pavement [ˈpeɪvmənt] *n.* 人行道
paw [pɔː] *n.* 爪
pay [peɪ] *v.* 支付；偿还 *n.* 工资；薪金
payment [ˈpeɪmənt] *n.* 支付；付款额
pea [piː] *n.* 豌豆
peace [piːs] *n.* 和平；平静；安宁

peaceful [ˈpiːsful] *adj.* 和平的；爱好和平的

peach [piːtʃ] *n.* 桃；桃树

peak [piːk] *n.* 山顶；巅峰 *adj.* 最高的；高峰时期的 *v.* 达到高峰

peanut [ˈpiːnʌt] *n.* 花生

pear [pεə] *n.* 梨子；梨树

pearl [pɜːl] *n.* 珍珠

peasant [ˈpezənt] *n.* 农民；佃农

pebble [ˈpebl] *n.* 卵石

pedal [ˈpedl] *n.* 踏板 *v.* 踩踏板；骑自行车

pedestrian [pɪˈdestrɪən] *n.* 步行者 *adj.* 行人的

peel [piːl] *v.* 削皮；剥皮 *n.* 果皮

peep [piːp] *v.* 偷看；窥视

peer [pɪə] *n.* 同辈 *v.* 凝视

pen [pen] *n.* 钢笔 *v.* 写；撰写

pencil [ˈpensəl] *n.* 铅笔 *v.* 用铅笔写

pendulum [ˈ pendʒələm] *n.* 摆；钟摆

penetrate [ˈpenɪtreɪt] *v.* 穿过；渗入；看穿

peninsula [pɪˈnɪnsjulə] *n.* 半岛

penny [ˈpenɪ] *n.* 便士；美分

people [ˈpiːpl] *n.* 人们；人民；民族

pepper [ˈpepə] *n.* 胡椒粉；胡椒；辣椒

per [pə] *prep.* 每；经；由

percent [pəˈsent] *n.* 百分之……；部分

percentage [pəˈsentɪdʒ] *n.* 百分数；百分比

perfect *adj.* [ˈpɜːfɪkt] 完美的；完全的 *v.* [pəˈfekt] 使完美

perfection [pəˈfekʃən] *n.* 尽善尽美；完美

perfume [pəˈfjuːm] *n.* 香水；香料 *v.* 抹香水

perhaps [pəˈhæps] *adv.* 可能；也许；大概

person [ˈpɜːsən] *n.* 人；人物；人称

personal [ˈpɜːsənl] *adj.* 个人的；私人的；亲自的

pest [pest] *n.* 害虫

pet [pet] *n.* 宠物；宠儿

petition [pɪˈtɪʃən] *n.* / *v.* 请愿（书）；请求

petrol [ˈpetrəl] *n.* 汽油

petroleum [pəˈtrəulɪəm] *n.* 石油

petty [ˈpetɪ] *adj.* 小的；不重要的；琐碎的

pharmacy [ˈfɑːməsɪ] *n.* 药房；药剂学；制药业；药剂学

philosopher [fɪˈlɔsəfə] *n.* 哲学家；哲人

phone [fəun] *n.* 电话 *v.* 打电话

photo [ˈfəutəu] *n.* 照片

physician [fɪˈzɪʃən] *n.* 内科医生

physicist [ˈfɪzɪsɪst] *n.* 物理学家

physics [ˈfɪzɪks] *n.* 物理（学）

physiological [ˌfɪzɪəˈlɔdʒɪkəl] *adj.* 生理学的；生理学上的

piano [pɪˈænəu] *n.* 钢琴

pick [pɪk] *v.* 拾；摘；挑选 *n.* 挑选

pickup [ˈpɪkʌp] *n.* 小卡车；好转；搭车者

picnic [ˈpɪknɪk] *n.* 野餐 *v.*（去）野餐

picture [ˈpɪktʃə] *n.* 画；图片 *v.* 画；描述

pie [paɪ] *n.* 馅饼

piece [piːs] *n.*（一）件；碎片 *v.* 拼合；拼凑

pierce [pɪəs] *v.* 刺穿；刺破

pig [pɪg] *n.* 猪；猪肉

pigeon [ˈpɪdʒɪn] *n.* 鸽子

pile [paɪl] *n.* 堆；大量 *v.* 堆；叠；堆积

pilgrim [ˈpɪlgrɪm] *n.* 旅游者；朝圣者

pill [pɪl] *n.* 药丸

pillar [ˈpɪlə] *n.* 柱；台柱；栋梁

pillow [ˈpɪləu] *n.* 枕头

pilot [ˈpaɪlət] *n.* 飞行员 *v.* 驾驶；领航

pin [pɪn] *n.* 大头针；别针 *v.* 钉住；别住

pinch [pɪntʃ] *v.* 捏；掐；拧；夹紧；节约

pine [paɪn] *n.* 松树

pink [pɪŋk] *n.* 粉红色 *adj.* 粉红色的

pint [paɪnt] *n.* 品脱

pipe [paɪp] *n.* 管子；导管；烟斗；笛

pirate [ˈpaɪərɪt] *n.* / *v.* 海盗；盗版（者）

pistol [ˈpɪstl] *n.* 手枪

piston [ˈpɪstən] *n.* 活塞

pit [pɪt] *n.* 坑；陷阱；煤矿；矿井

pitch [pɪtʃ] *n.* 场地；球场 *v.* 投掷；扔

pity [ˈpɪtɪ] *v.* 可怜；惋惜 *n.* 憾事；怜悯

place [pleɪs] *n.* 地方；名次；地位；寓所 *v.* 安排；放置

plain [pleɪn] *adj.* 明白的；朴素的；坦率的 *n.* 平原；旷野

plan [plæn] *n.* 计划；规划 *v.* 计划；组织

plane [pleɪn] *n.* 飞机；平面 *adj.* 平坦的

planet [ˈplænɪt] *n.* 行星

plant [plɑːnt] *n.* 植物；作物；工厂 *v.* 栽种

plantation [plænˈteɪʃən] *n.* 种植园

plaster [ˈplɑːstə] *n.* 灰泥；熟石膏；膏药

plastic [ˈplæstɪk] *n.*（常 pl.）塑料；塑料制品 *adj.* 塑料制的；可塑的

plate [pleɪt] *n.* 盘子；一盘 *v.* 电镀

platform [ˈplætfɔːm] *n.* 平台；站台；发射台

play [pleɪ] *v.* 玩（游戏）；参加比赛 *n.* 游戏；玩耍；剧本

playground [ˈpleɪgraund] *n.* 运动场；游戏场

plea [pliː] *n.* 抗辩；恳求；托词

pleasant [ˈplezənt] *adj.* 令人愉快的；惬意的

please [pliːz] *v.* 请；（使）愉快；满意

pleasure [ˈpleʒə] *n.* 愉快；快乐；乐趣

plentiful [ˈplentɪful] *adj.* 富裕的；丰富的

plenty [ˈplentɪ] *n.* 丰富；大量

plight [plaɪt] *n.* 困境 *v.* 保证；约定

plot [plɔt] *n.* 密谋；情节 *v.* 绘制；密谋

plough [plau] *n.* (plow) 犁；耕地 *v.* 犁地

plug [plʌg] *n.* 插头；塞子 *v.* 堵；塞

plumber [ˈplʌmə] *n.* 水管工人；水电工

plural [ˈpluərəl] *adj.* 复数的 *n.* 复数

plus [plʌs] *prep.* 加上 *adj.* 正的 *n.* 加号

pneumonia [njuːˈməunjə] *n.* 肺炎

pocket [ˈpɔkɪt] *n.* 口袋 *v.* 把……装入袋内

poem [ˈpəuɪm] *n.* 诗

poet [ˈpəuɪt] *n.* 诗人

poetry [ˈpəuɪtrɪ] *n.* 诗歌；诗集

point [pɔɪnt] *n.*（某物的）尖（端）；点论点；见解；重点 *v.* 指向；朝向

poison [ˈpɔɪzən] *n.* 毒物；毒药 *v.* 毒害；污染

poke [pəuk] *n.* / *v.* 刺；戳

polar [ˈpəulə] *adj.* 极地的；极性的 *n.* 极线

pole [pəul] *n.* 柱；杆；地极；磁极；电极

police [pəˈliːs] *n.* 警察；警察部门 *adj.* 警察的

policeman [pəˈliːsmən] *n.* 警察

polite [pəˈlaɪt] *adj.* 有礼貌的；客气的

pollute [pəˈluːt] *v.* 弄脏；污染

pollution [pɜːˈluːʃən] *n.* 污染

pond [pɔnd] *n.* 池塘

pool [puːl] *n.* 水池；游泳池 *v.* 集中资源

poor [puə] *adj.* 贫困的；可怜的；低劣的

pop [pɔp] *adj.* 流行的 *n.*（发出）砰的一声 *v.* 突然出现

pope [pəup] *n.* 罗马教皇；主教

popular [ˈpɔpjulə] *adj.* 流行的；通俗的；受欢迎的；普遍的

population [ˌpɔpjuˈleɪʃən] *n.* 人口

porcelain [ˈpɔːsəlɪn] *n.* 瓷器 *adj.* 瓷器的

porch [pɔːtʃ] *n.* 门廊；入口处

pork [pɔːk] *n.* 猪肉

port [pɔːt] *n.* 港口

porter [ˈpɔːtə] *n.* 守门人；行李搬运工；护工

portrait [ˈpɔːtreɪt] *n.* 肖像；画像

position [pəˈzɪʃən] *n.* 位置；职位；姿势；立场 *v.* 安置；使处于

possibility [ˌpɔsəˈbɪlətɪ] *n.* 可能；可能性

possible [ˈpɔsəbl] *adj.* 可能的 ；可能发生的 *n.* 可能适合的人（事物）

possibly [ˈpɔsəblɪ] *adv.* 可能地；也许

post [pəust] *v.* 贴出；投寄 *n.* 邮寄；职位

postage [ˈpəustɪdʒ] *n.* 邮费；邮资

postcard [ˈpəʊstkɑːd] *n.* 明信片

poster [ˈpəustə] *n.* 海报 *v.* 张贴海报

postman [ˈpəustmən] *n.* 邮递员

postpone [pəustˈpəun] *v.* 推迟；延期

posture [ˈpɔstʃə] *n.* 姿势；态度；看法

pot [pɔt] *n.* 罐；壶

potato [pəˈteɪtəu] *n.* 马铃薯；土豆

poultry [ˈpəultrɪ] *n.* 家禽

pound [paund] *n.* 磅；英镑 *v.* 猛击；敲打

poverty [ˈpɔvətɪ] *n.* 贫穷；贫困

powder [ˈpaudə] *n.* 粉末；药粉；火药

power [pauə] *n.* 权力；能源；功率

powerful [ˈpauəful] *adj.* 强大的；有权的

practically [ˈpræktɪkəlɪ] *adv.* 几乎；实际上

practice [ˈpræktɪs] *n.* 练习；实践

practise [ˈpræktɪs] *v.* 练习；实践

praise [preɪz] *v.* 赞扬；歌颂 *n.* 称赞；赞美

pray [preɪ] *v.* 祈祷；祈求

prayer [preə] *n.* 祈祷；祷告；祷文

precaution [prɪˈkɔːʃən] *n.* 预防；谨慎；警惕

prefer [prɪˈfɜː] *v.* 更喜欢；宁愿

pregnant [ˈpregnənt] *adj.* 怀孕的

preparation [ˌprepəˈreɪʃən] *n.* 准备；预备

prepare [prɪˈpɛə] *v.* 准备；预备

preposition [ˌprepəˈzɪʃən] *n.* 介词

present [ˈprezənt, prɪˈzent] *adj.* 出席的；现在的 *n.* 现在；礼物 *v.* 赠送；呈现；展示

presently [ˈprezəntlɪ] *adv.* 现在；不久

president [ˈprezɪdənt] *n.* 总统；主席

press [pres] *v.* 压；压榨；紧迫；催促 *n.* 报刊；通讯社；压榨机

presumably [prɪˈzjuːməblɪ] *adv.* 很可能；大概

pretext [ˈpriːtekst] *n.* 借口；托词

pretty [ˈprɪtɪ] *adv.* 相当；很 *adj.* 漂亮的

price [praɪs] *n.* 价格；价钱；代价 *v.* 标价

prick [prɪk] *n.* / *v.* 刺伤；刺痛；刺孔

pride [praɪd] *n.* 自豪 *v.* 使自豪

priest [priːst] *n.* 教士；神父

primitive [ˈprɪmɪtɪv] *adj.* 原始的；早期的

prince [prɪns] *n.* 王子；亲王

princess [prɪnˈses] *n.* 公主；王妃

print [prɪnt] *n.* 印刷；印刷品 *v.* 印刷；出版

prison [ˈprɪzən] *n.* 监狱

prisoner [ˈprɪzənə] *n.* 囚犯

prize [praɪz] *n.* 奖赏；奖品 *v.* 珍视；珍惜

probability [ˌprɔbəˈbɪlətɪ] *n.* 可能性；概率

probable [ˈprɔbəbl] *adj.* 很可能的；大概的

problem [ˈprɔbləm] *n.* 问题；疑难问题

procession [prəˈseʃən] *n.* 队伍；行列

produce [prəˈdjuːs] *v.* 生产；制造 *n.* 产品

product [ˈprɔdʌkt] *n.* 产品；制品

production [prəˈdʌkʃən] *n.* 生产；产品；作品

professor [prəˈfesə] *n.* 教授

programme [ˈprəugræm] *n.* (program) 节目；计划；规划；程序 *v.* 编程序

progress [ˈprəugres] *v.* / *n.* 进步；进展；前进

projector [prəuˈdʒektə] *n.* 放映机；投影仪

promise [ˈprɔmɪs] *v.* 承诺；保证；指望 *n.* 承诺；希望

pronoun [ˈprəunaun] *n.* 代词

pronounce [prəˈnauns] *v.* 发音；读音；正式宣布

pronunciation [prəˌnʌnsɪˈeɪʃ(ə)n] *n.* 发音；读法

proof [pruːf] *n.* 证据；证明；检验；证实；校样

prophet [ˈprɔfɪt] *n.* 预言家；先知；提倡者

proposition [ˌprɔpəˈzɪʃən] *n.* 主张；建议；命题

prose [prəuz] *n.* 散文 *adj.* 散文的

prospective [prəˈspektɪv] *adj.* 预期的

protein [ˈprəutiːn] *n.* 蛋白质

prototype [ˈprəutətaɪp] *n.* 原型；典型；范例

proud [praud] *adj.* 自豪的；得意的

prove [pruːv] *v.* 证明；证实；检验；结果是

provided [prəˈvaɪdɪd] *conj.* 假如；只要

province [ˈprɔvɪns] *n.* 省；领域；范围

psychiatry [saɪˈkaɪətrɪ] *n.* 精神病学；精神病疗法

pub [pʌb] *n.* 酒吧；酒馆；小旅馆

public [ˈpʌblɪk] *adj.* 公共的；公用的；公开的；公然的 *n.* 公众；民众

puff [pʌf] *n.* 吐气；吸烟 *v.* 吸；抽；喷出

pull [pul] *v.* 拉；拖 *n.* 拉；拖；拉力

pulse [pʌls] *n.* 脉搏；脉冲

pump [pʌmp] *n.* 泵 *v.* 用（泵）抽（水）；打气

punch [pʌntʃ] *v.* 拳打；以拳痛击；打孔；按（键或钮） *n.* 重拳击打；冲床；打孔机

pupil [ˈpjupəl] *n.* 学生；小学生；瞳孔

puppet [ˈpʌpɪt] *n.* 木偶；傀儡

pure [pjuə] *adj.* 纯的；纯洁的；完全的

purify [ˈpjuərɪfaɪ] *v.* 使纯净；提纯

purple [ˈpɜːpl] *adj.* 紫的 *n.* 紫色

purse [pɜːs] *n.* 钱包

push [puʃ] *v.* 推；按；促进 *n.* 推；推力

put [put] *v.* 放；搁；安置

puzzle [ˈpʌzl] *n.* 难题；拼图游戏 *v.*（使）困惑

pyramid [ˈpɪrəmɪd] *n.* 金字塔

Q

qualitative [ˈkwɔlɪtətɪv] *adj.* 定性的；质量的

quantify [ˈkwɔntɪfaɪ] *v.* 确定……的数量

quantitative [ˈkwɔntɪtətɪv] *adj.* 数量（上）的

quarrel [ˈkwɔrəl] *n.* 争吵；不和；口角

quart [kwɔːt] *n.* 夸脱（容积单位）

quarter [ˈkwɔːtə] *n.* 四分之一；一个季度；一刻钟

v. 把……四等分
quarterly [ˈkwɔːtəlɪ] *n.* 季刊 *adj.* 每季的
quartz [kwɔːts] *n.* 石英
queen [kwiːn] *n.* 女王
queer [kwɪə] *adj.* 古怪的；可疑的
quench [kwentʃ] *v.* 止渴；扑灭；抑制
question [ˈkwestʃən] *n.* 问题 *v.* 问问题
questionnaire [ˌkwestʃəˈnɛə] *n.* 调查表；问卷
queue [kjuː] *n.* 队；行列 *v.* 排队（等候）
quick [kwɪk] *adj.* 快的；迅速的
quiet [ˈkwaɪət] *adj.* 安静的 *v.*（使）安静
quilt [kwɪlt] *n.* 被子
quit [kwɪt] *v.* 辞职；停止；离开
quite [kwaɪt] *adv.* 相当；很；非常
quiver [ˈkwɪvə] *v.* 微颤；抖动 *n.* 抖动；颤音
quiz [kwɪz] *n.* 问答比赛（游戏）；小测验
quote [kwəut] *v.* 引用；报价 *n.* 引文；报价

R

rabbit [ˈræbɪt] *n.* 兔子
race [reɪs] *n.* 人种；种族；速度竞赛
rack [ræk] *n.* 挂物架；搁物架 *v.* 使痛苦
racket [ˈrækɪt] *n.* 球拍
radar [ˈreɪdɑː] *n.* 雷达
radiant [ˈreɪdɪənt] *adj.* 发光的；辐射的；容光焕发的
radio [ˈreɪdɪəu] *n.* 收音机
radioactive [ˌreɪdɪəuˈæktɪv] *adj.* 放射性的
radius [ˈreɪdɪəs] *n.* 半径；半径范围
rag [ræg] *n.* 抹布；破布；碎布
rage [reɪdʒ] *n.* 愤怒
raid [reɪd] *n.* / *v.* 袭击；搜查
rail [reɪl] *n.* 栏杆；围栏 (pl.) 铁轨；栏杆
railroad [ˈreɪlrəud] *n.* 铁路 *v.* 由铁道运输
rain [reɪn] *n.* / *v.* 下雨
rainbow [ˈreɪnbəu] *n.* 彩虹
raise [reɪz] *v.* 举起；增加；饲养；提出
rake [reɪk] *n.* 耙子 *v.* 耙；搜索
range [reɪndʒ] *n.* 范围；一系列；山脉 *v.* 排列
rap [ræp] *n.* 叩击；说唱音乐 *v.* 敲；说唱
rape [reɪp] *n.* / *v.* 掠夺；蹂躏；强奸
rapid [ˈræpɪd] *adj.* 快；急速的 *n.* 急流；湍滩
rare [reə] *adj.* 稀有的；珍奇的；半熟的
rarely [ˈreəlɪ] *adv.* 很少；难得；非常地
rash [ræʃ] *adj.* 轻率的；鲁莽的 *n.* 皮疹
rat [ræt] *n.* 鼠
rate [reɪt] *n.* 速率；等级；价格 *v.* 估价；评级
rather [ˈrɑːðə] *adv.* 相当；宁愿；宁可
ratio [ˈreɪʃɪəu] *n.* 比；比率
raw [rɔː] *adj.* 生的；未加工过的；无经验的
ray [reɪ] *n.* 光线；射线
razor [ˈreɪzə] *n.* 剃刀
reach [riːtʃ] *v.* 抵达；伸手；够到 *n.* 伸出；能达到的范围
read [riːd] *v.* 朗读；阅读；理解
reader [ˈriːdə] *n.* 读者；读本；读物
readily [ˈredɪlɪ] *adv.* 容易地；乐意地；欣然地
reading [ˈriːdɪŋ] *n.* 读书；读物；阅读
ready [ˈredɪ] *adj.* 准备好的；现成的；乐意的
real [ˈriːəl; ˈrɪəl] *adj.* 真的；真实的；实际的
realise [ˈrɪəlaɪz] *v.* (realize) 认识到；实现
really [ˈriːəlɪ] *adv.* 确实；实在；真正地
reap [riːp] *v.* 收割；收获
rear [rɪə] *n.* 后面；后方 *v.* 饲养；抚养；栽培
reason [ˈriːzən] *n.* 原因；理智 *v.* 推理
reassure [ˌriːəˈʃuə] *v.* 使安心；使放心
rebel *v.* [rɪˈbel] 反抗；反叛 *n.* [ˈrebəl] 叛逆者
rebellion [rɪˈbeljən] *n.* 叛乱；反抗；叛逆
recall [rɪˈkɔːl] *v.* 回忆；回想；召回
recede [rɪˈsiːd] *v.* 后退；渐渐退去
receive [rɪˈsiːv] *v.* 收到；接到；接待
reciprocal [rɪˈsɪprəkəl] *adj.* 相互的；互利的
recite [rɪˈsaɪt] *v.* 背诵；朗诵
reckon [ˈrekən] *v.* 估计；计算；认为
reclaim [rɪˈkleɪm] *v.* 要求归还；收回；开垦
recognition [ˌrekəgˈnɪʃ(ə)n] *n.* 认出；辨认；承认
recollect [ˌrekəˈlekt] *v.* 回忆；想起
record *n.* [ˈrekɔːd] 记录；唱片 *v.* [rɪˈkɔːd] 记录；录音
recorder [rɪˈkɔːdə] *n.* 记录员；录音机
rectangle [ˈrektæŋgl] *n.* 矩形；长方形
rectify [ˈrektɪfaɪ] *v.* 纠正；矫正；精馏

red [red] *adj.* 红的；红色的 *n.* 红色
reed [riːd] *n.* 芦苇；苇丛；芦笛；牧笛
reel [riːl] *n.* 卷筒；线轴 *v.* 卷；绕
refreshment [rɪˈfreʃmənt] *n.* (pl.) 点心；饮料；恢复精力
regard [rɪˈɡɑːd] *v.* 把……看作为；考虑 *n.* (pl.) 敬重；问候
regret [rɪˈɡret] *v.* / *n.* 遗憾；懊悔；抱歉
refuse [rɪˈfjuːz] *v.* 拒绝；回绝 *n.* 废物；垃圾
refusal [rɪˈfjuːzəl] *n.* 拒绝；回绝
rejection [rɪˈdʒekʃən] *n.* 拒绝；拒绝接受
rejoice [rɪˈdʒɔɪs] *v.*（使）欣喜；（使）高兴
relativity [ˌreləˈtɪvətɪ] *n.* 相关（性）；相对论
relax [rɪˈlæks] *v.*（使）松驰；放松
relay [ˈriːleɪ, rɪˈleɪ] *v.* 接力；转播 *n.* 接力赛
religion [rɪˈlɪdʒən] *n.* 宗教；信仰
relish [ˈrelɪʃ] *n.* 享受；喜爱；开胃小菜；调味品 *v.* 享受；渴望
rely [rɪˈlaɪ] *v.* 依赖；依靠；信赖；信任
remainder [rɪˈmeɪndə] *n.* 剩余物；剩下的
remains [rɪˈmeɪnz] *n.* 剩余；残余；遗迹
remember [rɪˈmembə] *v.* 记住；纪念
remnant [ˈremnənt] *n.* 剩余部分；零头布料 *adj.* 剩余的；残留的
removal [rɪˈmuːv(ə)l] *n.* 移动；迁居；开除
render [ˈrendə] *v.* 使得；致使；提供；提交
renew [rɪˈnjuː] *v.*（使）更新；恢复；重新开始
renovate [ˈrenəveɪt] *v.* 更新；修复；整修
rent [rent] *v.* 租；租赁 *n.* 租金
repair [rɪˈpeə] *n.* 修理；修补 *v.* 修理；补救
repay [rɪˈpeɪ] *v.* 偿还；报答
repeat [rɪˈpiːt] *v.* 重复；重说 *n.* 重现
repeatedly [rɪˈpiːtɪdlɪ] *adv.* 重复地；再三地
repertoire [ˈrepətwɑː] *n.* 全部剧目；全部技能
repetition [ˌrepəˈtɪʃn] *n.* 重复；反复
replacement [rɪˈpleɪsmənt] *n.* 取代；替换（物）
reply [rɪˈplaɪ] *v.* / *n.* 回答；答复
report [rɪˈpɔːt] *n.* / *v.* 报告；汇报
reporter [rɪˈpɔːtə] *n.* 报告人；通讯员；记者
repression [rɪˈpreʃən] *n.* 压抑；压制；镇压
reproach [rɪˈprəutʃ] *v.* / *n.* 责备；指责
reptile [ˈreptaɪl] *n.* 爬行动物
republic [rɪˈpʌblɪk] *n.* 共和国；共和政体
research [rɪˈsɜːtʃ] *v.* / *n.* 研究；调查
resemblance [rɪˈzembləns] *n.* 相似；相似性
reservation [ˌrezəˈveɪʃ(ə)n] *n.* 保留；保护；预订
resolute [ˈrezəluːt] *adj.* 坚决的；果断的
respect [rɪˈspekt] *n.* / *v.* 敬重；尊重 *n.* 方面
respective [rɪˈspektɪv] *adj.* 各自的；各个的
rest [rest] *n.* 休息；剩余部分 *v.* 休息
restaurant [ˈrestərənt] *n.* 餐馆；饭店
restless [ˈrestlɪs] *adj.* 坐立不安的；不耐烦的
result [rɪˈzʌlt] *n.* 结果；成绩 *v.* 由……导致
resultant [rɪˈzʌltənt] *adj.* 由此引起的
retire [rɪˈtaɪə] *v.* 退休；退役；出局
retort [rɪˈtɔːt] *n.* / *v.* 反驳；回嘴
retrieve [rɪˈtriːv] *v.* 取回；挽回；检索
return [rɪˈtɜːn] *v.* / *n.* 返回；归还；回答
review [rɪˈvjuː] *v.* 回顾；复习 *n.* 复习；评论
revolt [rɪˈvəult] *v.* / *n.* 反抗；起义
rib [rɪb] *n.* 肋骨；肋状物
ribbon [ˈrɪbən] *n.* 缎带；丝带；带状物
rice [raɪs] *n.* 稻；米
rich [rɪtʃ] *adj.* 有钱的；富饶的；丰富的
rid [rɪd] *v.* 使摆脱；使去掉
riddle [ˈrɪdl] *n.* 谜；谜语
ride [raɪd] *v.* / *n.* 骑；乘
ridge [rɪdʒ] *n.* 岭；山脉；屋脊
ridiculous [rɪˈdɪkjuləs] *adj.* 荒谬的；可笑的
rifle [ˈraɪfl] *n.* 步枪
right [raɪt] *adj.* 正确的；恰当的；右边的 *adv.* 正好；在右面 *n.* 正当；公正；权利
rim [rɪm] *n.*（圆物的）边；边缘；（眼镜）框
ring [rɪŋ] *n.* 戒指；环；铃声 *v.* 按（铃）；（打）电话；敲（钟）
riot [ˈraɪət] *n.* 暴（骚）乱；狂欢 *v.* 骚乱；暴动
rip [rɪp] *v.* 撕；撕裂 *n.* 裂口；裂缝
ripe [raɪp] *adj.* 熟的；成熟的；时机成熟的
rise [raɪz] *v.* 升起；起立；上涨 *n.* 上升
risk [rɪsk] *v.* 冒……的危险 *n.* 冒险；风险
river [ˈrɪvə] *n.* 河流
road [rəud] *n.* 路；道路；途径

roar [rɔː] *n.* / *v.* 吼叫；怒号；咆哮
roast [rəust] *v.* 烤；炙；烘 *n.*（大块）烤肉
rob [rɔb] *v.* 抢劫；盗取；非法剥夺
robe [rəub] *n.* 长袍；上衣
robot [ˈrəʊbɒt] *n.* 机器人；自动机械
robust [rəuˈbʌst] *adj.* 强壮的；健康的；耐用的；坚固的；强大的；稳固的
rock [rɔk] *n.* 岩石；摇滚乐 *v.*（使）摇晃
rocket [ˈrɔkɪt] *n.* 火箭
rod [rɔd] *n.* 杆；棒
role [rəul] *n.* 角色；作用；任务；职责
roll [rəul] *v.* 滚动；卷起 *n.* 卷；名单
romance [ˈrəumæns; rəuˈmæns] *n.* 浪漫史；爱情故事
romantic [rəuˈmæntɪk] *adj.* 浪漫的；爱情的 *n.* 浪漫的人；空想者
roof [ruːf] *n.* 屋顶；顶
room [ruːm] *n.* 房间；空间
root [ruːt] *n.* 根部；根本；根源 *v.*（使）生根
rope [rəup] *n.* 绳；索
rose [rəʊz] *n.* 玫瑰；蔷薇
rot [rɔt] *v.*（使）腐烂；（使）腐败；腐朽
rotary [ˈrəutərɪ] *adj.* 旋转的
rotate [rəuˈteɪt] *v.*（使）旋转
rotten [ˈrɔtən] *adj.* 腐烂的；腐朽的
rough [rʌf] *adj.* 粗糙的；粗略的；艰难的
round [raund] *adj.* 圆的 *prep.* 围绕 *adv.* 在周围 *v.* 绕行 *n.*（一）回合
roundabout [ˈraundəbaut] *adj.* 迂回的；转弯抹角的 *n.* 环状交叉路口
row [rəu] *n.*（一）排；（一）行 *v.* 划（船等）
royalty [ˈrɔɪəltɪ] *n.* 皇家；皇族
rub [rʌb] *v.* 擦；摩擦
rubber [ˈrʌbə] *n.* 橡皮；橡胶；橡胶制品
rubbish [ˈrʌbɪʃ] *n.* 垃圾；废物；废话
ruby [ˈruːbɪ] *n.* 红宝石
rude [ruːd] *adj.* 粗鲁的；无礼的；粗糙的
rug [rʌg] *n.*（小）地毯；垫子
ruin [ˈruːɪn] *v.* 毁灭 *n.* 毁坏；(pl.) 废墟
rule [ruːl] *v.* 统治；支配；裁定 *n.* 规章；条例；统治
ruler [ˈruːlə] *n.* 统治者；尺；直尺
rumor [ˈruːmə] *n.* (rumour) 传闻；谣言
run [rʌn] *v.* 奔；跑；流；淌；经营；运转
rust [rʌst] *n.* 铁锈 *v.*（使）生锈

sack [sæk] *n.* 袋；麻袋；解雇 *v.* 解雇
sad [sæd] *adj.* 悲哀的；忧愁的
saddle [ˈsædl] *n.* 鞍；马鞍
safe [seɪf] *adj.* 安全的；谨慎的 *n.* 保险箱
safety [ˈseɪftɪ] *n.* 安全；保险；安全场所
sail [seɪl] *n.* 帆；航行 *v.* 航行
sailor [ˈseɪlə] *n.* 水手；海员
saint [seɪnt] *n.* 圣人；基督教徒
sake [seɪk] *n.* 缘故；理由
salad [ˈsæləd] *n.* 沙拉；凉拌菜
salary [ˈsælərɪ] *n.* 薪金；薪水
sale [seɪl] *n.* 出售；销售；销售额
salesman [ˈseɪlzmən] *n.* 售货员；推销员
salt [sɔːlt] *n.* 盐 *v.* 腌；盐渍
salute [səˈluːt] *v.* / *n.*（向……）行军礼；敬礼；致敬；鸣礼炮
salvation [sælˈveɪʃən] *n.* 解救；拯救
same [seɪm] *adj.* 相同的 *adv.* 同样地
sample [ˈsɑːmpl] *n.* 样本；样品 *v.* 品尝；尝试；采样
sand [sænd] *n.* 沙 (pl.) 沙滩；沙地
sandwich [ˈsænwɪdʒ] *n.* 三明治；夹心面包片
sane [seɪn] *adj.* 神志清醒的；明智的
satellite [ˈsætəlaɪt] *n.* 卫星；人造卫星 *adj.* 卫星传送的
satire [ˈsætaɪə] *n.* 讽刺；讽刺文学；讽刺作品
satisfaction [ˌsætɪsˈfækʃən] *n.* 满足；满意
satisfactory [ˌsætɪsˈfæktərɪ] *adj.* 令人满意的；符合要求的
satisfy [ˈsætɪsfaɪ] *v.* 满意；使满意；使满足
Saturday [ˈsætədeɪ] *n.* 星期六
sauce [sɔːs] *n.* 酱汁；调味汁
saucer [ˈsɔːsə] *n.* 茶托；碟子
sausage [ˈsɔsɪdʒ] *n.* 香肠；腊肠
savage [ˈsævɪdʒ] *adj.* 野蛮的；残暴的 *n.* 野人；未开化的人

save [seɪv] v. 救助;储蓄;节省
saving [ˈseɪvɪŋ] n. 节省 (pl.) 储蓄金;存款
saw [sɔː] n. 锯子;锯床 v. 锯;锯开
say [seɪ] v. 说;讲 n. 发言权;决定权
scan [skæn] v. 细看;浏览;扫描 n. 扫描;快速查阅;浏览
scar [skɑː] n. 伤疤;创伤 v. 创伤
scarce [skeəs] adj. 缺乏的;稀有的
scare [skeə] n. 惊恐;恐慌 v. 惊吓;受惊
scarf [skɑːf] n. 围巾;头巾
scene [siːn] n. 现场;(戏剧的)一场;景色
scenery [ˈsiːnərɪ] n. 风景;舞台布景
scent [sent] n. 气味;线索 v. 嗅;发觉
school [skuːl] n. 学校;上学;学业;学派
science [ˈsaɪəns] n. 科学;学科
scientific [ˌsaɪənˈtɪfɪk] adj. 科学上的
scientist [ˈsaɪəntɪst] n. 科学家
scissors [ˈsɪzəz] n. 剪子
scold [skəuld] v. 责骂;训斥
scout [skaut] n. 侦察员;侦察机 v. 侦察
scramble [ˈskræmbl] n. / v. 攀登;爬;争夺
scrap [skræp] n. 碎片;废料 v. 废弃;报废
scrape [skreɪp] v. 刮(掉)擦伤;艰难地完成 n. 刮;擦痕;刮擦声
scratch [skrætʃ] v. 抓;挠;划破 n. 抓;划伤
scream [skriːm] v. / n. 尖声叫;大声叫
screen [skriːn] v. 检查;筛查 n. 屏幕;银幕
screw [skruː] v. 拧;拧紧 n. 螺旋;螺丝(钉)
script [skrɪpt] n. 剧本 v. 写剧本
sculpture [ˈskʌlptʃə] n. 雕刻;雕刻作品
sea [siː] n. 海;海洋
seal [siːl] n. 封条;印章;海豹 v. 封;密封
seam [siːm] n. 缝;接缝 v. 裂开;产生裂缝
search [sɜːtʃ] v. / n. 搜索;寻找;探查
seaside [ˈsiːsaɪd] n. 海滨;海边
season [ˈsiːzən] n. 季节;时节
seat [siːt] n. 座位;职位 v. 使坐下;使就职
second [ˈsekənd] adj. 第二 n. 秒
secret [ˈsiːkrɪt] adj. 秘密的;机密的 n. 秘密
secretary [ˈsekrətərɪ] n. 秘书;部长
see [siː] v. 看到;注意到;留意到;明白
seed [siːd] n. 种子 v. 播种
seek [siːk] v. 寻找;试图;征求
seem [siːm] v. 好像;似乎
seemingly [ˈsiːmɪŋlɪ] adv. 看似;似乎
segregate [ˈsegrɪgeɪt] v. 使分开;使隔离
seize [siːz] v. 抓住;逮住;夺取;占领
seldom [ˈseldəm] adv. 很少;不常
self [self] n. 自我;自己
selfish [ˈselfɪʃ] adj. 自私的;利己的
sell [sel] v. 卖;出售
semester [sɪˈmestə] n. 学期
semiconductor [ˌsemɪkənˈdʌktə] n. 半导体
senate [ˈsenət] n. 参议院;上院
senator [ˈsenətə] n. 参议员
send [send] v. 送;寄出;传达
sense [sens] n. 感官;感觉 v. 觉得;意识到
sentence [ˈsentəns] n. 句子;判决;宣判 v. 宣判;判决
September [sepˈtembə] n. 九月
serial [ˈsɪərɪəl] n. 连续剧;连载刊物 adj. 连续的
serious [ˈsɪərɪəs] adj. 严肃的;严重的 ;认真的
servant [ˈsɜːvənt] n. 仆人
service [ˈsɜːvɪs] n.服务;服侍;服役;仪式 v. 维修;满足……的需求
set [set] n. 一套;一副;装置 v. 放置;设置
session [ˈseʃən] n.(一届)会议;一段时间
setting [ˈsetɪŋ] n. 环境;场合;背景
seven [ˈsevən] num. 七;七个
several [ˈsevərəl] adj. 几个;若干;各自的
sew [səu] v. 缝;缝纫
sex [seks] n. 性别;性
shabby [ˈʃæbɪ] adj. 破旧的;破烂的;卑鄙的
shade [ʃeɪd] n. 阴凉处;遮光物 v. 为……遮阳(挡光)
shadow [ˈʃædəu] n. 阴影;影子;暗处
shady [ˈʃeɪdɪ] adj. 成荫的;多荫的;靠不住的
shaft [ʃɑːft] n. 轴;杆状物
shake [ʃeɪk] n. / v. 摇动;摇;颤抖;震动
shall [ʃæl] aux. 将要;会;应该
shallow [ˈʃæləu] adj. 浅的;肤浅的
sham [ʃæm] n. / adj. 假冒(的)虚伪(的) v. 假装;

冒充

shame [ʃeɪm] *n.* 羞耻；耻辱 *v.* 使羞愧

shampoo [ʃæmˈpuː] *n.* 香波 *v.* 用洗发剂洗

shape [ʃeɪp] *n.* 形状；外形 *v.* 成型；塑造

share [ʃɛə] *v.* 分享；分担 *n.* 股份；份额

shark [ʃɑːk] *n.* 鲨鱼

sharp [ʃɑːp] *adj.* 锋利的；锐利的；轮廓分明的 *adv.* 准时地

shatter [ˈʃætə] *n.* 碎片；粉碎 *v.* 粉碎；破坏

shave [ʃeɪv] *v.* 剃（须）；刮去 *n.* 刮脸

she [ʃiː] *pron.* 她

shear [ʃɪə] *v.* 剪；修剪

shed [ʃed] *v.* 去除；摆脱 *n.* 棚；小屋

sheep [ʃiːp] *n.*（绵）羊；易受人摆布的人

sheer [ʃɪə] *adj.* 纯粹的；陡峭的；险峻的

sheet [ʃiːt] *n.* 被单；（一）张；（一）片；纸张

shelf [ʃelf] *n.* 架子；搁板

shell [ʃel] *n.* 壳；贝壳；炮弹

shepherd [ˈʃepəd] *n.* 牧民；牧羊人

shield [ʃiːld] *n.* 防护物；护罩；盾 *v.* 保护；防护

shift [ʃɪft] *v.* 替换；转移 *n.* 转换；（轮）班

shilling [ˈʃɪlɪŋ] *n.* 先令

shine [ʃaɪn] *v.* 照耀；发光；擦亮 *n.* 光泽；光

ship [ʃɪp] *n.* 船舶；舰艇 *v.* 航运；运送；发货

shipment [ˈʃɪpmənt] *n.* 装运；装载的货物

shirt [ʃɜːt] *n.* 衬衫

shiver [ˈʃɪvə] *v.* / *n.* 战栗；发抖

shock [ʃɔk] *n.* 震动；触电 *v.*（使）震动；震惊

shoe [ʃuː] *n.* 鞋

shoot [ʃuːt] *v.* 射击；发射；拍摄 *n.* 幼苗；拍摄

shop [ʃɔp] *n.* 商店；车间 *v.* 买东西

shopkeeper [ˈʃɔpkiːpə] *n.* 店主；老板

shore [ʃɔː] *n.* 海滨；湖滨

short [ʃɔːt] *adj.* 短的；矮的；缺乏；不足 *n.* (pl.) 短裤

shortage [ˈʃɔːtɪdʒ] *n.* 不足；缺少

shortcoming [ˈʃɔːtkʌmɪŋ] *n.* 短处；缺点

shorthand [ˈʃɔːthænd] *n.* 速记

shortly [ˈʃɔːtlɪ] *adv.* 立刻；不久；简短地

shot [ʃɔt] *n.* 开枪；射击；投篮；子弹

should [ʃud] *aux.* 应该；应当

shoulder [ˈʃəuldə] *n.* 肩；肩部 *v.* 肩负；承担

shout [ʃaut] *v.* 大声叫；喊 *n.* 呼喊；叫

shove [ʃʌv] *v.* 乱推；乱塞；用力推 *n.* 猛推

show [ʃəu] *n.* 节目；表演 *v.* 上演（戏剧等）；放映（电影）

shower [ˈʃauə] *n.* 阵雨；沐浴 *v.* 洗澡

shrewd [ʃruːd] *adj.* 机灵的；敏锐的；精明的

shrug [ʃrʌg] *v.* / *n.* 耸肩

shut [ʃʌt] *v.* 关；关闭

shutter [ˈʃʌtə] *n.* 百叶窗；快门；关闭装置

shuttle [ˈʃʌtl] *n.* 航天飞机；往返于两地的交通工具；摆渡车 *v.* 往返；穿梭

shy [ʃaɪ] *adj.* 怕羞的；腼腆的 *v.* 惊退；畏缩

sick [sɪk] *adj.* 患病的；恶心的；想吐的

side [saɪd] *n.* 旁边；侧面；坡；岸；一边；一侧；一方 *v.* 支持

sideways [ˈsaɪdweɪz] *adv.* / *adj.* 从一边（的）；在一边（的）；斜着（的）

siege [siːdʒ] *n.* 包围；围攻；围困

sigh [saɪ] *n.* 叹息；叹息声 *v.* 叹息；叹气

sight [saɪt] *n.* 视力；视野；景色 *v.* 看到

sightseeing [ˈsaɪtsiːɪŋ] *n.* 观光；游览

sign [saɪn] *n.* 标记；招牌；征兆；迹象 *v.* 签名（于）；署名（于）

signal [ˈsɪgnəl] *n.* 信号；暗号 *v.* 发信号

silence [ˈsaɪləns] *n.* 寂静 *v.* 使沉默；使安静

silent [ˈsaɪlənt] *adj.* 寂静；沉默的

silicon [ˈsɪlɪkən] *n.* 硅

silk [sɪlk] *n.* 丝；绸

silly [ˈsɪlɪ] *adj.* 傻的；糊涂的；愚蠢的

silver [ˈsɪlvə] *n.* 银；银器；银币 *v.* 镀银

simply [ˈsɪmplɪ] *adv.* 简单地；完全；仅仅

sin [sɪn] *n.* 罪；罪恶 *v.* 犯罪

since [sɪns] *prep.* / *conj.* 自从

sincere [sɪnˈsɪə] *adj.* 诚挚的；真实的；诚恳的

sing [sɪŋ] *v.* 唱；演唱

single [ˈsɪŋgl] *adj.* 单人的；单一的；单身的

singular [ˈsɪŋgjulə] *adj.* 单数的；非凡的 *n.* 单数

sink [sɪŋk] *v.*（使）下沉；下落 *n.* 水槽；水池

sip [sɪp] *v.* 小口地喝；抿；呷 *n.* 一小口的量

sir [sɜː] *n.* 先生；长官

siren [ˈsaɪərən] *n.* 警报声；警报器

sister [ˈsɪstə] *n.* 姐妹；修女；女教士

sit [sɪt] *v.* 坐；坐下；位于；栖息；使就座

site [saɪt] *n.* 位置；场所；地点

situated [ˈsɪtʃueɪtɪd] *adj.* 位于……的；坐落在

situation [ˌsɪtʃuˈeɪʃən] *n.* 形势；状况；位置

six [sɪks] *num.* 六；六个

size [saɪz] *n.* 大小；尺寸；规模

skate [skeɪt] *v.* 溜冰；滑冰 *n.* 冰鞋

skeleton [ˈskelɪtən] *n.* 骨骼；轮廓；框架

ski [skiː] *n.* 雪橇 *v.* 滑雪

skill [skɪl] *n.* 技能；技巧

skilled [skɪld] *adj.* 熟练的；有技能的

skillful [ˈskɪlful] *adj.* 灵巧的；熟练的

skim [skɪm] *v.* 略读；浏览；轻轻掠过

skin [skɪn] *n.* 皮；皮肤；皮毛 *v.* 剥皮

skip [skɪp] *v.* 跳跃；跳绳 *n.* 跳跃

skirt [skɜːt] *n.* 裙子；边缘；郊区

skull [skʌl] *n.* 头盖骨；颅骨

sky [skaɪ] *n.* 天；天空

skyscraper [ˈskaɪskreɪpə] *n.* 摩天大楼

slam [slæm] *v.*（门、窗等）砰地关上 *n.* 猛然关闭的声音

slap [slæp] *n.* / *v.* 拍；掌击

slaughter [ˈslɔːtə] *n.* / *v.* 屠杀；屠宰

slave [sleɪv] *n.* 奴隶；苦工 *v.* 做苦工

sleep [sliːp] *v.* 睡；睡觉 *n.* 睡眠

sleeve [sliːv] *n.* 袖子

slender [ˈslendə] *adj.* 修长的；苗条的；微小的；微薄的

slice [slaɪs] *n.* 薄片；切块；小块 *v.* 把……切成薄片

slide [slaɪd] *v.*（使）滑动；下滑 *n.* 滑坡；滑道；幻灯片；下滑

slim [slɪm] *adj.* 苗条的；微小的 *v.* 变苗条

slip [slɪp] *v.* 滑；滑倒；溜走 *n.* 滑倒；疏忽

slipper [ˈslɪpə] *n.* 便鞋；拖鞋

slippery [ˈslɪpərɪ] *adj.* 滑的；滑溜的

slit [slɪt] *v.* 切开；割开 *n.* 狭长切口；狭缝

slogan [ˈsləugən] *n.* 标语；口号

slope [sləup] *n.* 斜坡；山坡 *v.*（使）倾斜

slot [slɔt] *n.* 狭缝；空档 *v.* 放入狭缝中

slow [sləu] *adj.* 慢的；慢速的 *v.* 减速

slum [slʌm] *n.* 贫民窟；贫民区；陋巷

sly [slaɪ] *adj.* 狡猾的；偷偷摸摸的

small [smɔːl] *adj.* 小的；不重要的；小规模的

smart [smɑːt] *adj.* 漂亮的；聪明的

smash [smæʃ] *v.* / *n.* 打碎；粉碎

smell [smel] *n.* 气味；嗅觉 *v.* 嗅；闻到

smile [smaɪl] *n.* / *v.* 微笑 *v.* 露出笑容

smog [smɔg] *n.* 烟雾

smoke [sməuk] *n.* 烟；烟雾；抽烟 *v.* 抽烟

smooth [smuːð] *adj.* 光滑的；顺利的 *v.* 弄平滑

smuggle [ˈsmʌgl] *v.* 走私；偷运

snack [snæk] *n.* 小吃；点心；快餐

snake [sneɪk] *n.* 蛇

snap [snæp] *v.* 断裂；（使啪地）打开（或关上）*n.* 啪嗒声；快照

snatch [snætʃ] *n.* / *v.* 攫取；抢夺

sneak [sniːk] *v.* 偷偷地走；偷带；偷偷地做

sneeze [sniːz] *v.* 打喷嚏；发喷嚏声 *n.* 喷嚏

sniff [snɪf] *v.* 嗅；闻；抽鼻子；对嗤之以鼻

snow [snəu] *n.* 雪；降雪 *v.* 下雪

snowstorm [ˈsnəustɔːm] *n.* 暴风雪

so [ˈsəu] *adv.* 如此 *conj.* 因此；以便

soak [səuk] *v.* 浸泡；浸湿；浸透

soap [səup] *n.* 肥皂

sob [sɒb] *v.* / *n.* 哭泣；呜咽

sober [ˈsəubə] *adj.* 清醒的；认真的；冷静的

so-called [ˌsəuˈkɔːld] *adj.*（贬）所谓的；号称的

soccer [ˈsɔkə] *n.* 足球

sociable [ˈsəuʃəbl] *adj.* 好交际的；友好的

social [ˈsəuʃəl] *adj.* 社会的；社交的

socialism [ˈsəuʃəlɪzəm] *n.* 社会主义

society [səˈsaɪətɪ] *n.* 社会；社群；协会

sociology [ˌsəusɪˈɔlədʒɪ] *n.* 社会学

sock [sɔk] *n.* (pl.) 短袜

soda [ˈsəudə] *n.* 苏打；汽水

sofa [ˈsəufə] *n.* 长沙发；沙发

soft [sɔft, sɔːft] *adj.* 软的；温柔的；柔软的

software [ˈsɔftwεə] *n.* 软件

soil [sɔɪl] *n.* 泥土；土地 *v.* 弄脏；（使）变脏

solar [ˈsəulə] *adj.* 太阳的；太阳能的

soldier [ˈsəuldʒə] *n.* 士兵；军人

sole [səul] *adj.* 单独的；唯一的 *n.* 鞋底

solemn [ˈsɔləm] *adj.* 庄严的；隆重的；严肃的

solid [ˈsɔlɪd] *adj.* 固体的；结实的 *n.* 固体

solo [ˈsəuləu] *n.* 独奏 *adj.* / *adv.* 单独的（地）

soluble [ˈsɔljub(ə)l] *adj.* 可溶的；可解决的

some [sʌm] *adj.* 一些；某个 *pron.* 一些

somebody [ˈsʌmbədɪ] *pron.* 某人；有人 *n.* 重要人物

somehow [ˈsʌmhau] *adv.* 以某种方式；用某种方法；不知怎么地

someone [ˈsʌmwʌn] *pron.* 某人

something [ˈsʌmθɪŋ] *pron.* 某事；某物

sometime [ˈsʌmtaɪm] *adv.* 将来（或过去）某个时候 *adj.* 以前的

sometimes [ˈsʌmtaɪmz] *adv.* 不时；有时；间或

somewhat [ˈsʌmwɔt] *pron.* / *adv.* 稍微；有点

somewhere [ˈsʌmweə] *adv.* 某地；在某处 *n.* 某个地方

son [sʌn] *n.* 儿子；孩子

song [sɔŋ, sɔːŋ] *n.* 歌唱；（虫、鸟等）鸣声；歌曲

soon [suːn] *adv.* 不久；即刻；马上

sophomore [ˈsɒfəmɔː] *n.*（高中、大学）二年级学生

sore [sɔː] *adj.* 疼痛的；痛心的 *n.* 痛处

sorrow [ˈsɔrəu] *n.* 悲哀；悲痛

sorry [ˈsɔrɪ] *adj.* 对不起；抱歉的；难过的

soul [səul] *n.* 灵魂；心灵；精神；精力

sound [saund] *n.* 声音 *v.* 发声；作响 *adj.* 健全的；合理的

soup [suːp] *n.* 汤

sour [ˈsauə] *adj.* 酸的；有酸味的；*v.*（使）变糟；变坏

south [sauθ] *n.* 南方；南部 *adj.* 南方的；南部的

southeast [ˌsauθˈiːst] *n.* / *adj.* 东南（的）；东南部（的）

southern [ˈsʌðən] *adj.* 南方的；南部的

southwest [ˌsauθˈwest] *n.* / *adj.* 西南（的）；西南部（的）

sow [səu] *v.* 播种

space [speɪs] *n.* 间隔；空地；空间 *v.* 隔开

spacecraft [ˈspeɪskrɑːft] *n.* 宇宙飞船

spaceship [ˈspeɪsʃɪp] *n.* 宇宙飞船

spade [ˈspeɪd] *n.* 铁锹；铲子

span [spæn] *n.* 持续时间；跨度 *v.* 横跨

spare [spɛə] *adj.* 多余的；备用的 *v.* 节约；节省；抽出（时间）

spark [spɑːk] *n.* 火花；火星 *v.* 发火花

sparkle [ˈspɑːkl] *v.* / *n.* 闪耀；闪烁；活力

speak [spiːk] *v.* 说话；演说；说某种语言

speaker [ˈspiːkə] *n.* 说话者；发言者；扬声器

spear [spɪə] *n.* 矛；枪

special [ˈspeʃəl] *adj.* 特殊的；特别的

specialist [ˈspeʃəlɪst] *n.* 专家

specification [ˌspesɪfɪˈkeɪʃən] *n.* 详述；（pl.）规格；说明书；规范

specimen [ˈspesɪmən] *n.* 标本；样本

spectacular [spekˈtækjulə] *adj.* 壮观的；引人注目的 *n.* 壮观的演出

spectator [spekˈteɪtə] *n.* 观众；旁观者

spectrum [ˈspektrəm] *n.* 光谱；范围；幅度

speech [spiːtʃ] *n.* 演说；讲话；语言

speed [spiːd] *n.* 速度 *v.* 快速移动；加速

spell [spel] *v.* 拼写

spelling [ˈspelɪŋ] *n.* 拼法；拼写法

spend [spend] *v.* 花费；消耗；度过

sphere [sfɪə] *n.* 球；球体；范围；领域

spicy [ˈspaɪsɪ] *adj.* 辛辣的；加很多香料的

spider [ˈspaɪdə] *n.* 蜘蛛

spill [spɪl] *v.* / *n.* 洒出（量）；溢出（量）

spin [spɪn] *v.* 旋转；织网 *n.* 旋转

spine [spaɪn] *n.* 脊柱；脊椎；书脊

spiral [ˈspaɪərəl] *adj.* 螺旋形的 *n.* 螺旋；螺线 *v.* 螺旋上升；盘旋

spirit [ˈspɪrɪt] *n.* 精神；心境；灵魂

spit [spɪt] *v.* 吐（唾沫）；吐痰 *n.* 唾液

spite [spaɪt] *n.* 恶意；怨恨

splash [splæʃ] *v.* / *n.* 飞溅（声）；溅落（声）

splendid [ˈsplendɪd] *adj.* 壮丽的；辉煌的

spoil [spɔɪl] *v.* 破坏；宠坏；溺爱

spokesman [ˈspəuksmən] *n.* 发言人

sponge [spʌndʒ] *n.* 海绵

spoon [spuːn] n. 匙；调羹
sport [spɔːt] n.（体育）运动 (pl.) 运动会
sportsman [ˈspɔːtsmən] n. 运动员
spouse [spaus] n. 配偶
spray [spreɪ] n. 喷雾；水花 v. 喷；喷射
spread [spred] v. / n. 伸开；伸展；传播
spring [sprɪŋ] n. 春；泉；弹簧 v. 跳；跳跃
sprinkle [ˈsprɪŋkl] n. 洒；喷；淋
sprout [spraut] v.（使）发芽；抽条 n. 新芽；嫩苗
spur [spɜː] n. 刺激；靴刺；马刺 v. 刺激；激励
spy [spaɪ] n. 间谍 v. 察觉；发现
square [skwɛə] n. 正方形；广场 adj. 正方形的 v. 使成方形
squirrel [ˈskwɪrəl] n. 松鼠
stab [stæb] v. / n. 刺；戳
stack [stæk] n. 堆；一堆 v. 堆积；堆起
stadium [ˈsteɪdɪəm] n. 体育场
stage [steɪdʒ] n. 舞台；戏剧；阶段；时期
stagger [ˈstægə] v. 摇晃着移动；蹒跚 n. 蹒跚
stair [steə] n. (pl.) 楼梯
staircase [ˈsteəkeɪs] n. (stairway) 楼梯
stale [steɪl] n. 不新鲜的；陈旧的；陈腐的
stalk [stɔːk] n. 茎；梗 v. 跟踪；阔步走
stall [stɔːl] n. 货摊 v.（使）停止；拖延
stamp [stæmp] n. 邮票 v. 跺脚；盖章
stand [stænd] v. 站立；忍受 n. 看台；货摊；立场
star [stɑː] n. 星；恒星；明星 v. 用星号标出；扮演主角
start [stɑːt] v. 开始；动身 n. 开端；开始
state [steɪt] n. 状态；情况；国；州 v. 陈述；说明
statement [ˈsteɪtmənt] n. 声明；陈述
statesman [ˈsteɪtsmən] n. 政治家；国务活动家
static [ˈstætɪk] adj. (statical) 静态的；静力的
station [ˈsteɪʃən] n. 车站；电视台；所；局 v. 安置；驻扎
stationary [ˈsteɪʃənərɪ] adj. 静止的；稳定的
stationery [ˈsteɪʃənərɪ] n. 文具；信纸
statistical [stəˈtɪstɪk(ə)l] adj. 统计的；统计学的
statue [ˈstætʃuː] n. 塑像；雕像
status [ˈsteɪtəs] n. 地位；身份；状况
stay [steɪ] v. 逗留；保持 n. 逗留；停留
steak [steɪk] n. 牛排；鱼排
steal [stiːl] v. 偷；窃取
steam [stiːm] n. 蒸汽；水蒸气 v. 冒蒸气
steamer [ˈstiːmə] n. 汽船；轮船
steel [stiːl] n. 钢
steep [stiːp] adj. 陡峭的；险峻的；急剧的
steer [stɪə] v. 驾驶；为……操舵；引导
step [step] n. 步；台阶；步骤 v. 踏；跨步走
stereo [ˈsterɪəu] n. 立体声音响；立体声装置 n. / adj. 立体声（的）
steward [ˈstjuːəd] n. 乘务员；服务员；管家
stick [stɪk] n. 棍；棒；手杖 v. 刺；戳；粘贴
sticky [ˈstɪkɪ] adj. 黏的；黏性的；棘手的
stiff [stɪf] adj. 硬的；不易弯曲的 adv. 非常；极其
still [stɪl] adj. 静止的；寂静的 adv. 还；仍然；静止地
sting [stɪŋ] v. / n. 刺；叮；蛰
stir [stɜː] v. / n. 搅拌；搅动；激动
stitch [stɪtʃ] n. 一针；针脚 v. 缝；缝补
stock [stɔk] n. 现货；库存；股票 v. 储备
stocking [ˈstɔkɪŋ] n. 长（统）袜
stomach [ˈstʌmək] n. 胃；腹部 v. 承受；忍受
stone [stəun] n. 石头；岩石；矿石
stool [stuːl] n. 凳子
stoop [stuːp] v. / n. 弯腰；俯身 v. 卑鄙
stop [stɔp] v. 停止；阻止 n. 停车站；停止
storage [ˈstɔrɪdʒ] n. 贮藏（量）；保管；库房
store [stɔː] n. 商店；贮藏；贮备品 v. 贮藏
storey [ˈstɔːrɪ] n. (story) 楼；层
storm [stɔːm] n. 暴风雨；暴风雪；风暴
story [ˈstɔːrɪ] n. 故事；传说；小说；楼层
stove [stəuv] n. 炉子；火炉
straight [streɪt] adj. / adv. 直的（地）；笔直的（地） adj. 直率的
strange [streɪndʒ] adj. 奇怪的；陌生的
stranger [ˈstreɪndʒə] n. 陌生人；外地人
strap [stræp] n. 皮带；带子 v. 用带束住
straw [strɔː] n. 稻草；麦秆；吸管
strawberry [ˈstrɔːbərɪ] n. 草莓
stream [striːm] n. 小河；溪流 v. 流出；涌
streamline [ˈstriːmlaɪn] adj. 流线型的 v. 使成流线

型;精简
street [stri:t] *n.* 街;街道
strength [streŋθ] *n.* 力量;实力;长处;人力
strenuous [ˈstrenjuəs] *adj.* 费力的;奋发的;努力的
stress [stres] *n.* 压力;重音 *v.* 强调;重读
strict [strɪkt] *adj.* 严格的;严谨的;严厉的
stride [straɪd] *v.* 大踏步走;跨越 *n.* 一大步 (pl.) 长足进步
strife [straɪf] *n.* 冲突;斗争
string [strɪŋ] *n.* 弦;线;细绳 *v.* 缚;捆
strip [strɪp] *n.* 条;带 *v.* 除去;剥夺
stripe [straɪp] *n.* 长条;条纹
stroke [strəuk] *n.* 击打;击球;中风 *v.* 抚摸
stroll [strəul] *n.* / *v.* 漫步;散步;游荡
strong [strɔŋ] *adj.* 强壮的;强大的;强烈的
stubborn [ˈstʌbən] *adj.* 顽固的;倔强的
student [ˈstju:dənt] *n.* 学生;学者
studio [ˈstju:dɪəu] *n.* 工作室;播音室
study [ˈstʌdɪ] *v.* / *n.* 学习;研究;调查
stuff [stʌf] *n.* 物品;东西 *v.* 填满;塞满
stumble [ˈstʌmbl] *n.* 跌倒;绊倒 *v.* 绊(摔)倒;结结巴巴说
stun [stʌn] *v.* 使震惊;使吃惊;使昏迷 *n.* 昏迷;惊倒
stupid [ˈstju:pɪd] *adj.* 愚蠢的;迟钝的
style [staɪl] *n.* 风格;式样;作风
submarine [ˈsʌbməri:n] *n.* 潜水艇 *adj.* 水底的;海底的
submerge [səbˈmɜ:dʒ] *v.* 沉没;淹没;潜入
subtract [səbˈtrækt] *v.* 减(去);扣掉
suburb [ˈsʌbɜ:b] *n.* 市郊;郊区
subway [ˈsʌbweɪ] *n.* 地铁;地下行人隧道
successor [səkˈsesə] *n.* 继承者;接替的事物
such [sʌtʃ] det. / *pron.* 这样的;那样的
suck [sʌk] *v.* / *n.* 吸;吮;啜
sudden [ˈsʌdən] *adj.* 出乎意料的;突然的
sue [su:] *v.* 控告;起诉
sugar [ˈʃugə] *n.* 糖;食糖 *v.* 加糖于
suggest [səˈdʒest] *v.* 建议;暗示;表明
suggestion [səˈdʒestʃən] *n.* 建议;提议;暗示
suit [su:t] *v.* 合适;相配 *n.* 一套西服;诉讼
suite [swi:t] *n.* 套间;套房;一套家具、产品
sulfur [ˈsʌlfə] *n.* (sulphur) 硫
sum [sʌm] *n.* 总数;金额 *v.* 合计;总计
summer [ˈsʌmə] *n.* 夏天;夏季 *adj.* 夏季的
summit [ˈsʌmɪt] *n.* 最高点;顶点;山顶
sun [sʌn] *n.* 太阳;恒星
Sunday [ˈsʌndeɪ] *n.* 星期日
sunrise [ˈsʌnraɪz] *n.* 日出;拂晓;朝霞
sunset [ˈsʌnset] *n.* 日落;傍晚;晚霞
sunshine [ˈsʌnʃaɪn] *n.* 日光;日照;晴天
super [ˈsu:pə] *adj.* 极好的;超级的
supermarket [ˈsu:pəmɑ:kɪt] *n.* 超市
supersonic [ˌsu:pəˈsɔnɪk] *adj.* 超音速的;超声波的 *n.* 超声波
supper [ˈsʌpə] *n.* 晚餐;宵夜
sure [ʃuə] *adj.* 肯定的;确信的 *adv.* 当然
surface [ˈsɜ:fɪs] *n.* 表面;外表 *adj.* 表面的
surgeon [ˈsɜ:dʒən] *n.* 外科医生
surname [ˈsɜ:neɪm] *n.* 姓
surprise [səˈpraɪz] *v.* 使诧异 *n.* 诧异;惊异
surround [səˈraund] *v.* 包围;环绕 *n.* 环绕物
surroundings [səˈraʊndɪŋz] *n.* 周围的事物;环境
survey *v.* [sɜ:ˈveɪ] / *n.* [ˈsɜ:veɪ] 审视;勘测(做)民意调查
swallow [ˈswɔləu] *v.* 吞;咽 *n.* 燕子;吞
swamp [swɔmp] *n.* 沼泽;湿地 *v.* 浸没;使疲于应对
swan [swɔn] *n.* 天鹅 *v.* 闲荡;游荡
swarm [swɔ:m] *n.* 一大群 *v.* 蜂拥;挤满
sway [sweɪ] *v.* 摇摆;说服 *n.* 摇动;影响力
swear [sweə] *v.* 诅咒;宣誓;发誓
sweat [swet] *n.* 汗 *v.*(使)出汗
sweater [ˈswetə] *n.* 毛衣;厚运动衫
sweep [swi:p] *v.* 打扫;清除;席卷 *n.* 打扫
sweet [swi:t] *adj.* 甜的; 可爱的 *n.*(pl.)糖果;甜食
swell [swel] *n.* / *v.* 肿胀;增大;增加
swim [swɪm] *v.* 游泳;漂浮 *n.* 游泳
swing [swɪŋ] *v.* 摇摆;摇荡 *n.* 秋千;摇摆
sword [sɔ:d] *n.* 剑;刀;武力
symmetry [ˈsɪmɪtrɪ] *n.* 对称(性);匀称;整齐

sympathize [ˈsɪmpəθaɪz] *v.* (sympathise) 同情；共鸣；赞成
syndrome [ˈsɪndrəum] *n.* 综合征；典型表现
system [ˈsɪstəm] *n.* 系统；体系；方法；体制

T

table [ˈteɪbl] *n.* 桌子；表格
tablet [ˈtæblɪt] *n.* 药片；碑；匾
tail [teɪl] *n.* 尾巴；尾部；跟踪者 *v.* 尾随；跟踪
tailor [ˈteɪlə] *n.* 裁缝 *v.* 缝制；订制
take [teɪk] *v.* 拿；带；乘坐；吃
tale [teɪl] *n.* 故事；传说
talent [ˈtælənt] *n.* 才能；天资；人才
talk [tɔːk] *n.* 谈话 *v.* 说话；交谈
tall [tɔːl] *adj.* 高的；高大的
tame [teɪm] *adj.* 驯服的；温顺的；乏味的 *v.* 驯服
tan [tæn] *n.* / *adj.* 棕褐色（的） *v.*（使）晒黑
tangle [ˈtæŋgl] *n.* 纠缠；缠结；混乱 *v.*（使）缠绕；变乱
tank [tæŋk] *n.* 罐；槽；箱；坦克
tanker [ˈtæŋkə] *n.* 油船
tap [tæp] *n.* 塞子；水龙头；轻打 *v.* 开发
tape [teɪp] *n.* 磁带 *v.* 录音；系；捆
tar [tɑː] *n.* 柏油；焦油 *v.* 涂焦油于
tariff [ˈtærɪf] *n.* 关税；收费
task [tɑːsk, tæsk] *n.* 任务；作业；工作
taste [teɪst] *v.* 品尝；体验 *n.* 滋味；味觉
tax [tæks] *n.* 税（款）；负担 *v.* 对……征税
taxi [ˈtæksɪ] *n.* 出租汽车
tea [tiː] *n.* 茶（叶）；午后茶点
teach [tiːtʃ] v 教；讲授；训练
teacher [ˈtiːtʃə] *n.* 教师；老师
team [tiːm] *n.* 小队；小组 *v.* 协同工作
tear [tɪə] *n.* (pl.) 眼泪；破洞 *v.* 撕裂；扯破
tease [tiːz] *v.* 取笑 *n.* 戏弄；玩笑
technician [tekˈnɪʃən] *n.* 技术员；技师；技工
tedious [ˈtiːdɪəs] *adj.* 乏味的；单调的；冗长的
teenager [ˈtiːneɪdʒə] *n.* 十几岁的青少年
telegram [ˈtelɪgræm] *n.* 电报
telegraph [ˈtelɪgrɑːf] *n.* 电报机；电报 *v.* 打电报；发电报
telephone [ˈtelɪfəun] *n.* 电话 *v.* 打电话
telescope [ˈtelɪskəup] *n.* 望远镜 *v.* 缩短
tell [tel] *v.* 告诉；讲述；辨别
temperature [ˈtempərɪtʃə] *n.* 温度；体温；气温
temple [ˈtempl] *n.* 庙宇；寺
tempo [ˈtempəu] *n.* 节奏；（音乐的）速度
temptation [tempˈteɪʃən] *n.* 引诱；诱惑（物）
ten [ten] *num.* 十；十个
tenant [ˈtenənt] *n.* 承租人；房客 *v.* 租借；承租
tender [ˈtendə] *adj.* 温柔的；嫩的 *v.* 提供；投标
tennis [ˈtenɪs] *n.* 网球
tense [tens] *n.* 时态 *v.* 拉紧 *adj.* 绷紧的；紧张的
tent [tent] *n.* 帐篷
term [tɜːm] *n.* 学期；期限；期间 (pl.) 条件；条款；术语
terminate [ˈtɜːmɪneɪt] *v.*（使）结束；（使）停止
terrible [ˈterəbl] *adj.* 很糟的；可怕的
terrific [təˈrɪfɪk] *adj.* 极好的；非常的；极度的
test [test] *n.* / *v.* 试验；检验；测验
text [tekst] *n.* 正文；文本；教科书
textbook [ˈtekstbuk] *n.* 课本；教科书
texture [ˈtekstʃə] *n.*（织物）质地；（材料）构造；肌理
than [ðæn] *prep.* / *conj.* 比
thank [θæŋk] *v.* / *n.* 感谢
Thanksgiving [ˌθæŋksˈgɪvɪŋ] *n.* 感恩节
that [ðæt] *adj.* / *pron.* 那；那个 *adv.* 那么
the [ðə; ðɪ] art. 这（那）个；这（那）些
theater [ˈθɪətə] *n.* (theatre) 戏院；戏剧
theft [θeft] *n.* 偷窃（行为）；偷窃罪
their [ðeə] *pron.* 他们的
theirs [ðeəz] *pron.* 他们的
them [ðem] *pron.* 他们
theme [θiːm] *n.* 题目；主题；主旋律；基调
themselves [ðəmˈselvz] *pron.* 他们自己
then [ðen] *adv.* 当时；在那时；然后；那么
theory [ˈθɪərɪ] *n.* 理论；原理；学说
there [ðeə] *adv.* 在那儿；往那儿
thereafter [ˌðeərˈɑːftə] *adv.* 此后；以后
thereby [ˌðeəˈbaɪ] *adv.* 因此；从而
therefore [ˈðeəfɔː] *adv.* 因此；所以 *conj.* 因此

thermometer [θəˈmɔmɪtə] *n.* 温度计

these [ðiːz] *pron.* / *adj.* 这些

thesis [ˈθiːsɪs] *n.* (pl. theses) 论文；论题

they [ðeɪ] *pron.* 他们

thick [θɪk] *adj.* 厚的；浓的 *adv.* 厚；浓；密

thief [θiːf] *n.* (pl. thieves) 贼；小偷

thigh [θaɪ] *n.* 大腿；股骨

thin [θɪn] *adj.* 瘦的；薄的；淡的

thing [θɪŋ] *n.* 东西；事情；物品

think [θɪŋk] *v.* 想；认为；考虑

third [θɜːd] *num.* 第三

thirst [θɜːst] *n.* 渴；口渴；渴望

thirsty [ˈθɜːstɪ] *adj.* 口渴的；渴望的

thirteen [ˈθɜːˈtiːn] *num.* 十三

thirty [ˈθɜːtɪ] *num.* 三十

this [ðɪs] *pron.* / *adj.* 这个 *adv.* 这（样）

thorn [θɔːn] *n.* 刺；荆棘

thorough [ˈθʌrə] *adj.* 彻底的；完全的；详细的

those [ðəuz] *pron.* / *adj.* 那些

though [ðəu] *adv.* 可是；然而 *conj.* 尽管；虽然

thought [θɔːt] *n.* 想法；思考；思维

thousand [ˈθauzənd] *num.* 一千

thread [θred] *n.* 线；思路 *v.* 穿线；穿过

threat [θret] *n.* 恐吓；威胁；凶兆

three [θriː] *num.* 三

throat [θrəut] *n.* 咽喉；嗓子

throne [θrəun] *n.* 御座；王位；王权

through [θruː] *prep.* / *adv.* 穿过；自始至终；透过 *adj.* 直达的

throughout [θruːˈaut] *prep.* 遍及；贯穿 *adv.* 到处；自始至终

throw [θrəu] *v.* 扔；抛 *n.* 投掷

thrust [θrʌst] *v.* 猛塞；猛推；刺；戳

thumb [θʌm] *n.* 拇指 *v.* 示意要求搭车；迅速翻阅

thunder [ˈθʌndə] *n.* 雷（声）；轰隆声 *v.* 打雷

Thursday [ˈθɜːzdeɪ] *n.* 星期四

thus [ðʌs] *adv.* 如此；像这样；于是；因此

tick [tɪk] *v.* 滴答响；打勾 *n.* 滴答声；勾号

ticket [ˈtɪkɪt] *n.* 票；入场券；罚单

tide [taɪd] *n.* 潮汐；潮流；趋势

tidy [ˈtaɪdɪ] *adj.* 整洁的；整齐的 *v.* 整理；收拾

tie [taɪ] *n.* 领带；联系；束缚 *v.* 扎；系；捆

tiger [ˈtaɪgə] *n.* 老虎

tight [taɪt] *adj.* 紧的；拉紧的 *adv.* 紧紧地

tighten [ˈtaɪt(ə)n] *v.*（使）变紧；（使）紧固

tile [taɪl] *n.* 瓦片；瓷砖 *v.* 铺瓦于；贴砖于

till [tɪl] *prep.* 直到；直到……为止

tilt [tɪlt] *n.* / *v.*（使）倾斜；（使）倾侧

timber [ˈtɪmbə] *n.* 木材；木料

time [taɪm] *n.* 时间；时刻；次数；倍

timely [ˈtaɪmlɪ] *adj.* 及时的；适时的

timid [ˈtɪmɪd] *adj.* 胆怯的；怯懦的

tin [tɪn] *n.* 罐头；锡 *adj.* 锡制的

tiny [ˈtaɪnɪ] *adj.* 极小的；微小的

tip [tɪp] *n.* 尖端；小贴士；小费 *v.* 轻击；倾斜；给小费

tire [ˈtaɪə] *v.*（使）疲倦；（使）厌倦 *n.* (tyre) 轮胎

tired [ˈtaɪəd] *adj.* 疲劳的；厌倦的

tiresome [ˈtaɪəsəm] *adj.* 使人厌倦的；讨厌的

tissue [ˈtɪʃuː] *n.*（动；植物的）组织；薄绢；纸巾

title [ˈtaɪtl] *n.* 书名；标题；头衔；称号

to [tuː] *prep.*（表示方向）到；向

toast [ˈtəust] *n.* 烤面包；吐司；祝酒（词）*v.* 烘；烤；（向……）祝酒

tobacco [təˈbækəu] *n.* 烟草；烟叶

today [təˈdeɪ] *adv.* 在今天；现今 *n.* 今天；现在

toe [təu] *n.* 脚趾；足尖

together [təˈgeðə] *adv.* 共同；一起；集拢地

toilet [ˈtɔɪlɪt] *n.* 厕所；盥洗室

tomato [təˈmɑːtəu] *n.* 西红柿

tomb [tuːm] *n.* 坟；冢

tomorrow [təˈmɔrəu] *n.* 明天；未来 *adv.* 在明天

ton [tʌn] *n.* 吨；(pl.) 大量；许多

tone [təun] *n.* 语气；音色；风格；气氛

tongue [tʌŋ] *n.* 舌；语言

tonight [təˈnaɪt] *adv.* 在今晚 *n.* 今晚

too [tuː] *adv.* 也；还；太；过于

tool [tuːl] *n.* 工具；用具；方法；手段

tooth [tuːθ] *n.* (pl. teeth) 牙齿；齿状物

top [tɔp] *n.* 顶端；顶点 *adj.* 最高的；顶部的

topic [ˈtɔpɪk] *n.* 话题；主题；题目

torch [tɔːtʃ] *n.* 手电筒；火炬；火把

torment *n.* [ˈtɔːment] 折磨；痛苦 *v.* [tɔːˈment] 折磨；纠缠
torrent [ˈtɔrənt] *n.* 激流；洪流；爆发
torture [ˈtɔːtʃə] *v.* / *n.* 拷问；磨难；痛苦
toss [tɔs] *v.* 向上掷、扔；摇摆 *n.* 掷硬币决定
total [ˈtəutəl] *n.* 总数；合计 *adj.* 总的；全部的
touch [tʌtʃ] *v.* 触；碰；摸；感动 *n.* 触摸
tour [tuə] *n.* 旅游；旅行；巡回演出、比赛 *v.* 旅游
tourist [ˈtuərɪst] *n.* 旅游者；观光客
tow [təu] *v.* 拖（车、船等） *n.* 拖；牵引
toward [təˈwɔːd] *prep.* (towards) 朝；向；将近；对于；为了
towel [ˈtauəl] *n.* 毛巾 *v.* 用毛巾擦或擦干
tower [ˈtauə] *n.* 塔 *v.* 高耸
town [taun] *n.* 市镇；集镇；闹市区
toy [tɔɪ] *n.* 玩具
tractor [ˈtræktə] *n.* 拖拉机；牵引车
trade [treɪd] *n.* 贸易；商业；行业 *v.* 交易
trademark [ˈtreɪdmɑːk] *n.* 商标；特征
traffic [ˈtræfɪk] *n.* 交通；交通量
tragedy [ˈtrædʒɪdɪ] *n.* 悲剧；惨事；灾难
train [treɪn] *n.* 列车 *v.* 训练；培养
training [ˈtreɪnɪŋ] *n.* 训练；培养
traitor [ˈtreɪtə] *n.* 叛徒；卖国贼
tram [træm] *n.* 有轨电车
tramp [træmp] *v.* 踩踏 *n.* 长途步行；流浪者
transistor [trænˈzɪstə] *n.* 晶体管；晶体管收音机
translate [trænzˈleɪt] *v.* 翻译；解释
translation [trænsˈleɪʃən] *n.* 翻译；译文
trap [træp] *n.* 陷阱；圈套 *v.* 诱捕；使中圈套；设圈套
trash [træʃ] *n.* 垃圾；废物；拙劣的作品
travel [ˈtrævəl] *n.* 旅行 *v.* 旅行；传播
tray [treɪ] *n.* 盘；碟；托盘
treason [ˈtriːzən] *n.* 谋反；通敌；叛国
treasure [ˈtreʒə] *n.* 财宝；财富 *v.* 珍爱；珍惜
treat [triːt] *v.* 对待；治疗；请客 *n.* 款待；请客
treaty [ˈtriːtɪ] *n.* 条约；协议
tree [triː] *n.* 树
tremble [ˈtrembl] *n.* 战栗；颤抖 *v.* 发抖；颤抖
trench [trentʃ] *n.* / *v.*（挖）沟；（挖）战壕
trend [trend] *n.* 倾向；趋势 *v.* 倾向
trial [ˈtraɪəl] *n.* 讯问；审讯；试验；试用；尝试
triangle [ˈtraɪæŋgl] *n.* 三角（形）
trick [trɪk] *n.* 诡计；恶作剧；窍门 *v.* 欺骗；哄骗
trifle [ˈtraɪfl] n 小事；琐事；少量
trim [trɪm] *adj.* 整齐的；整洁的 *v.* 修剪；修整 *n.* 饰物
trip [trɪp] *n.* 旅行；绊倒 *v.* 绊倒
trolley [ˈtrɔlɪ] *n.* 手推车；（英）无轨电车；（美）有轨电车
troop [truːp] *n.* (pl.) 部队；军队；（一）群 / 队 *v.* 群集；集合
tropic [ˈtrɔpɪk] *n.* 回归线；热带地区
tropical [ˈtrɔpɪkəl] *adj.* 热带的
trouble [ˈtrʌbl] *n.* 烦恼；问题；故障 *v.*（使）烦恼
troublesome [ˈtrʌblsəm] *adj.* 令人烦恼的；讨厌的
trousers [ˈtrauzəz] *n.* 裤子
truck [trʌk] *n.* 卡车；载重汽车
true [truː] *adj.* 真实；可靠的；正确无误的
trumpet [ˈtrʌmpɪt] *n.* 喇叭；小号
trunk [trʌŋk] *n.* 树干；象鼻；箱子；躯干
trust [ˈtrʌst] *v.* 信任；相信 *n.* 信任；信任
truth [truːθ] *n.* 真实；真相；真实性
try [traɪ] *v.* 尝试；试图；试验；审讯 *n.* 尝试
tub [tʌb] *n.* 盆；浴缸
tube [tjuːb] *n.* 管；电子管；显像管；地铁
tuck [tʌk] *v.* 卷起；塞进
Tuesday [ˈtjuːzdeɪ] *n.* 星期二
tug [tʌg] *v.* 用力拖（或拉）；苦干 *n.* 拖；苦干；拖船
tumble [ˈtʌmbl] *v.*（使）摔倒；打滚；翻腾 *n.* 摔跤；跌倒
tumour [ˈtjuːmə] *n.* (tumor)（肿）瘤；肿块
tune [tjuːn] *n.* 调子；曲调 *v.* 调音；调整
tunnel [ˈtʌnəl] *n.* 隧道；山洞
turbine [ˈtɜːbaɪn] *n.* 汽轮机；涡轮机
turkey [ˈtɜːkɪ] *n.* 火鸡（肉）
turn [tɜːn] *v.* / *n.*（使）转动；（使）转变 *n.* 转弯
tutor [ˈtjuːtə] *n.* 导师；家庭教师 *v.* 辅导
TV *n.* (television) 电视；电视机
twelve [twelv] *num.* 十二

twenty [ˈtwentɪ] *num.* 二十

twice [twaɪs] *adv.* 两次;两倍

twin [twɪn] *adj.* 成双的 *n.* 双胞胎之一

twinkle [ˈtwɪŋkl] *v.*(星等)闪烁;(眼睛)发亮 *n.* 闪烁;闪光

twist [twɪst] *v.* / *n.* 捻;拧;转动

two [tu:] *num.* 二;两个 *n.* 两个(人或物)

type [taɪp] *n.* 类型;字体 *v.* 打字

typewriter [ˈtaɪpraɪtə] *n.* 打字机

typhoon [taɪˈfu:n] *n.* 台风

typist [ˈtaɪpɪst] *n.* 打字员

U

ugly [ˈʌglɪ] *adj.* 丑陋的;难看的

ultraviolet [ˌʌltrəˈvaɪələt] *adj.* / *n.* 紫外线(的)

umbrella [ʌmˈbrelə] *n.* 伞

uncle [ˈʌŋkl] *n.* 伯父;叔父;舅父;姑父;姨父;叔叔

under [ˈʌndə] *prep.* / *adv.* 在……下面

underground [ˈʌndəgraund] *adj.* 地下的 *n.* 地铁 *adv.* 在地下

underneath [ˌʌndəˈni:θ] *prep.* 在……下面 *adv.* 在下面;在底下

understand [ˌʌndəˈstænd] *v.* 明白;理解;体谅

understanding [ˌʌndəˈstændɪŋ] *n.* 理解;了解;谅解 *adj.* 通情达理的

undo [ˌʌnˈdu:] *v.* 松开;解开

unfold [ˌʌnˈfəuld] *v.* 打开;展示;呈现

unfortunately [ʌnˈfɔ:tʃənətlɪ] *adv.* 不幸地

uniform [ˈju:nɪfɔ:m] *n.* 制服 *adj.* 相同的

unify [ˈju:nɪfaɪ] *v.* 使联合;使相同

unit [ˈju:nɪt] *n.* 单元;部件;科、室、部门;(计量)单位

unity [ˈju:nɪtɪ] *n.* 团结;统一

university [ˌju:nɪˈvɜ:sətɪ] *n.*(综合)大学

unless [ənˈles] *conj.* 除非 *prep.* 除……外

unlike [ˌʌnˈlaɪk] *adj.* 不同的;不相似的 *prep.* 不像;和……不同

unlikely [ˌʌnˈlaɪklɪ] *adj.* 不大可能发生的;靠不住的

unload [ˌʌnˈləud] *v.* 卸货;取出(子弹或胶卷等);推卸(责任)

until [ˌʌnˈtɪl] *conj.* / *prep.* 直到……为止

unusual [ˌʌnˈju:ʒuəl] *adj.* 不平常的;与众不同的

up [ʌp] *adv.* / *adj.* / *prep.* 向上

upon [əˈpɒn] *prep.* 在……上;在……旁

upper [ˈʌpə] *adj.* 上面的;上部的;较高的

uproar [ˈʌprɔ:] *n.* 骚动;喧嚣;鼎沸

upstairs [ˌʌpˈsteəz] *adv.* 在楼上;上楼 *adv.* 楼上地

up-to-date [ˌʌptəˈdeɪt] *adj.* 现代化的;最新的

upward [ˈʌpwəd] *adj.* 向上的;上升的 *adv.* 向上

urge [ɜ:dʒ] *v.* 催促;怂恿 *n.* 强烈欲望;迫切要求

us [ʌs] *pron.* 我们

usage [ˈju:zɪdʒ] *n.* 使用;用法;惯例

use [ju:z] *n.* 使用;用法 / 途;用处 *v.* 使用;消耗

used [ju:zd] *adj.* 习惯于;适应;二手的;旧的

useful [ˈju:sful] *adj.* 有用的;实用的;有益的;有帮助的

usual [ˈju:ʒuəl] *adj.* 通常的;平常的

usually [ˈju:ʒuəlɪ] *adv.* 通常;平常

utter [ˈʌtə] *v.* 说;发出(声音) *adj.* 彻底的;完全的

vacation [vəˈkeɪʃən] *n.* 休假;假期

V

valley [ˈvælɪ] *n.*(山)谷;流域

value [ˈvælju:] *n.* 价格;价值;实用性 *v.* 评价;估价;尊重

valve [vælv] *n.* 阀;活门;(心脏的)瓣膜

van [væn] *n.* 有篷汽车;有篷货运车厢

vapour [ˈveɪpə] *n.* (vapor) 汽;(水)蒸气

vase [vɑ:z] *n.* 花瓶;瓶

vast [vɑ:st] *adj.* 辽阔的;大量的

vegetable [ˈvedʒtəbl] *n.* 蔬菜;植物 *adj.* 植物的;蔬菜的

vegetarian [ˌvedʒəˈteərɪən] *n.* 素食主义者

vegetation [ˌvedʒəˈteɪʃən] *n.* 植物;草木

veil [veɪl] *n.* 面纱;遮蔽物 *v.* 用面纱掩盖;掩饰

vein [veɪn] *n.* 静脉;叶脉;矿脉

velocity [vəˈlɒsətɪ] *n.* 速度;速率

velvet [ˈvelvɪt] *n.* 丝绒;天鹅绒 *adj.* 丝绒制的;柔软的

ventilate [ˈventɪleɪt] *v.* 使通风;给……装通风设备
verb [vɜːb] *n.* 动词
versatile [ˈvɜːsətaɪl] *adj.* 通用的;多才多艺的;多方面的
verse [vɜːs] *n.* 韵文;诗;诗句
versus [ˈvɜːsəs] *prep.* 与……相比
vertical [ˈvɜːtɪkəl] *adj.* 垂直的;竖的 *n.* 垂线
very [ˈverɪ] *adv.* 很;非常 *adj.* 恰好;正是的
vest [vest] *n.* 背心;马甲
veto [ˈviːtəu] *n.* / *v.* 否决
via [ˈvaɪə] *prep.* 经;通过;凭借
vibrate [vaɪˈbreɪt] *v.*(使)振动;(使)摇摆
vice [vaɪs] *n.* 邪恶;恶习;罪行 *adj.* 副的
vicinity [vəˈsɪnətɪ] *n.* 邻近;附近
victory [ˈvɪktərɪ] *n.* 胜利;战胜
video [ˈvɪdɪəu] *n.* 视频;录像 *v.* 录下;拍摄
view [vjuː] *n.* 视野;风景;见解 *v.* 认为;观看
vigorous [ˈvɪgərəs] *adj.* 充满活力的;精力旺盛的
village [ˈvɪlɪdʒ] *n.* 村;村庄
vinegar [ˈvɪnɪgə] *n.* 醋;尖酸
violet [ˈvaɪələt] *n.* 紫罗兰;紫色 *adj.* 紫色的
violin [ˌvaɪəˈlɪn] *n.* 小提琴
virgin [ˈvɜːdʒɪn] *n.* 处女;新手 *adj.* 处女的;纯洁的;原始的
virus [ˈvaɪərəs] *n.* 病毒
visa [ˈviːzə] *n.* 签证 *v.* 签证
vision [ˈvɪʒən] *n.* 视力;洞察力;视野;幻想
visit [ˈvɪzɪt] *n.* / *v.* 访问;参观
visitor [ˈvɪzɪtə] *n.* 访问者;参观者;客人
vitamin [ˈvɪtəmɪn] *n.* 维生素
vocabulary [vəˈkæbjələrɪ] *n.* 词汇;词汇量
voice [vɔɪs] *n.* 声音;嗓音;想法;语态
void [vɔɪd] *adj.* 空虚的;没有的;无效的
volcano [vɔlˈkeɪnəu] *n.* 火山
volleyball [ˈvɔlɪbɔːl] *n.* 排球
volt [vəlt] *n.* 伏特
voltage [ˈvəultɪdʒ] *n.* 电压
volume [ˈvɔljuːm] *n.* 容积;卷;册;音量
vote [vəut] *v.* / *n.* 投票;表决 *n.* 选票
vowel [ˈvauəl] *n.* 元音;元音字母
voyage [ˈvɔɪɪdʒ] *n.* 航海;航行;旅行

W

wage [weɪdʒ] *n.* 工资;报酬
wagon [ˈwægən] *n.* 四轮运货车;敞篷车厢
waist [weɪst] *n.* 腰;腰部
wait [weɪt] *v.* / *n.* 等候;等待
waiter [weɪtə] *n.* 侍者;服务员
waitress [ˈweɪtrɪs] *n.* 女侍者;女服务员
wake [weɪk] *v.* 醒来;唤醒;唤起;激起
waken [ˈweɪkən] *v.* 醒;弄醒;唤醒
walk [wɔːk] *v.* / *n.* 走;步行;散步
wall [wɔːl] *n.* 墙;围墙 *v.* 筑墙围住
wallet [ˈwɔlɪt] *n.* 皮夹;钱包
want [wɔnt] *v.* 想要;需要 *n.* 需要;短缺
war [wɔː] *n.* 战争(状态);冲突 *v.* 作战
ward [wɔːd] *n.* 病房;被监护人 *v.* 接受(病人)入病房
wardrobe [ˈwɔːdrəub] *n.* 衣柜;衣橱;全部服装
warehouse [ˈweəhaus] *n.* 仓库;货栈
warfare [ˈwɔːfeə] *n.* 战争;斗争;冲突
warm [wɔːm] *adj.* 温暖的;热情的 *v.*(使)变暖
warmth [wɔːmθ] *n.* 温暖;热心;热情
warn [wɔːn] *v.* 警告;告诫
wash [wɔʃ, wɔːʃ] *n.* 洗 *v.* 冲刷;洗
waste [weɪst] *v.* 浪费 *adj.* 无用的;荒芜的 *n.* 浪费;废物
watch [wɔtʃ] *v.* 观看;注视;照看;当心 *n.* 手表;观察
water [ˈwɔːtə] *n.* 水 *v.* 浇灌;给……饮水
waterfall [ˈwɔːtəfɔːl] *n.* 瀑布
waterproof [ˈwɔːtəpruːf] *adj.* 防水的;耐水的
watt [wɔt] *n.* 瓦;瓦特
wave [weɪv] *n.* 波浪;挥手;卷发 *v.* 挥手;挥舞
wax [wæks] *n.* 蜡;蜂蜡 *v.* 打蜡
way [weɪ] *n.* 道路;路程;方法/式;手段
we [wiː] *pron.* 我们
weak [wiːk] *adj.* 虚弱的;无力的
wealth [welθ] *n.* 财富;财产
wealthy [ˈwelθɪ] *adj.* 富有的;丰裕的 *n.* 富人
weapon [ˈwepən] *n.* 武器;兵器
wear [ˈweə] *v.* / *n.* 穿着;戴着;磨损

weary [ˈwɪərɪ] *adj.* 疲倦的；令人厌烦的 *v.* 使疲倦；使厌倦
weather [ˈweðə] *n.* 天气；气象
weave [wiːv] *v.* 编（织） *n.* 编织法；编织式样
web [web] *n.* 网；蜘蛛网
wedding [ˈwedɪŋ] *n.* 婚礼
wedge [wedʒ] *n.* 楔；楔形 *v.*（将……）楔入
Wednesday [ˈwenzdeɪ] *n.* 星期三
weed [wiːd] *n.* 杂草；野草 *v.* 除草；锄草
week [wiːk] *n.* 星期；周
weekday [ˈwiːkdeɪ] *n.* 平常日；工作日
weekend [ˌwiːkˈend] *n.* 周末
weekly [ˈwiːklɪ] *adj.* 每星期的；一周的 *adv.* 每周一次 *n.* 周刊；周报
weep [wiːp] *v.* 哭泣；流泪 *n.* 哭泣
weigh [weɪ] *v.* 称……重量；重达；考虑；权衡
weight [weɪt] *n.* 重量；体重；重要性；权重
weird [wɪəd] *adj.* 古怪的；离奇的
welcome [ˈwelkəm] *int.* 欢迎 *adj.* 受欢迎的 *v.* / *n.* 欢迎；迎接
weld [weld] *v.* 焊接 *n.* 焊接；焊缝
well [wel] *adv.* 好；令人满意地 *adj.* 健康的
n. 井 int. 嗯；好
well-known [ˌwelˈnəun] *adj.* 有名的；著名的
west [west] *n.* / *adj.* 西方（的）；西部（的） *adv.* 向西
western [ˈwestən] *adj.* 西方的；西部的 *n.* 西部电影；西方人
wet [wet] *adj.* 湿的；潮湿的；多雨的 *v.* 弄湿；沾湿
whale [weɪl] *n.* 鲸；庞然大物
what [wɔt] *pron.* / det. / *adj.* / *int.* 什么；多么
whatever [wɔtˈevə] *pron.* 无论什么 *adj.* 无论什么样的
whatsoever [ˌwɒtsəʊˈevə] *adv.*（用于否定句中以加强语气）任何
wheat [wiːt] *n.* 小麦
wheel [wiːl] *n.* 轮；车轮
when [wen] *adv.* / *pron.* 什么时候 *conj.* 在……时候
whenever [wenˈevə] *conj.* 无论何时；随时；每当
where [wɛə] *adv.* / *pron.* 哪里 *conj.* 然而
whereas [wɛəˈæz] *conj.* 而；却；反之
wherever [ˈwɛəˈevə] *conj.* / *adv.* 无论在哪里
whether [ˈweðə] *conj.* 是否；无论
which [wɪtʃ] *adj.* / *pron.* 哪个；哪些
whichever [wɪtʃ ˈevə] *pron.* / *adj.* 无论哪个；无论哪些
while [waɪl] *conj.* 当……的时候；然而；虽然；尽管 *n.* 一段时间
whip [wɪp] *n.* 鞭子；鞭打 *v.* 鞭打
whirl [wɜːl] *v.*（使）旋转；猛地转动 *n.* 旋转；短暂的旅行
whisky [ˈwɪskɪ] *n.* 威士忌酒
whisper [ˈwɪspə] *v.* / *n.* 耳语；低语耳语
whistle [ˈwɪsl] *n.* 口哨；口哨声 ；汽笛；鸟鸣 *v.* 吹口哨；鸣笛
white [waɪt] *adj.* 白色的；苍白的 *n.* 白色；白种人
who [huː] *pron.* 谁；什么人
whoever [huːˈevə] *pron.* 无论谁；任何人
whole [həul] *n.* 全部 *adj.* 全体的；完整的
wholesome [ˈhəulsəm] *adj.*（食物）有益健康的
wholly [ˈhəulɪ] *adv.* 完全地；全部地
whom [huːm] *pron.* 谁；哪个人
whose [huːz] *pron.* 谁的
why [waɪ] *adv.* / *conj.* 为什么
wicked [ˈwɪkɪd] *adj.* 邪恶的；令人厌恶的
wide [waɪd] *adj.* 宽阔的；广泛的 *adv.* 广阔地；充分地
widespread [ˈwaɪdspred] *adj.* 分布广泛的；普遍的
widow [ˈwɪdəu] *n.* 寡妇
width [wɪdθ] *n.* 宽度；广度
wife [waɪf] *n.* 妻子；太太
wild [waɪld] *adj.* 野生的；狂热的；荒芜的 *n.* 偏远地区
will [wɪl] *v.* 将；会；愿意 *n.* 意志；决心
willing [ˈwɪlɪŋ] *adj.* 愿意的；乐意的
win [wɪn] *v.* 赢得；获胜 *n.* 胜利
wind [wɪnd] *n.* 风 *v.* 缠绕；上发条；蜿蜒而行
window [ˈwɪndəu] *n.* 窗；窗口
wine [waɪn] *n.* 葡萄酒；果酒
wing [wɪŋ] *n.* 翅膀；机翼；派别
wink [wɪŋk] *v.* 眨眼 *n.* 眨眼；眼色；小睡

winter [ˈwɪntə] *n.* 冬季；冬天
wipe [waɪp] *v.* / *n.* 擦；拭 *n.* 抹布；纸巾
wire [ˈwaɪə] *n.* 金属线；电线 *v.* 用金属丝捆扎；为接上电线
wisdom [ˈwɪzdəm] *n.* 智慧；明智
wise [waɪz] *adj.* 有智慧的；聪明的
wish [wɪʃ] *v.* / *n.* 希望；祝愿
wit [wɪt] *n.* 智力；才智；智慧
witch [wɪtʃ] *n.* 女巫；巫婆；巫师
with [wɪð] *prep.* 跟……一起；用；随着；关于
within [wɪˈðɪn] *prep.* 在……以内 *adv.* 在内
without [wɪˈðaut] *prep.* / *adv.* 缺乏；没有
wolf [wulf] *n.* 狼
woman [ˈwumən] *n.* 妇女；成年女子
wonderful [ˈwʌndəful] *adj.* 奇妙的；极好的
wood [wud] *n.* 木材；木头 (pl.) 森林；林地
wooden [ˈwudən] *adj.* 木制的；（行为）呆板的
wool [wul] *n.* 羊毛；毛线；毛织品
word [wɜːd] *n.* 词；词语；息 *v.* 措辞；用词
work [wɜːk] *n.* 工作；作品 *v.* 工作；运转
worker [ˈwɜːkə] *n.* 工人；工作人员
workshop [ˈwɜːkʃɔp] *n.* 车间；作坊；工作室
world [wɜːld] *n.* 世界；地球 ；领域
worldwide [ˌwɜːldˈwaɪd] *adj.* 全世界的；世界范围的 *adv.* 遍及全世界
worm [wɜːm] *n.* 虫；蠕虫
worry [ˈwʌrɪ] *n.* / *v.*（使）焦虑；（使）烦扰
worse [wɜːs] *adj.* / *adv.* 更坏；更差（的 / 地）
worship [ˈwɜːʃɪp] *n.* / *v.* 敬神；崇拜；敬奉
worst [wɜːst] *adj.* / *adv.* 最坏；最差（的 / 地）
worth [wɜːθ] *n.* 价格；价值 *adj.* 值得的；价值……的；值……钱的
would [wud] aux. 将会；想；会
wound [wuːnd] *n.* 创伤；伤口 *v.* [waund] 伤；伤害
wrap [ræp] *v.* 包；裹 *n.* 披肩；围巾
wreath [riːθ] *n.* 花环；花圈
wreck [rek] *n.* 失事船（或飞机） *v.*（船等）失事；遇难；破坏
wrench [rentʃ] *v.* 猛拧；扭伤；使痛苦 *n.* 扳手；痛苦；难受
wretched [ˈretʃɪd] *adj.* 可怜的；悲惨的；讨厌的；恶劣的
wrinkle [ˈrɪŋkl] *n.* 皱纹 *v.* 起皱；起褶
wrist [rɪst] *n.* 腕；腕关节
write [raɪt] *v.* 写；写作；写信
writing [ˈraɪtɪŋ] *n.* 写作；著作；作品
wrong [rɔŋ] *adj.* 错的 *adv.* 错误地 *n.* 坏事；错误的行为 *v.* 冤枉

X

X-ray [ˈeks reɪ] *n.* X 射线；X 光

Y

yard [jɑːd] *n.* 院子；场地；码（长度单位）
yawn [jɔːn] *v.* 打呵欠 *n.* 呵欠
year [jɪə] *n.* 年；年度；学年；年龄；年代
yearly [ˈjɪəlɪ] *adj.* 每年的；一年一度的
yell [jel] *v.* 大叫；呼喊 *n.* 叫喊；呐喊
yellow [ˈjeləu] *adj.* 黄的；黄色的 *n.* 黄色
yes [yes] *adv.* 是的
yesterday [ˈjestədeɪ] *n.* / *adv.* 昨天；不久前
yet [jet] *adv.* 还；仍然 *conj.* 然而；但是
you [juː] *pron.* 你；你们
young [jʌŋ] *adj.* 年轻的 *n.* 青年人
your [jɔː] *pron.* 你的；你们的
yours [jɔːz] *pron.* 你的；你们的
yourself [jɔːˈself] *pron.* 你自己；你亲自
youth [juːθ] *n.* 青年；年轻人

Z

zebra [ˈziːbrə] *n.* 斑马
zero [ˈzɪərəu] *n.* 零；零度 *num.* 零
zigzag [ˈzɪgzæg] *n.* / *adj.* 之字形（的） *v.* 使曲折；曲折行进
zinc [zɪŋk] *n.* 锌
zip [zɪp] *n.* 拉链；拉锁 *v.* 拉拉链
zoo [zuː] *n.* 动物园
zoom [zuːm] *v.* 快速移动；猛涨 *n.*（车辆等）疾驰的声音；变焦镜

索 引 表

Aa

Bb

Cc

Dd

Ee

Ff

Gg

Hh

Ii

Jj

Ll

Mm

Nn

Oo

Qq

Rr

Ss

Tt

Uu